GST ACCOUNTING WITH TALLY.ERP 9

Accountants' Hand Book for GST

by

Asok K Nadhani

BPB PUBLICATIONS

FIRST EDITION 2018

Copyright © BPB Publications, INDIA

ISBN:

Distributors:

BPB PUBLICATIONS
20, Ansari Road, Darya Ganj
New Delhi-110002
Ph: 23254990/23254991

BPB BOOK CENTRE
376 Old Lajpat Rai Market,
Delhi-110006
Ph: 23861747

DECCAN AGENCIES
4-3-329, Bank Street,
Hyderabad-500195
Ph: 24756967/24756400

MICRO MEDIA
Shop No. 5, Mahendra Chambers, 150
DN Rd. Next to Capital Cinema, V.T.
(C.S.T.) Station, MUMBAI-400 001 Ph:
22078296/22078297

COMPUTER BOOK CENTRE
12, Shrungar Shopping Centre,
M.G.Road, BENGALURU–560001
Ph: 25587923/25584641

Published by Manish Jain for BPB Publications, 20, Ansari Road, Darya Ganj, New Delhi-110002 and Printed by Repro India Ltd., Mumbai

UPDATES

Salient points of latest updates on GST

Interception of Conveyance for Inspection of goods in movement

As per GST Circular 49 dt 21 Jun 2018,only such goods and/or conveyances should be detained/confiscated in respect of which there is a violation of the provisions of the GST Acts or the rules made thereunder.

Illustration: Where a conveyance carrying several consignments (e.g 25 consignments) is intercepted and valid e-way bills and/or other relevant documents are produced only in respect of few consignments (say 20 consignments), detention/confiscation can be made only with respect of consignments in violation of the Act / Rules (i.e the balance 5 consignments).

Unique Common Enrolment Number for Transporter

As per amendment dt 19 Jun 2018, A transporter who is registered in multiple States / UT having same PAN, may apply for a *Unique Common Enrolment Number* (UEN) by submitting Form GST ENR-02, using any of the his GSTIN. Upon validation of details furnished, a Unique Common Enrolment number will be generated and communicated to the said transporter. On obtaining the Unique Common Enrolment Number, they will use UEN for their pan-India activities, and no more use any of the GSTIN for e-way Bill (Chapter VI).

- **Extension of Time for Final Report in Part B of Form EWB-03 :**As per Notification # 28/2018,Rule 138C(1), the following proviso are added, extending the time by *3 days* :

  The commissioner or any authorized officer, on sufficient cause being shown, extend the time for recording of Final report in Part B of Form EWB-03, for a further period not exceeding *3 days (counted from midnight of the date on which the vehicle is intercepted).*

- **Notice & Order for demand of Amount payable** : Rule 142 : In addition to s.73(9), s. 74(9)s & s.76(3), under existing rule, *s. 129 & 130* are also inserted.

GSTR-4 for Composition Dealer : For the Quarterly Returns from Jul17 to Jun 18, Serial 4A of Table (Inwards details) need not be filed.

Enhancement of e-way Bill threshold

- As per notification dt 15 Jun 2018, e-way Bill to be generated where the consignment value exceeds Rs 1 Lakh (Applicable for Delhi), for intra state goods movements in Delhi, without passing through any other State.
- Effective 1st July 2018, e-way Bill to be generated where the consignment value exceeds Rs 1 Lakh, for intra state goods movements in Maharashtra.
- More States are gradually announcing threshold limit for Intra State movement, to Rs. 1 Lakh

Change in e-mail id & mobile number in GST Registration

As per Press Release dt 14 Jun 2018,The Jurisdictional tax authority may update the e-mail id & mobile number of the authorised signatory. The tax payer is to approach concerned jurisdictional authority to get the password for the GSTIN, providing valid documents as proof of identity, validating the business details. The Tax official will upload the necessary documents on GST Portal. He will then record the new email id and mobile number, and reset the password.

The temporary password as set by tax official would be communicated through email and SMS. Now the taxpayer should login through the option *First Time login* link. The user will enter Username & temporary password and then set his user name and password.

RCM waiver extended upto 30th Sep 2019

As recommended by 28th GST council meeting dt 21st Jul 2018, the waiver on RCM u/s 9(4), on purchases from unregistered dealer is extended till 30.9.2019.

Simplified Return Filing

As recommended by 28th GST council meeting dt 21st Jul 2018, Regular taxpayers with a turnover of up to Rs 5 crores can opt to file GST return on a quarterly basis (earlier limit Rs. 1.5 crores).However these taxpayers would pay taxes monthly through a challan.

Such Taxpayers (upto 5 Crore Turnover), having only B2C supplies may file Return in SAHAJ Form, while taxpayers having both B2B & B2C supplies, may file Return in SUGAM Form, under UPLOAD-LOCK-PAY TAX process.

- Amendments shall be carried out in amendment return with additional payment
- NIL Return (no purchase and no sale) may be filed just by sending a SMS.

The new GST return would be simple with two main tables. In one table, the taxpayer would have to report sales and in another report purchases for availing ITC. Invoices can now be uploaded continuously by the seller and continuously viewed and locked by the buyer for availing input tax credit. This process would ensure that for the most part, return is automatically filled based on the invoices uploaded by the buyer and the seller

Composition dealers may provide supply of services: As recommended by 28th GST council meeting dt 21st Jul 2018, Composition Dealers may supply services to the extent of 10% of the turnover **or** Rs 5 lakhs, whichever is higher (except Restaurant).

Threshold limit enhanced for 6 States

As recommended by 28th GST council meeting dt 21st Jul 2018, GST exemption increased to 20 lakhs (from earlier 10 lakhs) for 6 States (Sikkim, Arunachal Pradesh, Himachal Pradesh, Uttarakhand, Assam & Meghalaya).

Multiple GST Registration

As recommended by 28th GST council meeting dt 21st Jul 2018, Taxpayers may opt for multiple registrations within a State/Union territory in respect of multiple places of business located within the same State/Union territory (earlier restricted to multiple businesses in the separate States)

Registration for e-commerce operators : As recommended by 28th GST council meeting dt 21st Jul 2018,E-commerce operators need to have compulsory GST registration only for certain goods.

Consolidated credit/debit Notes : As recommended by 28th GST council meeting dt 21st Jul 2018, registered persons may issue consolidated credit/debit notes in respect of multiple invoices issued in a Financial Year.

Tally. erp9 updates
Important Updates in Tally ERP.9 rel 6.4.4

- Supports the latest changes made in GSTR-3B Offline Tool Version 4.0.
- Fixed Assets purchases may be made in account invoice mode also (apart from usual voucher mode).

Important Updates in Tally ERP.9 rel 6.4.6 of 5ᵗʰ July 2018

- The latest offline tool ver 2.3, for GSTR-4 (for Composite Dealer) is now supported
- The latest e-way Bill & Consolidated e-way Bill JSON preparation tool v.1.0.0618, is now supported
- Provision of separate threshold limit for Intra-state & Inter-state e-way Bill
- GST UIN validation checks on UN, Embassy bodies & Government
- Additional validation traps and notification of errors

Important Updates in Tally ERP.9 rel 6.4.7

- Enhanced GSTIN validation
- Option to avail Input Credit under Reverse Charge in current or future period.
- Taxpayers may view the Details of liability or input credit to be booked or claimed, on purchases under reverse charge, and import of goods and services, in the report provided for Input Credit to be Booked in GSTR-3B.
- Summary of Input Tax Credit
- Raise liability in one tax period and claim input credit in the subsequent period
- Eligible Input Credit - Capture from purchases or journal vouchers
- Supports latest e-Way Bill and Consolidated e-Way Bill JSON Preparation Tools, Ver. 1.0.0618

Preface

This book is aimed for readers who like to know practical aspects of implementing & maintaining GST Accounts, Statutory Returns filing on GST Portal & various compliance under GST Acts & Rules. It explains steps of GSTN Portal management & Returns filing with illustrations of each operational step, in simple language.

This book specifically explains maintenance of GST Accounts with Tally.ERP9, the most popular accounting software of the country. Comprehensive sets of business scenario illustrated with relevant screen components and explanation of detailed operational steps are included. Even first time users would be able to perform the tasks, without any external help.

Apart from Business Executives, Owners and Accountants and business, *Part 4: Assignments (p.592)*, of the book, containing Quiz, Tests & Business projects would be useful for aspiring candidates for Accounting jobs in business organisations, and get prepared for competitive examinations.

Readers successfully completing the Quiz, Tests and Projects, under Assignments section, would get *Distinction Certificate* (FREE of Cost), which would help them in getting employment and rising to higher echelon, in their professional career.

I request readers to give their feedback on how to make the book more useful to readers

Asok K Nadhani

September 2018

Table of Contents

Invoice for supply of Goods **36**, Tax Invoice for supply of Services **37**, Contents of Bill of Supply **37**, Advance Payment **38**, Receipt Voucher **38**, Refund Voucher **38**, Supply under reverse charge **38**, Sale on Approval **38**, Export Invoice **38**, Credit Notes **39**, Debit Notes **39**, Revision of Invoice **39**, Invoice in Special Cases **40**, Delivery Challan **40**, Way Bill **41**, Goods transported in knocked down condition **41**

09   Input Tax Credit 42-45

Inputs for a Business **42**, Rules of ITC **42**, Input Tax credit on stock held **42**, Set off of ITC **43**, Ineligible ITC **43**, Special circumstances of ITC **44**, ITC Claim Procedure **45**, ITC Claims process **45**, Documents needed to claim ITC **45**, Input Tax Credit on Import **45**

10   Reverse Charge Mechanism 46-48

Reverse Charge **46**, Self-invoicing **46**, Cases where Reverse Charge is applicable **46**, Time of Supply under Reverse Charge **47**, Rules relating to Reverse Charge **47**, Supplies of Goods under Reverse Charge **47**, Supplies of services under Reverse Charge **47**

11   Advance Receipt 49-50

Receipt of Advance against supply **49**, Receipt Voucher **49**, Tax on Advance Received **49**

12   Tax Payments & Refunds 51-56

GST Payment Liability **51**, GST Portal Tax Accounts **51**, Accounting entries in GST portal Tax Accounts **51**, Set off of Tax Liability **51**, Tax Payment Process **51**, GST Payment Forms **52**, Taxes Payable under GST **52**, Persons liable to pay GST **52**, Pre Registration of Credit Card **52**, Tax Payment Challan Generation **53**, Counter payment of GST **53**, Tax payment of earlier period **53**, Tax Refunds **54**, Refunds Forms **54**, Refund of unutilized input tax credit **54**, Time limit for Refunds Claims **55**, Documents for Refunds claims **55**, Refund Application Processing **55**, Notice of Rejection of Refunds Claim **55**, Refund Order **55**

13   Returns Filing 57-58

GST Returns **57**, List of GST Returns **57**, Late Fees **58**

14   Movement of Goods 59-63

Delivery Challan **59**, Carriage Services **59**, Issue of Delivery Challan **59**, E-WAY BILL **60**, Objective of e-way Bill **60**, Applicability of e-way Bill **61**, e-way bill non-applicability **61**, Generation of e-way bill **61**, Persons responsible for generation of e-way Bill **61**, e-way Bill Forms **62**, Multiple Consignments **62**, Multiple Vehicles **62**, Transfer of goods from one vehicle to another **62**, Acceptance of Goods by Recipient **63**, Validity of e-way bill **63**, Cancellation of e-way Bill **63**, e-way Bill Administration **63**

15   Input Service Distributor 64-67

Centralised Business Operations **64**, Registration of ISD under GST **64**, Modes of ITC Distribution **64**, ISD Returns Forms **64**, Distribution of ITC by an ISD **65**, Addition / Reduction in ITC **66**, Apportionment of reduction amount **66**, Method of ITC distribution **66**

16   Import & Export 68-71

Import of Goods **68**, Valuation of Imported Goods **68**, Place of Supply **68**, ITC on Imported Goods **68**, GST on Imports by EOUs/EHTPs/STPs **68**, Import of Services **69**, GST on Ocean Freight **69**, Imports initiated under previous regime **69**, Export of Goods **70**, Export of Services **70**, Supply of Service out of India **70**, ITC Refund on Export **70**, ITC Refund Process for Exports **70**

17   Books of Accounts 72-73

Specified Books of Accounts **72**, Contents of Books of Accounts **72**, Place of Accounts Maintenance **73**, Period for preservation of accounts **73**, Electronic Records **73**, Maintenance of Records by warehouse /

Part 3 : GST Accounting using Tally.ERP 9 381-591

PART 1
GST OVERVIEW

Introduction to GST

GST in other countries

Several countries have already established the Goods and Services Tax. In Australia, the system was introduced in 2000 to replace the Federal Wholesale Tax. In New Zealand GST was implemented in 1986. Manufacturer's Sales Tax was replaced by GST in Canada, in 1991. In Singapore, GST was implemented in 1994. In Malaysia GST came into effect in 2015.

GST Milestones in India

- **2000**: GST was first conceived by the Atal Bihari Vajpayee Government in 2000. An Empowered Committee (EC) was formed to create GST structure.
- **2004**: A task force that was headed by Vijay L. Kelkar to study the existing tax structure, to be mitigated by the GST system.
- **2005**: P. Chidambaram, FM suggested to implement a uniform GST structure across the country, covering the whole production-distribution chain, as discussed in the budget session of FY 2005-06.
- **2006**: States were asked to prepare and make reforms for upcoming GST regime, as proposed
- **2008**: At the union budget session for 2008-09, FM announced the roadmap for GST to be implemented from 1 April 2010.
- **2009**: Pranab Mukherjee, FM, announced the basic skeleton of the GST system. The EC First Discussion Paper (FDP), describing the proposed GST regime.
- **2010**: The government introduced the mission-mode project laying foundation for GST, with a budgetary outlay of Rs.1,133 crore, computerised commercial taxes in states.
- **2011**: Constitution (115th Amendment) Bill for the introduction of GST was sent to a standing committee for a detailed examination.
- **2012**: FM and ministers of states hold meetings to resolve issues of States.
- **2013**: Report created by the standing committee is submitted to the parliament, which approved the regulation with few amendments
- **2014**: The new FM, Arun Jaitley, submits the Constitution (122nd Amendment) Bill, 2014 in the parliament.
- **2015**: The Lok Sabha passes the Constitution Amendment Bill. But the Bill is not passed in Rajya Sabha. Jaitley mentions that the disruption had no specific cause.

- **2016**: The Ministry of Finance releases the draft model law on GST to the public, inviting suggestions and views. The Bill passed in the Rajya Sabha. President of India gives his consent for the Constitution Amendment Bill to become an Act.

- **2017**: Four Bills (Central GST Bill, Integrated GST Bill, Union Territory GST Bill, GST (Compensation to States Bill), related to GST become Act. Finally, Government declares that the GST Bill will be applicable from 1 July 2017.

Tax Structure before GST : Before the implementation of GST, taxation laws between the Centre and states were clearly demarcated. The Centre would levy tax on goods manufacture, except alcohol for consumption, narcotics, opium, etc. The states had the power to charge tax on the sale of goods. The Centre was levying Central Sales Tax on Inter State sales, collected by originating states. The Centre was also levying service tax on services. Additionally, the Centre was charging and collecting additional duties of customs on Import / Export of goods

Amendments to Constitution empowered both Centre and states to levy and collect GST. Joint decisions are taken about the structure and operation of GST.

Constitution (One Hundred and First) Amendment Act, 2016 : To address prevalent issues in taxation, the Constitution 122nd Amendment Bill was put forth on 19 Dec 2014, with following recommendations:

– Levy of GST on all goods and services, except alcohol that humans consume.

– Dual GST by the Centre (CGST) and states/union territories (SGST/UTGST)

– Centre would levy the GST on inter-state trade or imports of services and goods as IGST

– Central Government will also levy excise duty on tobacco products, in addition to GST.

– Tax on five petroleum products (HSD, crude, petrol, natural gas, and ATF) will be outlined later after a decision is made by the GST Council

Goods and Services Tax Council (GSTC) was created by union finance minister, revenue minister, and ministers of state to take decisions on GST rates, thresholds, taxes to be subsumed, exemptions, and other features of the taxation system. EC would be the platform for states to hold discussions of regional issues. The GST Council is a separate entity that would oversee the implementation of the GST system.

Goods and Services Tax Network : Goods and Services Tax Network (GSTN) was set up as a private company in 2013 by the Government u/s 25 of the Companies Act, 1956, to offer front-end services of registration, payment, and returns to taxpayers. GSTN also identified IT and financial technology companies (GST Suvidha Providers) to develop applications for use by taxpayers to interact with GSTN.

GST Model: A dual tax model like Canada (which has a federal government like India) is introduced in India, having taxation power to both the Centre and the State. GST shall have two components: CGST (levied by Centre), and SGST/ UTGST (levied by States / Union Territories). The existing taxes would subsume within the CGST or SGST / UTGST.

Acts under GST: Following Acts under GST were passed and received the President's assent on 12th April, 2017 : (1) The Central Goods and Service Tax Act, 2017(CGST), (2) The Integrated Goods and Service Tax Act, 2017(IGST), (3) The Union Territory Goods and Service Tax Act, 2017(UTGST), (4) The Goods and Service Tax(Compensation to States) Act, 2017(Compensation Cess).

Twenty eight states excluding Jammu & Kashmir, Union Territories with legislature- Delhi and Puducherry and the remaining five Union Territories passed their respective State Goods and Service Tax Act (SGST) and UTGST Act by 30th June, 2017.The State of Jammu & Kashmir passed their SGST Act on 5th of July, 2017.The CGST and IGST Acts extends to the whole of India except the State of Jammu & Kashmir. All the acts are effective from 1st day of July, 2017

GST Rates : The various rates of IGST and (CGST+SGST/UTGST) are Nil,5%,12%,18% and 28%. There is a special rate of 0.25% for rough diamonds, 3% for Gold, silver and jewellery, platinum, imitation jewellery, pearl, diamond, synthetic stone. In addition, GST Compensation cess is applicable on Aerated waters, cigarettes, tobacco and tobacco products, coal, peat, lignite and motor vehicles.

GST

GST is a destination based tax on consumption of goods and services (which means that the tax would accrue to the taxing authority which has jurisdiction over the place of consumption i.e place of supply). It is proposed to be levied at all stages right from manufacture up to final consumption with credit of taxes paid at previous stages available as setoff. Only value addition will be taxed and burden of tax is to be borne by the final consumer.

GST is a consumption based tax, i.e. tax will be payable in the State in which goods and services or both are finally consumed. Exports are not taxable, because the place of consumption is outside India. Imports are taxable, because the place of consumption is in India. Thus, the States from which goods are supplied will not get any tax where goods are consumed in another State.

Central & State Levy

GST is levied on *Taxable Supply*. Since India is a federal country, it has Central as well as State as its participants. The GST also has two components such as CGST (Central Goods and Services Tax) and SGST (State Goods and Services Tax), these are levied by Central and State respectively and are applied on supply of Goods or Services. In case of Union Territories, UTGST is applicable in place of SGST.

Taxes subsumed by GST: GST eliminates following Taxes

- **Taxes currently levied and collected by the Centre:**
    - Central Excise duty
    - Duties of Excise (Medicinal and Toilet Preparations)
    - Additional Duties of Excise (Goods of Special Importance)
    - Additional Duties of Excise (Textiles and Textile Products)
    - Additional Duties of Customs (commonly known as CVD)
    - Special Additional Duty of Customs (SAD)

- – Service Tax
- – Central Surcharges and Cesses so far as they relate to supply of goods and services
- • **Taxes currently levied and collected by the Centre:**
  - – State VAT
  - – Central Sales Tax
  - – Luxury Tax
  - – Entry Tax (all forms)
  - – Entertainment and Amusement Tax (except when levied by the local bodies)
  - – Taxes on advertisements
  - – Purchase Tax
  - – Taxes on lotteries, betting and gambling
  - – State Surcharges and Cesses so far as they relate to supply of goods and services

Imports & Exports: Customs is outside GST and hence would continue on imports. GST is not charged on exported goods and services

Non GST Items: Certain Items like Alcohol for human consumption, Petroleum Products viz. petroleum crude, motor spirit (petrol), high speeddiesel, natural gas, aviation turbine fuel & Electricity, are kept outside the purview of GST. The existing taxation system (VAT & Central Excise) will continue in respect of these commodities. Tobacco and tobacco products would be subject to GST. In addition, the Centre would have the power to levy Central Excise duty on Tobacco and tobacco products

Goals of GST Implementation
- – Reduce cascading effect of taxes;
- – Reduce Compliance cost;
- – Fewer rate slabs;
- – Removal / merging of many taxes;
- – Reduction of corruption;
- – Simplification of tax collection and administration;
- – Lower burden of taxes on end consumers;
- – Industry competitiveness on their foreign competitors;
- – Easy flow of resources across the country;
- – Reduction in inflation;
- – Widening tax base and tax collection

Transition to GST

Taxpayers already Registered under old Tax Regime

Taxpayers already Registered under old Tax Regime (i.e before 1st July 2017) must not suffer for the Tax already paid and credits available to them under old Tax regimes, while moving to new GST regime. GST consolidates multiple taxes into one.

To guard existing Taxpayers, GST Model Law has made transition provisions for closing balance of input tax credit with taxpayers under the old indirect tax regime. To ensure that the transition to the GST regime is very smooth and hassle-free and no ITC (Input Tax Credit)/benefits earned in the existing regime are lost, transition provisions are made in respect of:

- Input Tax Credit
- Refunds and Arrears
- Other Cases : Job Work, Input Service Distributor, Composition Scheme

Input Tax Credit

Important provision in respect of transition of Input Tax Credit available under VAT, Excise Duty or Service Tax to GST, are summarized below (registered dealer opting for composition scheme will not be eligible to carry forward ITC available in previous regime).

- **Closing balance of credit on Inputs:** Closing balance of ITC as per the last return filed (under the respective regime) before GST can be taken as credit in the GST regime, if the returns for the last 6-months (January 2017 to June 2017) were filed in the previous regime (i.e. VAT, Excise and Service Tax returns had been filed). Form TRAN-1 must filed (by 27th Dec 2017) to carry forward the Input Tax Credit

- **Credit on Capital Goods:** Carried over part of ITC Capital Goods can be carried forwarded to GST by entering the details in Form TRAN-1.

- **Credit on Stock:** A manufacturer or a service provider who has goods lying in the closing stock (for less than 1 year as on 1.7.17 and must possess the Invoice) on which duty has been paid can avail the credit, on the stock of such goods.

  When invoice of earlier purchase is unavailable, Traders (not manufacturers or service providers) can claim credit, if the stock are identifiable separately, and if the benefit is passed on to the final consumer.

  - **Persons not registered under previous law**: Registered persons who were not registered under previous law, and:
    - o was engaged in the manufacture of exempted goods or provision of exempted services
    - o was providing works contract service and was availing abatement

o   was a first stage dealer or a second stage dealer, or a registered importer

can also enjoy ITC of inputs in stock held on 1st July, on following conditions

o   Inputs or goods are used for making taxable supplies

o   Such benefit is passed on by way of reduced prices to the recipient

o   Taxable person is eligible for input tax credit on such inputs

o   The person is in possession of invoices evidencing payment of duty under the earlier the law

o   The invoices are not older than 12 months

o   The supplier of services is not eligible for any abatement under GST

- **Goods Sent Before 1st July:** Input Tax Credit can be claimed by the manufacturer/dealer for those goods received after the appointed day, the tax on which has already been paid under previous law, if the invoice/tax paying document is recorded in the accounts of such person within 1ˢᵗ August 2017.

ITC in case of Centralised Registration under Service Tax

Such Registered Person can take credit of the amount of CENVAT carry forwarded in return furnished under the existing law, if the return under the existing law has been filed within three months. Such credit may be transferred to any of the Registered Persons having the same PAN for which the centralised registration was obtained.

Reversed Input Service credit

CENVAT credit reversed on account of non-payment of consideration within three months can be reclaimed if the payment is made to the supplier of service within 3 months from the appointed day.

Goods belonging to the principal lying at the premises of the agent

This provision is specific to SGST law. In such cases, agent shall be entitled to take credit, if:

- The agent is a registered taxable person
- Both the principal and the agent have declared the details of stock
- The invoices are not older than twelve months
- The principal has either reversed or not been availed on the input tax credit

Refunds and Arrears

Claims/appeals pending for the refund on the due amount of CENVAT credit, tax or interest paid before 1st July shall be disposed of according to the previous laws. Any amount found to be payable under previous law will be treated as arrears of GST and be recovered according to GST provisions.

Job Work

No tax shall be payable in Inputs, semi-finished goods removed for job work for carrying certain processes and returned on or after 1st July, under following conditions:

- Goods are returned to the factory within 6 months from 1st July 2017
- Goods held by job worker are declared in Form TRAN-1

– Supply of semi-finished goods is done only on payment of tax in India or the goods are exported out of India within 6 months from 1st July 2017.

Taxes are not applicable if finished goods were removed before 1st July for carrying certain processes and are returned within 6 months from 1st July. Input tax credit will be recovered if the goods are not returned within 6 months

Goods removed before appointed Day

Following rules apply for Goods removed before 6 months of the appointed day, but returned within 6 months from the appointed day:

– **Goods are returned by an unregistered person**: Refund of the duty/VAT paid under the existing law can be claimed.
– **Goods returned by a Registered Person**: Return of goods shall be treated as supply of goods (ITC can be claimed).

Goods sent on Approval

No tax is payable by the person returning the goods, if Goods sent on approval basis before 6 months of the appointed day are returned within 6 months from the appointed day:

– If such goods returned afterwards, tax is payable by the recipient
– If such goods are not returned, tax is payable by the person who sent the goods on approval basis.

Credit Distribution by Input Service Distributor

Transition provisions will apply in cases where the service was received prior to 1st July 2017, and the invoices received on or after 1st July 2017. ISD will be eligible to distribute input tax credit under GST.

Composition Dealer

A registered dealer who was paying tax under composition scheme under old regime, but is a normal tax payer under GST, can claim credit of inputs available as on 1st July by in following conditions:

– The Input are used for taxable supply
– Registered Person is eligible for ITC under GST
– Invoice or other duty payment documents (Invoices not more than twelve months old) are available

Types of GST

Central & State Levy

India is a federal country where both the Centre and the States have been assigned powers to levy and collect taxes through appropriate legislation. Both the levels of Government (Central & State) have distinct responsibilities to perform according to the division of powers prescribed in the Constitution. So, separate GST will be charged for Central & State GST.

Types of GST: Accordingly, following types of GST are charged

— **SGST (State Goods & Service Tax):** Different indirect taxes like State Sales Tax, VAT, Luxury Tax, Entertainment tax (unless it is levied by the local bodies), Taxes on lottery, betting and gambling, Entry tax not in lieu of Octroi, State Cess and Surcharge related to in supply of goods and services, are subsumed with SGST.

  The tax revenue collected under SGST is meant for State Government. For Union Territories, UTGST(Union Territory Goods and Service Tax) is applicable (in place of SGST).

— **CGST (Central Goods and Service Tax):** Central taxes of Central Excise Duty, Central Sales Tax CST, Service Tax, Additional excise duties, excise duty levied under the medical and toiletries preparation Act, CVD (Additional Customs duty – Countervailing Duty), SAD (Special Additional Duty of customs) surcharges and cesses are subsumed.

  CGST is charged on the movement of goods and services of standard commodities and services. The revenue collected under CGST is for Centre.

— **IGST (Integrated Goods and Service Tax):** IGST is charged when movement of goods and services from one state to another (irrespective of sale or stock transfer). For example, if goods are moved from Tamil Nadu to Kerala, IGST is levied on such goods. The revenue out of IGST is shared by state government and central government.

  So, for inter state transaction (between 2 states), IGST will be applicable, while for intrastate transaction (within the state), CGST & SGST / UTGST and will be applicable. Interstate stock transfer (materials belonging to same assesse) will also be subject to GST.

— **Union Territory GST (UTGST):** A union territory is directly under the governance of the Central Government. This differentiates them from the states, which have their own elected governments. Currently, there are 7 union territories in India, viz: Chandigarh, Lakshadweep, Daman and Diu, Dadra and Nagar Haveli, Andaman and Nicobar Islands, Delhi, Puducherry

  Among these, Delhi and Puducherry have their own legislature, with elected members and a Chief Minister, functioning as semi-states.

Under GST, the SGST Act applies to all the states in India. The definition of 'States' in the Indian Constitution includes union territories with their own legislature. Hence, the SGST Act also applies to the union territories of Delhi and Puducherry. So, on supplies within the union territories of Delhi and Puducherry, the taxes levied will be CGST +SGST, and on supplies from Delhi/Puducherry to another state/union territory, IGST would be levied.

As the SGST Act cannot be applied on a union territory without its own legislature, the GST Council has introduced the UTGST Act, to levy a tax, called UTGST, in the union territories of Chandigarh, Lakshadweep, Daman and Diu, Dadra and Nagar Haveli and Andaman and Nicobar Islands. UTGST will be levied in place of SGST in these union territories.

Types of Invoices

In the GST regime, broadly two types of invoices will be issued – Tax Invoice and Bill of Supply.

–   **Tax invoice**: Tax invoice is to be issued by a registered taxable person for the supply of taxable goods or services.

–   **Bill of Supply**: Bill of Supply is to be issued by a Registered Taxable Person for the supply of exempted goods or services, and for supplies by a Composition Tax Payer.

GST Rates

Rate structure as agreed upon by GST council

–   0%: Zero tax rate will apply to 50% of the items present in the consumer price index basket, including foodgrains such as rice and wheat, etc.
–   5%: Items of mass consumption like spices, tea, mustard oil etc.
–   12% : Items of processed food items, etc
–   18%: Items such as soaps, oil, toothpaste, refrigerator, and smartphones
–   28%: Sin products such as luxury cars, tobacco products, pan masala, aerated drinks, etc.
–   GST Rates are changed from time to time, by government notification

Taxable value

GST is charged on sale value, irrespective of MRP value. X supplies Y some genuine Maruti auto parts @ Rs 2000, whose MRP value is Rs 2800. X would charge GST on Rs 2000 at the prevailing rate.

Incidental charges like delivery, packing charges etc, included in the bill would be chargeable to GST. X supplies some glassware costing Rs 12,000, and charges Rs 1000 for wooden packing boxes and Rs 500 for delivery charges. X would charge GST on 12000+1000+500=13500, at prevailing GST rate on glassware.

Discount allowed in the bill, or known at the time of sale / purchase would be allowed. But discount allowed later conditionally, not known at the time of trade, would not be allowed.

X sold goods to Y for Rs. 10000, and allowed trade discount @ 1% in the bill. X also agreed to allow another 1% cash discount on the due amount if the payment is made through net banking within 7 days. In this case, X would charge GST on 10000 -100 (1% on 10000) = on 9900. Though the Discount was committed and made known at the time of deal, X would not give any GST benefit on additional cash discount, as it was conditional on timely payment through net banking.

In case of transaction involving exchange of goods (or service), in part or in whole, GST would be charged on the value of goods (or services) exchanged also.

X supplied an Air Conditioner to Y, at Rs. 20,000 after taking back his old AC. Now GST would be charged on Rs. 20000 + value of old AC taken back (as old AC taken is also a part of price taken for supply of new AC). The value of old AC be computed on following rules:

– Open Market Value of such supply.

– If the open market value is not available, the sum total of consideration in money and the monetary value of consideration not in money, if such monetary value is known at the time of supply.

– If the value cannot be determined by applying above rules, the value of supply of goods or/and services of like kind and quality will be considered.

In this case, GST would be valued on the normal sale value of similar AC, where no old AC is taken back, or if the value of old returned AC can be determined fairly (e.g. Rs 2000), then its value would be added to the met cash price received (i.e on 20000+2000=22000).

XYZ offered a new model of phone 'Alisa' before pre launch (price not yet fixed) to its first customer of its VEEVA model of Phone costing Rs 29000, on the launch day. As price of Alisa was not known (as its price was not fixed yet), the price of a phone similar in feature of Alisa (e.g 4000) would be added to the price of VEEVA. GST would be charged on Rs.29000+4000=Rs.33000 at the prevailing GST rate.

Advance Payments Received

When a registered dealer receives an advance payment for a supply, the Receiver should issue a *Receipt Voucher* for the advance paid.

As per GST rule, if advance is received before the issue of the invoice the time of supply would be the date of receipt of advance. So, GST would have to be paid by the receiver, on receipt of Advance.

Example: S entered into a contract for supplying goods to B, for Rs. 11,20,000 (Goods Rs. 10,00,000 + GST rate @ 12%) in January 2018. He received advance of Rs.2,24,000 on 10th January and balance payment of Rs.9,76,000 on 20th February after receiving goods. The invoice was also raised on 20th February 2018.

The payment would be adjusted as follows

Jan: Total Rs 2,24,000: Rs. 2,00,000 for Goods value & Rs 24,000 for GST. So, GST of Rs 24000 would be paid by seller in Jan

Feb: Total Rs 8,96,000: Rs. 8,00,000 for Goods value & Rs 96,000 for GST. So, GST of Rs 96000 would be paid by seller in Feb. So, total goods value paid 2,00,000 + 8,00,000 = 10,00,000. Total GST paid = 24000 +96,000 = 1,20,000. Total payments made: 2,24,000 (Advance) + 9.76,000 (Final) = 11,20,000

So, when lump sum advance is received, the total amount received would be split up into Supply Value & GST components and the GST would be deposited accordingly.

After a dealer issues a receipt voucher, if the supply does not take place, the dealer can issue a refund voucher to the recipient against the advance received. The receipt voucher should indicate the amount adjusted against value of goods / services, and the Tax component, like an Invoice.

ITC can not be claimedon advance paid. ITC can be claimed only after raising Invoice for supply of goods or services.

Note: GST on Advance for supply of *Goods* is not payable (but Payable on Supply of Services). It is Payable on issue of Invoice (not on advance received), as per notification effective from 15 Nov 17.

GST Registration

All businesses having turnover above threshold limit, must register under GST. GST registration is mandatory for some entities irrespective of Turnover.

Threshold Limit for GST Registration

Any person having Aggregate Turnover of threshold limit (currently reported as Rs 20 Lakhs / 10 lakhs in North East), across all locations in India will need to obtain registration in the States from where they make a supply.

–   **Liability to Register**: The threshold amount for liability of register is Total Turnover of Rs 19 Lakhs (Rs 9 Lakhs for North East India), while The threshold amount for liability to pay Tax is Rs 20 Lakhs (Rs 10 Lakhs for North East India)

–   **North East States**: Under GST rules, the states of Arunachal Pradesh, Assam, Jammu and Kashmir, Manipur, Meghalaya, Mizoram, Nagaland, Sikkim, Tripura, Himachal Pradesh and Uttarakhand are considered under North East States for whom the threshold limit is lower.

–   **Statewide separate Registration**: One registration for each State is required. A Tax payer may choose to obtain separate registrations for its different business verticals within a State.

–   **Free Registration**: There is no fee for registration under GST.

–   **On-line Registration**: Registration will be done online through GSTN (Goods and Services Tax Network) portal. Applicant may register themselves, or get it done through GSPs (GST Suvidha Providers)

–   **Aggregate Turnover**: Aggregate Turnover includes the aggregate value, computed on all India basis (excluding taxes charged under the CGST Act, SGST Act and the IGST Act) consisting of All taxable and non-taxable supplies, Exempt supplies & Exports of goods and/or service of a person having the same PAN. Aggregate turnover does not include value of supplies on which tax is levied on reverse charge basis, and value of inward supplies.

Compulsory Registration

In following cases, GST registration is compulsory, irrespective of Turnover

–   Person registered under Pre-GST laws (Excise, VAT, Service Tax etc.), now subsumed by GST

–   Registered Business transferred to someone, the transferee shall take registration with effect from the date of transfer.

–   Business doing inter-state supply of goods

–   Casual taxable person

–   Non-Resident taxable person

- Agents supplying on behalf of other registered taxable persons
- Person paying tax under Reverse Charge Mechanism
- Input Service Distributor (ISD)
- Persons responsible to deduct TDS
- E-commerce operator or aggregator
- Person who supplies via e-commerce aggregator
- Person supplying online information and database access or retrieval services from a place outside India to a person in India, other than a registered taxable person
- Aggregator who supplies services under his brand name / trade name
- Other person as may notified by Government

Special Exemption by Notification: However, as per subsequent notifications, following are exempt from registration

- E-commerce sellers/aggregators need not register if total sales are less than Rs. 20 lakh (Notification No. 65/2017dt 15.11.2017)
- Service providers providing Inter State through e-commerce services, having turnover below 20lakhs (10 lakhs for Special states. 20 lakhs for J&K vide notification # 10/2017 dt 15.11.17),
- Job workers making inter-state supply of services to a registered person are exempted from registration if their turnover is below 20lakhs (10 lakhs for Special states (Notification No. 7/2017 dated 14.9.2017)

Voluntary Registration

Registration carries business authenticity and more credibility. So, a business entity, even not compulsorily liable for registration, may opt for suo-moto voluntary registration. On registration, they may avail benefit of Input Credit, make Inter State Transaction, do e-commerce or open e-commerce site.

Such organisation will make application for GST registration like a normal new applicant. All the provisions of GST applicable to a registered taxable person will similarly apply to such a voluntarily registered person also, i.e., he will be treated as a normal taxable person.

Registration under Composition scheme

Small dealers with turnover below the threshold limit, as notified from time to time, have the option of adopting the Composition scheme and pay at flat rate on turnover.

Government Bodies

In case of specified government, UN, Embassy Bodies, *Unique Identification Number* (UID) would be allotted by respective state tax authorities (instead of GSTIN), who are not making outwards supplies of GST goods (and thus not liable to obtain GST registration), but making inter-state purchases.

Casual & Non Resident Taxable Person

– **Casual Taxable Person:** It means a person who occasionally undertakes transactions in a taxable territory where he has no fixed place of business.

– **Non-resident Taxable Person:** It means a taxable person residing outside India and coming to India to occasionally, undertake transaction in India, but has no fixed place of business in India

– **Validity of Certificate:** The certificate of registration issued to a "casual taxable person" or a "non-resident taxable person" shall be valid for 90 days from the effective date of registration. However, the proper officer, at the request of the said taxable person, may extend the validity of the aforesaid period by a further period not exceeding 90 days.

Effective Date of Registration

– **Application submitted within thirty days:** In case of Application for registration submitted within thirty days of becoming liable for registration, the effective date of registration shall be date of his liability for registration.

– **Application submitted after thirty days:** In case of Application for registration submitted after thirty days of becoming liable for registration, The effective date of registration shall be the date of grant of registration.

– **Suo moto (Voluntary) registration**: The effective date of registration shall be the date of order of registration.

Penalty for Non Registration: If a person liable to register, do not apply for registration, or not paying tax or making short payments (genuine errors) has to pay a penalty of 10% of the tax amount due, subject to a minimum of Rs.10,000.The penalty of 100% of the tax amount due will be charged, when the offender deliberately evades tax payment.

Auto Migration of Existing Tax Payers

All existing dealers registered with central or state tax authorities (e.g State VAT, Central Excise / Service Tax) and having a valid PAN will be auto-migrated and allotted with a provisional certificate of registration in Form GST REG-21. Within 6 months, such dealers should submit Form GST REG-20 in GST Portal with prescribed documents.

– **Final Registration**: If the information provided is complete and satisfactory, final registration certificate will be issued in Form GST REG-06.

– **Cancellation of Provisional Registration**: If the details submitted are not satisfactory, a show cause notice will be issued in Form GST REG-23, and there will be a hearing before cancelling the provisional registration. If the show cause hearing is not successful, or if the details are not provided within the stipulated period, the provisional registration allotted in Form GST REG-21 will be cancelled by issuing an order in Form GST REG-22.

During transition, if a taxable person is not required to register under GST, but was previously registered (Central and State law), he has an option to cancel the provisional registration issued by submitting the Form GST REG-24.

GST Registration Process

Registration of GST is mostly digital process and normally can be finished in 5 working days, provided the concerned officer find the application or documentation in order. PAN is mandatory for GST Registration (except in case of Non Resident)

Submission of Application

– **GST REG -01 (Part A):** Submit the following particulars

   o   Legal Name of the Business (As mentioned in PAN)

   o   PAN (PAN of business or PAN of Individual for Proprietorship business)

   o   E-mail address

   o   Mobile Number

   On successful verification of e-mail / mobile number on OTP, the application reference number would be generated and communicated to the applicant.

– **GST REG -01 (Part B):** Using the Application Reference number as received, submit the desired particulars, along with documents specified in the Form, at the common portal (directly or through a facilitation centre). On receipt of the Application, an acknowledgement shall be issued to the applicant in Form GST REG -02

Applicants for Casual Registration shall be given a temporary identification number by the common portal for making advance deposit of tax.

The following persons shall submit the application in other forms (in lieu of GST-REG-01).

– Non Resident Taxable person - GST-REG-09,

– Person required to deduct TDS u/s 51 or u/s 52- GST-REG-07,

– Person supplying online information and data base access or retrieval services from outsideIndia to a non taxable on line recipient - GST-REG-09A

There is no fee for GST registration.

Documents to be submitted alongwith Form GST REG -01

•   **Photograph of key persons as applicable:** (a) Proprietary Concern – Proprietor (b) Partnership Firm / LLP – Managing/Authorized/Designated Partners (personal details of all partners is to be submitted but photos of only ten partners including that of Managing Partner is to be submitted) (c) HUF – Karta (d) Company – Managing Director or the Authorised Person (e) Trust – Managing Trustee (f) Association of Person or Body of Individual –Members of Managing Committee (personal details of all members is to be submitted but photos of only ten members including that of Chairman is to be submitted) (g) Local Authority – CEO or his equivalent (h) Statutory Body – CEO or his equivalent (i) Others – Person in Charge

•   **Constitution of Taxpayer**: Partnership Deed in case of Partnership Firm, Registration Certificate/ Proof of Constitution in case of Society, Trust, Club, Government Department, Association of Person or Body of Individual, Local Authority, Statutory Body and Others etc.

- **Proof of Principal/Additional Place of Business:**

  o **For Own premises:** Any document in support of the ownership of the premises like Latest Property Tax Receipt or Municipal Khata copy or copy of Electricity Bill.

  o **For Rented or Leased premises:** A copy of the valid Rent / Lease Agreement with any document in support of ownership of the premises of the Lessor like Latest Property Tax Receipt or Municipal Khata copy or copy of Electricity Bill.

  o **Other premises not covered as above:** A copy of the Consent Letter with any document in support of the ownership of the premises of the Consenter like Municipal Khata copy or Electricity Bill copy. For shared properties also, similar documents may be uploaded.

- **Bank Account Related Proof**: Scanned copy of the first page of Bank passbook / one page of Bank Statement Opening page of the Bank Passbook held in the name of the Proprietor / Business Concern – containing the Account No., Name of the Account Holder, MICR and IFSC and Branch details.

- **Authorization Form**: For each Authorised Signatory mentioned in the application form, Authorization or copy of Resolution of the Managing Committee or Board of Directors to be filed.

Issue of Certificate

- **Approval of Application**: On receipt of Application, if the particulars and attached documents are found in order, the concerned officer would approve the Application with 3 working days. If deficiencies found, the officer will intimate the applicant in Form GST-REG-03, within 3 days. The Applicant would respond to the deficiencies, electronically in Form GST-04, within 7 working days.

- **Deemed Approval:** If the officer fails to take any action (a) Within three working days from the date of submission of application, or (b) Within seven working days from the date of receipt of clarification, information or documents furnished by the applicant, the application for grant of registration shall be deemed to have been approved.

- **Issue of Certificate**: On approval of the application, the officer would issue certificate of registration in Form REG-GST-06.

- **Rejection of Application**: If not satisfied with the response received from applicant in Form GST-REG-04, the officer would reject the application in Form GST-REG -05 within 7 working days.

Separate Registration for multiple business verticals within a state or in Union territory

Any person having multiple business verticals within a State, may opt for separate registration for any of its business verticals.

GSTIN: On registration, unique 15 letter GSTIN (GST Identification Number) is allotted. Having following structure

2 digit State Code, 10 Letter PAN, 1 letter entity serial number for the PAN, 1 letter alphabet (currently Z), 1 checksum digit

Composition Scheme

Small businesses having annual turnover less than '1.5 crore' can opt for Composition scheme. Composition dealers will pay nominal tax rates as follows:

Manufacturer: 2%, Trader of Goods – 1%, Supplier of Food & Drink for human consumption (other than alcoholic drinks) – 5%

- Composition dealers are required to file only one quarterly return (instead of three monthly returns filed by normal tax payers).
- Composition dealers cannot issue taxable invoices, i.e., collect tax from customers (i.e bear the tax themselves). They will prepare Bill of Supply.
- Composition dealers cannot claim any input tax credit.

However, Service providers, Inter-state sellers, E-commerce sellers, Supplier of non-taxable goods, Manufacturer of Notified Goods, cannot get registered under Composition Scheme,

Other important provisions regarding Registration

- **Signatory of the Application Form**: The application form shall be signed by – **1. Individual**: By himself or by other person authorized by him. **2. HUF:** Karta or by adult member of family duly authorized by Karta **3. Company:** CEO or authorized signatory thereof **4. Government, Government Agency, Local authority** - Officer authorized in this behalf. **5. Partnership firm:** Any Partner (not being minor) or Authorized signatory. **6. Trust:** Any Trustee (not being minor) or Authorized signatory. **7. Any other person:** By a person competent to act on his behalf, or by a person authorised u/s.48

- **Verification of business premises:** The proper officer may make physical verification of the place of business, if considered necessary. Such verification report along with other documents, including photographs, shall be uploaded in FORM GST REG-29 on the Common Portal within fifteen working days following the date of such verification.

- **Amendment to Registration:** Where there is any change in any of the particulars furnished in the application for registration, at the time of obtaining registration or afterwards, the registered taxable person shall, within fifteen days of such change, submit an application electronically, duly signed, in FORM GST REG-11, along with documents relating to such change..

  o **Change in key info**: In case of change relating to: **1.** Name of business, **2.** Principal Place of Business, **3.** Details of Partners or directors, Karta, Managing Committee, Board of Trustee, CEO, or person responsible for day to day affairs of business, The officer after proper verification, issue order in Form GST REG- 12 electronically.

  o **Change in other particulars:** In case of change relating to another than key info, the certificate of registration shall stand amended upon submission of the application in FORM GST REG-11 on the Common Portal.

  o **Change in constitution of firm or PAN**: In case the change in constitution of any business results in change of PAN, a fresh application for registration in to be submitted in FORM GST REG-01.

– **Suo Moto Registration:** Where, during the course of any survey, inspection, search, enquiry or any other proceedings, the proper officer finds a person liable to registration under the Act, has failed to apply for such registration, such officer may register the said person on a temporary basis and issue an order in FORM GST REG-13.

– **Cancellation of Registration:** A registered taxable person seeking cancellation of his registration shall electronically submit an application in FORM GST REG-14 including the details of closing stock and liability thereon andfurnishing, relevant documents. Cancellation of registration cannot be considered for the person who has taken voluntary registration.

Every taxable person, other than a person paying tax under Lump sum Scheme, seeking cancellation of registration under sub-rule (1) shall furnish a final return under GST REG-19**.**

– **Display of registration certificate and GSTIN:** Every registered taxable person shall display his certificate of registration in a prominent location at his principal place of business and at every additional place or places of business.

Exemption from GST Registration

Following persons are not required to register under GST

– **Agriculturists:** Person who supplies the products out of his cultivation land. Agro-inputs like fertilizers, seeds, irrigation (electricity), machinery and all other agricultural services are also exempted under GST.

– **Persons making Nil-Rated/ Exempt supplies of goods and services:** Persons engaged in supplying of exempted items (which are in the exemptions list of GST), like:

   o   Unprocessed food like rice, wheat, bread, milk, vegetables, cereals, eggs, meta fish, salt etc

   o   Train travel by local and sleeper classes

   o   Education

   o   Healthcare (but not medicines)

   o   Hotels, lodges with room rent less than Rs 1,000

   o   Kid's colouring /drawing books

   o   Bindis, sindoor, bangles, etc

– **Persons making Non-Taxable/ Non-GST supplies of goods and services**: Dealers of Items not coming under purview of GST, like:

   o   Petroleum Crude & petrol

   o   High Speed Diesel

   o   Natural Gas

   o   Electricity

   o   Alcohol for Human Consumption

   o   Aviation Turbine Fuel

- **Activities other than Supply of Goods or Services:**
    - o Services by an employee.
    - o Services by any Court or Tribunal.
    - o Functions and duties of:
        - – MPs, MLAs, Members of Panchayats, Municipalities and other local authorities;
        - – Person holding any Constitutional Post;
        - – Person as a Chairperson or a Member or a Director in a body.
    - o Funeral Services.
    - o Sale of land and building.
    - o Actionable claims (other than lottery, betting, and gambling).

- **Persons making only supplies covered under reverse charge:** The Central Government has, by Notification No. 5/2017 dt.19th June 2016 (effective from 22nd June 2016), exempted persons from obtaining registration who are only engaged in making supplies of taxable goods or services, the total tax on which is liable to be paid on reverse charge basis by the recipient of such goods or services.

Supply of Goods & Services

The taxable event under GST is *Supply* of goods and services. The term *Supply* includes all forms of supply, such as sale, transfer, barter, exchange, license, rental, lease or disposal made in the course of business, and importation of service. Transactions between principal and agents are deemed to be supplies. Even supply without any consideration will also amount to sale.

Supply also includes specified transactions such as permanent transfer of business assets, temporary application of business assets to a non-business use, services put to non-business use, assets retained after deregistration. Hire purchase transactions are considered as Supply.

Lottery tickets are goods and GST will be payable. GST will also be payable on services relating to betting and gambling.

Activities not considered as Supply

– Services by employee to employer in the course of or in relation to his employment;

– Services of funeral, burial, crematorium or mortuary including transportation of the deceased.

– Actionable claims, other than lottery, betting and gambling

– Sale of land / Sale of building after occupation or completion will not attract GST, but sale of building before completion or before occupancy will attract GST

– Activities or transactions undertaken by the Central Government, a State Government or any local authority in which they are engaged as public authorities, as may be notified by the Government on the recommendations of the Council.

– Supply of goods to a job worker would not be treated as supply.

– Sale of properties under construction, temporary transfer of intellectual property rights, works contracts (including transfer of property in goods involved in execution of works contracts), transfer of right to use any goods and development, upgradation, customisation etc., of software would be supply of service.

Illustrations of Supply

Type of Transaction	Nature of Supply
Any transfer of the title in goods (e.g Sale of Refrigerator)	Supply of Goods
Any transfer of goods without transfer of title (Renting of Refrigerator)	Supply of Services
Any transfer of title of goods where property in goods to pass at a future date upon payment of full consideration as agreed (Hire Purchase)	Supply of Goods
Any lease, easement, tenancy, and licence to occupy land	Supply of Services
Any lease or letting out of the building including a commercial, industrial or residential complex for business or commerce, wholly or partly	Supply of Services
Job work – Any treatment or process which is being applied to another person's goods	Supply of Services
Permanent transfer or disposal of business assets transferred with or without consideration	Supply of Goods
Business assets put to private use or non- business use whether or not for a consideration	Supply of Services
Renting of immovable property	Supply of Services
Development, design, programming, customisation, adaptation, up-gradation, enhancement, implementation of information technology software	Supply of Services
Works contract, including transfer of property in goods (whether as goods or in some other form) involved in the execution of a works contract of immovable property	Supply of Services

Deemed Supply of Goods & Services

Following activities will be considered as deemed supply of goods and services and will attract GST:

- **Transfer:** Any Transfer of title in goods, Right in goods, undivided share in goods without the transfer of title, transfer under an agreement which stipulates that property will pass at a future date upon payment of full consideration

- **Land & Building**: Any lease, tenancy, easement, license to occupy land or building (either for commercial or residential purpose, fully or partly)

- **Treatment or Process:** Any Treatment or Process applied to another person's goods

- **Transfer of Business Assets:**

  o Goods forming part of the assets of a business are transferred or disposed of, and are no longer forming part of business

  o Goods held for business are put to use for any private use, in such a way, as not for business

  o Any person ceases to be a taxable person, any goods earlier forming part of business, unless (a) the business is transferred as a going concern to another person, or (b) the business is carried on by a personal representative who is deemed to be a taxable person (with or without consideration)

– **Supply of Services** – Following shall be treated as deemed *Supply of Services*:

o renting of immovable property;

o construction of a complex, building, civil structure or a part thereof, including a complex or building intended for a sale to a buyer, wholly or partly, except where the entire consideration has been received after issuance of completion certificate;

o Temporary transfer or permitting the use or enjoyment of any intellectual property right;

– **Composite Supply** – Following shall be treated as deemed "supply of Services":

o Works contract as defined in section 2 (119) of CGST Act

o Supply, by way of or as part of any service or in any other manner whatsoever, of goods, being food or any other article for human consumption or any drink (other than alcoholic liquor for human consumption), where such supply or service is for cash, deferred payment or other valuable consideration.

– **Supply of goods**: Supply of goods by any unincorporated association or body of persons to a member thereof for cash, deferred payment or other valuable consideration.

o **Inward Supply or Purchases**: *"Inward Supply"* in relation to a person, shall mean receipt of goods and/or services whether by purchase, acquisition or any other means and whether or not for any consideration

o **Outward Supply or Sales:** *"Outward Supply"* in relation to a person, shall mean supply of goods and/or services, whether by sale, transfer, barter, exchange, license, rental, lease or disposal made or agreed to be made by such person in the course or furtherance of business

o **Continuous Supply:** Means a supply of services which is provided, or agreed to be provided, continuously or on recurrent basis, under a contract, for a period exceeding three months with periodic payment obligations and includes supply of such services as the Government may specify.

Supply of Goods & Services between Related Person

Supply of Goods or Services between related persons will be supply even if made without consideration, and is taxable under GST

– **Fringe Benefits to Employees & Directors:** Supply of Goods or Services between Employer & employee are considered as Taxable Supply, like benefits provided to employee (such as transport, meals, telephone).

– **Gifts to Employees:** Gifts of value more than Rs 50,000 per year to an employee would be subject to GST, when made without consideration, in the course or furtherance of business

– **Use of Goods by related Person**: Where Goods held or used for the purposes of the business, put to any private use or are used, or made available to any person for use, for any purpose other than a purpose of the business, whether or not for a consideration, the usage or making available of such goods is a supply of services. Supply by principal to agent is subject to GST. Commission agent has to pay GST only on his commission.

- **Transactions between group companies**: Activities like deputation of persons, supply of goods on loan basis, common facilities shared by group companies, transactions between branches, considered as Taxable supply.

- **Import of Services**: Import of services from related persons or from business establishment outside India is subject to GST even if there is no consideration. Branch / Head office in India receiving free services from Head Office / Outside India will be subject to GST.

Mixed Supply

Two or more individual supplies of goods or services, or any combination thereof, made in conjunction with each other by a taxable person for a single price where such supply does not constitute a composite supply.

Taxability: The tax liability on a mixed supply comprising two or more supplies shall be treated as supply of that particular supply which attracts the highest rate of tax .

Example: Supply of a Tour package of Travel (Transportation) and Accommodation (Hotel). Each of these items can be supplied separately and is not dependent on any other. It shall not be a mixed supply if these items are supplied separately.

Composite Supply & Principal Supply

- **Composite Supply:** Supply made by a taxable person to a recipient comprising two or more supplies of goods or services, or any combination thereof, which are naturally bundled and supplied in conjunction with each other in the ordinary course of trade, one of which is a principal supply

    Example: Where goods are packed and transported with insurance, the supply of goods, packing materials, transport and insurance is a composite supply (here supply of goods is the principal supply).

- **Principal Supply:** Supply of goods or services which constitutes the predominant element of a composite supply. Any other supply forming part is ancillary and does not constitute, for the recipient an Item in itself, but a provides means for better enjoyment of the principal supply.

Zero Rated Supply

Export of goods or services or both; or supply of goods or services or both to a Special Economic Zone developer or a Special Economic Zone unit (eligible for ITC).

Place of Supply

The place of supply of goods is the place where the goods are delivered, except in few cases. The place of supply of services to a registered person, is the location of such registered person. For services provided to an unregistered person, it is the address of recipient, and if it is not available, the location of the supplier of services.

[There are various exceptions provided to these principles, such as services pertaining to immovable property, training and appraisal, admission to events and organisation of events, transportation, telecom, financial services etc.]

Example:

–   **Intra-State Sale**: M of Mumbai (Maharashtra) supplies goods to N of Nagpur (Maharashtra). The place of supply is Nagpur (Maharashtra). Since the movement is in same state, CGST & SGST will be applicable.

–   **Inter State Sale**: M of Mumbai (Maharashtra) supplies goods to B of Bangalore (Karnataka). The place of supply is Bangalore (Karnataka). Since the movement is in different state, IGST will be applicable.

–   **Delivery to 3rdParty:** L in Lucknow (UP) buys goods from M of Mumbai (Maharashtra). The buyer (L of Lucknow - UP) requests the seller (M of Mumbai - Maharashtra) to send the goods to Nagpur (Maharashtra). In this case, movement would be considered as if buyer in Lucknow has received the goods. So, IGST will be charged.

–   **Receiver takes Delivery from seller**: B of Bangalore (Karnataka) arranges its own transport and takes delivery of goods from M of Mumbai (Maharashtra). The movement of goods terminates at Mumbai, Maharashtra, the place of supply would be Mumbai (Maharashtra). Since the movement is in same state, CGST & SGST will be applicable. It is immaterial whether the receiver further transports the goods or not.

–   **E-commerce**: M of Mumbai (Maharashtra) orders Amazon for a mobile set, which is supplied by A of Ahmedabad (Gujrat). Here the goods are received by M of Mumbai. So, place of supply would be Mumbai (Maharashtra) and IGST will be charged.

–   **Installation:** R of Ranchi (Jharkhand) asks K of Kolkata (WB), to install Boiler at their Ranchi plant. Although K of Kolkata (WB) has supplied goods (Boiler), but the goods are installed at site in Ranchi. So, the pace of supply would be Ranchi. Hence it is considered as Intra State supply and CGST+SGST would be charged. So, in case of installation by seller, place of supply would be place of installation, irrespective of the place of registration of seller.

–   **Goods sold in Transit:**

    o   A traveler in a flight from Mumbai to Delhi buys foods in the plane (the Airlines is registered both in Delhi & Maharashtra). Here the food items were loaded in Mumbai (Maharashtra). The place of supply is considered Mumbai (as the plane has not yet reached Delhi). So, it is considered as Intra State sale and CGST+ SGST would be charged.

    o   In a train starting from Chandigarh (to Kolkata WB), having loaded Food Items at Chandigarh, X boards in intermediate station in Patna (Bihar) and buys food in the train. Here the place of supply is considered as Chandigarh (as the train has not yet reached Kolkata), as the foods were loaded in Chandigarh. So, UTGST+CGST would be charged.

–   **Import:** The place of supply for Goods imported into India, by an organisation registered in India, would be the location of Importer. In such case, IGST would be applicable. M of Mumbai (registered in Maharashtra) imports goods from China. So, the place of supply is Mumbai, and so IGST would be applicable.

– **Export:** For exports from India, Place of supply would be the place of registration of the Indian Exporter. K of Kolkata exports Jute Bags to L of London (UK). The place of supply is Kolkata. There would be no GST, as exports are exempted from GST

The place of supply of services to a registered person, is the location of such registered person. For services provided to an unregistered person, it is the address of recipient, and if it is not available, the location of the supplier of services.

– ABC Caterers of Mumbai, Maharashtra, gives catering service to PQR of Ahmedabad. In this case, the place of supply is Ahmedabad, Gujrat. So, it is considered an Inter State supply (IGST applicable).

– ABC Event Management of Mumbai, Maharashtra, organises the Annual Event of PQR Limited of Bangalore, Karnataka, at Jaipur, Rajasthan. The place of supply is Jaipur, Rajasthan. So, it is considered an Inter State supply (IGST applicable).

– ABC Event Management of Mumbai, Maharashtra, organises the Annual Event of PQR Limited of Pune, Maharashtra, at Port Blair, Andaman & Nicobar Islands. The place of supply is Port Blair, Andaman & Nicobar Islands. So, it is considered Inter Union Territory supply (CGST+UTGST applicable).

Time of supply

– **Time of supply of goods:** It is the earliest of: (i) date of removal/ making available goods by the supplier; (ii) date of issue of invoice; (iii) date of receipt of payment by the supplier; or (iv) date on which the recipient shows the receipt of goods in his books of accounts.

– **Time of supply of services:** It is the earliest of: (i) date of issue of invoice or date of receipt of payment, if invoice is issued within prescribed period, (ii) date of completion of service or date of receipt of payment, if invoice not issued within the prescribed period, (iii) date on which recipient shows the receipt of services in his books of accounts, where (i) or (ii) above does not apply.

– **Time of supply under reverse charge:** It is the earliest of: (i) date of receipt of supply; (ii) date of payment; (iii) date of receipt of invoice; (iv) Thirty Days from Date of Invoice by the supplier of Goods (60 days in case of services).

If for some reason, time of supply could not be determined as per above rules, then date of entry in books of Receiver would be considered as Time of Supply.

Receipt of Advance Payments for Supply

Liability for payment of GST would arise at the *Time of Supply* of goods and service. As per definition of the term supply, Receipt of *Advance Payments for Supply* of goods and/or services would be considered as 'time of supply' and tax liability would arise on such advance receipt. Even though GST would be paid on advance payments, credit for the same would be available only on receipt of goods and services.

Value of supply

Transaction Value is the basis to compute the value of supply of goods/ services for levy of GST.

To determine transaction value, specific additions are prescribed to be made to the price charged. Such additions include value of goods/ services supplied free/ at concessional rates by the recipient to the supplier, subsidies linked to the supply, reimbursable expenditure, etc. In addition, royalties or license fees related to the supply of goods and/ or services are to be added to the value of taxable supplies.

The discounts, including the post-sale discounts known at the time of supply (and linked to specific invoices), are allowed as deduction from transaction value.

Composition Scheme

GST for Small Taxpayers

Composition Scheme is a simple and easy scheme under GST for taxpayers. Small taxpayers can get rid of tedious GST formalities and pay GST at a fixed rate of turnover.

Threshold Limit for Composition Scheme: Small Taxpayer, having turnover less than Rs. 1.5 crore (75 lakhs for NE States), (as per GST meeting dt 10 Nov 2017), may opt for Composition Scheme. For Traders, Turnover means supply of Taxable Supplies of Goods / Services. Composition Dealers need to pay GST at a fixed rate of turnover.

Persons not eligible for composition scheme

- Persons making Inter State supplies of goods or services
- Supplier of services other than restaurant related services
- Manufacturer of ice cream, pan masala, or tobacco
- Casual taxable person or a non-resident taxable person
- Businesses supplying goods through e-commerce operator
- Taxpayer supplying GST exempted supplies

Rules applicable for composition scheme

- No Input Tax Credit can be claimed by composition dealer
- The taxpayer cannot make inter-state supply, or transact between Branches / Agents / Principals situated in other States.
- Taxpayer has to pay tax at normal rates for transactions under Reverse Charge Mechanism
- Person having multiple segments of businesses (such as textile, electronic accessories, groceries, etc.) under same PAN, must collectively register all such businesses under the scheme
- The taxpayer must mention the words 'composition taxable person' on every notice or signboard
- Can issue Bill of Supply (not Taxable Invoice), mentioning 'composition taxable person, not eligible to collect tax on supplies' on supply bills. Cannot charge Tax in the Bill from customer (has to pay Tax on their own).
- The goods held in stock by the taxpayer on the date GST came into force should not have been purchased in the course of inter-state trade, imported, or received from a branch / agent situated outside the State

- The goods held in stock by the taxpayer should not have been purchased from an unregistered supplier (if purchased from an unregistered supplier, the taxpayer must then have paid GST on the purchase on reverse charge basis).

- On the inward supply of goods or services or both, taxpayer should have paid tax under reverse charge basis

- The taxpayer should not have been engaged in the manufacture of goods notified u/s 10(2)(e), during the preceding financial year.

Transition from Composition scheme from old regime to GST regime

Taxpayers registered under composition scheme under VAT will be allowed to take credit of input in stock, or in semi-finished goods or in finished goods held on the day before the day of opting out of composition scheme, on fulfilling following conditions

- Inputs or goods will be used for making taxable supplies.

- The CENVAT Credit was eligible to be claimed in the previous regime, however, couldn't claim it being under composition scheme.

- ITC is eligible for availing under GST regime.

- The taxpayer has bills of input tax paid on such goods.

- Invoices should not be older than 1 year from 1st July 2017 (i.e. not dated before 1st July 2016)

A Composition Dealer may switch between the Composition Scheme and the normal scheme based on turnover. The rules of Invoicing & returns would be applicable as per as per scheme in force at time

GST Rates for Composition Dealer on sale: Manufacturers – 2%. Traders (Goods) - 1%, Supplier of Drinks (without alcohol) for human consumption – 5%. (50% of the Tax is charged under CGST and 50% under SGST / UTGST). Service Providers cannot opt for Composition Scheme.

Registration Process under Composition Scheme

- **Person already registered under current tax regime:** A person who is registered under the current regime and applying for the Registration under GST will be given Provisional Certificate first. To opt for composition scheme, shall file on-line FORM GST CMP-01 / GST CMP-02, through GST Portal.

  o   He should submit details of stock, held by him before he opting for composition scheme in on-line FORM GST CMP-03 within 60 days.

  o   He shall not collect any tax from the appointed day but shall issue bill of supply for supplies made after the said day.

- **Person applying for fresh registration:** Person applying for the fresh Registration under GST should file FORM REG-01 and under Part B of the form, select the option for Composition scheme. To opt for Composition Scheme for a financial year or during the middle of a financial year, he has to inform the government about their choice, by filing GST CMP-02. If CMP-02 is filed in the middle of the financial year, the rules of the scheme are applicable from the month immediately succeeding the month in which CMP-02 is file (e.g If CMP-02 is filed on Nov, composition scheme would be applicable from Dec). Both CMP-01 and CMP-02 are to be filed online on the GST Portal

Returns to be filed: Quarterly return GSTR-4 by 18th of the month following the Quarter end, and annual return GSTR-9A has to be filed by 31st December of next financial year.

A composition dealer need not maintain detailed records under GST rules.

De-registration Process: A Composition Dealer may opt out of Composition Scheme, in following cases, by filing GST CMP-04 on-line in GST portal.

– Wants to opt out of Composition Scheme voluntarily

– Turnover exceeds limits

– Fails to fulfill any of the conditions for availing the scheme.

When a dealer opts out of composition scheme all the normal rules are applicable from the day of opting out. For example, a composition dealer opting out of composition scheme on 15th October 2017, has to file two GSTR-4 for the quarters July – September 2017, and October (15 days), and also file GSTR-1, GSTR-2, and GSTR-3 for the period of 15th to 31st October 2017

Rules for filing GST CMP-04.

– GST CMP-04 has to be filed within 7 days from the date on which the taxpayer plan to opt out of Composition Scheme or is ineligible to be covered in the scheme**.**

– A dealer has to opt out the day on which they fail to fulfill all the conditions to be complied by a Composition Dealer. For example, Composition Dealer's turnover exceeds the Rs 1.5 crore on 15th December 2017. The dealer will have to file CMP-04 by 22nd December 2017.

– CMP-04 has to be filed on the GST Portal

Reverse Charge Liability

A Composition Dealer has to pay tax under Reverse Charge Mechanism wherever applicable, as per applicable rate at which GST has to be paid (not at the rate under composition scheme). No ITC is available for tax paid under reverse charge for a composition dealer.

Tax on Purchase from Unregistered Dealer: Tax at normal rates has to be paid on purchases from an unregistered dealer only for the months of July and August 2017. From September 2017, there is no need to pay tax on purchases from Unregistered Dealer.

Computation of Tax

A composition dealer is required to pay tax at a specific rate on total sales. Also, the dealer has to pay tax under reverse charge on specified purchases, purchase form unregistered dealer and import of services.

So, composition dealer would pay GST (as applicable) on:

– Tax on supplies (net of advance and goods returned)

– Tax on B2B transactions where Reverse Charge is applicable

– Tax on B2B purchases from Unregistered suppliers (July and August 2017 only, not from Sep 17 onwards)

−　Tax on Import of Services

The Rate of Tax on transactions under Reverse Charge, purchased from an unregistered dealer and import of services will be at GST normal rates, i.e. the rates applicable to the supplies. Rates under Composition Scheme are applicable only to Sales of a composition dealer.

Advantage of Composition Scheme

−　Lesser compliance (returns, maintaining books of record, issuance of invoices)

−　Lower Tax Rate

Disadvantage of Composition Scheme

−　Limited territory of business, as the dealer cannot undertake inter-state transactions

−　No Input Tax Credit available to composition dealers

−　The taxpayer will not be eligible to supply exempt goods or goods through an e-commerce portal.

Composition scheme is favoured by small dealers doing local business only, not dealing with GST exempt goods.

e-Commerce

E-commerce (electronic commerce) means the commercial transaction of buying and selling of goods and services, or transmitting of funds or data, over an electronic network, primarily the internet. These business transactions occur either as business-to-business, business-to-consumer, consumer-to-consumer or consumer-to-business. The terms e-commerce and e-business are often used interchangeably.

Special features of e-commerce:

– Enables third-party sellers to sell online on the e-commerce platform.

– E-commerce operator charges subscription fees/ commission on transaction value.

– Third-party sellers gain access to a larger customer base

– Customer gain access to multiple sellers and competitive prices

– Merchandise are shipped by Merchant/Third-party seller directly or through the fulfillment center

Considering the continuous increase in e-commerce, GST has specifically come out with rules & regulations specific to this segment.

e-commerce operators

GST Law defines Electronic Commerce Operator (Operator) as every person who, directly or indirectly, owns, operates or manages an electronic platform which is engaged in facilitating the supply of any goods and/or services. A person providing any information or any other services incidental to or in connection with such supply of goods and services through electronic platform would also be considered as an Operator.

A person supplying goods/services on his own account, however, would not be considered as an Operator. For instance, Amazon and Flipkart are e-commerce Operators because they are facilitating actual suppliers to supply goods through their platform (popularly called Market place model or Fulfilment Model). However, Titan supplying watches and jewels through its own website would not be considered as an e-commerce operator for the purposes of GST.

Aggregator

Aggregator is a person, who owns and manages an electronic platform, and by means of the application and communication device, enables a potential customer to connect with the persons providing service of a particular kind under the brand name or trade name of the said aggregator (e.g Ola cabs). Aggregators are liable to be registered irrespective of the value of supply made by them.

GST Rules applicable to e-commerce operators

– **Registration:** e-commerce operators having total sales 20 lakhs or above must register under GST. They cannot avail Composition Scheme.

– **Tax to be paid by e-commerce operator on notified services:** Certain service categories may be notified, on supply of which, tax shall be paid by the e-commerce operator, and not the supplier. If the e-commerce operator does not have an establishment in a state, any person representing the e-commerce operator for any purpose in the state will be liable to pay the tax (if it does not have a representative in the state, a person must be appointed in the state for the purpose of paying tax, who shall be liable to pay the tax.

– **Returns and tax payment process:** An e-commerce operator has to furnish Form GSTR-8 containing details of *outward supplies* made through the platform in the previous month, including supplies returned by 10th of the month. Form GSTR-8 should contain invoice-wise details of supplies to registered taxable persons and aggregate value of supplies to unregistered persons. The e-commerce operator also has to pay the tax collected from suppliers.

Any discrepancy between supplies reported by the e-commerce operator and suppliers on the platform must be submitted in Form GST ITC-1. The discrepancy must be rectified in the return for the month in which it is communicated

Suppliers on e-commerce platforms: Suppliers on e-commerce platforms are persons who supply goods or services on an e-commerce platform.

– **Mandatory registration:** All suppliers on e- commerce platforms are mandatorily required to register under GST, Hence, even e-commerce suppliers whose aggregate turnover does not exceed the threshold limit for registration will have to compulsorily register.

– **Non-eligibility for Composition Scheme:** A person who supplies goods or services through an e-commerce operator will not be eligible for registration under composition Scheme. Hence, even if the person's aggregate turnover does not cross the threshold limit, such person does not have the option to become a composition tax payer

– **Returns process:** A supplier on an e-commerce platform, must follow the GST return process as applicable to regular dealer. In addition, following are the details to be provided with respect to supplies through e-commerce platforms:

o Form GSTR-1 containing details of *outward supplies* made through e-commerce platforms, by 10th of the month, containing invoice-wise details of supplies to registered taxable persons and aggregate value of supplies to unregistered persons made through the e-commerce platform, during the previous month.

o Form GSTR-2A showing the figures of aggregate amount of tax collected by e-commerce operators in the previous month will be auto populated, based on Form GSTR-8 filed by the e-commerce operators, by 11th of the month.

o The supplier has to furnish Form GSTR-2, by 15th of a month, in which the details of tax collected by the e-commerce operator can be accepted or modified. The tax collected will be credited to the supplier's electronic cash ledger on provisional basis, which can be set-off against the tax liability.

o   By 20th of the month, the return must be filed clearing all the tax liabilities

Form GST ITC-1 is made available to a supplier by 21st of a month. Any discrepancy in supplies furnished with supplies reported by the e-commerce operator will be shown. The discrepancy must be rectified in the return for the month in which it is communicated. If not rectified and the value of supplies furnished by the operator is more than the value furnished by the supplier, the differential amount along with interest will be added to the tax liability of the supplier for the succeeding month.

Special Exemption by notification: e-commerce sellers need not register if total sales is less than Rs. 20 lakh (Notification dated 15.11.2017)

Tax at Source (TCS) collected by E-commerce operator

–   **Registration for TCS**: Any person required to collect tax at source, shall electronically submit an application, duly signed or verified through electronic verification code, in *FORM GST REG-07* for the grant of registration through the common portal, either directly or through a Facilitation Centre notified by the Commissioner.

–   **TCS Rate**: Every e-commerce operator should collect TCS @ 2% on the net value of taxable supplies made through their platform, where the consideration, with respect to such supplies, has to be collected by the operator, and deposited to the government.

–   Net value of taxable supplies = Value of taxable supplies made by all registered taxable persons through the operator, other than notified supplies on which tax is paid by the operator -(Value of taxable supplies returned to the suppliers)

–   **Statement:** Every e-commerce operator is required to furnish a statement, electronically, of all amounts collected as TCS towards outward supplies of goods and/or services effected through it, during a calendar month within ten days after the end of such calendar month. The statement shall contain, inter alia, the details of the amount collected on behalf of each supplier in respect of all supplies of goods and/ or services effected through the operator and the details of such supplies during the said calendar month.

–   **Credit to Original Supplier**: Such TCS which is deposited by the operator into government account will be reflected in the cash ledger of the actual registered supplier (on whose account such collection has been made) on the basis of the statement filed by the operator. The TCS can be used at the time of discharge of tax liability in respect of the supplies by the actual supplier.

Note: As per the notification dated 26th June 2017, the provisions of TCS has been put on hold and it will come into force from a date to be communicated later.

Tax Invoice

Invoice

Under GST, Invoice means a document issued in respect of transaction of goods or service. Normally, Invoice is issued by supplier, but in some cases, receiver of supply may need to issue self-invoice.

Supply

Under GST, *Supply* means a transfer, exchange, rental, lease, barter, disposal or license of goods or services.

– A providing supply of goods or services has to issue Tax Invoice on supply of Goods or Services.

– A person registered receiving supply of goods or services from an unregistered person also needs to issue Tax invoice

Types of Invoice

– **Tax Invoice**: All registered persons, other than supplier of exempted goods, exempted service and composite dealer, shall issue *Tax Invoice*.

– **Bill of Supply**: A registered person supplying exempted goods or services or both or paying tax under composition scheme shall issue a *Bill of Supply*, instead of a Tax Invoice,.

– **Receipt voucher**: A registered person, on receiving advance payment with respect to any supply of goods or services , shall issue a *Receipt Voucher*.

– **Refund Voucher**: A registered person, having issued a receipt voucher in respect of advance payment received in relation to any supply of goods or services, on making refund of the advance money (as subsequently no supply is made and no tax invoice is issued), would issue a *Refund Voucher* against such payment refunded.

– **Payment voucher**: A registered person liable to pay tax under reverse charge, shall issue a *Payment Voucher* at the time of making payment to the supplier.

– **Credit Note**: Where in the tax invoice issued for a supply, the value or tax charged is more than what is actually payable/chargeable, or where the recipient of goods has returned the goods (or recipient of services has found the services deficient), the supplier should issue a credit note to the recipient.

– **Debit Note**: Where in the tax invoice issued for a supply, the value or tax charged is less than what is actually payable/chargeable, the supplier can issue a Debit Note (also known as *Supplementary Invoice*) to the recipient

– **Revised Invoice**: A dealer may revise Invoice issued before GST registration, and issue a *Revised Invoice* under GST, within one month of date of Registration.

Tax invoice: A registered person making a supply should issue *Tax Invoice*

- **Supply of Goods**: In the case of Supply of goods, the invoices shall be raised within the prescribed time as enumerated below.

  – **Actual movement of goods**: When there is actual movement of goods, then before or at the time of removal of such goods.

  – **No movement involved**: Earlier of delivery or making available of such goods.

  – **Successive issuance of goods**: Earlier of each such issuance.

  – **Receipt of goods on reverse charge**: When GST is applicable on reverse charge basis

  – **Sale on approval basis**: Before or at the time of supply or six months from the date of removal, whichever is earlier

- **Supply of Services**: In the case of supply of services, the invoice has to be issued within specified time, as follows:

  – **Actual Supply**: Within 30 days from the actual supply

  – **Continuous supply**: 30 days from due date (where due date can be ascertained), or 30 days from actual payment date (where due date can not be ascertained),

  – **Cessation of supply**: In case of cessation of supply before the contract ends, at the time of such cessation.

  In case of banks and other financial institutions, the due date would be 45 days (instead of 30 days).

Bill of Supply: A Composition Dealer or a person dealing with exempted goods only, or a Composition Dealer, should issue Bill of supply (in lieu of invoice)

Number of Copies of Invoices to be issued

– **Supply of goods**: Invoices to be issued in TRIPLICATE (original for the recipient, duplicate for transporter, triplicate copy for supplier).

– **Supply of services**: Invoices have to be issued in DUPLICATE (original for the recipient, duplicate for supplier).

Contents of Tax Invoice for supply of Goods

A model Invoice Format is suggested by GST. However, Invoice may be issued in slightly different format, provided all the essential applicable information as given in the model Invoice Format, as specified below, are available in proper and complete manner.

– Name, address and GSTIN of the supplier

– A consecutive serial number, in one or multiple series, containing alphabets or numerals or special characters like hyphen or dash and slash symbolised as "-" and "/" respectively, and any combination thereof, unique for a financial year, upto 16 characters

– Date of its issue

- Name, address and GSTIN or UIN, if registered, of the recipient [Name and address of the recipient and the address of delivery, along with the name of State and its code, if such recipient is un-registered and taxable supply is fifty thousand rupees or more]

- HSN code of Goods /Accounting Code of Services

- Description of goods or services

- Quantity in case of goods and unit or Unique Quantity Code there of

- Total value of supply of goods or services or both

- Taxable value of supply of goods or services or both, taking into account the discount or abatement, if any

- Rate of tax (Central tax, State tax, Integrated tax, union territory tax or cess)

- Amount of tax charged in respect of taxable goods or services (Central tax, State tax, Integrated tax, union territory tax or cess)

- Place of supply along with the name of State (in case of inter-State supply)

- Address of delivery where different from the place of supply

- Whether the tax is payable on reverse charge basis

- Signature or digital signature of the supplier or his authorized representative

Tax Invoice for supply of Services

A registered person supplying taxable services shall, before or within 30 days of providing service, issue a tax invoice, showing the description, value, tax charged thereon and such other particulars as prescribed in the Invoice Rules.

The Government may specify the categories of services in respect of which: (a) Any other document issued in relation to the supply shall be deemed to be a tax invoice; or (b) Tax invoice may not be issued.

Contents of Bill of Supply

A bill of supply shall be issued by the supplier containing the following details:

- Name, address and GSTIN of the supplier

- A consecutive serial number, in one or multiple series, containing alphabets or numerals or special characters like hyphen or dash (""-") and ("/"), and any combination there of, unique for a financial year, upto 16 characters

- Date of its issue

- Name, address and GSTIN or UIN, if registered, of the recipient

- HSN Code of goods or Accounting Code for Services (for organisation with turnover above 1.5 crores)

- Description of goods or services or both

- Value of supply of goods or services or both taking into account discount or abatement, if any

– Signature or digital signature of the supplier or his authorized representative

Advance Payment

Whenever a registered person receives payment in advance, with respect to any supply of goods or services or both, he has to issue a receipt voucher or any other document, evidencing the receipt of such payment, containing following particulars:

Receipt Voucher: A receipt voucher needs to contain the following particulars:

(a) Name, address and GSTIN of the supplier

(b) Unique Consecutive serial number

(c) Date of its issue

(d) Name, address and GSTIN or UIN, if registered, of the recipient

(e) Description of goods or services

(f) Amount of advance taken

(g) Rate of tax (Central tax, State tax, Integrated tax, Union territory tax or cess). If Rate of tax is not determinable, the tax may be paid@18%;

(h) Amount of tax charged in respect of taxable goods or services (Central tax, State tax, Integrated tax, union territory tax or cess);

(i) Place of supply along with the name of State and its code, in case of a supply in the course of inter-State trade or commerce. If nature of supply is not determinable, it shall be treated as inter-State supply.

(j) Whether the tax is payable on reverse charge basis

(k) Signature or digital signature of the supplier or his authorized representative

Refund Voucher: Where any such receipt voucher is issued, but subsequently no supply is made and no tax invoice is issued, the registered person who has received the advance payment can issue a refund voucher against such payment.

Supply under reverse charge

A registered person liable to pay tax under reverse charge (both for supplies on which the tax is payable under reverse charge mechanism and supplies received from unregistered persons) has to issue an invoice in respect of goods or service received (he is also to issue a payment voucher at the time of making payment to the supplier).

Sale on Approval basis

Where the goods being sent or taken on approval for sale or return, are removed before the supply takes place, the invoice shall be issued before or at the time of supply or six months from the date of removal, whichever is earlier.

Export Invoice

In case of export of goods or services, invoice shall carry an endorsement "SUPPLY MEANT FOR EXPORT ON PAYMENT OF IGST" or "SUPPLY MEANT FOR EXPORT UNDER BOND OR LETTER OF UNDERTAKING

WITHOUT PAYMENT OF IGST" and shall contain the following details:

- name and address of the recipient
- address of delivery
- name of the country of destination
- number and date of application for removal of goods for export

Credit Notes

Where in the tax invoice issued for a supply, the value or tax charged is more than what is actually payable/chargeable, or where the recipient of goods has returned the goods (or recipient of services has found the services deficient), the supplier can issue a credit note to the recipient.

A registered person has to declare details of such credit note in the return for the month during which such credit note has been issued, within September following the end of the financial year in which such supply was made, or within filing relevant annual return, whichever is earlier.

The tax liability of the registered person will be adjusted in accordance with the credit note issued, if the incidence of tax and interest on such supply has not been passed on to any other person.

Debit Notes

Where in the tax invoice issued for a supply, the value or tax charged is less than what is actually payable/chargeable, the supplier can issue a Debit Note (also known as supplementary Invoice) to the recipient.

A registered person has to declare details of such debit note in the return for the month during which such debit note has been issued, and tax liability shall be adjusted in prescribed manner

Revision of Invoice: A dealer may revise Invoice issued before GST registration, and issue a revised invoice, within one month of date of Registration.

Contents of credit or debit note / revised invoice

- The word "Revised Invoice", wherever applicable, indicated prominently
- Name, address and GSTIN of the supplier
- Nature of the document
- A consecutive unique serial number
- Date of issue of the document
- Name, address and GSTIN or UIN, if registered, of the recipient [Name and address of the recipient and the address of delivery, along with the name of State and its code, if such recipient is un-registered]
- Serial number and date of the corresponding tax invoice (or bill of supply)
- Value of taxable supply of goods or services, rate of tax and the amount of the tax
- Signature or digital signature of the supplier or his authorized representative.

Invoice in Special Cases

*   **ISD**: An ISD should issue invoice / credit note containing the following details:

    o   Name, address and GSTIN of the Input Service Distributor

    o   Invoice serial number

    o   Date of its issue

    o   Name, address and GSTIN of the recipient to whom the credit is distributed

    o   Amount of the credit distributed

    o   Signature or digital signature of the Input Service Distributor or his authorized representative

*   **ISD of Banking /Insurance Company**: ISD of a banking company or a financial institution, including a non-banking financial company, a tax invoice shall include any document in lieu thereof, by whatever name called, whether or not serially numbered but containing the prescribed information.

    Where the supplier of taxable service is an insurer or a banking company or a financial institution, including a nonbanking financial company, the said supplier shall issue a tax invoice or any other document in lieu thereof, by whatever name called, whether or not serially numbered, and whether or not containing the address of the recipient of taxable service but containing other information as prescribed

*   **Goods Transport Agency**: Goods Transport Agency shall issue a tax invoice or any other document in lieu thereof, by whatever name called, containing the gross weight of the consignment, name of the consignor and the consignee, registration number of goods carriage in which the goods are transported, details of goods transported, details of place of origin and destination, GSTIN of the person liable for paying tax whether as consignor, consignee or goods transport agency, and also containing other information as prescribed.

*   **Passenger Transporter:** Where the supplier of taxable service is supplying passenger transportation service, a tax invoice shall include ticket in any form, by whatever name called, whether or not serially numbered, and whether or not containing the address of the recipient of service but containing other prescribed information

Delivery Challan

In following cases, Delivery Challan may be issued in lieu of invoice, at the time of removal of goods:

–   Supply of liquid gas, where the quantity is not known, at the time of removal

–   Transportation of goods for job work

–   Transportation of goods for reasons other than by way of supply

–   Such other supplies as may be notified by the Board

Contents of Delivery Challan: Delivery Challan should contain Date, Serial Number, Name, address and GSTIN of the consigner, Name, address and GSTIN or UIN of the consignee (if registered), HSN code and description of goods, Quantity (provisional, where the exact quantity being supplied is not known), Taxable value, Tax Rate and Tax Amount (Central tax, State tax, Integrated tax, Union territory tax or cess, as applicable) where the transportation is for supply to the consignee, Place of supply in case of inter-State movement, Signature

Copies of Delivery Challan: In case of supply of goods, the delivery challan shall be prepared in Triplicate: Original copy marked as ORIGINAL FOR CONSIGNEE, The duplicate copy marked as DUPLICATE FOR TRANSPORTER, Triplicate copy marked as TRIPLICATE FOR CONSIGNER.

Way Bill: Where goods (valued Rs 50000 or more) are being transported, WAYBILL FORM should be issued, in prescribed manner.

Issuing Tax Invoice: Where the goods being transported are for the purpose of supply, but the tax invoice could not be issued at the time of removal, the supplier shall issue a tax invoice after the delivery of goods.

Goods transported in knocked down condition

Where the goods are being transported in *knocked down condition* (semi knocked down or completely knocked down):

– The supplier shall issue the complete invoice before dispatch of the first consignment

– The supplier shall issue a delivery challan for each of the subsequent consignments, giving reference of the invoice

– Each consignment shall be accompanied by copies of the corresponding delivery challan along with a duly certified copy of the invoice

– The original copy of the invoice shall be sent along with the last consignment

Input Tax Credit

Inputs for a Business

Inputs (Goods or Services) used or intended to be used in the course or furtherance of business, classified as:

- **Input Goods:** Any goods (other than capital goods) used or intended to be used in the course or furtherance of business.

- **Input Services:** Services used or intended to be used in the course or furtherance of business.

- **Capital Goods:** Goods which have been capitalized in the books of account of the person claiming the credit., and are used or intended to be used in the course or furtherance of business.

Input Tax Credit: Input Tax Credit means, adjustment (reduction) of tax you already paid on inputs, from the tax liability payable on output.

Rules relating to ITC

- No interest is paid on input tax balance by the government

- Input tax credit cannot be taken on purchase invoices more than one year old, from the date of the tax invoice.

- Input credit can be availed on both goods and services (except those which are on the exempted / negative list).

- Input tax is not allowed for goods and services for personal use.

- No input tax credit shall be allowed after GST return has been filed for September following the end of the financial year to which such invoice pertains or filing of relevant annual return, whichever is earlier

- The Buyer should pay the supplier, the value of the goods or services along with the tax within 180 days from the date of issue of invoice, failing which the amount of credit availed by the recipient would be added to his output tax liability, with interest. However, once the amount is paid, the recipient will be entitled to avail the credit again. In case part payment has been made, proportionate credit would be allowed.

- The credits claimed need to be matched with the tax liability of the supplier. In case of any discrepancies, the amount of excess credit claimed will be added in the tax liability of the recipient. The time limit for claim of credit is one year from the date of the invoice.

Input Tax credit on stock held: Input Tax credit held in your closing stock may be availed if:

- The closing stock is held in the form of raw materials, semi-finished goods, or finished goods, and must be used or intended to be used for taxable supplies,

- The date of invoices or any other prescribed duty / tax paying documents is within 12 months from the date of transitioning,

- The supplier of services is not eligible for any abatement under the act, the benefit of such credit must be passed on, by way of reduced prices, to the recipient.

Set off of ITC

Input Tax Credit would be set off against the respective liabilities for Tax Payable, for each Tax element, as follows:

- CGST would be first utilized towards the payment of output CGST, and then towards the payment of output IGST.

- SGST shall be first utilized towards the payment of output SGST, and then towards the payment of output IGST.

- IGST shall be first utilized towards payment of IGST; then towards the payment of output CGST; and then towards the payment of output SGST

However, CGST credit will not be allowed to be set-off against SGST and vice versa.

Unclaimed Tax Credit (when Input Tax paid is more than Output Tax Liability), would be carried forward to next period for subsequent period set off.

Items on which ITC not allowed (Ineligible ITC)

- Motor vehicles and conveyances except the below cases

- Such motor vehicles and conveyances are further supplied i.e. sold

- Transport of passengers

- used for imparting training on driving, flying, navigating such vehicle or conveyances

- Transportation of goods

- Food and beverages, outdoor catering, beauty treatment, health services, cosmetic and plastic surgery

  (Note: If the goods and/or services are taken to deliver the same category of services or as a part of a composite supply, credit will be available

  Example: D purchases cosmetic creams to supply it to a customer, then credit of ITC paid on purchases will be allowed.

- Sale of membership in a club, health, fitness centre.

- Rent-a-cab, Health Insurance and Life Insurance, except the following:

  o   Government makes it obligatory for employers to provide it to its employees

  o   goods and/or services are taken to deliver the same category of services or as a part of a composite supply, credit will be available

    Example: Dev takes the service of rent-a-cab to supply to his customer Mr, then credit of ITC paid on purchases will be allowed.

- Travel benefits extended to employees on vacation such as leave or home travel concession.

- Works contract service for construction of an immovable property (except plant & machinery or for providing further supply of works contract service)

- Goods and/or services for construction of an immovable property (whether for personal or business use

- Goods and/or services where tax have been paid under composition scheme

- Goods and/or services used for personal use

- Goods or services received by non-resident taxable person, except for goods imported by him.

- Goods lost, stolen, destroyed, written off or disposed of by way of gift or free samples

- ITC will not be available in the case of any tax paid due to non payment or short tax payment, excessive refund or ITC utilized or availed by the reason of fraud or willful misstatements or suppression of facts or confiscation and seizure of goods.

- ITC cannot be claimed beyond September of the following FY to which invoice pertains or date of filing of annual return, whichever is earlier

Special circumstances under which ITC is available

- A person who has applied for registration within 30 days of becoming liable for registration is entitled to ITC of input tax in respect of goods held in stock (inputs as such and inputs contained in semi-finished or finished goods) on the day immediately preceding the date from which he becomes liable to pay tax.

- A person who has taken voluntary registration, is entitled to ITC of input tax in respect of goods held in stock (inputs as such and inputs contained in semi-finished or finished goods) on the day, immediately preceding the date of registration.

- A person switching over to normal scheme from composition scheme is entitled to ITC in respect of goods held in stock (inputs as such and inputs contained in semi-finished or finished goods) and capital goods on the day immediately preceding the date from which he becomes liable to pay tax as normal taxpayer.

- Where an exempt supply of goods or services or both become taxable, the person making such supplies shall be entitled to take ITC in respect of goods held in stock relatable to exempt supplies. He shall also be entitled to take credit on capital goods used exclusively for such exempt supply, subject to reductions for the earlier usage as prescribed in the rules.

- In case of change of constitution of a registered person on account of sale, merger, demerger etc, the unutilised ITC shall be allowed to be transferred to the transferee.

- A person switching over from composition scheme to normal scheme or where a taxable supply become exempt, the ITC availed in respect of goods held in stock, as well as capital goods will have to be paid.

- In case of supply of capital goods or plant and machinery, on which ITC is taken, an amount equivalent to ITC availed minus the reduction as prescribed in rules (5% for every quarter or part thereof) shall have to be paid. In case the tax on transaction value of the supply is more, the same would have to be paid.

ITC Claim Procedure: Aregistered taxable person can claim ITC, in the following process

- The goods and services received is used for business purposes.

- Input Tax Credit can be claimed on exports/zero rated supplies and are taxable.

- If the constitution of the taxpayer changes due to merger, sale or transfer of business, then the Input Tax Credit which is unused shall be transferred to the merged, sold or transferred business.

- All Supporting documents like debit note, tax invoice, supplementary invoice, must be available

- Input Tax Credit can be claimed on actual receipt of goods and services,

- All related GST returns u/s 27 such as GST-1, 2, 2A, 6, 6A, 7, 7A must be filed

- During bulk receipt of goods (multiple receipt of one purchase), Input Tax Credit can be claimed after the final lot is received.

ITC Claims process

- Supplier uploads all his tax invoices details as issued in GSTR-1.

- The details uploaded by Supplier is automatically populated or reflected in GSTR-2A, when the buyer files the GSTR-2 returns of his (buyer) purchase.

- The details of the sale are then accepted and acknowledged for by Buyer, and subsequently, the purchase tax is credited to Buyer's 'Electronic Credit '

- The Buyer would use ITC against his Tax Liability

Documents needed to claim ITC

- Invoice issued by a supplier of goods or services or both

- Invoice issued by recipient along with proof of payment of tax

- A debit note issued by supplier

- Bill of entry or similar document prescribed under Customs Act

- Revised invoice

- Document issued by Input Service Distributor

The above documents prepared as per the GST invoice rules should be furnished while filing the GSTR-2 form. ITC claim would be rejected in case of fraud, suppression of facts or wilful misstatement.

Input Tax Credit on Import

For Imports, Input Tax Credit of IGST& GST Compensation Cess is allowable, on declaring GSTIN on Bill of Entry. However, ITC on Basic Customs Duty is not available.

Reverse Charge Mechanism

Reverse Charge

Normally, the supplier of goods or services pays the tax on supply (normally referred as *Forward Charge*). In certain cases, called as *Reverse Charge*, the receiver becomes liable to pay the tax, i.e., the chargeability gets reversed. So, under Reverse Charge mechanism, the recipient of the goods / services (or a third party like e-commerce operator) is liable to pay GST instead of the supplier. Reverse Charge is not applicable for supply of exempted goods / services

A Taxable person liable to pay tax under the reverse charge mechanism, must take mandatory registration under GST, irrespective of turnover (no threshold limit applicable).

The recipient (i.e., who pays reverse tax) can avail the tax paid as input tax credit, if the goods / services purchased are used for business.

Self-invoicing: In case purchase of goods / services by registered person, from unregistered supplier, as the unregistered supplier cannot issue a GST-compliant invoice, the registered buyer would create a self-invoice

GST provides 2 kinds of Reverse Charges:
– **Specified nature of supply and/or nature of supplier**: This is specified u/s 9 (3) of the CGST/ SGST (UTGST) & u/s 5 (3) of the IGST Act.

– **Supplies by Unregistered person to a registered person**: This is covered u/s 9 (4) of CGST Act and u/s 5 (4) of IGST Act, where taxable supplies is made by any unregistered person to a registered person

As per Notification dt 29.6.18, RCM u/s 9(4) in respect of purchases from unregistered dealer has been deferred till 30th September 2018.

Cases where Reverse Charge is applicable
• **Supply from Unregistered Dealer to Registered Dealer:** If a vendor, not registered under GST, supplies goods to registered person Reverse Charge would apply. The GST will have to be paid directly by the registered receiver instead of the supplier.

  The registered dealer who has to pay GST under reverse charge has to do self-invoicing for the purchases made from unregistered dealer.

  However, supplies of goods / services by a registered person from any or all the unregistered suppliers less than five thousand rupees in a day are exempted.

• **Services through an e-commerce operator:** If an e-commerce operator supplies services, then reverse charge will be applicable to the e-commerce operator (not the supplier of service). So, e-commerce service operator (like, Urban Clap provides services of plumbers, electricians, teachers, beauticians etc), would be liable to pay GST.

- **Supply of certain specified goods and Services:** On some supplies of Goods (like Bidi Unpeeled or Unshelled Cashew Nuts, Tendu Bidi Wrapper Leaves , Tobacco Leaves, Silk Yarn, Lottery) and services (like GTA, Advocate, Sponsor, Company Director, Insurance Agent, Author), specified by Government, reverse charge is applicable.

- **Import of Goods / Services:** If the supplier is located in a non-taxable territory and cannot collect and deposit taxes from the recipient then the recipient would be liable to deposit tax under reverse charge mechanism.

A supplier cannot take ITC of GST paid to make supplies on which the recipient is liable to pay tax.

The supplier, must mention in the related Invoice / Receipt Voucher / Refund Voucher, whether the tax mentioned in the document is payable on Reverse Charge.

Time of Supply under Reverse Charge

- **Time of supply of Goods:** In case of reverse charge, the Date of receipt of goods or 30 days from the date of issue of Invoice by the supplier; whichever is earlier, shall be considered as Time of Supply

- **Time Of Supply of Services:** In case of reverse charge, the date of Payment, or 60 days from the date of issue of **invoice**, whichever is earlier, shall be considered as Time of Supply

Note: If time of supply cannot be determined, then date of entry in the books of recipient would be considered as Time of Supply).

Rules relating to Reverse Charge

- Every registered person must maintain records of all supplies attracting Reverse Charge

- Payment of Reverse Charge shall be made through electronic cash ledger (Reverse Charge liability cannot be discharged by using input tax credit)

- Invoice level information in respect of all supplies attracting reverse charge, rate wise, are to be furnished separately in Table 4B of GSTR-1.

- Advance paid for reverse charge supplies is to be paid by person making advance payment

Supplies of Goods under Reverse Charge Mechanism

- Cashew nuts (not shelled or peeled)

- Bidi wrapper leaves (Tendu Leaves)

- Tobacco leaves

- Lottery Tickets

- Silk yarn

Supplies of services under Reverse Charge Mechanism

- Goods Transport Services (GTA Services)

- Legal Services by Advocate

- Services supplied by an arbitral tribunal to a business entity

- Services provided through Sponsorship to a Body Corporate or Partnership Firm

- Services supplied by Government or local authority, to a Business entity (excluding some specified services)
- Services supplied by Director to the said company
- Services supplied by an Insurance Agent
- Services supplied by Recovery Agent to a banking company / financial institution
- Supply of services by an author, music composer, photographer, artist etc, on copyrighted work

Advance Receipt

As per GST Rules, Tax is payable at the earliest of (i) Date of issue of invoice, (ii) Date of receipt of payment/ advance, (iii) Date on which invoice should be issued. So, if advance is received before issue of Invoice, Tax is payable by recipient of Advance, on receipt of Advance.

However, as per Notification dated 13/10/2017, Registered Persons (other than composition dealers) having turnover during FY 16-17 less than 1.5 crore, are not required to pay GST on outward supply of goods, at time of receipt of advance. So, as per notification:

– GST will not be payable at time of receipt of advance for outward supply of goods by registered persons having turnover less than 1.50 Crore during last FY, w.e.f. 13th October 2017. However, GST on advance is payable if advance received during period 01/07/2017 to 12/10/2017.

– In case of Persons having turnover more than 1.50 crore during last FY, GST is payable on advance received on outward supply of Goods, if advance is received during the period 01/07/2017 to 14/11/2017. No GST is payable on advance if it is received on or after 15/11/2017.

– This relief is not available on outward supply of services. So, GST is payable on advance received in case of outward supply of services.

– This relief is not available if tax is payable on reverse charge. So, in case of reverse charge, GST will be payable at time of payment, if payment made before receipt of goods.

Issue a Receipt Voucher: The supplier has to issue a receipt voucher to the person paying advance. The receipt voucher will contain details like amount of advance, the rate of tax applicable, description of goods or services, etc**.**

Pay Tax on Advance Received: The recipient of Advance (i.e. Supplier) has to pay Tax on Advance received during the Tax period. ITC cannot be claimed on Tax paid on Advance received.

The Rate of Tax would be as per rate applicable for supply of Goods / Services for which Advance Received. If the Rate cannot be fixed, tax @18% on Advance received is to be paid.

The Tax component of Advance received is to be computed as $A \times r /(100+r)$ [A= Amount of Advance Received. r = Tax rate applicable in %]

The balance of amount after deducting tax would be treated as Advance against supply. So, if the applicable Tax rate is 18 and total advance received is Rs 2,00,000, then GST on Advance would be [(200000 x 18) / (100+18)] = 3600000/118=30,508. So, the amount of Advance would be Rs 2,00,000 – 30508 = 169492

Adjustment of Advance &Tax paid: On issue of Invoice, the proportionate amount of tax already paid on Advance adjusted against the Invoice would be eligible for Tax Credit. So, in the above example, if the Invoice is later issued for Rs 3,00,000+ Tax 54000, then Tax on advance paid would be adjusted against Tax Liability on supply. So, further Tax of 54000- 30508 = 23492 would have to be paid.

Reporting in GSR-1: The amount of Advance for which Invoice has not been issued would be added to Tax Liability. This has to be reported separately for Intra State supply (under column 11A) and Inter State supply (under column 11B) of Table 11.

Tax Payments & Refunds

GST Payment Liability

Every registered regular tax payer must pay the tax due by the 20th of the month. Delay Interest on the tax due will be applicable for delayed payment of Tax, from the day on which the tax was due to be paid.

Any monthly return submitted by dealer, without paying tax due, will be considered Invalid. Monthly Return cannot be submitted before submitting the previous month's return & Tax payment. So, tax liabilities under GST must cleared to avoid the penalties of non-payment of tax.

GST Portal Tax Accounts: Every registered dealer will have following ledgers in GST portal:

– **Electronic tax liability register:** All liabilities of a person towards tax, interest, penalty, late fee or any other amount will be debited here. The total net tax liability for the month would be displayed.

– **Electronic cash ledger:** Every deposit made by a person towards tax, interest, penalty, late fee or any other amount will be credited here. All deposits made in cash, TDS, TCS would be reflected here. The amount may be used for making any payment on account of GST.

– **Electronic credit ledger:** Input tax credit, as self-assessed and claimed in Form GSTR-2, will be credited here. This can be used only for paying tax, but not for other amounts (like Interest, late fee, etc)

To pay the liabilities shown in the Electronic tax liability register, a person can use the balance in the Electronic cash ledger and Electronic credit ledger.

Accounting entries in GST portal Tax Accounts: The Electronic credit ledger will be debited by credit used for making the payment. The Electronic cash ledger will be debited by the amount deposited, and the Electronic tax liability register will be credited by the corresponding amount.

For example, the tax liability was Rs 1,00,000 in Electronic tax liability register, Input Tax credit balance was Rs 20,000 in Electronic credit ledger. Rs 80,000 is deposited in Electronic cash ledger. On deposit of Rs 80,000, the amount would be adjusted against liability of Rs 1,00,000 in Electronic tax liability register, and the balance of Rs 20,000 input Tax credit would be adjusted in Electronic credit ledger. Now all the 3 accounts would be adjusted showing NIL balance.

Set off of Tax Liability: However, set off of Input Tax credit can be made as per set off rules for each component of GST (IGST, CGST & SGST / UTGST) as explained under set off of Tax Liability.

Tax Payment Process

– **Generate Tax Challans**: Challan for the payment can be generated from the GST portal using Form GST PMT-06, entering respective details of tax, interest, penalty, fees & other amount, if any. The challan generated will be valid for 15 days.

- **Payment Modes**: Having generated the Challan, the payment with reference to the challan can be made through various payment modes, through authorised Bank:

  o   Internet Banking through the customer's Net banking facility

  o   Bank Debit / Credit Cards

  o   NEFT or ITGS (by generating a mandate, valid for 15 days)

  o   OTC (over the Counter) of the authorised Bank (for payment upto Rs 10000 per challan), by Cash, Cheque, DD etc

- **CIN / Credit in Electronic Cash Register:** Upon credit of the Tax deposited in bank, to the Government account by the Bank, a CIN (Challan Identification Number) would be generated, posted in GST portal, and credited to Electronic cash ledger account of tax payer.

Forms related to GST Payment: The GST forms related to Payment have prefix GST-PMT and numbered from 01 to 07, as below:

- GST-PMT-01: Electronic Tax liability
- GST-PMT-02: Electronic credit ledger
- GST-PMT-03: Rejection of claim for refund in Electronic credit /Electronic cash ledger
- GST-PMT-04: Discrepancy in Electronic credit ledger
- GST-PMT-05: Electronic Cash Ledger
- GST-PMT-06: Payment Challan
- GST-PMT-07: CIN not generated / not posted in GST Portal

Taxes Payable under GST

- **Central GST (CGST)**: Going into the account of the Central Government
- **State GST (SGST / UTGST)**: Going into the account of the concerned State Government / Union Territory).
- **Integrated GST (IGST)**: Components of both CGST and SGST (For Inter-state supply),
- **Others:** Tax Deducted at Source (TDS), Tax Collected at Source (TCS), Interest, Penalty, Fees and any other payment as required by law.

Persons liable to pay GST

- **Supplier**: In general, the supplier of goods or service is liable to pay GST.
- **Recipient**: Under Revere Charge Mechanism, the payment liability is cast on the recipient.
- **Others**: Liability to pay is on the third person (e.g. e-commerce operator responsible for TCS or Government Department responsible for TDS).

Pre Registration of Credit Card: The taxpayer should pre-register his credit card, from which the tax payment is intended, with the Common Portal maintained on GSTN. GSTN may get the credit card verified by taking a confirmation from the credit card service provider.

Generation of Challan for Payment of Tax

• **Registered Tax Payers**

 – **By Registered tax payer**: Log on to GSTN Common Portal where basic details (such as name, address, email, mobile no. and GSTIN) of the tax payer will be auto populated in the challan;

 – **By authorized representatives of tax payers**: Log on to the GSTN Common Portal and select the tax payer on whose behalf he proposes to pay GST. Challan details for such tax payer will be auto populated;

• **Others**

 – Using temporary Registration number allotted by any one Tax authority, for tax payments on behalf of an unregistered person.

 – By creation of a challan without requirement of USER ID and Password, for enabling payment of GST by a registered or an unregistered person on behalf of a taxpayer as per the directions of the tax authority using the GSTIN.

The challan can even be partially filled and temporarily saved the challan for completion at a later stage. A saved challan can be edited before finalization. After the tax payer has finalized the challan, he will generate the challan, for use of payment of taxes and may print the challan for record.

The challan so generated will have a 14-digit (yymm followed by 10-digit) Unique Common Portal Identification Number (CPIN), assigned only when the challan is finally generated. After the challan is generated, it will be frozen and will not be allowed to be modified (another challan can be generated)

The CPIN/challan so generated would be valid for a period of seven days. In case of payment through NEFT/RTGS, CPINs would remain live with RBI for a period of 30 days. GSTN would purge all unused CPINs on the day immediately after the date on which the validity period is over (i.e. 7 days if CC/DC and OTC payment is selected and 30 days if NEFT/RTGS is selected for payment)

After successful completion of a transaction, the concerned bank will create a 17-digit CIN (Challan Identification Number) generated by GSTN for the challan (14-digit number & and 3-digit Bank code). The date of credit to the Government account is considered the date of Tax Payment

Counter payment of GST

A tax payer to pay tax (upto Rs. 10,000/- per challan), over the Bank Counter will generate draft challan, accessing GSTN. The taxpayer will fill in the details of the taxes to be paid. The taxpayer would select option (of cheque, DD or cash). name of authorized bank and its location (city/town/village). The challan so generated will have a Unique Common Portal Identification Number (CPIN). Upon generation of challan, the taxpayer would pay the Tax on the specified branch of the Bank.

Tax payment of earlier period

Where Tax of earlier period is due, the tax should be paid in following sequence:

(i) First self-assessed tax and interest for the previous period

(ii) Thereafter self-assessed tax and interest for the current period;

(iii) Thereafter any other amounts payable / confirmed demands

REFUNDS

Refunds can be claimed on following accounts, within specified period, by submitting Refund application RFD – 1 (No Refund claim for amount less than Rs 1000):

- Excess payment of GST, within 2 years from date of payment

- Claim of rebate or Refund on Exports, supplies to SEZ, Deemed Exports, within 2 years from date of desptach / loading/ passing the frontier

- ITC accumulation due to output being tax exempt or nil-rated, within 2 years from the last date of financial year to which the credit belongs

- In case of reverse charge, where the input tax credit cannot be used completely against the output tax.

- Refund of tax paid on purchases made by Embassies or UN bodies, within 6 months from the end of quarter in which such goods/service were received, in Form RFD-10

- Refund due to Casual / Non Resident Taxable persons where at the end of the registration period tax paid in advance exceeds the actual tax liability.

- Tax Refund for International Tourists.

- Refund of pre-deposit

- Refund of Tax paid by treating the supply as intra-State supply which is subsequently held as inter-State supply and vice versa

- Finalization of provisional assessment, within 2 years from the Date on which tax is adjusted

- Refund arising on account of judgment, decree, order or direction of the Appellate Authority, Appellate Tribunal or any court

- Suppliers receiving discounts or credits through the issuance of credit notes

On submission of RFD-01, an acknowledgement in Form RFD-02 will be auto-generated for future references and sent across through an email and an SMS. In case of any deficiencies in the Refund Application, then Form RFD-03 shall be sent to the taxpayer to make rectification in Refund application

Other Forms related to Refund

- Show cause notice for complete rejection of a refund application - RFD-07

- Payment advice - RFD-08:

- Order for interest on late payments - RFD-09

Refund of unutilized input tax credit: It can be claimed in the following cases:

- Unutilized input tax credit on zero-rated goods/services on which no payment of tax was made

- Accumulation of unutilized ITC due to higher tax rate on inputs than the output supplies (other than zero-rated/exempted goods)

No refund of unutilized ITC would be allowed under the following cases:

- If the unutilized ITC is for GST paid on goods exported out of India attract excise duty.

- If the supplier of goods has availed duty drawback on the excise duty paid or claims the refund on the integrated tax paid on such supply.

Time limit for claiming Refunds

- **Excess Payment of GST :** 2 years from date of payment
- **Export (including deemed export) of goods or services**: 2 years from date of desptach / loading/ passing the frontier

Documents to be furnished for claiming refund

The applicant must furnishdocumentary evidence as may be prescribed to establish that a refund is due to the applicant.

- **Refund application below Rs. 5 lakhs**: Applicant must make a declaration that the amount of refund has not been utilised by or transferred to any other person.
- **Refund application Rs. 5 lakhs or above**: Apart from the declaration, document evidencing that the amount was paid by the taxpayer shall also be attached

Processing of Refund Application

Normally it would take about 30 days to process a refund application. Where the refund claim exceeds prescribed amount, it will be subjected to an audit process.

- On qualifying for refund, order shall be passed accordingly
- If it meets the criterion for being "unjustly enriching" the taxpayer (presumption that the person will shift the incidence of tax to final cosumer), the amount shall be transferred to the Consumer Welfare Fund.

Notice of Rejection of Claim: if Proper Officer seeks to reject the claim, a notice has to be given online to the applicant stating the ground on which the refund is sought to be rejected. The applicant needs to respond online within 15 days from the receipt of such notice.

Refund Order

When the taxpayer claims refund of monies arising out of exports of goods or services, then an authorised officer can issue a provisional refund order in Form RFD-04 of an amount of 90% of the refund claim., in following circumstances:

- Has not been prosecuted for evading taxes for an amount exceeding Rs. 250 lakhs over a period of 5 years.
- Has a GST compliance rating of more than 5 out of 10
- Has no appeal or review pending with respect to refunds.

In all other cases, the refund application shall be processed within 60 days from the application date.

- The authorised officer will issue a final order in Form RFD-05 within a period of 60 days from the application date.
- If the officer fails to pass an order within the said 60 days, then the taxpayer shall receive an interest @ 6% p.a. for the period exceeding the expiry of 60 days until the receipt of refund.

- When the refund has to be adjusted against the taxable amount, then Form RFD-06 shall be issued to that effect.

The refund amount will be directly credited to the bank account of the applicant.

Power with the Commissioner to Withhold Refund

Where an order giving rise to a refund is the subject matter of an appeal or further proceedings or where any other proceedings under this Act is pending, and the Commissioner is of the opinion that grant of such refund is likely to adversely affect the revenue, he may, after giving the taxable person an opportunity of being heard, withhold the refund till such time as he may determine.

However, if the applicant becomes eligible for refund, payment of interest @ 9% p.a on the refund amount would also be paid.

Returns Filing

GST Return

GST Return is a document containing details of transactions related to GST, like Purchases, Sales, Output GST (On sales), Input tax credit (GST paid on purchases), etc. This is used by tax authorities to calculate tax liability.

All entities registered under GST will have to file a GST Return. A Nil return has to be filed even if no purchase-sales activities have been carried out during the return period.

GST return cannot be revised. Any changes in details can however be made in the amendment section of the Return Form of next period

The taxpayers having turnover exceeding the prescribed limit will also be required to get their accounts audited by a Chartered / Cost Accountant, and submit a copy of the audited annual accounts with the annual return. They would submit a reconciliation statement, reconciling the value of supplies declared in the return furnished for the year with the audited annual financial statement, and any other documents as may be prescribed.

List of GST Returns

Return Form	Description	Due Date
GSTR 1	Outward supplies made by taxpayer (other than compounding taxpayer and ISD)	10th of next month
GSTR 2	Inward supplies received by a taxpayer (other than a compounding taxpayer and ISD)	15th of next month
GSTR 3	Monthly return (other than compounding taxpayer and ISD)	20th of next month
GSTR 3B	Provisional return for the months of July 2017 to March 2018	20th of next month
GSTR 4	Quarterly return for compounding Taxpayer	18th of next month
GSTR 5	Periodic return by Non-Resident Foreign Taxpayer	20th of next month
GSTR 6	Return for Input Service Distributor (ISD)	13th of next month
GSTR 7	Return for Tax Deducted at Source	10th of next month
GSTR 8	e-commerce operator	10th of next month
GSTR 9	Annual Return by Taxpayer	31st December of next financial year
GSTR 9A	Annual Return under Composition scheme	31st December of next financial year

| GSTR 10 | Final Return on registration canceled or surrendered | Within three months of the date of cancellation |
| GSTR 11 | Details of inward supplies to be furnished by a person having UIN and claiming refund | 28th of the month following the month |

Some of the Returns are auto generated by the GSTN system and the dealer is expected to validate the data (and fill missing data, if any).

If a taxpayer submits a Return without paying the tax liability in full, the return is considered invalid. A taxable person who has not furnished a valid return shall not be allowed to utilize such credit till he discharges his tax liability.

Late Fees: The taxpayer is liable to pay interest and a late fee, if GST Returns are not filed within time.

- **Interest**: Interest is 18% per annum, on the amount of outstanding tax to be paid. The time period will be from the next day of filing to the date of payment.

- **Late fee**: Rs. 100 per day per Act (Rs 100 under CGST & Rs. 100 under SGST maximum is Rs. 5,000 (Late fee for GSTR 3B & GSTR -4 has been reduced to Rs 50 per day / Rs 20 per day for NIL Return)

Movement of Goods

Delivery Challan

Normally, an Invoice should be issued at the time of movement of goods. In following cases, the consigner should issue a *Delivery challan* in place of an invoice at the time of removal of goods for transportation, and goods may be transported without issue of an invoice:

– Supply of liquid gas, where the quantity at the time of removal from the place of business of the supplier is not known

– Transportation of goods for job work

– Transportation of goods for reasons other than supply

– Any other notified supplies

The Delivery Challan should contain the details of Goods supplied. It should also contain the details of Tax in case of Supplies. If the exact quantity is not available, the delivery challan should show estimated quantity.

When a delivery challan is issued in place of Tax Invoice, the reference should be made in e-way bill. In case of supply, the corresponding tax invoice should be issued later on.

Delivery Challan / Invoices are printed in 3 copies. Original for Consignee / Buyer, Duplicate for Carrier, Triplicate for Seller / Consignor.

Carriage Services

– **Supply of Goods Carriage services by a carrier:** The goods carrier should issue a document for supply of carriage service, showing the details and value of services, and each component of Tax Applicable, Reverse Tax Applicable, if any.

– **Supply of Passenger Carriage services by a carrier:** The Passenger carrier should issue a Ticket in any form (with or without serial number), but should contain some mandatory info like GSTIN of transporter, GSTIN of service receiver (if registered), details of service value, each component of Tax,

Rules of Issue of Delivery Challan

Under Rule 10, goods may be transferred without raising invoice, both Intra State or Inter State, in following manner. Delivery Challans (in lieu of Invoice) should be issued in triplicate, 1. For Consignee, 2. Transporter, 3. Consignor.

– **Liquid Gases**: As Quantity is not known at the time of removal of goods from the place of supply (So quantity can not be specified , Invoice after Final Supply)

- **Transportation for Job Work**: Goods sent for Job Work for Intermediate / Final Processing or Packaging (as goods for Job work would be returned to the principal after job work). The movement of goods is not for sale.

- **Transportation of goods other than for supply**: Supplies for approval, inter godown transfer etc, under same registration,

- **Cases as notified by Government**

Essential Contents of Delivery Challan: Though no specific format for Delivery Challans is prescribed by government, Delivery Challan should contain following info:

- Challan Number: Unique challan ID, serially numbered, not exceeding 16 letters, in one or multiple series.

- Challan date: Date of issue of delivery challan.

- Details of Consignor (Supplier of Goods), such as Consignor Name, Consignor Address, GSTIN of Consignor (if applicable),

- Details of Consignee (Receiver of Goods), such as Consignee Name, Consignee Address, GSTIN of Consigne (if applicable),

- Details of goods moved: HSN Code, Description, Quantity (provisional quantity where exact quantity is not known), Unit, Taxable Value, Tax rate, Tax Amount (CGST / SGST / IGST)

- Place of supply: In case of Inter State movement of goods

The challan must be signed.

Where the goods are transported for supply but Invoice could not be issued at the time of removal of goods, the supplier would issue a Tax Invoice after delivery of goods.

Where challans are issued in lieu of Invoice, in such case, details of Challan is to be entered in e-way bill.

E-WAY BILL

E-way Bill is a compliance mechanism by way of a digital interface. The person causing the movement of goods uploads the relevant information prior to the commencement of movement of goods and generates e-way bill on the GST portal.

Transport of goods (of more than Rs 50,000 in value) cannot be made by a registered person without an e-way bill. which can be generated on the e-Way Bill Portal (can also be generated / canceled through SMS).

Objective of e-way Bill: 1. Reduce number of check posts across the country, eliminate friction in movement of goods to ensure smooth movement of goods, and reduce friction corruption. 2. Provide one e-way bill for movement of goods throughout the country. 3. Prevent evasion of Tax. 4. Tracking Movement of Goods through e-way Bill Number. 5. Speedy verification.

Through GST, states have removed the physical barriers at State Border for transport of goods, to speed up movement of goods.So, in one hand, e-way bill eliminates friction of movement of goods at various stages and level, On the other hand, E-way Bill aims to place control in the hands of government to check clandestine activities on movement and transactions of goods

Applicability of e-way Bill

It is applicable for movement of goods for supply or for reasons other than supply (like Job Work, Testing, Goods sent on Approval etc), of value exceeding Rs.50,000. Generation of e-way Bill for consignment of lower value is optional. In case of intra state movement of goods within Delhi, e-way bill is mandatory for value exceeding Rs 1 Lakh.

However, e-way Bill mandatory irrespective of value of goods (even for value lower than Rs 50000) for Inter-State movement of goods for Job Work (except for Inter State movement of Handicrafts goods for Job Work by small dealers having turnover 20 lakhs / 10 lakhs). In case of further intra state transportation to a distance upto 50km, only part A of the e-way bill may be filled up.

e-way bill is not applicable in following cases

- Goods transported in non-motorised conveyance

- Goods transported from port, airport, air cargo complex or land customs station to Inland Container Depot (ICD) or Container Freight Station (CFS) for clearance by Customs.

- Transport of specified goods [under rule 138(14)]

- Movement of goods within notified areas [under rule 134(14)(d)]

Generation of e-way bill: The e-way bill is to be generated before the commencement of movement of goods. On generation of e-way bill is generated a unique e-way bill number (EBN) is allocated and is available to the supplier, recipient, and the transporter.

Persons responsible for generation of e-way Bill:

- **Registered Person**: When goods are transported by registered person, either acting as a consignee or consignor in his own (or hired) vehicle, the supplier or recipient of the goods should generate the e-way Bill. If the consignor does not generate the e-way bill, the transporter must generate the e-way bill based on info submitted in the related documents submitted (like Invoice / Delivery Note etc)

- **Unregistered Person**: In case of supplies by unregistered person, the movement shall be said to be caused by the recipient i.e. the registered dealer, provided the recipient is known at the time of commencement of the movement of goods.

  o **Registered Recipient is known at the time of movement of goods**: The registered dealer will be liable to generate the e-way bill. The Unregistered Dealer or Transporter have option to generate e-way Bill

  o **Registered Recipient is not known at the time of movement of goods**: Sometimes, unregistered suppliers manufacture goods at their place, and then bring the goods for sale to a common market, where many buyers are available. In such a situation, the unregistered supplier may not know the recipient at the time of movement of goods, In such a situation, the e-way bill is not mandatory. However, the unregistered dealer may generate the e-way Bill through the option *Enrolment for Citizen* (to be made available soon)

- **Transporter**: When the goods are handed over to a transporter, the e-way bill should be generated by the transporter. In this case, the registered person should declare the details of the goods in a common portal.

Handicraft goods: In case of inter state purchase from unregistered dealer, e-way bill is to be mandatorily generated irrespective of the value of the consignment. The unregistered dealer supplying such goods is liable to generate e-way Bill.

Persons involved in e-way bill cycle

- **Suppliers**: Generate the e-Way Bills, reject the e-Way Bills generated by other party against his name, if it does not belong to him.

- **Recipients**: Generate the e-Way Bills (if not generated by supplier), reject the e-Way Bills generated by other party against his name, if it does not belong to him/her.

- **Transporters**: Generate the e-Way Bills (if not generated by supplier / recepient), consolidated e-Way Bills and update the vehicle numbers for the e-Way Bills assigned to him for transportation by the taxpayers.

- **Department Officers**: Verify the e-Way Bills and consignments carried with the e-Way Bills.

Forms related to e-way Bill:

- **GST ENR-01**: Used by un registered person for enrolment under e-way Bill.

- **GST EWB-01:** GST EWB-01 is used as e-way bill form. Part-A contains details of the goods, and Part-B contains details of transporter. GST-02 is used for consolidated e-way bill.

- **GST EWB 03** – It is used for Verification Report

- **EWB 04** isused for Detention Report

- **GST INV-1**: A registered person may obtain an Invoice Reference Number from the common portal by uploading, on the said portal, a tax invoice issued by him in FORM GST INV-1 and produce the same for verification by the proper officer in lieu of the tax invoice and such number shall be valid for a period of thirty days from the date of uploading.

  In such case, the registered person will not have to upload the information in Part A of FORM GST EWB-01 for generation of e-way bill and the same shall be auto populated by the common portal on the basis of the information furnished in FORM GST INV-1.

Multiple Consignments: The transporter should generate a consolidated e-way bill in the Form GST INS 02 and separately indicate the serial number of e-way bills for each of the consignment.

Multiple Vehicles: Sometimes, multiple vehicles may used for carrying the same consignment to its destination or due to unforeseen exigencies, consignments to be carried in a different conveyance than the original one. For such situations, the transporter transferring goods from one conveyance to another in the course of transit shall, before such transfer and further movement of goods, update the details of the conveyance in the e-way bill on the common portal in FORM GST EWB-01

Transfer of goods from one vehicle to another: Before transferring the goods to another vehicle and making any further movement of such goods, a transporter should generate new e-way bill in Form GST EWB 01 by specifying the details of the mode of transport.

Acceptance of Goods by Recipient: The recipient of goods (registered person) should communicate acceptance or rejection of the consignment covered by the e-way bill within 72 hours of the details being made available. If the recipient of goods does not communicate acceptance or rejection within 72 hours, it will be deemed as accepted by the recipient.

Validity of e-way bill: The validity of e-way bill would depend on distance covered, upto 100 km, - 1day, 100-300 km – 3 days, 300-500 km – 5 days, 5-1000 km – 10 days & more than 1000 km-15 days. However, the validity period of specific goods may be extended by Commissioner by notification.

Cancellation of e-way Bill: If e-way bill is generated but goods are not transported, the e-way bill may be cancelled. An e-way bill cannot be cancelled after being verified by an officer during transit.

Administration:

– The transporter or the person in charge of a conveyance should carry the copy of Invoice / Bill / Delivery Challan, e-way bill (or the e-way bill number).

– At the place of verification, the officer may intercept any vehicle to physically verify the e-way bill / e-way bill number, for all movement of goods (interstate and intrastate).

– To avoid verification of the physical copy of the e-way bill, RFID (Radio Frequency Identification Device) may be fixed to the vehicle, mapping the e-way to the device. At the place of verification, the e-way bill mapped to this device will be verified through RFID readers. For certain class of transporters, fixing of RFID devices to the vehicle and mapping of e-way bill to device are mandated, as notified by commissioner.

– On the ground of suspicion of tax evasion, a physical verification of the vehicle can be carried out by an officer after obtaining necessary approval from the commissioner (or an officer authorized on his behalf). Once a physical verification of vehicle is done at any place (*within the state or in any other state*), no further physical verification will be carried out again during the transit, unless specific information of tax evasion is reported subsequently.

– After every inspection, the officer needs to record the details of the inspection of goods in Part- A of Form GST INS-03 within 24 hours of inspection and the final report must be recorded in Part B of Form GST INS 03 within 3 days of inspection. If the vehicle is detained for more than 30 minutes, the transporter may complain by uploading the details in Form GST INS 04.

– With GST, e-way bill becomes the ultimate mode of verification and the functions of numerous check post across the country would be done away with, resulting easier movement of goods.

Input Service Distributors

Centralised Business Operations

Large multi location Organisations may have their head office at one place and units at other places, each registered separately. The Head Office would be procuring certain services for common utilization of multiple units. The bills for such expenses would be raised on the Head Office. But the Head Office itself would not be providing any output supply to utilize the credit. So, the ITC on inputs get accumulated. Since the common expenditure is meant for multiple units, credit of input services in respect of such common invoices should be apportioned between the consuming units. ISD mechanism enables such proportionate distribution of credit of input services

ISD mechanism is meant only for distributing the credit on common invoices pertaining to input services only and not goods (Raw materials or Capital goods).

An ISD cannot accept any invoices on which tax is to be discharged under reverse charge mechanism (to take reverse charge supplies, ISD has to separately register as Normal taxpayer).

The ISD itself cannot discharge any tax liability (as person liable to pay tax) and remit tax to government account.

So, as per GST:

- ISD is an office (like head office, administrative office, corporate office, regional office, depot) belonging to registered taxable person who intends to distribute the credit
- It receives tax towards the receipt of inward supply of services
- It distributes the tax credit paid of inward supplies of services to the branch units (having same PAN), which have consumed the services, and issues invoices for the distribution of credit.

Registration of ISD under GST

ISD registration is for one office of the taxpayer, which will be different from the normal registration.

Businesses who are already registered as an ISD under the existing regime (i.e. under Service Tax), will be required obtain a new ISD registration under GST (as existing ISD registration will not be migrated to the GST regime).

Mode of ITC Distribution

The unit to which the input tax credit is distributed is referred to as the 'recipient of credit'.

- **ISD and recipient of credit are located in the same state:** When the ISD and recipient of credit are located in the same state/union territory, the input tax credit of IGST, CGST, SGST, and UTGST should be distributed to the recipient in same category. This means that IGST with ISD would be distributed to IGST of Recipient, CGST with ISD would be distributed to CGST of Recipient, SGST with ISD would be distributed to SGST of Recipient, UTGST with ISD would be distributed to UTGST of Recipient.

- **ISD and recipient of credit are located in different state:** When the ISD and recipient of credit are located in different state/union territory, the input tax credit of IGST, CGST, SGST, and UTGST should be distributed to the IGST of recipient. This means that IGST, CGST, SGST & UTGST with ISD would be distributed to only IGST of Recipient

Return Forms for ISD

- **Form GSTR-6A**: This monthly return showing the Details of inward supplies made available to the ISD recipient, on the basis of FORM GSTR-1 furnished by the supplier, should be submitted by 11th of the next month.

- **Form GSTR-6:** Monthly Return showing the details of Input Credit distributed should be submitted by 13th of the next month

An ISD shall not be required to file Annual return.

Conditions for distribution of input tax credit by an ISD

- An ISD invoice is issued only for distribution of input tax credit, by the distributor to the unit to which the input tax credit is distributed (referred as the 'Recipient of credit'), contain following details;

    o   Name, address, and GSTIN of the Input Service Distributor

    o   A consecutive unique serial number (only alphabets and/or numerals), for a financial year

    o   Date of its issue

    o   Name, address, and GSTIN of the supplier of services for which credit being distributed, serial number and date of invoice issued by such supplier.

    o   Name, address, and GSTIN of the recipient to whom the credit is being distributed

    o   The amount of credit distributed

    o   Signature or digital signature of the supplier or his authorized representative

- The amount of credit distributed shall not exceed the amount of credit available for distribution.

- The input tax credit available for distribution in a month shall be distributed in the same month, and the details of the same shall be furnished in Form GSTR -6.

Addition / Reduction in Input Credit

- **Supplementary Input Credit**: Any additional amount of input tax credit on account of issuance of a 'debit note' by a supplier to the ISD shall be apportioned to each recipient in the same ratio in which the input tax credit contained in the original invoice was distributed.

- **Reduction in Input Credit**: In case the input tax credit already distributed gets reduced for any reason, an ISD credit note should be issued for the reduction of credit. The following details have to be captured in the ISD credit note:

  o Name, address, and GSTIN of the ISD

  o A consecutive SL.No containing alphabets or numerals or special characters such as hyphen or dash or slash, symbolized as, "-" "/" respectively, and any combination thereof, unique for a financial year

  o Date of its issue

  o Name, address, and GSTIN of the recipient to whom the credit is distributed

  o The amount of credit distributed, and

  o The signature or digital signature of the ISD or his authorized representative

Apportionment of reduction amount:

  o Reduced from the amount to be distributed in the month in which the credit note is included in the return in FORM GSTR – 6 and

  o Added to the output tax liability of the recipient, in case the amount so apportioned is negative.

Method of input tax distribution

- **Distribution to Single Receiver**: The input tax credit should be distributed only to that branch which has consumed the input services.

  Example: ABC Ltd, located in Bangalore, Karnataka, have branches in Mysore (Karnataka), Chennai (Tamil Nadu), and Mumbai (Maharashtra). The unit in Bangalore is the Head office and they procure common services in bulk which are used by the other branches too.

  ABC Ltd receives an input invoice of Rs.1,00,000 + GST of Rs.18,000 towards services provided exclusively to the Mysore branch. The total credit of Rs. 18,000 will be distributed only to the Mysore branch.

- **Distribution to Multiple Receiver** The credit of tax paid on input services, availed by more than one recipient of credit or all, should be distributed only amongst such recipients or all recipients.

  The distribution shall be on pro rata basis based on the turnover for the previous year of such recipients. In the absence of turnover in previous financial year, the turnover of the last quarter of the month in which ITC is distributed, will be considered

Example:

- – Amount of credit to be distributed: Rs.90,000

- – Aggregate turnover of Mysore unit in previous financial year (PY): Rs.60 Lakhs

- – Aggregate turnover of Chennai unit in previous financial year (PY): Rs.90 Lakhs

- – Aggregate turnover of all recipients of credit: Rs.150 Lakhs

The credit of Rs.90,000 will be distributed in the following manner:

- – Mysore: (60,00,000 / 1,50,00,000) x 90,000 =36,000

- – Chennai: (90,00,000 / 1,50,00,000) x 90,000 = 54,000

Import & Export

Import of Goods: Import of goods means bringing goods into India from a place outside India. GST subsumes Countervailing Duty (CVD) and Special Additional Duty (SAD). However, Basic Customs Duty (BCD) has been kept outside the purview of GST and will be charged as per the current law. All imports shall be deemed as inter-State supplies and accordingly Integrated Tax shall be levied in addition to the applicable Custom duties.

– **Customs Duty:** The integrated tax on goods shall be in addition to the applicable Basic Customs Duty (BCD) levied under Customs Tariff Act. In addition, GST compensation cess, may also be leviable, as applicable (on certain luxury and demerit goods). Imported goods can be removed from a customs station only after payment of Customs Duty and the Integrated GST tax payable.

– **Passenger Baggage:** Full exemption from IGST has been provided on import of passenger baggage. However, Basic Customs Duty shall be leviable.

Valuation of Imported Goods for levying Tax

– **IGST:** The value of the goods for the purpose of levying integrated tax shall be, assessable value plus Customs Duty levied under the Act, and any other duty chargeable on the said goods under any law for the time being in force as an addition to, and in the same manner as, a duty of customs.

– **Cess:** The value of the imported article for the purpose of levying cess shall be, assessable value plus Basic Customs Duty levied under the Act, and any sum chargeable on the goods under any law for the time being, in force as an addition to, and in the same manner as, a duty of customs. The integrated tax paid shall not be added to the value for the purpose of calculating cess.

Place of Supply: Place of supply of goods imported into India shall be the location of the importer. Thus, if an importer, say is located in Rajasthan, the state tax component of the integrated tax shall accrue to the State of Rajasthan.

Input Tax Credit on Imported Goods: Integrated Tax (IGST) paid at the time of import shall be available to the importer and the same can be utilized by him as Input Tax credit for payment of taxes on his outward supplies. The Basic Customs Duty (BCD), shall not be available as input tax credit. HSN (Harmonised System of Nomenclature) code would be used for the purpose of classification of goods under the GST

GST on Imports by EOUs/EHTPs/STPs

– EOUs/EHTPs/STPs will be allowed to import goods without payment of Basic Customs Duty (BCD) as well additional duties leviable under Section 3 (1) and 3(5) of the Customs Tariff Act.

– GST would be leviable on the import of input goods or services used in the manufacture by EOUs, which can be taken as input tax credit (ITC). This ITC can be utilized for payment of GST taxes payable on the goods cleared in the DTA. Refund of unutilized ITC can be claimed under Section 54(3) of CGST Act.

- In GST regime, clearance of goods in DTA will attract GST besides payment of amount equal to BCD exemption availed on inputs used in such finished goods. DTA clearances of goods, which are not under GST would attract Central Excise duties as before.

Import of Services

Import of Services means supply of any service where the supplier is located outside India, the recipient is located in India, and the place of supply of service is in India.

The importer of services will have to pay tax on reverse charge basis.

However, in respect of import of online information and database access or retrieval services (OIDAR) by unregistered, non-taxable recipients, the supplier located outside India shall be responsible for payment of taxes. Either the supplier will have to take registration or will have to appoint a person in India for payment of taxes.

In general, imports of services without consideration shall not be considered as supply. So, import of free services from Google and Facebook by all of us, without any consideration, are not considered as supply. However, Import (Downloading) of a song for consideration for personal use would be a service, even though the same are not in the course or furtherance of business. Import of some services by Indian branch from their parent company, in the course or furtherance of business, even if without consideration, will be a supply.

GST on Ocean Freight

Ocean freight in relation to transportation of goods by a vessel from a place outside India up to the customs station of clearance in India is liable to IGST. The accountability of the discharging the GST liability is on the Importer.

Accordingly, the Importer pays IGST on ocean freight under Reverse charge basis. However, in most cases, exporter sells on CIF basis (Cost, Insurance & Freight), where the value of each element is not separately known.

Freight is considered as service. As per GST rule, where value of taxable service person located in non Taxable area is not available with the person liable to pay Integrated Tax, it would be deemed to be 10% of CIF value of imported goods (so on 10% of CIF value, IGST @5%, i.e effective amount of IGST @ 0.5% of CIF value)

Imports initiated under previous regime

All imports of services made on or after the appointed day will be liable to integrated tax regardless of whether the transactions for such import of services had been initiated before the appointed day. However, if the tax on such import of services had been paid in full under old regime, no tax shall be payable on such import under the IGST Act.

In case the tax on such import of services had been paid in part under the existing law, the balance amount of tax shall be payable on such import under the IGST Act.

For example, In case of a supply of service for rupees one crore was initiated prior to the introduction of GST, a payment of Rs. 20 lacs has already been made to the supplier and service tax has also been paid on the same, the. integrated tax shall have to be paid on the balance Rs. 80 lacs.

Export of Goods

Under GST, exports will be zero rated. A registered taxable person exporting goods or services shall be eligible to claim refund under one of the following two options:

– **Export under Bond**: Export under bond or letter of undertaking without payment of Integrated Tax and claim refund of unutilized input tax credit.

– **Export under Rebate Claim:** Export on payment of Integrated Tax and claim refund of the Integrated Tax so paid on goods and services exported.

The aforesaid refunds will be subject to rules, safeguards and procedures as may be prescribed.

Export of Services

Export of Services means services delivered from a supplier located in India, to a service receiver located outside India, for services received outside India, for which Payment is received in convertible foreign exchange

GST rate on Export of Service is zero, provided the supplier & receiver of service are not related to same entity.

Supply of Service out of India not considered as exports: Following services are not considered as export of service

– **Supply of service to a person located outside India where place of supply of service is in India:** For example, a property rented out in Mumbai to a person residing in Dubai; agent located in India providing service to a New York based exporter for selling goods to China.

– **Supply of services where consideration is not received in Indian currency / convertible currency**: For example supply of consultancy service by an Indian consulting firm to an overseas entity, payment for which is made in Indian rupees by Indian branch of overseas entity.

– **Services provided to overseas Branch**: Such services would not be eligible as export of service

ITC Refund on Export

– In case of zero rated supplies made without payment of tax, refund of input tax credit will be available u/s 54(2) of CGST Act.

– No refund of unitized input tax credit shall be allowed in cases other than exports including zero rated supplies or in cases where the credit has accumulated on account of rate tax on inputs being higher than the rate of tax on output supplies, other than nil rated or fully exempt supplies (first proviso to section 54(3) of CGST Act).

– No refund of unutilized input tax credit shall be allowed in cases where the goods exported out of India are subjected to export duty (second proviso to section 54(3) of CGST Act).

– No refund of input tax credit shall be allowed if the supplier of goods or services avails duty drawback of CGST / SGST / UTGST or claims refund of IGST paid on such supplies (third proviso to section 54(3) of CGST Act).

Drawback: Drawback in relation to any goods manufactured in India and exported, means the rebate of duty, tax or cess chargeable on any imported inputs or on any domestic inputs or input services used in the manufacture of such goods

ITC Refund Process for Exports

- Application form for claiming refund can be filed through the GSTN portal, at the end of each quarter.

- An acknowledgement number would be shared with applicant via SMS or e-mail, once the application is filed electronically.

- Adjustment would be made to return and cash ledger and increase the amount of "carry-forward input tax credit" automatically.

- Refund application and documents submitted shall be scrutinized within a period of 30 days of filing the refund application.

- Refund will be credited electronically to the account of applicant via ECS, RTGS or NEFT.

- No refund shall be provided for an amount of less than Rs 1000.

Books of Accounts

All registered persons and owner or operator of warehouse/godown/any other place used for storage of goods, must maintain proper books of account as specified u/s 35, 36 of CGST Act and rules.

Specified Books of Accounts: The following Books of Account must be maintained separately for every activity undertaken (such as manufacturing, trading, provisions of service etc):

– Inward/Outward supply of goods and/or services

– Names & complete addresses of the inward/outward suppliers

– Stock of goods for each commodity received/ supplied

– Particulars of good lost, stolen, destroyed, written off or disposed of by way of gift or free samples

– Stock of scrap and wastage

– Input tax credit availed

– Output tax payable and paid

– Goods or services imported or exported

– Supplies attracting tax on reverse charge

– Advances received and paid and adjustments relating thereto

– Goods or services imported or exported

– Supplies attracting payment of tax on reverse charge

– All related documents like, invoices, bills of supply, delivery challans, credit notes, debit notes, receipt vouchers, payment vouchers, refund vouchers and e-way bills.

The Commissioner may add more records to be maintained.

Contents of Books of Accounts

– Accounts of stock in respect of goods received and supplied; showing particulars of the opening balance, receipt, supply, goods lost, stolen, destroyed, written off or disposed of by way of gift or free samples and balance of stock including raw materials, finished goods, scrap and wastage thereof

– Separate account of advances received, paid and adjustments made thereto

– Details of tax payable, tax collected and paid, input tax, input tax credit claimed together with a register of tax invoice, credit note, debit note, delivery challan issued or received during any tax period

– Names and complete addresses of suppliers from whom taxable goods or services received

– Names and complete addresses of the persons to whom supplies made

- Complete addresses of the premises where the goods are stored (including goods stored during transit) along with the particulars of the stock stored therein

- Monthly production accounts showing the quantitative details of raw materials or services used in the manufacture, quantitative details of goods manufactured including the waste and by products thereof

- Accounts showing the quantitative details of goods used in the provision of services, details of input services utilised and the services supplied,

- separate accounts for works contract showing the names and addresses of the persons on whose behalf the works contract is executed

  o description, value and quantity (wherever applicable) of goods or services received for the execution of works contract

  o description, value and quantity (wherever applicable) of goods or services utilized in the execution of works contract

  o the details of payment received in respect of each works contract and

  o the names and addresses of suppliers from whom he has received goods or services

Any entry in registers, accounts and documents shall not be erased, effaced or overwritten and all incorrect entries, other than those of clerical nature, shall be scored out under attestation and thereafter the correct entry shall be recorded and where the registers and other documents are maintained electronically, a log of every entry edited or deleted shall be maintained. Each volume of books of account maintained manually, shall be serially numbered.

Place of Maintenance: The books of account shall be kept at the principal place of business and at every related place(s) of business mentioned in the certificate of registration and such books of account shall include any electronic form of data stored on any electronic devices. The data so stored shall be authenticated by way of digital signature.

Period for preservation of accounts: All accounts maintained together with all invoices, bills of supply, credit and debit notes, and delivery challans relating to stocks, deliveries, inward supply and outward supply shall be preserved for seventy two months (six years) from the due date of furnishing of annual return for the year pertaining to such accounts and records and shall be kept at every related place of business mentioned in the certificate of registration.

Records under litigation to be retained till 1 year from the date of final disposal of proceeding, or until the expiry of 6 years from the due date of the annual return, whichever is later

Electronic Records: Proper electronic back-up of records must be kept. The relevant records or documents, duly authenticated, in hard copy or in any electronically readable format must be produced on demand

Maintenance of Records by warehouse / transporters

The transporters, owners or operators of godowns, warehouse, etc, if not already registered under the GST, shall submit the details regarding their business electronically on the Common Portal in FORM GST ENR-01. A unique enrolment number shall be generated and communicated to them.

- Every person engaged in the business of transporting goods shall maintain records of goods transported, delivered and goods stored in transit by him and for each of his branches.

- Every owner or operator of a warehouse or godown shall maintain books of accounts, with respect to the period for which particular goods remain in the warehouse, including the particulars relating to dispatch, movement, receipt, and disposal of such goods.

- The goods shall be stored in such manner that they can be identified item wise and owner wise and shall facilitate any physical verification or inspection, if required at any time.

Maintenance of Records by Agent

Agent means person, including a factor, broker, commission agent, arhatia, del credere agent, an auctioneer or any other mercantile agent, by whatever name called, who carries on the business of supply or receipt of goods or services or both on behalf of another

Every agent shall maintain records of:

- particulars of authorisation received by him from each principal to receive or supply goods or services on behalf of such principal separately

- particulars including description, value and quantity (wherever applicable) of goods or services received on behalf of every principal

- particulars including description, value and quantity (wherever applicable) of goods or services supplied on behalf of every principal

- details of accounts furnished to every principal;

- tax paid on receipts or on supply of goods or services effected on behalf of every principal

Audit

GST Audit

Audit means examination of records, returns and other documents maintained or furnished by the registered person, to verify the correctness of turnover declared, taxes paid, refund claimed and input tax credit availed, and to assess compliance with the provisions of the GST Acts or the rules made thereunder (s.2(13) of CGST Act 2017)

Audit by Registered Person

A Registered taxable person having turnover during exceeding Rs 2 crore in a Financial Year, shall get his accounts audited by a chartered accountant or a cost accountant, and shall electronically file:

- Annual Return in Form GSTR 9B, while filing GSTR-9, along with the reconciliation statement by 31st December of the next Financial Year,

- Audited copy of the annual accounts,

- Reconciliation statement of the value of supplies declared in the return with the audited annual financial statement,

- Any other particulars as prescribed.

Rectifications after Return Based on Results of Audit under GST: If any taxable person, after furnishing a return discovers any omission/incorrect details (from results of audit), he can rectify subject to payment of interest. However, Rectification will not be allowed where results are from scrutiny/audit by the tax authorities

Audit by Tax Authorities

- The Commissioner or any officer authorised by him, may conduct audit of a taxpayer.

- A notice will be sent to the auditee at least 15 days before, in Form GST ADT-01

- The Audit can be carried out at auditee's business premises or at the office of the proper officer

- The audit will be completed within 3 months from date of commencement of the audit (of the date when information are called for are provided, or audit initiated at the auditee's business premises).

- The Commissioner can extend the audit period for a further six months with reasons recorded in writing.

The Auditee will provide necessary facility to verify the books of account/other documents as required, and give information and assistance for timely completion of the audit.

- **Audit Findings**: The audit findings would be reported to the auditee, within 30 days of conclusion of audit, in Form ADT-02.

- **Recovery Actions**: If the audit results in detection of unpaid/under paid tax or wrong refund or wrong input tax credit availed, then demand and recovery actions will be initiated.

Special Audit

During scrutiny, investigation, or other proceeding, if the Assistant Commissioner (or an higher officer), is of the opinion that the value has not been correctly declared or the wrong credit has been availed, may direct Special Audit (with the prior approval of the Commissioner), in Form ADT-03. Special audit can be conducted even if the tax payers books have already been audited before.

- **Auditor for special audit**: The special audit will be carried out by a chartered accountant or a cost accountant nominated by the Commissioner.

- **Time limit for special audit:** The auditor will have to submit the report within 90 days (or as extended by Tax Officer), under Form GST ADT-04, to the Assistant Commissioner.

- **Cost :** The expenses for examination and audit including the auditor's remuneration will be determined and paid by the Commissioner.

- **Findings of special audit:** The taxable person will be given an opportunity of being heard in findings of the special audit.

- **Recovery Action**: If the audit results in detection of unpaid/ short paid tax, wrong refund or input tax credit wrongly availed, then demand and recovery actions will be initiated.

GST Audit Forms

- GST ADT -01: Notice of Audit u/s 65(3)
- GST ADT -02: Audit Findings u/s 65(6)
- GST ADT -03: Special Audit directive u/s 66
- GST ADT -04: Special Audit findings by Auditor

Assessment

Assessment under GST

Assessment means determination of tax liability under GST law. There are different types of Assessment under GST. During Assessment, dealer is to furnish the information asked for, within specified time.

Types of Assessment

- **Self Assessment**: Every registered taxable person must assess the tax payable by himself/herself and furnish the relevant return for each tax period (s.59). It is important to furnish accurate information and pay tax due on a timely basis, as per the due dates laid down. Self-assessment done appropriately ensures that assessment is not initiated by the tax authorities.

- **Assessment by the Tax Authorities**: In following cases, assessment may be initiated by the tax authorities(s.60)

  o **Provisional Assessment:** If a taxable person is unable to determine the value of goods and/or services or determine the rate of tax applicable, the person can request an officer (in writing) to allow payment of the tax on a provisional basis (submitting a Bond to pay the difference in tax, if any). The officer will pass an order allowing the person to pay the tax on a provisional basis.

    – **Final Assessment**: The Final assessments will be done within 6 months of Provisional Assessment.

    – **Interest on delayed Tax payment**: The tax payer will have to pay interest (@18%pa max) on tax not paid within the due date.

    – **Refund of Excess Tax paid and Interest**: If the tax as per final assessment is less than provisional assessment then the taxable person will get a refund along with Interest (@6%pa max)

  o **Scrutiny Assessment:** Under scrutiny assessment, an officer can examine the return and other information furnished by a person, to verify the correctness of the return (s.61). If any discrepancy is noticed, the officer will inform the person and seek his explanation (scrutiny of returns is not a legal or judicial proceeding, so, no order can be passed). If the explanation is satisfactory, no further action will be taken. In case no satisfactory explanation is given within 30 days of being informed or if the person does not make corrections in the return after accepting the discrepancies, the officer will initiate appropriate action (like Audit u/s 65, Special Audit u/s 66, Inspect & Search, Initiate demand & recovery provisions).

  o **Best Judgement Assessment:** In following circumstances, an officer may assess the tax liability of a person to the best of his/her judgement.

- **Assessment of non-filers of returns**: If a person fails to furnish a return, even after a notice is served to the person, an officer will assess the tax liability of the person to the best of his judgement, on the basis of all relevant material available to him(s.62).

- **Assessment of unregistered persons**: If a taxable person fails to obtain registration even though he/she is liable to do so, an officer will assess the tax liability of the person to the best of his judgement for the relevant tax periods, and issue an assessment order (s.63)

o **Summary Assessment:** In certain special cases, an officer may, on finding any evidence showing tax liability of a person, with the permission of the Additional/Joint Commissioner, assess the tax liability of the person to protect the interest of revenue, and issue an assessment order(s.64)

Demands & Recovery

Demand

Demand means notice issued by appropriate authority for Payment of Tax due.

The Goods and Service Tax is payable on a self-assessment basis. If there is any short payment, or wrongful utilisation of input credit, GST authorities will initiate demand and recovery provisions against the assessee.

Show Cause Notice

Show Cause Notice (SCN) is an order issued by appropriate Tax authority to explain why legal action as per provisions of law, would not be taken against the Taxpayer. Under GST, a show cause notice may be issued in various circumstances

Show Cause Notice when there is No Fraud (s.73)

When Tax is unpaid/short paid or, Refund is wrongly made or, Input tax credit has been wrongly availed/ utilized, without committing any fraud (no motive to evade tax), the proper officer will serve a show cause notice on the taxpayer, to pay the amount due, along with interest and penalty, in Form GST DRC-01

– **Time limit for adjudication of Show cause Notice**: The Show Cause Notice has to be adjudicated within a period of three years from the due date of filing of annual return.

– **Time limit for issue of Show cause Notice**: The Show Cause Notice is to be issued at least three months prior to the time limit set for adjudication.

– **Serving of Statement for other period**: On serving the notice, proper officer can serve statement of any unpaid tax/wrong refund etc. for other periods not covered in the notice, in Form GST DRC-02. No separate notice need to be issued for each tax period.

Voluntary Tax Payment: A person can pay tax along with interest, based on his own calculations (or the officer's calculations), before issue of notice/statement, and inform the officer in Form GST DRC -03. The officer will issue acknowledgement of payment in Form GST DRC 04. The officer will issue order in Form GST DRC 05.

The officer will not issue any notice in this case. However, if short payment found, officer can issue a notice for the balance amount.

Penalty: The tax officer, after considering the taxpayer's representation (in Form GST DRC-06), will issue order (in FORM GST DRC 07), within three years from the due date for filing of relevant annual return, to pay interest and penalty (10% of tax subject to a minimum of Rs. 10,000). Any rectification of the order shall be made by the officer in Form GST DRC 08.

Penalty will even be payable where any self-assessed tax etc. has not been paid within thirty days from the due date of payment of the tax.

Show Cause Notice When there is Fraud (s.74)

In case of Tax unpaid / short paid, wrong refunds, or wrong utilization of Input credit through fraud, willful misstatement or suppression of facts, the proper officer will serve a show cause notice to the taxpayer, to pay the amount due along with interest and penalty.

- **Time limit for adjudication of Show cause Notice**: The Show Cause Notice has to be adjudicated within a period of Five years from the due date of filing of annual return.

- **Time limit for issue of Show cause Notice**: The Show Cause Notice is to be issued at least six months prior to the time limit set for adjudication.

Voluntary Tax Payment: If the person pays tax along with interest and penalty @15%, based on their own calculations (or the officer's calculations) before issue of the notice/statement, and informs the officer in writing, then the officer will not issue any notice. However, if any short payment is found, the officer can issue a notice for the balance amount.

- If the taxpayer pays all their dues and a penalty of 25% within 30 days from the date of notice, all proceedings (except for prosecution u/s 132) regarding the notice will be closed.

- If the taxpayer pays all their dues and a penalty of 50% within 30 days from the date of order, then all proceedings (including prosecution) regarding the notice will be closed.

Payment of Tax and other Amounts in Instalments

- On an application filed electronically by a taxable person, in FORM GST DRC- 20, seeking extension of time for the payment of any amount due or for allowing payment in instalments the Commissioner shall call for a report from the jurisdictional officer about the financial ability of the taxable person to pay the said amount.

- Upon consideration of the request of the taxable person and the report of the jurisdictional officer, the Commissioner may issue an order in FORM GST DRC- 21, allowing further time to make payment and/or to pay the amount in monthly instalments (not exceeding twenty-four), as he may deem fit.

- Such facility shall not be allowed where:

  o the taxable person has already defaulted on the payment of any amount for which the recovery process is on

  o the taxable person has not been allowed to make payment in instalments in the preceding financial year

  o the amount for which instalment facility is sought is less than Rs 25,000

Rules of Tax / Penalty (s.75)

- If the service of notice or issue of the order has been stayed by a Tribunal/Court order, then the stay period will be excluded from the time limits of 3 and 5 years.

- If the Appellate Authority/Tribunal/Court decides that charges of fraud are not sustainable (not a fraud case), then the notice issued earlier will be assumed to be a notice u/s 73 (non-fraud case). The tax officer will calculate the tax accordingly.

- If the Tribunal/Court directs that an order has to be passed, then such order will be issued within two years from the date of the direction.

- An opportunity of a personal hearing will be given to the taxpayer (when such request is made in writing OR a penalty or any adverse decision is proposed against such person).

  The proper officer can adjourn the personal hearing if the person provides sufficient cause in writing. But adjournment will be allowed for a maximum of 3 times.

- The amount of tax, interest and penalty demanded in the order will not exceed the amount specified in the notice. All demands will be only on grounds specified in the notice.

- The Appellate Authority/Tribunal/Court can modify the amount of tax determined by the officer.

- Interest unpaid/short paid tax will have to be paid whether or not specified in the order.

- If the order is not issued within 3 or 5 years then it is assumed that the adjudication proceedings are completed. No order will be issued afterwards.

- Pending cases where the decision was against the interest of revenue, might be appealed to a higher authority. For these, the period between the date of the decision (aggrieved order) and the date of appeal decision of higher authority) will be excluded from the period of 3/5 years.

- Recovery provisions for unpaid/short paid tax and interest is applicable irrespective of demand provisions.

- When penalty is imposed u/s 73 or 74, no other penalty can be imposed. However, charges for offences u/s 132 facing prosecution will not be dropped.

Recovery

Recovery means the action taken by tax authorities to recover the Tax due from the Assessee. The Tax authority may take recourse to following means of recovery process.

- **Recovery by Deduction from money owed:** Where any amount payable by to the Government is not paid, the proper officer may require, in FORM GST DRC-09, a specified officer to deduct the amount from any money owing to such defaulter u/s 79 (1).

- **Recovery by Sale of Goods under the Control of Proper Officer**

  - Where any amount due from a defaulter is to be recovered by selling goods belonging to such person u/s 79 (1)(b), the proper officer shall prepare an inventory and estimate the market value of such goods and proceed to sell only so much of the goods as may be required for recovering the amount payable along with the administrative expenditure incurred on the recovery process.

  - The said goods shall be sold through a process of auction, including e-auction, for which a notice shall be issued in FORM GST DRC-10 clearly indicating the goods to be sold and the purpose of sale.

  - The last day for submission of bid or the date of auction shall not be earlier than fifteen days from the date of issue of the notice. However, where the goods are of perishable or hazardous nature or expenses of keeping them in custody are likely to exceed their value, the proper officer may sell them forthwith.

- The proper officer may specify the amount of pre-bid deposit to be furnished, to make the bidders eligible to participate in the auction. Such amount may be returned to the unsuccessful bidders, forfeited in case the successful bidder fails to make the payment of the full amount.

- The proper officer shall issue a notice to the successful bidder in FORM GST DRC-11, to make payment within fifteen days from the date of auction.

- On payment of the full bid amount, the proper officer shall transfer the possession of the said goods to the successful bidder and issue a certificate in FORM GST DRC-12.

- Where the defaulter pays the amount under recovery, including any expenses incurred on the process of recovery, before the issue of the notice of auction, the proper officer shall cancel the process of auction and release the goods.

- where no bid is received or the auction is considered to be non-competitive due to lack of adequate participation or due to low bids, the officer may cancel the auction process and proceed for re-auction

- **Recovery From a Third Person:** The proper officer may serve upon a third person u/s 79(1)(c), a notice in FORM GST DRC-13 directing him to deposit the amount specified in the notice. Where the third person makes the payment of the amount specified in the notice issued, the proper officer shall issue a certificate in FORM GST DRC-14 to the third person clearly indicating the details of the liability so discharged.

- **Recovery through Execution of Decree:** Where any amount is payable to the defaulter in the execution of a decree of a civil court for the payment of money or for sale in the enforcement of a mortgage or charge, the proper officer shall send a request in FORMGST DRC- 15 to the said court and the court shall (subject to provisions of the Code of Civil Procedure, 1908), execute the attached decree, and credit the net proceeds for settlement of the amount recoverable.

- **Recovery by Sale of Movable or Immovable Property**

  - The proper officer shall prepare a list of movable and immovable property belonging to the defaulter, estimate their value as per the prevalent market price and issue an order of attachment or distraint and a notice for sale in FORM GST DRC- 16 prohibiting any transaction with regard to such movable and immovable property, for recovery of the amount due. However, attachment of any property in a debt not secured by a negotiable instrument, a share in a corporation, or other movable property not in the possession of the defaulter except for property deposited in, or in the custody of any Court, shall be attached in the manner provided in rule 151.

  - The proper officer shall send a copy of the order of attachment or distraint to the concerned Revenue Authority or Transport Authority or any such Authority to place encumbrance on the said movable or immovable property, to be removed only on the written instructions from the proper officer to that effect. Where the property subject to the attachment or distraint is:

    o *immovable property*, the order of attachment or distraint shall be kept affixed on the property till the confirmation of sale.

    o *movable property*, the proper officer shall seize the said property, and the custody of the said property shall either be taken by the proper officer

– The property attached or distrained shall be sold through auction / e-auction, for which a notice shall be issued in FORM GST DRC- 17 clearly indicating the property to be sold and the purpose of sale.

– Where the property to be sold is a negotiable instrument or a share in a corporation, the proper officer may, instead of selling it by public auction, sell such instrument or a share through a broker and the said broker shall deposit to the Government so much of the proceeds of such sale, reduced by his commission, as may be required for the discharge of the amount under recovery and pay the amount remaining, if any, to the owner of such instrument or a share.

– The proper officer may specify the amount of pre-bid deposit to be furnished in the manner specified by such officer, to make the bidders eligible to participate in the auction, which may be returned to the unsuccessful bidders or, forfeited in case the successful bidder fails to make the payment of the full amount, as the case may be.

– The last day for the submission of the bid or the date of the auction shall not be earlier than fifteen days from the date of issue of the notice. However, where the goods are of perishable or hazardous nature or where the expenses of keeping them in custody are likely to exceed their value, the proper officer may sell them forthwith.

– Where any claim is preferred or any objection is raised with regard to the attachment or distraint of any property on the ground that such property is not liable to such attachment or distraint, the proper officer shall investigate the claim or objection and may postpone the sale for such time as he may deem fit.

– The person making the claim or objection must adduce evidence to show that on the date of the order issued under sub-rule (1) he had some interest in, or was in possession of, the property in question under attachment or distraint.

– Where, upon investigation, the proper officer is satisfied that, on the said date, such property was not in possession of the defaulter or of any other person on his behalf or that, being in the possession of the defaulter on the said date, it was in his possession, not on his own account or as his own property, but on account of or in trust for any other person, or partly on his own account and partly on account of some other person, the proper officer shall make an order releasing the property, wholly or to such extent as he thinks fit, from attachment or distraint.

– Where the proper officer is satisfied that the property was, on the said date, in the possession of the defaulter as his own property and not on account of any other person, or was in the possession of some other person in trust for him, or in the occupancy of a tenant or other person paying rent to him, the proper officer shall reject the claim and proceed with the process of sale through auction.

– The proper officer shall issue a notice to the successful bidder in FORM GST DRC-11 to makepayment within 15 days of such notice. After the said payment is made, he shall issue a certificate in FORM GST DRC-12 specifying the details. On issue of such certificate, the rights, title and interest in the property shall be deemed to be transferred to such bidder: Where the highest bid is made by more than one person and one of them is a co-owner of the property, he shall be deemed to be the successful bidder.

- Any amount, including stamp duty, tax or fee payable in respect of the transfer of the property, shall by the person to whom the title in such property is transferred.

- Where the defaulter pays the amount under recovery, including any expenses incurred on the process of recovery, before the issue of the notice, the proper officer shall cancel the process of auction and release the goods.

- Where no bid is received or the auction is considered to be non-competitive due to lack of adequate participation or due to low bids, the proper officer shall cancel the process and proceed for re-auction.

- **Recovery Through Land Revenue Authority**: Where an amount is to be recovered/s 79(1)(e), the proper officer shall send a certificate to the Collector or Deputy Commissioner of the district or any other officer authorised in this behalf in FORM GST DRC-18 to recover specified amount from as an arrear of land revenue.

- **Recovery Through Court:** Where an amount is to be recovered as fine imposed under the Code of Criminal Procedure, 1973, the proper officer shall make an application before the appropriate Magistrate u/s 79(1)(f), in FORM GST DRC- 19 to recover the specified amount as if it were a fine imposed by him.

- **Recovery From Surety:** Where any person has become surety for the amount due by the defaulter, he may be proceeded against as a defaulter.

- **Recovery from Company in Liquidation**:Where the company is under liquidation, the Commissioner shall notify the liquidator, in FORM GST DRC -24. for recovery of any amount representing tax, interest, penalty or any other amount due.

Continuation of Certain Recovery Proceedings: The order for the reduction or enhancement of any demand, shall be issued in FORM GST DRC- 25.

Attachment of Properties & Interest in Partnership

- **Attachment of Debts, Shares & other movable properties**:

  - A debt not secured by a negotiable instrument, a share in a corporation, or other movable property not in the possession of the defaulter except for property deposited in, or in the custody of any court shall be attached by a written order in FORM GST DRC-16 prohibiting.-

    o in the case of *debt*, the creditor from recovering the debt and the debtor from making payment thereof until the receipt of a further order from the proper officer;

    o in the case of *share*, the person in whose name the share may be standing from transferring the same or receiving any dividend thereon;

    o in the case of any other *movable* property, the person in possession of the same from giving it to the defaulter.

  - A copy of such order shall be affixed on some conspicuous part of the office of the proper officer, and another copy shall be sent, in the case of debt, to the debtor, and in the case of shares, to the registered address of the corporation and in the case of other movable property, to the person in possession of the same.

   – Such debtor may pay the amount of his debt to the proper officer, and such payment shall be deemed as paid to the defaulter.

- **Attachment of Property in Custody of Courts or Public Officer:** Where the property to be attached is in the custody of any court or Public Officer, the proper officer shall send the order of attachment to such court or officer, requesting that such property, and any interest or dividend becoming payable thereon, may be held till the recovery of the amount payable.

- **Attachment of Interest in Partnership:** Where the property to be attached consists of an interest of the defaulter, being a partner, in the partnership property, the proper officer may make order charging the share of such partner and profits in the partnership property, with payment of the amount due under the certificate. The officer may appoint a receiver of the share of such partner in the profits, whether already declared or accruing, and of any other money which may become due to him in respect of the partnership, and direct accounts and enquiries and make an order for the sale of such interest or such other order as the circumstances of the case may require. The other partners shall be at liberty at any time, to redeem the interest charged or, in the case of a sale being directed, to purchase the same.

Provisional Attachment of Property

– Where the Commissioner decides to attach any property, including bank account, he shall pass an order in FORM GST DRC-22, giving the details of property attached.

– The Commissioner shall send a copy of the order of attachment to the concerned Authority, to place encumbrance on the property, which shall be removed only on the written instructions from the Commissioner to that effect.

– Where the property attached is of perishable or hazardous nature, and if the taxable person pays an amount equivalent to the market price of such property (or the amount payable by the taxable person, whichever is lower), then such property shall be released forthwith, by an order in FORM GST DRC-23, on proof of payment.

– Where the taxable person fails to pay the amount of the said property of perishable or hazardous nature, the Commissioner may dispose of such property and the amount realized thereby shall be adjusted against the tax, interest, penalty, fee or any other amount payable by the taxable person.

– Any person whose property is attached may, within seven days of the attachment, file an objection to the effect that the property attached was or is not liable to attachment. The Commissioner may, after affording an opportunity of being heard to the person filing the objection, The Commissioner may, upon being satisfied that the property is not liable for attachment, release such property by issuing an order in FORM GST DRC- 23.

Appropriation and Disposal of Sales Proceeds

The amounts realised from the sale of goods, movable or immovable property, for the recovery of dues from a defaulter shall be appropriated s follows:

– first, against the administrative cost of the recovery process;

– next, against the amount to be recovered;

- next, against any other amount due from the defaulter GST rules
- any balance, be paid to the defaulter.

GST Demand & Recovery Forms

GST DRC – 01: Summary of Show Cause Notice

GST DRC - 02: Summary of Statement

GST DRC - 03: Intimation of payment made voluntarily or made against the show cause notice (SCN) or statement

GST DRC - 04: Acknowledgement of acceptance of payment made voluntarily

GST DRC - 05: Intimation of conclusion of proceedings

GST DRC - 06: Reply to the Show Cause Notice

GST DRC - 07: Summary of Order

GST DRC - 08: Rectification of Order

GST DRC - 09: Order for recovery through specified officer u/s79

GST DRC - 10: Notice for Auction of Goods u/s 79 (1) (b)

GST DRC - 11: Notice to successful bidder

GST DRC - 12: Sale Certificate

GST DRC - 13: Notice to a third person u/s 79(1) (c)

GST DRC – 14: Certificate of Payment to Third Person

GST DRC – 15: Application before civil court requesting execution for decree

GST DRC – 16: Notice for attachment and sale u/s 79

GST DRC – 17: Notice for Auction u/s 79(1) (d)

GST DRC – 18: Certificate action u/s 79 (1) (e)

GST DRC – 19: Application to Magistrate for Recovery as Fine

GST DRC – 20: Application for Deferred Payment/ Payment in Instalments

GST DRC – 21: Order for acceptance/rejection of application for deferred payment / payment in instalments

GST DRC – 22: Provisional attachment of property u/s 83

GST DRC – 23: Restoration of provisionally attached property / bank account u/s 83

GST DRC – 24: Intimation to Liquidator for recovery

GST DRC – 25: Continuation of Recovery Proceedings

Penalties & Prosecution

Offences & Penalties

- **Offence:** Offence is a breach of a law
- **Penalty:** Penalty is a punishment imposed by law for committing an offence or failing to do something that was the duty of a party to do. Under GST rules, both corporal (jail) or pecuniary monetary), civil or criminal Penalty, may be imposed

Offences under GST

- **Fake/wrong invoices**

    o   Supplies any goods/services without any invoice or issues a false invoice.

    o   Issues any invoice or bill without supply of goods/services in violation of GST rules

    o   Issues invoices using the identification number of another bonafide taxable person

- **Fraud**

    o   Submits false information while registering under GST

    o   Submits fake financial records/documents or files fake returns to evade tax

    o   Does not provide information/gives false information during proceedings

- **Tax evasion**

    o   Collects GST but does not submit it to the government within 3 months

    o   Obtains refund of any CGST/SGST by fraud.

    o   Avails or utilizes input tax credit without actual receipt of goods and/or services

    o   Deliberately suppresses his sales to evade tax

- **Supply/transport of goods**

    o   Transports goods without proper documents

    o   Supplies/transports goods liable for confiscation

    o   Destroys/tampers goods which have been seized

- **Others**

    o   Does not file return, as prescribed under law

    o   Does not file return within specified time, as prescribed under law

    o   Has not registered under GST although he is required to by law o   Does not deduct TDS where applicable, or deducts less amount

o   Does not collect TCS where applicable, or collects less amount

o   Being an Input Service Distributor, takes or distributes input tax credit in violation of rules

o   Obstructs proper officer during his duty

o   Does not maintain all books as required by law

o   Destroys any evidence

Common Offences - Fines / Penalties

–   **Delay in filing GSTR**: Late fee is Rs. 100 per day per Act (Rs 100 under CGST & 100 under SGST) & Interest @18% pa, for delayed period. Maximum late fee Rs. 5,000. No late fee on IGST.

–   **Not filing GSTR**: Penalty of 10% of tax due or Rs. 10,000, whichever is higher

–   **Fraud**: Penalty 100% of tax due or Rs. 10,000, whichever is higher. For High value fraud, in addition to Penalty, Jail Term upto1 year (Rs 100-200 Lakhs), upto 2 year (Rs 200 - 500 Lakhs), Upto 5 Years (above Rs.500 Lakhs)

–   **Non-fraud Offence**: Penalty of 10% of tax due or Rs. 10,000, whichever is higher

–   **Helping a person to commit fraud**: Penalty extending upto Rs. 25,000

–   **Wrongly opting for composition scheme**: Demand & Recovery u/s 73 & 74

–   **Wrongfully charging GST Rate**: Penalty of 100% of tax due or Rs. 10,000, whichever is higher (if additional GST collected is not deposited with govt)

–   **Not issuing invoice**: Penalty of 100% of tax due or Rs. 10,000, whichever is higher

–   **Not registering under GST**: Penalty of 100% of tax due or Rs. 10,000, whichever is higher

–   **Incorrect invoicing**: Penalty of Rs. 25,000

–   **General Offence**: Any other offence under GST for which penalty not specifically mentioned, penalty upto Rs. 25,000.

–   **Minor Breaches:** For Minor breaches (tax amount less than Rs.5000) or unintentional rectifiable errors: No substantial penalties (tax authority may issue a warning).

–   **Third Party Offences:** Penalty may be imposed even on persons other than Taxable person, where the person:

o   Helps any person to commit fraud under GST

o   Deals with goods subject to confiscation

o   Fails to appear before the tax authority on receiving a summons

o   Fails to issue an invoice according to GST rules

o   Fails to account/vouch any invoice appearing in the books

Notice of Penalty: Every person, on whom the penalty is imposed, will be served Show Cause Notice, offering reasonable opportunity of being heard. The tax authority will explain nature of offence and reason for penalty. When a person voluntarily discloses a breach of law, the tax authority may reduce the penalty

Prosecution: Prosecution is conducting legal proceedings for criminal charges.

Offences liable for Prosecution: Any person committing the following offences (deliberate intention of fraud) becomes liable to prosecution on criminal charges. Apart from prosecution, the offender can also be arrested.

– Supplies any goods/services without an invoice to evade tax

– Issues any invoice without supplying any goods/services, to avail input credit or refund by fraud

– Collects any GST but does not submit it to the government within 3 months.

– Obtains refund of tax by fraud.

– Submits fake financial records/documents or files fake returns to evade tax

– Obstructs the proper officer during his duty

– Acquires/receives goods/services liable for confiscation (having knowledge)

– Destroys any evidence

– Does not provide information/gives false information during proceedings

– Helps any person to commit fraud under GST

Compounding of offences: Compounding means forbearance from prosecution (payment of Tax & Penalty) to evade litigation. Penalty of 50% of the tax involved (minimum Rs. 10,000), Maximum 150% of the tax, or Rs. 30,000, whichever is higher. On payment of the compounding amount, no further proceedings shall be initiated against the accused person for the same offence and any criminal proceedings, if already initiated, will be abated.

Presumption of "Mens Rea" or Guilty Mind: When prosecuting an offender, the court shall assume that the accused had a guilty mind, or the law was intentionally broken. The accused will have to prove it otherwise.

Cognizance of Offence: Offences where the evasion of tax is less than Rs.5 crores shall be non-cognizable and bailable, while offences where the evasion of tax exceeds Rs.5 crores shall be cognizable and non-bailable.

Inspection Under GST

The Joint Commissioner (or a higher officer) having reasons to believe that a person has suppressed any transaction or claimed excess input tax credit etc, to evade tax,can authorize any other officer (in writing) to inspect places of business of the suspected evader.

Search & Seizure under GST

- **Goods with Tax payer**: The Joint Commissioner, having reasons to believe, that there are goods liable to confiscation, may order for search of any premises. Any incriminating goods, documents or books, or any hidden things hidden may be seized

- **Goods with carrier:** The person in charge of a vehicle carrying goods exceeding Rs. 50,000 is required to carry Invoice / bill of supply / delivery challan / Copy of e-way bill (hard copy or via RFID). The proper officer may intercept Goods-in-transit, inspect goods and documents.

Goods found in contravention, related documents and the vehicle carrying them may be seized. The goods will be released only on payment of Tax and Penalty.

Before confiscating the goods, the tax officer shall give an option of paying a fine instead of confiscation.

Arrest Under GST

If the Commissioner believes a person has committed any grave offense liable for arrest, he can be arrested under GST by any authorized officer

The arrested person will be informed of the grounds for his arrest. He will appear before the magistrate within 24 hours in case of a cognizable offense (offenses where the police can arrest a person without an arrest warrant)

Offenses u/s 132 attracting arrest provisions

- A taxable person supplies any goods/services without any invoice or issues a false invoice

- He issues any invoice or bill without supply of goods/services in violation of the provisions of GST

- He collects any GST but does not submit it to the government within 3 months

- Even if he collects any GST in contravention of provisions, he still has to deposit it to the government within 3 months. Failure to do so will be an offense under GST

- He has already been convicted of an earlier u/s 132 i.e., this is his 2nd offense

A person can be arrested only where the tax evasion is more than Rs.100 lakhs rupees or where a person has earlier been convicted of an offence u/s 132.

Appeals

Appeals to Higher Authority

At the conclusion of a proceeding in a court, a Party may feel that the case has not been properly interpreted and is not satisfied with the court decision. The aggrieved Party may think that something went wrong with the first decision and that it should be changed. In such case, the aggrieved Party may request higher authority (i.e Appeal) to relook into the case.

In legal terms, Appeal is a legal proceeding by which a case is brought before a higher court for review of the decision of a lower court.

Appeals Under GST: Any person unhappy with any decision or order passed by an adjudicating authority under GST, can appeal to the First Appellate Authority. GST law provides 4 tiers for appeals

- 1st Appeal – Appellate Authority

- 2nd Appeal – Appellate Tribunal

- 3rd Appeal – High court

- 4th Appeal – Supreme Court

Appeal Procedure: All appeals should be filed as per prescribed forms with requisite fees. Fee for an appeal shall be100% of the tax amount, interest, fee, penalty, arising from such challenged orderAND10% of the disputed amount (upto 25% where the disputed tax amount is above Rs 25 Crores). However, where the GST officer is the appealing person, no such prepayment of fees is required.

Any person required to appear before a GST Officer/First Appellate Authority/Appellate Tribunal can assign an authorized representative to appear on his behalf, unless he is required by the Act to appear personally

Appeals cannot be made for the following decisions:

- An order to transfer the proceedings from one officer to another officer

- An order to seize or retain books of account and other documents;

- An order sanctioning prosecution under the Act;

- An order allowing payment of tax and other amount in installments

Appeals pre-deposit

- An appellant before AA would pre-deposit full amount of tax, interest, fine, fee and penalty, as is admitted by him, arising from the impugned order and a sum equal to 10% of the remaining amount of tax in dispute arising from the impugned order.

- In case of appeals to Tribunal, appellant should deposit in full, such part of the amount of tax, interest, fine, fee and penalty arising from the impugned order, as is admitted by him, and a sum equal to 20% of the remaining amount of tax in dispute, in addition to the amount deposited before the AA.

- If the pre-deposit made by the appellant before the AA or Tribunal, is required to be refunded consequent to any order of the AA or of the Tribunal, interest shall be payable from the date of payment of the amount till the date of refund of such amount.

Appeal to First Appellate Authority

- A person unhappy with the order passed by an adjudicating can appeal within 3 months (extendable up to 1 month) from the date of the order in FORM GST APL-01.

- The First Appellate Authority may adjourn the hearing of the appeal if there is sufficient cause, by recording the reasons in writing. Adjournment will be allowed only three times.

- The First Appellate Authority can confirm, modify or annul the decision, but will not refer the case back to the authority

- Any order increasing any fee/penalty/fine or confiscating higher value goods or decreasing the refund or input tax credit will be passed only after a reasonable opportunity of showing cause.

- Any order for payment of unpaid/short-paid tax or wrong refunds or input tax credit wrongly availed will be passed only after the appellant is given show cause notice.

- The order must be passed within 1 year from the date of filing the appeal. If the order is stayed by an order of a Court or Tribunal, the period of such stay shall be excluded in from the one year period

- The First Appellate Authority shall communicate the order passed to the appellant and to the adjudicating authority. A copy of the order will also be sent to the jurisdictional Commissioners of CGST and SGST.

- The Revision Authority can, on his own, or on request from the Commissioner, examine the records of any proceeding. He will examine the records if he considers that any decision by any subordinate officer is prejudicial to the interest of the revenue, Illegal, Improper, some facts were ignored, or some observation was made by the C&AG. It can stay the order for a time period as he deems fit. The person concerned will be given an opportunity of being heard. Chief Commissioner or Commissioner can enhance or modify or annul the order.

Appeals before Tribunal

The Tribunal is the second level of appeal, where appeals can be filed by any person aggrieved by such an Order-in-Appeal/ Order-in-Revision, against the orders-in-appeal passed by the AA or order in revision passed by revision authority.

- **Jurisdiction**: If place of supply is one of the issues in dispute, then the National Bench/ Regional benches of the Tribunal will have jurisdiction to hear the appeal.

  If the dispute relates to issues other than the place of supply, then the State/Area Benches will have the jurisdiction to hear the appeal.

An appeal from the decision of the National Bench will lie directly to the Supreme Court and an appeal from the decision of the State Bench will lie to the jurisdictional High Court on substantial questions of law.

- **Time Limit**: Appeal to the Tribunal is to be filed within 3 months from the communication of the order under appeal. Further, Tribunal has the power to condone delay (of up to 3 months in case of appeals or 45 days in case of cross objections, beyond the mandatory period).

- **Threshold Amount**: The Tribunal has the discretion of not admitting any appeal involving an amount of Rs. 50,000 or less.

- **Cross Objection**: Cross-objections by the respondent against such part of the order against which the respondent may initially not have chosen to file an appeal.

  On receipt of notice of filing appeal by the appellant, the party against whom the appeal has been preferred (respondent) may, notwithstanding, that he may not have appealed against such order or any part thereof, file memorandum of cross-objections, within 45 days, against any part of the order appealed against. Such memorandum shall be disposed of by the Appellate Tribunal as if it were an appeal presented within the time specified for the initial appeal.

  Condonation of delay (on sufficient cause) applies here also, but only to the extent of further 45 days from the date of expiry of the period for filing cross objections.

- **Form &Fees**: The form, fees, etc. for the appeals to Tribunal shall be as prescribed by Rules.

- **Orders:** The Tribunal, after hearing both sides, may pass such orders confirming, modifying or annulling the decision. It may also refer the case back to the AA or to the revision authority, or to the original adjudicating authority. The Tribunal may grant up to 3 adjournments to either side.

Appeal to the High Court

- The Party (department or party), aggrieved by any order passed by the Tribunal, may file an appeal to the High Court. High Court, satisfied that the case involves a substantial question of law, may admit such appeal. Appeals to the High Court are to be filed within 180 days (HC may condone delay on sufficient cause).

- The High Court will only allow appeals in cases involving a substantial question of law.

- The High Court shall formulate the substantial question of law involved in any case and hear the appeals on the basis of the question. However, the respondents can argue that the case does not involve such question at the hearing.

- The High Court can decide on any issue which has not been determined by the State Bench or Area Benches, or has been wrongly determined by the State Bench or Area Benches, due to the question of law raised.

However, appeals cannot be made to the High Court where 2 or more states or when the state and Centre have different views. These cases will go straight to Supreme Court.

Decisions: The appeal will be heard by a bench of at least 2 High Court Judges. Decision will be on the basis of majority. If there is no majority, then one or more other High Court Judges will hear the different points and decide the verdict on a majority basis, considering the opinions of both the original and new judges.

Appeal to Supreme Court

Any person unhappy with the High Court, National Bench or Regional Benches can appeal to the Supreme Court if the High Court certifies to be fit for appeal to the Supreme Court. Cases where 2 states or State and Centre have different views will be automatically appealed to the Supreme Court.

The costs of the appeal shall be at the discretion of the Supreme Court

All sums due under order passed by the Appellate Tribunal or High Court must be paid even if appealed to Supreme Court.

Advance Ruling

Expert Interpretation of Law

Sometimes a party going into a business transaction, may like to understand proper interpretation and tax implication of the transaction, to safeguard from unforeseen loss or legal dispute. In such case, the party may approach an empowered proper authority to give written opinion on the issue.

Advance Ruling

Advance tax ruling is a written interpretation of tax laws. It is issued by tax authorities in response to request by taxpayer for clarification of certain tax matters (when the taxpayer is confused and uncertain about certain provisions). Advance ruling helps the applicant in planning his activities which are liable for Tax, well in advance. Advance tax ruling is applied for, before starting the proposed activity.

Authority for Advance Rulings under GST

It is an independent quasi-judicial body outside the Tax department, consisting of senior officers of the Government of India, and headed by retired Judge,

- The Authority for advance ruling constituted under the provisions of State Goods and Services Tax Act or Union Territory Goods and Services Tax Act shall be deemed to be the Authority for advance ruling in respect of that State or Union territory under the CGST Act, 2017 also.

- The Appellate Authority for Advance Ruling constituted under the provisions of a State Goods and Services Tax Act or a Union Territory Goods and Services Tax Act shall be deemed to be the Appellate Authority in respect of that State or Union territory under the CGST Act, 2017 also.

- Both the Authority for Advance Ruling (AAR) & the Appellate Authority for Advance Ruling (AAAR) are constituted under the respective State/Union Territory Act (and not the Central Act). So, ruling given by the AAR & AAAR will be applicable only within the jurisdiction of the concerned state or union territory. So, questions on determination of place of supply cannot be raised with the AAR or AAAR.

Advance ruling in GST

An advance ruling helps the applicant in planning his activities which are liable for payment of GST, well in advance. It also brings certainty in determining the tax liability, helps in avoiding future litigation as the ruling is binding on the applicant as well as Government authorities.

- **Objective of advance ruling**:

  - Provide certainty for tax liability in advance, to a future activity to be undertaken by the applicant

  - Clarifying taxation and showing a clear picture of the future tax liability for Investors / non-residents

  - Reduce litigation and costly legal disputes

- Give decisions in a timely, transparent and inexpensive manner
- Attract Foreign Direct Investment (FDI)

- **Request for Advance ruling:** A non-resident (individual, company, firm, association of persons or other body corporate) can request an Advance Ruling with respect to tax liability in relation to a transaction, which has been undertaken or proposed to be undertaken. A resident of India can also request for an advance ruling, if the transaction involves a non-resident.

- **Matters for GST Advance Ruling:** Advance ruling can be requested about:
  - Classification of any goods and/or services
  - Applicability of a notification which affects the rate of tax
  - Determination of time and value of supply of goods/services
  - Admissibility of input tax credit paid (or deemed to be paid)
  - Determination of the liability to pay tax on any goods/services
  - Whether the applicant has to be registered under GST
  - Whether any particular act regarding goods/services will result in a supply.
  - On receipt of an application, a copy will be forwarded to the prescribed officer to furnish the necessary relevant records.

- **Process of Advance Ruling under GST:** A request for advance ruling is first sent to Authority for Advance Ruling (Authority), FORM GST ARA-01, along with fees Rs. 5,000

  The Authority can by order, either admit or reject the application. Advance ruling decision will be given within 90 days from application. If the members of the Authority differ in opinion on any point, they will refer the point to the Appellate Authority. Advance Ruling will have prospective effect only.

- **Rejection of Advance Ruling:** The Authority will NOT admit the application when same matter has already been decided in an earlier case for the applicant, or is pending in any proceedings for the applicant. Applications will be rejected only after giving an opportunity of being heard. Reasons for rejection shall be given in writing. Any person unhappy with the advance ruling can appeal to the Appellate Authority for Advance Ruling (Appellate Authority).

Validity of Advance Ruling

- Though law does not provide for a fixed time period for which the ruling shall apply, advance ruling shall be binding till the period when the law, facts or circumstances supporting the original advance ruling have not changed.

- The advance ruling will be binding only on the specific applicant and on the jurisdictional tax authorities in respect of the applicant. If the law, facts of the original advance ruling change then the advance ruling will not apply. Advance ruling will not be valid if the facts of the transaction actually executed are materially different from the facts on the basis of which the ruling was pronounced.

Appeals against order of AAR

- If the applicant is aggrieved with the finding of the AAR, he can file an appeal with AAAR.

- Similarly, if the prescribed or jurisdictional officer of CGST/SGST does not agree with the finding of AAR, he can also file an appeal with AAAR.

- Any appeal must be filed within thirty days from the receipt of the advance ruling, in form GST ARA -02.

- The Appellate Authority must pass an order after hearing the parties to the appeal,within 90 days of the filing of appeal.

- If members of AAAR differ on any point referred to in appeal, it shall be deemed that no advance ruling is issued in respect of the question under appeal.

Rectification of Mistakes

AAR and AAAR may amend their order to rectify any mistake apparent from the record within a period of six months from the date of the order. Such mistake may be noticed by the authority on its own accord or may be brought to its notice by applicant or GSTofficer. If a rectification has the effect of enhancing the tax liability or reducing the quantum of input tax credit, the applicant must be heard before the order is passed.

Powers and procedure of AAR and AAAR

AAR and AAAR have powers of a civil court for discovery and inspection, enforcing the attendance of a person, examining him on oath, and compelling production of books of account and other records. Any proceeding before the authority shall be deemed to be judicial proceeding.

Advance Ruling Forms

- GST ARA 01 - Application Form for Advance Ruling

- GST ARA 02 - Appeal to Appellate Authority for Advance Ruling [Rule 106(1)]

- GST ARA 03 - Appeal to Appellate Authority for Advance Ruling [Rule 106(2)]

PART 2
GSTN PORTAL

On line GST Registration

GST on line New Registration Process

We have explained the legal provisions related to Registration under GST and the rules of Registration.

Now we explain the on-line GST New Registration process, through GST portal. In web browser, type *www.gst.gov.in* to get GST Portal homepage(F-1A).

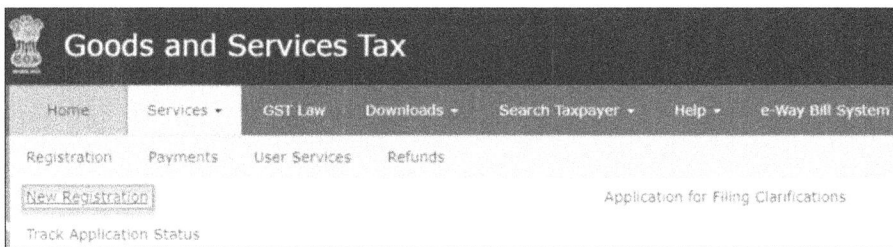

F-1A: GST Homepage – New Registration

At GST Portal homepage (F-1A). select *Services>Registration> New Registration* to get the New Registration Form (F-1B), to enter the details as follows (F-1B):

– **Status**: In the drop-down under I am a – select *Taxpayer* [For registration by other types of persons, select the appropriate option from the list, like: GST Practitioner, Tax Deductor (TDS), Tax Collector (e-commerce), Non Resident Taxable Person]

– **State / District / UT**: Select *State / District* (or Union Territory), as applicable, from the drop down list

– **District:** Select the District from the drop down list of selected State

– **Legal Name of Business**: Enter the Name of Business and PAN of the business (in case of proprietorship Firm, enter the name of Proprietor, as written in the PAN card)

– **PAN:** Enter the PAN correctly (each letter in sperate cell).

– **E-mail address**: Enter the email Address (e-mail OTP would be sent to this e-mail). This e-mail ID becomes your registered e-mail for all communication by GST authorities. So, it is very important and specify it correctly.

– **Mobile Number**: Enter Mobile Number. (mobile OTP would be sent to this Mobile. So, it is very important and specify it correctly.

The registered email id and mobile number will receive the OTPs.

– **Captcha**: Type the Captcha (an image showing some specially formatted number) displayed (click on the resend icon to change the Captcha if you cannot read it properly

– **Proceed**: Click on Proceed button, to get *OTP Verification* screen (F-1C)

F-1B: On-line GST New Registration Form

OTP Verification: At OTP verification screen (F-1C), enter as follows:

– **e-mail OTP**: At e-mail OTP, enter the OTP received (better copy paste to ensure correctness) in your e-mail (check the Junk / Spam folder if you do not get the e-mail), sent from donotreply@gst.gov.in from the GST e-mail (read the instructions in the e-mail.

– **Mobile OTP**: At Mobile OTP, enter the OTP received in your Mobile Phone

Enter the two OTP separately, as received in e-mail and OTP (they are different). Click on *Continue* button. If you have not received the OTP click on *Resend OTP*.

F-1C: OTP Verification for GST On-line Registration

Temporary Reference Number (TRN): The Temporary Reference Number (TRN) auto allotted by the Portal (F-2A), would be shown. Note down the TRN. The TRN will also be sent to by email and SMS to mobile.

F-2A: Temporary Registration Number allotment

You will get a message (F-2A) showing the date by which the Application can be filed using the allotted TRN (otherwise the Temporary Registration will expire and you will have to submit the Application again). You can access the Application form the Portal from *My Saved Application* and then submit on GST Portal

Application Reference: Go to the Portal again (www.gst.gov.in) and get the New Registration Form as stated (F-1A). In the Form, click on the *Temporary Reference Number (TRN)* radio button. Now enter the following details obtained earlier:

– **TRN:** Enter the TRN

– **Captcha**: Enter the Captcha code exactly as displayed on the screen (if you cannot read the Captcha properly, click the round arrow icon to get a new Captcha Code).

Having entered the Captcha (F-2B), Click on *Proceed* button. You will get another mail from donotreply@ gst.gov.in showing OTP in your mobile and e-mail (same OTP). Enter the OTP (F-2C). Type the OTP at Verify OTP screen. Click PROCEED button.

F-2B: Temporary Registration – Captcha Entry

F-2C: Temporary Registration - OTP verification

You get the *My Saved Application* screen (F-3A), where you see the reference of Applications showing the Creation date (date of submission), Form Number &(GST-REG-01) and Form Description, Expiry Date of submission of Application (by which you must submit the application) and Status (as DRAFT).

F-3A: saved GST-REG01 applications

Submission of Application with Documents: Against the application reference shown on the screen, Click Edit (Pencil Icon) button (F-3A) to get Part B of the Application form and details of Documents (F-4A).

F-4A: GSTR Application form GST-REG-01 submission: Part B

Part B of Application Form: It shows a Tab bar with 10 sections (F-4A). Click on each section and fill up the respective details. After entering data at each section, click *Save & Continue* button at the end of each section, to proceed to select Tab of another section to enter data.

As you complete a section, the Tab colour changes to Blue and a tick mark appears, indicating filing the details of the respective section, for your reference. As you enter the details under each tab section, the last modified date is shown and the Profile updation percentage increases (F-4A).

F-4B: GST Registration Application – Business Details section

F-4C: GST Registration Application - Business Details section

Details to be filled up under each Tab of the Part B of Application Form

1. Business Details

Click on the *Business Details* Tab and enter the following Details (F-4B):

– **Legal Name of the Business**: It will be carried from the PAN by default.

– **Permanent Account Number**: PAN will be carried as entered in Part – A

– **Trade Name**: Enter the Trade name. Trade name may be different from Legal Name

– **Constitution of Business:** Select the Constitution of your business from the list. This will be validated with the CBDT Database for a match with the PAN entered in Part A of the form.

– **State Jursidiction**: Select the State where the business is situated, from the list

– **District**: Select the District where the business is situated, from the list

– **State Jurisdiction**: Enter the Jurisdiction

– **Sector / Circle/ Ward / Charge / Unit**: Select from the list, as per District of the State selected. VAT registered Taxpayers will find the details in their VAT registration certificate. You can get the list from respective State Tax website, or search from google.

– **Commissioner ate Code / Division Code / Range Code**: Select the Centre Jurisdiction applicable one from the list. Taxpayers registered under Central Excise / Service Tax find the details in their registration certificate.

Sector / ward / Charge/ Unit

You get the list as per District selected, but you often do not know the appropriate one applicable to your business. Click on the link for *Centre Jurisdiction*, to get the site of Central Board of Excise & Customs, from which you successively select the State, District / ward etc, note down and select the appropriate one from the respective list.

Application Type: At *Are you applying for Casual Taxable Person*, select *Yes* for Causal Application, Select *No* for permanent Registration (F-4C).

– **Composition Dealer:** At *Option for Composition*, select Yes if the application is for Composition Registration, else select No

– **Reason for Registration:** Select from the list of Reasons for Registration (you get the option depending on Type of Dealer selected). Depending on selection of type of Business from the list, you have to enter respective details for the specific type of Business.

– **Date of Commencement of Business:** Enter the Date when the business commenced (for exiting Business) or to commence from (for new Business).

– **Date on which liability to register arises:** Enter the Date when you become liable for Registration (you have to apply for registration within 30 days of such date)

    o   The registration for a normal taxpayer shall be effective from the date on which the person becomes liable for registration if he files the application for new registration within 30 days from the date on which the liability to register arises. however, in case of delay in filing of application of

New Registration, the date of liability to register remains same but effective date of registration shall be the date of grant of registration.

    o   A casual taxable person shall submit application at least five days prior to the commencement of business. For Casual Taxpayer, date on which liability to register arises is auto filled.

− **Existing Registration Details:** Enter the details of exiting registration with statutory authority (like VAT, Service Tax, Excise etc, Trade License etc)

    o   **Registration Type:** Select the Registration type from the list

    o   **Registration Number:** Enter the Registration number for the selected Type

    o   **Registration Date:** Enter the Registration Date for the selected Type

Click *Add* button to enter a new record for each existing Registration Type. Click *Cancel* button if you do not like to select any option at Existing Registration to come out of the list.

2. Promoter / Partners Details

Click on the *Promoter / Partners Details* Tab (F-4A) and enter the personal details of Proprietor (for Proprietorship Firm) / Partners (for Partnership firm) / Promoter / Director (for Company), as the case may be. The following details of Proprietor, for instance, are to be submitted, in 3 sections: (i) Personal Info, (ii) Identity Information (iii) Residential Address

Personal Information: Enter the personal details as follows (F-5A):

− **Name:** Enter the First / Middle & last Name of the applicant in respective cells

− **Father Name**: Enter the First / Middle & last Name of the applicant's father, in respective cells

− **Date of Birth**: Date of Birth of the Applicant in DD/MM/YYYY format

− **Mobile Number**: Enter the personal Mobile Number of the applicant

− **e-mail**: Enter the personal e-mail id of the applicant

− **Gender**: Select the Gender from the list

− **Telephone Number**: Enter the telephone number (landline with STD Code), if any

F-5A: GST Registration Application – Personal Info of Promoter Partner

F-5B: GST Registration Application –
Identity Info of Promoter Partner

Identity Details: Enter the following ID details of the person (F-5B)

– **Designation / Status**: Designation / Status of the person in respect of the organisation for which registration is being sought.

– **Director DIN**: Enter Director ID in case the person is Director in the Company. DIN is mandatory for Private Limited Company, Public Limited Company, Public Sector Undertaking, Unlimited Company, Foreign Company registered in India

– **Citizenship:** At *Are you citizen of India*, select *Yes* if Indian Citizen, else select *No*

– **Permanent Account Number**: PAN of the person

– **Passport Number**: Passport Number if foreigner (not Indian Citizen)

– **Aadhar Number**: Aadhar Number in case of Indian Resident.

Residential Address: Enter the Residence Address details like, i) Building / Flat Number, ii) Floor Number, iii) Name of Premises / Building, iv) Road / Street, v) City / Town / Locality / Village, Country, State, District, PIN Code.

Document Upload: Upload the Photograph / Document image (F-6A)

– **Photograph**: Upload the photograph of the person (whose details are submitted), in JPEG format (file not exceeding 100 KB), by selecting the image file

– **Documents**: Upload the authorization document (in PDF or JPEG format with 100KB size) like Letter of Authority, Board Resolution, as selected from the list (F-6B). Apart from Photograph, following documents are to be uploaded

o   Constitution of the taxpayer

o   Proof for the place of business

o   Bank account details

o   Authorization form

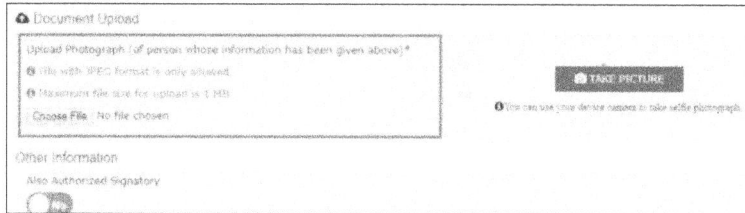

F-6A: Document upload

Authorised Signatory: Under the head *Other Information* (F-6A), at *Also Authorised Signatory*, select *Yes* if the person is also authorised signatory under GST Rules, else select *No*.

3. Authorised Signatory

You may specify the person whose details are submitted, as authorised signatory as explained. To specify any other person as Authorised Signatory, click Authorised Signatory Tab (F-4A) to get the entry screen similar to the Personal Details info discussed above.

You may also check the check box *Primary Authorised Signatory*, if the authorised Signatory is be made as Primary Authorised Signatory.

– **Photograph Upload**: As explained, upload the photograph of authorised signatory (or Click TAKE PICTURE button to capture photograph directly from device camera and upload therefrom).

– **Multiple Signatories**: To add another signatory, click ADD NEW button and enter details, upload document & photograph of another signatory, as explained (you should specify one of them as Primary Authorised Signatory, as explained)

4. Authorised Representative

Authorised Representative is a person appointed to represent the Tax Payer before the GST Officer, Appellate Authority or the Appellate Tribunal, in connection with any proceedings under the Act.

To add any Authorised Representative, click on the Tab *Authorised Representative*(F-4A).Select Yes at *Do you have any Authorised Representative*(F-7A). Select the option *GST Practitioner* or *Others*, as the case may be (F-7A) and accordingly, enter the details of appointed Authorised Representative (F-7B).

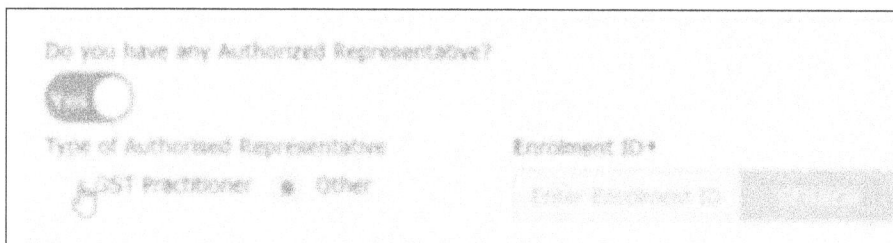

F-7A: Authorised Representative option

F-7B: Authorised Representative details entry

In case of GST practitioner, the Enrolment ID and the details are auto carried in the Form (F-7B). In case of Others persons appointed (other than GST Practitioner), enter the details in the Form (F-7B).

5. Principal Place of Business

Click on the Tab *Principal Place of Business* (F-4A). You get the entry screen with 3 major sections: i) Address (F-8A / 8B) ii) Contact Information (F-9A) iii) Nature of Business Activity (F-9B).

F-8A: Address details of Principal Place of Business

F-8B: Search for latitude & Longitude of place of business

Address: Enter the Address details like Building / Flat Number, Floor, Building name, Road / Street, City / Town / Village, as shown in the entry Form (F-9A).

– **State / District / PIN Code**: Select the State from list. Next select the District from list, as per State selected. Next select PINCODE from list, as per District selected.

– **Latitude &Longitude**: To enter Latitude & Longitude of the place of Business, you search for any website which provides the details of Latitude & Longitude of places (like latlong.net). Enter the name of the place and the latitude & longitude would be shown (alternatively, you may select the place on google map and get the Latitude & Longitude)

– **Nature of possession**: Select the *Nature of Possession* from the list

– **Documents Upload**: At *Documents Upload* section, select the Document type from the list (as per Nature of Possession) and then select the Document file (in PDF or JPEG format, within 1 MB), as documentary evidence of place of business.

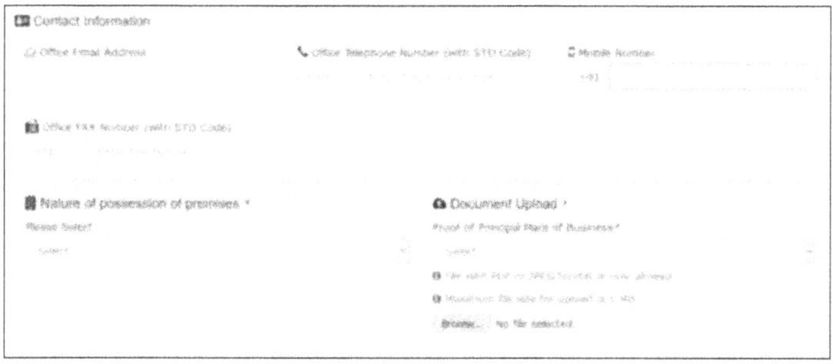

F-9A: Contact Details of Principal Place of Business

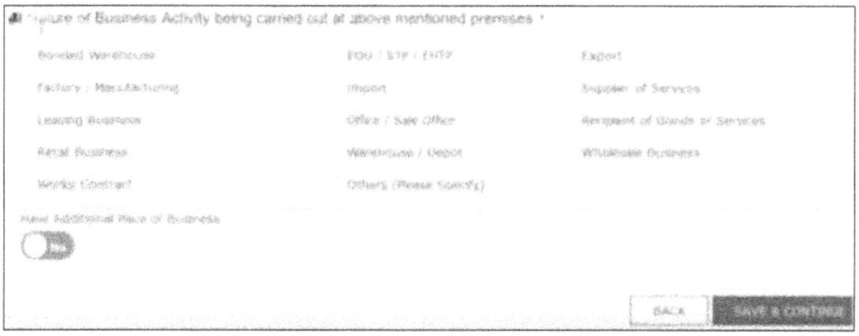

F-9B: Nature of Business Activity details of
Principal Place of Business

Nature of Business Activity: Tick the appropriate check box(F-9B) for the nature of activity being carried at the specified place of Business (you may check multiple check boxes as applicable)

6. Additional place of Business: To enter details of additional place of activity, Type *Yes* at *Have additional Place of* Activity (F-9B) to get another form to enter similar details of additional places (like branch etc). Type *No* if you do not have any additional Place of Business. You may also click the Tab *Additional Places of Business* at Part-B of the Form (F-4A) to get the entry screen for Additional Place of Business.

7. Goods & Services

At Part-B of the Form (F-4A) screen, Click Goods & Services Tab to get the Goods (F-10A) & Services (F-10B) entry screen**.**

– **Goods Details:** To enter details of Goods sold, enter the HSN Code (F-10A). The details of the Goods for the entered HSN is displayed and shown below. This way, you may select upto 5 HSN Code of top Items sold. The Items selected in this manner are listed next (click Delete button to delete any added item)

– **Services Details:**To enter details of Services provided, enter the SAC Code (F-10B). The details of the Services for the entered SAC is displayed and shown below. This way, you may select upto 5 SAC Code of top Services provided. The Services selected in this manner are listed next (click Delete button to delete any added item)

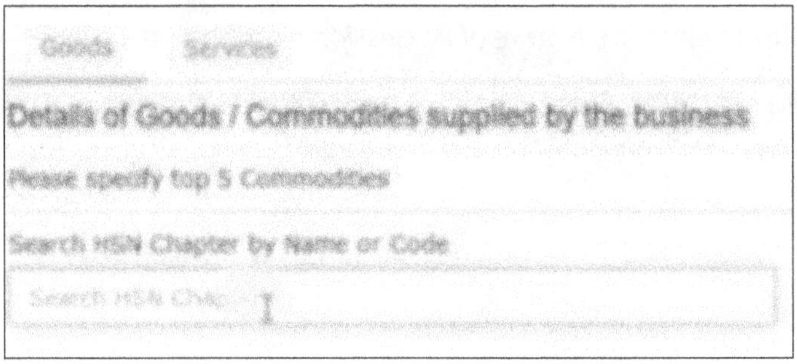

F-10A: Goods details

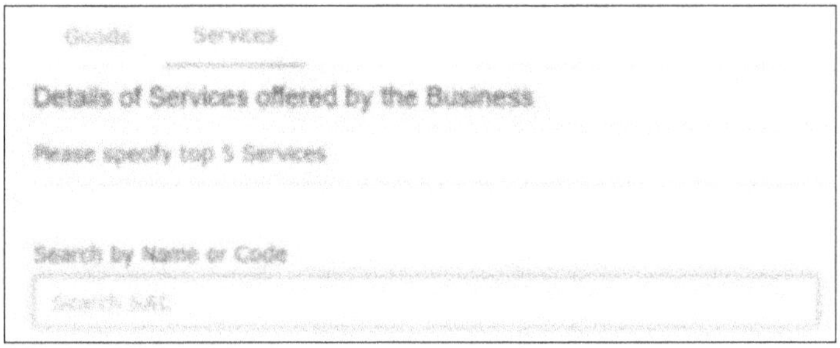

F-10B: Services details

8. Bank Accounts

At Part-B of the Form (F-4A) screen, click Bank Accounts Tab to get Details of Bank Account screen (F-11A) to enter the following details:

– **Account Number:** Enter the Bank Account Number

– **Type of Account:** Select the Account Type from the list

– **Bank IFSC:** Enter Bank IFSC as printed on the cheque book / bank statement (you may click and get IFSC Code of the Bank & Branch)

– **Branch Address:** Click on the GET ADDRESS button to display the Address of the branch of the Bank as per IFSC Code.

– **Upload Documents:** To Upload the documents as evidence of the Bank Account select the file like Bank Statement, Cheque etc. .

F-11A: Bank Account Details entry

9. State Specific Information Tab:

At Part-B of the Form (F-4A) screen, click State Specific Information Tab to enter the details related to State, as applicable (F-12A)

– **Professional Tax Employer Code (EC) No**: Enter professions tax E.C number.

– **Professional Tax Registration Certificate (RC) No**: Enter Professions tax R.C number.

– **State Excise License No**: Enter state excise license number.

– **Name of the person in whose name Excise License is held**: Enter the name of the person in whose name excise license is held.

Click SAVE & CONTINUE button.

F-12A: State Specific Information

10. Verification

After entering all details, at Part-B of the Form (F-4A) screen click on the *Verification Tab* (last Tab) to get the Verification screen to enter following info (F-13A):

– **Signatory**: At *Name of Authorised Signatory*, enter the Name of the Authorised Signatory

– **Place**: Place of signing the document

– **Designation / Status**: Enter the Designation / Status of the Signatory

– **Date**: Date of Signing

F-13A: Verification of GSTR Application form GST-REG-01

Declaration: Tick on the declaration check box (F-13A), enter the required info and click the respective button to submit the application using e-sign (submit with e-signature) or EVC (submit with EVC)

– Using e-Sign – OTP will be sent to Aadhaar registered number

– Using EVC – OTP will be sent to the registered mobile

Companies (including LLP) must submit application using DSC

Confirmation Message: On submission of the Application and verification, a SUCCESS message is displayed (F-14A). The Application Reference Number (ARN) is sent to registered email and mobile after sometime after validation & verification.

F-14A: GST Registration Application submission – Success message

You can then check the ARN status of registration by entering the ARN in GST Portal (www.gst.gov.in).

Registration for Casual Taxable Person

Casual taxable person means a person who occasionally undertakes transactions involving supply of goods and/ or services in a taxable territory where he has no fixed place of business. A person applying for registration as a casual taxable person while submitting the Application form creates a Challan and a Provisional GSTIN is generated by the GST Portal for making advance deposit of tax and the acknowledgement is issued electronically only after the deposit is made in the electronic cash ledger

For Casual taxable person, at *Are you applying for Casual Taxable Person* (F-4C), set *Yes* you to fill up additional info and details of Tax Deposit (F-15A).

F-15A: Application details for Casual Taxable person

Cancellation of Provisional Registration

A person registered under Pre GST regime (like VAT / Service tax / Excise Duty etc), gets Provisional Registration. If he is not liable to be registered under GST, he may cancel the provisional registration

F-16A: Cancellation of Provisional Registration – option selection

First create User ID and Password using credential of Provisional Registration, as explained. Login to the GSTIN portal using the User ID / Password. After login, at Dashboard (F-16A), select the option *Cancellation of Provisional Registration* and click *Continue* to get *Cancellation of Provisional Registration* screen (F-16B)

F-16B: Cancellation of Provisional Registration – Declaration

At Cancellation of Provisional Registration screen (F-16B), check the declaration check box. Click SUBMIT button. A warning message is displayed that once the form is submitted, Provisional Registration will be cancelled and migrated taxpayer will not able to restore Provisional Registration (F-16C). Click PROCEED button to cancel the Provisional Registration

F-16C: Cancellation of Provisional Registration – Warning screen

Cancellation of Registration

Login to GST Portal with user-ID and password. At Dashboard, select *Services>Registration>Application for Cancellation of Registration* to get Cancellation of Registration screen (F-17A) with 3 Tabs (F-17B).

F-17A: Application for Cancellation of Registration – Option selection

At Application for Cancellation of Registration screen (F-17B), select the respective tab to enter the details.

F-17B: Application for Cancellation of Registration – Tabs

Basic Details: Click *Basic Details* Tab (F-17B) to get the Basic Details screen (F-17C)

– **Address for Principal Place of Business**: These details are shown pre filled.

– **Address for Future correspondence:** Enter the details in the respective fields, or click the check box Address same as above if the address for future correspondence is same as Principal Place of Business as was filed in the registration certificate

Click Save & Continue

F-17C: Application for Cancellation of Registration – Basic Details

Cancellation Details: At Application for Cancellation of Registration Tabs (F-17B), click the next tab *Cancellation Details* to get Cancellation Details screen (F-17D)

F-17D: Registration Cancellation details screen

F-17E: Entry of Reason for Cancellation of Regsitration.

Reason for Cancellation: Select the applicable reason from drop down list (F-17E), as follows:

– Change in constitution of business leading to change in PAN

– Ceased to be liable to pay tax

– Discontinuance of business / Closure of business

– Others

– Transfer of business on account of amalgamation, merger, demerger, sale, leased or otherwise

Depending on the reasons for cancellation, you have to enter further details;

In case of *Change in constitution of business leading to change in PAN* and *Transfer of business on account of amalgamation, merger, demerger, sale, leased or otherwise*:

– Enter the date from which registration is to be cancelled.

– Provide the GSTIN of the transferee entity under the Details for Transfer, Merger or Change in Constitution section.

System will validate the same, and based upon it's Legal Name of Business, will auto-populate the Trade Name.

For all Other Reasons as specified in drop down list, enter the following details

– **Date from which Registration is to be cancelled**: Enter the date from which registration is to be cancelled.

– **Tax payable on Stock**: Enter the value of stock and the corresponding tax liability on the stock (F-17F)

– **Tax payment**: Enter the value to offset the liability (tax payable) that you wish to offset from either the Electronic Cash Ledger & Electronic Credit Ledger (F-17G)

Click Save & Continue. On submitting the form, the amount will be deducted from the respective Electronic Cash Ledger, or the Electronic Credit Ledger, or both, and debit entries will be made.

17F: Tax payable on Stock

17G: Tax paid.

Verification

Click the last tab Verification (F-17B), to get Verification screen (F-17H).

F-17H: Verification

Check the Verification statement box. Select the name of the authorised signatory from the Name of Authorized Signatory drop-down. Enter the Place of making this declaration.

Submit the form by using either Digital Signature Certificate (DSC), or the EVC option.

OTP verification

Next you will get OTP verification screen and you will get OTP in your registered mobile. Enter the OTP and click Validate OTP.

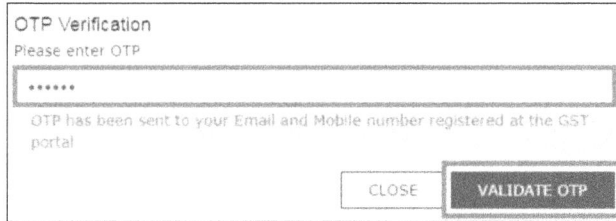

F-17I: OTP Verification

On successful filing for cancellation of registration, the system will generate the ARN and display a confirmation message. A confirmation message will also be sent by GST Portal on your registered mobile phone number and e-mail-ID.

After this stage, the concerned Tax Official will review your application and take a decision accordingly.

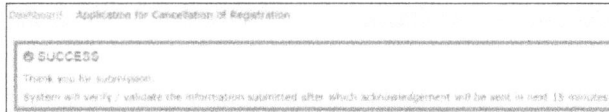

F-17J: Successful submission for application for
cancellation of registration

To view the ARN, at dashboard, select Services > Registration > Track Application Status option (F-17K), to get *Application Status Tracking* screen (F-17L).

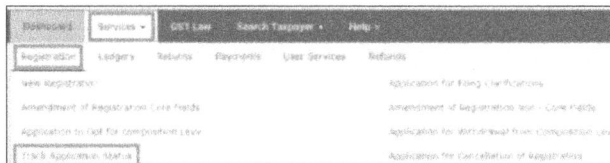

F-17K: Application Status Tracking option

At Application Status Tracking screen (F-17L), select Submission Period radio button and then enter the Return Period at From & To dates.

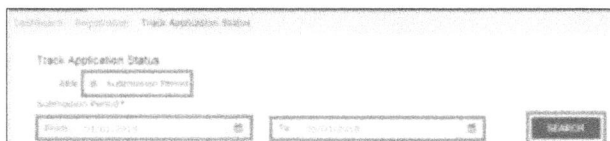

F-17L: Application Status Tracking

Click the *SEARCH* button to view Application Status for the specified period (F-17M).

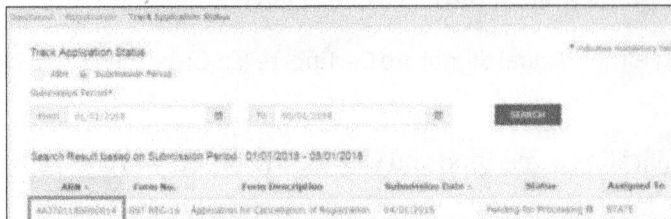

F-17M: Registration cancellation Application status

Registration for Composition scheme

To register as Composition Dealer, at Business details section (F-4C), set Yes at *Option for Composition*. Alternatively, after registering as regular dealer, you may opt for Composition, as described next.

Changing from Regular to Composition Scheme: After logging in to your account, from dashboard, select *Services>Registration>Application to opt for Composition scheme* (F-18A), to get *Composition Declaration* screen (F-18B).

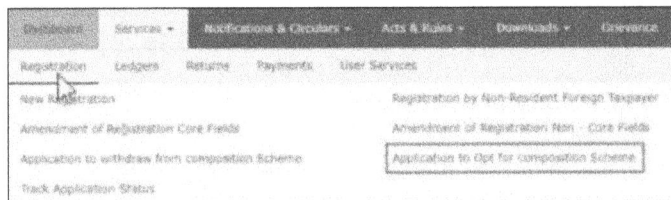

F-18A: Change to Composition scheme

At *Composition Declaration* screen (F-18B), click the check boxes regarding composition scheme (F-18B) and file the Application as usual.

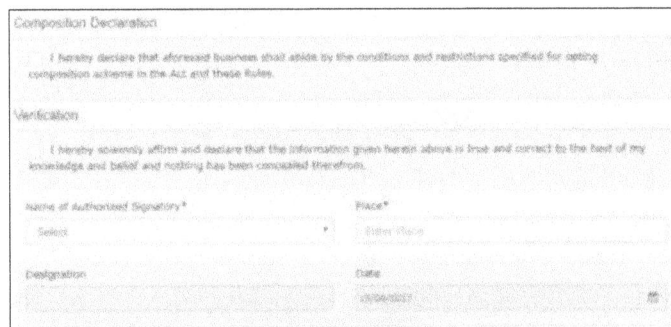

F-18B: Declaration for Composition scheme

User Account Management

In this chapter, we discuss about some important functions of in GSTIN portal User Accounts Management.

Creation of Username / Password in GST Portal

Only existing tax payers are invited to enroll into the new GST common portal. To create a user name and password you need to have one Provisional ID and Password (a temporary username and password, commonly referred as *Temporary Registration Number -TRN*), as communicated by the existing tax payment department like State VAT Department, Central Excise through your email- id or registered mobile number.)

Obtaining Temporary Registration Number (TRN)

You need to have the Temporary Registration Number (TRN) to create Username & password.

- **Existing Taxpayer**: If you are an existing Taxpayer under State VAT / Central Excise / Service, you will be getting TRN form the department, as per their procedure

- **New Applicants**: New applicants for GST registration, get the TRN on submission of Registration Application.

Having obtained the TRN, you can proceed to get Username / password as described later.

Provisional ID for Existing Tax Payers

Existing Tax payers (like Local VAT, Central Excise / Service Tax) should obtain provisional ID from the statutory bodies under which they are registered. In case of State bodies, the tax payer (like State VAT) should login to their State Tax website (which are different for each state / UT). Taxpayer under Central Scheme (like Central Excise / Service Tax) can get the provisional ID from.

Login to www.gst.gov.in to get GST Homepage. At GST Homepage, at the links (F-1A), click *State Tax Websites* to get the list of State Website of the selected State, or Click *Central Board of Excise & Customs* to get CBEC website.

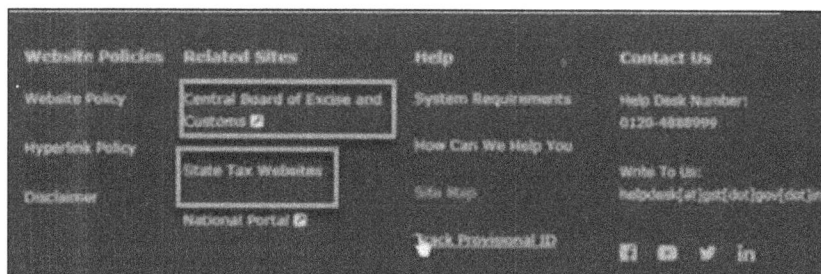

F-1A: GST Homepage

Provisional ID for Excise & Service Tax Dealers from Central Board of Excise & Customs

Login to Central Excise portal using your existing User ID and Password (F-2A), to get *Provisional ID access* screen (F-2B)

F-2A: CBEC login

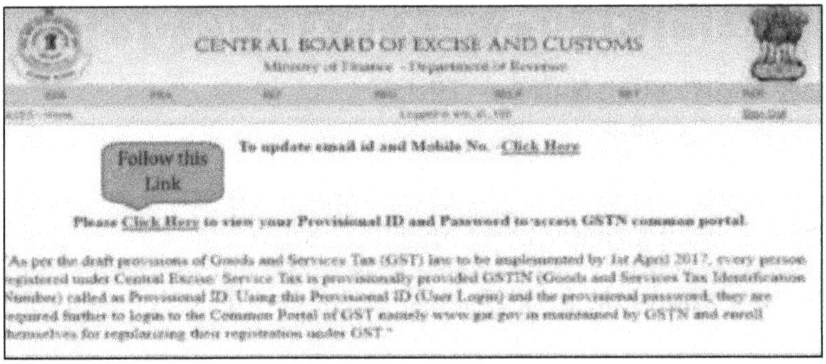

F-2B:GST Provisional ID link

At *Provisional ID access* screen (F-2B), either follow the link to get the new GST Provisional ID and Password or navigate using the Menu on the site (F-3A).

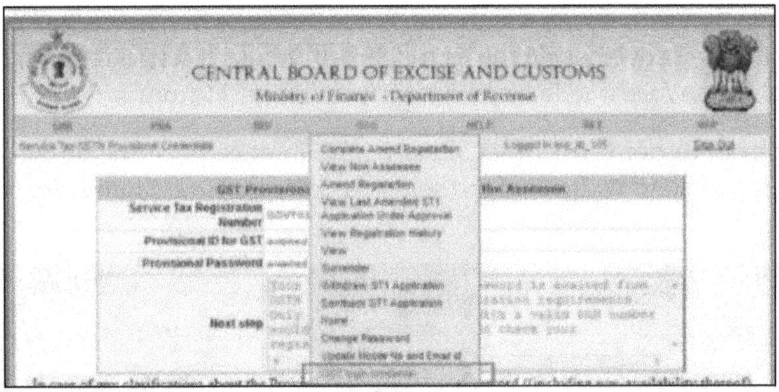

F-3A: GST Login Credential

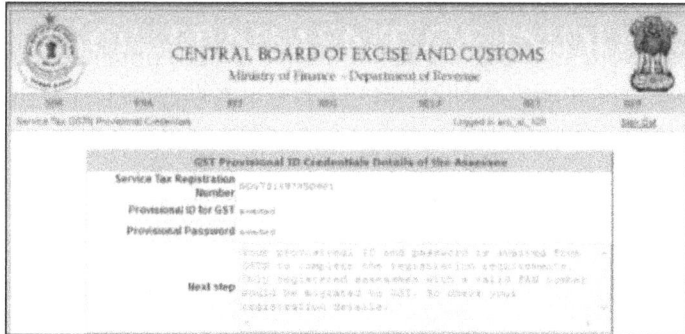

F-3B: GST Provisional ID Credential

Note the Provisional ID and password that is provided (F-3B) In case a Provisional ID is not provided, please refer the Next Step section on the screen.

Provisional ID from Delhi VAT Board

The screen for each State Government Tax site differs. We show you an example for Delhi State. Consult your State Tax site for the steps.

Dealers registered under VAT in Delhi should login to Delhi VAT site with User ID & password (F-4A) to get *GST Credential details* screen, where the Provisional User ID and Password is displayed (F-4B).

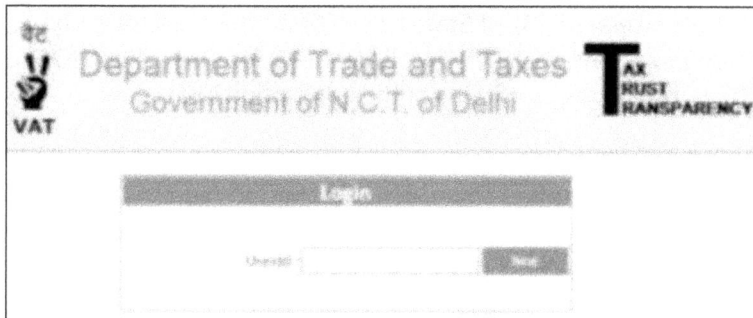

F-4A: Login screen

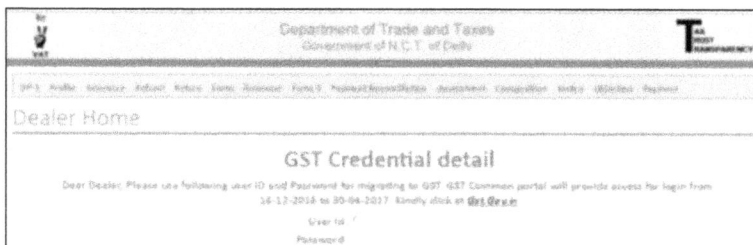

F-4B: GST Credential Screen

The Dealer/Trader should now login to the GST Common Portal (https://www.gst.gov.in) or may follow the link provided in above screen, to fill and submit Form 20 with necessary supporting documents. The link will take to GST website to migrate to GST.

Track Provisional ID

The provisional ID and password for the GST registrations are directly obtained from State (VAT) or Central authorities (Central Excise). The provisional ID is required for enrolling for GST (to login).

To track Provisional ID, type www.gst.gov.in browser to get GST Home page (F-1A). Click *Track Provisional ID* to get *Check Registration Status* screen (F-5A)

F-5A: Registration Status screen

At *Check Registration Status* screen (F-5B), at State, select State from List. At ID Type, select ID Type from the List (Registration Number, Provisional ID, PAN). Type the ID for the selected ID Type. Type the Captcha displayed. Click SUBMIT button to get the Status of the application just below.

Creation of User Name & Password

After getting *Provisional id & Password* (Temporary Registration Number -TRN) from the existing tax paying department, create a Username & Password of the GST Portal, through following steps. You must have a valid e-mail ID and Mobile Number of authorised signatory.

At browser, type www.gst.gov.in to get GST Common portal home page (F-6A).

F-6A: GST Portal home page

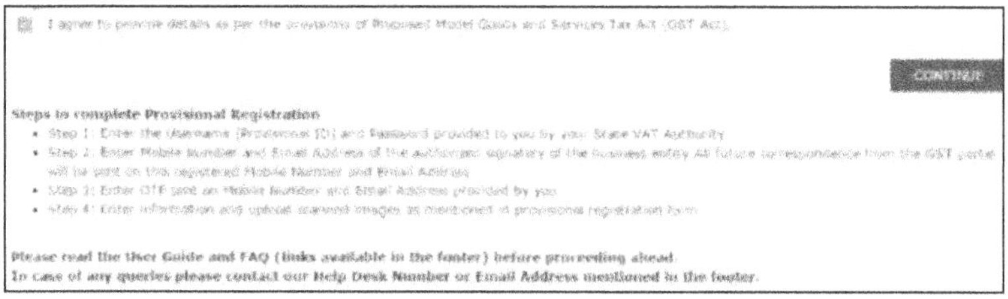

F-6B: Consent to proceed to get Temporary user name

Àt GST home page (F-6A), click NEW USER LOGIN (F-6A)button. Check the check box and click CONTINUE button (F-6B). Read and follow the instructions displayed on screen (F-6B), as illustrated next.

You get the login page (F-6C). Enter the Provisional ID and Password provided by the department in to the form. Type the Captcha (formatted number in image) displayed and click LOGIN button (F-6C) to get *User Info* screen (F-6D)

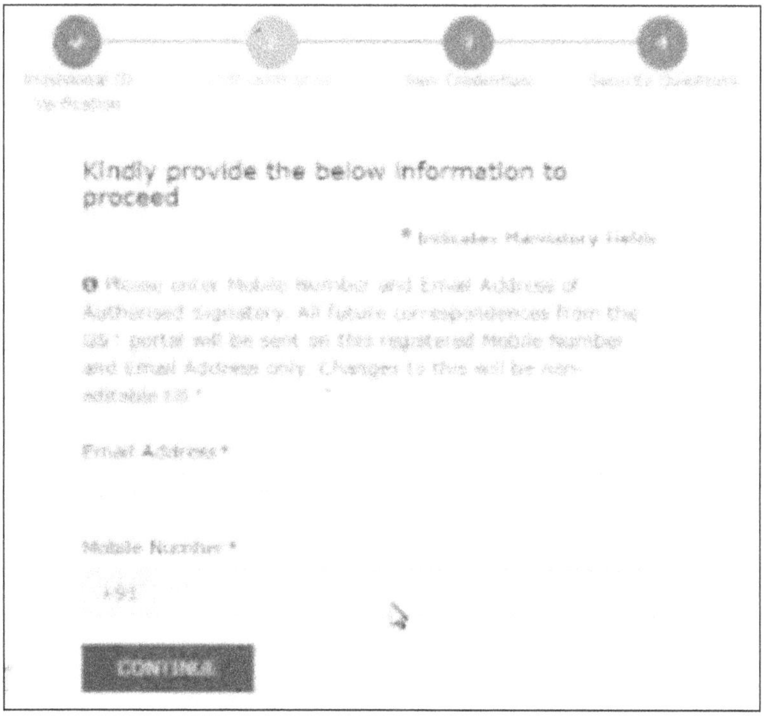

F-6C: Login screen for User Name

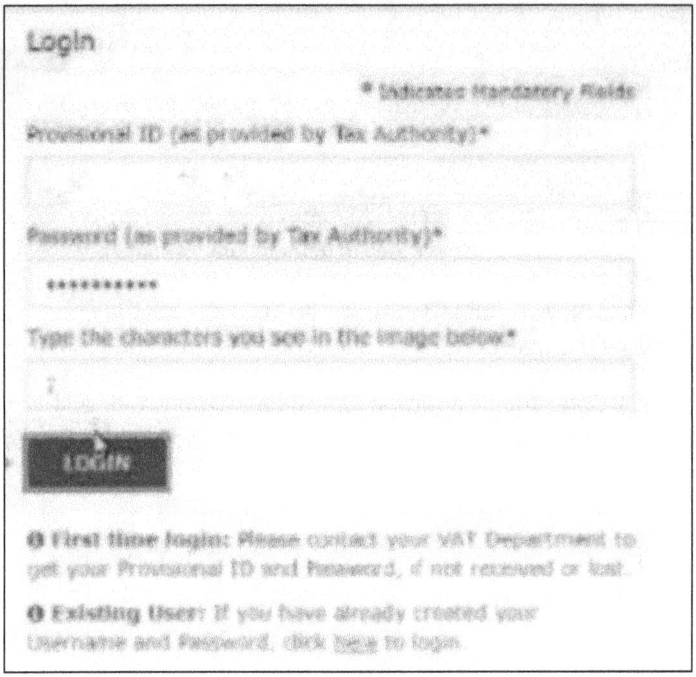

F-6D: User Info screen

At User Info screen (F-6D), enter a valid Mobile Number and e-mail address. Click CONTINUE button, to get OTP Verification screen (F-6E). You will get two OTP, one at your email id (email OTP) and another one at your mobile (mobile OTP), to be entered at OTP Verification screen (F-6E)

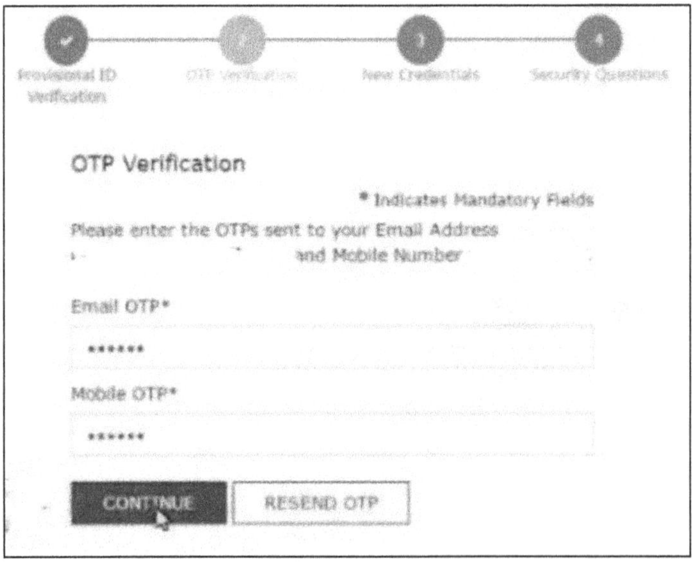

F-6E: OTP Verification

At OTP Verification screen (F-6E), enter the two OTP received at the respective OTP verification field. Make sure that you are entering two different OTP (click RESEND OTP to get another OTP, if the previous OTP expired). Click CONTINUE button, to get Password Set Up screen (F-6F).

At Password Set Up screen (F-6F), enter a Username for yourself and enter a Password (as per criteria guidelines shown). Type again the new password to re-confirm. Click on CONTINUE button to get Security Questions screen (F-6G)

F-6F: Password set up Screen

F-6G: Security Questions screen

At Security Questions screen (F-6G), enter the answers of each of the question. Note down the questions and their respective answer entered in this screen. These questions would be asked to retrieve lost password (in case you forget password). Click SUBMIT button to get the message of successful creation of Username & Password (F-6H).

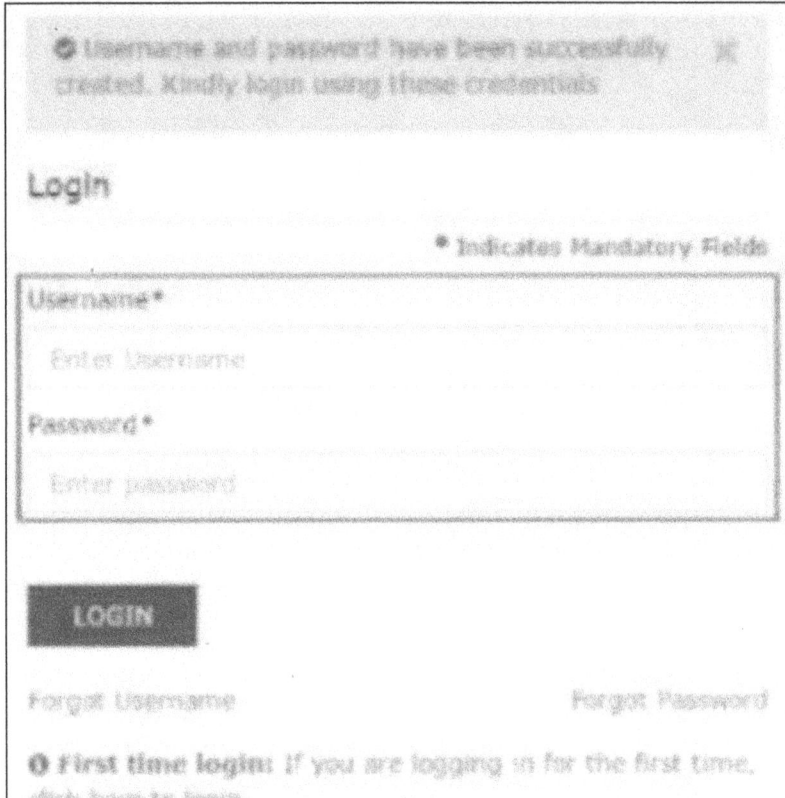

F-6H: Login screen t login to GST Portal

You can now login to GST Common portal using the Username / Password set by you (F-6H).

Creation of Username password for New applicant

Login to GST Portal: Typewww.gst.gov.in, to get the GST Home page (F-7A). Click *Login* link at top right-hand corner of the GST Home page (F-7A), to get Login screen (F-7B). Regular user should enter User Name &password .

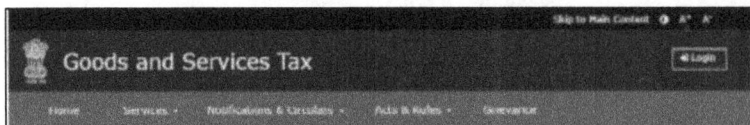

F-7A: GST Home Page login link

First time Login: Migrated taxpayers need to login first time to the GST Portal (www.gst.gov.in) with Provisional ID and Password. Click the *here* link (F-7B) in the instruction at the bottom of the page that says "First time login: If you are logging in for the first time, click at *here*link to login, to get *New User Login* screen (F-7C).

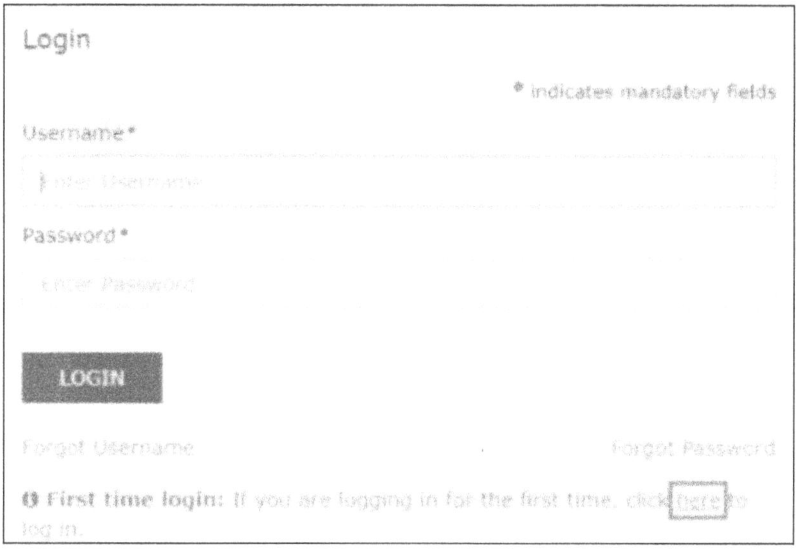

Login

* indicates mandatory fields

Username*

[Enter Username]

Password*

[Enter Password]

[LOGIN]

Forgot Username   Forgot Password

ⓘ First time login: If you are logging in for the first time, click here to log in.

F-7B: Login screen

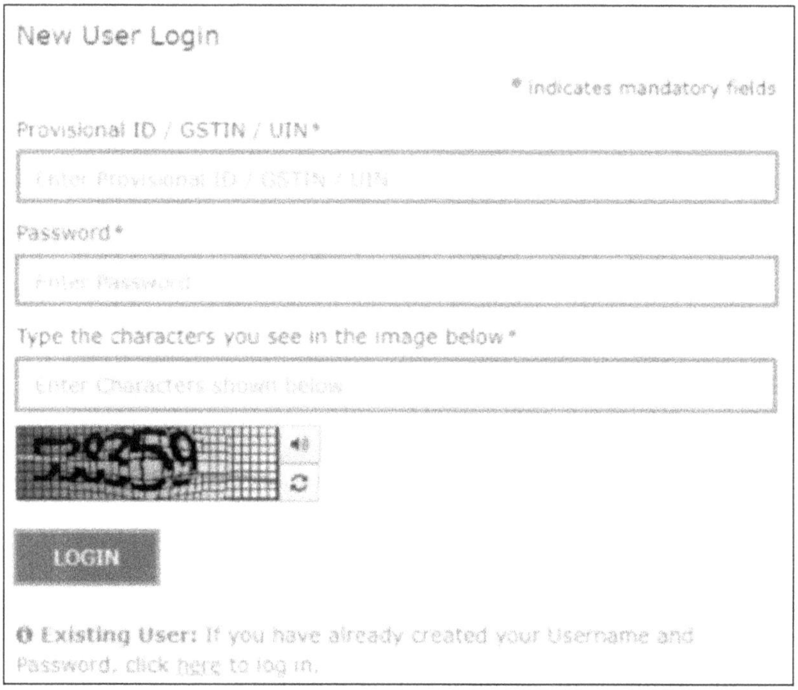

New User Login

* indicates mandatory fields

Provisional ID / GSTIN / UIN*

[Enter Provisional ID / GSTIN / UIN]

Password*

[Enter Password]

Type the characters you see in the image below*

[Enter Characters shown below]

[LOGIN]

ⓘ Existing User: If you have already created your Username and Password, click here to log in.

F-7C: New User Login screen

At *New User Login* screen (F-7C), at *Provisional ID / GSTIN/ UIN*, type the Provisional ID/ GSTIN/ UIN received by e-mail. At *Password*, type the password received by e-mail. Type the Captcha (formatted number in image). Click *LOGIN* button, to get Password set up screen (F-7D).

F-7D: Password Set Up screen

F-7E: Login screen with Username / Password

At Password set up screen (F-7D), at *New Password*, enter a Password of your choice (that you will be using from next time onwards). At *Re-Confirm Password*, re-enter the new password. Click SUBMIT button. Click on submit button to get the message of successful creation of Username & Password.

You can now login to GST Common portal using the Username / Password set by you (F-7E)

Retrieval of forgotten Username

To retrieve username, type www.gst.gov.in at browser URL to get GST Home Page. Click login link to get Login screen (F-8A).

F-8A: Login screen

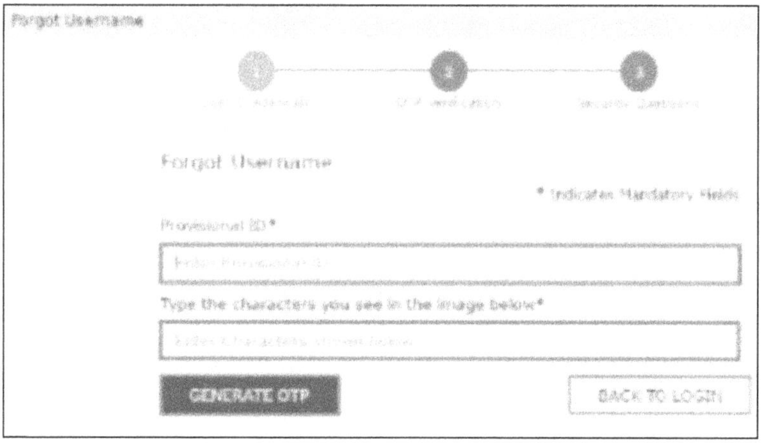

F-8B: Forgot Username screen

At Login screen (F-8A), click *Forgot User name* to get *Forgot Username* screen (F-8B). At *Forgot Username* screen (F-8B), at *Provisional ID*, type the Provisional ID received earlier. Type the Captcha displayed. Click GENERATE OTP button. The One Time Password (OTP) will be sent to your registered e-mail address and mobile number. You get OTP Entry screen to enter the OTP received (F-8C).

F-8C: OTP entry screen

F-8D: Security Questions screen

At OTP Entry screen (F-8C), at *Enter OTP*, enter the OTP received in e-mail / SMS. Click CONTINUE button (click RESEND OTP button to get a new OTP again, if the OTP is expired), to get Security Questions page (F-8D). Enter the answers to security questions that you entered during first-time GST enrollment. Click SUBMIT button (F-8D).

F-8E: Login with retrieved Username

The message "Username had been emailed to your registered Email address. Kindly check your email "is displayed (F-8E). Check your e-Mail to retrieve the username. Now login using the Username, in usual way.

Retrieval of forgotten Password

Type www.gst.gov.in at browser URL to get GST Home Page. Click login link to get login screen (F-9A)

F-9A: User login screen

At login screen (F-9A), click *Forgot Password* to get Forgot Password screen (F-9B)

F-9B: Forgot Password screen.

F-9E: OTP Verification screen

At Forgot Password screen (F-9B), enter the User name and Captcha displayed. CLICK GENERATE OTP button. OTP would be sent to your registered mobile & e-mail. You will get OTP Verification screen, where you enter the OTP received (F-9E) and click CONTINUE button (click RESEND OTP button to get a new OTP again, if the OTP is expired), to get New Password screen (F-9F) to set up New Password.

F-9F: New Password set up screen

F-9G: Security Questions screen

At New Password screen (F-9F), at New Password, enter the new password to be used, as per guidelines displayed on screen. At Re-confirm Password, re -enter the Password correctly, to get Security Question screen (F-9G).

At Security Question screen (F-9G), enter the answers to security questions that you specified during first-time GST enrollment. Click SUBMIT button. Having entered the answers to security questions, the new password would be set and you will get confirmation message (F-9H). Now login using your new password.

F-9H: Password set up message

Changing Login Password

First login using existing User name / password to get the Dashboard. Select *Change Password* link at Dash Board to get Change password screen (F-10A)

F-10A: Change Password screen

F-10B: Password Change message.

At Change Password screen (F-10A), enter the existing password to be changed, Click Change Password button. A message is then displayed confirming change of password (F-10B).

View Saved Application

While entering info for GST Registration application, you may save the entered data, if all data are available or the complete form entry is not finished. Later on, you may retrieve the application and fill up the rest of the portion. This saves time as you do not have redo the work that is already done.

Login to your account through Username Password to get Dashboard (F-11A)

F-11A: Saved Application option

F-11B: Saved Application for editing

At Dashboard Click *My Saved application* button (F-11A) to get My Saved Application screen (F-11B). Click on the Pencil icon against the Application you like to edit. You will get the application opened in Edit Mode. Now you may modify / enter data in Part B of the Application Form, as required. Having done, save the Application and submit it as explained. Application Form will be available for 15 days from the date of generation of TRN.

Track Enrolment Application status

Stages of Application Status: Following List shows the status of different stages of application at the time of application for Registration and amendments to Registration info.

- **Registration**

  o **ARN Generated** - On submission of the Registration Application

  o **Pending for Processing** - Registration Application successfully filed

  o **Provisional** - Status of GSTIN, when create challan is initiated (in case of Casual Taxable Person) till Registration Application is approved

  o **Pending for Validation** - On submission of the Registration Application until ARN is generated

  o **Validation Error** – When validation fails on submission of the Registration Application, until ARN is generated

- **Amendments to Core Fields**

  o **Pending for Processing** - Amendment Application of Registration application successfully filed and ARN generated

  o **Pending for Validation** - On submission of the Amendment Application until ARN is generated

  o **Validation Error** – When validation fails, on submission of the Amendment Application until ARN is generated

You may track Application Status in 3 modes: i) Pre login ii) Post Login iii) Login using TRN

Pre login: On submission of the Enrolment Application for New Registration (GST-REG-01), you get Application Reference Number (ARN).

To track application status of Enrolment Application, at GST portal (gst.gov.in), click Services> Registration> Track Application Status (F-12A) to get *Track Application Status* screen.

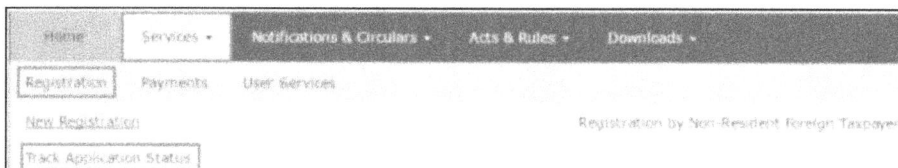

F-12A: Track Application Status – pre login

Enter the ARN and captcha and click Search button to view the Application status (F-12B)

F-12B: Application Status

Post login: Login to the GST Portal with valid credentials. At dashboard, select *Services > Registration > Track Application Status* command (F-13A)

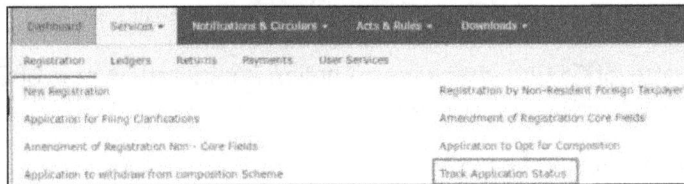

F-13A: Track Application Status – post login

Click ARN radio button and enter the ARN and click Search Button (F-13B). Next click *Submission Period* radio button and enter the Submission period (at From& To) and click Search Button.

F-13B: ARN entry

F-13C: Submission period entry

Login using TRN: Type www.gst.gov.in at URL to get GST Home page. Click REGISTER NOW link to get Registration screen (F-14A)

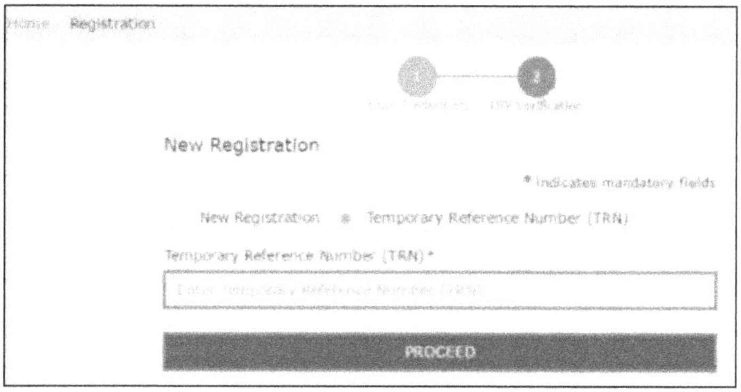

F-14A: Login using TRN

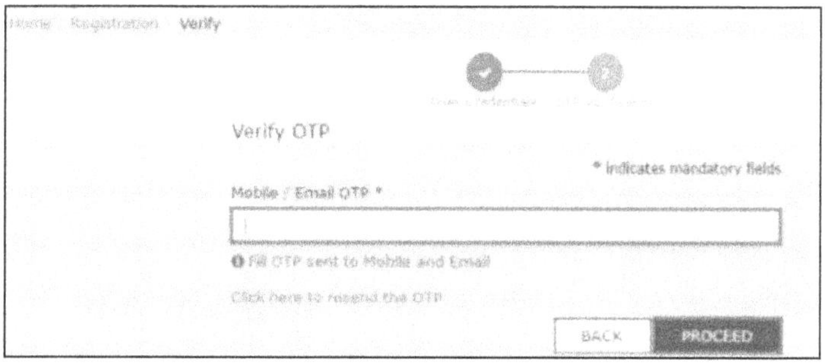

F-14B: OTP entry

At Registration screen (F-14A), Click *Temporary Reference Number* (TRN) radio button. At *Temporary Reference Number (TRN)*, enter the TRN received. Click *PROCEED* button to get Verify screen (F-14B) In the *Mobile / Email OTP* field, enter the OTP you received (same number is received in SMS and e-mail). Click the PROCEED button to get *My saved Application* screen, showing the status of Application '(F-14C)' at the end of sentence.

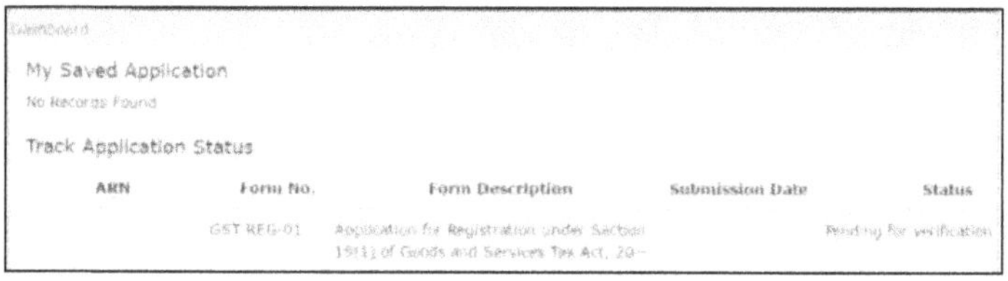

F-14C: Application Status

GSTIN Details

To check the details of any GSTIN, at GSTIN website, select *Services > User Services> Search Taxpayer* to get Search Taxpayer screen (F-15A). At GSTIN / UIN of the Tax payer, enter the GSTIN / UIN. Enter the Captcha displayed and click Search. The GSTIN details heads are displayed (F-15B).

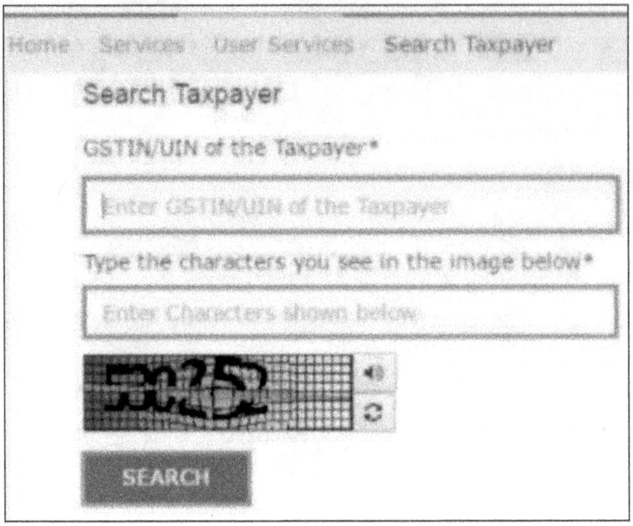

F-15A: GSTIN query

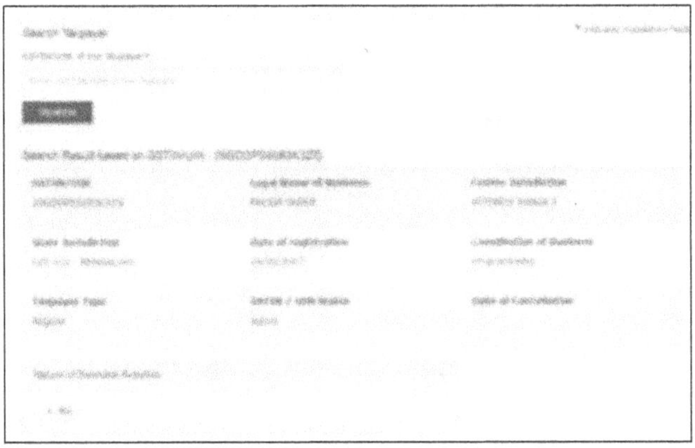

F-15B: GSTIN Details

User Authentication Methods: There are three methods for user authentication on the GST Portal.

– **Digital Signature Certificate (DSC):** Digital Signature Certificates (DSC) are the digital equivalent (electronic format) of physical or paper certificates. A Digital Certificate can be presented electronically to prove one's identity, to access information or services on the Internet or to sign certain documents digitally. In India, DSC are issues by authorized Certifying Authorities (GST Portal accepts only PAN based Class II and III DSC).

– **Electronic Signature (E-Sign):** Electronic Signature (E-Sign) is an online electronic signature service in India to facilitate an Aadhar holder to digitally sign a document.

A One Time Password (OTP) will be sent to mobile phone number that is registered with Aadhar at the time of digitally signing documents at the GST Portal.

– **Electronic Verification Code (EVC):** The Electronic Verification Code (EVC) authenticates the identity of the user at the GST Portal by generating a OTP. The OTP will be sent to the user via SMS on the registered mobile number and e-mail address of Authorized Signatory at the Portal.

To avail this service, the user must have a valid Aadhaar Card and valid mobile phone number that is registered in the Aadhar Database.

Digital Signature Certificate (DSC)

DSC or Digital Signature Certificate is used to establish one's identity while filing documents online through the internet. It is the digital equivalent to a normal hand written signature.

DSC is mandatory for companies and limited liability partnerships (LLPs), and optional for other taxpayers. Digital Signature Certificate (DSC) can be obtained directly from any Certifying Authorities (CAs) in India by filling requisite application form, attaching supporting documents, and payment of specified fees.

A DSC is linked to the Permanent Account Number (PAN) of the signatory, whose PAN is encrypted in a DSC token. To obtain a DSC, signatories must provide a copy of their PAN and proof of address (like Aadhar card) to a Certifying Authority (CA), along with an application form and a nominal fee. The CA then issues the DSC with software that allows the DSC to be installed on the user's computer or on the business' system.

After installing the token, the DSC needs to be registered on GST Portal (click *Register Digital Signature Certificate* link).

During registration, the portal prompts the user to select the PAN of the person whose DSC is being registered. The system then validates the PAN against the DSC. If it matches, the registration is complete, and the DSC can be used to sign and file online GSTR.

A DSC is typically valid for one to two years. Upon renewing a DSC, taxpayers will also need to update it within the GST Common Portal to avoid any mismatch or interruption.

Certifying Authorities (CA) for DSC: The following Certifying Authorities (CA) are authorised to grant license (Class 2 or 3 certificates) to issue a digital signature certificate u/s 24 of the Indian IT-Act 2000.

– Tata Consultancy Services (TCS) "http://www.tcs-ca.tcs.co.in"

– National Informatics Center (NIC) "http://nicca.nic.in/"

– IDRBT Certifying Authority "http://idrbtca.org.in"

– SafeScrypt CA Services, Sify Communications Ltd. "http://mcacert.safescrypt.com"

– Code Solutions CA "https://www.ncodesolutions.com"

– E-MUDHRA "http://www.e-mudhra.com"

Msigner Signing Utility: Msigner (www.emsigner.com) from *e-mundhra.com* is an DSC enabling utility, which may be downloaded from GST system portal. Download, right click on the icon and select *Run as administrator* option.

e-sign

E-sign (electronic signature) is linked to the Aadhar card of the signatory. It's designed for small entrepreneurs, such as proprietors, who do not have digital signature certificates (DSC). While filing a return within the GST Common Portal, authorized signatories click on "E-Sign" and receive a prompt to enter their Aadhar number. This sends a request to the UIDAI system to generate a one-time password (OTP), which is then sent to the email address and mobile number associated with that Aadhar number. The user then inputs the OTP into the portal. If the OTP matches, the action (e.g filing) is complete.

Signing GSTR with e-sign is a quick and easy process compared to using DSC.

Registering Digital Signature Certificate (DSC)

To register DSC, you must have downloaded and installed the DSC client installer from the DSC Registration page of the GST common Portal, in your computer (otherwise click on the signer utility to install, following the instructions: F-16D).

At GST website (www.gst.gov.in), login using username / password and click My Profile at dashboard to get My Profile screen (F-16A).

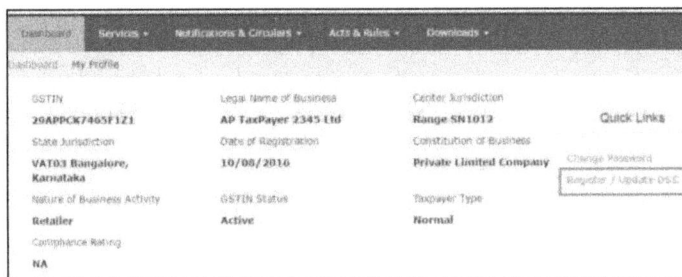

F-16A: Register / Update DSC

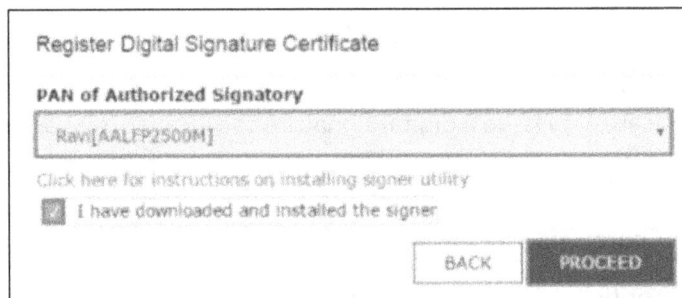

F-16B: PAN entry for DSC registration

At My Profile screen (F-16A), at *Register / Update DSC* to get *Register Digital Signature Certificate* screen (F-16B). At PAN of Authorized Signatory drop-down list, select the PAN of the authorized Signatory that you want to register (Only PAN specified in the Registration form can be used for registering DSC). Select the *I have downloaded and installed the signer* checkbox. Click PROCEED button to get the Digital Signature signer screen listing the certificate details.

Select the certificate (and click *View Certificate* button to view) and click Sign button (F-16C:).

A message "Your DSC has been successfully registered" is displayed (F-16D:).

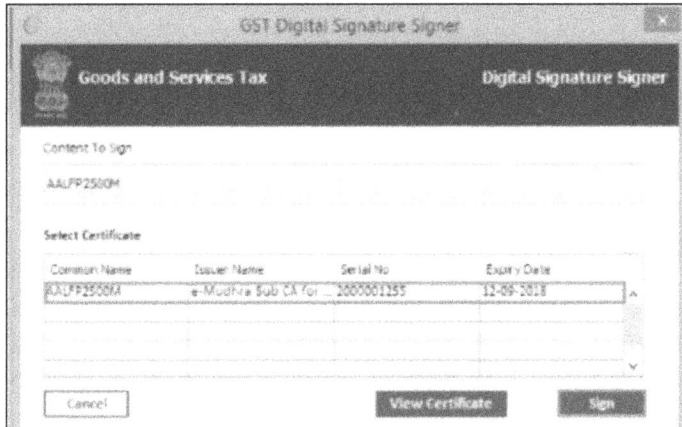

F-16C: Selection of Certificate

F-16D: Registration of DSC

Commonly used Services Available on GST Portal: Here is a list of some services available on the GST Portal.

– Application for Registration for Normal Taxpayer, ISD, Casual Dealer

– Application for GST Practitioner

– Opting for Composition Scheme (GST CMP-02)

– Stock intimation for Composition Dealers (GST CMP-03)

– Opting out of Composition Scheme (GST CMP-04)

– Filing GST Returns

– Payment of GST

– Filing Table 6A of GSTR-1 (Export Refund)

– Claim Refund of excess GST paid (RFD-01)

– Transition Forms (TRAN-1, TRAN-2, TRAN-3)

– Viewing E-Ledgers

GSTR-1 Outwards Supplies Physical Form

Form GSTR-1

Form GSTR-1 is a statement containing all the outward supplies. Outward supplies made to registered businesses (B2B) are required to be captured at invoice level. Supplies made to unregistered business or end consumers are required to be captured GST Rate-wise. In certain cases, even B2C invoice details are to be captured.

Method of Filing: GSTR-1 may be filed on line or offline.

- **On-line Entry**: Invoices may be uploaded directly into the GSTN system. However, only 500 B2B invoices may be entered on- line during a month, but any number of B2C Invoices may be uploaded on-line.

- **Off line uploading**: Organisation having more than 500 B2B invoices in a month, would upload through off line method. Invoices may be uploaded off line through Offline utility (available on download from GSTN network), Excel Utility, 3rd party software (like Tally, Busy etc,), or through GSP (GST Service provider). Anyone (even organisation having less than 500 B2B Invoices), can use the offline method.

The physical Form GSTR-1 is described here for clear understanding the data to be entered / uploaded.

GSTR-1 contains details of all outward supplies. From GST point of view of submission of returns, the outward supplies may be broadly classified as follows.

- **Intra State Supply** (Seller & Buyer in same state)

  o **B2B**: Business to Business, where good are sold to registered customer (having GSTIN) for business. Details of these invoices are uploaded invoice wise, so that the recipient can claim ITC, on matching the invoices.

  o **B2C**: Business to Consumer, where good are sold to unregistered customer not (having GSTIN). Consolidated figures of these invoices are uploaded.

- **Inter State Supply** (Seller & Buyer in different state)

  o **B2B**: Business to Business, where good are sold to registered customer (having GSTIN) for business. Details of these invoices are uploaded invoice wise, so that the recipient can claim ITC, on matching the invoices.

  o **B2C Large**: Business to Consumer, where good valued over 2,50,000 are sold to unregistered customer not (having no GSTIN). Details of these invoices are uploaded invoice wise, to track large transactions with unregistered parties.

o   **B2C**: Business to Consumer (upto Rs 2,50,000) sale to unregistered customer (having no GSTIN). State wise break up of consolidated figures of these invoices are uploaded, to track state wise share of government revenue through IGST.

o   **Export**: Goods sold for export (considered Inter State for the purpose of GST classification). Details of these invoices are uploaded invoice wise.

Multi Tax Rate Invoice: In case of multi tax rate invoice (multiple tax rate items in one invoice), the Tax rate wise break up figures (of taxable amount for each tax rate) should be compiled in respect of each multi tax Invoice, to enter the details (often total amount of SGST / SGST or IGST for the entire invoice is mentioned in Invoice).

Inter State & Intra State transactions: In on-line system, the system automatically recognizes Inter State & Intra State transactions, comparing the first 2 digit State Code of the organisation and that of the Recipient. Accordingly, the tax amount in the respective tax rate row would be posted in IGST / SGST+CGST columns.

Format of GSTR-1 Physical form

We discuss the contents of data elements in the Tables of GSTR-1 Physical Form. The data input form in Offline or On-line methods are aligned with the GSTR-1 Physical Form. To link the contents of Physical form and on-line entry, we explain the format and contents of each table of physical Form and on-line Form, simultaneously. So, understanding On line entry alongwith GSTR-1 Physical Form together, you will be able to easily fill up the forms data and file the return correctly & properly.

Form GSTR-1

[See Rule ----]

Details of outward supplies of goods or services

			Year	
			Month	

1.		GSTIN	
2.	(a)	Legal name of the registered person	
	(b)	Trade name, if any	
3.	(a)	Aggregate Turnover in the preceding Financial Year	
	(b)	Aggregate Turnover - April to June, 2017	

GSTR-1: Part Table 1-3

1. GSTIN

2. (a) Legal name of the registered person

   (b) Trade name, if any

3. (a) Aggregate Turnover in the preceding Financial Year

   (b) Aggregate Turnover - April to June, 2017

Figures for 3a & 3b, to be submitted in first Return only.

Table 4: Taxable outward supplies made to registered persons (including UIN-holders) other than Zero Rated supplies and Deemed Exports

4. Taxable outward supplies made to registered persons (including UIN-holders) other than supplies covered by Table 6										
									(Amount in Rs. for all Tables)	
GSTIN/ UIN	Invoice details			Rate	Taxable value	Amount				Place of Supply (Name of State)
	No.	Date	Value			Integrated Tax	Central Tax	State / UT Tax	Cess	
1	2	3	4	5	6	7	8	9	10	11
4A. Supplies other than those (i) attracting reverse charge and (ii) supplies made through e-commerce operator										
4B. Supplies attracting tax on reverse charge basis										
4C. Supplies made through e-commerce operator attracting TCS (operator wise, rate wise)										
GSTIN of e-commerce operator										

GSTR-1: Part Table 4

In Table 4, all B2B supplies (outward supplies made to a registered person) both inter-State and intra-State outward supplies should be captured at invoice level rate-wise details.

Parts of Table 4: This table has 3 sections, as follows:

— 4A. Supplies other than those (i) attracting reverse charge (as entered in Table 4B) and (ii) supplies made through e-commerce operator (as entered in Table 4C)

— 4B. Supplies attracting tax on reverse charge basis

— 4C. Supplies made through e-commerce operator attracting TCS (operator wise, rate wise)

Contents of Table 4

1.GSTIN/ UIN: 15 digit GSTIN/ UIN of the organisation

Invoice Details: Enter the following detail of Invoice

2. No.: Invoice Number 3.Date: Invoice Date in DD/MM/YYY format 4.Value: Value of Invoice in INR

Invoice Sub Details: Enter Rate wise break up of following column, in the sub details of Invoice

5. Rate: GST Tax Rate

6 Taxable Value: Taxable Value on which GST is charged. Any amount on which GST is not charged would be excluded from this amount.

Tax Amount: Tax component charged in the Invoice, in respective column

7. Integrated Tax: Amount of Integrated Tax 8. Central Tax: Amount of Central Tax 9. State / UT Tax: Amount of State / UT Tax. 10. Cess: Amount of Cess.

11. Place of Supply (Name of State): Enter name of State of the receiver, in case of Inter State Sale

In Table 4C, enter the GSTIN of the e-commerce operator also, in an additional column at the end.

Table 5: Taxable outward inter-state supplies to un-registered persons where the invoice value is more than Rs 2.5 Lakh

In Table 5, invoice-wise and rate-wise details of all inter-State B2C large supplies (supplies made to unregistered dealer or end consumer exceeding Rs 2,50,000), are to be submitted. Enter the details separately for supplies other than e-commerce (in Table 5A) and through e-commerce (in Table 5B)

Place of Supply (State)	Invoice details			Rate	Taxable Value	Amount	
	No.	Date	Value			Integrated Tax	Cess
1	2	3	4	5	6	7	8
5A. Outward supplies (other than supplies made through e-commerce operator, rate wise)							
5B. Supplies made through e-commerce operator attracting TCS (operator wise, rate wise)							
GSTIN of e-commerce operator							

5. Taxable outward inter-State supplies to un-registered persons where the invoice value is more than Rs 2.5 lakh

GSTR-1- Part Table 5

Parts of Table 5: This table has following additional sections:

– 5A. Outward supplies (other than supplies made through e-commerce operator, rate wise)

– 5B. Supplies made through e-commerce operator attracting TCS (operator wise, rate wise)

Contents of Table 5

1. Place of Supply (State)

   Invoice details

2. No. 3.Date 4.Value

5. Rate

6. Taxable Value

   Amount

7. Integrated Tax 8.Cess

Table 6: Details of Zero Rate supplies and Deemed Exports

Table 6, contains information related to exports, like Exports out of India , supplies to SEZ unit or SEZ developer, and deemed exports.

6. Zero rated supplies and Deemed Exports								
GSTIN of recipient	Invoice details			Shipping bill/ Bill of export		Integrated Tax		
	No.	Date	Value	No.	Date	Rate	Taxable value	Amt.
1	2	3	4	5	6	7	8	9
6A. Exports								
6B. Supplies made to SEZ unit or SEZ Developer								
6C. Deemed exports								

GSTR-1: Part Table 6

Parts of Table 6: This table has 3 sections, as follows:

- 6A. Exports

- 6B. Supplies made to SEZ unit or SEZ Developer

- 6C. Deemed exports

Contents of Table 6
1. GSTIN of Recipient

Invoice details:2.No. 3.Date 4.Value

Shipping bill / Bill of export: 5.No. 6.Date

Integrated Tax: 7.Rate 8.Taxable value9.Amt.

Notes:

1. Shipping bill and its Date (col 5 & 6): The details of Shipping Bill shall be furnished in 13 digits capturing port code (six digits) followed by unique reference number of shipping bill and its date. If the shipping bill details are not available at the time of filing GSTR-1, the same can be left blank and can be updated as amendment in Table 9 in the next tax period in which the details are available but before claiming any refund/rebate related to the said invoice. 2. Any supply made by SEZ to Domestic Tariff Area (DTA), without the cover of a Bill of Entry is required to be reported by SEZ unit in GSTR-1. The supplies made by SEZ on cover of a Bill of Entry shall be reported by DTA unit in its GSTR-2 as Imports in GSTR- 2. 3. In case of export transactions, GSTIN of recipient will not be applicable and may be left blank.

4. For Export transactions effected without payment of IGST (under Bond/Letter of Undertaking (LUT)), Tax amount would be zero (Table 6A and 6B).

Table 7: Details of Taxable supplies (Net of debit notes and credit notes) to unregistered persons other than the supplies covered in Table 5

7. Taxable supplies (Net of debit notes and credit notes) to unregistered persons other than the supplies covered in Table 5					
Rate of tax	Total Taxable value	Amount			
		Integrated	Central Tax	State Tax/UT Tax	Cess
1	2	3	4	5	6
7A. Intra-State supplies					
7A (1). Consolidated rate wise outward supplies [including supplies made through e-commerce operator attracting TCS]					
7A (2). Out of supplies mentioned at 7A(1), value of supplies made through e-Commerce Operators attracting TCS (operator wise, rate wise)					
GSTIN of e-commerce operator					
7B. Inter-State Supplies where invoice value is upto Rs 2.5 Lakh *[Rate wise]*					
7B (1). Place of Supply (Name of State)					
7B (2). Out of the supplies mentioned in 7B (1), the supplies made through e-Commerce Operators (operator wise, rate wise)					
GSTIN of e-commerce operator					

GSTR-1: Part Table 7

Parts of Table 7: This table has following sections:

− **7A. Intra-State supplies**

   o **7A (1). Consolidated rate wise outward supplies [including supplies made through e-commerce operator attracting TCS]:** Consolidated rate-wise details of all intrastate outward supplies made to unregistered persons, including supplies made through e-commerce operator.

   o **7A (2). Out of supplies mentioned at 7A(1), value of supplies made through e-Commerce Operators attracting TCS (operator wise, rate wise):** Details of supplies made through e-commerce operator attracting TCS out of gross supplies reported in 7A (1).

− **7B. Inter-State Supplies where invoice value is upto Rs 2.5 Lakh *[Rate wise]***

   o **7B (1). Place of Supply (Name of State):** Details of inter-state outward supplies having invoice value up to Rs 2.5 lakh need to be captured state-wise and rate-wise in 7B (1).

   o **7B (2). Supplies made through e-Commerce Operators (operator wise, rate wise):** Details of supplies made through e-commerce operator attracting TCS, out of gross supplies reported in 7B (1).

Contents of Table 7

1. Rate of Tax

2. Total Taxable Value

Tax Amount: 3.Integrated Tax. 4.Central Tax 5.State Tax/UT Tax 6.Cess

GSTIN of e-commerce operator: In case of export transactions through e-commerce operator, enter GSTIN of e-commerce operator, in other cases, it would be left blank.

Note: In Table 7, all the above values should be Net of Debit Note and Credit Note. If there are any debit note or credit note is issued pertaining to the supplies mentioned under this Table, only the net taxable value and corresponding tax, after adjusting such Debit / Credit Notes to be furnished.

Table 8: Details of Nil rated, exempted and non GST outward supplies

In Table 8, enter the Nil rated, exempted and Non GST outward supplies made during the period.

8. Nil rated, exempted and non GST outward supplies			
Description	Nil Rated Supplies	Exempted (Other than Nil rated/non-GST supply)	Non-GST supplies
1	2	3	4
8A. Inter-State supplies to registered persons			
8B. Intra- State supplies to registered persons			
8C. Inter-State supplies to unregistered persons			
8D. Intra-State supplies to unregistered persons			

GSTR-1: Part Table 8

Parts of Table 8: This Table has 4 sections, as follows:

– 8A. Inter-State supplies to registered persons

– 8B. Intra- State supplies to registered persons

– 8C. Inter-State supplies to unregistered persons

– 8D. Intra-State supplies to unregistered persons

Contents of Table 8

1. Description

2. Nil Rated Supplies

3. Exempted (Other than Nil rated/non-GST supply)

4. Non-GST supplies

Table 9: Details of debit notes, credit notes, refund vouchers issued during current period and any amendment to GSTR-1 filed for earlier tax periods in Table 4, 5 and 6

In Table 9, enter the details of debit note, credit note and refund voucher (return of advance received) issued against the supplies already reported in Table 4 (b2B Supplies), Table 5 (B2C Large supplies) & Table 6 (exports/SEZ unit or SEZ developer/deemed exports)

9. Amendments to taxable outward supply details furnished in returns for earlier tax periods in Table 4, 5 and 6 [including debit notes, credit notes, refund vouchers issued during current period and amendments thereof]															
Details of original document			Revised details of document or details of original Debit/Credit Notes or refund vouchers						Rate	Taxable Value	Amount				Place of supply
GSTIN	Inv. No.	Inv. Date	GSTIN	Invoice		Shipping bill		Value			Integrated Tax	Central Tax	State / UT Tax	Cess	
				No	Date	No.	Date								
1	2	3	4	5	6	7	8	9	10	11	12	13	14	15	16
9A. If the invoice/Shipping bill details furnished earlier were incorrect															
9B. Debit Notes/Credit Notes/Refund voucher [original]															
9C. Debit Notes/Credit Notes/Refund voucher [amendments thereof]															

GSTR-1: Part Table 9

Parts of Table 9: This Table has 3 sections, as follows:

– 9A. If the invoice/Shipping bill details furnished earlier were incorrect

– 9B. Debit Notes/Credit Notes/Refund voucher [original]

– 9C. Debit Notes/Credit Notes/Refund voucher [amendments thereof]

Contents of Table 9

Details of original document - 1. GSTIN 2. Inv. No. 3.Inv. Date

Revised details of document or details of original Debit/Credit Notes or refund vouchers

4 GSTIN 5.Invoice No. 6. Invoice Date 7. Shipping bill No. 8. Shipping bill Date 9.Value

10.Rate 11.Taxable Value

Tax Amount - 12. Integrated Tax. 13 Central Tax 14. State / UT Tax 15. Cess

16. Place of supply

Notes:

– These details are to be captured rate-wise along with the original invoice number against the debit note or credit note issued. In the first three columns, enter the details of original invoice, followed by the rate-wise details of credit note/debit note/refund voucher issued during the return period.

– If shipping pertained to export transactions effected during earlier return and Shipping bill number and date was not declared in earlier returns due to non-availability, now enter such details In Table 9A, as amendments. If the export transactions are related to current month, the shipping details should be entered in Table 6

– In Table 9B, enter rate-wise details of credit note/debit note/refund voucher issued during the return period.

– In table 9C, enter the details of amendments made through credit note/debit note/refund voucher against the invoice/advance receipt pertaining to pervious return period.

– Any debit/credit note pertaining to invoices issued before the appointed day must also to be reported in this table.

Table 10: Details of Debit Note and Credit Note issued to unregistered person

Rate of tax	Total Taxable value	Amount			
		Integrated Tax	Central Tax	State/UT Tax	Cess
1	2	3	4	5	6
Tax period for which the details are being revised	\<Month\>				
10A. Intra-State Supplies [including supplies made through e-commerce operator attracting TCS] [Rate wise]					
10A (1). Out of supplies mentioned at 10A, value of supplies made through e-Commerce Operators attracting TCS (operator wise, rate wise)					
GSTIN of e-commerce operator					
10B. Inter-State Supplies [including supplies made through e-commerce operator attracting TCS] [Rate wise]					
Place of Supply (Name of State)					
10B (1). Out of supplies mentioned at 10B, value of supplies made through e-Commerce Operators attracting TCS (operator wise, rate wise)					
GSTIN of e-commerce operator					

10. Amendments to taxable outward supplies to unregistered persons furnished in returns for earlier tax periods in Table 7

GSTR-1: Part Table 10

In Table 10, enter the consolidated rate-wise details of debit note/credit note issued against the intra-State supplies to unregistered person and inter-State supplies having invoice value less than Rs. 2.5 Lakhs to unregistered person in previous return period, as amendment to the details declared in Table 7 of earlier return.

Parts of Table 10

–   10A. Intra-State Supplies [including supplies made through e-commerce operator attracting TCS] [Rate wise]

–   10A (1). Out of supplies mentioned at 10A, value of supplies made through e-Commerce Operators attracting TCS (operator wise, rate wise)

–   10B. Inter-State Supplies [including supplies made through e-commerce operator attracting TCS] [Rate wise]

–   10B (1). Out of supplies mentioned at 10B, value of supplies made through e-Commerce Operators attracting TCS (operator wise, rate wise)

In case of Inter State, Place of Supply (Name of State) is also to be mentioned.

In case of e-commerce operation, GSTIN of e-commerce operator to be mentioned.

Contents of Table 10

1. Rate of tax

2. Total Taxable value

Tax Amount: 3.Integrated Tax 4.Central Tax 5.State/UT Tax 6.Cess

Table 11: Details of Advances Received/Advance adjusted in the current tax period or Amendment to GSTR-1 furnished in earlier tax period

Rate	Gross Advance Received/adjusted	Place of supply (Name of State)	Amount			
			Integrated	Central	State/UT Tax	Cess
1	2	3	4	5	6	7
I Information for the current tax period						
11A Advance amount received in the tax period for which invoice has not been issued (tax amount to be added to output tax liability)						
11A (1) Intra-State supplies (Rate Wise)						
11A (2) Inter-State Supplies (Rate Wise)						
11B Advance amount received in earlier tax period and adjusted against the supplies being shown in this tax period in Table Nos. 4, 5, 6 and 7						
11B (1) Intra-State Supplies (Rate Wise)						
11B (2) Inter-State Supplies (Rate Wise)						
II Amendment of information furnished in Table No. 11[1] in GSTR-1 statement for earlier tax periods [Furnish revised information]						
Month		Amendment relating to information furnished in S. No (select)	11A(1)	11A(2)	11B(1)	11B(2)

11. Consolidated Statement of Advances Received/Advance adjusted in the current tax period/ Amendments of information furnished in earlier tax period

GSTR-1: Part Table 11

In Table 11, enter consolidated state-wise and rate-wise details related to advances received in the current period, and also the details of advances received in earlier period but adjusted in the current period.

Parts of Table 11

– **Section I: Information for the current tax period**

o   11A. Advance amount received in the tax period for which invoice has not been issued (tax amount to be added to output tax liability)

•   11A (1). Intra-State supplies (Rate Wise)

•   11A (2). Inter-State Supplies (Rate Wise)

o   11B. Advance amount received in earlier tax period and adjusted against the supplies being shown in this tax period in Table Nos. 4, 5, 6 and 7

•   11B (1). Intra-State Supplies (Rate Wise)

•   11B (2). Inter-State Supplies (Rate Wise)

– **Section II: Amendment of earlier Tax period:** Furnish revised information in relation to info furnished in Table No. 11[1] in GSTR-1 for earlier tax periods

Contents of Table 11

1. Rate

2. Gross Advance Received/adjusted

3. Place of supply (Name of State)

Tax Amount: 4. Integrated Tax. 5. Central Tax. 6.State/UT Tax 7.Cess

Notes:

–   In Table 11A, enter the details of advance received for which the invoice has not been be issued, categorised into intra-State supplies in table 11A (1) and inter-State supplies in table 11A (2).

–   In table 11B, enter details related to adjustment of tax paid on advance received and reported in earlier tax periods against invoices issued in the current tax period, categorised into intra-State supplies in Table 11B (1) and inter-State supplies in table 11B (2).

–   If there are any changes pertaining to details declared in table 11A to 11B in earlier return, it can be amended by furnishing the changes in Part II of Table 11.

–   Details relating to advances received to be submitted in Table 11, only if the invoice has not been issued in the same tax period in which the advance was received. If the advance and invoice is issued in the same month, such advance & adjustment details need not be included in Table 11.

Table 12: HSN-wise summary of outward supplies

Sr. No.	HSN	Description (Optional if HSN is provided)	UQC	Total Quantity	Total value	Total Taxable Value	Amount			
							Integrated Tax	Central Tax	State/UT Tax	Cess
1	2	3	4	5	6	7	8	9	10	11

12. HSN-wise summary of outward supplies

GSTR-1: Part Table 12

Contents of Table 12

1. Sr. No.

2. HSN

3. Description (Optional if HSN is provided)

4. UQC

5. Total Quantity

6. Total value

7. Total Taxable Value

Tax Amount: 8. Integrated Tax. 9. Central Tax. 10. State/UT Tax. 11. Cess

Notes:

–   HSN code must be be reported. It will be optional for taxpayers

–   Organisation having annual turnover up to Rs. 1.50 Crore in preceding year, may omit HSN Code (However, description of goods is mandatory and must be mentioned). Organisations having annual turnover between Rs. 1.5 Cr. but up to Rs. 5 Cr. in the preceding year, may enter first 2 digits of HSN, and Organisations having annual turnover exceeding 5 crores, should write the full HSN Code.

– Unit of measure (UOM) must be expresses in terms of corresponding UQC (unit quantity code) to maintain uniformity in UoM.

List of UQC			
BAG-BAGS	CTN-CARTONS	MTS-METRIC TON	TGM-TEN GROSS
BAL-BALE	DOZ-DOZENS	NOS-NUMBERS	THD-THOUSANDS
BDL-BUNDLES	DRM-DRUMS	PAC-PACKS	TON-TONNES
BKL-BUCKLES	GGK-GREAT GROSS	PCS-PIECES	TUB-TUBES
BOU-BILLION OF UNITS	GMS-GRAMMES	PRS-PAIRS	UGS-US GALLONS
BOX-BOX	GRS-GROSS	QTL-QUINTAL	UNT-UNITS
BTL-BOTTLES	GYD-GROSS YARDS	ROL-ROLLS	YDS-YARDS
BUN-BUNCHES	KGS-KILOGRAMS	SET-SETS	OTH-OTHERS
CAN-CANS	KLR-KILOLITRE	SQF-SQUARE FEET	
CBM-CUBIC METERS	KME-KILOMETRE	SQM-SQUARE METERS	
CCM-CUBIC CENTIMETERS	MLT-MILILITRE	SQY-SQUARE YARDS	
CMS-CENTIMETERS	MTR-METERS	TBS-TABLETS	

List of UQC

Table 13: Documents Issued during Tax Period

In Table 13, enter the details of documents issued during the return, along with the starting and ending number of the document, cancelled document and net number of documents actually issued.

Sr. No	Nature of document	Sr. No.		Total number	Cancelled	Net issued
		From	To			
1	2	3	4	5	6	7
1	Invoices for outward supply					
2	Invoices for inward supply from unregistered person					
3	Revised Invoice					
4	Debit Note					
5	Credit Note					
6	Receipt voucher					
7	Payment Voucher					
8	Refund voucher					
9	Delivery Challan for job work					
10	Delivery Challan for supply on approval					
11	Delivery Challan in case of liquid gas					
12	Delivery Challan in cases other than by way of supply (excluding at S no. 9 to 11)					

13. Documents issued during the tax period

GSTR-1: Part Table 13

Contents of Table 13

1. Sr. No.

2. Nature of document

   Sr. No

3. From 4.To

5. Total number

6. Cancelled

7. Net issued

Declaration

Verification
I hereby solemnly affirm and declare that the information given herein above is true and correct to the best of my knowledge and belief and nothing has been concealed there from and in case of any reduction in output tax liability the benefit thereof has been/will be passed on to the recipient of supply.

Signatures

Place
Signatory ....

Name of Authorized

Date
/Status...

Designation

GSTR-1 Declaration

GSTR-1 Outwards Supplies Offline Data Upload

Offline Data upload in GSTN Portal

Businesses generating a large number of invoices in a tax period may find on-line entry of invoice details one-by-one, cumbersome & time consuming. So, GSTN provides facilities to upload Invoice data (entered in Excel Sheet, or created by external Invoicing / Accounting software) of invoices in bulk, in one go, as if these data have been entered on line in the Portal.

Returns Offline Tool

Returns Offline Tool is utility provided by GSTIN to upload data offline into GSTIN stored in a specific format. Taxpayers can download the Returns Offline Tool from GSTN and upload data for each Tax period.

Downloading Offline Data Upload Tool for GSTR-1 Return

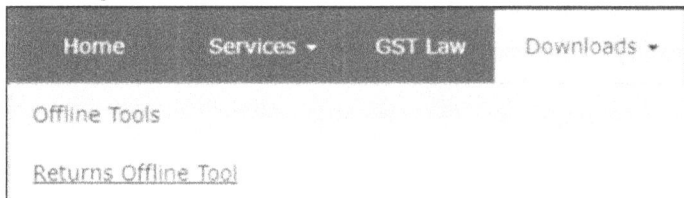

F:1A: Returns Offline Tool option

At GSTIN homepage, select Downloads>Offline Tools>*Returns Offline Tools* (F-1A), to get Returns Offline Tools screen (F-1B).

F-1B: Download Offline Tool

At Returns Offline Tools screen (F-1B), click *Downloads* link to get Download confirmation screen 'Click PROCEED button (F-1C) to download offline tool zip file'.

F-1C: Download Confirmation screen

F-1D: Downloaded GST Offline Tool Zip file

The downloaded file (gst_offline_tool.zip) is saved in specified (or default) folder (F-1D). On unzipping the downloaded file (F-1D), you get following files (F-1E):

– *GST Offline tool.exe* file for the Returns Offline tool to be installed in the specified folder

– *Section_wise_CSV_*files folder which contains .csv file with the sample data which should be deleted before filling the actual data to the template

– *GSTR1_Excel_Workbook_Template.xlsx* file to upload invoice data entered in the respective worksheets for all sections at one go

– *Readme.txt* file that explains in detail the prerequisites for the Returns Offline tool

– *Invoice Upload Offline tool User Manual* User Manual detailing out the guidance for taxpayers to use Returns Offline tool.

F- 1E: Extracted files

The folder gst_offline_toolcontains various types of files

– **Excel File**: In the folder, open the Excel file (like GSTR1_Excel_Workbook_template-v.1.3.xlsx). It contains tabs for data for B2B, B2CL, B2CS, CDNR etc.

– **CSV Files**: The folder contains another folder for CSV files (section_wise_CSV_files). This folder contains CSV files for each section (F-1F)

F-1F: Section wise CSV Files

Installation of GST Offline Tool

Double click the GST Offline tool file (F-1E). Click Yes (F-2A) and click Next (F-2B) at *Offline Tool installation wizard* to install offline tool (F-2A).

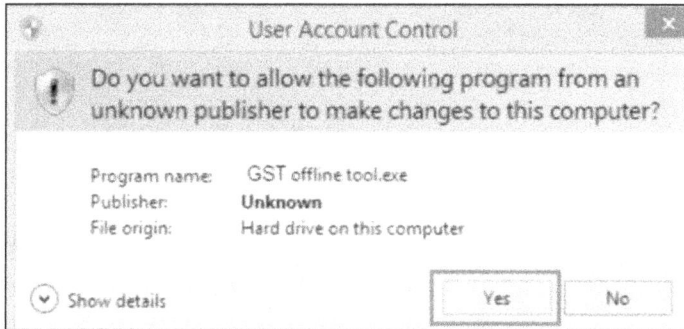

F-2A: Installation of Offline Tool

F-2B: Offline Tool installation wizard

Click *Browse* and specify the Folder where the offline tool would be installed (F-2C). You should select a different folder (F-2C) other than the folder where you have placed the gst_offline_tool folder (normally installed in C: drive).

F-2C: Offline Set Up Tool folder

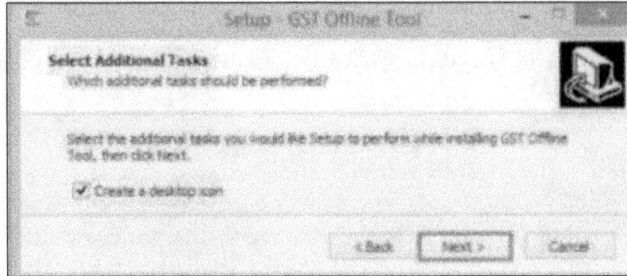

F-2D: Creation for desktop icon for Offline Tool

Select the checkbox at Create a desktop icon (F-2D) to create an icon for the Returns Offline tool on the desktop as a short cut. Click the Next button (F-2D).

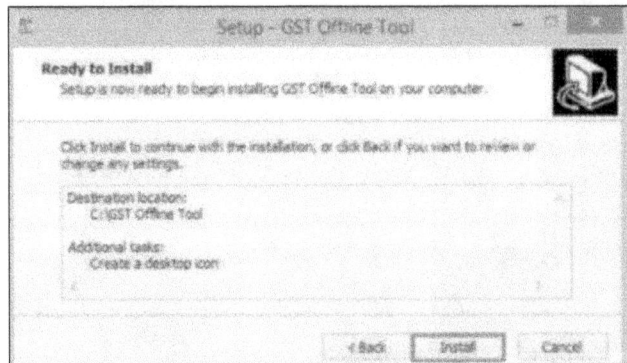

F-2E: Installation of Offline Tool

F-2F: Installation completion

F-2G: Desktop icon

Click the *Install* button to install the offline tool (F-2E). Returns Offline tool set up is completed. Ensure that both the checkboxes are selected in order to start the tool. Click the Finish button (F-2F). A shortcut icon is created in desktop (F-2G). DoubleClick on the icon to launch the tool.

Re-Installation: If for any reason, you need to re-install the tool again, first un-install the tool and then re-install at the same location (if re-installed in different location, restart the system so that tool refers to new location).

Running the off line tool application

Now click on the shortcut to run the application in the GST portal (F-5A). The first Tab (New) is used to upload New Data and the last Tab (Open) is used to open the error file on uploading.

Uploading Invoice Data: Double click the Offline tool icon on desktop, to get Offline tool Home Page, having three tabs:

- **Upload new invoice/ other data for return**: Click NEW button to Upload New Invoice/ upload other data. (Return will be prepared on the GST Portal, based on the data uploaded using the tool)

- **Open Downloaded Return file from GST portal**: Click OPEN button to open Downloaded pre-auto populated Return file (like GSTR-1,1A, 2A..etc) which was downloaded from GST Portal.

- **Open Downloaded Error File from GST portal**: Click OPEN button to open error file to get details of errors occurred on the portal while uploading the JSON file to the portal, to rectify the rejected invoices

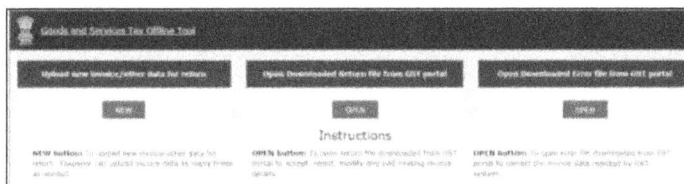

F-5A: GST offline application screen

Uploading invoice details: Click the NEW button to get File Returns page (F-5B). Now enter as follows:

- At *GST Statement/Returns* drop-down list, select the GSTR 1

- In the *GSTIN of Supplier*, enter your GSTIN

- At *Financial Year* drop-down list, select the financial year for which the return has to be filed.

- At Tax period, select the period of the return to be filed.

Enter the following details, for the first Tax Return period (e.g July 2017). In subsequent period returns, these need not be filled up.

- At Aggregate Turnover for the preceding financial Year, enter the Total aggregate turnover for previous year (enter zero if no turnover in previous year)

- At Aggregate Turnover for Apr – Jun 2017, enter the aggregate turnover for Apr – Jun 17 (enter zero if no turnover during Apr -Jun 2017)

Click Proceed button to get Invoice upload screen (F-5C)

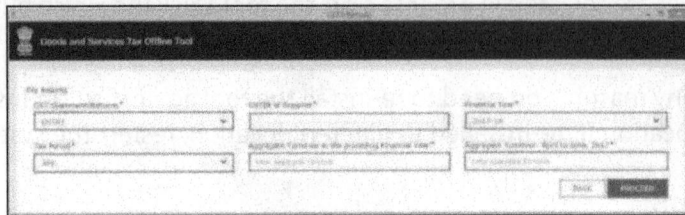

F-5B: GST Return screen

At Invoice Upload screen (F-5C), select the relevant Return section form the drop down list. You will select the relevant Tabs (of the Excel file) or the relevant CSV file, to upload relevant Invoices. Now you may enter / upload invoice data in any pf the following:

– Manual Entry of Invoice Data directly into the Portal

– Import Full Excel File of multiple sheets

– Copy & paste from Excel Sheet

– Import from CSV file

You may upload upto 19000 Invoice line items at a time.We now describe each of the process.

Manual Entry of Invoice Data

Enter the invoice data manually in the Returns Offline tool directly (one invoice at a time),

– At *Select Section* drop-down list (F-5B), select the applicable section where the invoice data needs to be entered.

– Enter the invoice details in each column like Receiver GSTIN/UIN, Invoice No. etc.

  Click the Plus icon (Highlighted in Red square under Actions column) on the right side and then enter the Item Level Details.

– Click save button after entry of each Invoice data. A success massage is displayed indicating that the Invoice data is saved in the file.

The added invoices are shown in the screen.

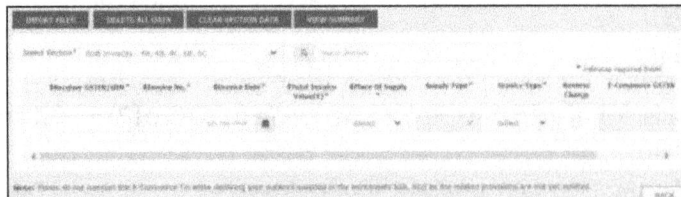

F-5C: Invoice Entry screen

To modify any data of any invoice, or delete any Invoice, check the Invoice the respective checkbox against the Invoice and then:

– Click EDIT icon (pencil) to edit Invoice data, to make correction in any field

– Click Delete button to delete any wrongly entered Invoice (all data of the selected Invoice will be deleted)

Import of data in Multiple Excel Sheet of all sections

At Invoice Entry screen (F-5C), click *Import Files* button (F-5C) to get data Import screen (F-6A). Click *Import Excel* (F-6A) and then select the GSTR1_Excel_Workbook template file from the saved downloaded files folder (F-6B), to import data from Excel Worksheet. Click Yes to proceed. A success message is displayed on successful import of the Excel file. Click Back button to view the populated invoice data.

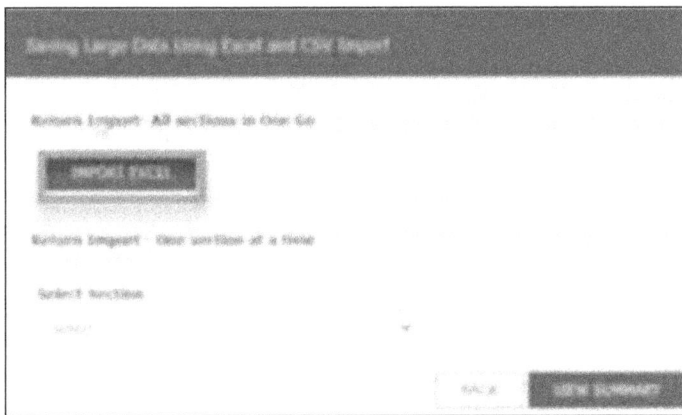

F-6A: Data import from Excel File

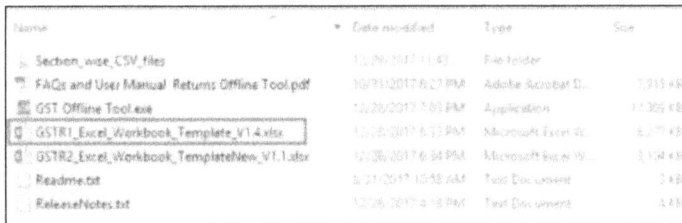

F-6B: Opening of GSTR-1 Excel Worksheet template

An error message is shown in case of any error encountered during Import. In case of import of Duplicate Invoice (multiple invoice having same invoice number in the current Tax period), the older one is overwritten. The error message shows the list of duplicate Invoice, Invalid Invoices Rejected, Record showing invalid data (like Invalid date format etc (F-6C). Note down the details if needed, and click OK

F-6C: Import Invoice error messages

It is suggested that you name the worksheet files for each month to keep data for each month separately, else all will go onto one file and create confusion. You may even create separate sub folder for each month data.

Copy and Paste from Excel Workbook

You may copy data from any Excel Sheet compatible with GSTIN format. Open the excel sheet (in same format as prescribed in the respective Return Forms). Copy the header part (first 3 rows) of data (select the rows and press Ctrl+C to copy). Click the IMPORT FILES button in the Returns Offline tool screen (F-5C).

F-7A: Copy Paste from Excel

F-7B: Copy & Paste pop up screen

From the *Select Section* drop-down list (F-7A), select the section for which you want to upload the invoices. Click the COPY EXCEL button (F-7A). The copy paste pop up appears (F-7B). Click on *Click here* and press Ctrl & V Keys together to paste the data copied from the excel sheet. The Returns Offline tool validates the data copied. Data failing these validations can't be processed further. On getting the data pasted into the worksheet, a success message is displayed. Click the *BACK* button to view the invoices from the Excel sheet, being populated in the screen. You may now EDIT / DELETE specific records as explained earlier. To Delete all data copied, click DELETE ALL DATA button (F-5C)

Import CSV file

Use CSV template downloaded in the exploded Zip file folder to create the CSV file for the applicable section of the return. Click IMPORT FILES button (F-5C), At *Select Section*, select the section from drop down list. (F-7A), click Import CSV button (F-7A). Now select the CSV files saved in the folder to import data from CSV file. A confirmation message is displayed. Click Yes to import data. On successfule import of data, a success mesaage is displayed. An error message is shown in case of any error encountered during Import, as explained earlier. Click Back button to view the data populated in the screen, from CSV file. You may edit /delete selected record, as explained.

Creation of JSON file

Having imported data, to generate compatible .JSON file, in the section wise summary screen, click GENERATE FILE button (F-8A).

F-8A: JSON file generation option

Save the JSON file in your computer, at specified location. This saved .JSON file is to be uploaded on the GST Portal. The system would create JSON file with same name each time. So, rename the file properly for each month / GSTIN.

Uploading the JSON file

In GSTR-1 File Return menu, Click Upload Offline, Click Choose File link and select the saved JSON file. A message appears, showing the refence number, on successful uploading of JSON file. GSTN system would validate GSTIN of buyers, Duplicate Invoice, Reference of Credit /Debit Notes, and other sanity checks to trap apparent errors. Now you will find the Invoice records in the respective sections.

The Excel Template

We now explain the contents of Excel Sheet so that you understand data of each section, to enter data correctly in each section. The multi excel sheet includes 11 worksheets covering different tables in GSTR-1, with a header in each sheet along with sample data. Delete the sample data in each section and enter data manually in these sheets.

GST data Classification: The excel template file / CSV files is portal created file in its own format for following transaction types:

- **B2B:** Taxable Supplies to other registered Suppliers
- **B2Ba:** Amended details of B2B invoices in current tax period, in respect of Invoices issued in previous periods
- **B2CL:** Business to Consumer Large (CL) – Taxable outward supplies where:
  - o Place of Supply is outside the State where the supplier is registered
  - o Recipient is unregistered.
  - o Invoice value more than 2,50,000
- **B2CLa:** Amended details of B2CL invoices in current tax period, in respect of Invoices issued in previous periods
- **B2CS:** Business to Consumers Small (CS) – Taxable outward supplies to unregistered Consumer where:
  - o Place of supply is same State (any value)
  - o Outside State Rs 2,50,000 or less
- **B2CSa:** Amended details of B2CS invoices in current tax period, in respect of Invoices issued in previous periods
- **CDNR:** Credit / Debit Note Registered ; Credit / Debit Note / Refund vouchers issued to registered taxpayers during the tax period.
- **CDNRa:** Amended details of CDNR Credit / Debit Notes, in current tax period, in respect of Notes issued in previous periods
- **CDNUR: :** Credit / Debit Note Un Registered ; Credit / Debit Note / Refund vouchers issued to unregistered taxpayers during the tax period.
- **CDNURa:** Amended details of CDNUR Credit / Debit Notes, in current tax period, in respect of Notes issued in previous Tax periods
- **EXP:** Supplies exported
- **EXPa:** Amended details of EXP invoices in current tax period, in respect of Invoices issued in previous Tax periods
- **AT:** Advance Tax - Tax liability arising on receipt of advance before issuance of invoice in the same period excluding tax amounts (Gross advance received).
- **Ata:** Amended details of Tax Liability in respect of receipt of advance in current period, in respect of advance receipts of previous Tax periods
- **ATADJ:** Advance Adjustments - Adjustment of Tax Liability for tax already paid on advance receipt of consideration and invoices issued in the current period
- **ATADJa:** Amendments in Adjustment of Tax Liability for tax advance receipt during current period, in respect of adjustments made in previous Tax periods.
- **EXEMP:** Nil Rated, Exempted and Non GST supplies
- **HSN:** Harmonized System Nomenclature (HSN) wise summary of goods/services
- **DOCS:** Details of various documents issued by the taxpayer

In amended records, reference of original invoice of earlier period (original document ID and original document date) are also to be entered apart from amended data.

Sample data in Excel format for each section

B2B data

4	GSTIN/UIN of Recipient	Invoice Number	Invoice date	Invoice Value	Place Of Supply	Reverse Charge	Invoice Type	E-Commerce GSTIN	Rate	Taxable Value	Cess Amount
5	05ABCDE1234E1ZF	1000	14-Jul-17	50000.00	37-Andhra Pradesh	N	Regular		12.00	45000.00	756.00
6	05ABCDE1234E1ZF	A1001	14-Jul-17	50000.00	37-Andhra Pradesh	N	Regular		5.00	40000.00	
7	05ABCDE1234E1ZF	1000A	14-Jul-17	52000.00	36-Telangana	N	Regular		12.00	40000.00	
8	05ABCDE1234E1ZF	A 1005	14-Jul-17	50000.00	31-Lakshdweep	Y	Regular		23.00	50000.00	6700.00

F-9A: B2B Sample data in Excel Sheet

B2CL data

4	Invoice Number	Invoice date	Invoice Value	Place Of Supply	Rate	Taxable Value	Cess Amount	E-Commerce GSTIN
5	10001	14-Jul-17	250000.01	37-Andhra Pradesh	5.00	345600.00	20756.00	12AJIPA1572E1C7
6	10002	14-Jul-17	250000.01	37-Andhra Pradesh	0.00	255000.00	20756.00	
7	10003	14-Jul-17	250000.01	32-Kerala	12.00	255000.00	20756.00	
8	10004	14-Jul-17	250000.01	37-Andhra Pradesh	5.00	265000.00	20756.00	
9	10005	14-Jul-17	250901.00	04-Chandigarh	5.00	250000.00	20756.00	12AJIPA1572E1C7

F-9B: B2CL Sample data in Excel Sheet

B2CS data

4	Type	Place Of Supply	Rate	Taxable Value	Cess Amount	E-Commerce GSTIN
5	E	37-Andhra Pradesh	5.00	-500000.00		12AJIPA1572E1C7
6	OE	37-Andhra Pradesh	28.00	50000.00	20756.00	
7	E	32-Kerala	12.00	250000.00		12AJIPA1572E1C7
8	OE	37-Andhra Pradesh	5.00	76000.45		
9	E	36-Telangana	12.00	350004.56		12AJIPA1572E1C7

F-9C: B2CS Sample data in Excel Sheet

At type field, E stands for E Commerce, OE stands for other than E Commerce.

CDNR Data

4	GSTIN/UIN of Recipient	Receiver Name	Invoice/Advance Receipt Number	Invoice/Advance Receipt date	Note/Refund Voucher Number	Note/Refund Voucher date	Document Type	Reason For Issu
5	12GEOPS0823BBZH	Kumar	1000	14-Jul-17	96001	15-Jul-17	C	01-Sales Return
6	12GEOPS0823BBZH	Kumar	A1001	14-Jul-17	90002	15-Jul-17	C	02-Post Sale Dis
7	12GEOPS0823BBZH	Kumar	1000A	14-Jul-17	90003	15-Jul-17	C	03-Deficiency in
8	12GEOPS0823BBZH	Kumar	A 1005	14-Jul-17	90004	15-Jul-17	D	04-Change in PO

F-9D: CDNR Sample data in Excel Sheet

CDNUR Data

UR Type	Note/Refund Voucher Number	Note/Refund Voucher date	Document Type	Invoice/Advance Receipt Number	Invoice/Advance Receipt date	Reason For Issuing document
B2CL	9009	15-Jul-17	C	10001	14-Jul-17	01-Sales Return
B2CL	90010	15-Jul-17	D	10002	14-Jul-17	02-Post Sale Discount
EXPWP	90011	15-Jul-17	C	81512	14-Jul-17	03-Deficiency in services
EXPWOP	90012	15-Jul-17	C	81511	14-Jul-17	04-Correction in Invoice

F-9E: CDNUR Sample data in Excel Sheet

In UR Type, B2CL means supply to Consumer, EXPWP indicates Export with payment of Tax, EXPWOP Export without payment of Tax. Document Type D means Debit Note, C means Credit Note, R means Refund Voucher.

EXP data

4	Export Type	Invoice Number	Invoice date	Invoice Value	Port Code	Shipping Bill Number	Shipping Bill Date	Rate	Taxable Value
5	WOPAY	81510	14-Jul-17	80048.36	INB995	184298	15-Jul-17	5.00	78788.00
6	WOPAY	81511	14-Jul-17	50990.00	INB996	184299	15-Jul-17	12.00	44545.00
7	WPAY	81512	14-Jul-17	50048.36	INB997	184300	15-Jul-17	12.00	48644.00

F-9F: EXP Sample data in Excel Sheet

At Export Type, WOPAY means Without Payment of Tax, WPAY means With Payment of Tax

AT Data

4	Place Of Supply	Rate	Gross Advance Received	Cess Amount
5	32-Kerala	12.00	87515.00	6819.00
6	02-Himachal Pradesh	5.00	15445.00	5901.00
7	36-Telangana	3.00	87515.00	

F-9G: AT Sample data in Excel Sheet

ATADJ Data

4	Place Of Supply	Rate	Gross Advance Adjusted	Cess Amount
5	01-Jammu & Kashmir	12.00	30000.00	2300.00
6	04-Chandigarh	18.00	15000.00	2200.00
7	36-Telangana	12.00	30000.00	

F-9H: ATADJ Sample data in Excel Sheet

EXEMP data

4	Description	Nil Rated Supplies	Exempted(other than nil rated/non GST supply)	Non-GST Supplies
5	Inter-State supplies to registered persons	21143.00	51235.00	5213.00
6	Intra-State supplies to registered persons			
7	Inter-State supplies to unregistered persons	1234.00	512.00	5123.00

F-9I: EXEMP Sample data in Excel Sheet

HSN data

4	HSN	Description	UQC	Total Quantity	Total Value	Taxable Value	Integrated Tax Amount	Central Tax Amount	State/UT Tax Amount	Cess Amount
5	3401	Copper	BAG-BAGS	2.05	-200.00	-10.23	214.52	600.00	500.00	200.00
6	1001	Cashew	BAL-BALE	2.05	99876.36	10.23	14.52	600.00	590.00	300.00
7	10083214	Fabric	NOS-NUMBERS	3.05	99877.36	11.23	678.00	601.00	501.00	301.00
8		Biscuit	BDL-BUNDLES	3.05	99877.38	11.23	895.00	701.00	561.00	301.00
8	3456721	Aerated Drinks	CAN-CANS	3.05	99877.36	11.23	345.00	5601.00	9769.00	301.00

F-9J: HSN Sample data in Excel Sheet

DOCS data

4	Nature of Document	Sr. No. From	Sr. No. To	Total Number	Cancelled
5	Invoices for outward supply	A1	A100	51235	6123
6	Invoices for outward supply	B1	B100	62356	234
7	Debit Note	C1	C50	723741	734
8	Debit Note				
9	Delivery Challan for job work				
10	Invoices for inward supply from unregistered person				
11	Refund Voucher				
12	Invoices for outward supply	Abc10	Xyz100	1234	512

F-9K: DOCSSample data in Excel Sheet

For multiple Item invoice, multiple rows should be added with common Document ID, Document Date, PoS etc.

GSTIN/UIN of Recipient	Invoice Number	Invoice date	Invoice Value	Place Of Supply	Reverse Charge	Invoice Type	E-Commerce GSTIN	Rate	Taxable Value	Cess Amount
05AEJPP9087R1ZF	A/1003	10-Apr-17	100000.00	37-Andhra Pradesh	N	Regular		12.00	10000.00	
05AEJPP9087R1ZF	A/1003	10-Apr-17	100000.00	37-Andhra Pradesh	N	Regular		5.00	85000.00	
05AEJPP9087R1ZF	A/1003	10-Apr-17	100000.00	37-Andhra Pradesh	N	Regular		18.00	12455.00	
05AEJPP9087R1ZF	A/1003	10-Apr-17	100000.00	37-Andhra Pradesh	N	Regular		1.00	33000.00	
05AEJPP9087R1ZF	A/1003	10-Apr-17	100000.00	37-Andhra Pradesh	N	Regular		28.00	10000.00	

F-9L: Multiple Line Item Invoice data

GSTR-1 Outwards Supplies On Line Entry

GSTR-1 Return

GSTR-1 is a statement containing all the outward supplies. Data of Outward supplies made to registered businesses (B2B) are required to be uploaded at invoice level. Data of Supplies made to unregistered business or end consumers (B2C) are required to be captured GST Rate-wise consolidated figures. However, for large transactions, invoice details are to be captured even for B2C transactions.

Method of Filing

GSTR-1 may be filed on line or offline. On-line entry means direct data entry in GSTN System. Off line entry means prime data is first entered into some system outside the GSTN System. Such data is uploaded and populated in GSTN System through some process.

- **On-line Entry**: Invoices may be uploaded directly into the GSTN system. However, only 500 B2B invoices may be entered on- line during a month, but any number of B2C Invoices may be uploaded on-line.

- **Off line Uploading**: Organisation having more than 500 B2B invoices in a month, would upload through off line method. Invoices may be uploaded off line through Offline utility (available on download from GSTN network), Excel Utility, 3rd party software (like Tally, Busy etc,), or through GSP (GST Service Provider). Anyone (even organisation having less than 500 B2B Invoices), can use the offline method.

Here we discuss about GSTR-1 on line entry & filing process to GSTN Network. However, irrespective of method of filing, the data is ultimately stored in GSTN system, in same way. Here we discuss stepwise process about on-line GSTR-1 entry & filing

Types of Outwards Supplies

GSTR-1 contains details of all outward supplies. From GST point of view of submission of returns, the outward supplies may be broadly classified as follows.

- **Intra State Supply** (Seller & Buyer in same state)

  o **B2B**: Business to Business, where good are sold to registered customer (having GSTIN) for business. Details of these invoices are uploaded invoice wise, so that the recipient can claim ITC, on matching the invoices.

  o **B2C**: Business to Consumer, where good are sold to unregistered customer not (having GSTIN). Consolidated figures of these invoices are uploaded.

– **Inter State Supply** (Seller & Buyer in different state)

o **B2B**: Business to Business, where good are sold to registered customer (having GSTIN) for business. Details of these invoices are uploaded invoice wise, so that the recipient can claim ITC, on matching the invoices.

o **B2C Large**: Business to Consumer, where good valued over 2,50,000 sold to unregistered customer not (having no GSTIN). Details of these invoices are uploaded invoice wise, to track large transactions with unregistered parties.

o **B2C**: Business to Consumer (upto Rs 2,50,000) sale to unregistered customer (having no GSTIN). State wise break up of consolidated figures of these invoices are uploaded, to track state wise share of government revenue through IGST.

o **Export**: Goods sold for export (considered Inter State for the purpose of GST classification). Details of these invoices are uploaded invoice wise.

Multi Tax Rate Invoice

In case of multi tax rate invoice (multiple tax rate items in one invoice), the Tax Rate wise break up figures (of taxable amount for each tax rate) should be compiled in respect of each multi tax Invoice, to enter the details

Inter State & Intra State transactions

In on-line system, the system automatically recognizes Inter State & Intra State transactions, comparing the first 2 digit State Code of the supplier and that of the Recipient. Accordingly, the tax amount in the respective tax rate row would be posted in IGST / SGST+CGST columns.

To make entry correctly and quickly, it is advisable to note the State of Supply in case of Inter-State supply Invoices, and tax rate wise summary of Taxable Value & Tax amount, for each tax component, so that the figures may be correctly and quickly entered in the Form.

Login to GSTN

First login to your GST account by entering your login ID and Password at GSTN website gst.gov.in, as usual (F- 1A).

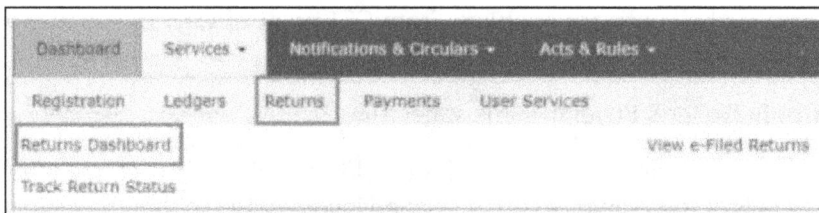

F- 1A: Returns Dash board selection

F-1B: Retrun Period

Select *Services>Returns>Return Dashboard* (F-1A), to get *File Returns* page (F-1B). Enter Financial Year and Return Filing Period for which the GSTR-1 Return is being filed (F-1B). Click *SEARCH* button.

Periodicity of Filing

Small taxpayer with turnover upto Rs 1.5 Crore may file Returns Quarterly. Accordingly, set the Periodicity option (F-1B):

– At *Do you expect your aggregate Turnover during FY 17-18 upto Rs 1.5 Crore*, set Yes in case of small taxpayer, whose turnover would remain within 1.5 crore, to get option to file *Quarterly Return* instead of Monthly Return

– Having set *Yes* at the above option, at *Would you like to opt for Quarterly Return*, set *Yes* to file *Quarterly Return* instead of Monthly Return

Quarterly Return Filing: Having set Yes at both the options, you get a message for Quarterly Return (F-1C), otherwise you get message for Monthly Return filing (F-1D).

F-1C: Confirmation for Quarterly Return

F-1D: Confirmation for Monthly Return

Accordingly, you select the Return File Period (for a Month / Quarter), to get Return Filing Main Menu (F-2A). GSTR-1 Filing Menu. On selection of period, you get GSTR-1 Menu (F-2A).

F-2A: GSTR-1 Menu

GSTR-1 General Information

At GSTR-1 Menu (F-2A), click PREPARE ON LINE under GSTR-1 Tab to enter data on line directly into GST Network, to file GSTR-1 (Details of Outwards Supply of Goods or Services) Return

You get the on-line entry screen showing the organizational info like GSTIN, Legal Name etc, followed by GSTR-1 Dashboard (F-4A) to enter data. The due of the filing of return for the selected month is shown (F-3A).

F-3A - GSTR-1: Organisation Info details

Now enter the following initial data for GSTR-1 (F-3A) to get GSTR-1 Dashboard.

– **Aggregate Turnover of the preceding Financial Year**: At Aggregate Turnover of the preceding Financial Year, enter the aggregate turnover of previous financial year

– **Aggregate turnover of the last quarter (April to June, 2017**): Enter the Aggregate Turnover of the preceding Quarter.

These info are entered in first Return only. These data would be carried to next returns automatically and need not be entered again in subsequent Returns.

GSTR-1 Dashboard

GSTR-1 Dashboard contains 11 Blocks to access the entry forms to enter Invoice data relating to outward supplies details, under 2 sections: *Invoice Details* containing 5 Blocks (F-4A) and *Other Details* containing 6 Blocks (F-4B). Based on the nature of business and the nature of supplies made during the month, only relevant data are to be submitted.

GSTR-1 Dashboard for Invoice Details section

This section (F-4A) contains 5 blocks, in which Invoice wise details are to be entered. As details of each Invoice is to be entered, the number of entries may be large. As no summarised figures are be entered, entries can be readily made from Invoices, at the respective Form.

F-4A: GSTR-1 Tiles for Invoice Details Blocks

GSTR-1 tiles for Invoice Details (F-4A)

– **4A, 4B, 4C, 6B, 6C - B2B Invoices**: To add Invoice for taxable outwards supplies to registered person

– **5A, 5B - B2C (Large) Invoices**: To add Invoice for taxable outwards supplies to consumer, where place of supply is other than the State where supplier is located (Inter-state supplies) and invoice value is more than Rs. 2.5 lakh

– **9B - Credit / Debit Notes (Registered)**: To add details of credit or debit notes issued to the registered recipients

– **9B - Credit / Debit Notes (Unregistered)**: To add details of credit, debit notes or refund voucher issued to the unregistered recipients

– **6A - Exports Invoices**: To add an invoice for supplies exported

– **Amended Invoices**: To make amendments of Invoices entered in earlier tax period (applicable for Period after July 17 only)

　o **9A - Amended B2B Invoice**: To make amendments to details of outward supplies to a registered person of earlier tax periods

　o **9A - Amended B2C (Large) Invoice**: To make amendments to taxable outward supplies to an unregistered person of earlier tax periods

　o **9A - Amended Exports Invoices**: To make amendments to supplies exported

　o **9C - Amended Credit/ Debit Notes (Registered):** To make amendments to details of credit or debit notes issued to the registered recipients of earlier tax periods

o **9C - Amended Credit/ Debit Notes (Unregistered):** To make amendments to details of credit or debit notes issued to the unregistered recipients of earlier tax periods

GSTR-1 Dashboard for Other Details sections

Other Details section (F-4B), contains 6 blocks to enter consolidated info pertaining to outwards supplies. Here only consolidated figures (not invoice wise details) are entered, which are to be first compiled from Invoice record. The data compilation may be a tough task depending on volume and pattern of business. Normally the summarized figures are compiled using Excel Sheet or using some other tools (or manually for small volume of data).

F-4B: GSTR-1 Tiles for consolidated Invoice Data

GSTR-1 Tiles for Consolidated Details (F-4B)

– **7- B2C Others**: To add consolidated details of taxable outwards supplies to a customer where invoice value is less than Rs. 2.5 lakh and all intra state supplies to unregistered customers

– **8A, 8B, 8C, 8D - Nil Rated Supplies**: Nil Rated Supplies: To add consolidated details of nil rated, exempted and Non-GST Outward supplies

– **11A(1), 11A(2) - Tax Liability (Advances Received)**: Tax Liability (Advances Received): To add details of transactions attracting tax liability arising on account of Time of Supply (like receipt of advances)

– **11B(1), 11B(2) - Adjustment of Advances**: To add the advance amount received in earlier tax period and adjusted against the supplies being shown in this tax period

– **12 - HSN-wise-summary of outward supplies:** To furnish the summarized details of all outward supplies HSN and rate wise along with quantitative details.

– **13 - Documents Issued**: To add the details of documents issued during the tax period

– **Amended Details**: To make amendments of details entered in earlier tax period (applicable for Period after July 17 only)

o **11A - Amended Tax Liability (Advance Received):** Consolidated statement for amendments of information furnished in earlier tax period

o **11B - Amended of Adjustment of Advances**: Consolidated statement for amendments of information furnished in earlier tax period

o **10 - Amended B2C (Others):** To make amendments to details of B2C of earlier tax periods

Invoice Entry Interface

The interface of on-line entry is similar for all forms

– **Addition:** For Addition of new records (Click ADD button), The uploaded data is listed in the table after each record entry for viewing. Review the entered record immediately after each entry.

– **Modification**: If there is any error in any entry, click the *Blue Pencil* square to get the record in edit mode. Now you can modify the data as required, in the same way as entry.

– **Deletion**: If any record has been wrongly entered, Click the *Red* square button to Delete the record.

Invoice Details Block

B2B Invoice entry

At Invoice details Block of GSTR-1 Dashboard (F-4A), select the block 4A, 4B, 4C, 6A, 6B – B2B Invoices block to get B2B Invoice entry screen (F-5A).

Here enter all the Invoice details of B2B Taxable transactions (deliveries to Registered Parties having GSTIN), during the specified month.

F-5A: GSTR-1 Form to enter on-line Invoice details of B2B Invoices (corresponding to Table 4A,4B,4C,6B,6C)

Now enter the following details in respect of each B2B Invoice

Invoice Details section

Receiver GSTIN/UIN: Enter the 15 digit GSTIN/UIN of the receiver (Buyer). The Receiver name would be shown beside.

– **Invoice Details**: Enter the following detail of Invoice

– **Invoice No.**: Enter the Invoice Number (unique serial number within 16 digits, including special characters like -, / etc)

– **Date**: Select the Invoice Date from the Date wizard.

- **Place of Supply**: Select the State where the goods are despatched to. From the first 2 digit of the GSTIN of the buyer as entered, State would be auto selected by default and shown from the list of States. Just click it to select. However, you may select any other State if the goods are despatched to any other State, on behalf of the Receiver.

Total Invoice Value: Value of Invoice (including all taxes and charges) payable by the buyer.

Supply Type: The nature of Transaction (supply type) is displayed as *Inter State Sale* (when State of despatcher & receiver is different) and *Intra State* Sale (when place of supply is same as home State of the seller).

Checkboxes: Click the respective checkboxes for following Invoices (otherwise do not tick any checkbox)

- **Deemed Export:** In case of Deemed Export (exports in which goods do not move physically out of India, but payment may be received either in INR or in convertible foreign currency), click on the check box *Deemed Export*. These data correspond to Table 6C

- **Supply against Reverse Charge:** In case of Outward supplies attracting reverse charges u/s 9(3),click on the check box *Supply Attract Reverse charge*. The Tax amount of the Invoice would not be added in the Tax liability (as the liability to pay tax on RCM is on Receiver). These data correspond to Table 4B

- **Supplies eligible for differential tax rate :** in case supply is eligible to be taxed at a differential percentage of the existing rate of tax, check the checkbox Is *the supply eligible to be taxed at a differential percentage (%) of the existing rate of tax, as notified by the Government?*

Item Details section: Having entered the Invoice details, at *Item Details* section, enter the Tax Rate wise figures for Taxable Amount and Tax Amount, the respective Tax rate row.

If one Invoice contains several multi rate items, then you have to compile the Taxable Value and Tax Amount for each Tax rate. So, it is advisable, to write the Tax Rate wise consolidated figures of Taxable Value and Tax Amount in case of multi tax rate invoice, to enter data quickly & correctly in GSTR-1.

- **Taxable Amount**: Enter Taxable Amount on which Tax is computed

- **Tax amount**: The computed Tax amount (on Taxable Amount) for the respective Tax Rate respective columns under IGST (for Inter state Sale) or CGST/ SGST (for Intra State Sale) and Cess, if any, are displayed

B2B supplies entered through this block correspond to the following Table of GSTR-1 Physical form

- Normal B2B Supplies (other than B2B, e-commerce, Deemed Export) – Table 4A

- Supplies attracting Reverse Charges- Table 4B

- Through e-commerce operator – Table 4C

- Supplies to SEZ unit / SEZ developer – Table 6B

- Deemed Export – Table 6C

B2C Large Invoices

At Invoice details Block of GSTR-1 Dashboard (F-4A), select the block 5A, 5B, B2C (Large) Invoices block to get B2C (large) Invoice entry screen (F-6A).

Here enter all the Inter State supplies (Items sold to other than home State) Invoice details of B2C Large Invoices (deliveries to Unregistered Parties not having GSTIN), for Invoice value exceeding Rs. 2,50,000 (including Tax and all other charges).

Invoice Details section: Enter the following details in respect of each B2C large Invoice

- **Place of Supply**: Select the Sate where the goods are despatched to (since only Inter State supplies can be entered here, the home State of the seller will not be available for selection)

- **Invoice No.**: Enter the Invoice Number (unique serial number within 16 digits)

- **Invoice Date**: Select the Invoice Date from the Date wizard .

- **Supply Type:** The nature of Transaction is displayed as Inter State Sale

- **Total Invoice Value**: Value of Invoice (including all taxes and charges) payable by the buyer.

- **Supplies through e-commerce operator:** In case of such sale through e-commerce operator,click on the check box *Supplies through e-commerce operator*, and then enter the GSTIN of e-commerce operator, in the text box appearing.

Tax Details section: Having entered the Invoice details, at *Item Details* section, enter the Tax Rate wise figures for Taxable Amount and Tax Amount.

- **Taxable Amount**: Enter Taxable Amount on which Tax is computed

- **Tax amount**: The computed IGST amount (on Taxable Amount) for the respective Tax Rate and Cess (if any) is displayed.

B2C Large supplies exceeding 2,50,000 entered through this block correspond to the following Table of GSTR-1 Physical form

- Other than through e-commerce: Table 5A

- Through e-commerce: Table 5B

Debit / Credit Notes (Registered Recipient)

At Invoice details Block of GSTR-1 Dashboard (F-4A), select the block 9B Credit / Debit Notes (Registered), to get Credit / Debit Notes (Registered) entry screen (F-7A).

Here enter all the Debit / Credit Notes issued by the organisation to Registered Parties, related to outward supplies.

Normally, Credit notes are raised on customers in respect of goods returned. Credit notes may also be issued in respect of supplies of defective goods, rebates etc (the original sales invoice, in effect, is reduced through issue of credit note). The customer's account is credited by the amount of Credit Note issued. So, such Credit notes would reduce the Tax Liability.

Sometimes, Debit note may be issued for Additional charges, supplementary bills for Rate Difference or any other adjustments / amendment of the original sales invoice (the original sales invoice, in effect, is increased through issue of Debit Note). So, such Debit notes would increase the Tax Liability.

A Credit / Debit Note will always be in reference to a sales invoice issued earlier. The reference of such earlier invoice of original supply should be recorded in the Debit / Credit Note.

F-7A: GSTR-1- On line entry for Credit / Debit Notes (Registered) Recipient)

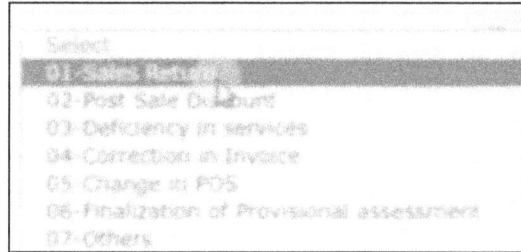

F-7B: List of Reasons of issue of Debit / Credit Notes

Receiver GSTIN/UIN: Enter the 15 digit GSTIN/UIN of the receiver (Buyer). The Receiver name would be carried beside.

Debit / Credit Note Details: Enter the following detail of Invoice.

–   **Debit / Credit Note No.**: Enter the Debit / Credit Note Number (unique serial number within 16 digits)

–   **Debit / Credit Note Date**: Select the Debit / Credit Note Date from the Date wizard.

–   **Original Invoice No.**: Enter the original invoice number against which the Debit / Credit note is issued

–   **Original Invoice Date**: Select the original invoice date, from the Date wizard.

–   **Note Type:** Select Debit (for Debit Note) / Credit (for Credit Note) Note from the list.

–   **Note Value**: Value of Debit / Credit by which the Customer Account is Debited (for Debit Note), or Credited (for Credit Note).

–   **Supply Type:** Select the supply type (Inter State / Intra state), depending on the State in which the supplier is situated.

–   **Reason for Issuing the Note:** Select the applicable reason from the list (F-7B), for which the Note was issued (like Sales Return, Post sale Discount, Deficiency in Service, Correction in Invoice, Change in PoS, Finalisation of Provisional Assessment, Others), etc.

–   **Pre GST Regime**: If the original invoice (against which the debit / credit note is being issued) relates pre GST regime, click the check box *Pre GST Regime*.

Tax Details section: Having entered the Debit / Credit Note details, at *Item Details* section, enter the Tax Rate wise figures for Taxable Amount and Tax Amount.

–   **Taxable Amount**: Enter Taxable Amount on which Tax is computed

–   **Tax amount**: The computed IGST amount (on Taxable Amount) for the respective Tax Rate and Cess (if any), is displayed

Debit / Credit Notes issued on Registered dealer entered through this block correspond to the Table 9B. However, Table 9B also contains data of Refund Voucher for Refund of Advance (not captured through this Form)

Reference of Original Invoice

Specify the reference of Original Invoice and Invoice Date in the Debit / Credit Note. In case of goods returned (whole or Part of a supply relating to one specific Invoice), due to some reason (rejection / defective) etc., the original Invoice Number may be mentioned. However, often, goods relating to several invoices may be retuned, at a time (normally good re returned only after some correspondence between supplier & customer). In such, reference number & date of original invoice cannot be entered correctly (as there is provision of entry of only one invoice number & date of original invoice).

Sometimes, Credit Note may be issued for lump sum discount, rebate etc., is allowed on various invoices. Debit Note may be issued for supplementary charges in respect of several invoices. In such cases, reference of one invoice cannot be given. You may enter some relevant reference at Original Invoice No & Date.

Reasons of Issue of Debit Credit Notes: You have to select the most appropriate reason of issuing the Debit / Credit Note, from the following list of Reasons.

– **Sales Return**: This is the most common reason of issuing credit note issued by seller on return of goods by the buyer to seller. The buyer returns the goods giving reference of the original supply. On receiving the goods, the original seller receiving back the goods,

– **Post Sales Discount**: This may be allowed on specific sales or as general discount as Sales policy. So, Original single Invoice reference may not be available.

– **Deficiency in Services**: Such Credit Note are issued against service invoice. This may be allowed against specific service invoice or general discount as Sales policy

– **Correction in Invoice**: A debit note may be issued by seller on the buyer, if the original sale invoice was undercharged in respect of value or Tax, for adjustment of under charge. Similarly, a Credit note may be issued by seller on the buyer, for return of goods, or if the original invoice was over charged in respect of value or Tax, for adjustment of over charge.

– **Change in place of Supply**: Due to change in place of supply, the nature of supply may change and consequently, a debit / credit note may be issued

– **Finalisation of Provisional Assessment**: A debit / credit note may be issued on revision of assessment (additional tax or refunds)

– **Others**: Any other reason

While issuing credit note / debit note, the seller adds GST in the Debit / Credit Note, as per the GST rate specified in the original sale invoice, with reference to which the Debit / Credit Note is being issued.

Credit & Debit Notes may be issued in relation to sale (credit note to reduce sale value, debit note to increase sale value). A Debit Note is also sometimes called as Supplementary Sales Invoice, as it increases seller's Tax liability and buyer's dues, like a sales Invoice.

However, the Debit / Credit note issued by seller in respect of sale only are to be reported in GSTR-1 (A buyer would also issue / record Debit / Credit note issued in respect of Purchase by buyer, to make accounting adjustments. Such Debit / Credit Notes related to Purchase transactions are not to be entered in GSTR-1).

So, the organisation must clearly distinguish Debit Notes / Credit Notes issued relating to Sale, from those relating to Purchase.

Tax liability of Credit Note can be adjusted within September of next financial year, or the due date of filing of Annual Return, whichever is earlier, provided that the recipient has reversed ITC.

Debit / Credit notes (Unregistered Recipient)

F-8A: GSTR-1 In line entry for Debit / Credit notes (Unregistered Recipient)

At Invoice details Block of GSTR-1 Dashboard (F-4A), select the block 9B Credit / Debit Notes (Unregistered), to get Credit / Debit Notes (unregistered) entry screen (F-8A). Credit notes related to B2CL are entered here. Credit notes issued in respect of B2CS invoices are reported in B2CS as negative value (not reported here). Credit Notes issued against Export Sales are also entered here (Exports are treated as unregistered parties as foreign buyers do not have GSTIN)

Debit / Credit Note Details: Enter the following detail of Invoice.

- **Type**: Select the type of transaction from the list:

  o **B2CL**: When the credit note is issued in respect of sale to unregistered party, for invoice value exceeding 2,50,000

  o **Exports with payment of Tax**: When debit / credit note is issued in respect of original export sale with payment of Tax)

  o **Exports without Payment of Tax**: When debit / credit note is issued in respect of original export sale without charging Tax, e.g in cases like LUT - Letter of Undertaking or Bond).

- **Debit / Credit Note No.**: Enter the Debit / Credit Note Number.

- **Debit / Credit Note Date**: Select the Debit / Credit Note Date from the Date wizard.

- **Original Invoice No.**: Enter the original invoice number against which the Debit / Credit note is issued

- **Original Invoice Date**: Select the original invoice date, from the Date wizard.

- **Note Type:** Select Debit (for Debit Note) / Credit (for Credit Note) Note from the list.

- **Note Value**: Value of Debit / Credit by which the Customer Account is Debited (for Debit Note), or Credited (for Credit Note).

- **Supply Type:** The supply type (Inter State) would be displayed (Credit Note against B2CL & SEZ, are Inter State supplies)

- **Reason for Issuing the Note:** Select the applicable reason from the list, for which the Note was issued (like Sales Return, Post sale Discount, Deficiency in Service, Correction in Invoice, Change in PoS, Finalisation of Provisional Assessment, Others)

- **Pre GST Regime**: If the original invoice (against which the debit / credit note is being issued) relates pre GST regime, click the check box *Pre GST Regime*

Tax Details section: Having entered the Debit / Credit Note details, at *Item Details* section, enter the Tax Rate wise figures for Taxable Amount and Tax Amount.

- **Taxable Amount**: Enter Taxable Amount on which Tax is computed

- **Tax amount**: The computed Tax amount (on Taxable Amount) for the respective Tax Rate &Cess (if any) is displayed in IGST column.

Debit / Credit Notes issued on Unregistered dealer entered through this block correspond to the Table 9B. However, Table 9B also contains data of Refund Voucher (not captured through this Form)

Exports

At Invoice details Block of GSTR-1 Dashboard (F-4A), select the block Export Invoices 6A to get Exports entry screen (F-9A).

F-9A: GSTR-1 - On line entry for Exports

Here enter all the Export Invoice details as follows:

– **Invoice No.**: Enter the Invoice Number

– **Invoice Date**: Select the Invoice Date from the Date wizard.

– **Port Code:** Enter the 6 digit Port Number, if available

– **Shipping Bill Number / Bill of Export No**: Enter the Shipping Bill or Bill of Export number, if available.

– **Shipping Bill / Bill of Export Date**: Enter the Shipping Bill or Bill of Export number

– **Total Invoice Value**: Value of Invoice (including all taxes and charges) payable by the buyer.

– **Supply Type:** The Nature of Transaction is displayed as Inter State Sale (exports are treated as Inter State sales in GST system)

– **GST Payment:** Select With payment of Duty, when Tax is paid. Select Without Payment of Duty, when Tax is not paid (for example, in case of Exports under Bond / LUT (Letter of Undertaking)), as the case may be, from the list.

Tax Details section: If the Export Invoice is with Payment of Duty, at *Item Details* section, enter the Tax Rate wise figures for Taxable Amount and Tax Amount.

– **Taxable Amount**: Enter Taxable Amount on which Tax is computed

– **Tax Amount**: The computed Tax amount (on Taxable Amount) for the respective Tax Rate is displayed in IGST column.

Export Invoices entered through this block correspond to the Table 6A.

GSTR-1 Other Details

In this section, you get 6 blocks. Unlike blocks under Invoice Details section, you need not enter Invoice wise details in Forms through various blocks under Other details section. Rather you enter Tax rate wise consolidated figures for the month.

GSTR-1 - On line entry for B2C (Others)

At Other Details Block of GSTR-1 Dashboard (F-4B), select the block 7- B2C (Others) to get B2C (Others) Tab screen (F-10A), to enter B2C Invoices other than those entered at B2CL, explained earlier. So, here you enter Invoices relating to:

– Intra State Sales to Unregistered Parties

– Inter State Sales to unregistered Parties for value upto 2,50,000.

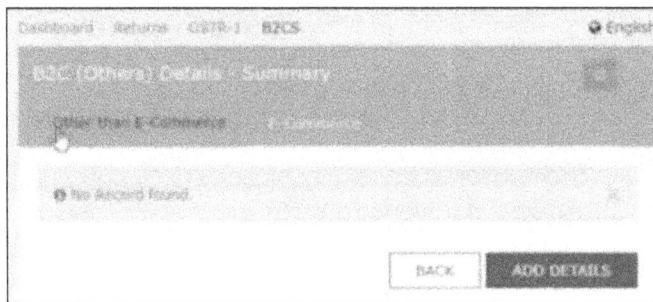

F-10A: B2C Others (Tabs)

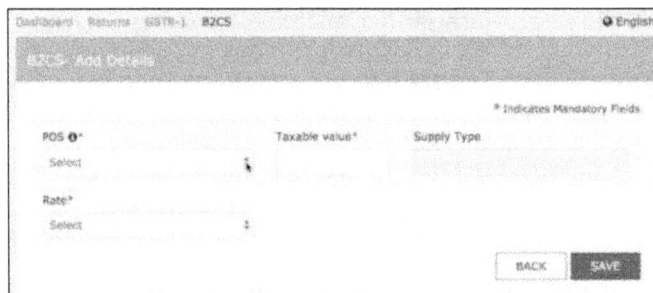

F-10B: B2CS (other than e-commerce)

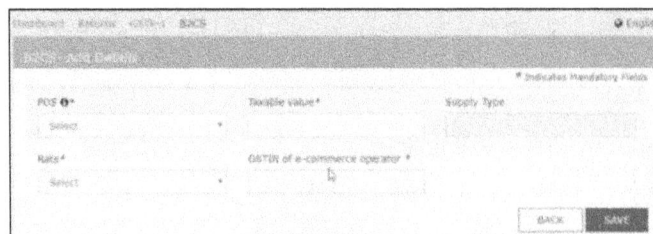

F-10C: B2CS (e-commerce)

You get 2 Tabs (F-10A):

– **Other than e-commerce**: To record Invoices not sold through e-commerce

– **e-commerce**: To record Invoices sold through e-commerce operators

Here, you enter the consolidated figures of all Invoices for the period.

– Select the Tab *Other than e-commerce* (F-10A) to get the B2C Others (other than e-commerce) entry screen (F-10B).

– Select the Tab e-commerce (F-10A) to get the B2C Others (e-commerce) entry screen (F-10C).

Now enter as follows:

– **PoS:** Select the State from list of States.

– **Taxable Value:** Enter the Taxable Value of Sale for that State

– **Supply Type:** Depending on the State selected, the nature of supply would be displayed (Inter State - when the State selected at PoS is different from Home State), (Intra State - when Home State is selected at PoS)

– **Rate:** Select the Tax Rate from the list of Rates

– **Tax Amount**: Depending on Supply Type (Inter State or Intra State) , computed Tax Amount at respective Tab (Integrated Tax for Inter State supply) or Central Tax / State Tax (for Intra State supply) and cess, if any, would be displayed as the respective Tax rate row.

This way, enter the consolidated details for each Tax rate, for each State, for transactions other than e-commerce operator.

Sale through e-commerce Operator: For sale through e-commerce operator, select the tab e-commerce (F-10A). Enter the GSTIN of the e-commerce operator and enter the Invoice details in the same way , for each tax rate, for each State, for the respective e-commerce operator.

This way, enter the Invoice details for sale through e-commerce operator, for each Tax rate, for each state, for each e-commerce operator.

It is recommended to create separate Invoice series for each e-commerce operator, so that you can easily compile the figures, for each State, for each rate.

B2CS supplies entered through this Block correspond to following Tables:

– B2CS Intra State Supplies other than e-commerce 7A(1)

– B2CS Intra Sate supplies, through e-commerce: Table 7A(2)

– B2CS Inter State Supplies upto 2,50,000, other than e-commerce: Table 7B(1)

– B2CS Inter State Supplies upto 2,50,000, through e-commerce: Table 7B(2)

NIL Rated Supply

At Other Details Block of GSTR-1 Dashboard (F-4B), select the block 8A, 8B, 8C- NIL rated Supply to get NIL Rated Supplies screen (F-11A). Enter the details of Invoices of NIL rated Items only (Invoices in which No Tax is charged).

Here you enter Inter State & Intra state consolidated Invoice figures, separately for Registered & Non Registered persons:

- **NIL Rated Items Sale**: Gross Sales Value for Items where GST rate is zero (like Eggs, News paperetc)

- **ExemptedItems Sale**: Gross Sales Value for Items exempted under GST rate is zero (like Rice, Wheat etc)

- **Non GST Supplies Sale**: Gross Sales Value for excluded from the ambit of GST (like Petroleum, Alcohol)

Since only NIL Tax supplies are recorded here, Tax figures need not be entered in these cases.

F-11A- GSTR-1 - On line entry for NIL rated supply

Enter the consolidated sales figures in respect of each element in respective columns, as follows:

- **Inter State Supplies to Registered person**. Total Inter State Sales to registered persons for NIL rated, Exempted & Non-GST goods / services (corresponding to Table 8A), in the respective columns.

- **Inter State Supplies to unregistered person**: Total Inter State Sales to unregistered persons for NIL rated, Exempted & Non-GST goods / services (corresponding to Table 8C), in the respective columns.

- **Intra State Supplies to Registered person**: Total Intra State Sales to registered persons for NIL rated, Exempted & Non-GST goods / services (corresponding to Table 8B), in the respective columns.

- **Intra State Supplies to unregistered person**: Total Intra State Sales to unregistered persons for NIL rated, Exempted & Non-GST goods / services (corresponding to Table 8D),, in the respective columns.

Though the report appears to be simple and small, it may be substantial work to compile the figures (there are 12 summarised figures in all). Planning and segregating Invoice series, as per their trade pattern, may be helpful, if number of such invoices are large.

Advances Received

As per GST rules, Tax is to be paid on advance received (even if supply is not made or Invoice not issued). The seller receiving advance against supply to be made, should enter the details of such Advance Received.

Applicable Rate of Tax on Advance Received: Tax is to be paid at same rate applicable on goods to be supplied against receipt of advance. So, the rate of advance depends on the rate of Goods to be supplied (where the rate of goods supplied is known).

If the rate of Tax of goods to be supplied is not known, cannot be ascertained at the time of taking advances, then GST should be charged @ 18%. For example, if the buyer gave orders and advances for some supplies for which GST rate is not exactly known at that time, 18% GST will have to be paid on those advances.

If the type of supply (Intra State or Inter State), not known then at advance should be deemed to be considered as Inter State supply (so IGST would be charged).

Allocation of Advance &Tax: Tax is to be computed on amount of Advance (excluding Tax). Sometimes Advance is received in lump sum, including Tax amount. In such case, you should back calculate the Advance & Tax amount. For example, if the amount of Rs 50,000 received in advance, is to be split up into Advance and Tax thereon, then you have to compute the Advance & tax as:

Advance portion P=: A/(1+r/100), Tax portion T=A-P

So, for Amount of Rs 50,000 received in advance, the Advance and Tax element at Tax Rate 12% would be computed as:

Advance (P) = 50000 / (1+12/100) = 50000/1.12 = 44643. So, the Tax (T) would be computed on 44643@ 12% = 5357 .

So, 50,000 (Total Amount received: A) is to be accounted for as Rs.44643 (Advance: P) and Rs.5357 (Tax on Advance: T)

Advance against Multi Rate supplies: When advance is received in respect of supply of multiple tax rate items, the amount must be segregated properly, for each Tax rate slab. For example, If Rs. 50000 is received for supply of goods of Tax rate 5% and 12%, the amount should be proportionately split up making an estimate of the value of expected supply and entered accordingly. This is very important, as when sale Invoice is created in subsequent period, the corresponding figure of Advance adjusted must be accounted for respective Tax rate (explained next).

Entry of Advance Received: At Other Details Block of GSTR-1 Dashboard (F-4B), select the block 11A (1), 11A (2) (Tax Liability) – Advances received to get Advanced Received screen (F-12A).

Here you enter details of Tax Liability in respect of Advances received from Customers for supply of goods / services

F-12A: GSTR-1 - On line entry for Tax Liability (Advances Received)

Now Enter as follows:

- **PoS:** Select the State of the Party from whom advance was received, from list of States.

- **Supply Type:** Depending on the State selected, the nature of supply would be displayed (Inter State -when the State selected at PoS is different from Home State), (Intra State - when Home State is selected at PoS)

At Item details screen, enter the details of Advance received and Tax Liability thereon, in the respective Tax Rate slab.

- **Gross Advance Received**: Enter the Amount of Advance Received(Amount on which Tax is computed, excluding Tax Amount), against the applicable Tax Rate.

- **Tax Amount**: : Depending on Supply Type (Inter State or Intra State) , computed Tax Amount at respective Tab (Integrated Tax for Inter State supply) or Central Tax / State Tax (for Intra State supply) would be displayed against respective Rate.

Advances received as entered through this Block correspond to following Tables

- Advances received from Parties within home State – Table 11A(1)

- Advances received from Parties from outside State – Table 11A(2)

Adjustment of Advances

At Other Details Block of GSTR-1 Dashboard (F-4B), select the block 11B (1), 11B (2) (Adjustment of Advances) to get Advanced Received screen (F-13A).Here you enter details of Adjustment of pending Advances received in earlier period, on which Tax was already paid.

F-13A: GSTR-1 - On line entry for Tax Liability (Adjustment of Advances)

Now Enter as follows:

– **PoS:** Select the State of the Party from whom advance was received, from list of States**.**

– **Supply Type:** Depending on the State selected, the nature of supply would be displayed (Inter State -when the State selected at PoS is different from Home State), (Intra State - when Home State is selected at PoS)

At Item details screen, enter the details of Advance received and Tax Liability thereon

– **Gross Advance Adjusted**: Enter the Amount of Advance Adjusted (Amount on which Tax is reversed computed), against the applicable Tax Rate

– **Tax Amount**: Depending on Supply Type (Inter State or Intra State) , computed Tax Amount at respective Tab (Integrated Tax for Inter State supply) or Central Tax / State Tax (for Intra State supply) and Cess (as applicable) would be displayed against respective Rate.

Advances adjusted as entered through this Block correspond to following Tables

– Advances received from Parties within home State – Table 11B (1)

– Advances received from Parties from outside State – Table 11B (2)

As explained earlier, the GSTR system keeps track on Advances received & adjusted, separately for Inter State & Intra state, for each rate. The adjustment figures must be properly matched against the advances received. This is based on assumption that the buyer exactly knows the Item (to determine the Tax rate) and also the nature of Supply (Inter State or Intra State). Accordingly the Tax on advance is computed and accounted for.

However, complexity and problem would arise when materials of different tax rate is supplied than planned at the time of making advances, or supplied from different State.

For example, the buyer paid advance for supply of materials of GST rate 12% but the materials of different tax rate was supplied. At the time of supply, the tax would be computed @ 12% but in the Invoice, tax rate would be different. It is not clear how the adjustment would be reported under this table.

Take another example, Rs 30,000 advance was paid for supply of Item 1 (GST @12%) and Rs 15000 was paid for supply of Item 2 (GST @ 18%). Subsequently, Item -1 for 15000 and Item -2 of Rs 30000 were supplied. The adjustment of Tax for the respective Tax Rate would be difficult in the given format.

The complexity would also arise, when the nature of supply changes. For example advance was given for Intra State supply to be made from a factory in the same state, but Inter State supply was made from factory of another state. In such case, reporting of adjustment of advance in this Form may pose problem.

HSN wise summary

At Other Details Block of GSTR-1 Dashboard (F-4B), select the block 12 HSN wise summary of Outward supplies to get HSN wise summary of Outward supplies entry screen (F-14A).

Here you enter HSN wise summary of Outward Supplies and Tax charged thereon

F-14A: GSTR-1 - On line entry for HSN wise summary of outward supplies

Now enter the following details of all outward supplies, in respect of each HSN Code

- **HSN**: Enter the HSN Code (2/4 digits) as per applicable rules for the organisation.

- **Description**: Enter the Description of supplies

- **UQC:** Select the Unit Quantity Code (UQC) as per the Unit of measurement.

- **Quantity**: Enter the Quantity in terms of the UQC

- **Total Value**: Enter the total value of Invoice (including all taxes and other charges)

- **Total Taxable value**: Enter the total Taxable value of Invoice (on which Tax is charged)

- **Integrated Tax**: Enter the respective amount of Integrated Tax

- **Central Tax**: Enter the respective amount of Central Tax

– **State / UT Tax**: Enter the respective amount of State / UT Tax

– **Cess**: Enter the respective amount of Integrated Tax

So, one record would be entered for each HSN Code. HSN summary entered through this Block correspond to Table 12

Documents Issued: At Other Details Block of GSTR-1 Dashboard (F-4B), select the block 13 Documents issues during the Tax period to get Documents issued screen (F-14A).

Document Numbering: Document Number is consecutive serial number not exceeding sixteen characters, in one or multiple series, containing alphabets or numerical or special characters hyphen or dash symbolized as "-" and "/" respectively, and any combination thereof, unique for a financial year.

GST specifies that for each document series, serial numbered document must be issued. So, GST does not allow to insert document like 21A between 21 and 22.

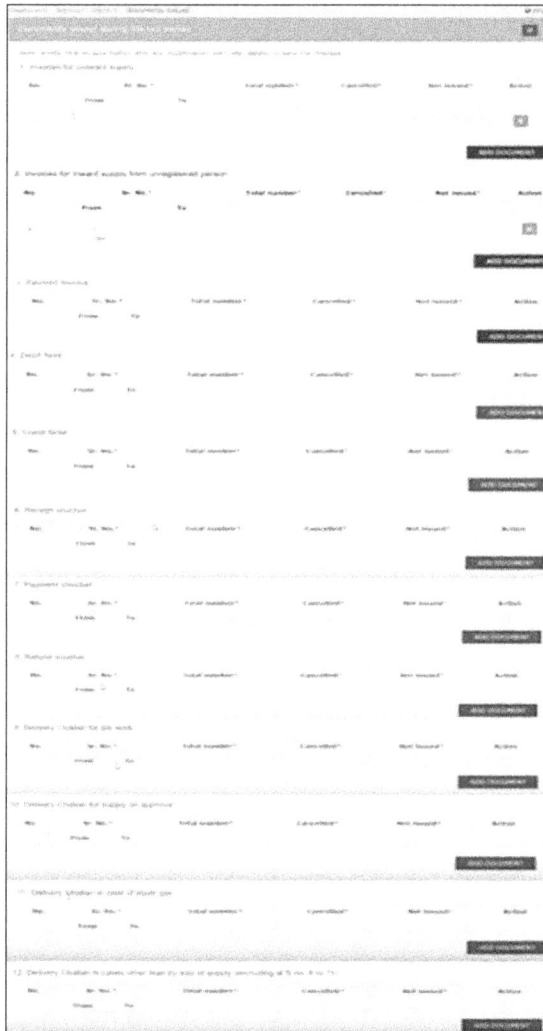

F-15A: Documents issued during Tax Period

Now enter the following details for each series of the 12 types of Documents, as listed next

- **From**: Enter the Series & Start Number of Invoice

- **To**: Enter the Series & Start Number of Invoice

- **Total Number**: Total Number of Invoice issued within the specified range (including cancelled invoices)

- **Cancelled:** Number of cancelled invoices within the range of issued invoices

- **Net issued**: Number of invoices actually issued (excluding the cancelled invoices)

Types of Documents: The above details in respective columns are to be submitted for following types of documents

1. **Invoices for Outwards Supply**: In respect of all types of supply such Inter State / Intra State, Taxable / Nil rated, Exempted, Non GST etc.

2. **Invoices for inward supply from unregistered person**: Invoices of inward supply from unregistered person (only subject to reverse charges), which are to be created by buyer.

3. **Revised Invoice**: Invoices of outward supply issued in lieu of provisional invoice issued during effective date of registration and date of issue of registration certificate.

4. **Debit Note**: Debit Notes issued by seller in relation to previous supply.

5. **Credit Note**: Credit Notes Issued by seller in relation to previous supply.

6. **Receipt voucher**: Receipt Voucher for receipt of advance against supply of goods or services.

7. **Payment Voucher**: Payment Voucher for tax payment under reverse charge u/s. 9(3) or s. 9(4) of CGST Act 2017.

8. **Refund voucher**: Refund Voucher for refund of Advance received (full or part)

9. **Delivery Challan for job work**: Delivery Challan for job work issued during the month

10. **Delivery Challan for supply on approval**: Delivery Challan for supply on approval issued during the month

11. **Delivery Challan in case of liquid gas**: Delivery Challan in case of liquid gas issued during the month

12. **Delivery Challan in cases other than by way of supply other than above**: Other delivery challan (other than specified above).

Number of documents: Specify the number of documents under the following columns, for each document type:

- **Total Number**: Total Number of documents issued. It would normally be according to the starting and ending serial number of the document. For example, 21 to 30 means 10 documents.

–   **Cancelled**: Number of documents cancelled (invalidated within the specified range of issued document. For example, if after issuing Invoice 21-30, the Invoice number 27 is cancelled, then number of issued documents would be 10, Cancelled document would be 1 and Net Issued would be 9.

–   **Net Issued**: the number would be difference between Total Number of documents issued and Cancelled.

Document details entered through this Block correspond to Table 13

Revised Invoice

Under GST, all the taxable dealers will have to apply for provisional registration. On completion of all formalities, they will get the permanent registration certificate.

Now, against all Invoices, issued between the effective date of registration and Date of issue of Registration certificate, the dealers will have to issue a revised invoice against the invoice already issued between the said period. The revised invoice will have to be issued within one month from the date of issue of the registration certificate. The word "Revised Invoice", wherever applicable, be indicated prominently

Having entered all the details, check each of the Form to ensure correctness. Click checkbox at the declaration, click on the Submit button and file with DSC or EVC. After filing, you cannot modify any data in the Form

Declaration & Filing

GSTR-1 on-line For entry - Declaration

Invoice Details summary

After entry of Invoice details under each tile (like B2B, B2C large etc), you get list of the Invoices under various Tabs:

–   **Uploaded by Taxpayer:** The "Uploaded by Taxpayer" tab shows all the invoices that you have uploaded for a given tax period.

–   **Uploaded by Receiver:** The "Uploaded by Receiver" tab displays the invoices that you missed from your GSTR-1, but were uploaded by the Receiver Taxpayer for taking appropriate actions.

–   **Modified by Receiver:** If the receiver Taxpayer has modified any invoice that you uploaded in your GSTR-1, it will show-up under the "Modified by Receiver" tab for taking appropriate actions.

–   **Rejected by Receiver:** The "Rejected by Receiver" tab displays invoices from your GSTR-1 that were rejected by the receiver Taxpayer for taking appropriate actions

B2B invoices uploaded in GSTR-1 as a supplier will reflect in the B2B Invoices of the receiver in GSTR-2A/GSTR-2. However, no action can be taken by receiver unless the Supplier files GSTR-1

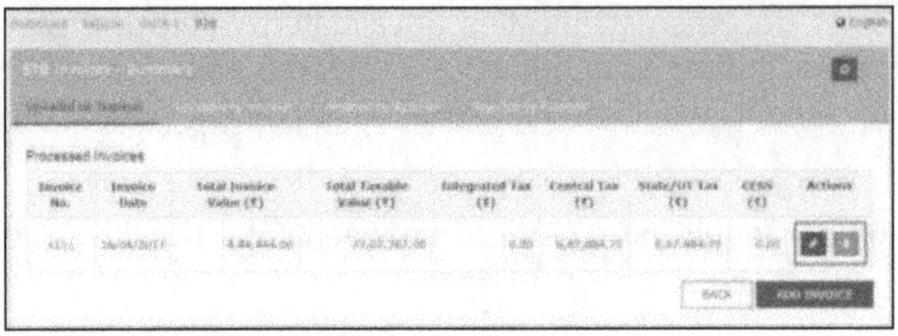

Invoice Details Summary

This way, you may view the record entered during entry and add, edit or delete records during entry time.

Receiver-Wise-Summary: Click the *BACK* button to go back to the Invoices - Receiver-Wise-Summary page, to view receiver wise summary of invoices. You may add invoice of the particular receiver by clicking on the particular receiver and then clicking on the *ADD INVOICE* button at the bottom of the page. Click the *BACK* button to go back to the GSTR-1 page.

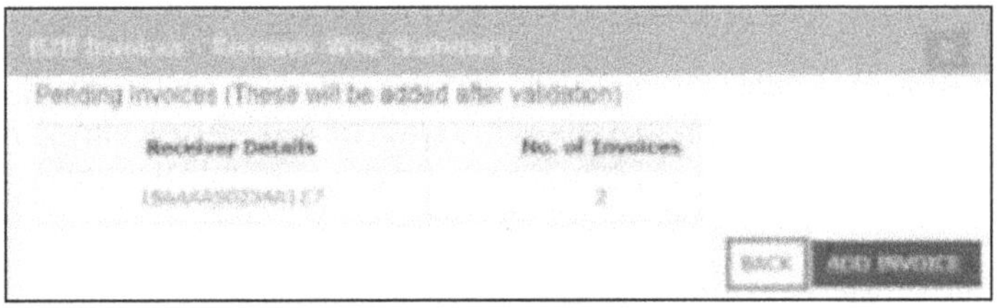

Receiver wise Summary

Amended Invoice Entry

To make amendments to details of outward supplies furnished in returns of earlier tax periods, select the respective tile for Amended Invoice block to get Amended Invoice list summary screen.

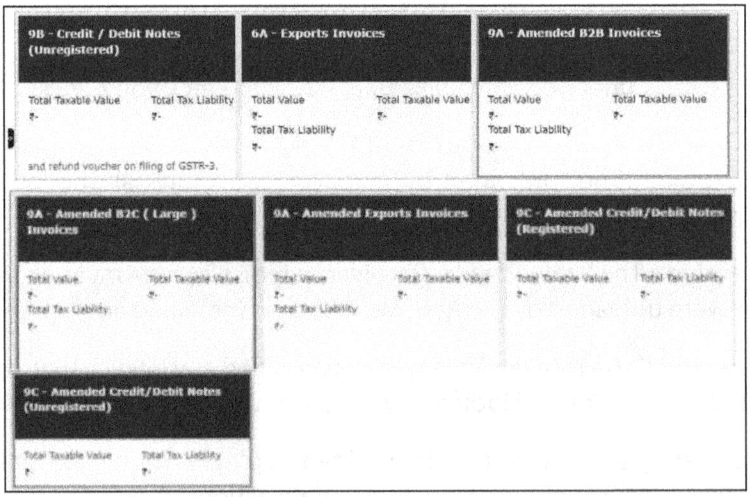

Previous period amended invoice entry block

Select the *Financial Year* from the drop-down list. In the *Invoice No.* field, enter the invoice number which you want to amend from earlier tax period.

Amended Invoice summary

Click the *AMEND INVOICE* button to get the Amended Invoice entry screen, similar to Invoice entry screen, discussed earlier

Amended Invoice entry screen, you get 2 additional fields

– **Revised Invoice No: E**nter the revised invoice number for the previous invoice.

– **Revised Date** : Enter the date using calendar.

Now Make amendments to the details as required. You cannot amend the GSTIN of the invoice furnished earlier. Click *SAVE* button.

This way, you may make amendments selecting the tiles for invoice wise details

GSTR-1 Modification

As explained, on submitting the JSON file, it will be validated. If OK, Processed remark would be reported in Status column. Here we discuss about modification of errors encountered in GSTR-1.

However, if the GSTR-1 was filed off line, on encountering any error, you should delete the GSTR-1 data before submission. Modify the basic data to remove all errors inconsistency. Upload again till the data is uploaded error free.

Now we explain how to locate the errors in uploaded GSTR-1, rectify data to make error free and submit GSTR-1 for filing.

Downloading Error Report: If any error encountered, *Process with Error* would be reported at Status column and *Generate Error Report* would be displayed at Error Report Column. To view the errors, click on *Generate Error Report*. After a few minutes, Download Error Report would be shown at Error Report columns. Click on the link (meanwhile, a message Error Report generation requested would be reported) to Download Error Report (a zip file),

Opening Error File: Open it (zip file) with GST offline tool ONLY (do not explode the file) to view the contents (error notes) and carry out modifications. Click Proceed. The errors would be reported in Error Messages column. To edit, click the pencil icon. Click Open at the tab Open Downloaded Error File from GST Portal (to accept, reject, modify and add missing invoice details).

Modification of entry: Now you may modify, delete or insert invoices in the GSTR-1 file.

– **Adding New Records:** To add missing Invoice, click Add Details button and enter the missing Invoice data, as explained at Online Entry.

– **Modification:** To modify Click the EDIT (Pencil Icon) button under *Action* column to edit the invoices and make the required corrections in the invoices/details uploaded/added earlier by you in GST Portal.

  To modify the details or records at Rate level, click on the' +' button and navigate to the rate level records. Do the necessary corrections and click the UPDATE button.

  On *Modification*, a success message is displayed. The status is changed to Modified (M). Similarly, any invoice and other returns data may be modified from other sections.

– **Deletion**: To Delete Invoices, select the checkbox at left side for the invoice to be deleted. Click the DELETE button.

  To delete all invoices in one go, select the top left checkbox for all invoice to be deleted in the *Particulars* section. Click*DELETE* button.

  On Deletion, a success message is displayed. The status is changed to Deleted (D). Similarly, user can delete the other invoice and other returns data from other sections.

  Delete operation does not physically delete the invoices/details from offline. It changes the status flag to "D". Invoices get deleted online after uploading the JSON.

GSTR-1: Review of B2B Invoices in GSTR-1

Summary Generation

After making all entries, Scroll down to the bottom of the *GSTR-1 – Details of outward supplies of goods or services* page and click the *GENERATE GSTR1 SUMMARY* button to include the auto drafted details pending for action from recipients. The invoices that were missed to be included by you, may have been added in the *Uploaded by Receiver* while filing his GSTR-2.

GSTR-1 Summary Generation

You will receive a message of initiation of summary generation process

Message of Summary Generation process

After the summary is generated, you will notice a success message on top of the page. The summary is generated by the GST Portal automatically at an interval of every 30 minutes. If you attempt to view summary too early, you may get an error message. Wait for more time

Summary Preview

At Generate Summary screen, click PREVIEW button, todownload the PDF draft Summary page (with DRAFT watermark) of your GSTR-1 for your review. Now carefully review the summary of entries made in different sections before submitting the GSTR-1.

GSTR-1 Form Submission

Having checked the GSTR-1 Form data, at Generate Summary screen, click the checkbox and click Submit button to Submit and freeze the GSTR-1 Form to get GSTR-1 Summary submission message. You will be not able to upload any further invoices for that month. If any invoice is missed, you can upload such missing invoices in the next month or you can wait for receiver to add it in receiver GSTR-2.

GSR-1 Summary Submission message

Click *PROCEED* button. A success message is displayed. The status will get changed to Submitted

Summary Submission success message

Filing of GSTR-1 with Signature

At Generate Summary screen, click *FILE RETURN* button, to get *Returns Filing for GSTR1* page. Check the *Declaration* checkbox.

In the *Authorised Signatory* drop-down list, select the authorized signatory. Click the *FILE WITH DSC* or *FILE WITH EVC* button to file GSTR-1. On filing of the GSTR-1, notification through e-mail and SMS is sent to the Authorized Signatory.

GSTR-1A

GSTR-1A allows a registered taxpayer to update the details of sales for GSTR-1 filed in earlier Tax period.

Invoices uploaded by seller in GSTR-1 is reflected in GSTR-2 of Buyer.

The Invoices modified by buyer in GSTR-2. Any changes made in GSTR-2 by the Buyer would be reflected in GSTR-1A of the seller. The seller must accept or reject the changes

Example: (a) Buyer B buys 100 Boxes of Pencil worth Rs. 5000 from Seller S. (b). Seller S erroneously showsit as Rs. 500 sales in his GSTR-1. (c) The erroneous data (Rs 500) from Seller S's GSTR-1 will flow into GSTR-2A (and then to GSTR-2) of Buyer B. (d) Buyer B corrects the erroneous data (Rs 500 to 5000) in his GSTR-2. (e) This correction is reflected in Seller S's GSTR-1A (Rs 5000). (f) Seller S accepts this correction and his GSTR-1 gets automatically updated (Rs 5000).

All changes in GSTR-1A must be accepted/rejected between the 15th and 17th of the next month. Changes made in GSTR-1A by seller will be automatically reflected in his GSTR-1.

GSTR-1A Summary Generation

Login to *www.gst.gov.in* through Username / password credential. Click *Services > Returns > Returns Dashboard* command (or click the *Returns Dashboard* link on the Dashboard), to get File Return page. Enter the Financial Year, Return filing period and click SEARCH to get the GSTR Returns Menu. Click *PREPARE ON LINE* button at Details of *Auto Drafted Supplies GSTR1A* tile to get GSTR1A page. Scroll down to the bottom of the GSTR1A page and click the *GENERATE GSTR1A SUMMARY* button. The *Details of auto drafted supplies of goods or services* page is displayed.

Action on Auto populated details in GSTR-1A

You get following tiles for each Tables. Click on the respective tile to take action on the relevant Invoices

o **3,4 – B2B Invoices** – To view and take actions on the auto-populated details of changes and additions made by the recipients of taxable outward supplies made to registered persons (including supplies attracting reverse charge and zero rated suppliesto SEZ / deemed exports)

o **5 – Credit / Debit Notes (Registered)** – To view and take action on the auto-populated details of changes and additions made by the recipients, of Debit Notes and Credit Notes (including amendments) issued during current period.

Select the Invoice (click the checkbox) and then click the respective button to take action as follows:

– **ACCEPT:** To accept the changes. The status changes to ACCEPTED

– **REJECT:** To accept the changes. The status changes to REJECTED

– **PENDING:** To keep the changes pending, to take action in later Return filing period. The status changes to PENDING (but before filing of Annual Return or Return for September month following the end of Financial year).

Preview GSTR-1A: Having generated GSTR-1A Summary, click *PREVIEW* button to download the GSTR-1A draft Summary (watermarked PDF). Now review each section of the draft summary to make sure everything is correct, before submission of GSTR-1A.

Submission: Having reviewed the Draft preview, Click on the acknowledgement checkbox and Click SUBMIT. Click PROCEED at pop up. The submission success message is displayed (now the data is frozen and cannot be modified). The Status changes to *Submitted*. You may download the Final PDF to preview the submitted page (click PREVIEW button again).

Filing GSTR-1A: Click the *FILE RETURN* button to file GSTR-1A (a notification through e-mail and SMS is sent to the Authorized Signatory). Click the *Declaration* checkbox. At *Authorised signatory* drop-down list, select the authorized signatory. Click the *FILE WITH DSC*(and click Proceed at pop up**)** or *FILE WITH EVC* button (and enter OTP) to file GSTR-1A, as applicable. A success message is displayed. The status of GSTR-1A changes to *Filed* (notification is sent through e-mail and SMS to the Authorized Signatory).

GSTR-2 Inward Supplies Off line Upload

GSTR-2 Return

After filing of GSTR-1 (details of outward supplies), the taxpayers should file GSTR-2. After suppliers file GSTR-1, the details of respective inward supplies from registered buyer, get auto-populated in GSTR-2A. The GSTR-2A may be reviewed by Buyer to ensure that the entries are correct, but cannot make any changes in GSTR-2A. All additions / modifications are to be done in GSTR-2.

> The GST 23rd meeting dt 10th Nov 17 deferred filing of GSTR-2 returns until 31st March 2018. Accordingly, uploading, saving, and submitting of GSTR-2 are temporarily suspended on the GST portal.

So, only details of purchases not reflecting in GSTR-2A (like purchases from unregistered dealers, missing entries etc.), have to be entered while filing GSTR-2. Thus, GSTR-2 Return contains details of all inward supplies. Based on this return, the eligible Input Tax Credit taxpayer is determined.

Double click the Offline tool icon on desktop to get *Offline Tool* Home Page, with following Tabs :

- **Upload new invoice/ other data for return** : Click *NEW* to Upload New Invoice/ other data. (Return will be prepared on the GST Portal based on the data uploaded using the tool. You may upload invoice data multiple times)

- **Open Downloaded Return file from GST portal** : Click *OPEN* to open auto populated pre filed Return (like GSTR-1, 2, 1A, 2A.) downloaded from GST Portal.

- **Open Downloaded Error File from GST portal** : Click OPEN to open error file to review the errors occurred on the portal while uploading the JSON file to the portal and take necessary action to rectify offending invoices rejected by GST Portal.

Like off line data upload in GSTR-1, you may upload the data in GSTR 2 in any of the following ways :

- 1 : Manual Entry of Invoice Data

- 2 : Import full Excel Workbook (multiple sheets)

- 3 : Copy and Paste from Excel Workbook

- 4 : Import CSV file

Here we discuss about GSTR-2 entries and filing through off line utility. We have already explained the process of downloading offline tool and installing in your computer, while discussing GSTR-1 Off Line uploading in earlier chapter.

Adding Missing Entries

Double click on the offline tool icon at desktop to get the offline tool menu (F-1A)

You have to add missing entries (Invoices/ Debit / Credit Notes), not uploaded by supplier in GSTR-1

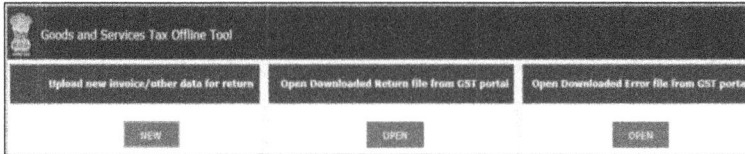

F-1A : GSTR Offline tool homepage

F-1B : Selection of GSTR-2 Return details

At *GSTR-2 offline Tool* menu, click NEW button (F-1A), to get Files Return screen (F-1B).Now enter as follows

–   At *GST Statement/Returns* drop-down list, select GSTR2

–   At *GSTIN of receiver,* enter GSTIN (submitting the GSTR-2 Return).

–   At Financial Year drop-down list, select the financial year for which the return has to be prepared and filed.

–   At Tax Period drop-down list, select the Tax Period (Month / Quarter as applicable) for which return for which the return has to be prepared.

Now you get GSTR-2 off line entry screen (F-2A)

You may upload data offline in following ways :

–   Manual Entry of Invoice Data

–   Import full Excel Workbook consisting of multiple sheets

–   Copy and Paste from Excel Workbook

–   Import the CSV file

We now discuss each of the methods. The process is similar to GSTR-1 off line entries discussed in earlier chapter. We briefly explain the relevant points.

Manual entry of Invoice Data

Enter Invoice data manually one by one, for each Invoice.

– **Table Section** : At *Select Section* select the applicable section where the invoice data needs to be entered, from drop-down list.

– **Invoice Details** : Enter the invoice details in each column (Supplier's GSTIN, Invoice No. Invoice Date, Total Invoice value, select Place of Supply from list, select Supply Type from list, Click if Reverse Charge applicable). Wrong GSTIN format entry will elicit error message

– **Tax Details** : Click rightmost Plus icon to get *Add Items* screen to enter Tax details

At GSTR-2 off line entry screen (F-2A), *Select Section* drop-down list and select the applicable section where the invoice data needs to be entered (F-2A). Enter the invoice details in each column like Supplier's GSTIN, Invoice No. etc.

F-2A : Invoice entry in GSTR-2

Click the Plus icon under *Actions* column (on the right side) to get Add Items screen (F-2B) and fill the item level details for the invoice.

F-2B : Item level details of Invoice entry in GSTR-2

Click *Save* button to save each Invoice entry (a success message is displayed indicating saving). This way, enter all the new Invoice in GSTR-2 to get the list of all Invoices entered (F-2C). Just review and edit / delete any entry as required.

F-2C : GSTR-2 New Invoices updation

You may further Modify or Delete the saved invoice if required. Select the desired Invoice (click on the checkbox) to be modified / deleted (click the Invoice checkbox) and perform as follows :

– **Invoice Modification** : Click the right most Pencil icon to get the Invoice in Edit mode to make correction

– **Invoice Deletion** : Click Delete button (at the bottom left on the screen) an type Yes to confirm deletion.

Import Full Excel Workbook

You may Import auto populated workbook containing all section Table to work on the Invoice (accept, Reject, ITC eligibility etc). It would be helpful to understand the auto populated data structure in the downloaded Excel Files of auto populated Invoice data, arranged in Table sections

GSTR-2 Excel Template Worksheet format

We now explain the format of Excel Sheet of each section of GSTR-2 off line Excel Sheet so that you may enter data properly for each section

The multi excel sheet includes 11 worksheets covering different Tables in GSTR2, with some sample data for illustration. Just delete the sample data, keeping the Header (first 3 rows in each Table) intact. Now enter data manually in these sheets.

The format of each Table, with sample data is shown :

Table B2B : B2B Inward supplies from registered Supplier (F-3A)

1. GSTIN of Supplier : Enter the GSTIN of the supplier. Check that the registration is active on the GST portal

2. Invoice number : Enter the Invoice number of invoices issued by registered supplier in proper format

3. Invoice Date : Enter date of invoice in DD-MMM-YYYY (like 24-May-2017).

4. Invoice value : Enter the total value indicated in the invoice with 2 decimal Digits.

5. Place of Supply (POS) : Select the code of the State of the supplier, from drop down list for the place of supply.

6. Reverse Charge : Please select Y if the supplies/services are subject to tax as per reverse charge mechanism, else select N.

7. Invoice Type : Select from the drop down (regular, SEZ unit/developer with or without payment of tax, deemed export).

8. Rate : Enter the combined (State tax + Central tax) or the integrated tax, as applicable.

Enter the following value for each Rate line :

9. Taxable Value : Enter the taxable value of the received goods or services for each Rate line item (computed as per GST valuation provisions), with 2 decimal Digits,

10. Integrated Tax Paid : Enter Integrated Tax Paid

11. Central Tax Paid : Enter Central Tax Paid ; not applicable if Integrated Tax is paid

12. State/UT Tax : Enter State/UT Tax Paid ; not applicable if Integrated Tax is paid

13. CessPaid : Enter the total Cess amount paid.

14. Eligibility For ITC : Select the eligibility from dropdown (input, input services, capital goods or ineligible).

15. Availed ITC Integrated Tax : Enter the Amount of ITC available for Integrated Tax paid

16. Availed ITC Central Tax : Enter the Amount of ITC available for Central Tax paid

17. Availed ITC State/UT Tax : Enter the Amount of ITC available for State/UT Tax paid

18. Availed ITC Cess : Enter the Amount of ITC available for Cess paid

GSTIN of Supplier	Invoice Number	Invoice date	Invoice Value	Place Of Supply	Reverse Charge	Invoice Type	Rate	Taxable Value	Integrated Tax Paid	Central Tax Paid	State/UT Tax Paid
10GDJDPF5186PDZR	1001	12-Aug-17	100200.00	21-Odisha	N	Regular	12.00	90000.00	23.00	0.00	0.00
10GDJDP5186PDZR	1002	15-Aug-17	100201.00	03-Punjab	N	Regular	12.00	90000.00	10800.00	0.00	0.00
12GDJDP5516PDZR	1003	15-Aug-17	100201.00	31-Lakshadweep	N	Regular	5.00	10000.00	500.00	0.00	0.00
10GDJDP5516PDZR	1004	15-Aug-17	100004.00	12-Arunachal Prd	N	Regular	5.00	94000.00	0.00	4700.00	4700.00
10GDJDP5516PDZR	1005	16-Aug-17	100004.00	08-Rajasthan	N	Regular	5.00	94000.00	4700.00	0.00	0.00

F-3A : GSTR-2 - B2B offline data Worksheet sample data

Table B2BUR : B2B Inward supplies received from unregistered Supplier (F-4A)

1. Supplier Name : Enter the name of supplier from whom supplies have been received

2. Invoice number : Enter the Invoice number for supplies received in proper format.

3. Invoice Date : Enter date of invoice in DD-MMM-YYYY (like24-May-2017).

4. Invoice value : Enter the total value, with 2 decimal Digits.

5. Place of Supply(POS) : Select the code of the state of place of supply, from drop down list of States

6. Supply Type : Select from drop down to declare the supply type (as inter state or intra state)

7. Rate : Enter the applicable Tax Rate (State tax + Central tax combined) or the integrated Tax

Enter the following value for each Rate line :

8. Taxable Value : Enter the taxable value for each rate line item with 2 decimal digits (computed as per GST valuation provisions).

9. Integrated Tax Paid : Enter Integrated Tax Paid, as applicable

10. Central Tax Paid : Enter Central Tax Paid ; not applicable if Integrated Tax is paid

11. State/UT Tax : Enter State/UT Tax Paid ; not applicable if Integrated Tax is paid

12. CessPaid : Enter the total Cess amount payable, as applicable

13. Eligibility For ITC : Select the eligibility of ITC (Eligible / Ineligible) from the dropdown list

14. Availed ITC Integrated Tax : Enter the Amount of ITC available for Integrated Tax paid

15. Availed ITC Central Tax : Enter the Amount of ITC available for Central Tax paid

16. Availed ITC State/UT Tax : Enter the Amount of ITC available for State/UT Tax paid

17. Availed ITC Cess : Enter the Amount of ITC available for Cess paid

F-4A : GSTR-2 - B2BUR offline data Worksheet sample data

Table IMPS (Import of Services) : Details of services imported (F-5A)

1. Invoice number : Enter the Invoice number of invoices for import of services, as per format.

2. Invoice Date : Enter date of invoice in DD-MMM-YYYY (e.g. 24-May-2017).

3. Invoice value : Enter the total value of invoice of received services, with 2 decimal Digits.

4. Place of Supply(POS) : Select the code of the state from drop down list for the place of supply.

5. Rate : Enter the integrated tax rate , as applicable.

6. Taxable Value : Enter the taxable value of the received services for each rate line item - with 2 decimal Digits (computed as per GST provisions).

7. Integrated Tax Paid : Enter Integrated Tax Paid

8. CessPaid : Enter the total Cess amount paid.

9. Eligibility For ITC : Select from the dropdown list (Input Services / Ineligible)

10. Availed ITC Integrated Tax : Enter the Amount of ITC available for Integrated Tax paid

11. Availed ITC Cess : Enter the Amount of ITC available for Cess paid

F-5A : GSTR-2 - IMPS offline data Worksheet sample data

Table IMPG (Import of Goods) : Details of Goods imported (F-6A)

1. Port Code : 6 digit Port code of port through which goods were imported.

2. Bill Of Entry Number : 7 digit Bill of entry number

3. Bill Of Entry Date : Bill of Entry date in DD-MMM-YYYY (e.g 24-May-2017).

4. Bill Of Entry Value : Total value of Bill of Entry

5. Document type : Select from the drop down

6. GSTIN Of Supplier : Enter the GSTIN of the supplier. Validate the registration number

7. Rate : Enter the integrated tax rate, as applicable.

8. Taxable Value : Enter the taxable value of the received inputs/capital good for each rate line item - with 2 decimal Digits, The taxable value has to be computed as per GST valuation provisions.

9. Integrated Tax Paid : Enter Integrated Tax Paid

10. CessPaid : Enter the total Cess amount paid.

11. Eligibility For ITC : Select from the dropdown list (Input, capital goods, ineligible)

12. Availed ITC Integrated Tax : Enter the Amount of ITC available for Integrated Tax paid

13. Availed ITC Cess : Enter the Amount of ITC available for Cess paid

F-6A : GSTR-2 - IMPG offline data Worksheet sample data

Table CDNR - Credit / Debit Note issued by Registered Supplier : Details of Debit / Credit Notes issued by Registered supplier (F-7A)

You have to enter the reference of original Invoice in respect of which supply was made.

1. GSTIN of Supplier : GSTIN of the supplier. This should be validated.

2. Invoice/Advance Payment Voucher Number : Credit/debit note (or the refund voucher) number, in proper format

3. Invoice/Advance Payment date : Enter credit/debit note/Refund voucher date in DD-MMM-YYYY (e.g. 24-May-2017).

4. Invoice/Advance Payment Voucher Number : Original invoice number as reported in B2B section of earlier period/current tax period or pre-GST period, against which the credit/debit note is issued.

5. Invoice/Advance Payment Voucher date : Original invoice/advance voucher date in DD-MMM-YYYY (e.g 24-May-2017).

6. Pre GST : Yes if credit/debit note is related to pre-GST supplies (original Invoice is dated before 1st Jul 2017), else No

7. Document Type : D for Debit noteC for credit note, R for Refund voucher.

8. Reason For Issuing document : Select Reason for issue of the document, from list

9. Supply Type : Intra State or Inter State

10. Note/Refund Voucher value : Debit / Credit Note / Refund Voucher Amount with 2 decimal digits.

11. Rate : Tax Rate (State tax + Central tax) or integrated tax.

12.Taxable value : Taxable value for each rate line item with 2 decimal Digits

13. Integrated Tax Paid : Integrated Tax Paid

14. Central Tax Paid : Central Tax Paid (not applicable if Integrated Tax is paid)

15. State/UT Tax : State/UT Tax Paid (not applicable if Integrated Tax is paid)

16. CessPaid : Total Cess amount.

17. Eligibility For ITC : Select from the dropdown list (input, input services, capital goods or Ineligible).

18. Availed ITC Integrated Tax : Amount of ITC available for Integrated Tax paid

19. Availed ITC Central Tax : Amount of ITC available for Central Tax paid

20. Availed ITC State/UT Tax : Enter Amount of ITC available for State/UT Tax paid

21. Availed ITC Cess : EnterAmount of ITC available for Cess paid

4	GSTIN of Supplier	Note/Refund Voucher Number	Note/Refund Voucher date	Invoice/Advance Payment Voucher Number	Invoice/Advance Payment Voucher date	Pre GST	Document Type	Reason For Issuing document
5								

F-7A : GSTR-2 - CDNR offline data Worksheet sample data

Table CDNUR (Credit / Debit Note issued by Unregistered Supplier) : Details of Debit / Credit Notes issued by Unregistered supplier (F-8A)

You have to enter the reference of original Invoice in respect of which supply was made.

1. Note/Voucher Number : Credit/ Debit note number or the refund voucher number

2. Note/ Voucher date : Enter credit/debit note/Refund voucher date in DD-MMM-YYYY (e.g 24-May-2017).

3. Invoice/Advance Payment Voucher number : Enter original invoice number (Refund Voucher number) as entered in earlier period/current tax period or pre-GST Period against which credit/debit note is issued.

4. Invoice/Advance Payment Voucher date : Enter the original invoice/advance receipt date in DD-MMM-YYYY (e.g 24-May-2017).

5. Pre GST : Select Y if the credit/debit note relates to pre-GST supplies (i.e the original Invoice is dated earlier than 1st July 2017)

6. Document Type : D for Debit note, C if note is credit note or enter "R" for refund voucher.

7. Reason For Issuing document : Select the applicable reason for issue of the document from the dropdown.

8. Supply Type : Inter State / Intra State. This would be validated with original invoice upon upload to portal.

9. Note/Refund Voucher value : Credit / Debit Note / Refund Voucher Amount, with 2 decimal digits.

10. Rate : Enter Tax Rate (State tax + Central tax) / integrated tax rate.

11.Taxable value : Taxable value of for each rate line item with 2 decimal Digits,computed as per GST valuation provisions.

12. Integrated Tax Paid : Integrated Tax Amount

13. Central Tax Paid : Central Tax Amount ; not applicable if Integrated Tax is paid

14. State/UT Tax : State/UT Tax Amount ; not applicable if Integrated Tax is paid

15. CessPaid : Enter the Total Cess amount, if applicable.

16. Eligibility For ITC : Select from dropdown list (input, input services, capital goods or ineligible)

17. Availed ITC Integrated Tax : Amount of ITC available for Integrated Tax paid

18. Availed ITC Central Tax : Amount of ITC available for Central Tax paid

19. Availed ITC State/UT Tax : Amount of ITC available for State/UT Tax paid

20. Availed ITC Cess : Enter the Amount of ITC available for Cess paid

Invoice/Advance Payment Voucher	Invoice/Advance Payment Voucher date	Pre GST	Document Type	Reason For Issuing document	Supply Type	Invoice Type	Note/Voucher Value	Rate	Taxable Value	Integrated Tax Paid	Central Tax Paid
1006	12-Aug-17	N	C	06-Finalization of Provisional	Inter State	B2BUR	20000.00	12.00	17600.00	2112.00	0.00
1007	12-Aug-17	N	D	02-Post Sale Discount	Inter State	IMPS	20000.00	28.00	22500.00	6300.00	0.00

F-8A : GSTR-2 - CDNUR offline data Woksheet sample data

Table AT (Advance Received) : Advance Amount paid for Reverse Charge Supplies (F-9A)

1. Place of Supply(POS) : Select the state of the place of supply, from drop down list.

2. Rate : Enter the Tax rate (State tax + Central tax) or integrated tax rate.

3. Gross advance received : Amount of advance received excluding the tax portion.

4. CessAmount : Cess amount collected/payable.

4	Place Of Supply	Supply Type	Gross Advance Paid	Cess Amount
5	02-Himachal Pradesh	Inter State	30000.00	2300.00
6	08-Rajasthan	Inter State	45000.00	0.00
7	08-Rajasthan	Intra State	50000.00	500.00

F-9A : GSTR-2 – AT offline data Worksheet sample data

ATADJ (Advance Adjusted) : Adjustment of Advance Amount paid in earlier period, adjusted in current period (F-10A).

4	Place Of Supply	Supply Type	Gross Advance Paid to be Adjusted	Cess Adjusted
5	03-Punjab	Inter State	12341.00	1234.00
6	10-Bihar	Inter State	61324.00	6131.00
7	07-Delhi	Intra State	5000.00	

F-10A : GSTR-2 – ATADJ offline data Worksheet sample data

Table EXEMP : Supplies from Composition Dealer, Nil rated Exempted & Non GST supplies (F-11A)

1. Description : Type of supply (Intra State / Inter State)

2. Composition Taxable person : Value of Intra State supplies received from composition taxable person.

3. Nil rated supplies : **Value** of supplies received under "Nil Rated" category Items.

4. Exempted : **(Other than Nil rated/non-GSTsupply)** : Value of supplies received under"Exempted "category Items.

5. Non GST Supplies : Value of supplies received under "Non GST" category Items.

	Description	Composition taxable person	Nil Rated Supplies	Exempted (other than nil rated/non GST supply)	Non-GST supplies
4					
5	Inter-State supplies		6000.00	34000.00	12000.00
6	Intra-State supplies	23000.00	56000.00	12000.00	14000.00

F-11A : GSTR-2 – EXEMP offline data Worksheet sample data

Table ITCR : ITC Reversal / Reclaim(F-12A)
1. Description of Reversal :

2. To be Added or Reduced from Output Liability : To be Added / To be reduced

3.ITC Integrated Tax Amount : Amount of ITC Integrated Tax amount

4.ITC Central Tax Amount : Amount of ITC Central Tax

5.ITC State/UT Tax Amount : Amount of ITC State/UT Tax

6.ITC CessAmount : Amount of ITC Cess

4	Description for reversal of ITC	To be added or reduced from output liability	ITC Integrated Tax Amount	ITC Central Tax Amount	ITC State/UT Tax Amount
5	(a) Amount in terms of rule 37 (2)	To be added	10000.00	20000.00	15000.00
6	(b) Amount in terms of rule 42 (1) (m)	To be added	50000.00	50000.00	50000.00
7	(c) Amount of rule 43(1) (h)	To be added	50000.00	50000.00	50000.00
8	(d) Amount in terms of rule 42 (2)(a)	To be added	50000.00	50000.00	50000.00
9	(e) Amount in terms of rule 42(2)(b)	To be reduced	50000.00	50000.00	50000.00
	(f) On account of amount paid subsequent				
10	to reversal of ITC	To be reduced	50000.00	50000.00	50000.00
11	(g) Any other liability (Specify)		50000.00	50000.00	50000.00

F-12A : GSTR-2 – ITCR offline data Worksheet sample data

Table HSNSUM : HSN wise Summary of Goods(F-13A)

1. HSN : HSN Code for the received goods or Services.

2. Description : Description of the received goods or Services (mandatory field HSN not provided)

3. UQC : Unit Quantity Code from drop down.

4. Total Quantity : Total quantity in terms f the UQC, with 2 decimal Digits.

5. Total Value : Value of the goods or services with 2 decimal Digits.

6. Taxable Value : Taxable value with 2 decimal Digits.

7. Integrated Tax Amount : Integrated tax amount.

8. Central Tax Amount : Central Tax amount

9. State/UT Tax Amount : State/UT Tax amount.

10. Cess Amount : Cess Amount.

HSN	Description	UQC	Total Quantity	Total Value	Taxable Value	Integrated Tax Amount	Central Tax Amount	State/UT Tax Amount	Cess Amount
1234		MLT-MILILITRE	345.00	564564.00	345656.00	115466.00	22867.00	22132.00	7876.00
	Butter	KGS-KILOGRAMS	187.00	56656.00	22332.00	11866.00	1124.00	4234.00	423.00
	1234 Mango	KGS-KILOGRAMS	1500.00	350000.00	50000.00	250.00	250.00	250.00	512.00

F-13A : GSTR-2 – HSNSUM offline data Worksheet sample data

Import multiple sheets Excel Workbook

Open the GSTR2_Excel_Workbook_TemplateNew_V1.1.xlsx sheet available in downloaded zip folder. Using *Return Import – All sections in one Go* option, you can upload invoice data entered in the respective worksheets for all sections at one go. Enter relevant data from invoices and other documents in the relevant sheets of the Workbook, in the applicable sections. Do not delete any worksheet (inapplicable worksheet should be left blank)

In the *Returns offline Tool* screen, Click the *IMPORT FILES* button and select the *GSTR2_Excel_Workbook_ TemplateNew_V1.1.xlsx* file to import. Click IMPORT EXCEL button. Click YES button to import. A successful message would be displayed on Import of data. Click *Back* button to view the populated data. You may use the Edit (using pencil icon) / Delete (using Delete button) to modify, Delete any imported record, as necessary, to make the data correct and complete. During Import, apparent errors encountered are displayed. Make the necessary corrections in the Excel Worksheet and re-upload Excel Sheet. Records having same Invoice Number will be overwritten by new data uploaded.

Copy and Paste from Excel Workbook

Open the excel sheet containing Missing Invoice data in the desired format. Copy the header part of the worksheet (press Ctrl+C) to copy. Header begins from 1st Row, Column A (1st column) covering first 3 rows (rows 1 to 3). You must copy / paste each section separately.

Click the IMPORT FILES button in the Returns Offline tool. From the *Select Section* drop-down list, select the section for which you want to upload the invoices. Click COPY EXCEL button (F-13B). In the pop up window, click at *Click here*link and press the Ctrl+V Keys to paste data from Excel sheet (F-13C). Click Proceed BUTTON to add Invoices. The off line tool validates data copied. The data failing validation cannot be processed further. A success message is displayed on copy of validated data. Click BACK button to view populated data. You may use the Edit / Delete button to modify, Delete any imported record, as necessary, to make the data correct and complete.

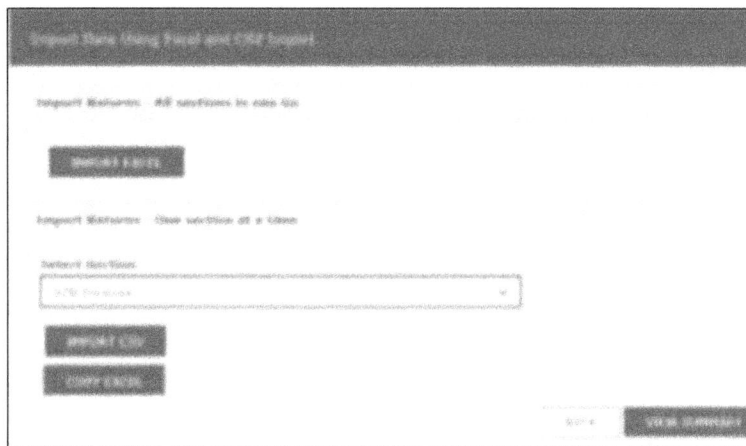

F-13B : Excel file Import

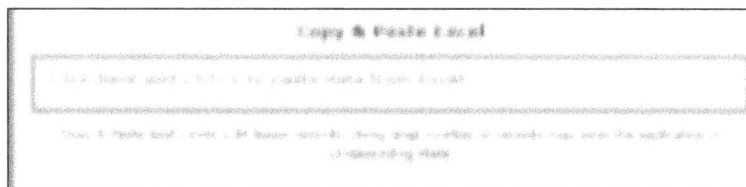

F-13C : pasting Excel data

Import CSV file

Import the invoice data from the CSV file to create GST compliant file (JSON). Click the IMPORT FILES button to import the CSV file in the Returns Offline tool. At *Select Section* drop-down list, select the appropriate section. Under *Return Import - One section at a time* section, select the *IMPORT CSV* button and select the appropriate CSV file from the CSV files folder. Click Yes to save the imported data. On successful import, a SUCCESS message is displayed.

Click the BACK button to view the Invoice data of excel sheet populated in the screen. You may use the Edit / Delete button to modify, Delete any imported record, as necessary, to make the data correct and complete. Click the VIEW SUMMARY button to display the Invoice Summary, for review.

Creation of JSON file : After review of GSTR-2 Summary, GENERATE FILE button to get the file in GST Compliant .JSON format. Click save button to save the file to be uploaded in GST portal.

Uploading the JSON file into GSTN Portal : Login to GSTN portal using the User credentials. At Services > Returns page, select Financial Year and Return filing period. Now click PREPARE OFFLINE button under Inward Supplies received by tax payer – GSTR-2 tile. Click Choose file link under *Invoice upload* and select the file to be uploaded. You get the upload history screen showing a generated reference of upload. After a while, the stats of uploaded file would get updated.

Deleting data from Offline Tool

You may delete data from offline tool of GSTR-1, GSTR-2, GSTR-2A, In the summary screen, in following ways :

- **Deleting specific Records** : Click the check box against the records to be deleted and click *Delete* button. The selected records would be deleted at one stroke.

- **Deleting all Data** : To delete all data uploaded to offline tool in one go, click DELETE ALL DATA button at the top

- **Deleting Data of a specific Section** : At select section, select the section from the drop down list. To delete all data of the selected section, click CLEAR SECTION DATA button. Click DELETE SECTION DATA button to mark all the data of the selected section with D status.

Opening Downloaded Error File

If data uploaded through JSON (For GSTR-1 & GSTR-2) on the portal fails validation, an Error File will be created for failed records. The error file will be available in a hyperlink as given in the below screen on the upload off line page in the portal. Initially the Status of the error file will be shown as In-Progress and will subsequently changed to Processed or Processed with Error (F-14A). In case of error, click the *Generate Error Report* in the Error Report column(F-15A) to generate Error file.

F-14A : Error status on JSON upload

F-15A : Error File generation

On Error file generation, click the link *Download error Reort* (F-15A) to view error offline. From the Select Section drop-down list, select the desired section and proceed to rectify the errors. The errors are indicated in the Error Message column against each invoice. Read the error message. To make correction, click the Edit (Pencil) button to edit the Invoice (make corrections). Click UPDATE button. The status is changed to *Modified*. This way, make correction for each section having errors. Click VIEW SUMMARY button to view the corrected records. After corrections, click GENERATE FULE button to create a new JSON file in same way. It will be validated again, as before. Save the JSON file is desired folder.

Login to GSTN portal and upload the JSON file.

Operation on GSTR-2 File

The GSTR-2 return file can be downloaded from GSTN portal and opened in Offline tool to view invoices and credit/debit notes uploaded by supplier in his GSTR-1, or uploaded by Recipient in GSTR-2. The Invoices may be modified, accepted, rejected or kept pending, as explained in on-line GSTR-2 entry in earlier chapter.

Downloading GSTR-2 Return Files : To download The GSTR-2 return file, click the *Services > Returns > Returns Dashboard* command to get File Returns page. Select Financial Year and Return Filing period from drop down list, Click Search button to get the Return of the selected tax period. At Inward Supplies received by taxpayer, GSTR2 tile, click the PREPARE OFFLINE button. The offline Upload & Download for GSTR-2 screen is displayed (F-16A).

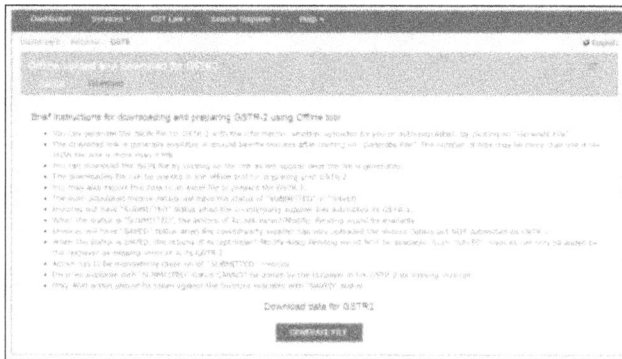

F-16A : Offline Upload & Download for GSTR-2

Click GENERATE FILE button to get the Return file downloaded in ZIP format, within some time (about 20 mins).

Opening the Offline downloaded file : At desktop click offline tool icon to get Offline Tool homepage (F-17A).

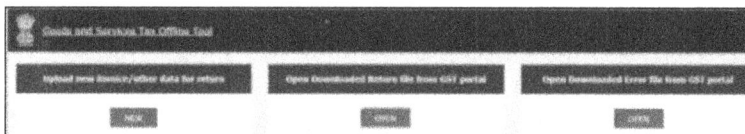

F-17A : Opening GSTR-2 Offline downloaded file

Click OPEN button under the tile Open Downloaded Return file from GST portal. Browse and select the downloaded return file in zip format and click the OPEN button. The file info are shown. Click PROCEED button (F-18A) to get Summary page (F-19A)

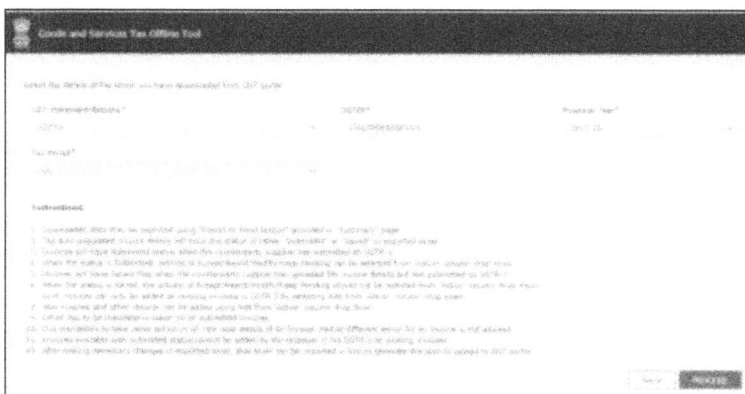

F-18A GSTR-2 Offline downloaded file details

At Summary page (F-19A),click on desired Section link to view the details of the Invoices of the selected section.

F-19A : GSTR-2 off line download file section details

Operation on GSTR-2 file : Now you can perform following operations on the Invoices, as explained in On-line entry in previous chapter

– **Modify Invoice** : To view and edit the details or records at rate level, click the edit button (pencil icon) and navigate to the rate level records (F-20A). The Rate detail are displayed (F-20B). Modify and click UPDATE button. By default, the system marks B2B invoices as inputs with ITC equal to tax paid for ITC eligible invoices. You may, however, verify and edit the system calculated ITC details. On saving of edited data, a success message is displayed and the status changes to M (N indicates No action taken).You may modify Total Invoice value, Taxable value and rates.

– **Accept Invoice** : To accept the invoice, select the checkbox against the invoice and click ACCEPT. Click YES at the popup to proceed. Invoice status changes from "N" to "A".

– **Reject Invoice :** To Reject the invoice, select the checkbox against the invoice and click REJECT button. Click YES at the popup to proceed. Invoice status changes from "N" to "R".

– **Keep Invoice Pending** : To Keep the invoices Pending, select the checkbox against the invoice and click PENDING button (F-20A). Click YES at the popup to proceed. Invoice status changes from "N" to "P".

F-20A : Modification of Invoice data

F-20B : Modification of Rate data of Invoice

Creating JSON file : Having done the necessary action on the Invoices (Accept, Reject or Modify), click the VIEW SUMMARY button. The summary page is displayed. Click GENARATE FILE button to get the GST compliant (JSON) file. Click *Save* button to save the .JSON file in selected folder.

Uploading the JSON file : Login to GST portal with your credentials and upload the JSON file as explained in earlier chapter.

Export to Excel

Alternatively, you may export the GSTR-2 offline downloaded file to Excel and perform the operations on Excel File. Then import back the Excel file to offline tool.

At sectionwise GSTR-2 offline screen, click EXPORT TO EXCEL button and click SAVE at the pop up screen showing the default Excel filename (you may change the filename). Having saved the file, open the Excel Worksheet (F-21A) to take actions on the Invoices (Accept, Reject, Modify, Pending, Add, Delete)

F-21A : Action on GSTR-2 offline Excel file

At the column Action, select the action Click and select the desired action on each Invoice (F-21A)

Importing the updated Worksheet : Having taken the actions on Invoices, click IMPORT FILES (F-22A) in Offline Tool and then click IMPORT EXCEL button (F-22A) to Import the file in Offline Tool

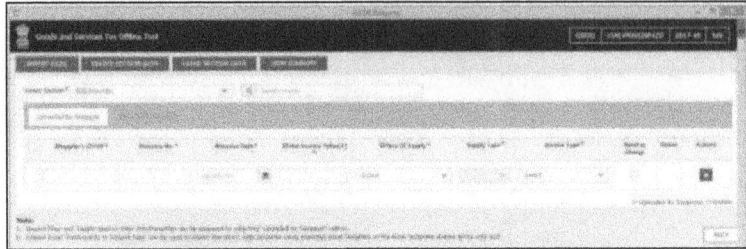

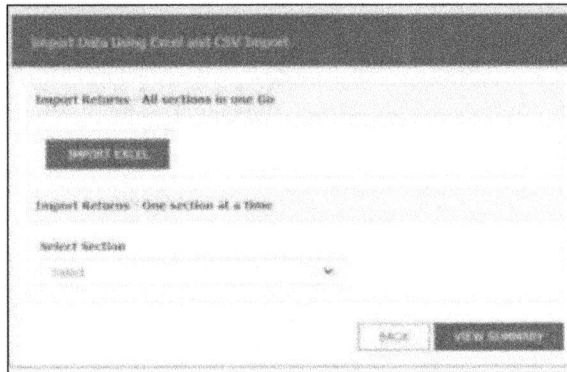

F-22A : Importing Action taken Excel worksheet

GSTR-2 Inward Supplies On-line Entry

GSTR-2 Return

GSTR-2 Return is to be filed by every Registered person, in respect of inward supplies (Purchases) of Goods & Services (file NIL Return, even if no transaction in the period).

However, following Persons not required to file GSTR-2

– Input Service Distributors

– Composition Dealers

– Non-resident taxable person

– Persons liable to collect TCS

– Persons liable to deduct TDS

– Suppliers of online information and database access or retrieval services (OIDAR), liable to pay IGST themselves

> The GST council deferred filing of GSTR-2 returns until 31st March 2018. Accordingly, the uploading, saving, and submitting of GSTR-2 are temporarily suspended on the GST portal.

After filing of GSTR-1 (details of outward supplies), the taxpayers should file GSTR-2.

– After suppliers file GSTR-1, the details of respective inward supplies from registered buyer, get auto-populated in GSTR-2A.

– Hence, only details of purchases not reflected in GSTR-2A (like purchases from unregistered dealers, missing entries etc) have to be entered while filing GSTR-2.

– GSTR-2 Return contains details of all inward supplies. Based on this return, theeligible Input Tax Credit taxpayer is determined.

Note: As per notification vide 23rdGST Council meeting held on10thNov 17, GSTR-2 (and GSTR-3) need not be filed upto Mar 18.

Data flow from GSTR-1 to GSTR-2
– **Auto uploaded Inwards Data**: GSTR-1 is submitted in respect of outward supplies made by Registered Dealer (B2B Invoices, Debit/ Credit Notes issued by registered supplier), as explained in earlier chapters. The outward supplies entered in GSTR-1 by supplier are auto-populated in in Auto drafted Details GSTR-2A in GSTR Reports Dashboard of the respective registered Recipient.

No action can be taken in GSTR-2A. GSTR-2A is for review (download / View) before filing GSTR-2. All modification (addition / modification etc) are to be done in GSTR-2 only.

– **Review of Inwards data**: In GSTR-2, the recipient can Accept, Modify, Reject (or keep pending).

If supply not received yet in respect of any Invoice, mark the record as Pending to be accepted in next period after receipt of goods. For example, a supplier delivered goods on 31st July. The receiver received the goods from carrier on 1st Aug. The supplier would file the sales in GSTR-1 in July, which would be reflected in GSTR2A of receiver in July 2A. However, the receiver would mark it pending in its GSTR-2A of July, and would accept it in GSTR-2 of Aug. The credit would be available by the receiver in Aug only.

– **Importing data from GSTR-2A to GSTR-2:** Inwards supplies data auto populated into GSTR-2A are to be imported in GSTR-2.

GSTR-2 Summary preview of Auto drafted documents

Login to the GST Portal *www.gst.gov.in* with valid credentials. Select *Services > Returns > Returns Dashboard* command (or click the *Returns Dashboard* link on the Dashboard). The *File Returns* page is displayed. Select *Financial Year* & *Return Filing Period* (Month /Quarter) from the drop-down list, for which you want to file the return. Click *SEARCH* button to get *GSTR Return* menu for various Returns. In *GSTR-2* tile, click the *PREPARE ONLINE* button to make entries for GSTR-2.

Operations in GSTR-2

You can either edit, accept, delete or keep the invoices in pending state, which are added by the supplier.

• **Action on Invoices Upload by Supplier:** Click the *Supplier's GSTIN* link under Supplier Details column to get list of invoice line items under the *Uploaded by Supplier* tab. Now click the checkbox against the Invoice, to take any of the following actions, as desired:

  o **Modify Invoices added by Supplier**: Click EDIT button. You may edit Total invoice value, Taxable value for various tax rates, ITC eligibility and Amount, but cannot modify non-editable details as the recipient of invoice. Edit the invoice details and click the *SAVE* button. In case, non-editable details need to be changed, you may reject the invoice and ask supplier to do the amendment.

  o **Accept Invoices added by Supplier**: Click the *Supplier's GSTIN* link under Supplier Details column to get list of invoice line items under *Uploaded by Supplier* tab. Now modify if necessary as explained, otherwise you may Accept or Reject. To accept the Invoices. Select the checkbox for the invoice and click the *ACCEPT* button (in case of any system issue with acceptance of invoice, you may put it in the bucket of non-submitted invoice). A success message (*Done! Invoice is accepted*) is displayed that the invoice is accepted and status changes to *ACCEPTED*. You may claim input tax credit after accepting the invoice.

  o **Reject Invoices added by Supplier**: Click the *Supplier's GSTIN* link under Supplier Details column to get a list of invoice line items under the *Uploaded by Supplier* tab. Select the checkbox for the invoice and click the *REJECT* button. A success message (*Done! Invoice is Rejected*) is displayed confirming that the invoice is rejected and status changes to "REJECTED". Your rejection shall be communicated to supplier through GSTR-1/1A for acceptance/rejection upon filing of GSTR-2.

o **Keep Pending Invoices added by Supplier**: Click the *Supplier's GSTIN* link under Supplier Details column to get a list of invoice line items under the *Uploaded by Supplier* tab. Select the checkbox for the invoice and click the *PENDING* button. A success message (*Done! Invoice is in Pending State*) and status changes to *PENDING*. You can take action on such invoice in next tax periods.

• **Entry of Missing Invoices:** In case, some invoices have been missed by the registered suppliers, you can add them here. Click the *ADD MISSING INVOICE DETAILS* button to add the missing invoices, as explained next.

Entry of Missing Invoice

Upto 500 record can be viewed / added through On-line method. Organisations having more records may use GST Offline Tool to upload unlimited data, as discussed in next chapter.

Click the *ADD MISSING INVOICE DETAILS* button to get Invoice entry Menu, to add the missing invoices. Alternatively, you may add through GST Offline tool, if number of Invoices are more than 500.

• **GSTR 2 - Invoice Details:** You have to add Invoice wise details through following Tiles (F-A)

  – **3,4A - Inward supplies received from Registered person including reverse charge supplies** - Inward supplies from registered person including supplies under RCM.

  – **5 - Import of Inputs/Capital goods and Supplies received from SEZ** - Inputs/ capital goods Imported / received from SEZ units on a bill of entry and eligible credits.

  – **4C - Import of service** - Import of service and eligible credits.

  – **6C - Debit/Credit Notes for supplies from registered person** - Debit / Credit Notes / Refund Voucher for supplies from registered person.

  – **4B - Inward supplies from an unregistered supplier** - Inward supplies from unregistered supplier under RCM.

  – **6C - Debit Notes/Credit Notes for Unregistered Supplier** - Debit / Credit Notes / Refund voucher for unregistered Supplier or import of services.

• **GSTR 2 - Consolidated Details:** You have to add Consolidated details through following Tiles

  – **7 - Supplies from composition taxable person and other exempt/nil rated/non GST supplies** - Supplies received from Composition Dealer and Exempt/nil rated/non GST Items.

  – **10A - Advance amount paid for reverse charge supplies** - Advance paid and the tax liability for reverse charge supplies.

  – **10B - Adjustment of advance amount paid earlier for reverse charge supplies** - Adjustment of advance amount paid earlier for reverse charge supplies, on receipt of goods / services / issue of Invoice

- **13 - HSN summary of inward supplies** - HSN summary of inward supplies of goods and services.

- **11 - Input Tax Credit Reversal/Reclaim** - Input Tax Credit reversal or reclaim.

You may edit, accept, delete or keep in pending state, of Invoices added by supplier. We describe the process to Add Invoice. However, you may carry on other type of actions by clicking the relevant buttons.

You may change status of the invoice from modify, accept, reject any number of times till submission. If, after the invoice has been modified and you wish to revert to original details, you need to first Reject the modified invoice. The status would now be changed to Rejected with original details. Same can be accepted now.

In case of Edit, you may modify editable fields (like Taxable Value, eligibility etc), but cannot change restricted details (to modify restricted details, reject the Invoice and ask the supplier to enter amended details which you may accept). Click SAVE after editing.

After editing, you will get to the previous page and a message is displayed that invoice is modified (status changes to MODIFIED). Such Modified Invoice would be reflected in supplier GSTR-1/1A upon filing of GSTR-2 for acceptance, rejection or keep pending the modifications made by you. ITC would be available on the basis of modified details.

Click *Add Missing Invoicedetails*button to add missing Invoice, not uploaded by some registered supplier. The seller will get a notification in his GSTR-1A for the addition / modification and may accept or reject it.

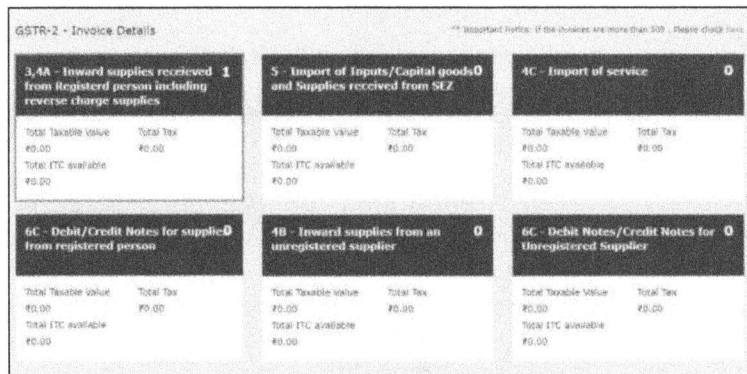

F-A: GSTR-2 Invoice Details menu

GSTR-2: B2B- Inward Supplies received from Registered person including Reverse Charge Mechanism (Table 3, 4A)

At GSTR-2 Menu (F-A), click on the Tab 3.4A- Inward Supplies received from Registered person including Reverse Charge Mechanism to get GSTR-2: B2B screen (F-1A).

F-1A: Add B2B Missing Invoice in GSTR2

Now enter the details as explained in on-line entry of B2B Invoices in GSTR-1.

– At Invoice Type, select from the list (Regular B2B Invoice, Deemed Export, SEZ supplies with Payment, SEZ supplies without Payment),

– Depending on the state selected in POS, *Supply Type* is auto-populated (Intra State / Inter State)

– Click the checkbox Supply Attract Reverse charge for Invoices attracting Reverse Charges.

– At Eligibility for ITC, select form the 4 options – Inputs (for Materials Purchase), Input Services (for Service Purchase), Capital Goods (for Capital Goods Purchase), Ineligible (where ITC is not eligible).

– Enter the Amount ITC available, in respective ITC column (depending on Type of Supply). In case of ineligible ITC, the amount would be zero in these columns. The Amount of ITC available may be equal or less than Amount of Tax, but cannot exceed the Amount of Tax (a message would be displayed if higher amount is attempted to be entered at ITC available column).

The data saved would be added in Table 3 of GSTR-2. If the check box *Supply against Reverse Charge* is ticked, then the data is posted in Table 4A of GSTR-2, for which recipient is liable to pay Tax (like Service supply by Goods Transport Agency, Supply of Tobacco Products etc).

IMPG- Import of Inputs / Capital Goods & Supplies received from SEZ (Table 5)

Any kind of import of inputs (items used to manufacture finished goods) or capital goods received against a Bill of Entry must be reported under this head. Goods received from SEZ are also reported here. Such data will not be entered by supplier. So, buyer must enter the details.

- **5A. Imports:** Any kind of import of inputs (items used to manufacture finished goods) or capital goods received against a Bill of Entry will be reported here. Details of bills of entry, along with 6-digit port Codes and 7-digit bill of Entry numbers must be mentioned.

- **5B. Received from SEZ:** Inputs or capital goods received from sellers in a SEZ will be reported here.

At GSTR-2 Main Menu (F-A), click on the Tab 5- Import of Inputs / Capital Goods & Supplies received from SEZ. To get the entry screen.

Entry of Missing Invoice for Import of Goods / Capital Goods in GSTR2: Now click *Add BOE* button to add Bill of Entry Invoice, if any (F-2A).

F-2A: Import of Inputs / Capital Goods & Supplies
received from SEZ entry in GSTR-2

The details are to be uploaded by Taxpayer (recipient of supply). Since Import is considered as Inter State purchase, only Integrated Tax would be applicable

In case of imports from SEZ, tick the checkbox *Imports from SEZ*. Imports from SEZ would be added in Table 5B. Other imports would be added in Table 5A

At Eligibility for ITC, select from the 3 options – Inputs (for Materials Purchase), Capital Goods (for Capital Goods Imports), Ineligible ITC (where ITC is not eligible). Enter the Amount ITC available. In case of ineligible ITC, the amount of ITC available would be zero.

GSTR-2 IMPG: Import of Goods / Capital Goods – Entry: You should enter Port Code Bill of Entry No, Bill of Entry Date, Bill of Entry Value (all the 3 info are mandatory).

– **Port Code**: Port Code is 5 letter alpha code, First 2 letters indicate Country Code (like IN for India) Code and next 3 letters indicate Port Name (like BOM for Bombay, CCU for Calcutta, COK for Cochin, IXE for Mangalore). So INIXE stands for Mangalore Port in India. INCCU refers to Calcutta Port in India.

– **Bill of Entry Number (BoE)**: Bill of Entry is a document filed by importers or customs clearance agents with the Customs Department. It is identified by unique 7 digit number called BoE Number.

Apart from Basic Customs Duty, IGST and GST Compensation Cess is applicable on Imports,

At *Eligibility for ITC*, select form the options – Inputs (for Materials Import), Capital Goods (for Capital Goods Import), Ineligible ITC (where ITC is not eligible). Enter the Amount of eligible ITC, in respective ITC column. In case of ineligible ITC, the amount would be zero.

IMPS- Import of Service (Table 4C)

At GSTR-2 Main Menu (F-A), Click on the Tab 4C- Import of Services. Here enter details of services purchased from services provider located outside India, while service recipient and place of supply is located in India. On line services are considered as Import of Service.

The details would be entered by Buyer of Service. Click *Add Details* button to get entry screen to enter details of Import of Services (F-3A).

F-3A: Import of Services

– At *Place of Supply* (PoS), select the State in where services (home state of importer) are received. Import would always be treated as Inter State Supply. So, IGST would be applicable.

– At *Eligibility for ITC*, select form the options – Input Services (for Services Import eligible for ITC), Ineligible ITC (where ITC is not eligible). Enter the Amount of eligible ITC, in respective ITC column.

If the place of supply is other than home state of buyer, then ITC would be ineligible. In case of ineligible ITC, the amount would be zero.

The details entered would be shown under the Tab Uploaded by Taxpayer (i.e Recipient of Supplies)

Debit / Credit Note for supplies from Registered Person (Table 6C)

At GSTR-2 Main Menu (F-A), click on the Tab *6C- Debit / Credit Note for supplies from Registered Person*.

Debit / Credit Notes issued by registered supplier would be reported in their GSTR-1 and would be reflected in auto-drafted GSTR-2A of receiver. However, on review of the auto-drafted report GSTR-2A, any missing Debit / Credit Note has to be added by the receiver, through this form. If all the debit credit notes reflected in GSTR-2A is found tallied by the recipient, then there is no need to add any record and this table will remain blank.

Now click *Add Debit Credit Note* button to get the entry screen to add Debit / Credit Note issued by Registered supplier (F-4A)

F-4A: Debit / Credit Notes issued by Registered Supplier

- At *Note type*, select from the 3 options from the list: Refund (in case of earlier Advance received, now Refunded by Registered Supplier), Credit (in case of Credit note issued by Registered supplier), Debit (in case Debit note issued by Registered Supplier).

- At *Original Invoice&Invoice Date*, enter the reference of Original Invoice Number and date against which the current Debit Note / Credit Note or Refund has been made by the supplier.

- At *Supply Type*, select the option Intra-State / Inter State. It is not auto selected.

– At *Reason*, select from the 7 reasons, as explained for Issue of Debit / Credit Note, earlier (01- Sales Return, 02 – Post sales Discount, 03 – Deficiency in Services, 04 - Correction in Invoice, 05 – Change in PoS, 06 -Finalisation of Provisional Assessment, 07 – Others).

– Check the checkbox *Pre GST Regime,* if the Refund / Debit / Credit Note relates to Pre GST period (The original Invoice Date should be of Pre GST period).

– At *Eligibility for ITC*, select from the 4 options – Inputs (for Materials Import), Input Services (for Purchase of Services) Capital Goods (for Capital Goods Import), Ineligible ITC (where ITC is not eligible). Enter the Amount of eligible ITC, in respective ITC column. In case of ineligible ITC, the amount would be zero.

Such added Debit / Credit Notes must be accepted by the supplier.

Inward Supplies from unregistered supplier (Table 4B)

At GSTR-2 Menu (F-A), click 4B-Inward Supplies from unregistered supplier tab to get *B2B Unregistered Supplier* screen

Here enter the details like Purchases from unregistered dealers (F-5A). The buyer of supplies from Unregistered person is liable to pay Tax and upload the details. Enter only those purchase on which Tax is to be paid (e.g Purchases from Unregistered person exceeding Rs 5000 per day).

– At *Place of Supply*, select Home State of the Buyer..

– At *Eligibility for ITC*, select form the options – Inputs (for Materials Purchase), Input Services (for Service Purchase), Capital Goods (for Capital Goods Purchase), Ineligible ITC (where ITC is not eligible). Enter the Amount of eligible ITC, in respective ITC column. In case of ineligible ITC, the amount would be zero.

F-5A: Inward Supplies from unregistered supplier

At *Place of Supply* (PoS), you should normally select buyer's Home State, as unregistered dealers cannot make Inter State supplies. However, if any Interstate purchase is ever made from Unregistered supplier (place of supply is other than Buyer's Home State), no ITC would be available and the option Ineligible would be auto carried at the Eligibility for ITC column.

Debit / Credit Notes from Unregistered Supplier (Table 6C)

At GSTR-2 Menu (F-A), click 6C-Inward Supplies from unregistered supplier tab to get *B2B Unregistered Supplier* screen. Click on Add Credit Note / Debit Note button to add records of Debit / Credit Note issued by Unregistered supplier, entered by the Registered Buyer (F-6A).

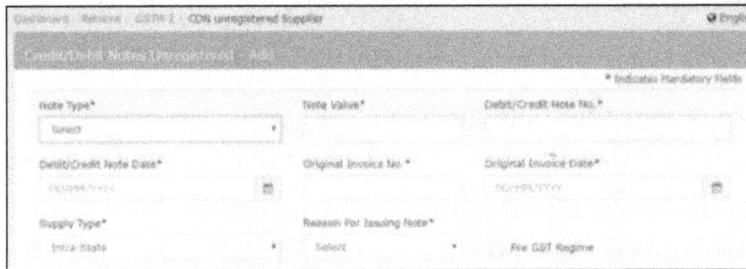

F-6A: Debit / Credit Note from unregistered supplier

At *Note Type*, select from the 3 options from the list Refund (in case of earlier Advance received, now Refunded by unregistered Supplier), Credit (in case of Credit note issued by unregistered supplier), Debit (in case Debit note issued by unregistered Supplier).

At Original Invoice & Invoice Date, enter the reference of Original Invoice Number and date against which the current Debit Note / Credit Note or Refund has been made by the supplier.

At Supply Type, select the option Inter sate / Inter State. It is not auto selected.

At Reason, select from the 7 reasons, as explained for Issue of Debit / Credit Note, earlier (01- Sales Return, 02 – Post sales Discount, 03 – Deficiency in Services, 04 Correction in Invoice, 05 – Change in PoS, 06, Finalisation of Provisional Assessment, 07 – Others).

Check the checkbox if the Refund / Debit / Credit Note relates to Pre GST period (The original Invoice Date should be of Pre GST period).

At Eligibility for ITC, select form the 4 options – Inputs (for Materials Import), Input Services (for Purchase of Services) Capital Goods (for Capital Goods Import), Ineligible ITC (where ITC is not eligible). Enter the Amount of eligible ITC, in respective ITC column. In case of ineligible ITC, the amount would be zero.

GSTR-2: Other Details: The Other details section of GSTR -2 Menu contains 5 Tabs for entry of consolidated figures of group of Invoices (F-7A).

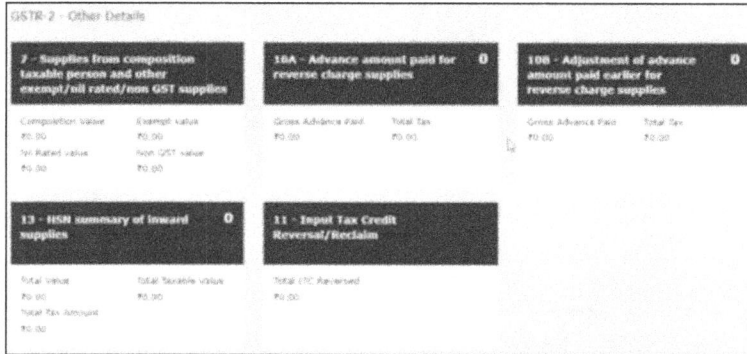

F-7A: GSTR-2: Other Details Tabs (Consolidated Invoice details)

Supplies from Composition Taxable Person and other Exempt / Nil Rated / Non GST supplies received (Table 7)

At GSTR-2 Other details Menu (F-7A), click on the *7-Supplies from Composition Taxable Person and other Exempt / Nil Rated / Non GST supplies received* Tab to get NIL rated supply entry screen. The details are to be uploaded by Tax payer (i.e Registered Recipient). Here enter the consolidated Amount of supplies received in respect of each of the supplier type (Composition, Exempt, Nil Rated, Non GST), in the respective field.

In case of Composition Dealer, data cannot be entered at Inter State supplies field, as Composition Dealers cannot make Inter State supplies.

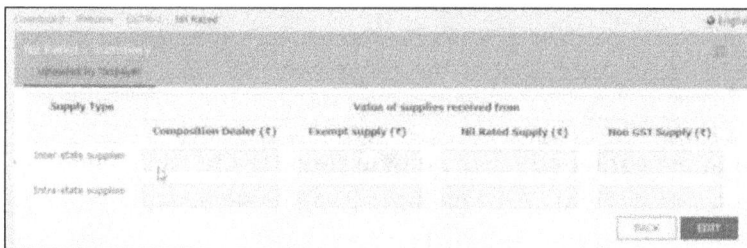

F-8A: Nil Rated supply summary

The data would be uploaded in following tables:

– **Table 7A: Inter State Supplies:** Supplied by supplier of Outside State of Buyer

– **Table 7B: Intra State Supplies:** Supplied by supplier of Home State of the Buyer

Advance paid for Reverse Charge supplies (Table 10A)

At GSTR-2 Other details Menu (F-7A), click *Advance paid for Reverse Charge supplies* to get the entry screen (F-9A). Here enter the consolidated figures of advance paid by buyer to supplier, for supplies subject to Tax under Reverse charge mechanism. You may recall the advance received by supplier and Tax paid thereon as reported in Table 11 of GSTR-1. Such advance need not be reported in Table 10 of GSTR-2. The advances paid for supplies subject to Reverse Charge (excluding the advances reported under Table 11 of GSTR-1), are to be entered in Table 10A of GSTR-2

F-9A: Advance paid for Reverse Charge supplies

At *Place of Supply*, select the State of the Supplier. Supply Type (Inter State / Intra state) would be auto populated accordingly.

Now enter the Amount of Advance paid at the respective rate sab. The Tax amount would be auto computed.

Advance Adjusted against earlier advance paid for Reverse Charge supplies (Table 10B)

At GSTR-2 Other details Menu (F-7A), click 10B-*Advance Adjusted against earlier advance paid for Reverse Charge supplies* to get the entry screen (F-10A). Invoices issued for Supplies made under Reverse Charge mechanism and earlier Advance adjusted are to be reported here.

Advance paid for supplies attracting Reverse Charges (Tax paid thereon and reported in Table 10A earlier), are subsequently adjusted against the Invoice for supplies made under Reverse Charge Mechanism. On issue of Invoice and adjustment of earlier advance, the details are to be entered here, to be populated in Table 10B. The balance of tax to be paid after adjusting the amount earlier paid on Advance, are to be paid on issue of invoice for supply.

F-10A: Advance adjusted against earlier advance paid for Reverse Charge supplies

At *Place of Supply*, select the State of the Supplier. Supply Type (Inter State / Intra state) would be auto populated accordingly. Now enter the Amount of Advance adjusted at the respective rate sab. The Tax amount would be auto computed, which would be adjusted against the total tax liability for the supply made under Reverse Charge.

Input Tax Credit Reversal / Reclaim (Table 11)

At *GSTR-2 Other details* Menu (F-7A), click *11- Input Tax Credit Reversal / Reclaim* to get the entry screen (F-11A)

F-11A: Input Tax Credit Reversal / Reclaim

ITC can be availed for goods / services used for Business Purpose only, but cannot be claimed for purpose other than business or for making Exempt Supplies. Such ineligible ITC must be reversed by entering in the Table under the respective fields, as below:

- **Amount in Terms of rule 37(2)**: Amount of Tax for Invoices not paid within 180 days.

- **Amount in Terms of rule 39(1)(j)(ii)**: In case of credit note issued by ISD, the ITC would be reduced

- **Amount in Terms of rule 42(1)(m)**: If any ITC is availed for *inputs on supplies* for Business & Non Business purpose, the proportionate amount of ITC in respect of Non-Business part would have to be reversed. So, the part relating to non-Business purpose would be entered in the respective field.

- **Amount in Terms of rule 43(1)(h)**: If any ITC is availed for *Inputs on Capital* Goods purchased for Business & Non Business purpose, the proportionate amount of ITC in respect of Non-Business part would have to be reversed. So, the part relating to non-Business purpose would be entered in the respective field.

- **Amount in Terms of rule 42(2)(a)**: After filing Annual Return, if total ITC on inputs of exempted / non business purpose is more than the ITC actually reversed during the year, the difference amount to be added to output liability. Enter the amount of liability to be added in such instance (and Interest would be applicable).

- **Amount in Terms of rule 42(2)(b)**: After filing Annual Return, if total ITC on inputs of exempted / non business purpose is less than the ITC actually reversed during the year, the difference amount to be reclaimed. Enter the amount of ITC to be reclaimed in such instance.

The instances under rule 42(2)(a) and rule 42(2)(b) are opposite to each other

The taxpayer can manually amend any details of ITC under 11A of earlier month, selecting the appropriate Item from the drop down list

HSN summary of Inward Supplies (Table 13)

At *GSTR-2 Other details* Menu (F-7A), click 13 - *HSN summary of Inward Supplies* to get the entry screen (F-12A).

F-12A - HSN summary of Inward Supplies

The consolidated figure for each HSN Code / Description is to be supplied, separately in respect of each UQC, as follows:

– **HSN Code & Description**; In case of tax payer having turnover less than 1.5 crores in previous year, HSN Cod is not mandatory, but Description has to be entered (if HSN Code is not entered). In case of turnover more than 1.5 crore but upto 5 crores in previous year, 2 digit HSN Code is to be provided. For organisation having Turnover more than 5 crores, 4 digit HSN Code are to be entered

– **UQC:** Enter the Unit Quantity from the list

– **Total Quantity**: Enter the total quantity in respect of the UQC

– **Total Value**: Enter the total value (including Tax) in respect of the UQC

– **Total Taxable Value**: Enter the total Taxable value (excluding Tax) on which Tax is charged, in respect of the UQC

– **Integrated Tax**: Enter the Integrated Tax in respect of the UQC

– **Central Tax**: Enter the Central Tax in respect of the UQC

– **State / UT Tax**: Enter the State / UT Tax in respect of the UQC

– **Cess**: Enter the Cess in respect of the UQC

GSTR-2 Summary Generation

Scroll down to the bottom of the GSTR-2 – Inward Supplies received by the Taxpayer page and click the GENERATE GSTR-2 SUMMARY button, to update the summary and view auto-drafted invoices/ credit note / debit notes etc.

Preview of GSTR-2 Summary

Once you have generated the GSTR-2 Summary, click the checkbox and click *PREVIEW* button to download the draft Summary page of GSTR-2, in watermarked PDF pages. Review the summary of entries made in different sections carefully.

Submit GSTR-2 Summary

Having checked the Summary data (and having made correction, if any, as described), click the checkbox and click *SUBMIT* button, to freeze the GSTR-2 data for the specific month. You will no more be able to upload any further invoices for that month (in case you have missed adding any invoice, you can upload those invoices in the subsequent month or you can wait for supplier to add it in supplier GSTR-1). Click *PROCEED* button. On successful submission, a success message is displayed at the top of the page.

Filing GSTR-2

After submission of GSTR-2, check the *Declaration* checkbox. At *Authorised Signatory* drop-down list, select the authorized signatory. Click the *FILE GSTR-2 WITH DSC* or *FILE GSTR-2 WITH EVC* button (and enter OTP), as applicable, and file GSTR-2. On filing of the GSTR-2, notification through e-mail and SMS is sent to the Authorized Signatory.

Filing GSTR-2 NIL Return

Even if there is no entry in GSTR-2 (i.e no purchases in any specific tax period), you have to file NIL Return. We briefly state the steps for filing NIL Return.

Login to your GST account using GST user id and password. Select the *Financial Year* and *Return Filing* period. Click on *Auto Drafted GSTR-2A* Tab. GSTR-2A contains auto populated Invoices uploaded by supplier. If there are no purchases for the month, the GSTR-2A would not contain any record. Go to *Returns Dashboard* and Click VIEW under *Auto Drafted Details* to see that there are no records in GSTR-2A.

Now Click PREPARE ON-LINE button at the tile *Inward Supplies received by TaxpayerGSTR-2*. The GSTR-2 Summary figures in all the sections would be shown as NIL. Download and Preview the GSTR2 Return, as explained. Submit and file the NIL GSTR-2 Return as explained.

GSTR 2A Sales Purchase Matching

GSTR-2A

GSTR 2A is an auto-generated read only document for information purpose only. When a seller files his GSTR-1, the information is captured (auto populated) in GSTR 2A of the respective Buyer.

GSTR 2A need not be filed. It is merely for an intimation to the counter-party for viewing and reconciliation of Outwards Invoice uploaded by seller with corresponding Inwards receipts by the Buyer

GSTR 2A will be auto-populated from the following returns of the sellers/counter party:

- GSTR 1: Regular registered seller

- GSTR-5: Non-resident

- GSTR 6: Input Service Distributor

- GSTR 7: Person liable to deduct TDS

- GSTR 8: Ecommerce

GSTR 2A Reconciliation & ITC acceptance

- **Auto flow from Supplier**: Registered Supplier submits outward supply details in *Form GSTR-1* by the 10th of the subsequent month. This include Sales Invoice, Credit Notes and Debit Notes (in respect of Sales only).

- **Review:** On 11th, Inward supplies may be viewed by respective recipient (i.e Buyer) in the auto-populated *GSTR-2A*, which may viewed or download (no amendments can be done in GSTR-2A).

- **Approval:** The buyer would approve the verified entries. The approved data would be included in GSTR-2. Updated *GSTR-2* would be submitted by 15th.

- **Editing**: The corrections (addition, modification and deletion) made by the recipient (during 16th to 17th) in *Form GSTR-2* will be made available to supplier in *Form GSTR-1A*. The supplier either accept or reject (but cannot Add or Modify) the adjustments made by the recipient. The *Form GSTR-1* will be amended as per corrections accepted by supplier.

If any Item is not disapproved, it would be treated as Auto Approved, and would be updated in GSTR-2

Example

The steps followed by ABC Supplier at the end of month, for submission of Returns, having entered following Sales / Purchase transactions:

Sales Bill to: Customer C1- Bill 1, Customer C1- Bill 2, Customer C2- Bill 3

Purchase Bill from: Supplier S1 – Bill 13, Bill 29, Supplier S2 – Bill 25, Bill 30,

ABC supplier uploads the 3 bills 1,2 & 3 on 10th of the following month in GSTR-1

Supplier S1 uploads the Bill 13 & 29 and supplier S2 uploads the Bills 25 by 10th, in their GSTR-1

On 11th, ABC supplier views the auto populated inwards bills in GSTR-2A. On reconciliation of GSTR-2A with their purchase records, it finds Bill 30 of Supplier S2 missing in GSTR-2A. So, ABC supplier uploads missed purchase Bill 30 of S2 in GSTR-2.

Subsequently, Bill 30 of S2 added by ABC supplier in their GSTR-2 is reflected in GSTR-1A of Supplier S2.

Supplier S2 then verifies and accepts the Bill 30. This bill will be amended in their GSTR-1

Now GSTR-1, GSTR-2 would be updated and GSTR-3 would be ready for submission and Tax payment.

Additional entries by Buyer

Apart from that, buyer would suo moto add Invoices not reported in GSTR-1 like Purchase from Unregistered Dealer, Composite Dealer, Imports etc (these need not be approved by seller), in GSTR-2, as explained in earlier chapter.

Auto-drafted GSTR-2A

Purchases from registered supplier will be auto-populated in GSTR-2A, from GSTR-1 filed by the seller. It will have all details of type, rate and amount of GST, whether ITC is eligible, amount of ITC.

Certain transactions may not be auto-populated, where *Seller did not file GSTR-1 or missed the transaction in their GSTR-1 filing*. In such case, buyer can manually add these transactions in GSTR-2. The respective registered seller will get a notification to accept this addition/modification in his GSTR-1A return.

If the supply is received in more than one lots, the invoice must be reported in the return of the month in which the last lot is received and recorded in books of accounts.

In ideal condition, where the seller has filed all sales correctly, the buyer would get all the auto-drafted records in GSTR-2A, tallied with his own records.

Review

Login to your account using Username & password. Select *Services > Returns > Returns Dashboard* to get File Returns screen. Enter Financial Year and Return Filing period to get File Returns Menu (F-1A).

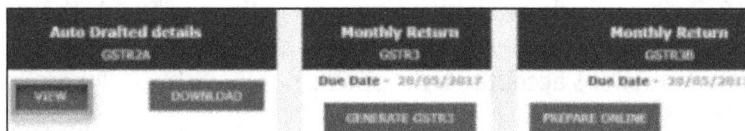

F-F1A: File Returns menu

At *Auto Drafted Details* GSTR-2A tile, click VIEW button to get GSTR-2A: Auto Drafted details screen (F-2A). You may only review the records of GSTR-2A, but cannot make any amendments, additions or deletion of any record in 2A. All modifications are to be done through GSTR-2 only.

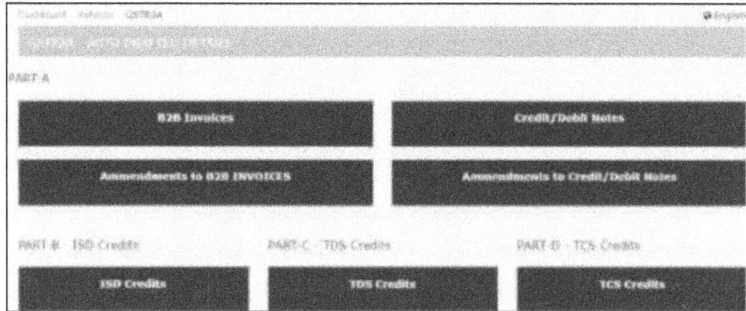

F-2A: GSTR-2A: Auto Drafted details

Review of Invoices, Debit / Credit Notes: In Part -A, you get following Tabs to review and make amendments of Invoices, Debit / Credit Notes (F-1B)

– **B2B Invoices:** Click on B2B Invoices. You will get the list of GSTIN of the supplier who has uploaded invoices. Click on the supplier GSTIN to get the list of Invoices uploaded by the selected supplier. Just review them and check with your records. Any missing or mismatch data are to be noted during the review. These are to be reported in GSTR-2 for proper updating.

– **Debit Credit Notes:** Click on Debit Credit Notes to view Debit Credit Notes issued by supplier. You may review the details in same way as B2B invoices and note down omission or discrepancy, if any.

Here, you will view Invoices / Debit / Credit notes uploaded by supplier through GSTR-1, only after due date of filing of GSTR-1.

Review of Amendment to previous period Invoices, Debit Credit Notes

– **Amendments to B2B Invoices:** Click on *Amendments to B2B Invoices* to view the details of any amendments of earlier period in their GSTR-1 or GSTR -5

– **Amendments to Debit Credit Notes:** Click on *Amendments to Debit Credit Notes* to view the details of any amendments of earlier period.

Review of Credits

Apart from the above, you may view the Credits in respect of ISD (ITC distributed by ISD filed under GSTR 6 in Part B), TDS (filed under GSTR-7 in Part C) & TCS (filed under GSTR-8 in Part D), from this menu.In Part B,C& D click the following Tabs to view the respective credit details uploaded (F-1B)

– **ISD Credits:** The details show auto-populated records of ISD credits distribution, based on GSTR 6 filed by Input Service Distributor.

– **TDS Credits**: The details show auto-populated records of TDS deducted, based on GSTR 7 filed by the dealers deducting TDS.

– **TCS Credits**: The details show auto-populated records based TCS collected, on GSTR 8 filed by TCS collector

Review Process: The steps of Review are explained briefly

Part A: B2B Invoices: B2B Invoices displays all the invoices added by the supplier through their GSTR-1 and GSTR 5. The B2B section of PART A of GSTR-2A is auto-populated on uploading or saving of invoices by the Supplier in their respective returns of GSTR 1 and GSTR 5.

To view the details, click the *B2B Invoices* button (F-2B) to get *B2B Invoices - Supplier Details* page (F-3A). Click on the GSTIN of the supplier link to get the Invoice details of the selected supplier (F-3B).

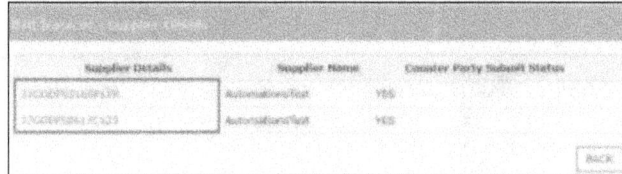

F-3A: B2B Invoices – Supplier Details

Click on the Invoice link (F-3B) to get the Item (Rate wise Tax) details.

F-3B: B2B Invoice Summary

Part A: Amendments to B2B Invoices: Here you view the Invoices amended by supplier in their GSTR-1 / GSTR-5 Returns. Click *Amendments to B2B Invoices* button (F-2A) to get *Amended B2B Invoice* page, showing the amended Invoices. Click the GSTIN link to view the Invoices related to the GSTIN

PART- A: Credit/Debit Notes: Here you view the Credit/Debit notes added by the supplier in their respective returns (GSTR-1/5). Click Credit/Debit Notes button (F-2A) and click the GSTIN link to view the Credit/Debit Notes related to the GSTIN (F-4A).

PART- A: Amendments to Credit/Debit Notes: Here you view the Credit / Debit Notes amended by supplier in their GSTR-1 / GSTR-5 Returns. Click *Amendments to Credit/ Debit Notes* button (F-2A) to get *Amended Credit / Debit Note*page, showing the amended Invoices. Click the GSTIN link to view the Invoices related to the GSTIN

F-4A: Credit / Debit Note summary

Part B: ISD Credits: Here you view the ISD Credits Received details as submitted in GSTR-6 Returns.

Part C: TDS Credits: Here you view the TDS Credits Received details as submitted in GSTR-7 by TDS deductors.

Part D: TCS Credits: Here you view the TCS Credits Received details as submitted in GSTR-8 by TCS collectors.

GSTR-3 Monthly Tax Return

GSTR-3 Return

GSTR-3 is a Monthly Return with the summarized details of sales (as filed under GSTR-1), purchases (as filed under GRST-2), along with the amount of GST Tax liability. This return is auto-generated pulling information from GSTR-1 and GSTR-2 filed for the respective month. The taxpayer must pay the tax and file the Return (NIL Return to be filed even if there is no transaction during a period). However, following registered persons need not file GSTR-3:

- Input Service Distributors
- Composition Dealers
- Non-resident taxable person
- Persons liable to collect TCS
- Persons liable to deduct TDS
- Suppliers of online information and database access or retrieval services (OIDAR), who have to pay tax themselves.

If GSTR-3 return is not filed, GSTR-1 of the next month cannot be filed. So, non filing of GSTR-3 will have cascading effect leading to heavy fines and penalty.

Interest @18% per annum has to be paid for late payment of Tax (16th of the month to the date of payment). Late fee is Rs. 100 per day per Act (Rs100 / day under CGST & Rs. 100 / day under SGST, i.e Total will be Rs. 200/day. Maximum Late fee is Rs. 5,000. There is no late fee on IGST.

Any mistake made in the return can be revised in the next month's GSTR-1 and GSTR-2 returns (not in the current month), as GSTR-3 is auto-generated which cannot be edited

There are 2 steps for GSTR-3 filing

- Utilisation of ITC and payment of Tax
- Filing of GSTR-3 after payment of Tax

First the Tax liability is to be relinquished by adjusting the ITC and payment of Tax. Having paid tax, the GSTR-3 Return is to be filed.

However, in case of extension of due dates of filing of GSTR-1 & GSTR-2, GSTR-3B is to be filed first. GSTR-3 need to be filed on further notification.

Note: As per notification vide 23rd GST Council meeting held on 10th Nov 17, GSTR-2 (and GSTR-3) need not be filed upto Mar 18.However, GSTR-1 &GSTR-3B are to be filed.

Utilisation of ITC and Tax Payment

At GST portal, login to your account. Select Services>ledgers>Utilise ITC / Cash to get Utilise Cash & Cash screen (F-2A).

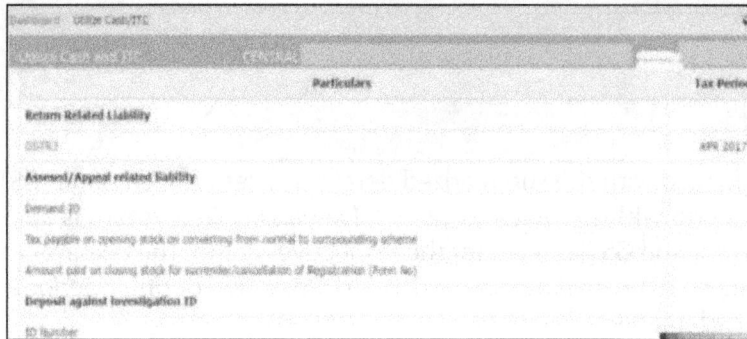

F-2A: GSTR-3 Return - Utilise Cash / ITC screen

Here you get the details under following heads (F-2A)

— Return Related Liability

— Assessed / Appeal related Liability

— Deposit against Investigation ID

Click on *GSTR-3* link under *Return related Liability* head (F-2A), to get Return Related Liability screen (F-3A)

Tax Details: In the upper part (F-3A) , you get Return Liability details showing total liability under various heads, with columns for IGST, CGST, SGST &Cess,

F-3A: Utlise Cash & ITC screen

Payment Options: In the lower part (F-3B), you get following payment options

— **Pay through Provisional ITC**: To use ITC balance available as on current month.

— **Pay through ITC upto previous month**: To use ITC balance available in electronic credit ledger, till previous month (recommended)

– **Pay through Cash**: Pay Tax through challan (challan should be printed first)

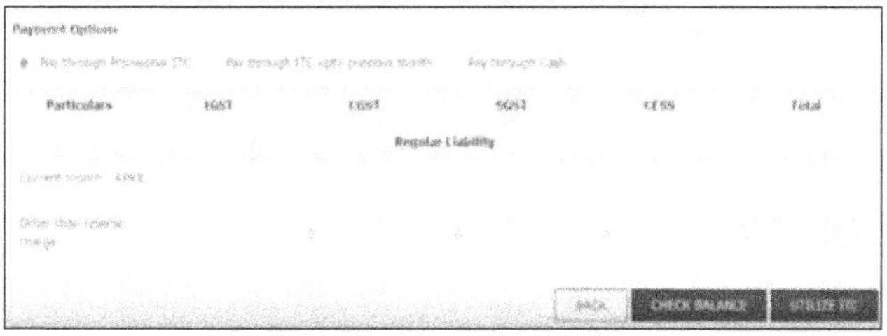

3B: Payment options

Utilisation of ITC: It is recommended to utilise balance till previous month, rather than provisional ITC, as there might be occasion when some ITC is rejected for the current month (out of the provisional ITC), which may lead to pay difference amount with Interest.

Before adjusting the ITC, click on *Check Balance* button (F-3B) to display the details of ITC balance available under each head (F-3C)

ITC Balance check

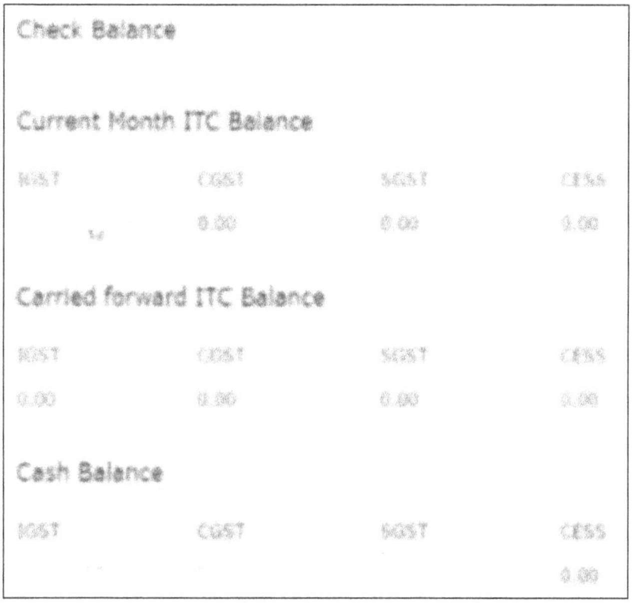

F-3C: ITC Balance Check

F-3D: ITC adjustment confirmation

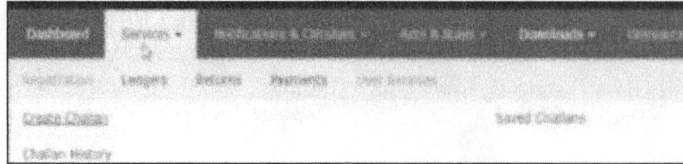

F-4A: Challan creation

Rules of ITC Utlisation against Tax Liability: The ITC adjustment would be done according to following rule:

– IGST balance should be used first against IGST, then against CGST and then against SGST liability

– CGST balance should be used first against CGST and then against IGST liability

– SGST balance should be used first against SGST and then against IGST liability

Utilisationof ITC balance of CGST & SGST against liability of each other is not permissible.

Adjustment of ITC Balance: To adjust the ITC balance, click on *Utilise ITC* (F-3B) to get a message displaying the adjustment of balance, for your confirmation (F-3D). Adjustment once done cannot be reversed. So, check the massage (F-3D) first and then click *Confirm* button to make the adjustment of ITC.

Payment through Cash: To discharge balance tax liability (after adjustment against ITC) on payment, first create a challan.

Challan Creation: Click on *Services* tab in the GST portal and then click on *Create Challan* link to get Challan Creation screen (F-4A). Click on Payment Tab.

Click on *Create Challan* link (F-4A) to get Challan entry screen (F-4B) to enter data to create a new challan to make payment of Tax.

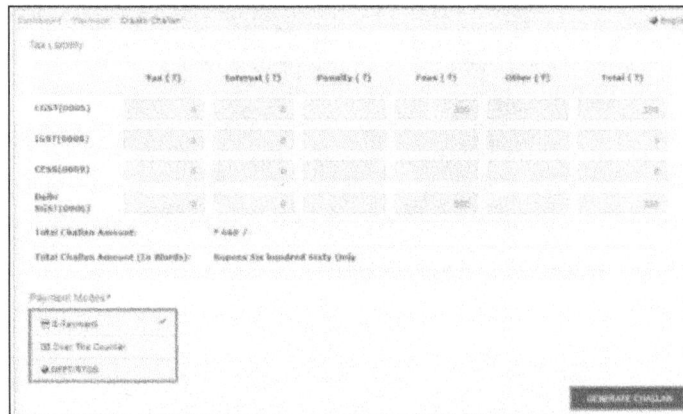

F-4B: Challan data entry screen

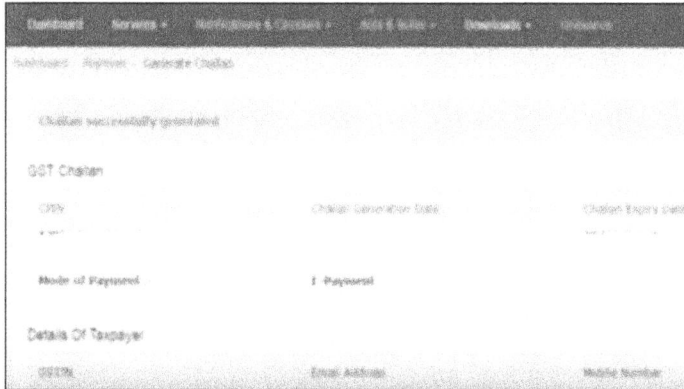

F-4C: Generated challan details

Now enter the amount under respective Tax Head (Tax Code), under respective columns for amount Tax, Interest, Penalty, Fees and others, as the case may be.

On entry under the respective amount the total challan amount in figures and in words would be displayed.

Payment Mode: Now tick on the desired payment mode (F-4B) and Click on *Generate Challan*. to view the details of challan (F-4C).

The challan is then displayed for payment of Tax. The next screens and details would depend on mode of payment and other options selected.

In case of digital payment (Net Banking etc), you get the bank's secured gateway where you enter the details.

After the payment is successful, you get an acknowledgement of receipt of payment, and a message from GSTN regarding receipt of payment is displayed.

Depending on the payment mode selected, you have to select Method (net Banking, Credit Card), Bank etc, and other details. Click on make payment button to make payment (for on line payment mode)

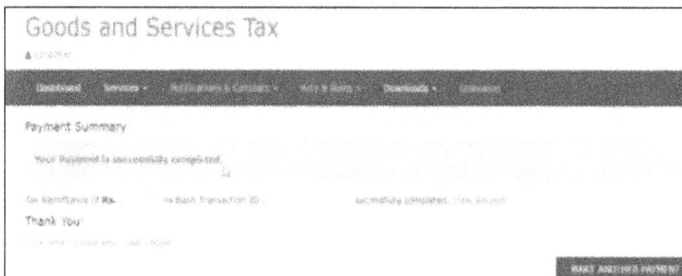

F-4E: Acknowledgement of Payment

Having made the payment, now you can adjust the balance tax liability against the cash payment made, as reflected in your cash ledger. At payment options screen (F-3B), click *Pay through Cash* link. Click on utilize Cash button to get message for adjustment screen (F-3D) & Click Confirm button, as explained earlier.

Filing of GSTR-3 Return

Having adjusted the ITC and having paid Tax in Cash, if any, you may file the GSTR-3 Return.

Login to your account. At Dashboard, click Services>RETURNS and then click Return Dashboard link to get File Returns screen. Enter the period, click GSTR-3 link under Monthly Return GSTR-3 Tab (F-5A) to get GSTR-3 generate screen (F-5B)

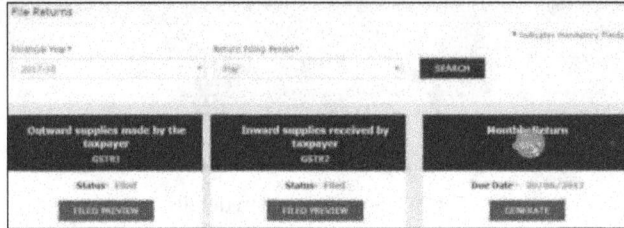

F-5A: GSTR-3 Filing

At File Returns screen (F-5A), at GSTR-3 Tile, Click GENERATE button to get GSTR-3 Return menu (F-5B)

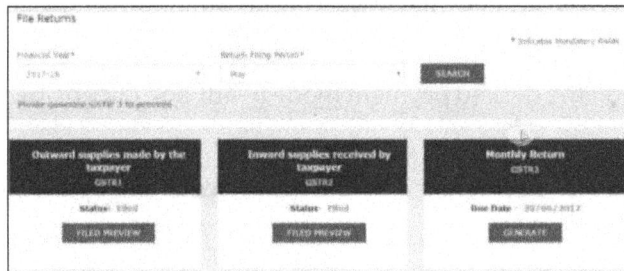

F-5B: GSTR3 Report generation

Now click Monthly Return link (F-5B) to get GSTR-3 Monthly Return screen (F-5C)

GSTR-3 Monthly Return Details

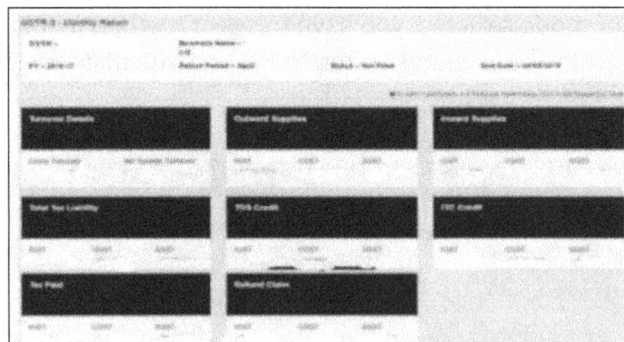

F-5C: GSTR-3 Monthly Return

Turnover Details

At GSTR-3 Monthly Return screen (F-5C), click on *Turnover details* link, to get Turnover Details screen, showing the previous Financial Year turnover details under each head (F-5D)

F-5D: GSTR-3: Turnover Details

F-5E: GSTR-3: Outward Supplies Details

Outward Supplies

At Monthly Return screen (F-5C), select *Outward Supplies* link to get Outward Supplies screen (F-5E), auto updated from GSTR-1 Return filed.

Inwards Supplies

At Monthly Return screen (F-5C), select *Inward Supplies* link to get Inward Supplies screen (F-5F), auto updated from GSTR-2 Return filed.

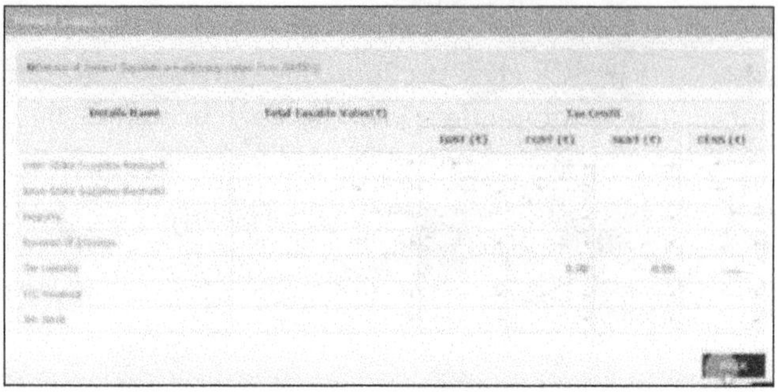

F-5F: GSTR-3: Inwards Supplies Details

Total tax Liability

At Monthly Return screen (F-5C), select *Total Tax Liability* link to get Total Tax Liability screen (F-5G),

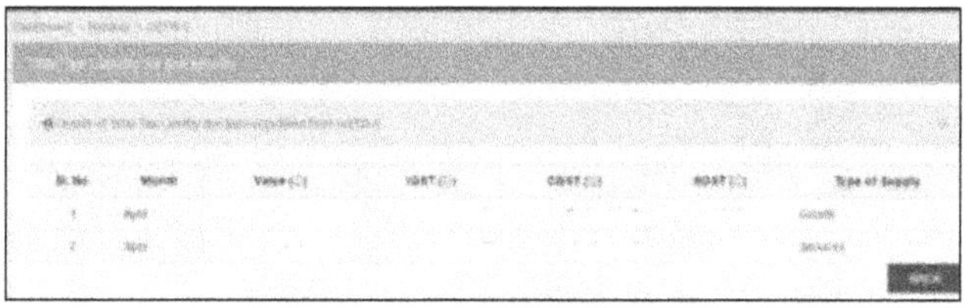

F-5G: Total Tax Liability for the month

TDS Credit: At GSTR-3 Monthly Return screen (F-5C), click *TDS Credit* to get TDS Credit screen (F-5H),auto populated as per GSTR -2 return.

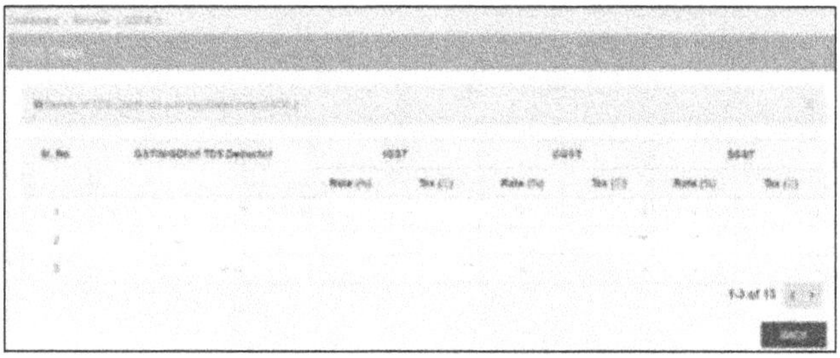

F-5H: TDS Credit

ITC Credit: At GSTR-3 Monthly Return screen (F-5C), click *ITC Credit* to get ITC Credit screen (F-5I)

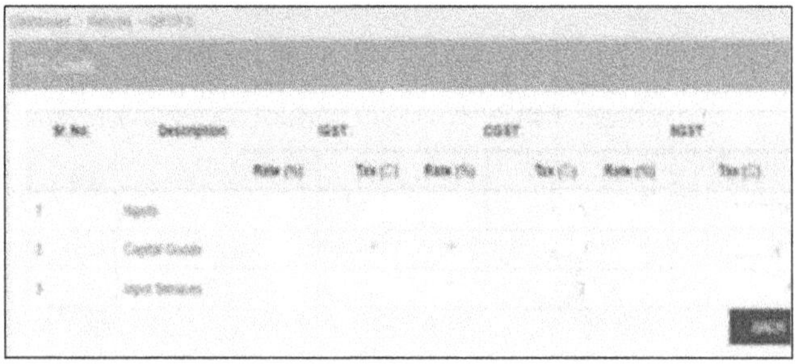

F-5I: ITC Details

Tax Paid: At GSTR-3 Monthly Return screen (F-5C), click *Tax Paid* to get Tax Paid screen (F-5J)

F-5J: Tax Paid

Refunds Claim: At GSTR-3 Monthly Return screen (F-5C), click *Refunds Claim* to get ITC Refunds Claim screen (F-5K)

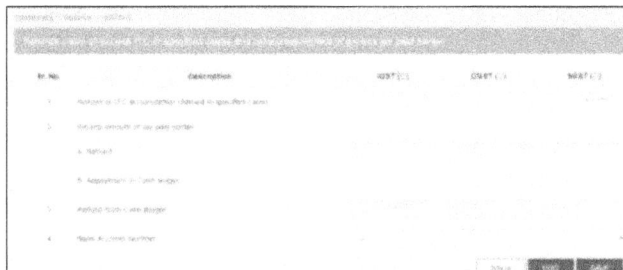

F-5K: Refunds Claim

Preview GSTR-3

At GSTR-3 Monthly Return screen (F-6A), Click PREVIEW button to download draft PDF file of GSTR-3. Check each table of the Return thoroughly.

Return Filing

Having checked the draft GSTR-3, at GSTR-3 Monthly Return screen (F-6A), Click *File GSTR-3* to file the Return with EVC or DSC signature, as usual. On filing the GSTR-3, the liability (Tax, Interest, Late Fees, Penalty) of the Taxpayer & ITC would be computed and updated in Tax Liability Register & Electronic Credit Ledger

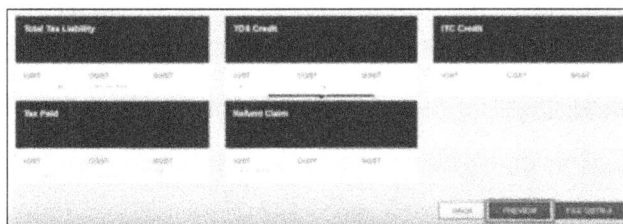

F-6A: GSTR-3 Preview / Filing

If GSTR-3 is filed with short/ no payment of liability, it will be treated as invalid (a mismatch report would be generated), as if GSTR-3 has not been filed for that period.

GSTR-3B Monthly Tax Return Off line Filing

GSTR-3B Offline Utility

The Excel based GSTR-3B Offline Utility helps to prepare GSTR-3B return offline.

Details of data for sections of GSTR-3B are to be entered as follows:

– Details of Outward Supplies and inward supplies liable to reverse charge (Table 3.1)

– Details of inter-State supplies made to unregistered persons, composition taxable persons and UIN holders [Of the supplies shown in 3.1 (a) above] (Table 3.2)

– Eligible ITC (Table 4)

– Values of exempt, nil-rated and non-GST inward supplies (Table 5)

– Interest & late fee payable (Table 5.1)

Steps of Filing GSTR-3B using Off line Excel Utility & JSON file

1. Download and Open GSTR-3B Off line Utility

2. Validate the Details (Click *Validate* button in the Excel Sheet)

3. Generate JSON File (Click *Generate File* button in the Excel Sheet)

4. Upload the generated JSON on GST Portal

1. Download GSTR-3B Off line Utility

– **Download File**: Login to the GST Portal www.gst.gov.in. Select Downloads > Offline tools > GSTR3B Offline Utility. The *Returns Offline Tool* page is displayed. Click the Download button (and Click PROCEED button) to download the ZIP file.

– **Unzip the Downloaded File**: Unzip the downloaded Zip file which contain GSTR3B_Excel_Utility excel sheet. Use the latest version of the offline utility available in the Portal.

– **Open GSTR-3B Off line Utility:** Double the Excel file GSTR3B_Excel_Utility_3.0.xls to open

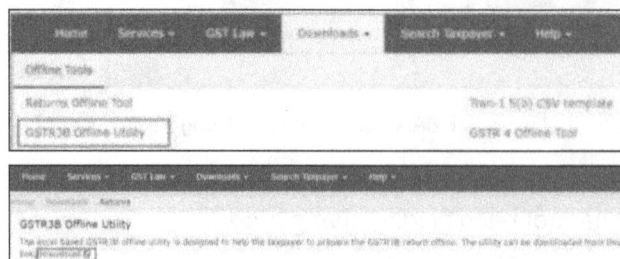

GSTR-3B Excel File: The Excel Sheet contains 2 Tabs.

– **Help Instructions**: It contains the operational instruction to file GSTR-3B using the Excel File to create JSON file and upload in the GST Portal

– **GSTR-3B Excel Format**: It contains the formats of the respective Table sections of GSTR-3B

Click *Enable Editing* button in the excel sheet.Click the *Clear All button* (and then Click *Yes*) to clear any data present in the sheet and to reset the Worksheet.

Contents of Excel Sheet GSTR-3B Table Formats
The Header part

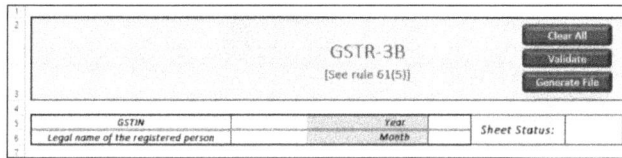

GSTR-3B Excel Sheet – Header part

Header data Entry

– **GSTIN:** Enter the GSTIN. GSTIN would be validated for correct structure.

– **Year:** Select *Year* drop-down list.

– **Legal name of registered person**: Enter the legal name of registered person

– **Month**: Select Month from drop-down list

GSTR-3B Excel Sheet: Details of Outwards Supplies - Table 3.1

GSTR-3B Excel Sheet: Details of Outwards Supplies - Table 3.1

In *Table 3.1: Details of Outward Supplies and inward supplies liable to reverse charge*, enter the respective details. Only CGST amount needs to be entered for applicable sections. Equal SGST amount would be populated based on CGST amount. If the value of SGST amount is not equal, one can change it on the portal.

GSTR-3B Excel Sheet: Interstate Supplies to Unregistered, Composition Dealer & UIN Holders – Table 3.2

GSTR-3B Excel Sheet: Interstate Supplies to Unregistered, Composition Dealer & UIN Holders – Table 3.2

Enter details of inter-State supplies made to unregistered persons, composition taxable persons and UIN holders [out of the supplies shown in 3.1 (a) above] in Table 3.2. Amount entered in Table 3.2 cannot be more than amount entered in Table 3.1 (a). Table 3.2 is placed in GSTR-3B worksheet as last Table

In Place of Supply (State/ UT) column, select the Place of Supply (State/UT) from the drop-down list.

GSTR-3B Excel Sheet: Eligible ITC – Table 4

	4. Eligible ITC			
Details	Integrated Tax	Central Tax	State/UT Tax	Cess
1	2	3	4	5
(A) ITC Available (Whether in full or part)				
(1) Import of goods	₹ 0.00			₹ 0.00
(2) Import of services	₹ 0.00			₹ 0.00
(3) Inward supplies liable to reverse charge (other than 1 &2 above)	₹ 0.00	₹ 0.00	₹ 0.00	₹ 0.00
(4) Inward supplies from ISD	₹ 0.00	₹ 0.00	₹ 0.00	₹ 0.00
(5) All other ITC	₹ 0.00	₹ 0.00	₹ 0.00	₹ 0.00
(B) ITC Reversed				
(1) As per Rule 42 & 43 of SGST/CGST rules	₹ 0.00	₹ 0.00	₹ 0.00	₹ 0.00
(2) Others	₹ 0.00	₹ 0.00	₹ 0.00	₹ 0.00
(C) Net ITC Available (A)-(B)	₹ 0.00	₹ 0.00	₹ 0.00	₹ 0.00
(D) Ineligible ITC				
(1) As per section 17(5) of CGST//SGST Act	₹ 0.00	₹ 0.00	₹ 0.00	₹ 0.00
(2) Others	₹ 0.00	₹ 0.00	₹ 0.00	₹ 0.00

GSTR-3B Excel Sheet: Eligible ITC– Table 4

In Table 4, enter amount of Eligible ITC, under the sections: A. ITC Available & 2. ITC Reversed, in respective rows & columns. The NET ITC Available is computed as (A-B). Under section D: Ineligible ITC, enter the amount of Ineligible ITC.

GSTR-3B Excel Sheet: Values of Exempt, Nil Rated & Non GST Inward Supplies – Table 5

5. Values of exempt, Nil-rated and non-GST inward supplies		
Nature of supplies	Inter-State supplies	Intra-state supplies
	1	2
From a supplier under composition scheme, Exempt and Nil rated supply	₹ 0.00	₹ 0.00
Non GST supply	₹ 0.00	₹ 0.00
Total	₹ 0.00	₹ 0.00

GSTR-3B Excel Sheet: Values of Exempt,
Nil Rated & Non GST Inward Supplies – Table 5

In Table 5. 1, enter Values of exempt, nil-rated and non-GST inward supplies, in respective rows & columns

GSTR-3B Excel Sheet: Interest & Late Fee Payable – Table 5.1

5.1 Interest & late fee payable			
Description	Integrated Tax	Central Tax	State/UT Tax	Cess
1	2	3	4	5
Interest	₹ 0.00	₹ 0.00	₹ 0.00	₹ 0.00

GSTR-3B Excel Sheet: Interest & Late Fee Payable – Table 5.1

In Table 5.1, enter only interest amount.

2. Validate Details

Having entered all the applicable details, click the *Validate* button (in the header part in the worksheet) to validate the GSTR-3B worksheet.

- **Successful validation**: On successful validation, click OK button at pop up message displayed (error message is displayed if any error encountered). On case of successful validation, at *Sheet Status* cell at the header, *Validation Successful* is displayed.

- **Validation Failure**: In case of Validation Failure, check for cells that have failed validation and correct errors as per help text. To view the comments for fields with errors, click the Review tab > Show All Comments link.

  After all errors are rectified, click the *Validate* button again to validate the GSTR-3B worksheet. Repeat the process till validation is successful.

3. Generate JSON File

After successful validation, Click Generate button (at the Header), to generate JSON file to upload on GST Portal. A confirmation message is displayed on JSON file generation. Click the OK button. JSON would be generated and a folder *GSTR* is shown in Desktop (JSON is generated only if the worksheet has been successfully validated). Double Click the GSTR folder in desktop to extract the JSON file (it is named as per GSTIN and Return Period for easy identification).

4. Upload Generated JSON on GST Portal

Access gst.gov.in to get GST Home page

Click *Services > Returns > Returns Dashboard* command to get *File Returns* page

At *Financial Year* drop-down list, select the financial year for which the return has to be uploaded.

In the Return Filing Period drop-down list, select the return filing period for which the return has to be uploaded. Click the SEARCH button. The Tiles of Returns are displayed. At *Monthly Return GSTR-3B* tile, click PREAPRE OFFLINE to get *Off line Upload for GSTR-3B* Page

Return details for Offline filing of GSTR-3 Return

Offline filing of GSTR-3 Return

At *Off line Upload for GSTR-3B* page, Click the Choose File button. Select the JSON file to be uploaded and click Open button to upload the JSON file.

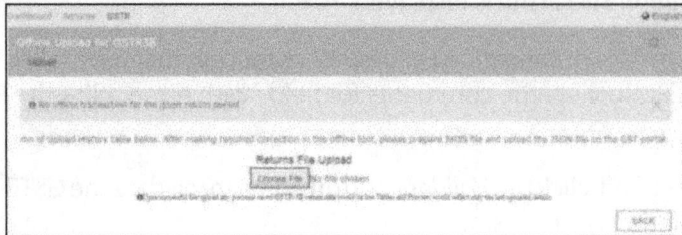

JSON file upload for Offline filing of GSTR-3 Return

The uploaded JSON file would be validated and processed. Upon successful validation and processing the details entered would be populated in respective Tables (error message would be displayed if any error is encountered) in the GSTN portal.

JSON file may be uploaded multiple times on GST portal till submission (earlier uploaded data would be overwritten) and the latest uploaded data would be shown in Preview would shown. After successful upload of GSTR-3B Return on GST Portal, you may preview the Form, Submit, Offset Liability and finally file the GSTR-3B Return.

GSTR-3B Monthly Tax Return on line filing

GSTR-3B

GSTR-3B is a temporary quick format Return of GSTR-3, currently to be filed for the period upto March 2018, before filing of GSTR-3. GSTR-3B form is introduced as the Government, the GSTN platform and the taxpayers were not fully equipped to submit detailed Info of GSTR-3. In GSTR-3B, a few key summary figures are filed instead comprehensive details to be filed in GSTR-3.

GSTR-3B is not in lieu of GSTR -3, but an additional Return to be submitted upto March 2018, on self-assessment basis. However, GSTR-3 are also to be submitted for which taxpayer is allowed some extra time.

GSTR-3B contains Summary of Outwards & Inwards Supply, Eligible ITC Claim & Net Taxes payable. The consolidated figures of Taxable Value and each components of Tax (IGST, CGST, SGST/UTGST, Cess) are submitted. No invoice wise details need to be submitted.

NIL GSTR-3B need to be filed, even if there is no transaction in any month.

Persons not liable to submit GSTR-3B

Every person registered under GST (except the following persons), must file separate GSTR 3B for each GSTIN

- Input Service Distributors

- Taxable Person Registered under Composition scheme

- Suppliers of online information and database access or retrieval services (OIDAR), who pay tax themselves

- Non-resident taxable person

GSTR-3B On line entry

We will now show each component of the GSTR-3B on-line entry screen in the portal and the respective table in the GSTR-3B form. You have to keep the data ready in the GSTR-3B Physical Form (print the Form and manually fill up or get a digital copy and enter data into it) before you login to the on-line form entry. The on-line form and the physical form are aligned. Just enter the data in the on-line form from the filled up Physical GSTR-3B Form, compiled from GSTR-1 & GSTR-2 Return.

On-line Form

After your account login in GSTN portal, select *Returns* and then enter the *Financial Year* and *Month* to get Returns dashboard (F-1A). You have to enter all data on-line in the portal. There is no provision to.

You must keep all the figures for GSTR-3B Return ready to be entered in respective forms, compiled from GSTR-1 & GSTR-2 returns filed.

F-1A: Returns Dash Board

Click on PREPARE ON-LINE button of Monthly Return GSTR-3B tile, to get GSTR-3B – Monthly Return menu. Click OK button to get the latest changes notification screen, describing the recent changes to make GSTR-3B filing simpler (F-1B). Read the instructions. Click OK to proceed.

F-1B: GSTR-3B Simplification message

F-1C: GSTR-3B Questionnaires

You get a set of Questionnaires with Yes / No option (F-1C). Click the relevant radio button (Yes / No) against each question, as relevant in your case. You may click Back button to go to the previous page. Having checked the questionnaires properly, click Next button to get GSTR 3B Monthly Return Menu (F-2A)

GSTR 3B Monthly Return Menu

At GSTR 3B Monthly Return Menu (F-2A), you get following tiles for the respective Tables to enter relevant details. Click on the respective tile to get the screen of the selected Table:

o **3.1 Tax on outward and reverse charge inward supplies**: Outward supplies, Inward supplies liable to reverse charge, and tax liability thereon.

o **3.2 Inter-state supplies**: Inter-state supplies made to unregistered persons, composition dealers and UIN holders, and tax thereon.

o **4. Eligible ITC**: Eligible ITC claimed, ITC Reversals and Ineligible ITC.

o **5. Exempt, nil and Non GST inward supplies**: Exempt, Nil and Non GST inward supplies.

o **5.1 Interest and Late Fee**: Interest and Late fee payable.

o **6. Payment of Tax**: Payment of Taxes, Interest and Late Fee.

After entry of data in each Table, click *SAVE GSTR3B* button at the bottom to save the data in the GST system. You will not loose data of a Table entered and may even exit after entry of a Table and come back later to complete the filing.

F-2A: GSTR-3B Monthly Returns Menu

Outwards & Reverse Charge inwards supplies (Table 3.1)

At GSTR-3B – Monthly Return menu, click at *3.1 Tax on Outwards & Reverse Charge Inwards supplies* tab to get the Table 3.1 on-line instruction screen (F-3C). Click OK button to get input screen (F-3B). The input screen refers to physical Form Table 3.1 (F-3A)

Nature of Supplies	Total Taxable value	Integrated Tax	Central Tax	State/UT Tax	Cess
1	2	3	4	5	6
(a) Outward taxable supplies (other than zero rated, nil rated and exempted)					
(b) Outward taxable supplies (zero rated)					
(c) Other outward supplies (Nil rated, exempted)					
(d) Inward supplies (liable to reverse charge)					
(e) Non-GST outward supplies					

3.1 Details of Outward Supplies and inward supplies liable to reverse charge

F-3A: GSTR-3B Physical Form - Table 3.1 :
Outwards & Reverse Charge inwards supplies

In on-line form, cells for which data is not applicable are shaded and the cursor will not move into those cells to prevent wrong entries.

F-3B: Outwards & Reverse Charge supplies –
Table 3.1 – on-line entry screen

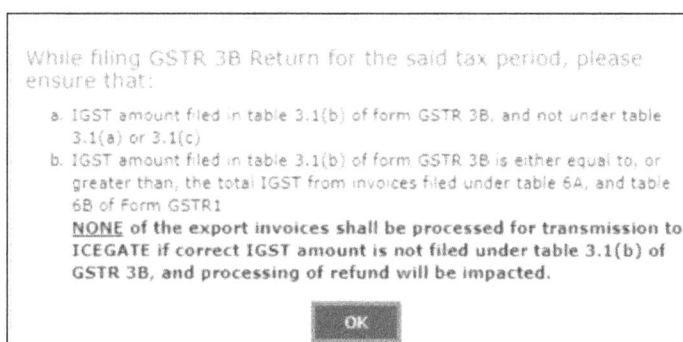

F-3C: Table 3.1 On-line filing instructions

Details of data to be filled up in Table 3.1

– **Outward Supplies**: Goods & Services sold / supplied or services within India (both inter-state and intra-state) :

– **Inward supplies liable to reverse charge**: Notified goods and services supplied for which the recipient pay the tax, instead of supplier

Value of Taxable Supplies : It is computed as : Value of invoices + value of Debit Notes – value of credit notes + value of advances received for which invoices have not been issued in the same month – value of advances adjusted against invoices.

a. Outward taxable value &taxes in respect of Inter-state and intra-state supplies (other than zero rated, nil rated and exempted) & amount of respective tax components &cess

b. Outward taxable supplies (zero rated) in respect of supplies outside India, supplies to notified SEZ within India & amount of respective tax components &cess

c. Other outward supplies of Nil rated and Exempted Items

d. Inward supplies (liable to reverse charge), where onus of payment of tax falls on the receiver & amount of respective tax components &cess

e. Non-GST outward supplies, covering Value of sales of goods which do not fall under the ambit of GST

The Tax components of IGST, CGST, SGST/UTGST and Cess are to be filled up in separate columns. For Intra Sate supplies, CGST & SGST/UTGST are applicable, For Inter State supplies, IGST is applicable. Cess is applicable only on few notified products (like Tobacco, Pan Masala etc).

Inter-State supplies made to unregistered persons, composition taxable persons and UIN holders (Table 3.2)

At GSTR-3B – Monthly Return menu, click at *3.2 Inter State Supplies* to get the input screen (F-4B), conforming to Physical form (F-4A).

F-4A: GSTR-3B Physical Form: Inter State supplies to Unregistered, Composition dealers & UIN holder – Table 3.2

Now enter data into the on-line Form in Table 3.2, separately in respect of *Inter State Supplies* to the following persons (already included in Table 3.1)

F-4B: GSTR-3B On-line Form: Inter State supplies to Unregistered, Composition dealers & UIN holder – Table 3.2 Menu

The Table has 3 components. Click on the + button (F-4B) to expand the relevant section and get the entry screen for the selected section, to enter data (F-4C).

F-4C: GSTR-3B On-line Form: Inter State supplies to Unregistered, Composition dealers & UIN holder – Table 3.2 – entry form sections

Click on the respective checkbox, enter the data (F-4C). At Place of supply, select the State form the drop down list of States. Enter the Taxable Value and the amount of IGST (no Cess Amount to be entered), in separate lines in respect of inter-state taxable supplies as per Table 3.2:

- **Supplies made to Unregistered Persons**: Taxable Supplies made to unregistered dealers and respective Tax components

- **Supplies made to Composition Taxable Persons**: Taxable Supplies made to Composition Dealers

- **Supplies made to UIN holders** : Taxable Supplies made to UIN holders

State wise outwards Taxable Inter State supplies value and IGST figures for each of the above sections, are to be entered. Click ADD button to add another record line for another State, in respective section.

Select the checkbox and click the *REMOVE* button to remove the data added. The system will accept only one entry for each place of supply. The details of tax paid on exports may not be entered here.

Having entered data, click CONFIRM button (F-5A)

ITC Details(Table 4)

At GSTR-3B – Monthly Return menu, click at *4 Eligible ITC* to get the input screen (F-5B), conforming to Physical Form (F-5A).

4. Eligible ITC				
Details	Integrated Tax	Central Tax	State/UT Tax	Cess
1	2	3	4	5
(A) ITC Available (whether in full or part)				
(1) Import of goods				
(2) Import of services				
(3) Inward supplies liable to reverse charge (other than 1 & 2 above)				
(4) Inward supplies from ISD				
(5) All other ITC				
(B) ITC Reversed				
(1) As per rules 42 & 43 of CGST Rules				
(2) Others				
(C) Net ITC Available (A) – (B)				
(D) Ineligible ITC				
(1) As per section 17(5)				
(2) Others				

F-5A: GSTR-3B Physical Form - Table 4 : Eligible ITC – Physical Form

Here enter the only the Tax Amount (not value of Inputs), under respective ITC claimed/ ITC reversed/ Ineligible ITC heads. Click CONFIRM

F-5B: GSTR-3B On-line Form: Eligible ITC – Table 4 – on line entry screen

A) ITC Available (whether in full or part)

1) **Import of goods**: IGST paid on goods imported and used only for business purposes

2) **Import of services**: IGST paid on import of services and used only for business purposes

3) **Inward supplies liable to reverse charge** (other than 1 & 2 above): For inward supply liable to reverse charge (onus of payment of tax falls on the receiver, tax paid will be provided as ITC in the subsequent month)

4) **Inward supplies from Input Service Distributor** (ISD) : Details of allocated input tax by input service distributor to respective unit.

5) **All other ITC**: Any other ITC as may be applicable (other than above). Figures for normal domestic inputs / services, would appear here (like B2B Purchases) etc.

B) ITC reversed (as per rules 42 & 43 of CGST Rules)

1) Total reversed amount for the period as per Rule 42 & 43

−   **Rules 42** : ITC in respect of inputs or input services, partly used for business the purposes and partly for other purposes, or for zero rated / exempted supplies. These rules have prescribed the formula for determination of input tax credit in such cases.

−   **Rule 43** : ITC eligible for Capital goods.

2) Any other reversed Amount

C) Net ITC Available (A) - (B)

Net ITC available for the tax period which is calculated as the difference of Total figures under (A) and (B), explained as above

D) Ineligible ITC :

1) ITC paid on following expenses / payment not available u/s 17(5):

o   Motor vehicles and conveyances (except where used for supply of specified services)

o   Services for food and beverages, outdoor catering, beauty treatment, cosmetic and plastic surgery (except where used for supply of specified services)

o   Membership of club, health and fitness center

o   Rent-a-cab services

o   Life insurance and health insurance (except obligatory under law or supplied as part of taxable composite or mixed supply)

o   Travel benefits to employees on vacation (like leave or home travel concession) o   Works contract services for construction of immovable property (other than plant and machinery)

o   Goods and services used for construction of immovable property on own account

o   Supplies on which tax paid under composition scheme

o   Goods and services received by non-resident person (except imports)

o   Goods lost, stolen, destroyed, written off or disposed of by way of gift or free samples

o   Goods and services used for personal consumption

2) Any other credit that may be ineligible

Exempt, Nil rated &Non GST Supplies Exempt, Nil rated & Non GST Supplies (Table 5)

At GSTR-3B – Monthly Return menu, click at *5* Exempt, Nil rated &Non GST Supplies Exempt, Nil rated & Non GST Supplies to get the input screen get Input Screen (F-6B) conforming to physical Form (F-6A)

5. Values of exempt, nil-rated and non-GST inward supplies		
Nature of supplies	Inter-State supplies	Intra-State supplies
1	2	3
From a supplier under composition scheme, Exempt and Nil rated supply		
Non GST supply		

F-6A:GSTR-3B Physical Form-Table 5:Exempt, Nil Rated & Non GST Inwards supply–Physical Form

Inward supplies from supplier under composition scheme, exempt and nil rated supply : Enter the following inward supplies (inter-state and intra-state separately):

–   Inward supply from a supplier under composition scheme

–   Inward supply of exempt Items / Services

–   Inward supply of Non-GST Items / Services

Dashboard Returns GSTR-3B Inward Supplies		◉ English
5. Values of exempt, nil-rated and non-GST inward supplies		
Nature of Supplies	Inter-State Supplies (₹)	Intra-State Supplies (₹)
From a supplier under composition scheme, Exempt and Nil rated supply	₹0.00	₹0.00
Non GST supply	₹0.00	₹0.00
	CANCEL	CONFIRM

F-6B: GSTR-3B on-line Form - Table 5 : Exempt,
Nil Rated & Non GST Inwards supply – on line Form

Interest & late Fee Payable (Table 5.1)

If Returns not filed / Payments not made in prescribed time, Interest & Late would have to be paid and accordingly. Otherwise figures for Interest & late fee would be left zero.

F-7A: GSTR-3B On-line Form - Table 5.1 : Interest & Late Fee Payable

At GSTR-3B – Monthly Return menu, click at *5*.1 Interest & late fee Payable to get the input screen (F-7A). The late fee would be system computed based on the number of days elapsed after the due date of filing. Late fee for the month includes previous month's late fee charged due to delay in filing of return, calculated as :

[Date of Filing –Due date of Filing)] * 25/day * per Act (CGST/SGST). Late fee is Rs. 10/- if no liability accrues during the month.

Click *CONFIRM* button.

Interest Liability: Click the check box of Interest Liability, if any, which is to be paid in cash in addition to Tax Liabilities for the month.

Saving Form GSTR-3B : Having entered data, at GSTR 3B Menu, click *SAVE GSTR3B* button to save data of GSTR-3B.

Preview Draft GSTR-3B : At bottom of GSTR 3B Menu, click *PREVIEW DRAFTGSTR3B* button and down load draft GSTR-3B form in PDF, in specified Folder. Open the Draft PDF and review each Table to ensure correctness.

Payment of Tax (Table 6.1)

At bottom of GSTR 3B Menu (F-2A), click *PROCEED TO PAYMENT* button to get Payment of Tax screen (F-8B), conforming to Physical Form (F-8A)

F-8A: GSTR-3B Physical Form - Table 6.1 : Payment of Tax – Physical Form

Tax liabilities as declared in the return along with the credits gets updated in the ledgers and reflected (auto populated) in the "Tax payable" column of the payment section. Credits get updated in the credit ledger and the updated balance is available and can be seen while hovering on the said headings of credit in the payment section. Provide the amount of credit to be utilized from the respective available credit heads to pay off the liabilities, so as the cash.

System auto-populates *Tax to be paid through ITC* fields with optimum utilization amounts based on provisions of the law relating to credit utilization, for your convenience (However, you may edit the ITC utilization). As you change ITC utilization, the cash to be paid will also get changed.

If available cash balance in Electronic cash ledger is not sufficient to offset the liabilities, additional cash required for paying liability is being reflected in the last column of the Table (Addition cash required). You may create challan for that amount directly by clicking on the *CREATE CHALLAN* button

F-8B: Payment of Tax – On line entry

Click the *MAKE PAYMENT / POST CREDIT TO LEDGER* button (F-8B) to pay off the liabilities or to claim credit in case of no liabilities. Now, you cannot make any changes to the Form GSTR-3B.

GST Portal will check the available Cash ledger balance. In case of insufficient balance, "You do not have sufficient balance in Electronic Cash Ledger. Do you want to Create challan?" pop-up message is displayed. Click *YES* button to get Create Challan screen (F-9A)

Liability Set Off Rules

Set Off rules are summarised below:

- **Primary Set Off : Initial set off should be made as follows:**

  o ITC of CGST will first set off the output tax liability of CGST.

  o ITCof SGST will first set off the output tax liability of SGST.

  o ITC of UTGST will first set off the output tax liability of UTGST.

  o ITC of IGST will first set off the output tax liability of IGST.

- **Balance Set off** : having made the primary set off as explained above, the balance, if any, would be set off as follows :

  o Balance ITC of CGST will be used to set off any output tax liability of IGST.

  o Balance ITC of SGST will be used to set off any output tax liability of IGST.

  o Balance ITC of IGST will be used to set off any output tax liability of CGST and further will be used to set off any output tax liability of SGST.

- CGST and SGST cannot set off each other.

Liability Set Off - Examples

Ex. Mr. X, a regular registered dealer (not falling under the composition scheme) has Tax liability against Sale, for a specified month -IGST : 34200, CGST: 9900, SGST: 9900

He has the following Input Tax Credit (ITC) against Purchase for the corresponding month :

IGST: 18000, CGST: 15600, SGST: 15600

The Tax Adjustments and Net Tax Liability payable computed as per rules are shown below

Tax Type	Output Tax Liability	Input Tax Credit (IGST)	Input Tax Credit (CGST)	Input Tax Credit (SGST)	Balance Payable by Cash
IGST	34200	(18000)	(5700) (15600-9900)	(5700) (15600-9900	4800 [34200 – (18000+5700+5700)]
CGST	9900		(9900)		-
SGST	9900			(9900)	-

Ex. Ms. Y, a regular registered dealer (not falling under the composition scheme) has Tax liability against Sale, for a specified month – IGST : 10000, CGST : 24000, SGST : 24000

She has following input tax credit against Purchase for the corresponding month – IGST : 36000, CGST : 8000, SGST : 8000

The Tax Adjustments and Net Tax Liability payable computed as per rules are shown below

Tax Type	Output Tax Liability	Input Tax Credit (IGST)	Input Tax Credit (CGST)	Input Tax Credit (SGST)	Balance Payable by Cash
IGST	10000	(10000)			-
CGST	24000	(16000)	(8000)		-
SGST	24000	(10000) [(36000-(10000+16000)]		(8000)	6000

Challan Entry

In the Challan Entry Form (F-9A) *Total Challan Amount* and *Total Challan Amount* (In Words) are auto-populated with total amount of payment to be made. You cannot edit the amount.

F-9A: Challan Entry screen

Select the *Payment Modes* (E-Payment/ Over the Counter/ NEFT/RTGS).Click the *GENERATE CHALLAN* button (F-9A).The Challan is generated.

– **Payment by Net Banking:** You get the Net Banking page of the selected Bank. The payment amount is shown at the Bank's website (to change the amount, abort the transaction and create a new challan). On successful payment, you will be re-directed to the GST Portal displaying the transaction status.

– **Over the Counter Payment:** Take a print out of the *Challan* and visit the selected Bank. Pay using *Cash/ Cheque/ Demand Draft* within the Challan's validity period. Status of the payment will be updated on the GST Portal after confirmation from the Bank.

– **Payment by NEFT/ RTGS:** Take a print out of the *Challan* and visit the selected Bank. Mandate form will be generated simultaneously. Pay using Cheque through your account with the selected Bank/ Branch. You can also pay using the account debit facility. The transaction will be processed by the Bank and RBI shall confirm after a few hours. Status of the payment will be updated on the GST Portal after confirmation from the Bank.

After payment, a *warning message* is displayed. Click Yes (F-9B) to proceed

Warning

WARNING: You are about to agree to credit claim and utilization, as indicated. Relevant amounts will be deducted from Electronic Cash and Credit ledgers and accordingly liability will be reduced. Also, amount of credit claimed will be credited to Electronic Credit ledger. Once these entries are made, these can NOT be reversed. Are you sure you want to continue?

NO   YES

F-9B: Tax Payment Warning Message

At payment of Tax screen (F-8B), click PROCEED TO FILE button to get Filing of Tax screen (F-9C)

F-9C: GSTR-3B Filing

At *Filing of Tax screen* (F-9C), select the checkbox for declaration. At *Authorised Signatory* drop-down list, select the authorized signatory. Click the *FILE GSTR-3B WITH DSC* or *FILE GSTR-3B WITHEVC* button, as applicable. At next Warning message, click PROCEED button to file the GSTR-3B Return. On successful filing, a success message with filing Reference details is displayed (F-9D). The status of GSTR-3B is changed to *Filed*. A message is also sent to registered e-mail ID and mobile number.

Filing Successful

GSTR-3B of GSTIN **97AJIPA1572E7Z8** for the month **December - 2017** has been successfully filed on **12/02/2018 at 11:38**.
The Acknowledgment Reference Number: is **AA971217000001X**.
The GSTR-3B can be viewed on your Dashboard Login=>Taxpayer Dashboard=>Returns=>View e-filed return.
This message is sent to your registered Email ID and Mobile Number.

OK

F-9D: GSTR-3B Filing Confirmation

F-9E: GSTR-3B Filed Return Download

Click *Download Filed GSTR-3B*button (F-9E) to download Final Return (Watermarked PDF). Now you may also view the filed GSTR-3 Return from Dashboard (refer F-9D).

Filing GSTR-3B NIL Return

GSTR-3B must be filed, even if there is no transaction for any Return period.

At the GSTR 3B Questionnaires as discussed earlier (F-1C), set Yes at the option *Do you want to file NIL Return* (F-10A). Consequently, you get *Filing of Tax* page directly (F-9C). Click *PREVIEW DRAFT GSTR-3B* to view and download the Draft NIL Return (with Zero values) in PDF (watermarked DRAFT)

F-10A: GSTR 3B NIL Return Filing option

As no payment is involved, Table 6.1 will not appear. Now set the checkbox and file the Return as explained (F-9E)

Changes made in GSTR-3B Form

The salient points of changes announced in GSTR-3B, as per GSTN Council meeting dt 21Feb 2018, are listed below :

– **Payment of tax :** Earlier, a taxpayer was required to submit the return to ascertain Tax Liability amount. Once the return was submitted, no changes were allowed.

   Now, the entire details – current balance of input tax credit i.e. ITC, current balance of cash registers, tax head wise liability, suggested best way to utilise ITC and the amount of tax liability to be paid in cash or credit – will be displayed in a single table view, before the return is submitted. Thus it will be easier for taxpayers to keep track of ITC and compute pending tax liability.

– **Generation of challan :** Earlier, a taxpayer had to manually fill in the input tax credit utilization amount, as well as the amount to be paid in cash, and then generate the challan.

   The new revised GSTR 3B form now provides option to edit ITC amount to be utilized (not to consider auto-generated and suggested credit utilisation amount). On changing the ITC utilization, the amount required to be paid gets automatically changed. So, the tax payment challan can now be auto-generated, after offsetting the input tax credit available in the credit ledger. So, chances of error in entry of Tax Amount under proper head, is eliminated.

– **Facility for downloading draft return :** Now the draft return at any stage of the return filing process may be downloaded, enabling tax payer to verify the saved details in offline mode.

– **Tax amount auto-filled :** The tax payer needs to fill in either the CGST amount or the SGST/UTGST amount, other amounts would accordingly be computed and auto-populated.

The changes indicate that GSTR 3B returns are likely to stay for longer time, till GST Council works out simplified GST return filing process.

GSTR-4 Composition Dealer Return

A dealer registered under composition scheme of GST is required to furnish GSTR-4 Quarterly Return. GSTR 4 is a consolidated form of purchases and supplies. filed in the same form

GSTR-4 Return cannot be revised after filing on the GSTN Portal. Any mistake in the return can be revised in the next quarter return. GSTR-4 cannot be filed unless the GSTR-4 due for previous month is filed.

Initially, GSTN -4 can be filed off-line, till on-line entry option is provided. GSTN offers off line tool. You can enter the data in Excel Sheet in the format provided by GSTN and then upload the data in GST portal.

Download Offline Tool

At GSTBN portal dashboard, click *Downloads > offline Tools> GSTR offline tool.* A zip file GSTR-4_offline_ utility would be downloaded in specified (or default folder). Extract the zip file to get 4 files (F-1B), GSTR_4_offline utility.xls (we explain here GSTR_4_offline utility_v2.2.xls), the Excel sheet in which GSTR-4 Return data would be entered and 3 files (one PDF and two Text files) related to GSTR-4. GSTN regularly updates the Utility Files. So, you must use the latest one otherwise you may encounter error during data work.

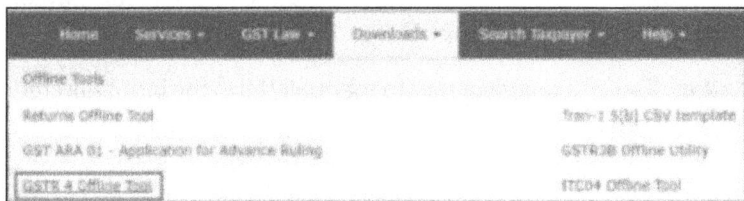

F-1A : GSTR-4 Offline tool download

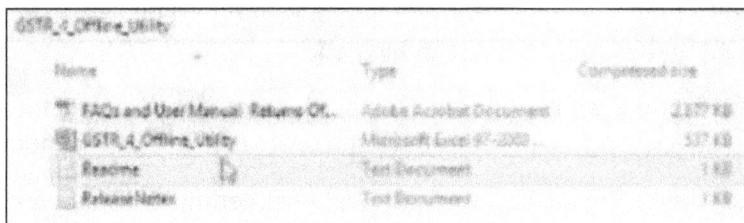

F-1B: GSTR-4 offline tool files

Open the Excel File. In the Excel File, Click *Enable Content* at the top, to enter / modify data in the Excel file (enabling the Macros)

Prepare GSTR4 Return Tool

Preparation of GSTR4 Return involves following steps

– Enter details in the GSTR4 worksheet of GSTR4 Return Tool.

– Validate the details entered using 'Validate Sheet' button.

– Generate JSON (.json) file using 'Generate JSON File to upload'.

– Upload the generated JSON on GST Portal. Preview the details uploaded, submit, offset liability and File return on the GST Portal.

First click the README Tab and read all the instructions to fill up each section in the worksheet.

F-1C: Instruction for Data entry in Excel Sheet

Data entry in Excel Sheet

Click on the excel sheet file to open and enter the data in the respective cells (F-2A). GST department has for the time being, waived off certain sections of the return (e.g 4A, 5A, 5C, 7, 8(ii) etc) for Q2 / Q3 of FY 17-18. So, these tab pages are not shown in the Excel Sheet currently being provided by GSTN. However, all sections would have to be filled up for later period.

F-2A : GSTR-4 Section wise Summary

Click on the respective Tab to add details, as explained for each sheet.

Error Trapping

After data entry of each row or after entry of a Tab, you may click *Validate Sheet* button (F-2A/F-3A). Any apparent detectable errors (inconsistent data), violating the data rules, is entered, error message would displayed (F-3B), and the cell containing wrong data would and be shown as red.

– **Sheet Validation Error** : Errors of data found in any cell in the specific sheet would be reported in in the respective row Sheet Validation Error column (F-3A)

– **GST Portal Validation Error** : Errors in respect inconsistent data having considered data of all the Tabs. Such errors are shown only after entry in individual Tabs

In case of any error reported, check the data and rectify the errors. On validation after ectification, the error free message would be displayed (F-3C)

F-3A: Error trapping

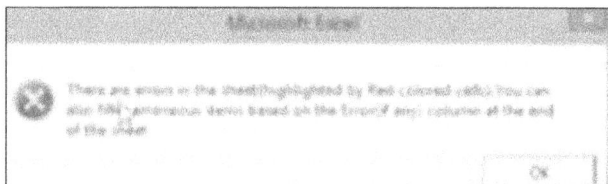

F-3B : Error Message

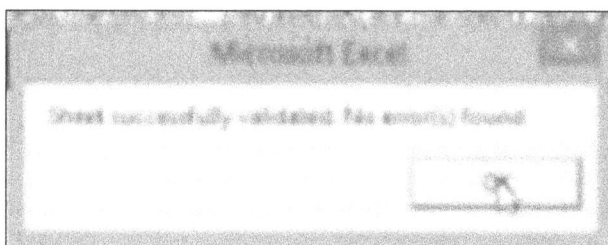

F-3C : Error-free entry Message

Now we describe the process of data entry in respective tab for each section of the GSTR-4 Return

General Info

Click on Home Tab to get 3 cells GSTIN in the main sheet (F-4A), to enter i) GSTIN, ii) Financial Year (like 2017) and iii) Period (like July-Sep, to be selected from drop down).

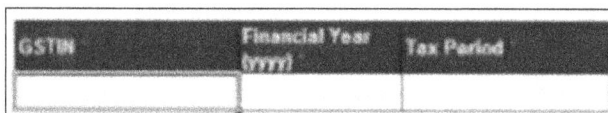

F-4A: General Info (Home Tab)

Inward Supplies received from Registered Supplier attracting Reverse Charge (Table 4A & 4B (B2B))

At GSTR-4 Section wise Summary (F-2A), click *Summary of 4A &B(B2B)* Tab to get the worksheet (F-5B). Read the instructions to know about data to be entered in respective cell (F-5A). Enter the details of goods & Services received from Registered Supplier attracting Reverse Charge (like services of registered GTA / Advocate etc) in respective cells (F-5A).

GSTIN of Supplier	Enter the GSTIN of the supplier. E.g. 05AEJPP8087R1ZF. Please check that the registration is active on the date of the invoice from GST portal
Invoice Number	Enter the invoice number of invoices issued by registered supplier. Ensure that the format is alpha-numeric with allowed special characters of slash(/) and dash(-). The total number of characters should not be more than 16.
Invoice date (dd-mm-yyyy)	Enter date of invoice in DD-MM-YYYY. E.g. 24-07-2017. The date should not be earlier than 01-07-2017 or registration as composition dealer and later than last date of selected Tax period or the Opting-out of composition whichever is earlier.
Invoice Value	Enter the total value indicated in the invoice of the received goods or services- with 2 decimal Digits.
Place Of Supply	Select the code of the state from drop down list for the place of supply.
Reverse Charge	Select 'Yes' for supplies attracting reverse charge and 'No' for inward supplies other than reverse charge.
Invoice Type	Select invoice type as Regular
Rate	Select the combined (State tax + Central tax) or the integrated tax, as applicable
Taxable Value	Enter the taxable value of the received goods or services for each rate line item - with 2 decimal Digits. The taxable value has to be computed as per GST valuation provisions.
Integrated Tax	It is auto calculated based on the Place of Supply, Rate and Taxable value
Central Tax	It is auto calculated based on the Place of Supply, Rate and Taxable value
State/UT Tax	It is auto calculated based on the Place of Supply, Rate and Taxable value
Cess	Enter the total Cess amount paid

F-5A: 4A &B(B2B) : Inward Supply received from Registered Supplier attracting Reverse Charge

In this sheet, you will select *Yes* at *Reverse Charge* column. At *Invoice Type*, select *Regular* (as this sheet contain data of supplies from Registered Dealer only). The Tax (CGST, SGST, IGST) would be auto computed from the Rate and Taxable value (shaded Blue), and would be shown in proper Tax column (you cannot enter / edit these figures). Enter Cess , if any.

F-5B: Inward Supply received from Registered Supplier attracting Reverse Charge

Note : Inward supplies from Registered Dealer (other than Reverse Charge) is not to be filled up for QE Jul-Sep & QE Oct-Dec (as per notification). From Q4 (Jan Mar 2018), these will be entered in Table 4A(B2B), which would be made available at that time.

Amendment of Inward Supplies received from a Registered supplier (attracting Reverse Charge) 5A(B2BA)

At GSTR-4 Section wise Summary (F-2A), click *Summary of 5A(B2BA)* Tab and enter the details of *Amendment of Inward Supplies received from a Registered supplier (attracting Reverse Charge)*

Import of Services (F-6D).

Original GSTIN of Supplier *	Enter the GSTIN of the supplier for which invoice is issued in previous quarter. E.g. 05AEJPP9087R1ZF. Please check
Original Invoice Number *	Enter the Invoice number of invoices issued by registered supplier which taxpayer wants to revise. Ensure that the format is alpha-numeric with allowed special characters of slash(/) and dash(-) .The total number of characters should
Original Invoice date (dd-mm-yyyy) *	Enter date of invoice in DD-MM-YYYY. E.g. 24-07-2017. The date should not be earlier than 01-07-2017 or registration as composition dealer and later than last date of selected Tax period or the Opting-out of composition whichever is earlier
Invoice Number *	Enter the Invoice number of invoices issued by registered supplier. Ensure that the format is alpha-numeric with
Invoice date(dd-mm-yyyy) *	Enter date of invoice in DD-MM-YYYY. E.g. 24-07-2017. The date should not be earlier than 01-07-2017 or registration
Invoice Value *	Enter the total value indicated in the invoice. of the received goods or services- with 2 decimal Digits.
Place Of Supply *	Select the code of the state from drop down list for the place of supply.
Reverse Charge *	Select Yes for supplies attracting reverse charge and No for inward supplies other than reverse charge.
Invoice Type *	Select invoice type as Regular.
Rate *	Select the combined (State tax + Central tax) or the integrated tax, as applicable.
Taxable Value *	Enter the taxable value of the received goods or services for each rate line item - with 2 decimal Digits. The taxable
Integrated Tax *	It is auto calculated based on the Place of Supply , Rate and Taxable value
Central Tax *	It is auto calculated based on the Place of Supply , Rate and Taxable value
State/UT Tax *	It is auto calculated based on the Place of Supply , Rate and Taxable value.
Cess	Enter the total Cess amount paid.

F-6C: Amendment of Inward Supplies received from a Registered supplier (attracting Reverse Charge) – Worksheet Format

Read the instructions (F-6C) to know about data to be entered in respective cell (F-6D).

F-6D: Amendment of Inward Supplies received from a Registered supplier (attracting Reverse Charge) Worksheet

Inward Supply received from Un-registered Supplier -Table 4C (B2BUR)

At GSTR-4 Section wise Summary (F-2A), click *Summary of 4C(B2BUR)* Tab and enter the details of Inward supply (self invoice) of Goods & Services received from Un-registered suppliers (F-6F), on which Reverse Charge is applicable.

F-6E: Inward supply of Goods & Services received from Un-registered suppliers – Worksheet Format

Read the instructions (F-6D) to know about data to be entered in respective cell (F-6E). In this sheet, there is no column for GSTIN of the supplier (as the supplier is unregistered)

F-6F: Inward supply of Goods & Services received from Un-registered suppliers Worksheet

Here enter the details of Invoice amount of Taxable supplies (exclude exempted supplies) of Rs 5000 or above (in one day) purchased from Unregistered Dealers, during 1st July 17 to 12 October 17, attracting Reverse Charge (From 13th October, it is withdrawn). At Supply Type, select from drop down list. So, in Q2 Return (Jul – Sep), you have to enter purchases of Rs 5000 and above. In Q3 Return (Oct - Dec), you have to enter purchases of Rs 5000 and above for the period upto 12th Oct 17.

Reverse Charges u/s 9(3) is still applicable (only Reverse Charge us/ 9(4) is waived from 13.10.17). So, details of specified services like services from Advocate, sponsorship, are to be reported here and tax be paid by the recipient.

At Invoice number & date, you should give the reference of self-invoice created by you (you may create a composite invoice in respect of small purchases) for purchases from unregistered supplier.

Amendment of Inward Supplies Received from Unregistered Supplier (5A(B2BURA)

At GSTR-4 Section wise Summary (F-2A), click *Summary of (5AB2BURA)* Tab and enter the details of Amendments of Inward Supplies Received from Unregistered Supplier (F-6G)

6G: Amendments of Inward Supplies Received from Unregistered Supplier – Worksheet Format

Read the instructions (F-6E) to know about data to be entered in respective cell (F-6F).

6H: Amendments of Inward Supplies Received from Unregistered Supplier – Worksheet

Import of Services (Table 4D)

At GSTR-4 Section wise Summary (F-2A), click *Summary of 4D(IMPS)* Tab and enter the details of *Import of Services* (F-7B). Read the instructions (F-7A) to know about data to be entered in respective cell (F-7B).

F-7A:Import of Services – Worksheet Format

Integrated Tax (IGST) will apply. Place of supply is the place (State) where the Service is received.

F-7B:Import of Services

Amendment of Import of Services -Table 5A(IMPSA)

At GSTR-4 Section wise Summary (F-2A), click *Summary of 5A(IMPSA)* Tab and enter the details of *Amendments ofImport of Services* (F-7D).

F-7C: Amendment of Import of Services- Worksheet Format

Read the instructions (F-7C) to know about data to be entered in respective cell (F-7D).

F-7D: Amendment of Import of Services- Worksheet

Debit Note / Credit Note from Registered Supplier (Table 5B)

At GSTR-4 Section wise Summary (F-2A), click *Summary of5B(CDNR)* Tab to enter Credit Note / Debit Note issued by Registered Supplier.

F-8A: Credit Note / Debit Note issued by Registered Supplier- Worksheet Format

Read the instructions (F-8A) to know about data to be entered in respective cell (F-8B).

F-8B: Credit Note / Debit Note issued by Registered Supplier- Worksheet

At Invoice /Payment voucher Number, enter the reference of original purchase against which the Debit / Credit Note is issued. At the next column, Invoice /Payment voucher date, entre the date of Original Voucher. At *Pre GST*, select *Yes*, If the original supply relates to Pre GST period (earlier than 1st July 2017), else select *No*. At Document Type, select Debit note / Credit Note from the drop down list, as the case may be. At Reason, select the appropriate Reason from drop down list (F-8C). At Supply Type select Intra State / Inter State from drop down list, as the case may be. At *Reverse Charge* column, select *Yes* from drop down list (Debit / Credit Notes related to inward supplies not attracting Reverse charges are not to be included here).

Amendment of Debit Note / Credit Note from Registered Supplier - Table 5C(CDNRA)

At GSTR-4 Section wise Summary (F-2A), click *Summary of5C(CDNR)* Tab to enter Credit Note / Debit Note issued by Registered Supplier (F-8D).

F-8C: Amendment of Credit Note / Debit Note issued by Registered Supplier -Worksheet Format

Read the instructions (F-8C) to know about data to be entered in respective cell (F-8D).

F-8D: Amendment of Credit Note / Debit Note issued by Registered Supplier -Worksheet Format

Debit Note / Credit Note from Un-registered Supplier -Table 5B(CDNUR)

At GSTR-4 Section wise Summary (F-2A), click *Summary of 5B(CDNUR)* Tab to enter Credit Note / Debit Note issued by Un-registered Supplier (F-9B).

F-9A: Credit Note / Debit Note issued by Unregistered
Supplier – Worksheet Format

Read the instructions (F-9A) to know about data to be entered in respective cell (F-9B). In this sheet, there is no column for GSTIN of the supplier (as the supplier is unregistered)

F-9B: Credit Note / Debit Note issued by Unregistered Supplier Worksheet

At Inward Supply Type, select B2BUR (for Notes issued by Unregistered Supplier), or IMPS (for overseas supplier)

Amendment of Debit Note / Credit Note from Un-registered Supplier -Table 5C(CDNURA)

At GSTR-4 Section wise Summary (F-2A), click *Summary of 5C(CDNURA)* Tab to enter Amendments of Credit Note / Debit Note issued by Un-registered Supplier (F-9C).

F-9C: Amendment of Debit Note / Credit Note from Un-registered Supplier - Worksheet Format

Read the instructions (F-9A) to know about data to be entered in respective cell (F-9B). In this sheet, there is no column for GSTIN of the supplier (as the supplier is unregistered)

F-9D: Amendment of Debit Note / Credit Note from Un-registered Supplier - Worksheet

Tax on Outward Supplies – Net of Advance & Goods Returned -Table 6(TXOS)

At GSTR-4 Section wise Summary (F-2A), Click *Summary of 6(TXOS)* Tab to enter details of Tax on Outward Supplies. Read the instructions (F-10A) to know about data to be entered in respective cell (F-10B).

Rate of Tax *	Select the Rate of Tax as per the Business Type
Turnover *	Declare the total amount of outward supplies made(Net of advance and goods returned) till 2 decimal places
Central Tax *	It is auto calculated based on the Rate of Tax and Turnover
State/UT Tax *	It is auto calculated based on the Rate of Tax and Turnover

F-10A: Tax on Outward Supplies – Worksheet Format

Here enter the details of Net Sales (net of Advance & Goods Returned), in respect of applicable Tax Rate.

You should compute Turnover figures as: Sales + Advances Received – Goods Returned. The Tax would be computed at the specified Rate and the 50% amount would posted in CGST & SGST / UTGST column. Since Composition dealers are allowed to sell only within State, only CGST and SGST would be applicable (IGST column is not shown).

	6. Tax on outward supplies made
Go Home	**(Net of advance and goods returned)**
	Please Note : Fields marked with * (red asterisk) are mandatory fields

Rate of Tax *	Turnover *	Central Tax *	State/UT Tax *
1.00			
2.00			
5.00			

F-10B: Tax on Outward Supplies

Amendment of Tax on Outward Supplies – Net of Advance & Goods Returned -Table 7(TXOSA)

At GSTR-4 Section wise Summary (F-2A), Click *Summary of 7(TXOS)* Tab to enter details of *Amendments of Tax on Outward Supplies (F-10D)*.

Original Tax Period *	Select the tax period for which amendment needs to be made
Financial Year *	Select the financial year
Original Rate of Tax *	Select the Rate of Tax as per the Business Type which needs to be revised
Turnover *	Declare the total amount of outward supplies made(Net of advance and goods returned) till 2 decimal places
Central Tax *	It is auto calculated based on the Rate of Tax and Turnover
State/UT Tax *	It is auto calculated based on the Rate of Tax and Turnover

F-10C: Amendment of Tax on Outward Supplies – Worksheet Format

Read the instructions (F-10A) to know about data to be entered in respective cell (F-10B).

Original Tax Period*	Financial Year*	Original Rate of Tax*	Turnover*	Central Tax*	State/UT Tax*
	▾	1.00			
		2.00			
		5.00			

7. Amendment of Tax on outward supplies (Net of advance and goods returned)
*Please Note : Fields marked with * (red asterisk) are mandatory fields*

F-10D: Amendment of Tax on Outward Supplies – Worksheet

Advance Amount paid on Reverse Charge supplies - Table 8A(AT)

At GSTR-4 Section wise Summary (F-2A), click *Summary of 8A(AT)* Tab to enter details of Advance paid to unregistered supplier for Purchases attracting Reverse Charge. Payment other advances not be entered here.

Place of supply *	Select the code of the state from drop down list for the place of supply.
Supply Type *	Declare the type of supply as inter or intra state.
Rate *	Enter the combined (State tax + Central tax) or the integrated tax rate.
Gross Advance Paid *	Enter the amount of advance received excluding the tax portion.
Integrated Tax *	It is auto calculated based on the Supply Type, Rate and Gross Advance Paid
Central Tax *	It is auto calculated based on the Supply Type, Rate and Gross Advance Paid
State/ UT Tax *	It is auto calculated based on the Supply Type, Rate and Gross Advance Paid
Cess	Enter the total Cess amount paid.

F-11A : Advance paid on Reverse Charge supplies – Worksheet Format

Read the instructions (F-11A) to know about data to be entered in respective cell (F-11B).

Place of supply	Supply Type	Rate	Gross Advance Paid	Integrated Tax	Central Tax	State/ UT Tax *	Cess

8A. Advance amount paid for reverse charge supplies in the tax period
*Please Note : Fields marked with * (red asterisk) are mandatory fields and need to be filled up*

F-11B : Advance paid on Reverse Charge supplies

Amendment of Advance Amount paid on Reverse Charge supplies - Table 8AII(ATA)

At GSTR-4 Section wise Summary (F-2A), click *Summary of 8AII(ATA)* Tab to enter details of *Amendment of Advance paid to unregistered supplier for Purchases attracting Reverse Charge*(F-11D). Paymentsother advances not be entered here.

Original Tax Period*	Select the tax period for which amendment needs to be made.
Financial Year*	Select the financial year.
Original Place of supply *	Select the code of the state from drop down list for the place of supply.
Original Supply Type *	Declare the type of supply as inter or intra state.
Rate *	Enter the combined (State tax + Central tax) or the integrated tax rate.
Gross Advance Paid *	Enter the amount of advance received excluding the tax portion.
Integrated Tax *	It is auto calculated based on the Supply Type, Rate and Gross Advance Paid
Central Tax *	It is auto calculated based on the Supply Type, Rate and Gross Advance Paid
State/ UT Tax *	It is auto calculated based on the Supply Type, Rate and Gross Advance Paid
Cess	Enter the total Cess amount paid.

F-11C : Amendment of Advance paid on Reverse Charge supplies – Worksheet Format

Original Tax Period	Financial Year	Original Place of supply	Original Supply Type	State	Gross Advance Paid	Integrated Tax	Central Tax	State/ UT Tax *	Cess

8A. Amendment of Advance amount paid for reverse charge supplies in the tax period
*Please Note : Fields marked with * (red asterisk) are mandatory fields and need to be filled up*

F-11D : Amendment of Advance paid on Reverse Charge supplies – Worksheet

Advance paid in earlier period, Invoice received in current period (Table 8B)

Click 8B(ATADJ) Tab for adjustment of *Advance paid in earlier period but Invoice received in current period* (F-12B).

Place of supply *	Select the code of the state from drop down list for the place of supply
Supply Type *	Declare the type of supply as inter or intra state
Rate *	Enter the combined (State tax + Central tax) or the integrated tax rate
Gross Advance Paid *	Enter the amount of advance received excluding the tax portion
Integrated Tax *	It is auto calculated based on the Supply Type, Rate and Gross Advance Paid
Central Tax *	It is auto calculated based on the Supply Type, Rate and Gross Advance Paid
State/ UT Tax *	It is auto calculated based on the Supply Type, Rate and Gross Advance Paid
Cess	Enter the total Cess amount paid

F-12A : Adjustment of Advance paid in earlier period, on Invoice received in current period – Worksheet Format

ead the instructions (F-12A) to know about data to be entered in respective cell (F-12B).

F-12B : Adjustment ofAdvance paid in earlier period, on Invoice received in current period - Worksheet

Since tax on advance paid has already been paid in earlier period, as recorded in Table 8A (AT) and 8AII(ATA) of earlier period, now enter the details of Invoice received in respect of advance paid earlier, to adjust the tax already paid in earlier period.

At *Gross Amount Paid*, enter the Advance paid in earlier period, for which Invoice is received in current period.

Amendment of Advance paid in earlier period, Invoice received in current period (Table 8B-II(ATADJ)

Click 8B-II(ATADJ) Tab for adjustment of Amendment of *Advance paid in earlier period but Invoice received in current period* (F-12D).

Original Tax Period*	Select the tax period for which amendment needs to be made
Financial Year *	Select the financial year
Original Place of supply *	Select the code of the state from drop down list for the place of supply
Original Supply Type *	Declare the type of supply as inter or intra state
Rate *	Enter the combined (State tax + Central tax) or the integrated tax rate
Gross Advance Paid *	Enter the amount of advance received excluding the tax portion
Integrated Tax *	It is auto calculated based on the Supply Type, Rate and Gross Advance Paid
Central Tax *	It is auto calculated based on the Supply Type, Rate and Gross Advance Paid
State/ UT Tax *	It is auto calculated based on the Supply Type, Rate and Gross Advance Paid
Cess	Enter the total Cess amount paid

F-12C : Amendment of Adjustment of Advance paid in earlier period,
on Invoice received in current period – Worksheet Format

Read the instructions (F-12C) to know about data to be entered in respective cell (F-12D).

F-12D : Amendment of Adjustment of Advance paid in earlier period, on Invoice received in current period – Worksheet

Data Validation

Having entered data in the worksheet, click the *Validate Sheet* button (F-13A) to validate the GSTR4 worksheet. Each sheet needs to be validated separately. Errors found on validation are reported, as explained earlier.

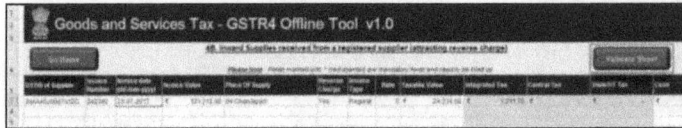

F-13A : Data validation

Summary

Having validated data and corrected errors, at Home Tab, click the button *Get Summary* button (F-2A), to view the summary in one sheet. You can verify the data form your records.

JSON file Generation

Upon successful validation, at Home page (F-14A), Click *Generate JSON File to upload* button to generate JSON file for upload on GST Portal. JSON would be generated only if the worksheet has been successfully validated. Click OK button.

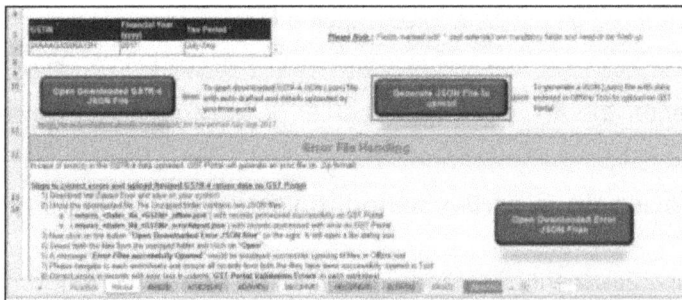

F-14A : GSTR-4 JSON File Generation

A confirmation message *The data in the sheets are successfully captured in the JSON file* is displayed. Click the OK button and save this file

Uploading the JSON file in GSTN Portal

Having saved the JSON file, at GSTN portalDashboard, click on the *Return Dashboard* button to get Return Dashboard screen (F-15A).

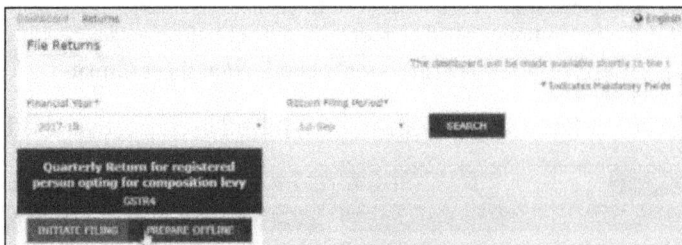

F-15A: File Return dashboard

JSON File Selection : At File Return Dash board screen (F-15A), click *Prepare Offline* button to get Offline GSTR-4 Upload screen (F-15B).

At Upload screen (F-15B) *Choose file* button and select the earlier saved JSON file from the respective location, to upload the JSON file.

F-15B : Offline GSTR-4 Upload screen

On JSON file upload, the details of JSON file uploaded will be displayed in the Upload History Table (F-15C). The system would validate the data (which would take about 15 minutes)

F-15C: JSON file upload details

Error File Generation: In case of any error encountered, *Error Occurred* message would be displayed. Click *Generate Error Report*(F-15C) button (it takes some time to Generate) and download the Generated Error Report (zip Format), at specified folder in your computer. Unzip the zip Folder to get 2 JSON files.

Under the 2nd error file, click Open Downloaded error JSON Files button. Select both error files and click OK.

Error Rectification : Go through the error shown under the column GST Portal Validation Errors, in each sheet Rectify all the errors. reported and repeat the process to get correct file uploaded.

You may upload JSON multiple times on GST portal till submission. However, earlier uploaded data would be overwritten. Tables and Preview would reflect only the last uploaded data.

After each sheet successfully validated, click the *Get Summary* button to update the summary on Home tab. Now follow the steps to Upload the JSON file on GSTN Poral.

You may download the records successfully processed on GST portal anytime through 'Returns Dashboard>Financial Year>Return Period>GSTR4Prepare Offline> Download' option.

Submission of GSTR4

At Dashboard screen (F-15A), click on the button *Initiate Filing* button (under Quarterly return for registered person opting for Composition levy GSTR-4) to get GSTR-4 Return screen (F-15D). For the first Return Period (July to Sep), at *Aggregate Turnover in the preceding Financial Year*, enter the Turnover of the previous year and at *Aggregate Turnover April – June 2107*, enter the turnover of the first quarter Apr-June 2017. Click Save button to save the data.

F-15D: GSTR-4 Return filing

F-15E : GSTR-4 Return filing Message

Click the check box. Click *Preview* button to view the Report and verify the data before filing.

Click *Submit* button. A message appears to check as you cannot change the Return after filing (F-15E). The Status changes to SUBMITTED. Tax Liability would be reflected in Table 10, to make payment of Tax accordingly

Tax Payment

At Dashboard, click the Tab *10, 11 - Tax Interest, Late fee* option to get the Tax Payment screen (F-16A), where the Tax liability is reflected.

F-16A : Tax Payment Menu

Tax details

On clicking the Tab 10, 11 - Tax Interest, Late fee payable & paid (F-16A), you get Tax Details screen showing the computed Tax figures (F-17A).

Click CASH LEDGER BALANCE button to check available balance in cash Ledger.

Click the UTILIZE CASH button to utilize cash ledger balance and adjust with the tax, interest and late fee.

F-17A: Tax Details entry screen

Challan Creation

If there is not sufficient Cash Balance you have to create Challan. At Dashboard, select *Services>Payment > Create Challan* option (F-18A) to get Payment Details screen (F-18B)

F-18A: Challan Creation option

Payment Details

Payment Details screen, the figures for Tax, Interest, Late Fee etc are displayed. Select the mode of payment and then click Generate Challan. Depending on mode of you, you get entry screen for entry of Payment details.

Enter the details and complete the payment process. A message *Your Payment is successfully completed* appears showing the amount and transaction ID. You may view the *Receipt* and view *Cash Ledger*.

GSTR-4 Return Filing

At Tax Payment screen (F-16A), click *File Return* button to get Return Filing screen (F-19A)

Enter the GSTIN, Financial Year & Return Filing Period. Click the check box, select the authorised signatory from the drop down list and click on the respective FILE WITH DSC / FILE WITH EVC button, as applicable in your case (and complete the verification process).

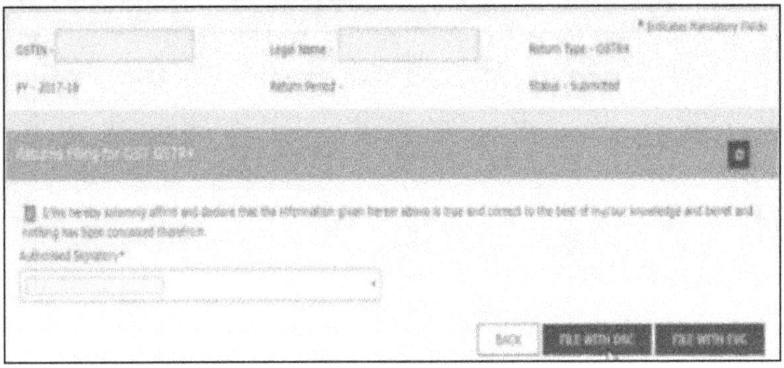

F-19A: Return Filing

A confirmation message of completion of filing with acknowledgment reference Number (ARN) is displayed (F-19B)

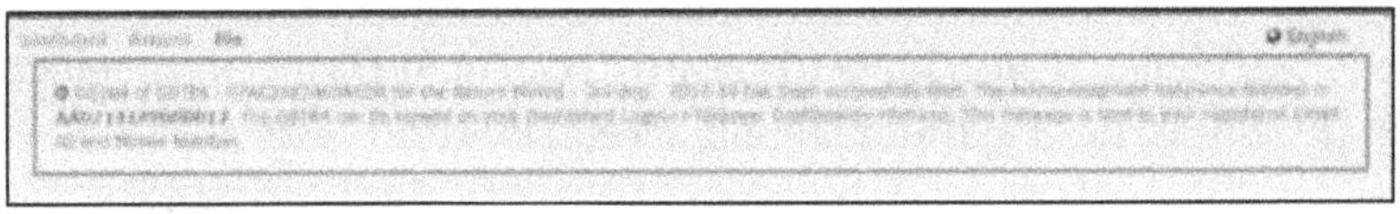

GSTR-4 Filing confirmation

In view of difficulties of small traders in submission of GSTR-4, the late fines are substantially reduced for GSTR-4 filing. As per Latest Notification No. 73/2017 late fees for GSTR-4 filing has been reduced to Rs. 50 per day, &late fees for NIL return reduced to Rs. 20 per day of delay of default.

GSTR-5 Non Resident Return Physical Form

Non-resident Taxable person

Any person who occasionally undertakes transactions involving supply of goods or services, as principal or agent or in any other capacity, but has no fixed place of business or residence in India.

Registration of Non-Resident Person

Every Non Resident individual or company, involved in (whether one-time transaction or frequent) taxable transactions, will have to obtain a registration under GST.

Such person must apply at at least five days prior to the commencement of business. Any person who makes a supply from the territorial waters of India shall obtain registration in the coastal state (or Union territory) where the nearest point of the appropriate baseline is located. For example, if highhigh-sea sale is carried out near the shore of Mumbai, the GST registration has to be obtained in Maharashtra.

Provisional Registration

- A non-resident taxable person will file electronically an application for registration using the *FORM GST REG-09* along with a self-attested copy of his valid passport, at least five days prior to the commencement of business. The application must be duly signed or verified through EVC. The non-resident (if it is a company) must submit its tax identification number of its original country (whatever is the equivalent of our PAN in that country).

- An advance deposit of tax (based on estimation) must also be submitted along with the application

The person will be given a temporary reference number electronically for making advance deposit of tax in his electronic cash ledger, and an acknowledgment will be issued thereafter.

Final Registration

Final registration will be made in the same way like resident taxpayers, as follows:

- If the person wishes to register under GST, then he will submit an application electronically using the *FORM GST REG–26*, within a period of three months.

- If information is correct and complete, final GST registration will be given in *FORM GST REG-06*, otherwise the officer will issue a show-cause notice using *FORM GST REG-27*. A reasonable opportunity of being heard will be given after which the provisional registration will be cancelled through the *FORM GST REG-28*.

- If the applicant's reply is satisfactory then the show cause notice issued can be nullified by issuing an order via the *FORM GST REG- 20*.

The application for registration made by a non-resident will be signed by his authorized signatory who must be a person resident in India with a valid PAN.

Advance Payment of Tax by Non-Resident Taxable Person

A non-resident taxable person must make an advance deposit of tax in an amount equivalent to the estimated tax liability of such person for the period for which registration is sought.

If the non-resident taxable person intends to extend the period of registration indicated in their application of registration, an application using the form GST REG-11 should be furnished before the end of the validity of registration granted to him.

Monthly Return GSTR-5

Every registered non-resident taxable person is required to furnish monthly return in GSTR-5 in GST Portal, by 20th of next month. If the Return is filed for less than 30 days, it should be filed within 5 days of expiry of the GSTN Registration. Information from GSTR-5 will flow into *GSTR-2* of buyers.

You have to file GSTR-5 on line, as described in next chapter. Here we describe the physical Form so that you understand the contents of the Form. It would be easier t file the GSTR-5 Return if you fill up the Physical Form, before filing GSTR-5 on – line

GSTR -5 Form

1. GSTIN : Enter GSTIN. Provisional id can also be used as GSTIN if Final Registration number is not allotted (F-1A)

2. Tax payer Details (F-1A)

–   **Name of the Taxpayer : Name of the taxpayer including legal and trade name (will be auto-populated)**

–   **Validity period of registration**– The validity period will also be auto populated.

–   **Month, Year –** Enter the relevant month and year for which GSTR-5 is being filed.

F-1A: For GSTR-5 : General Info

3. Inputs/Capital goods received from Overseas (Import of goods) : Enter details of inputs and capital goods imported into India, like details of Bill of entry along with rate of tax, IGST, cess paid and amount of ITC available, etc., (F-2A).

F-2A: Details of Import of Goods

4. Amendment in the details furnished in any earlier return : Enter the details of any amendment in data of imports, furnished in earlier period return (F-3A).

- Bill of entry

- Rate of IGST

- Taxable value

- Amount of IGST &Cess

- Amount of ITC now available

- Differential amount of ITC (if excess will be reversed and vice versa)

Both Original & Revised Details of Bill of Entry must be given.

4. Amendment in the details furnished in any earlier return												
Original details		Revised details									Differential ITC (+/_)	
Bill of entry		Bill of entry			Rate	Taxable value	Amount		Amount of ITC available			
No	Date	No	Date	Value			Integrated Tax	Cess	Integrated Tax	Cess	Integrated tax	Cess
1	2	3	4	5	6	7	8	9	10	11	12	13

F-3A: Amendment of previous period Import Data

5. Taxable outward supplies made to registered persons (including UIN holders)

Enter invoice wise details of B2B sales in India including sales to UIN holders (F-4A).Details of IGST/CGST & SGST &Cess along with State must be given.

GSTIN/ UIN	Invoice details			Rate	Taxable value	Amount				Place of Supply (Name of State/UT)
	No.	Date	Value			Integrated Tax	Central Tax	State / UT Tax	Cess	
1	2	3	4	5	6	7	8	9	10	11

5. Taxable outward supplies made to registered persons (including UIN holders)

F-4A: Taxable outward supplies made to registered persons

6. Taxable outward B2C inter-State Large value supplies to un-registered persons

Enter the details of inter-state B2C Large sales (Invoice value Rs. 2.5 lakh or more) to unregistered persons (F-5A).

6. Taxable outward inter-State supplies to un-registered persons where invoice value is more than Rs 2.5 lakh

Place of Supply (State/UT)	Invoice details			Rate	Taxable Value	Amount	
	No.	Date	Value			Integrated Tax	Cess
1	2	3	4	5	6	7	8

F-5A : Taxable outward B2C inter-State Large value supplies to un-registered persons

7. Taxable supplies (net of debit notes and credit notes) to unregistered persons other than the supplies mentioned at Table 6

Enter the details of sales to unregistered dealers (B2C), both intra-state and inter-State sales, which were not included in Table 6 above (F-6A).

The figures must be given separately for :

– Intra-state sales can be mentioned in a consolidated summary.

– Inter-state consolidated sales must be mentioned state-wise

Rate of tax	Total Taxable value	Amount			
		Integrated	Central	State /UT Tax	Cess
1	2	3	4	5	6
7A. Intra-State supply (Consolidated, rate wise)					
7B. Inter-State Supplies where the value of invoice is upto Rs 2.5 Lakh [Rate wise]					
Place of Supply (Name of State)					

F: 6A: Taxable supplies other than mentioned in Table 6

8. Amendments to taxable outward supply details furnished in Table 5 & 6of earlier periods

Enter any changes in details of B2B and B2C Large of previous months (F-7A). Also enter Original debit notes and credit notes issued during the month related to outward supplies. In case of revisions, original details also to mentioned.

8. Amendments to taxable outward supply details furnished in returns for earlier tax periods in Table 5 and 6 [including debit note/credit notes and amendments thereof]

Details of original document			Revised details of document or details of original Debit/Credit Notes				Rate	Taxable Value	Amount				Place of supply
GSTIN	No	Date	GSTIN	No	Date	Value			Integrated Tax	Central Tax	State / UT Tax	Cess	
1	2	3	4	5	6	7	8	9	10	11	12	13	14
8A If the invoice details furnished earlier were incorrect													
8B Debit Notes/Credit Notes [original)]													
8C Debit Notes/Credit Notes [amendment of debit notes/credit notes furnished in earlier tax periods]													

F-7A: Amendments to taxable outward supply of earlier period & Debit / Credit Notes

The figures must be given separately for :

- 8A: Amendments in respect of outwards supply in earlier period Invoices

- 8B: Debit / Credit note issued respect of outwards supply, during the period

- 8C: Amendments to Debit / Credit note issued respect of outwards supply, in earlier period

9. Amendments to Taxable outward supplies to unregistered persons reported in earlier tax periods in Table 7

Enter changes in details of B2C sales (F-8A) of previous months (earlier entered in Table 7).

The figures must be given separately for :

9A. Consolidated summary of Intra-state sales

9B. State-wise Inter-state sales

9. Amendments to taxable outward supplies to unregistered persons furnished in returns for Earlier tax periods in Table 7

Rate of tax	Total taxable value	Amount			
		Integrated Tax	Central Tax	State / UT Tax	Cess
1	2	3	4	5	6
Tax period for which the details are being revised					
9A Intra-State Supplies [Rate wise]					
9B Inter-State Supplies [Rate wise]					
Place of Supply (Name of State)					

F-8A : Amendments to Taxable outward supplies to unregistered persons of earlier period

10. Total Tax Liability

Enter the tax liability separately for (F-9A) :

- **10A. Outward supply:** Details of tax liability for outward supplies for the current month.

- **10B. On account of differential ITC being negative in Table 4:** Additional tax to be paid due to reversal of ITC (i.e., differential ITC being negative) on making changes in any imports of earlier months, as reported in Table 4.

10. Total tax liability

Rate of Tax	Taxable value	Amount of tax			
		Integrated Tax	Central Tax	State/UT Tax	CESS
1	2	3	4	5	6
10A. On account of outward supply					
10B. On account of differential ITC being negative in Table 4					

F-9A : Total Tax Liability

11. Tax Payable and Paid

Enter details of tax paid during the month (F-10A).Breakup of IGST, CGST, SGST &Cess will be shown. The Taxpayer can pay through cash or use ITC.

11. Tax payable and paid

Description	Tax payable	Paid in cash	Paid through ITC		Tax Paid
			Integrated tax	Cess	
1	2	3	4	5	6
(a) Integrated Tax					
(b) Central Tax					
(c) State/UT Tax					
(d) Cess					

F-10A : Total Tax Paid / Payable

12. Interest, late fee and any other amount payable and paid

Enter details of interest and late fee due / paid on account of late filing of return (F-11A).

12. Interest, late fee and any other amount payable and paid

Description	Amount payable	Amount paid
1	2	3
I Interest on account of		
(a) Integrated tax		
(b) Central Tax		
(c) State/UT Tax		
(d) Cess		
II Late fee on account of		
(a) Central tax		
(b) State / UT tax		

F:11A: Interest, late fee and any other amount payable / paid

13. Refund claimed from Electronic Cash Ledger

Enter details of all refunds received into electronic cash ledger (F-12A).

13. Refund claimed from electronic cash ledger

Description	Tax	Interest	Penalty	Fee	Other	Debit Entry Nos.
1	2	3	4	5	6	7
(a) Integrated tax						
(b) Central Tax						
(c) State/UT Tax						
(d) Cess						
Bank Account Details (Drop Down)						

F-12A: Refund claimed from Electronic Cash Ledger

14. Debit entries in electronic cash/credit ledger for tax/interest payment

The debit entries in electronic cash ledger, i.e., cash outflow for payment of tax/interest/late fee is populated after payment of tax and submissions of return (F-13A).

14. Debit entries in electronic cash/credit ledger for tax/interest payment [to be populated after payment of tax and submissions of return]

Description	Tax paid in cash	Tax paid through ITC		Interest	Late fee
		Integrated tax	Cess		
1	2	3	4	5	6
(a) Integrated tax					
(b) Central Tax					
(c) State/UT Tax					
(d) Cess					

F-13A: Debit entries shown in electronic cash/credit ledger for tax/interest payment

Verification

Finally, the return is verified by the authorized signatory, of the NR who must be a person resident in India with a valid PAN (F-14A).

Verification

I hereby solemnly affirm and declare that the information given herein above is true and correct to the best of my knowledge and belief and nothing has been concealed therefrom.

Signatures of Authorised Signatory

Place ....

Name of Authorised Signatory

Date ....

Designation /Status

F-14A: Verification for GSTR-5 Return filing

GSTR-5 Non Resident On-line Return Filing

GSTR-5 On line Form

We have described the GSTR-5 Physical form and related rules in earlier chapter. Here we describe the process of GSTR-5 on line entry and Return filing.

Login to GSTN portal with user name password credentials to get Return Dashboard. Click *Return Dashboard* to get *File Returns* screen (F-1A).

F-1A: GSTR5 Non Resident Monthly Return

Enter *Financial Year*, select *Return Filing Period* from drop down list and click SEARCH. Click PREPARE ON LINE button under Monthly Return by Non Resident Foreign Taxpayer GSTR-5 Tab to get to get GSTR-5 Return Menu (F-2A).

F-2A: GSTR5 Non Resident Monthly Return Menu

You get following Tiles to enter / view Invoices under each Table of GSTR-5 Return. Click on the tile names to view / enter details of Invoices under respective Table (F-2A).

- **3 : Import of Goods** - Inputs/ capital goods received from overseas

- **5 : Outward Supplies Made** - Taxable outward supplies made to registered persons (including UIN holders)

- **6 : B2C (Large) Invoices** - Taxable Inter-State outwards supplies to a consumer with invoice value above Rs. 2.5 lakh

- **7A,7B - B2C (Small) :**Taxable supplies to unregistered persons (other than mentioned at Table 6)

- **8B : Credit/Debit Notes** - Credit/ debit notes / refund voucher issued

- **8B - Unregistered Credit/Debit Notes** - Credit/ debit notes for B2C large details

Import of Goods (Table 3)

At GSTR-5 Return Menu (F-2A), click *3-Import of Goods* tile to get *Import of Goods* - Summary screen. Click Add BOE to get the *GSTR-5 – IMPG*entry screen to enter new Invoice (F-3A)

F-3A: GSTR-5 : Imported Goods Entry screen

Enter following details (F-3A)

- **Port Code :** At *Port Code,*enter the 6 digit port code.

- **Bill of Entry No :** At *Bill of Entry No.,* enter the bill of entry number.

- **Bill of Entry Date** : At *Bill of Entry Date*, select the **Bill of Entry Date** using the calendar wizard.

- **Tax Rate wise Details** : Now enter the following amount at respective columns, for each Tax rate, against the respective Rate rows

o **Bill of Entry Value** : At *Bill of Entry Value*, enter the total value of the BoE.

o **Taxable Value :** At*Taxable Value*, enter the taxable value of goods against the respective Rate rows

o **Integrated Tax** : AT *Integrated Tax*, enter the Integrated Tax Amount

o **Cess** : At *Cess*, enter the Cess amount, if any.

o **ITC Eligibility**: At *Eligibility for ITC,*Select *(Yes / No)* from the drop-down list.

o **Amount of ITC available :** At *Amount of ITC available*enter the amount of ITC claimed.

Click *SAVE* button to save the invoice details.

Outward Supplies (Table 5)

At GSTR-5 Return Menu (F-2A), click 5- *Outward Supplies Made*, to get *Outward Supplies Made* - Summary screen. Click *ADD DETAILS* button to get the *GSTR-5 – B2B* entry screen to enter new Invoice (F-4A)

F-4A : GSTR-5 – Outward Supplies (B2B Invoice) entry

Enter the following details (F-4A)

– At *Receiver GSTIN/UIN,* enter the GSTIN / UIN of Receiver.

– At *Invoice No., Invoice Date* and *Total Invoice Value,* enter the Invoice number, date of the invoice and value of the total invoice.

– On entry of *GSTIN, Receiver Name, POS* and *Supply Type* are auto-populated (however, place of Supply may be changed). Depending on Place of Supply, Supply Type gets auto populated.

- Depending on Supply Type (Inter State/ Intra State) the Tax columns (IGST or CGST+SGST/ UTGST) would get auto computed as per Rate and Taxable Amount, against each Tax Rate. At Cess, enter the amount of Cess, if any.

- If the supply is eligible to be taxed at a differential percentage of the existing rate of tax, check the checkbox *Is the supply eligible to be taxed at a differential percentage (%) of the existing rate of tax, as notified by the Government?*

Click *SAVE OUTWARD SUPPLIES* button to save the invoice details.

B2C Large Invoices (Table 6)

At GSTR-5 Return Menu (F-2A), click *6-B2C Large Invoices* to get *B2C Large Invoices – Summary* screen. Click ADD DETAILS to get *B2C Large Invoices- Add Invoice* screen (F-5A)

F-5A: GSTR- B2C Large Invoices entry

Now enter following details (F-5A):

- At *Place of Supply*, select the State from the drop-down list.

- At Invoice No., Invoice Date and Total Invoice Value fields, enter the Invoice number, date of the invoice and value of the total invoice.

- The Integrated Tax would be auto computed as per Taxable Value & Tax rate. At Cess, enter the Cess amount, if any.

- If the supply is eligible to be taxed at a differential percentage of the existing rate of tax, check the checkbox *Is the supply eligible to be taxed at a differential percentage (%) of the existing rate of tax, as notified by the Government?*

Click *SAVE* button to save the Invoice details.

B2C Small Invoices (Table 7A, 7B)

At GSTR-5 Return Menu (F-2A), click *7A,7B-B2C Small Invoices* to get *B2C Large Invoices – Summary* screen. Click ADD DETAILS to get *B2C (Small) - Add* screen (F-6A)

F-6A: GSR-5 - B2C Small Invoices

Now enter following details (F-6A):

– At *Place of Supply,* select the State from the drop-down list. Accordingly, *Supply Type* would get auto selected (Inter State / Intra State).

– At Invoice No., Invoice Date and Total Invoice Value fields, enter the Invoice number, date of the invoice and value of the total invoice.

– The Tax amount would be auto computed at the respective Tax Head, as per Supply Type, Taxable Value & Tax Rate. At Cess, enter the Cess amount, if any

– If the supply is eligible to be taxed at a differential percentage of the existing rate of tax, check the checkbox *Is the supply eligible to be taxed at a differential percentage (%) of the existing rate of tax, as notified by the Government?*

Click *SAVE* button to save the Invoice details.

Credit / Debit Notes of Registered Party (Table 8B)

At GSTR-5 Return Menu (F-2A), click *8B Credit / Debit Notes* to get *Credit / Debit NotesCounter Party wiseSummary* screen. Click ADD CREDIT / DEBIT NOTES Add screen (F-7A).

F-7A: GSR-5 –Debit / Credit Notes

Now enter following details (F-7A):

– At *Receiver GSTIN/UIN,* enter the GSTIN / UIN of Receiver. On entry of *GSTIN, Receiver Name,* is shown.

– At *Original Invoice No.* , enter the invoice number against which this Credit / Debit note has been issued. At *Original Invoice Date* , enter the date of the original invoice.

– At *Note Type,* select the type (Debit / Credit)

– At *Note Value,* enter the value of the note

– At *Debit / Credit Note No,* enter the serial number of the note

– At *Debit / Credit Note Date,* enter the date of this note.

– At*Supply Type* drop-down list, select supply type (Intra-State or Inter-State)

– In the Item Details screen, the relevant Tax columns will appear as per Supply Type and Tax amount would be auto computed at the respective Tax Head, as per Taxable Value & Tax Rate (tax Amount may be changed by Tax Payer). At Cess, enter the Cess amount, if any

– If the supply is eligible to be taxed at a differential percentage of the existing rate of tax, check the checkbox *Is the supply eligible to be taxed at a differential percentage (%) of the existing rate of tax, as notified by the Government?*

Click *SAVE* button to save the Invoice details

Credit / Debit Notes of Unregistered Party (Table 8B)

At GSTR-5 Return Menu (F-2A), click *8B-Unregistered Credit / Debit Notes* to get *Credit / Debit Notes Summary* screen. Click ADD CREDIT / DEBIT NOTES to get CREDIT / DEBIT NOTES - Add screen (F-8A).

F-8A: GSR-5 – Unregistered Credit / Debit Note

Now enter following details (F-8A):

– At *Note Type*, select Debit / Credit, from drop-down list.

– At*Debit / Credit Note No*, enter *Debit / Credit Note No*. At *Debit / Credit Note Date*, enter date of the note. At *Note Value*, enter Note Value.

– At *Original Invoice No.*, enter the original invoice number against which this Credit / Debit note has been issued. At *Original Invoice Date*, enter the date of the original Invoice.

– At Item Details screen, enter the Taxable Value at the respective Tax rate rows.

– If the supply is eligible to be taxed at a differential percentage of the existing rate of tax, check the checkbox *Is the supply eligible to be taxed at a differential percentage (%) of the existing rate of tax, as notified by the Government?*

Click *SAVE* button to save the Invoice details.

Modification / Deletion

You may edit any Invoice, before submission of GSTR-5. To edit, click Back button at the respective screen to get the summary screen showing individual Invoice record. Select the desired Invoice and click :

– **Edit** : Edit (pencil icon) to edit the Invoice. The Edit screen will appear showing the Invoice. Now edit the respective value and save the Edited Invoice

– **Delete** : Delete (Red Square) to delete the Invoice

Preview GSTR-5

Having entered the Invoices in GSTR-5, click the *PREVIEW* button to download watermarked Draft PDF of GSTR-5 for your review. Check each Table of the Return carefully (make editing if necessary, as explained).

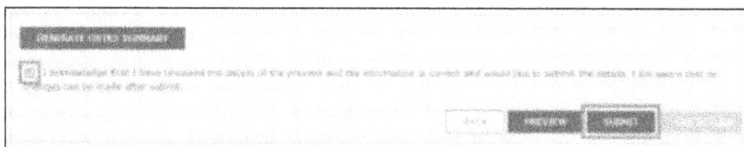

F-9A: Submission of GSTR-5 Return

Submit GSTR-5

Having checked the GSTR-5 Draft Return, Click Submit button to freeze the GSTR-5. Click PROCEED button. A success message is displayed on submission. No more changes can be done now. You may click Preview button again to download the Final watermarked PDF version of the GSTR-5 Return for your record.

Payment of Tax

Click payment of Tax Tile. The Tax labilities & credits get updated in the respective ledger account. You may click *CHECK LEDGER BALANCE* button(F-10A) to get *check ledger balance* screen to view the balance available for credit under each Tax Head (*Integrated Tax, Central Tax, State/UT Tax and Cess*).

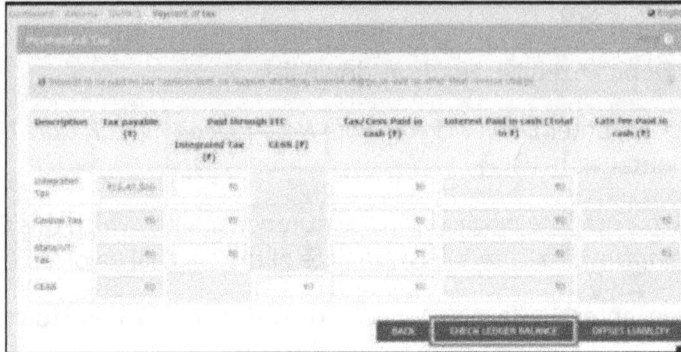

F-10A: Payment of Tax screen

Click *Offset Liability* button to pay off the Liabilities (a message *Offset Successful* appears). After making liability offset (and paying tax on deficit on any account), you may file the Return.

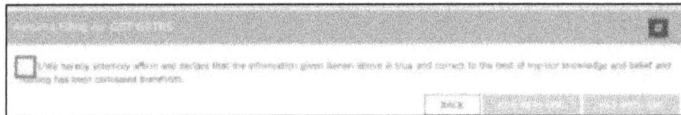

GSTR-5 Return Filing

At GSTR-5 Return Filing screen, check the checkbox and click File with DSC (and click Proceed and sign button) or File with EVC (and enter OTP and click Verify button), to file the Return. A success message with ARN is displayed and also sent by e-mail / SMS. The Status of GSTR-5 changes to *Filed*.

GSTR-5A OIDAR Return

Online information and database access or retrieval services'

Online information and database access or retrieval services (OIDAR) mean services whose delivery is mediated by information technology over the internet or an electronic network, whose supply is essentially automated, involving minimal human intervention, impossible to ensure in the absence of information technology and includes electronic services such as,

o   Advertising on the internet;

o   Providing cloud services;

o   Provision of movie, software, e-books, music, and other intangibles through telecommunication networks or internet;

o   Providing data or information, retrievable or otherwise, to any person in electronic form through a computer network;

o   Online supplies of digital content (movies, television shows, music etc.);

o   Digital data storage;

o   Online gaming.

Examples of Non OIDAR Service : Just using the internet to communicate or facilitate service does not always mean that a business is providing OIDAR services, It must be an automated process with minimal human intervention. Following are not considered as OIDAR service

–   Supplies of goods, where the order and processing is done electronically

–   Supplies of physical books, newsletters, newspapers or journals

–   Services of lawyers and financial consultants who advise clients through email

–   Booking services or tickets to entertainment events, hotel accommodation or car hire

–   Educational or professional courses, where the content is delivered by a teacher over the internet

–   Offline physical repair services of computer equipment

–   Advertising services in newspapers, on posters and on television

Salient Features of OIDAR Services

o   For Business-to-business (B2B) overseas transactions where receiver is located in India, place of supply for OIDAR services will be the location of service recipient. These services will be taxable under reverse charge mechanism.

o   For Business-to-consumer (B2C) overseas transactions where receiver is located in India, the liability to discharge tax is on overseas suppliers.

o   If supplier and recipient are in India, then normal registration rules will apply. Where supplier is located outside India and recipient is unregistered and located in India, such supplier has to take compulsory registration under simplified registration scheme.

o   Any OIDAR service provider supplying online information and database access or retrieval services from a place outside India, to a non-taxable online recipient is required to obtain GST registration by filing GST REG-01.

There are difficulties in compliances where supplier of OIDAR services is located outside India and recipient of service is not registered in India

OIDAR applicability Test

The following GST Test may be used to determine OIDAR service

−   **Test 1**: Whether Provision of service mediated by information technology over the internet or an electronic network

−   **Test 2**: Whether it is Automated and impossible to ensure in the absence of information technology

A Service is considered as OIDAR service, if both the above Tests are satisfied.

−   **PDF document manually e-mailed by provider** : Test 1 is satisfied but Test 2 is not Satisfied. So, it is not considered asOIDAR service

−   **PDF document automatically e-mailed by providers' system** : Here both Test 1 and Test 2 aresatisfied. So, it is considered asOIDAR service

−   **PDA document automatically downloaded from site** : Here both Test 1 and Test 2 aresatisfied. So, it is considered asOIDAR service

−   **Stock photographs available for automatic download** : Here both Test 1 and Test 2 is are Satisfied. So, it is considered asOIDAR service

−   **Online course consisting of pre-recorded videos and downloadable PDFs :** Here both Test 1 and Test 2 are Satisfied. So, it is considered asOIDAR service

−   **Online course consisting of pre-recorded videos and downloadable PDFs plus support from a live tutor** : Here Test 1 is satisfied but Test 2 is not Satisfied. So, it is not considered asOIDAR service

−   **Individually commissioned content sent in digital form, like photographs, reports, medical results** : Here Test 1 is satisfied but Test 2 is not Satisfied. So, it is not considered asOIDAR service

GST Registration for OIDAR Service Providers

– **Located in India** : OIDAR service providers with a place of business in India can obtain GST Registration through the normal method by applying as through the GST common portal

– **Located Outside India :** All OIDAR service providers supplying services to residents in India and not located in India are required to obtain GST registration by filing GST REG-10.

GSTR 5A Monthly Return

GSTR-5A is a Monthly Return to be furnished by Online Information and Database Access or Retrieval (OIDAR) services provider to un-registered person or customers, on the GST Portal for the services provided from a place outside India to a person in India, other than a registered person.

It contains details of taxable outward supplies made to non-taxable persons/ consumers in India, amendment to the details furnished in preceding tax period(s) and to view details of interest, or any other amount and offset the liabilities etc. in their GSTR-5A

GSTR-5A can be filed only after making full payment of taxes and other liabilities. GSTR-5A is to be filed even if there is no business activity (Nil Return) in the tax period. OIDAR services provider cannot claim any ITC in GSTR-5A.

If Tax payer has made payment of Tax on the GST Portal for GSTR-5A liabilities, the Payment Reference number and Date of the payment as generated in the CBEC Portal on the GST Portal, should be mentioned before filing GSTR-5A.

Click *Services > Returns > Returns Dashboard* command (or click the Returns Dashboard link on Dashboard) to get *File Returns* page. Select the *Financial Year & Return Filing Period* (Month) from the drop-down list. Click the *SEARCH* button. At GSTR-5A tile, click *PREPARE ONLINE* button (F-1A).

F-1A: GSTR-5A On-line Return Filing

Taxable outward supplies

To add details of Taxable outward supplies made to consumers in India, click the *5 - Taxable outward supplies made to consumers in India* tile (F-2A) to get *Taxable outward supplies made to consumers in India* screen (F-3A).

F-2A: Taxable outward supplies made to consumers in India

F-3A : Taxable outward supplies made to consumers in
India record addition.

F-4A : Taxable outward supplies made to consumers in
India record entry

At *Taxable outward supplies made to consumers in India* screen (F-3A), click *ADD DETAILS* button to get entry screen to add new record (F-4A). Select *Place of Supply* from the drop-down list. At *Taxable Value*, enter the Taxable Value. Select *Rate* from the drop-down list. Click *ADD* button to record the data entered. Having entered all Invoice, click SAVE to save the data entered. The GSTR-5 Tile will now show the updated figure in respect of Invoices entered. Click Preview Draft button (F-2A) to preview the Draft Report of GSTR-5A for review in PDF format.

Click *INITIATE FILING* button. Summary of information is displayed. Click *CONFIRM AND SUBMIT* button.

The information in GSTR5A would be freezed. Now offset the tax liability if sufficient balance in Electronic Cash Ledger is available. Otherwise create challan at GST portal and make payment which will be reflected in Electronic Cash Ledger. Thereafter, proceed to set off liabilities and file GSTR-5A.

After submission of GSTR-5A, *6 - Calculation of interest or any other amount, 7 - Tax, interest and any other amount payable and paid* tiles and *PAID AT CBEC PORTAL* button gets enabled. To view details of interest, penalty or any other amount, click *6 - Calculation of interest or any other amount* tile.

Liability Offset : You may set off the GSTR-5A liability in following modes**:**

* **Liability of GSTR-5A not paid the through CBEC Portal** : To view details of interest or any other amount payable, click *7 - Tax, interest and any other amount payable and paid* tile. Click the *CHECK LEDGER BALANCE* button to view the balance in the Electronic Cash Ledger. Click *OK* button. Fill up the amount to be paid in various heads and Click *OFFSET LIABILITY* button. Click *Close* button. Liability is offset and a Debit number is displayed. You may click *PREVIEW DRAFT* button to preview the draft for GSTR-5A.

* **Liability of GSTR-5A paid the through CBEC Portal :** If liability of GSTR-5A are already paid through CBEC Portal, click the *PAID AT CBEC PORTAL* button (no need to go for net banking for paying the liability through cash). Enter the Reference number and Date of the payment as generated in the CBEC Portal.

After the details are submitted, credit entry is posted to the Electronic Liability Register and taxpayer can file the return. After filing return, tax authorities of CBEC may verify the payment made.

Filing GSTR-5A with DSC/ EVC

Select *Declaration* checkbox (F-5A). At *Authorised Signatory* drop-down list, select the authorized signatory, enabling the buttons : *FILE GSTR-5A WITH DSC* and *FILE GSTR-5A WITH EVC*.

F-5A: Filing GSTR-5A

Click *FILE GSTR-5A WITH DSC* (you will confirm OTP) or *FILE GSTR-5A WITH EVC* button to file GSTR-5A. On filing of the GSTR-5A, The Report Status of GSTR-5A is shown as *Filed*, and acknowledgement through e-mail message and SMS is sent to the Authorized Signatory.

Downloading Filed GSTR-5A Return

Click the *DOWNLOAD FILED RETURN* button to download the Return (marked as Final) in PDF.

GSTR-6 ISD Return

GSTR 6A

Addendum Part -3 GSTR 6A Form is automatically generated from the details provided by the suppliers of an Input Service Distributor in their GSTR-1. GSTR-6A for a particular tax period show changes based on the details uploaded by the counter party supplier, till ISD taxpayer submits the GSTR-6 for the same tax period. GSTR-6A is a read-only form just for review (no editing can be done in GSTR-6A), which need not be filed.

As per Notification dt15th Sep 2017, The following entities also need to deduct TDS :

- Supplier uploads the B2B transaction details in GSTR-1& 5

- If Supplier submits the return before receiver submits his GSTR-6, then supplier's B2B details will be auto-populated in GSTR-6A of the Current tax period

- If supplier submits the return after receiver submits his GSTR-6, then supplier's B2B details will be auto-populated in the GSTR-6A of the next tax period

- Where ISD taxpayer has not submitted GSTR-6 and supplier has already submitted his GSTR-1, GSTR-1/ GSYR-5 data will be auto-populated to the corresponding tax period's GSTR-6A or open tax period GSTR-6A whichever is later.

- If the B2B details in GSTR-6 has been rolled over to next tax period, it would be included in GSTR-6 of next tax period (it will be not be part of GSTR-6A of next tax period).

Viewing GSTR-6A

Login to GSTN portal with user name password credentials to get Return Dashboard. Click *Return Dashboard* to get *File Returns* screen. Enter *Financial Year*, select *Return Filing Period* from drop down list and click SEARCH. Click PREPARE ON LINE button under Details of auto drafted supplies – GSTR-6A Tab (F-1A) to get GSTR-6A Return Menu (F-1B), showing get tiles for following Tables of GSTR-6A. Click on the tile to view invoice details under the respective Table:

- **Input tax credit received for distribution**: Input tax credit received for distribution.

- **Debit / Credit notes (including amendments thereof) received during current tax period**: Debit or credit notes received.

F-1A: GSTR-6A View

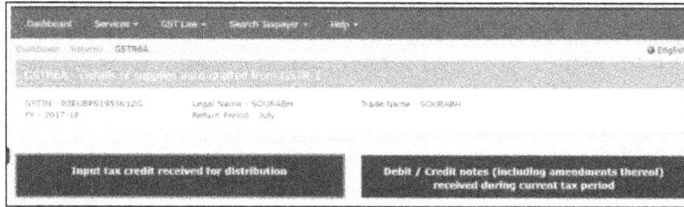

F-1B: GSTR-6A Menu

Input tax credit received for distribution

At GSTR-6A Menu (F-1B), click *Input tax credit received for distribution* to get the list of supplier GSTIN. (F-2A). Click on the Supplier GSTIN link to get the Invoice details of the selected supplier under "Uploaded by Supplier" Tab (F-2B). Click on the Invoice link (F-2B) to get the Item (tax) details of the Invoice.

F-2A: GSTR-6A Input tax credit received for distribution

F-2B: GSTR-6A Invoice details of Input tax
credit received for distribution

Debit / Credit notes received

At GSTR-6A Menu (F-1B), click *Debit Credit Note Received* to get the list of supplier GSTIN (F-3A). Click on the Supplier GSTIN link to get the Debit / Credit Note details of the selected supplier under "Uploaded by Supplier" Tab (F-3B). Click on the Invoice link (F-3B) to get the Item (tax) details of the Invoice.

F-3A: GSTR-6A - Debit / Credit notes received

F-3B: GSTR-6A - Debit / Credit notes received

GSTR-6

GSTR 6 is a monthly return to be filed by Input Service Distributor (ISD), by 13th of next month. It contains details of all the documents issued for distribution of Input Tax Credit, distribution of credit and tax invoice on which credit is received. GSTR -6, once filed, cannot be revised.

Login to *www.gst.gov.in* after entering Username & password. Click *Services > Returns > Returns Dashboard command* (or click the *Returns Dashboard* link on the Dashboard), to get *File Returns* screen (F-4A). Enter the Financial Year & Return filing period. At *Return for Input Service Distributor GSTR-6*, click the *PREPARE ONLINE* button to get GSTR – Menu (F-5A)

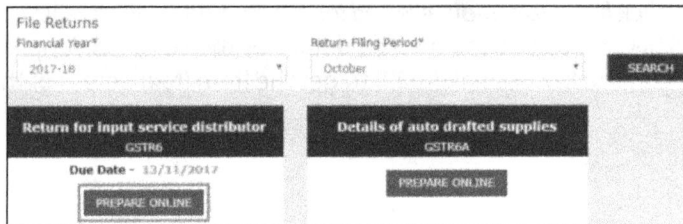

F-4A : GSTR-6 Filing menu

Generate GSTR-6 Summary

At GSTR-6 - Return Menu for Input Service Distributor (F-5A) click the *GENERATE GSTR6 SUMMARY* button (F-3A). The Details of auto drafted supplies of goods or services page is displayed. Initially, the Status should reflect *'Not Filed'*.

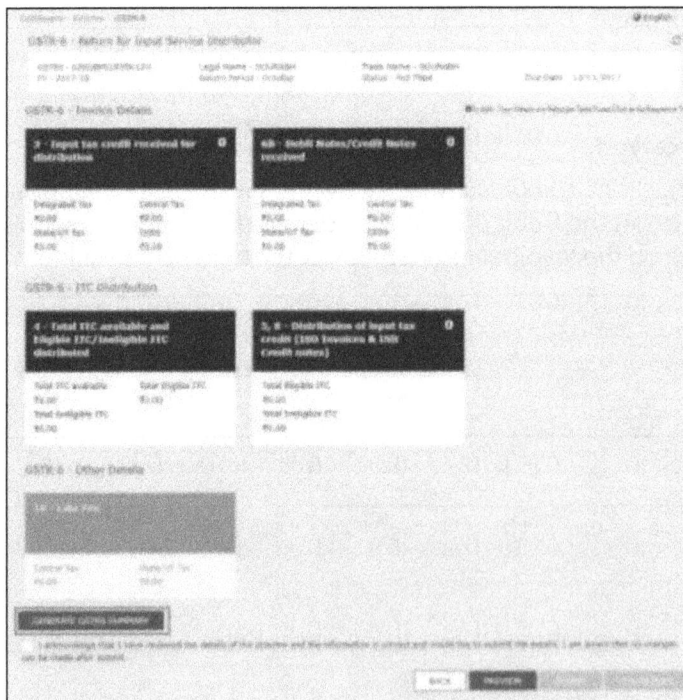

F-5A: GSTR-6 Menu

Entry of Invoice Details

Now click on the respective tile of GSTR-6 menu (F-5A), to enter data for each Table in GSTR-6 Physical Form:

– **3 - Input tax credit received for distribution**: Input tax credit received for distribution

– **6B - Debit Notes/ Credit Notes Received**: Debit / Credit notes received

– **5, 8 - Distribution of input tax credit (ISD Invoices & ISD Credit notes)**: Distribution of input tax credit for ISD invoices and ISD Credit notes

– **4 - Total ITC available and Eligible ITC/Ineligible ITC distributed**: ITC available, eligible and ineligible ITC distributed

– **10 - Late Fee**: Offset the late fee

Operation on Invoice Data in GSTR-6

Here you may edit, accept, delete or keep the invoices in pending state, which are added by the supplier. You may also add missing invoices not entered by the supplier. You may change status of the invoice from accept, reject, pending any number of times till submission.

– **EDIT :** When some details on the invoice are not correct. Click on the 'Edit' (Pencil) icon. Make the changes in the invoice details added by the supplier, as per your records. Click on 'SAVE' to save the changes made.

– **ACCEPT :** When the details of Invoice added by Supplier matches as per your records, select the checkbox beside the invoice and click on 'ACCEPT' button, to accept the Invoice data as entered by supplier.

– **REJECT :** When details in an invoice appear to be incorrect as per your records, click on the checkbox and click on the 'REJECT' button, to reject the invoice.

– **PENDING : :** When you are not sure about certain details on the invoice, select the Invoices and click on PENDING button, to keep the Invoice pending. You may change the status later on when you are sure about the Invoice

F-6A: GSTR-6: Operation on Invoice

We now explain the process of entering missing Invoice data in each Table

Input tax credit received for distribution (Table -3)

At GSTR-6 menu (F-5A), click *3-Input tax credit received for distribution* tile to get *Processed Invoice list* (F-7A).

Supplier Details	No Of Invoices	Integrated Tax (₹)	Central Tax (₹)	State/UT tax (₹)	CESS (₹)	Tax Paid (₹)	Total Taxable Value (₹)
29GGDDF8913921ZN	1	30.00	0.00	0.00	100.00	130.00	1,000.00
29AJRA1572RQZ5	1	10.53	0.00	0.00	10.20	20.73	4,211.00
07A3RA1572RM1Z	5	13,01,802.44	0.00	0.00	0.00	13,01,802.44	1,90,13,860.00

BACK ADD MISSING INVOICE DETAILS

F-7A: Processed Invoice List

At *Processed Invoice list* (F-7A), click ADD MISSING INVOICES, to get entry screen to add new Invoice details (F-8A). Fill in the details of Missing Invoice in the Form, as follows :

- **Invoice Details :** In the top part enter the following details of Invoice

    - **Supplier's GSTIN** : Enter the GSTIN of the supplier who supplied the goods or services. Supplier's name is shown.

    - **Invoice No :** Enter the invoice number.

    - **Invoice Date :** Select the date (using the calendar) of the invoice.

    - **POS** : Select the State of the Place of Supply (PoS) where the supplies were delivered. Based on the State selected in POS, *Supply Type* (Interstate or Intrastate) is shown.

    - **Total Invoice Value** : Enter the total value of invoice for which the goods or services are received.

- **Tax Details :** In case POS of the goods/ services is the same state, the transaction is an Intra-State transaction and the screen for Central Tax and State/UT Tax will appear. Enter as follows:

    - **Taxable Value** : Against respective Rates row, enter the taxable value of the goods or services.

    - **Amount of Tax** : Amount of Tax fields would be computed and shown (Tax amount may be edited)

    - **Cess** : Enter the Cess amount.

F-8A : New Invoice entry

After entry of data, click on 'SAVE' button (F-8A).

Uploading New Invoice Data : You will be directed to the previous page and a message is displayed that invoice is added. Click the Supplier's GSTIN link under Supplier Details column to get list of Pending Invoices (F-7A). Click the *Uploaded by Receiver Tab*. The missing invoice is added (you may even edit/delete the added invoices (under Actions) till the GSTR-6 is submitted. The invoice is added is reflected in GSTR-1/GSTR-1A of the supplier for action on the invoices.

6B – Debit Notes/ Credit Notes Received

At GSTR-6 menu (F-5A), click *6B - Debit Notes/ Credit Notes Received* tile. Click ADD CREDIT NOTE / DEBIT NOTE., to get the Debit / Credit Note entry screen (F-9A).

Enter the details of New Debit / Credit Note, are similar to Invoice. However, you also have to enter the original Invoice Number against which the Debt / Credit Note is issued, as shown in the entry screen (F-8A) :

F-9A: New Credit / Debit Note entry

Credit / Debit Note Details : In the upper part (F-9A), enter the Credit / Debit Note / Refund Voucher details, as follows:

- **Supplier GSTIN** : Enter supplier the name. At *Supplier Name*, Name of Supplier would be displayed.

- **Note Type** : Select from drop-down list (Debit Note / Credit Note / Refund voucher).

- **Note Value** : Value of the Note / Refund voucher.

- **Debit/Credit Note No :** Enter the Debit Note / Credit Note / Refund Voucher number

- **Debit/Credit Note Date : Enter** field, the Debit Note / Credit Note / Refund Voucher Date using the Calendar wizard (This Date cannot be earlier than original invoice date).

- **Original Invoice Number** : Enter the original Invoice against which the Debit / Credit Note / Refund Voucher is issued.

- **Original Invoice date** : Enter the date of original Invoice against which the Debit / Credit Note / Refund Voucher is issued

- **Supply Type :** Select Inter-state / Intra-state from drop down list

- **Reason for Issuing Note :** Select the reason of issuing Debit / Credit Note / Refund voucher from drop-down list.

Tax Details : In the lower part (F-9A), enter the Tax details of Credit / Debit Note / Refund Voucher, as follows:

- **Taxable Value** : Against respective Rates row, enter the taxable value of the goods or services.

- **Amount of Tax** : Amount of Tax fields would be computed and shown (Tax amount may be edited), as per nature of supply (CGST/SGST in case of Intra State, IGST in case of Inter State)

- **Cess** : Enter the Cess amount.

Like Invoice, click *SAVE* button to save the data entered and then upload the newly added missing Debit / Credit Notes. The Debit / Credit Notes gets reflected in GSTR-1/1A of the supplier for action on the invoices.

5, 8 - Distribution of input tax credit (ISD Invoices & ISD Credit notes)

At GSTR-6 menu (F-5A), click *5, 8 - Distribution of input tax credit (ISD Invoices & ISD Credit notes)* tileClick ADD DOCUMENT, to get the entry screen (F-10A).

F-10A: ISD Distribution for Intra State transaction

Enter the following details:

– **Eligibility of ITC**: Whether the ITC being distributed is eligible or ineligible for credit

– **Unit Type**: Select Registered or Unregistered unit

– **GSTIN** : GSTIN of the Registered recipient (in case of Registered)

– **ISD Document Type**: Invoice or Credit Note

– **Document Details** : Invoice Number, Date of Invoice, Credit Note Number and Date (if applicable)

– **Tax amount :** Depending on the State of recipient, the Tax heads appear (IGST or CGST/STGST) fields appear . Enter the Tax Amount in respective head

Click *SAVE* button after entering all the details.

4 – Total ITC available and Eligible ITC/Ineligible ITC distributed

At At GSTR-6 menu (F-5A), click *4 - Total ITC available and Eligible ITC/Ineligible ITC distributed*. Click 'CALCULATE ITC' to display figures of total ITC, eligible ITC and Ineligible ITC (F-11A).

F-11A: ITC Details

Preview of GSTR-6

Having viewed the ITC details, at GSTR-6 tiles screen, click the PREVIEW button (F-12A), showing the draft watermarked PDF Summary page of GSTR-6 for review. You may download (recommended) summary page and review the summary of entries made in different sections thoroughly before submitting the GSTR-6.

F-12A: GSTR 6 Preview & Submission

GSTR-6 Submission

Click on the check box (F-12A). Click*SUBMIT* button (the invoices uploaded in the GSTR-6 for that particular month would be freezed). Click *FILE RETURN* button to file GSR-6 by providing the required credentials. Click FILE WITH DSC (Click *PROCEED*, select Certificate and Click Sign button) or FILE WITH EVC (enter OTP and Click Verify), as the case may be, to file the Return.

F-13A: GSTR 6 Filing

On Filing the Return, status of the return on *Return Dashboard* gets changed to *Filed*. A notification through e-mail and SMS is sent to the Authorized Signatory.

GSTR7: TDS Return

As per GST law, following people/entities need to deduct TDS:

1. A department or establishment of the Central or State Government, or
2. Local authority, or
3. Governmental agencies, or

Persons or category of persons as may be notified, by the Central or a State Government on the recommendations of the Council.

GSTR 7 Return is to be to be filed by the persons deducting TDS (Tax deducted at source) under GST, showing details of TDS deducted, TDS liability payable / paid, TDS refund claimed if any etc.

The Deductee (person from whom TDS has been deducted) can claim such TDS deducted and utilize for the payment of output tax liability. The details of TDS deducted is available electronically to each of the Deductee in PART 'C' of Form GSTR 2A after the due date of filing of Form GSTR 7. The certificate for such TDS deducted shall be given to the deductee in Form GSTR 7A on the basis of return filed in GSTR 7.

As per 22nd GST Council meeting on 6th October 2017, the provisions of TDS have been currently put on hold, till further notification.

As per Notification dt15th Sep 2017, The following entities also need to deduct TDS :

-   Central or State Government department / establishment, Local authority, Governmental agencies, or other categories as may be notified
-   An authority or a board or any other bodyset up by Parliament or a State Legislature or controlled / owned by government
-   A registered society established by Central or State Government or a Local Authority
-   Public sector undertakings

TDS should be deducted @ 2% where the total value of supply under the contract exceeds Rs 2.5 Lakhs.

However, the TDS will *not* be deducted when the location of the supplier and place of supply is different from the registration place (State) of the recipient.

Any mistake made in GSTR-7 Return can be revised in the next month's Return.

Details of GSTR-7

DeductorDetails : Enter the GSTIN of the Deductor (F-1A). The Legal name & Trade Name (if any) would be displayed.

1.	GSTIN															
2.	(a) Legal name of the Deductor	Auto Populated													
	(b) Trade name, if any	Auto Populated													

F-1A: GSTR-7 - Deductor Details

Details of the tax deducted at source: Enter the details of TDS deducted (F-2A)

- GSTIN of the Deductee
- Total amount paid to Deductee
- TDS amount (Central/State/Integrated)

GSTIN of deductee	Amount paid to deductee on which tax is deducted	Amount of tax deducted at source		
		Integrated Tax	Central Tax	State/UT Tax
1	2	3	4	5

F-2A: TDS details

Revision of previous period TDS details

Enter the modification in respect of previous months, if any (F-3A). Enter the original figures previously submitted and the corresponding revised figures. TDS certificate (GSTR-7A) will get revised.

	Original details		Revised details				
Month	GSTIN of deductee	Amount paid to deductee on which tax is deducted	GSTIN of deductee	Amount paid to deductee on which tax is deducted	Amount of tax deducted at source		
					Integrated Tax	Central Tax	State/UT Tax
1	2	3	4	5	6	7	8

F-3A: Revision of previous period TDS details

TDS payment details

Enter details of the tax amount deducted from the deductee and the tax amount paid to the government (F-4A).

Description	Amount of tax deducted	Amount paid
1	2	3
(a) Integrated Tax		
(b) Central Tax		
(c) State/UT Tax		

F-4A: TDS Deduction & Payment details

Interest & Late Fee Details

Enter the details of Interest (@ 18% per annum) and late fees (Rs.100 / day for CGST + Rs.100 / per day for SGST) payable due to delayed deposit of TDS to government (F-5A).

Description	Amount payable	Amount paid
1	2	3
(I) Interest on account of TDS in respect of		
(b) Integrated tax		
(b) Central Tax		
(c) State/UT Tax		
(II) Late fee		
(a) Central tax		
(b) State / UT tax		

F-5A: Interest&Late Fee Details

Electronic cash ledger entries

On payment of TDS, with Late Fee / Interest, if any and submission of TDS return, the Debit entries in Electronic cash ledger would be shown.

Filing of TDS Return

After submission of Return, file the Return on verification under digital signature with the credentials, to authenticate the return (F-6A).

Verification

I hereby solemnly affirm and declare that the information given herein above is true and correct to the best of my knowledge and belief and nothing has been concealed therefrom.

Signature of Authorized Signatory ....

Place   Name of Authorized Signatory ....

Date   Designation /Status ....

F-6A: Verification & Filing

GSTR-8 TCS Return

Electronic Commerce Operator is liable to collect TCS for supply made through such Operator by other suppliers and the consideration is collected by the Electronic Commerce Operator. Supplies made by the electronic commerce operator on its own account are not subject to TCS requirements.

GSTR-8 is a return to be filed by persons deducting TCS (e.g. e-commerce operators) under GST, by 10th of following month. GSTR-8 contains the details of supplies and amount of TCS (Tax Collected at Source, on such supplies.

The supplier can take the input credit of such TCS deducted by the e-commerce operator after filing of GSTR-8 by the e-commerce operator. The amount of such TCS will be reflected in Part C of Form GSTR-2A of the supplier.

Currently, the Government has put the TCS provisions on hold, till further notice.

GSTR-8 once filed, cannot be revised. Any mistake made in the return can be revised in the next month's return.

e-commerce

- *Electronic Commerce* means supply of goods or services including digital products over digital or electronic network (s. 2(44) of CGST Act, 2017)

- *Electronic Commerce Operator* means any person who owns, operates or manages digital or electronic facility or platform for electronic commerce (s. 2(45) of CGST Act, 2017)

Registration of e-commerce Operator

Every e-commerce operators and are liable to be registered irrespective of the value of supply made by them. So, there is no threshold limit for e-commerce operators and registration is compulsory for them. However, where the e-commerce operators are liable to pay tax on behalf of the suppliers under notification issued u/s 9 (5) of the CGST Act, 2017, the suppliers of such services are entitled for threshold exemption.

Services notified u/s 9(5)

In case of following services notified u/s 9(5), tax shall be paid by the electronic commerce operator for services supplied through it, as if he is the supplier liable to pay tax in relation to the supply of such services.

- Services by way of transportation of passengers by a radio-taxi, motorcab, maxicab and motor cycle;

– Services by way of providing accommodation in hotels, inns, guest houses, clubs, campsites or other commercial places meant for residential or lodging purposes

Tax Collected at Source

Every e-commerce operator (other than an e-commerce operator who is required to pay tax under section 9(5) of the CGST Act, 2017) must collect TCS @ 1% (0.5% CGST + 0.5% SGST) of the net value of taxable supplies made through it , during the month in which the consideration amount is collected from the recipient. The TCS is to be paid to the Government within 10th of the following month

The amount of TCS will be reflected in the GSTR-2 of the actual registered supplier (on whose account such collection has been made) on the basis of the statement filed by the e-commerce operator. Actual supplier can use it to discharge his Tax Liability

GSTR- 8 Rules

The details of supplies furnished by every operator in his statement for the month will be matched with the corresponding details of outward supplies furnished in the GSTR-8. Any mismatch would be communicated to both persons. Additional liability arising due to mismatch, if any, would have to be paid with Interest

Contents of GSTR-8

GSTIN : Enter GSTIN (Enter provisional GSTN if is not available)

Legal name of the registered person: Name of the taxpayer will be displayed

Annual Return : The e-commerce operator is also required to file an annual statement by 31st day of December following the end of the financial year in which the tax was collected.

Details of supplies made through e-commerce operator :

Enter the gross value of supplies made to (to registered persons and unregistered persons, separately) and value of supplies returned (F-1A). The TCS would be charged on Net Amount (difference between the supplies made and supplies returned)

GSTIN of the supplier	Details of supplies made which attract TCS			Amount of tax collected at source		
	Gross value of supplies made	Value of supplies returned	Net amount liable for TCS	Integrated Tax	Central Tax	State /U/T Tax
1	2	3	4	5	6	7
3A. Supplies made to registered persons						
3B Supplies made to unregistered persons						

F-1A : Details of supplies made through e-commerce operator

Amendments of any earlier statement: Enter the details of modification made in previous period, showing original as well as revised figures.

Original details			Revised details						
Month	GSTIN of supplier	GSTIN of supplier	Details of supplies made which attract TCS			Amount of tax collected at source			
			Gross value of supplies made	Value of supply returned	Net amount liable for TCS	Integrated Tax	Central Tax	State/UT Tax	
1	2	3	4	5	6	7	8	9	
4A. Supplies made to registered persons									
4B. Supplies made to unregistered persons									

Amendments to details of supplies in respect of any earlier statement

Details of interest: Interest due to delayed payment of TCS to government

On account of	Amount in default	Amount of interest		
		Integrated Tax	Central Tax	State /UT Tax
1	2	3	4	5
Late payment of TCS amount				

Interest on late payment of TCS

Tax payable / paid: Total amount of tax payable and paid under each head (SGST/ CGST/ IGST)

Description	Tax payable	Amount paid
1	2	3
Integrated Tax		
Central Tax		
State / UT Tax		

Tax payable / paid

Interest payable and paid: Interest @ 18% (on outstanding tax amount) payable and paid for late payment of GST.

Description	Amount of interest payable	Amount paid
1	2	3
(a) Integrated tax		
(b) Central Tax		
(c) State/UT Tax		

Interest on late payment of GST.

Refund claimed: Refund claimed from electronic cash ledger. Refund can be claimed when all the TCS liability for that tax period has been discharged.

Description	Tax	Interest	Penalty	Other	Debit Entry Nos
1	2	3	4	5	6
(a) Integrated tax					
(b) Central Tax					
(c) State/UT Tax					
Bank Account Details (Drop Down)					

Refund claimed on account of TCS paid

Debit entries in cash ledger: Amount of TCS shown in Part C of GSTR-2A on filing of GSTR-8, after Tax Payment

Description	Tax paid in cash	Interest
1	2	3
(a) Integrated tax		
(b) Central Tax		
(c) State/UT Tax		

Debit entries in cash ledger on account of TCS

GSTR 9 Annual Return

GSTR 9 is annual return, to be filed by the registered taxpayers (including composition dealers), except the following persons :

- Casual Taxable Person
- Input service distributors
- Non-resident taxable persons
- Persons paying TDS under GST.

GSTR 9 contains details of outwards supplies made and inwards supplies received during the year and Tax under each tax heads. It is a consolidated report of all periodical returns (monthly/quarterly) related to the Financial Year. GSTR-9 should be filed on or before 31st December of subsequent financial year.

Types of Annual Returns:

- **GSTR 9** : By the *Regular Taxpayers* (other than Composition Dealers) filing GSTR 1, GSTR 2, GSTR 3.

- **GSTR 9A :** By Composition Dealers

- **GSTR 9B** : By *E-Commerce Operators* (who have filed GSTR 8 during the financial year).

- **GSTR 9C :** By the taxpayers whose *annual turnover exceeds Rs 2 crores* during the financial year. Such taxpayers should also file a copy of audited annual accounts and reconciliation statement of tax paid / payable as per audited accounts, along with GSTR 9C.

Contents of GSTR - 9

Taxpayer details : Enter the following details of the Taxable Person :

- **GSTIN:** On login, GSTIN of the taxpayer will be displayed at the time of return filing.

- **Legal name of the registered person**: Name of the taxpayer will be displayed at the time of return filing.

- **Whether liable to Statutory Audit:** Click Yes / No.Statutory audit is compulsory in case of companies and in case of individual/HUF if turnover exceeding Rs 1 crore.

- **Date of statutory Audit:** Enter the date of the statutory audit, where applicable

- **Auditors:** Enter the Name of the auditors (where applicable).

F-1A: GSTR-9: Details of Taxable Person

DETAILS OF EXPENDITURE

Enter Details of goods and services purchased during the financial year, along with the HSN/ SAC codes applicable and the taxable value of such goods and services, as submitted in GSTR 2, separately as follows:

— Inter State Purchases on which ITC availed

— intra-State Purchases on which ITC availed

— Imports on which ITC availed (Imports)

— Other Purchases on which no ITC availed

— Sales Return

— Other Expenditure (Expenditure other than purchases)

Inter-State Purchases on which ITC availed

F-2A: Inter State Purchases on which ITC availed

Intra-State Purchases on which ITC availed

F-2B: Intra State Purchases on which ITC availed

Imports on which ITC availed

Goods									
S.No.	Description	HSN Code	UQC	Quantity	Tax Rate		CIF Value	IGST	CustomDuty paid

Services					
S.No.	Description	SAC	Tax Rate	Taxable Value	IGST

F-2C: Imports on which ITC availed

Other Purchases on ITC not availed

S.No.	Goods/Services	Purchase Value

F-2D: Other Purchases on ITC not availed

Sales Returns

S.No	Goods	HSN Code	Taxable Value	IGST	CGST	SGST

F-2E: Sales Returns

Other Expenditure (Expenditure other than Purchases)

S. No.	Specify Head	Amount

F-2F: Other Expenditure (Expenditure other than purchases)

DETAILS OF INCOME

Details of all supplies and sales made during the year, as submitted under GSTR 1.

– **Inter-State supplies on which GST paid :** Supplies made in other states, on which IGST is paid.

– **Intra State Supplies on which GST Paid :** Supplies within the state, on which SGST and CGST is paid.

– **Exports on which GST Paid:** Export of goods and services made, on which IGST is paid

– **Exports without payment of GST:** Export of goods and services made, without paying IGST

– **Other Supplies on which no GST paid :** Supply of goods and services (other than Exports) made, without payment of GST

– **Purchase Returns :** Detail of Purchase return made during the year.

– **Other Income (Income other than from supplies) :** Any other income earned (supplies other than covered in any of the above heads)

Inter-State Supplies on which GST paid

Goods

S. No	Description	HSN Code	UQC	Quantity	Tax Rate	Taxable Value	IGST

Services

S. No	Description	Accounting Code	Tax Rate	Taxable Value	IGST

Inter-State Supplies on which GST paid

Intra State Supplies on which GST Paid

Goods

S No	Description	HSN Code	UQC	Quantity	Taxable Value	Tax Rate		Tax	
						CGST	SGST	CGST	SGST

Services

S No	Description	SAC	Taxable Value	Tax Rate		Tax	
				CGST	SGST	CGST	SGST

Intra State Supplies on which GST Paid

Exports on which GST Paid

Goods

S.No	Goods	HSN Code	UQC	Quantity	Tax Rate	FOB Value	IGST	Custom Duty

Services

S No	Services	SAC	Tax Rate	FOB Value	IGST

Exports on which GST Paid

Exports without payment of GST

Goods						
Sl.No	Goods	HSN Code	UQC	Quantity	Tax Rate	FOB Value

Services				
Sl.No	Services	SAC	Tax Rate	FOB Value

Exports without payment of GST

Other Supplies on which no GST paid

Sl. No.	Goods/Services	Value

Other Supplies on which no GST paid

Purchase Returns

Goods	HSN Code	Taxable Value	IGST	CGS

Services	SAC	Taxable Value	IGST	CGS

Purchase Returns

Other Income (Income other than from supplies)

Sl. No.	Specify Head	Amount

Other Income (Income other than from supplies)

Return Reconciliation Statement

The system will auto-reconcile the transactions and determine tax liability payable against Tax Actually paid, showing amount of tax difference, interest, penalty, if any.

A IGST						
Sl No.	Month	Tax Paid	Tax Payable (As per audited a/c)**	Difference	Interest	Penalty
	Total					

B CGST						
Sl No.	Month	Tax Paid	Tax Payable (As per audited a/c)**	Difference	Interest	Penalty
	Total					

C SGST						
Sl No.	Month	Tax Paid	Tax Payable (As per audited a/c)	Difference	Interest	Penalty
	Total					

Return Reconciliation Statement

Other Liabilities & Refunds

- **Other amount payable** : Other amount payable (like Arrears, Assessment etc), if any, will be displayed

- **Refunds :** Refunds payable would be displayed

A	Arrears (Audit Assessment etc)					
Sl No.	Details of Order		Tax Payable	Interest	Penalty	Current Status of the Order
	Total					

B	Refunds			
Sl No.	Details of Claim	Date of Filing	Amount of Refund	Current Status of the claim

This may be divided into parts :-
i) amount already paid / refund already received during the year.
ii) amount payable / refund pending.

Other Liabilities & Refunds

Profit / Loss as per Profit and Loss Statement

Enter the breakup of gross-profit, profit after tax and net profit

Profit as Per the Profit and Loss Statement
Gross Profit
Profit after Tax
Net Profit

Profit / Loss as per Profit and Loss Statement

Declaration

After submitting the details, the return is to be authenticated under digital signature as applicable, and filed.

I _____ hereby declare that the information given in this return is true, correct and complete in every respect. I further declare that I have the legal authority to submit this return.

Place:

Date: (Signature of Authorized Person)

Declaration for Filing

Electronic Ledger

Electronic Ledger (e-Ledger) is electronic form of passbook for GST, constituting following ledgers:

- **Electronic Cash Ledger** : GST deposited in cash to government in
- **Electronic Credit Ledger** : Input Tax Credit available (ITC)
- **Electronic Liability Register** : GST liability, Setoff of & Balance liability (if any)

We now describe each of them in details.

Electronic Cash Ledger

Electronic Cash Ledger shows head wise summary of all deposits/payments made by Taxpayer, in respect of each Major (like IGST, CGST, SGST/UTGST, and CESS) .& Minor Heads (like Tax, Interest, Penalty, Fee & Others).

It reflects the cash deposits in recognized Banks and payments of taxes and other dues made by the taxpayer. The Tax Deducted at Source (TDS) and Tax Collected at Source (TCS) are also shown accounted as cash deposits of the taxpayer.

A registered taxpayer can make cash deposits in the recognized Banks through the prescribed modes to the Electronic Cash Ledger using any of the Online or Offline modes permitted by the GST Portal. The Cash deposits can be used for making payment(s) like tax liability, interest, penalties, fee, and others.

Viewing Electronic Cash Ledger

It can be viewed by the taxpayers themselves, their authorized signatories & GST Practitioner. It can also be viewed by their Jurisdictional Officials (JO).

Login to the GST Portal with valid credentials to get Dashboard (F-1A). Click **S**ervices > Ledgers > Electronic Cash Ledger command to get Electronic Cash Ledger screen (F-2A)

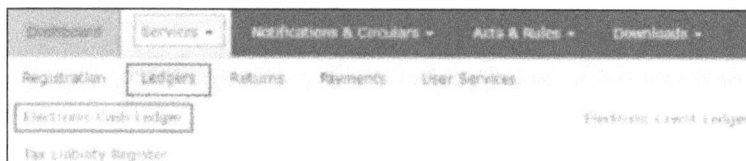

F-1A: Electronic Cash Ledger Tab

Electronic Cash Ledger page (F-2A), shows current Cash Balance at. Cash Balance as on date column (you may click the link for the amount displayed under Cash Balance as on date to view the summary of the Cash Balance under Minor & Major herds in a pop up window). Click Electronic Cash Ledger link to get Electronic Cash Ledger Display (F-3A)

F-2A : Electronic Cash Ledger screen

At *Electronic Cash Ledger Display* (F-3A), select the date at *From* and*To* date using the calendar to select the period (for maximum of 6 months) Electronic Cash Ledger. Click *GO* button to view details (F-3A)

F-3A: Electronic Cash Ledger Display

Click *SAVE AS PDF* button to save the Electronic Cash Ledger in the pdf format. Click *SAVE AS EXCEL* button to save the Electronic Cash Ledger in the excel format.

Notes

– Any additional amount deposited inadvertently will remain in the Electronic Cash Ledger and can be used to discharge liabilities in subsequent tax periods. Alternatively, the excess amount deposited in the Electronic Cash Ledger can be claimed as refund while filing the periodic return or via refund application.

– In exceptional circumstances, especially when the amount of additional demand is not stayed by the Appellate Authority, Tribunal, or Court, the amount can be debited from your Electronic Cash Ledger to the extent of the demand

Time of Reflection of Credits in Electronic cash Ledger : The instances of credit to Electronic Cash ledger in various scenarios are listed below:

– **Online payment through net banking in authorized Banks :** On receipt of CIN from the bank. (normally done instantly)

–   **OTC payment through cash and self-bank cheque in authorized banks:** On receipt of CIN from the bank (normally instantly on receipt of cash or realization of cheque)

–   **OTC payment through other bank cheques:** On receipt of CIN from the bank

–   **Online NEFT/RTGS payments though non-authorized but recognized Banks :** As soon as RBI shares CIN details (normally within same day or within 24 hours).

–   **Over the counter NEFT/RTGS payments through non-authorized Banks :** As soon as RBI shares CIN details.

–   **Payment through Credit Card/Debit Card** After 24 hours of Payment. But once amount is debited and Payment Gateway confirms the receipt of amount, Banks are given 45 days' time to confirm the payment and cash ledger will be updated after final confirmation from the bank.

Notes :

–   On successful payment CIN is communicated by the Bank to the GST System along with a unique reference number generated by the banking system, reflected in electronic cash ledger (updated on a near real time basis).

–   In case of outstation cheque in OTC mode, CIN and the bank reference number (BRN) is communicated by the Bank to GST System on realization of cheque and amount is credited to the Government account from the taxpayers account. On receipt of the CIN, the Cash Ledger gets updated on a near real time basis.

–   If payments made through challan are not reflected in Electronic Cash Ledger, the taxpayer should raise a grievance on the GST Portal (after 24 hours) using the GST PMT-06 form.

–   If wrong credit is shown in Electronic Cash Ledger, taxpayer can raise a grievance on the GST Portal using the GST PMT-04 form.

Electronic Credit Ledger

Electronic Credit Ledger shows all credits (with major head wise details : IGST, CGST, SGST, and CESS), accrued on account of inward supplies (referred as Input Tax Credit). Electronic Credit Ledger is not maintained for composition taxpayer, ISD taxpayer and Tax Deductor & E-commerce operator.

Utilisation of Credit available in Electronic Credit Ledger : The amount available in the Electronic Credit Ledger can be utilized for paying off tax liabilities as per the following rules:

–   ITC of IGST will first be utilised for payment of IGST output tax liability and then the balance can be utilized for payment of CGST and SGST in that order.

–   ITC of CGST will first be utilised for payment of CGST output tax liability and then the balance can be utilized for payment of IGST.

–   ITC of SGST will first be utilised for payment of SGST output tax liability and then balance can be utilized for payment of IGST.

–   ITC of CESS can be utilized only against CESS tax liability. CESS credit is not available for cross utilization with other tax liabilities.

Credit of SGST cannot be utilised for payment of CGST and vice versa.Credit availed on CESS will be available for setoff against any output tax liability of CESS only.

Notes:

- In exceptional circumstances as permitted in the Act and rules, especially when the amount of additional demand is not stayed by the Appellate Authority, Tribunal, or Court, the credit can be debited to the extent of the demand by the proper officer.

- Any excess amount remaining in Electronic Credit Ledgercan be utilised for any future liability. Refund can only be claimed for ITC accumulated for export of goods / services anddue to rate of tax on outward supplies being lower than inward supplies.

Provisional credit Table : Provisional credit tables display the balance of provisional and mismatch credit. Select *Services > Ledgers > Electronic Credit Ledger > Provisional Credit Balance* to view it.

Blocking of ITC in Electronic Credit Ledger : Jurisdiction Officer may scrutinize the amount of ITC claimed by a taxpayer, through GST TRAN-1 and GST TRAN-2 etc. for its authentication. The concerned Jurisdiction Officer may decide to temporarily block the ITC available to a taxpayer, wherever it is felt that further investigation is required in the interest of the revenue. The Jurisdictional Officer may block CGST, SGST, IGST & Cess balance in whole or in part. The Jurisdictional Officer, after investigation may unblock the ITC that was previously blocked. The Taxpayer is communicated through email and SMS on blocking or unblocking of ITC

Viewing Electronic Credit Ledger

Login to the GST Portal (www.gst.gov.in) with valid credentials.Click*Services > Ledgers > Electronic Credit Ledger* command to get Electronic Credit Ledger page showing the current balance on each head (F-4A).

F-4A: Electronic Credit Ledger

Electronic Credit Ledger: At *Electronic Credit Ledger* page (F-4A),Click *Electronic Credit Ledger* link.Select the **From** and **To** date using the calendar to select the period.Click *GO* button to view the details of Electronic Credit Ledger (F-5A)

F-5A: Electronic Credit Ledger

Click the *SAVE AS PDF* and *SAVE AS EXCEL* button (F-5A)to save the Electronic Credit Ledger in the pdf and excel format respectively.

Provisional Credit Balance: At *Electronic Credit Ledger* page (F-4A),Click the *Provisional Credit Balance* link to view Provisional Credit Balance details (F-6A)

Sr. No.	Tax Period,if any	Amount of provisional credit balance (₹)				
		Integrated Tax (₹)	Central Tax	State Tax	CESS	Total
1	Jul-17	20.00	20.00	20.00	20.00	80.00
2	Jun-17	41.00	40.00	31.00	31.00	143.00
3	May-17	30.00	30.00	30.00	30.00	120.00
4	Apr-17	1,040.00	22.00	11.00	1,020.00	2,093.00

F-6A: Provisional Credit Ledger

Click the *SAVE AS PDF* and *SAVE AS EXCEL* button (F-6A) to save the Provisional Credit Balance in PDF and Excel format respectively.

Blocked Credit Balance: At *Electronic Credit Ledger* page (F-4A),Click *Blocked Credit Balance* link to get Block Credit Balance details (F-7A)

Date	Amount of blocked credit balance (₹)				
	Integrated Tax	Central Tax	State Tax	CESS	Total
09-02-2018	41.00	37.00	36.00	41.00	155.00

F-7A: Blocked Credit Balance

Click *SAVE AS PDF* and *SAVE AS EXCEL* button (F-7A) to save the Blocked Credit Balance in PDF and Excel formatrespectively.

Electronic Liability Register

All return related liabilities accrued are displayed in the *Electronic Liability Register*, in 2 parts:

- **Part I** : It shows All Return related liabilities, Payments made from the Electronic Cash Ledger and/or credit utilized, Liabilities pertaining to GST CMP-03, GST ITC-03 and GST REG-16. It can be accessed in the post-login mode through *Services > Ledgers > Electronic Liability Register > Part-I: Return related liabilities.*

- **Part II** : It shows all liabilities other than return related liabilities. Payments made from the Electronic Cash Ledger and/or credit utilized to discharge the liabilities are also shown in the register. Liabilities not covered in Part-I are accounted for in Part-II. It can be accessed in the post-login mode through path *Services > Ledgers > Electronic Liability Register > Part - II: Other than return related liabilities.*

Viewing Electronic Liability Register

Login to the GST Portal with valid credentials to get Dashboard (F-8A).

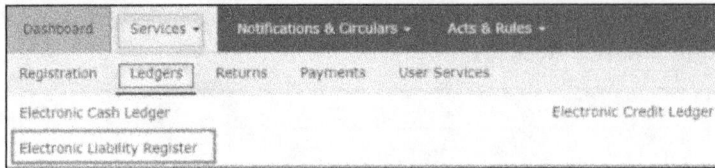

F-8A: Electronic Liability Register Tab

Click *Services* > *Ledgers* > *Electronic Liability Register* command to get *Electronic Liability Register* showing 2 links (F-9A)

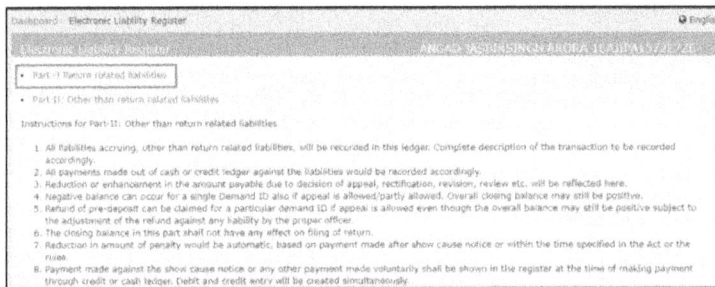

F-9A: Electronic Liability Register screen

Part I : Return Relates Liabilities

At Electronic Liability Register screen(F-9A), at *Financial Year* and *Month* drop-down list, select the financial year and month. Click *GO* button. Click *Part I : Return Relates Liabilities* link to get Electronic Liability Register (F-10A).

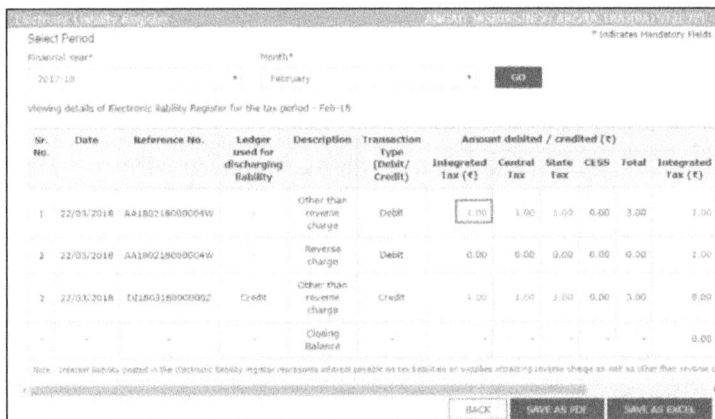

F-10A: Part I : Return Relates Liabilities

You may further click the link of any major head (*Integrated Tax, Central Tax, State Tax and Cess*) to view further details of minor heads (Tax, Interest, Penalty, Fee, Others and Total) in a pop up window.

Part II : Other than Return related Liabilities : At Electronic Liability Register screen(F-9A), click the link *Part II : Other than Return related Liabilities* link and select the Status option from drop down list (F-11A) to get the for the selected Status (F-11B). Use scroll bar to pan the report to view more details.

F-11A: Status list

F-11B: Electronic Liability Register

The amounts in Other than return related liability will be flowing from Assessment/Adjudication orders, Appeal orders (like GSTR-3, 3B, 4, 5, 5A, 6, 7, 8, 9, 10, ITC-03, surrender of registration etc). Other orders where demand is created also flows in the register.

Utilisation of Cash & ITC

Utilization of cash/ ITC for payment of demand is about payments of non-return related liabilities, created through Demand ID by tax officials, appearing in the Electronic Liability Register (Part-II).

Payments against the liabilities of a particular demand ID can be made from:

- Cash balance available in the Electronic Cash Ledger
- Input tax credit balance available in the Electronic Credit Ledger.

Making payment for demand appearing in Electronic Liability Register

Login to the GST Portal (www.gst.gov.in) with valid credentials. Click *Services > Ledgers > Payment towards Demand* command (F-1A) to get the *Outstanding Demand* page (F-2A).

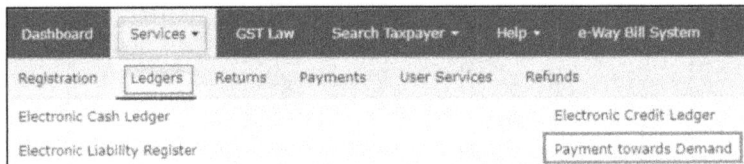

F-1A: Payment towards Demand Tab

At *Outstanding Demand* page (F-2A), showing Demand IDs for each Major Head (*Integrated Tax, Central Tax, State/UT Tax and Cess*).

F-2A : Outstanding Demand page

At *Outstanding Demand* page (F-2A), click the link of any Major Head to view Minor Head wise details (F-3A).

Integrated Tax (₹)

	Tax	Interest	Penalty	Fee	Others	Total
	₹61,89,189	₹8,768	₹978	₹0	₹878	₹61,99,813

F-3A : Minor head wise break up of selected Major Head

At *Outstanding Demand* page (F-2A), click Select button to select the Demand ID (for which to make payment) to get *Payment of Demand* screen (F-4A), for the selected Demand ID showing the Table of Outstanding Demand, Cash ledger Balance & Credit Ledger Balance with break up for each Major & Minor Head

F-4A: Payment of Demand screen

Under each screen component (Outstanding Demand, Cash ledger Balance & Credit Ledger Balance), use the scroll bar to pan right and enter the Amount (Amount intended to be paid, Amount intended to be paid through Cash, Amount intended to be paid through ITC) against the respective Demand ID (as per rules of utilization). Click *Set Off* button (F-4A). A confirmation message showing the adjustment figure is displayed. Click *OK* button. Once, set off, the amount cannot be reversed. A success message showing the Payment Reference Number is displayed. Click *OK*button.

Payment may be made in part in multiple installments, against a particular demand ID, till the outstanding balance becomes zero.

On utilization of Cash / ITC, Debit entry number will be generated and posted against the respective Demand ID in Electronic Liability Register Part-II as well as in the Electronic Credit Ledger.

Relief for Paying against Demand ID

In case Demand ID (u/s 74), the system allows reduced payment towards penalty, reduction in amount of penalty is allowed (a message is shown), if full Payment of Tax & Interest is made within 30 days from the date of order. 50% of the Penalty amount stated in the ordercan be paid and balance 50% of the penalty is waived off through credit entry automatically posted in liability ledger.

Tax Payments

Tax Payments for GST can be made only by the Challan/s generated through the GST Portal (www.gst.gov.in). Physical Challans will not be accepted for the payment of GST. A single Challan form is prescribed for all taxes, fees, penalty, interest, and other payments to be made under the GST.

Online Payment Mode : Payments may be made on line through following modes

- **Net Banking**

    o **Pre Login**

    o **Post Login**

- **Credit / Debit Cards**

    o **Pre Login**

    o **Post Login**

Off-line Payment Modes : Payments may be made off-line through following modes

- **Over the Counter (OTC)**

- **NEFT/ RTGS**

Challan IDs

- **Common Portal Identification Number (CPIN)**: Created for every Challan successfully generated by the taxpayer. Validity period for a CPIN is 15 days. GST payment cannot be made after CPIN date of expiry, as specified in the generated Challan

- **Challan Identification Number (CIN)** : Generated by the banks, after payment in lieu of a generated Challan is successful. CIN is proof that the payment has been made successfully and the amount paid will be credited to the cash ledger.

- **Bank Reference Number (BRN)** : Reference number given by the bank for a payment against a Challan

Challan Creation at Pre-login Stage

To generate Challan without logging onto the GST Portal, access GSTN URL (https://www.gst.gov.in) to get GST Home page (F-1A). Select *Services > Payments > Create Challan* command to get *Create Challan* page (F-2A).

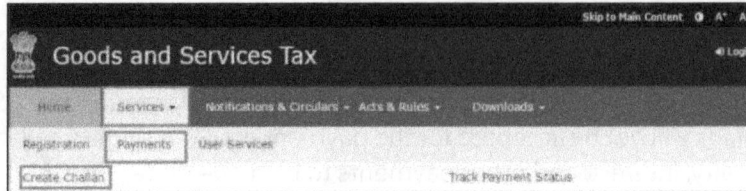

F-1A: GSTN login

ID entry : At *Create Challan* page (F-2A), at GSTIN/UIN/TMPID enter GSTIN, enter as follows:

−   In case of UN Bodies, Embassies, Government Offices or Other Notified persons provide Unique Identification Number (UIN).

−   In case of Tax Return Preparers, provide Tax Return Preparer Identification Number (TRPID).

−   In case of unregistered dealer, provide Temporary Identification Number (TMPID).

Type the Captcha characters. Click *PROCEED* button (F-2A) to get Challan details entry screen (F-3A). At Tax Payer details, the Taxpayer info are carried and displayed

F-2A: Challan creation

At Challan details entry screen (F-3A), at Tax Liability grid, enter the details of Payment. *Total Challan Amount* and *Total Challan Amount (In Words)* are displayed. At *Payment Modes*, select the appropriate option. Click *GENERATE CHALLAN* button

F-3A: Challan Details entry

In case of e-Payment mode, enter the OTP sent on registered mobile number. Click PROCEED button. The Challan is generated. Click *Download* button to download the challan in specified folder of your computer. Print the downloaded challan.

Notes:

– Unregistered persons can generate a Challan against the temporary ID allotted.

– GST payment may be made from any authorised bank in any other state.

– If a taxpayer enters the wrong GSTIN and the amount is debited from his account, it cannot be refunded. Taxpayers must ensure they enter the correct GSTIN at the time of generating the Challan.

– If a taxpayer has paid excess amount, he may file a refund application for the excess amount, or use to discharge liabilities in subsequent tax period/s.

– Even a third party can make payments on behalf of a taxpayer, mentioning proper GSTIN against which the payment is being made.

Challan Creation at Post-login Stage

Access GSTN URL (https://www.gst.gov.in). Click login link and enter the valid login credentials to get Dashboard.

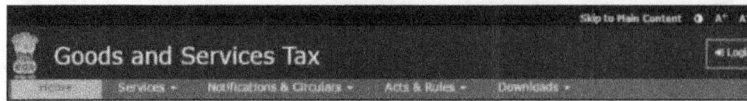

F-4A: Taxpayer Login at GSTN Portal

Click Services > Payments > Create Challan command to get Challan entry screen (F-5A)

	IGST (₹)	CGST(₹)	SGST (₹)
Liability related to Return	90,000	1,15,000	1,15,000
Cash	40,000	20,000	20,000
Input tax Credit	70,000	80,000	80,000
(Net Liability)/Net Credit	20,000	(15,000)	(15,000)
Liability other than Return	0	0	0

F-5A: Challan creation screen

In the Tax Liability Table, enter the details of payment to be made.

– To know the exact tax liability, check the Tax Liability Ledger.

– Enter amount which will get updated in your Electronic Cash Ledger. It can be utilized later.

– Amount entered under any Minor head (Tax, Interest, Penalty, Fee and Others) and Major Head (CGST, IGST, SGST/UTGST, Cess) can be utilized only for that liability. Cross-utilization among Major and Minor heads are not allowed.

The *Total Challan Amount* and *Total Challan Amount (In words)* are displayed as per amount entered

You may Generate challan, save in specified folder (upto 10 challans) and print the challan as explained.

Salient features of each Payment Mode : The challan creation process is almost similar in all the modes mentioned above. Salient features of each Payment are explained below

• **Net Banking** :

    o   User must have an account with any authorised bank with the Internet Banking (Netbanking) facility activated on it.

- o The bank details are available under Help > How can we help you > Payments > List of Authorised Banks.

- o The user is redirected to your bank's website to provide user credentials and make payment. Upon successful payment confirmation from Bank, the amount is instantly credited to Electronic Cash Ledger.

- o There is no surcharge (bank Charges) levied by any bank.

- **Credit / Debit Card :** The user is redirected to bank's website to provide user credentials and make payment. Upon successful payment confirmation from Bank, the amount is instantly credited to Electronic Cash Ledger

- **NEFT / RTGS :**

  - o Only Bank Account holder may make NEFT/RTGS payment through cheque to bank.

  - o Bank may levy NEFT/RTGS transaction charges (check respective bank website)

  - o Unique Transaction Reference (UTR) Number is provided by bank for each NEFT/RTGS transaction. UTR is used for reconciling the NEFT/RTGS transaction with the RBI. UTR has to be linked if the payment status has not been updated on the GST Portal within 2 hours of making the payment. In such case, link the UTR by opening NEFT/RTGS Challan available under Challan History, on the landing page of the NEFT/RTGS Challan.

  - o Normally NEFT transaction are limited to Rs.1,99,999 in many banks and RTGS are done for minimum of Rs.2,00,000 (no max limit Refer to RBI / Bank website for rules.

  - o NEFT / RTGS is an offline mode of payment. So, payments can be made only during bank branch's banking hours.

  - o Separate payment must be made for each NEFT payment. In case you have funds in more than one account, you can either transfer funds to one account and then make a single payment. Alternatively, you can generate separate Challans, breaking up the liability into smaller amounts based on available balances across the accounts.

- **OTC**

  - o OTC Challan payment/s can be made at any branch of the selected authorised bank. The details of these banks are available on the GST Portal.

  - o Total value of OTC payments within a tax period (calendar month/quarter) cannot not exceed Rs.10,000. So, maximum amount of a challan is Rs 10000.

  - o The date of cheque realization is treated as the payment deposit date. Cash payments get updated in the GST System Portal when updated by bank.

  - o The Payment Receipt is issued respective bank's branch

Notes:

– In online payment, though GSTIN is entered at the time of login and Taxpayer name is displayed, Credit would be given to the taxpayer on the basis of GSTIN. So, be careful about GSTIN entered, paying attention to Tax Payer Name displayed to avoid amount wrongly credit to any other credit person

– Change in the amount of the Challan not allowed after generation of CPIN. Create a new Challan for to change amount. The wrong Challan, if unused, will automatically expire after 15 days.

– All the historical Challan records may be traced at *Dashboard > Services > Payments > Challan History* section of GST Portal. A challan copy may be obtained therefrom any time.

Viewing Saved Challan

Saved Challans may be viewed (upto 7 days of creation), only in post-login mode as explained (even a partially filled challan may be saved). At Dashboard, Click *Services > Payments > My Saved Challans* command. The Saved Challans are displayed in descending order (most recently saved challan is shown first in the list). At *Action* column, click the *Edit* (pencil icon) to edit the specified challan.

Track Payment Status

Taxpayer is intimated regarding the payment status by SMS, E-mail. The Status is also updated on the GST Portal. To view Payment Status :

– Pre-login mode : Select *Services > Payments > Track Payment Status*.

– Post-login mode : Select *Services > Payments > Challan History*.

Challan status Types : List of Challan Status at various stages

– **Initiated :** No intimation yet received from Bank (during re-ping in case of E-payment)

– **Paid:** CIN received by taxpayer and status updated on portal as PAID

– **Not Paid**: Default status on challan generation

– **Failed** :Failure of any online transaction initiated by taxpayer

– **Paid at tax Office** : Taxpayer making payment at Commercial Tax Office counter (Enforcement Activity).

– **Awaiting Bank Confirmation**: In case of Internet Banking (Maker-Checker) till the time Checker authenticates the transaction

– **Awaiting Bank Clearance** : Instrument (cheque/DD) deposited in case of Over The Counter mode

– **Expired** :No payment initiated within 15 days of generation of challan

– **Cheque/DD Dishonored**: Instrument dishonored (due to insufficient funds or any other reason)

– **Transaction Failed** - On failure of transaction initiated through Internet Banking or Credit Card/ Debit Card.

– **MoE Reversal** – Memorandum of Error not in favor of taxpayer

Action on Challan status

– If the status of Challan is FAILED / NOT PAID and mode selected is E-Payment, Taxpayer can click VIEW CHALLAN button, select Bank, Terms and Conditions and click MAKE PAYMENT button to do the Payment again for the *Failed* or *Not Paid* challan.

– If Payment status is PAID, then VIEW RECEIPT button is enabled. Click it to view download the receipt. In case of any other Status of challan (other than PAID), Taxpayer may View the Challan.

Cancellation of OTC Challan

You may cancel a OTC Challan which is not paid from the Challan History. Log in to your account using the credentials. Click *Services > Payments > Challan History* command. Select the date range (at *From* and *To*) using the calendar (or select Search to cancel OTC challan through CPIN) to list the challans. Select the Challan and click Cancel button against the challan to be cancelled. To ensure that no payment is made against the OTC Challan, click *PROCEED* button. Status of the OTC Challan is changed to Cancelled.

Payment by OAIDAR at Non taxable territory

A person located in Non-Taxable Territory (NTT) supplying Online Information and Database Access or Retrieval (OIDAR) services to a non-taxable online recipient, is liable to pay IGST on such services provided. They may make their IGST payment through SWIFT payment network from their location outside India.

– Compute the tax liability to be paid in Indian Rupee. Calculate the amount to be transferred in foreign currency (including Bank Charges) through SWIFT mode. Challan should be generated using NEFT/RTGS mode.

– Access the SWIFT supporting Bank's portal.

– At selected Bank's webpage, initiate SWIFT transaction by providing GSTIN, Legal Name and breakup of tax liabilities.

– On remitting tax amount in foreign currency via SWIFT to the Bank in India, the overseas bank will send the message to credit the Centralized Account maintained by the Bank by giving the beneficiary account details and GSTIN.

– After tax amount is transferred in foreign currency, NTT Taxpayer should send an e-mail to the Banks (both Indian as well as overseas Bank) giving the SWIFT details.

– On receipt of funds, Bank will convert the same to Indian Rupees and send an acknowledgement to the Taxpayer (via Email) confirming the amount received in Indian Rupees.

– After receiving the confirmation of receipt of amount from the Bank in India, NTT taxpayer would generate a CPIN for the exact value of the Indian Rupee as intimated by the Bank, on the GST Portal and select the mode of Payment as NEFT/ RTGS(CPIN should be generated only after the money has been transferred by the NTT Taxpayer to the Bank in India, for the exact value of the Indian Rupee as communicated by the Bank)

- After CPIN is generated from the GST Portal, NTT taxpayer needs to send a soft copy of the generated challan to the Bank in India through e-mail.

- On receipt of the challan copy by e-mail, the Bank will remit the money to RBI for NEFT/ RTGS transaction and send acknowledgement to the NTT taxpayer.

- RBI shall send the payment details (signed CIN) to GSTN for updating the Electronic Cash Ledger.

- NTT taxpayer can login to the GST Portal to check the challan status. They may also check the status of challan from "Track Payment Status" service without logging to the GST Portal

Troubleshooting: Some common problems with GST payment related issues and solutions are discussed below:

- **Account Debit multiple times:**

  o   If the sum of both transactions is reflecting in the Electronic Cash Ledger, contact the Help Desk using the contact numbers/e-mail IDs given on the GST Portal.

  o   If only the original transaction amount is reflecting in the Electronic Cash Ledger, contact your bank because it may be a transaction error.

  o   If CIN is not generated but funds are debited or CIN is generated but not reported, use the Application (GST PMT 07) for *Credit of Missing Payment* under the Grievance Section of the GST Portal.

- **Payment accepted after Challan expiry date :** If Challan is wrongly accepted by Bank after expiry date, it would be rejected by GSTN Portal. Approach the bank branch and seek refund.

- **Payment Debited from Bank Account (in Net Banking payment Mode) but error generated as Server Down :** Check the payment status at Services > Payments > Challan History.

  o   If status shows *INITIATED*, then the payment is still in process.

  o   If status shows *FAILED*, create another challan.

Depending on the status of the challan, the debited money may either get updated in the Electronic Cash Ledger, or it may get returned to the Taxpayer's bank account (which may take up to 24 Hrs).

- **Wrongly Filled Challan submitted, which needs to be corrected:**

  o   If CPIN not generated, amendments in challan could be done within 7 days from the date of saving the challan for the first time.

  o   If the CPIN generated, create a new challan. The earlier wrong challan will automatically expire after 15 days of generation of CPIN.

- **Amount deducted twice but Cash Ledger credited by single entry :** GST Portal will update cash ledger on the basis of first information of CIN received from the Bank/ RBI. For same CPIN, cash ledger can't be updated more than once. Claim refund of the double deducted amount not credited to cash ledger, from the concerned bank.

Filing payment related Grievances

Grievances can be submitted either before or after logging-in to the GST Portal. However, payment related grievances can only be submitted by registered users or Taxpayers, on providing GSTIN.

Select *Services > User Services > Grievance / Complaints* command to get the Submit Grievance section of *Grievance / Complaints* page.

F-6A : Grievance Submission

- If already a grievance / complaint is filed and you are filing the grievance again, at Previous Grievance Number enter the previous grievance id.

- In the *Grievance Type* drop-down list, select the Grievance Against Payment (GST PMT 07) option.

- At *Grievance Related To* drop-down list, select one of the available two options, as applicable:

    o   Amount debited from the bank account, Cash ledger not updated

    o   NeFT/ RTGS related issue

– The details are displayed at *Details of Taxpayer(Person) who is reporting the grievance* are auto-populated (If not logged in, enter details).

    o   At *Discrepancy In Payments* section, enter the CPIN of the Challan (in case of pre-login, enter Capcha code).

    o   Select *Sign with Authorized Signatory's PAN* option and select the Authorized signatory.

    o   Click *SUBMIT WITH DSC* or *SUBMIT WITH EVC* button to submit the grievance form.

Click *PROCEED* button at *Warning* box. Select the certificate and click *SIGN* button. In case of *FILE WITH EVC*, enter the OTP sent on email and mobile and click *VALIDTATE OTP* button. On submitting grievance form, a *Grievance Tracking Number* would be generated and sent through e-mail. The grievance status may then be tracked using the 'Enquire Status' service.

– For issues related to Payments or Electronic Cash Ledger where money got deducted from the bank account but not reflecting in the Electronic Cash Ledger, or CIN not received, etc., users are advised to wait for 24 hours from the time of making the payment. Most cases get resolved automatically within 24 hours.

– If payment failed, the deducted money may either get rolled-back into your bank account, or it may get processed to generate a CIN and thereafter it will be reflected in your Electronic Cash Ledger.

If the situation doesn't automatically resolve in 24 hours, then you may go ahead and submit a grievance for your case on the GST Portal.

Grievance should not be raised in following situations:

– Before 24 hours of debit of amount from the bank account

– If payment status is PAID and amount is updated in Cash Ledger.

– In case of E-payment, payment not initiated from the GST Portal.

– If Memorandum of Error (MoE) is raised against the CPIN.

– Payment status is Failed and amount is not debited from bank account

– In case of OTC Payment, status is AWAITING BANK CLEARANCE and cheque/ Demand Draft is not realized.

Grievance Enquiry / Status Tracking

To see the status and details of earlier submitted grievance, Login to GST portal with credentials. Select *Services > User Services > Grievance /Complaints* command to display Grievance / Complaints page. Click *Enquire Status* tab. Enter Grievance Number or Date Range (if not logged in, search through *Grievance Number*). Click Search button. The submitted grievances are listed showing the status

Grievance Enquiry / Status Tracking

Click *Grievance Number* to view complete details and status of selected Grievance.

Grievance Follow up &Redressal : All grievances related to Payments are handled by the GST Portal. Based on the CPIN and Bank name entered by Taxpayer in the Grievance Form, on demand call will be sent to the concerned bank. Based on the response from the bank, the Electronic Cash Ledger will be updated with appropriate comments and the grievance will be closed.

– If no response is received from the concerned bank or incorrect response is received from the bank, Grievance ticket will be closed with appropriate remarks explaining the error occurred (e.g. "No details received from your bank for CPIN). Contact the bank to resolve this. You can also contact Bank Ombudsmen if the bank is not responding.

– The remarks will be sent by email and SMS.

Refunds

A Taxpayer may claim Refund when GST paid is more than the GST liability

Instances where Refunds may be claimed

- **Refund on Account of Export of Goods (With Payment of Tax) :** A taxpayer may claim Refund of IGST paid on Export of goods (with payment of tax), on Filing GSTR-1, providing Export details in Table 6A of GSTR-1 along with Shipping bill details having Integrated Tax levied, and on filing GSTR-3B of the relevant tax period for which refund is claimed.

  The taxpayer is not required to file separate refund application (Shipping Bill itself shall be treated as refund application). Refund will be credited to the account of the taxpayers. ICEGATE system shall share the payment information with the GST Portal and the GST Portal in turn shall share the information through SMS and e-mail with the taxpayers

- **Refund on Account of Assessment/ Provisional Assessment/ Appeal / Any Other Order :** The feature would be available shortly

- **Refund By Embassies/ International Organizations:** Refund Application FORM GST RFD-10 is to be submitted for claiming refund of tax paid by it on inward supplies of goods or services, within 6 months of last day of the quarter in which supply was made.

  - GST RFD-10 can be submitted only after filing statement of inward supplies in Form GSTR-11 of the corresponding tax period.

  - Application Reference Number (ARN) will be generated on successful submission of the refund application. Applicant would also be intimated through SMS & E-mail on successful submission of the Refund Application form RFD-10.

  - The refund sanctioned would be credited to the Bank account of the applicant, as mentioned in RDF-10

- **Refund Form RFD-01A:** To be filed in following cases of Refund

  o Refund of Excess Balance in Electronic Cash ledger

  o refund of ITC on account of exports of goods/services without payment of tax (accumulated ITC)

  o Refund on Account of Supplies made to SEZ Unit/ SEZ Developer (Without Payment of Tax)

  o Refund by Recipient of Deemed Export

  o Refund on Account of Supplies made to SEZ Unit/ SEZ Developer (With Payment of Tax) o   Refund on Account of Export of Services (With Payment of Tax)

RFD-01A Submission process : At GST Homepage, after login, select *Services > Refunds > Application for Refund* command to get Select Refund Type page, showing the list of each Refund Type. Click CREATE button against the desired Refund Type to get the respective Refund details screen. Enter the required Data and click SAVE to save the Return Form

Viewing saved Refund Application Forms

To view submitted application, navigate to *Services > Refunds > My Saved/Submitted Application* command. You may click ARN hyperlink to download the ARN receipt and print the ARN Receipt.

Tracking Refund Status

Select *Services > Refunds > Track Application Status* command. Enter ARN and click *SEARCH* button. The Application details, showing the Status of the specified ARN is displayed.

To track status of refund for IGST paid on account of Export of Goods, select *Services > Refunds > Track status of invoice data to be shared with ICEGATE* command (after logging to the GST Portal)

Letter of Undertaking

Any registered person wishing to supply goods or services for export without payment of Tax has to furnish, prior to export, a bond or a Letter of Undertaking (LUT), binding himself to pay Tax due along with interest in the event of failure to export the goods or services.

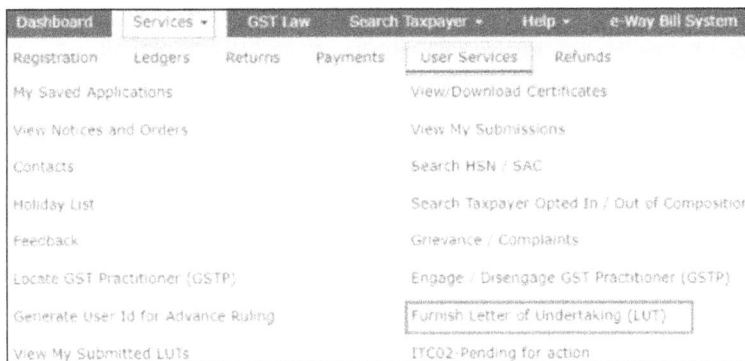

F-1A: LUT Tab selection

Login to GST Portal with valid credentials. Select*Services > User Services > Furnish Letter of Undertaking (LUT)* command to get Form GST RFD-11.

RFD_11 Filing : Select the financial year from *LUT Applied for Financial Year* drop-down list. Click *Choose File* button to upload the previous LUT file (in PDF / JPEG within 2 MB). Select the declaration checkboxes. At Name, Address and occupation of the independent and reliable witnesses section, enter the name and address of 2 witnesses. Enter the *Place of Filing LUT.* At *Name of Primary/ Other Authorized Signatory* drop-down list, select the name of authorized signatory. At *Place*, enter the place where the form is filed.

e-signature

Electronic Signature (e-signature), refers to data in electronic form, which is logically associated with other data in electronic form used by the signatory to sign. This type of signature provides the same legal standing as a handwritten signature in physical document. Following e-signing methods are available for GST Portal.

- **Digital Signature Certificate (DSC) :** Digital Signature Certificates (DSC) are the digital equivalent (electronic format) of physical or paper certificates. A digital certificate can be presented electronically to prove one's identity, to access information or services on the Internet or to sign certain documents digitally. In India, DSC are issues by authorized Certifying Authorities.

- **Electronic Signature (E-Sign) :** Electronic Signature (E-Sign) is an online electronic signature service in India to facilitate an Aadhar older to digitally sign a document. One Time Password (OTP) will be sent to mobile phone number (registered with Aadhar) at the time of digitally signing documents at the GST Portal.

- **Electronic Verification Code (EVC) :** Electronic Verification Code (EVC) authenticates the identity of the user through OTP sent to registered mobile phone of Authorized Signatory

We now explain each of these methods

emSigner

emSigner is a secure cloud based e-Signature solution using globally accepted legally valid e-signatures.

emSigner Installation : Access GST URL (https://www.gst.gov.in). Login with user credentials to get Homepage. Select *Register / Update DSC* link (F-1A) to get *Register Digital Signature Certificate* screen (F-2A).

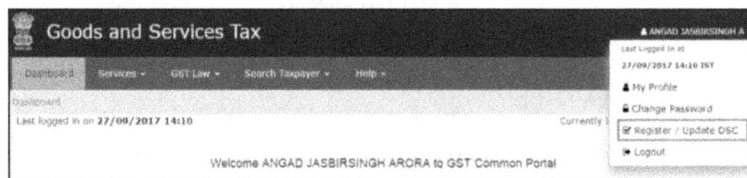

F-1A: DSC Registration link

At *Register Digital Signature Certificate* screen (F-2A), select *Click here for instructions on installing signer utility* link to get *Document Signer Install* page (F-3A) in a new tab.

F-2A: Register Digital Signature Certificate

At *Document Signer Install* page (F-3A), select the *Click here to download* link for the respective operating system.

F-3A: Document Signer Installation

The emSigner.msi file is downloaded on your machine. Double-click the emSigner.msi executable file to get *emSigner Setup* wizard. Click*Next* button and follow the instruction of the wizard assistant.

Digital Signature Certificate (DSC)

DSC is mandatory for companies and LLPs. All other entities can either use DSC or E-Sign. To obtain a DSC, contact an authorised DSC-issuing Certifying Authorities, at http://www.cca.gov.in/cca/?q=licensed_ca.html.

DSC Registration

Before DSC registration, mSigner utility must be installed in the machine as described. You should have DSC Dongle and DSC Software installed on the computer. For new registration of DSC, at GST Home page, click *REGISTER NOW* link to get *New Registration* screen (F-4A).

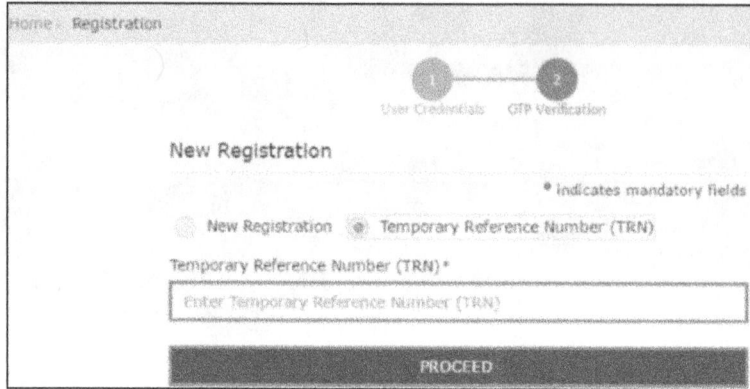

F-4A: New Registration

At *New Registration* screen (F-4A), select *Temporary Reference Number (TRN)* option. At *Temporary Reference Number (TRN)* field, enter TRN received.Click *PROCEED* button. Enter OTP sent to mobile and by email.Click *PROCEED* button.

Login to the GST Portal with valid credentials. Click *Services > User Services > Register / Update DSC* command. Go to *My Profile* link. Click *Register/ Update DSC* link (under *Quick link* section). Attach DSC dongle and open emSigner utility to get *Register Digital Signature Certificate* page (F-5A).

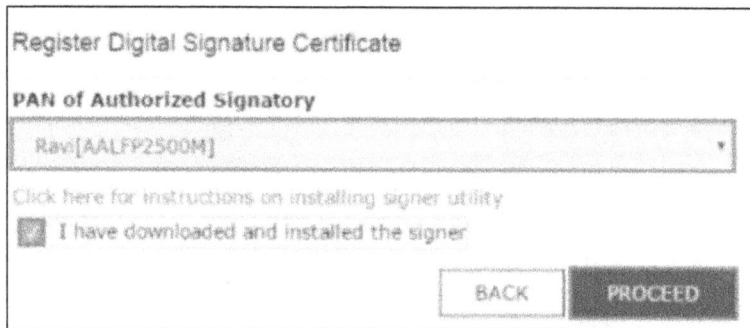

F-5A: Register Digital Signature Certificate

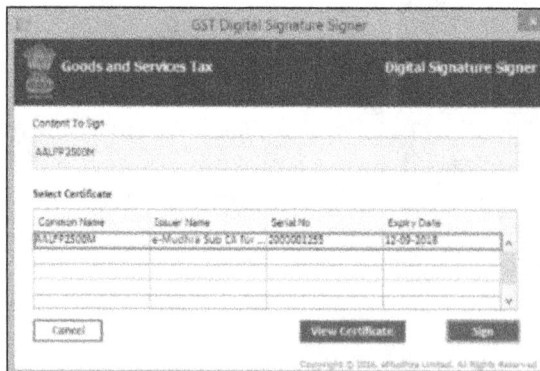

F-6A:GST Digital Signature Signer

Register Digital Signature Certificate page (F-5A), at *PAN of Authorized Signatory drop-down* list, select the PAN of the authorized Signatory to be registered. Select the *I have downloaded and installed the signer* checkbox. Click the *PROCEED* button to get *GST Digital Signature Signer* screen (F-6A).Select the certificate. Click *Sign* button (F-6A). A message *Your DSC has been successfully registered* is displayed.

Updating DSC : On renewal, update your DSC with the GST Portal. Login to the GST Portal with valid credentials.Go to *My Profile* link.Click *Register/ Update DSC* link to get *Register Digital Signature Certificate page*. At *PAN of Authorized Signatory* drop-down list, select the PAN of the authorized Signatory to be updated. Click *UPDATE* button. DSC RE-registration screen (F-7A) appears. Click *CONTINUE* button.

DSC Re-Registration

Re-Registering your Digital Signature Certificate will remove only your Digital Signature Certificate from GST System , but PAN will remain same

Are you sure you want to Re-Register your Digital Signature Certificate ?

CANCEL   CONTINUE

F-7A: DSC Re-registration

Select the certificate. Click *Sign* button. A message *DSC has been successfully updated* is displayed.

e-way Bill on-line

e-way Bill

e-way Bill is a compliance mechanism of movement of goods by way of a digital interface (digital record of Delivery Challan & transportation). The person causing the movement of goods uploads the relevant information, prior to the commencement of movement of goods and generates e-way bill on the GST portal.

Purpose & use of e-way Bill

– e-Way Bill is mandatory for Inter-State movement of goods of consignment value exceeding Rs.50,000/- in motorized conveyance.

– Registered GST Taxpayers can register in the e-Way Bill Portal using GSTIN. Unregistered Persons/ Transporters can enroll in the e-Way Bill System by providing their PAN and Aadhaar.

– Supplier/ Recipient/ Transporter can generate the e-Way Bill (EWB-01).

– Vehicle number can be entered/updated in PART - B of Form EWB - 01 by those who have generated the e-Way Bill or by the Transporter.

– QR code is provided in the e-Way Bill to facilitate quick verification.

– Certain goods are exempted from e-Way Bill (Rule 138 of CGST).

Generation of e-way Bill

E-way bill may be generated on-line through multiple modes, like *Web*, *Android App* – (using the IMEI of the phone and the registered mobile number), *SMS* (through registered Mobile Number) &*Excel based upload* (for bulk generation), before movement of goods. Alert messages are also issued to the Users through Online and SMS. Wrongly generated e-way bills may be cancelled, within 24 hours. Recipient can reject the e-Way Bill within 72 hours of generation. The Validity of e-Way Bill is fixed as one day for every 100 Kms or part thereof. The validity can be extended online before the expiry. Consolidated e-Way Bill can be generated for vehicle carrying multiple consignments.

Contents of e-way Bill

e-way bill (EWB-01) contains following info, in 2 parts. *Part A* can't be edited or modified once generated. *PART - B* can be updated with Vehicle details/ RR/Airway Bill etc.

PART-A

A.1 GSTIN of Recipient

A.2 Place of Delivery (PIN Code of place of delivery should be mentioned)

A.3 Invoice or Challan Number

A.4 Invoice or Challan Date

A.5 Value of Goods

A.6 HSN Code (2 / 4 digits as applicable)

A.7 Reason for Transportation (One digit Reason Code must be mentioned)

A.8 Transport Document Number (RR/#, L/R # etc)

PART-B

B. Vehicle Number (latest vehicle number carrying the consignment, should be recorded, where vehicles are changed).

Reason Code in e-way Bill : **1** Supply **2** Export or Import **3** Job Work **4** SKD or CKD **5** Recipient not known **6** Line Sales **7** Sales Return **8** Exhibition or fairs **9** For own use **0** Others

Registration for e-way Bill

Registration should be done by following persons

- Registered Suppliers
- Registered Transporters
- Unregistered Transporters
- Unregistered Suppliers

Registration under e-way Bill System by GST Registered Suppliers

To register, the supplier must have GSTIN with a registered mobile number. Login to e-way bill portal (ewaybill.nic.in) to get e-waybill login screen (F-1A).

F-1A: e-way Bill login screen

F-2A: Registration by Registered supplier

First time users should click e-way bill Registration link in the login screen (F-1A) to get e-Way Bill Registration Form' (F-2A).

Enter the GSTIN and click GO button (F-2A). The details are auto populated from the GSTIN database. Click Send OTP button to send an OTP in registered mobile. Now enter the OTP received in the mobile and click Verify OTP to verify the OTP.

Now enter User ID (unique User ID only accepted) and Password (8 to 15 alphanumeric characters including special characters) of your choice (and note it down). The system validates User name / password. If accepted, the requested user name with password is created (and a success message is displayed), else an error message is displayed and the applicant is to enter a valid Username / password acceptable to the system. Later on, you have to login to e-way Bill system, using the User Id & Password.

The user has to login by the Enrolment Number, User ID & Password (if user enters wrong password more than 3 times, the account would be temporarily freezed for 5 minutes, after which the user has to login using correct credentials).

– **Forgot Password** : If the Password is forgotten, click Forgot Password at login screen (F-1A) to get *Forgot Password* screen (F-2B). On entering the details, captcha &GSTIN, the password would be send to registered mobile number, through SMS

–   **Forgot Username** : If the User Name is forgotten, click Forgot Username at login screen (F-1A) to get *Forgot Password* screen (F-2C). On entering the details, captcha & GSTIN, the password would be send to registered mobile number, through SMS

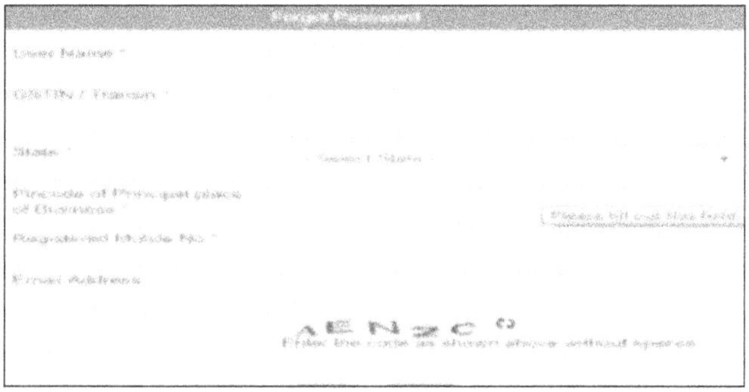

F-2B: Forgot Password

F-2C: Forgot Username

Enrolment by GST un-registered transporters

GST un-registered transporter cannot register as they do not have GSTIN. Such GST unregistered transporter should *Enrol* in e-way Bill System.

At e-way Bill login screen (F-1A), click Enrolment for Transporter button to get Enrolment screen (F-3A).

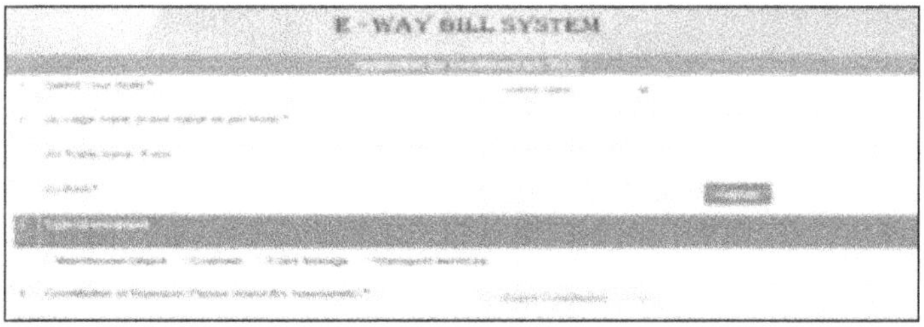

F-3A: Enrolment by unresgitered Transporters

Now enter the following details :

–   Select the State and enter his legal name as given in his PAN and PAN number and click 'Validate' button to validate the data

–   select the type of enrolment and constitution of business (Partnership, Proprietorship, Public/Private Limited etc.)

–   Enter business details and contact details.

–   Enter Aadhaar number related details and verify through OTP sent to his registered mobile

–   Clicking checkbox to consent to GSTN to use the Aadhaar details and declaration of enrolment(If Aadhaar number not available, enter the mobile number and validate by OTP)

–   Upload the Address and ID proofs (PoA and PoI) by clicking on respective 'Upload' buttons.

–   Create username and password (conforming to rules)

–   Clicking checkbox to confirm correctness of the given information by

–   Clicks 'Save' button. The system generates and displays the 15 digits TRANS ID

The TRANS ID has to be provided to clients to enter in the e-way bill so as to enable the transporter to enter the vehicle number for movements of goods.

e-Way Bill System Main menu

Login to e-way bill portal (ewaybill.nic.in). Enter username, password & captcha to get the e-way bill main menu, providing for following options:

*   In the left panel, you get following options for sub menu:

    –   **e-Way bill**: Generating, updating, cancelling and printing e-Way Bill.

    –   **Consolidated e-Way Bill** : Consolidating, updating and cancelling e-Way Bills

    –   **Reject** : Reject the e-Way Bill generated by others, not belonging to the user.

    –   **Reports** : Generating various e-way bill reports.

    –   **Masters** : Create masters like customers, suppliers, products, transporters, by the users.

    –   **User Management** : Create, modify and freeze the sub users.

    –   **Registration** : Register for SMS, Android App and API facilities

*   In the right panel, you get following options for Notifications, alerts and link to GST Portal.

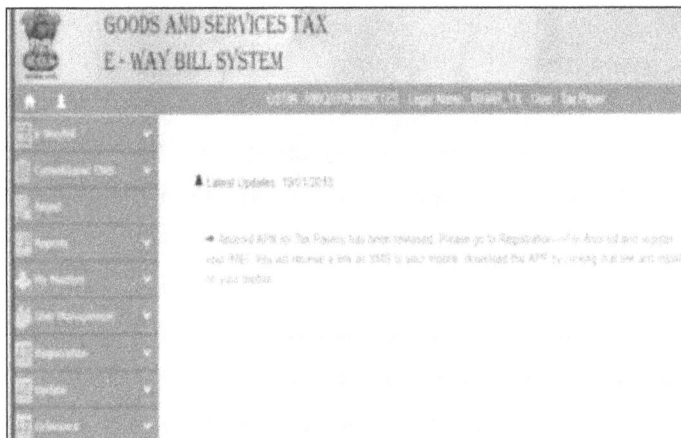

F-4A: e-way bill main menu

e-way Bill Main Menu Options

*   **e-Way bill** : Contains sub menus for generating, updating, cancelling and printing the e-Way Bill along with the option of extending the e-Way Bill.

*   **Consolidated EWB**:Sub Menu to generate, re-generate and print consolidated e-Way Bills.

*   **Reject**:To reject the e-Way Bill generated by others, if it does not belong to the user.

*   **Reports** : Sub Menu to generate various e-way Bill related reports

- **My Masters** : Sub menu to create the users masters like customers, suppliers, products, transporters

- **User Management:**Sub menu to create, freeze, update& change passwords for users

- **Registration**: Sub menu to register for SMS, Android App, GSP and API facilities

- **Update** : Sub Menu to update the details as Transporter/Taxpayer and GSTIN details from common portal.

- **Grievance**: Sub Menu for generating the Detention report based on E-way Bill number

e-Way bill Menu

At e-way Bill main menu (F-4A), click e-way Bill to get e-Way Bill menu

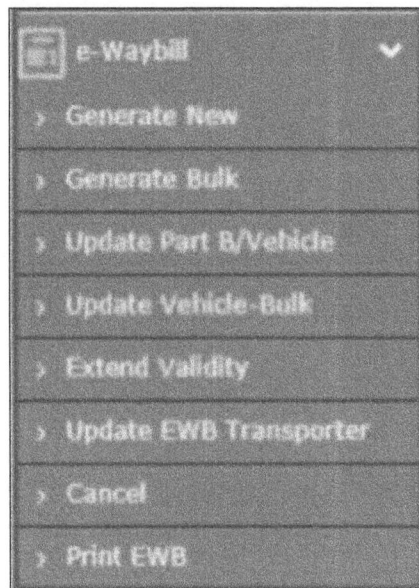

F-5A: e-way Bill sub menu

Generating new e-Way Bill

At e-way bill main menu (F-4A), select 'e-waybill' to get e-waybill sub menu (F-5A). At e-waybill' sub menu (F-5A), select Generate New' to get e-way Bill entry Form (F-5B), to create a new e-way Bill.

F-5B: e-way Bill entry

Now enter the following details

- **Transaction Type**: supplier of consignment would select 'Outward'. Recipient of consignment would select 'Inward'.

    - **Outward Consignment** : For outward consignment, select the appropriate option from the list : Supply, Export, Job Work, SKD/CKD, Recipient not known, For Own use, Exhibition or Fairs, Line Sales, Others

    - **Inward Consignment** : For Inward consignment, select the appropriate option from the list : Supply, Import, SKD/CKD, Job Work Returns, Sales Returns, Exhibition or Fairs, For Own use, Others

- **Document type**: Select from list - Invoice / Bill/ challan/ credit note/ Bill of entry, Others

- **Document No.** : Enter the document / invoice number

- **Document Date**: Select Invoice / Challan / Document date (future date is not allowed)

- **From/ To**: Enter the To / From section details about supplier (from) / recipient (To) and their address. If supplier / recipient unregistered, enter URP at GSTIN.

- **Item details** : Enter Item Details - Product Name, Description, HSN Code, Quantity, UoM, Value/ Taxable value, Tax Rates (in %), Cess Rate if any (in %)

- **Transporter details**: The mode of transport(Road/rail/ship/air), Approximate distance covered (in KM), Transporter name, transporter ID, transporter Doc. No. & Date (or Vehicle Number in alphanumeric form without any space or special character – like XX99XX9999).

    If transportation carried through a third party, then generate the E-way bill by entering the transporter id, transporter document number and date given by the transporter. The transporter ID can be auto populated if recorded in Master.

    If transportation details like vehicle number or transport document number is not entered, then the system generates the temporary unique number as 'Part-A Slip'.

    If the goods are being moved in the 'Over Dimensional Cargo' then select the Vehicle type as O to get additional validity period as per the rules.

    If a transporter is generating the e-Way Bill on behalf of the consignor/consignee, then the complete e-Way Bill entry form will be entered by him to generate the e-Way Bill. Here, the system allows him to enter both the consignor and consignee details without blocking any column.

- After the e-Way Bill is submitted with Part-B details, click SUBMIT button. The system validates the entered values and displays E-Way Bill in the EWB-01 form with unique 12 digit number (unless there is any error)

For ease of work and accurate entry, you may create masters of regularly used Products, Supplier / Customer / Client, Transporter and select from the list, at the respective field.

The e-Way Bill will not be valid for movement of the goods without the vehicle entry in the e-way bill form. Once the vehicle number is entered, the system will show the validity of the e-way bill. This indicates the user to get the goods moved within that valid date. The validity time is midnight of the validity date. Otherwise the movement of goods becomes illegal. The user can take the print out of the e-Way Bill from there.

Bulk Generation of e-way Bill

Bulk e-way Bill may be generated for multiple e-way Bills in one shot. A EWB bulk convertor or the excel file is needed to convert the multiple e-Way Bills excel file into a single JSON file.

At e-way Bill menu (F-5A), select 'Generate Bulk' to get Bulk Upload & generate e-way Bill screen (F-6G).

F-6G: Bulk e-way Bill Generation

Choose file and select the JSON to be uploaded (maximum allowed file size for upload is 5 MB), to upload in the e-Way Bill portal. Now the JSON file can be used to generate bulk e-Way Bill.

On processing the JSON file, the system generates the E-Way Bills and shows the EWB for each request (or displays error message if any error is encountered).

Update Part B/Vehicle

If vehicle number is not entered while generating e-Way Bill or vehicle has been changed for reasons like transit movement, vehicle breakdown etc), the present transporter may update the Part-B info. If the transporter has not been assigned to the e-way bill, the generator can update the Part-B.

At 'e-Waybill' menu, select 'Update Vehicle No' to get Update Vehicle Number screen (F-6H). Click respective radio button e-way bill No/ Generated Date/Generator GSTIN, as applicable. The e-way Bills are listed. Select the e-way Bill to be displayed on screen (F-6I). Now change / enter the vehicle number.

F-6H: Update Vehicle Number

F-6I: Update Vehicle Number screen

Update Vehicle-Bulk

To update vehicle details in bulk for multiple e-way bills in one go, EWB bulk convertor or the excel file is needed, to convert the multiple Part-B of e-Way Bills excel file into a single JSON file.

At e-Way Bills menu (F-5A),select "Update Vehicle Bulk' to get Update Vehicle-Bulk screen (F-6J). Click Choose File and select and upload the JSON (maximum allowed file size for upload is 5 MB) to upload in the e-Way Bill portal. The JSON file is then used to update bulk Part-B of e-Way Bills. After processing the JSON file, the system shows the list of e-way bills updated with Part-B for each request.

F-6J: Update Vehicle-Bulk

Extend Validity

In certain specified circumstances, the present transporter may extend validity of e-way Bill, by few hours. At e-way Bill menu (F-5A), select the option Extend validity and enter the e-way Bill number (for which validity to be extended) to get the screen showing the specified e-way Bill (F-6K)

F-6K : e-way Bill validity extension

In the form (F-6K), enter the required details like Form & To place, Distance, detailed reason for extension, extended period etc. The extended period is then updated.

Update Transporter

If the transporter is changed for the further movement of the goods, the present transporter can update the details for next transporter. Consequently, next transporter may update the Part-B info of e-way Bill. If the transporter is absent, the generator of the e-way bill can update the transporter.

At e-way Bill menu (F-5A), select the option *Update EWB Transporter*. Enter the the e-way Bill number (for which Transporter is to be updated) to get the screen showing the specified e-way Bill (F-6L)

F-6L : Update Transporter screen

Now change the Transporter details in the e-way Bill.

Cancel E-way bill

In case goods are not being moved, or e-way bill incorrectly generated, the e-way Bill may be canceled within 24 hours of generation. An e-way Bill verified by officer cannot be cancelled.

At e-way Bill menu (F-5A), select the option *Cancel e-Way Bill*. Enter e-way Bill number to be cancelled (F-6M) to get the e-way bill displayed on screen. View the Bill. Enter the reason for Cancellation.

F-6M: e-way Bill cancellation

Print E-Way Bill

To print the e-way Bill, at e-way Bill menu (F-5A), select the option *Print e-Way Bill*. Enter e-way Bill number (to be printed). The e-way Bill is displayed for viewing. Click Print button to print the e-way Bill (F-6N). e-Way Bill can be printed only by the generator and the transporter

F-6N: e-way Bill in print

To print complete details, click Detailed Print button.

Consolidated E-way bill

A consolidated E-way bill (EWB-02) is a single document that contains details of all the E-Way Bills related to multiple consignments carried in a single vehicle.

A transporter may generate consolidated E-way bill when transporter is carrying multiple consignments in a single vehicle, so that transporter need to carry a single document, instead of separate document for each consignment in a conveyance.

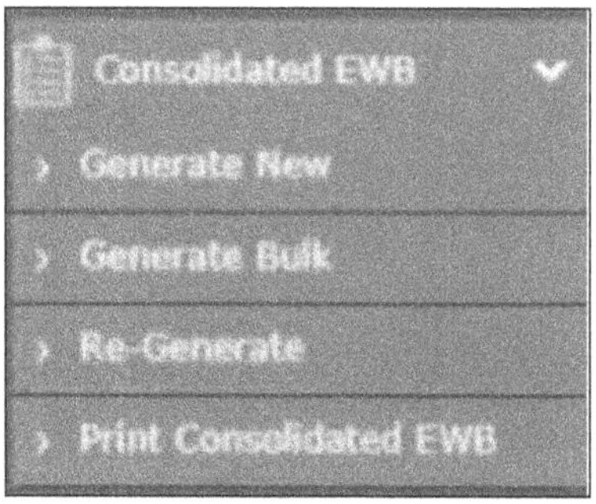

F-7A Consolidated e-way Bill menu

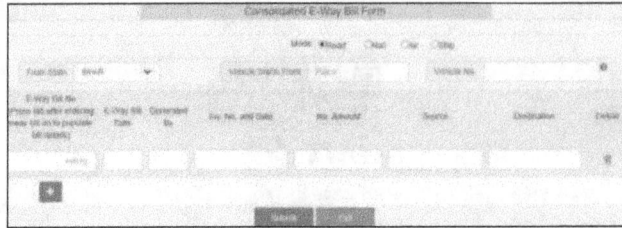

F-7A-1: Consolidated e-way bill creation

At e-way Bill main menu (F-4A), select *Consolidated EWB* to get Consolidated e-way Bill menu(F-7A). Select *Generate New* to get *Consolidated e-way Bill Form* to create Consolidated e-way Bill (F-7A-1).

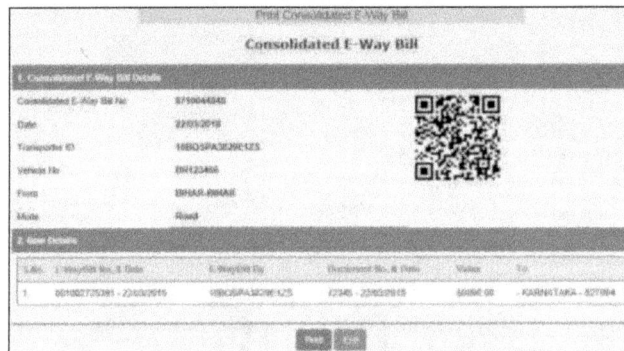

F-7B: Consolidated e-way bill in Print

Enter the details (F-7A-1). On entry of e-way Bill, the details of the e-way bill are carried. This way, enter all the individual e-way Bills (generated by the user) to be consolidated into one e-way bill (click + button to add multiple EBN). Click *Submit* to generate consolidated e-Way Bill with the consolidated EBN (F-7B).

To print the consolidated e-Way Bill, at Consolidated e-Way Bill sub menu, click *Print Consolidated e-Way Bill*. Enter the consolidated e-Way Bill number and click *Print* button to get the consolidated e-Way Bill in print (F-7B)

Bulk Consolidated E-way bill

Large-sized business houses or logistic operators having many consignments across the country on a single day may create bulk e-way bill combining multiple e-Way Bills/ consolidated e-way bills in one shot by a single upload

A Bulk consolidated bulk e-Way bill is used to generate multiple consolidated e-Way Bills at one shot, either using JSON template or using Excel template & Bulk Converter tool, and create JSON file. The 2nd method provides better error trapping facility to locate data errors.

To Generate Bulk Consolidated E-way bill, at Consolidated e-way Bill menu (F-7A), select Generate Bulk to get JSON file upload screen 9F-8A). Browse & Select the desired JSON file to upload in the e-Way Bill portal. This can be used to generate consolidated bulk e-Way Bill.

F-8A: JSON file upload for Bulk Generation of
Consolidated e-way Bill

F-8B: Bulk Consolidated E-way bill

At *Choose file*, select the JSON file (F-8B). Click *Upload & Generate* to generate Bulk consolidated e-way Bill.

Re-Generate Consolidated EWB

To update the transportation details (transportation or vehicle number etc) of consolidated EWB and re-generate the new Consolidated EWB (CEWB), at Consolidated e-way Bill menu (F-7A), select Regenerate Consolidated EWB to get Regenerate Consolidated EWB screen (F-8C)

F-8C: Regenerate Consolidated EWB

Select the appropriate option to list the e-Way Bill. Enter the 10 digit Consolidated EWB Number or enter the date of Consolidated EWB & select the EWB (F-8C). The EWB would be displayed to update the details like vehicle number, place, state, reason for the change in transportation, Transporter Doc. No. and Date etc. (F-8D)

F-8D : Vehicle updation in Consolidated e-way Bill

Print Consolidated EWB

At Consolidated e-way Bill menu (F-7A), select Print Consolidated e-way Bill to get Consolidated e-way Bill printing screen (F-8E). Enter the Consolidated e-way Bill Number and click GO button to get the Consolidated e-way Bill in print

F-8E: Print Consolidated e-way Bill

Rejection of e-Way Bills

EWB generated by others may be rejected within 72 hours of generation (when the e-way Bill is not relevant to the recipient or not getting the consignment mentioned in the e-Way Bill),

At e-way bill main menu (F-4A), select REJECT to get e-way Bill Rejection screen (F-8F). Enter the Date of EWB and click SUBMIT to get the list of EWB for the selected Date. Check the checkbox of the listed EWB for rejection.

F-8F: Rejection of e-way Bill

If the acceptance or rejection is not communicated within 72 hours from the time of generation of e-Way Bill, it is deemed to have been accepted.

Masters Creation

You may create often used your own business related Masters like Product, Customers, Suppliers, Transporteretc, for quick and correct entry of data in the system. Instead of entering complete data each time in e-way Bill and other forms, just select the Master Data from the list. The data of selected Master is pulled from the master record and populated in the screen.

At e-way bill main menu (F-4A), select Masters to get Masters sub menu.

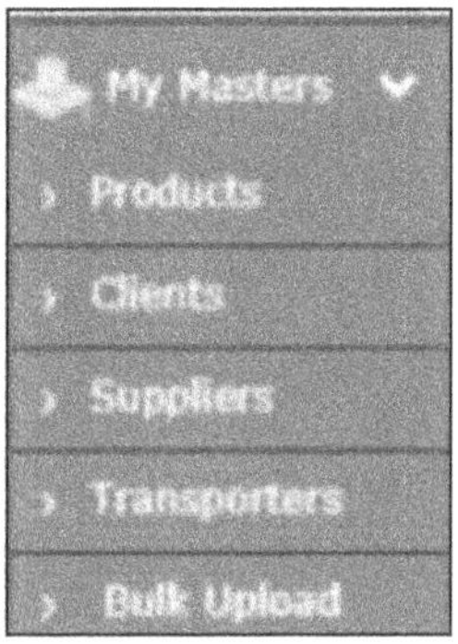

F-9A: Masters menu

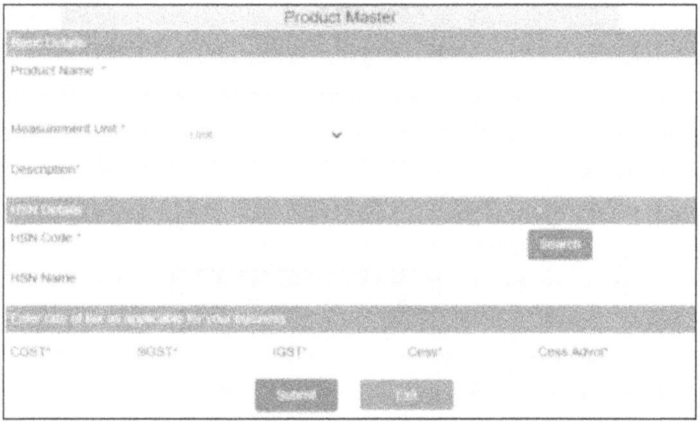

F-9B: Product master Entry

Product Master : At Masters sub menu, select *Products* to get Product master entry screen (F-9B). Enter product name, UoM (Unit of Measurement), brief Product Description, HSN Code (use search option to select HSN Code, if necessary), Tax Rate, Cess rate (or Cess Ad Valorem, as applicable). Click *Save* button after entry of each Product. Create separate Master record (with different name for identification) for different UoM and Tax Rate.

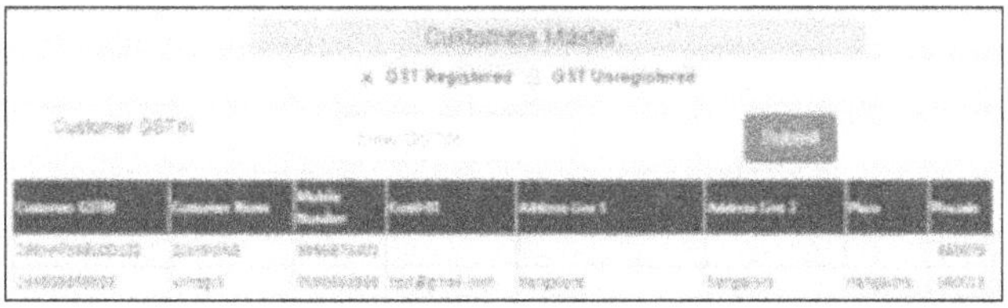

F-10A: Registered Customer master Entry

Customer Master : At Masters sub menu, select *Customers* to get Customer master entry screen. Click the radio button Registered / Unregistered(F- 10A / F-10B) to get respective entry screen. Enter the details of the Customer.Click *Submit* button.

F-10B: Unregistered Customer master Entry

Supplier Master : At Masters sub menu, select *Supplier* to get Supplier master entry screen, similar to Customer Master entry screen. Click the radio button Registered / Unregistered (F-11A), to get respective screen. Enter the details of the Supplier. Click *Submit* button.

F-11A: Registered Supplier Master

Transporter Master : At Masters sub menu , select *Transporter* to get Transporter master entry screen (F-12A). Enter the details of Transporter. Click *Submit* button.

F-12A: Transporter Master entry

Bulk Upload

Direct entry of numerous Master may be time consuming. You may upload bulk Masters for Product, Client, Supplier and Transporter

To upload a Bulk Master, at masters menu, select Bulk upload' and then select the option for the respective Master (F-12B), to get Bulk Master Upload screen (F-12C)

F-12B: Bulk master

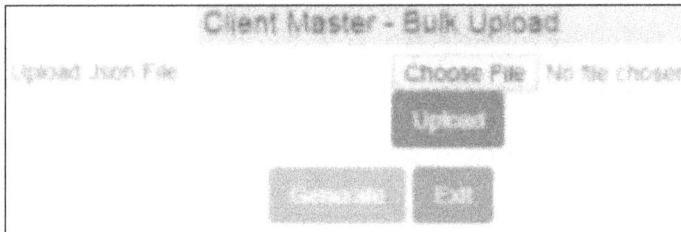

F-12C: Bulk master Upload

At Choose File (F-12C), select the JSON file and click UPLOAD to upload the Master in the Portal

e-way Bills Reports

At e-way bill main menu (F-4A), select Report to get Reports sub menu (F-13A)

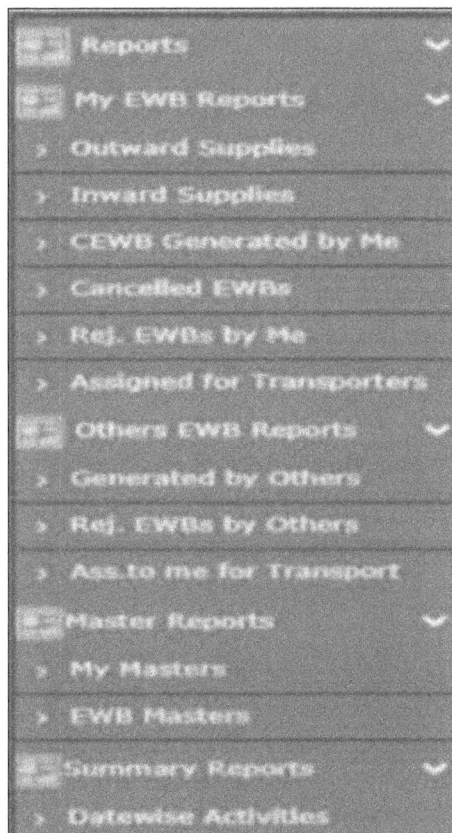

F-13A : e-way Bill Reports Menu

My EWB Reports : Reports of e-Way Bills generated by the user for a particular date:

o **Outward Supplies** : List of e-Way Bills which have been shown as outward supplies

o **Inward Supplies** : List of e-Way Bills which have been shown as inward supplies

o **CEWB Generated** : List of consolidated e-Way Bills.

o **Cancelled EWBs** : List of e-Way Bills cancelled.

o **Rejected EWBs** : List of e-Way Bills Rejected by.

o **Assigned for Transporters** : List of e-Way Bills assigned by the Transporters

Others' EWB Reports : List of e-Way Bills generated by the others against the user (as the other party) for a particular date

o EWBs generated by others : List of e-Way Bills generated by others for the user.

o Rejected EWBs by others : List of e-Way Bills assigned to others by the user but rejected by them.

o Assigned to me for Transport- List the e-Way Bills assigned to user for Transport by others.

Master Reports

o **My Masters** : List of master entries under different categories like Clients, Suppliers, Transporters and Products.

o **EWB Masters** : List the e-Way Bills based on Unit Quantity Code and State Code

Summary Reports : List the activities pertaining to particular e-Way Bill for a particular date. The user can export the populated details in an excel by clicking on 'Export to Excel" tab

e-way Bill User Management

Some users need to generate the e-Way Bill from multiple business places, multiple shifts or multiple e-way Bill Accounts. To facilitate such flexibility & security in e-way Bill System, you may create multiple Sub Users assigning different roles.At e-way bill main menu (F-4A), select *User Management* to get User Management sub Menu (F-13A).

F-13A : User Management Sub menu

F-13B: Sub User Creation screen

At User Management sub menu (F-13A), select *Create Sub User* and then enter the OTP sent to mobile, to get Sub user creation screen (F-13B).

Enter an unique 'suffix user id' for the sub user. Click *Check* button. The system will check the availability of the Suffix User Id (to prevent duplicate creation) and would proceed if available. System adds the main user Id (e.g ABCDEFGH) and Suffix User Id (XYZ) and checks for uniqueness of the combined Sub User login ID (ABCDEFGHXYZ) and proceed if validated. Next enter the name, designation, mobile number, email id. Check the option for All Offices / Specific Office (and then select the specific Office). Now the sub user may be authorised to generate specific type of EWB (Single / consolidated) and tasks (Rejection, Report generation, updation of Masters) by selecting the appropriate check boxes. After successful entry, the system will create a sub-user and send SMS message (with password) to the sub-user.

– **Freezing Sub user** : At *User Management* sub Menu, select *Freeze Sub user* and then enter the Sub User ID. Click *Freeze* button to freeze the sub user preventing the freezed sub user to login.

– **Update Sub user** : At *User Management* sub Menu, select *Update Sub User* and then enter the Sub User ID to get the Sub User Id screen like Create User. Now change the required data and click Submit button to update the sub user info.

– **Change Password** : At *User Management* sub Menu, select *Change Password* to get Password change screen. Enter User Name, Existing Password, New Password (and re-enter the new Password) and click Submit button to change the Password.

e-way Bill through SMS

We have explained registering for e-way Bill through e-way bill portal, using a desktop with Internet connection. Small Taxpayers, not having computer system with Internet, may alternately, register through SMS, using a mobile.

Registering e-way Bill for SMS : At e-way bill main menu (F-4A), select Registration to get Registration menu (F-14A). At e-way Bill registration sub menu (F-14A), select *For SMS* to get SMS registration screen (F-14B).

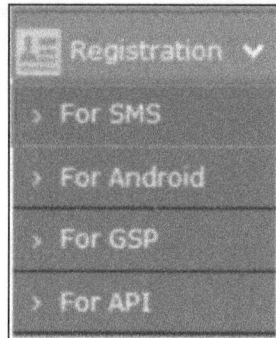

F-14A: Registration Sub menu

F-14B: SMS Registration

At SMS Registration screen (F-14B), select the User ID from drop down list showing Mobile Number. Click Send OTP and then enter the OTP . Click Verify OTP (You may register maximum of 2 mobile numbers for m-way). The system would validate the data before registration.

For Android : To generate an e -Way bill through android application, at Registration menu (F-14A), select 'For Android' to get Android Registration screen (F-14B)

F-14B: Android Registration

At Android Registration screen (F-14B), enter the email ID, select Mobile Number, Click Send OTP and then enter the OTP and click Verify OTP. On OTP verification, you get the Android Registration Form (F-14C)

F-14C: Android Registration form

Select the concern user from the drop down menu, Name and place will be auto populated by the system. Click Yes to enable the concern user with android app, enter the IMIE Number of the concern user and save the details in the e-Way Bill system. Once saved the concerned user will be able to generate e-Way Bill through android applications.

At SMS Registration screen (F-14B), GSP and API options (not yet activated) are under development.

Update : At e-way bill main menu (F-4A), select Update to get Update Menu (F-15A)

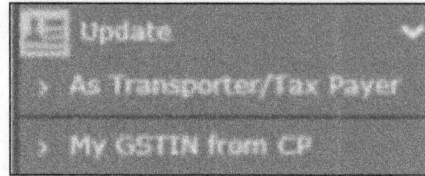

F-15A: Update Menu

F-15B : OTP verification for Transporter Registration

Transporter/Taxpayer : To generate an e-way bill for other parties (switching your role between Transporter/Taxpayer), at Update Menu, select *As Transporter/Taxpayer* to get OTP verification for Transporter Registration screen (F-15B). Enter the Mail ID, Mobile Number & OTP.

F-15C; Role switching *Transporter/Taxpayer*

On OTP verification (F-15B), you get the *Role switching* screen between Transporter/Taxpayer (F-15C). Select the appropriate option to change the role. Click SAVE button.

Grievance

Where a vehicle has been intercepted and detained for a period exceeding thirty minutes, user may fill up the *Detention Form* (F-16A)

At e-way Bill Main Menu (F-4A), select *Grievance* to get Grievance menu. Select Detention Report to get Detention Form (F-16A)

F-16A: Detention Form entry screen

Bulk EWB Generation process

Bulk EWB Generation has been briefly explained. Here we discuss about the tools used for Bulk Generation and the operational steps

Offline Method of e-Way Bill Generation : Through offline method, tax payers or transporters may generate the multiple e-way bills in one-go. This can be used by the two categories of tax payers.

– Tax payers who have automated their supplies but unable to use the API interface because of various reasons.

– Tax payers/transporters who want to generate the e-way bills in one shot by entering the e-way bill details in one excel file as order is received.

After finalization of the entries (sometimes with vehicle number), generate the EWB number. This avoids making separate entries for each order in the EWB system to generate the EWB Number. The taxpayer or transporter may download the formats provided from EWB portal, atHelp-> Tools-> Bulk Generation Tools'.

Download the excel file formats from Bulk Generation Tools for bulk upload of Bulk EWB Generation, Bulk Consolidated EWB Generation, Bulk Master Generation and Bulk Vehicle Number updation under 'JSON Preparation Tools' option. User may enter the requests in Excel file offline, validate and convert the same into JSON file for bulk upload in the system. Bulk Generation instructions are provided in the tool itself.

After entering the required data in the downloaded formats in 'Bulk Generation Tools' module, the tax payer or transporter logs in to the E-Way Bill system and uploads the file containing the multiple requests for EWB. On data validation, the system then generates the EWB number for all these requests one-by-one and shows the result in Table (else reports error details). The user may cut / paste table details into user's system for further use and action.

Bulk EWB request file preparation : Bulk EWB requests may be prepared in any of the two alternate methods

Method 1: Prepare Bulk EWB request file .

o   In the bulk EWB generation method, the request for e-way bill is accepted in the JSON format.

o   Ensure the codes are included in the JSON for the parameters as specified in the code list in the excel file.

o   JSON file with multiple requests are allowed (keep within 2000 requests to avoid uploading hassles).

o   Validate all the parameter value as per the format, codes and interlinked values before preparing the JSON file). Refer to the files from the web site: 1. EWB JSON Format.xlsx 2. Sample EWB JSON Format. xlsx

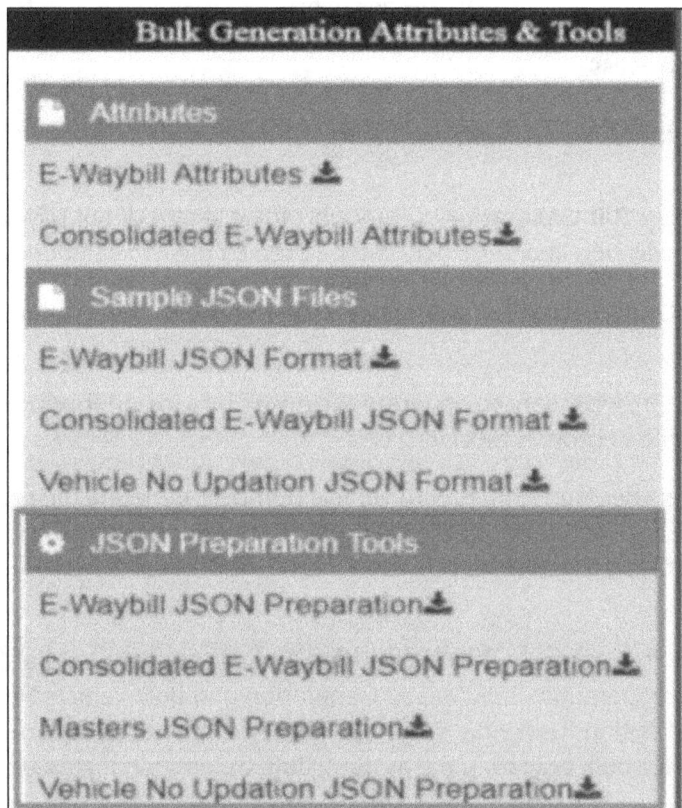

F-17A: Bulk EWB Generation Tools Menu

Method 2: EWB Preparation Tool

o   From EWB portal, at Help-> Tools-> Bulk Generation Tools (F-17A) Download EWB JSON preparation Tools (EWB_Preparation_Tool_.xlsx).

o   Use the tool to enter the requests in Excel file, validate and convert into JSON file (you may even prepare similar tool or use first method)

Generating the EWB from bulk file

*   Logins to e-way bill portal with valid credentials.

*   Select the 'Generate Bulk' option in the 'e-Waybill' menu.

*   At Upload JSON file, select the JSON file (F-17B)

*   Upload the EWB request file.

*   Click of 'Generate' button. The system generates the EWB showing the EWB Number in the grid (F-17B)

*   Click 'Export to Excel' (F-17B) to export the results in an excel file (if error encountered, rectify the error and generate the file again and re-process)

F-17B: Bulk EWB Generation & Upload

EWB Management through SMS

Through SMS, you may perform following Tasks

–   Generate the E-Way Bill

–   Update Vehicle details

–   Cancel the E-Way Bill

We now discuss the SMS Format for each of these tasks

e-way Generation Bill through SMS – Tax Payer : Generation of new E-Way Bill Number from the E-Way Bill system through SMS by the TaxPayer (Supplier / Receiver)

Format of SMS request : EWBG Type Rec GSTIN Del Pin Code Inv NoInv Date Total Value HSN Code Appr Dist Vehicle (there must a between the parameters)

Explanation of Parameters

–   **EWBG** - e-Way Bill Generate Key Word :   It is fixed for generation (so every SMS for e-way bill generation by Taxpayer must start with this word)

- **TranType** - Transaction Type : 4 character Transaction Code as per list

- **RecGSTIN** – 15 character Recipient's GSTIN (URP for UnRegistered Person)

- **DelPinCode** – 6 digit PIN Code of Place of Delivery of Goods

- **InvNo** - Invoice or Bill Number of the document of supplier of goods

- **InvDate** - Invoice or Bill Date of the document of supplier of goods, in DD/MM/YYYY format

- **TotalValue** - Total Value of goods (in Rs.) as per Invoice/Bill document

- **HSNCode** - HSN Code of the first Commodity

- **ApprDist** - Approximate distance in KMs between consignor and consignee

- **Vehicle** - Vehicle Number in which the goods is being moved (alphanumeric, in AB12AB1234, AB12A1234, AB121234 or ABC1234 Format)

List of 4 digit Transaction Type Code : OSUP – Outward Supply, OEXP – Outward Export, OJOB – Outward Job Work, OSCD – Outward SKD/CKD, ORNK – Outward Recipient Not Known, OFOU – Outward For Own Use, OEOF – Outward Exhibitions & Fairs, OLNS – Outward Line Sales, OOTH – Outward Others ISUP – Inward Supply, IIMP – Inward Import, ISCD – Inward SKD/CKD, IJWR – Inward Job Work Returns, ISLR – Inward Sales Returns, IEOF – Inward Exhibitions & Fairs, IOTH – Inward Others

List of Other Codes

- RecGSTIN–15 digitRecipient's GSTIN, as provided by GST or URP if he/she is UnRegistered Person,

- DelPinCode – 6 digitPIN Code of the Place of Delivery of the Goods as per Invoice

- InvNo-15 digit valid alphanumeric Invoice or Bill Number of the Document

- InvDate - Invoice or Bill Date ofthe Document of the goods Date in DD/MM/YYYY format

- TotalValue- Total Invoice / Bill Value of the Goods 15 numeric value with 2 decimal value

- HSNCode - HSN Code of the Goods (atleast 2 digit of HSN Code)

- ApprDist- Approximate Distance in KMs (Numeric)

- Vehicle - Vehicle Number carrying the goods (e.gAB12AB1234 or AB12A1234 or AB121234 Format

Example :
SMS : EWBG OSUP 19ABCX1234K1ZK 560026 592 30/09/2017 85000.00 1001 234 KA12AB9999

The SMS would generate following e-way Bill :

Outward Supply, Recipient GSTIN - 19ABCX1234K1Z, Pin Code of Place of Delivery – 560026, Invoice No – 592, Invoice Date : 30/09/2017, Total Invoice Value Rs 85000.00, HSN Code of first commodity – 1001, Approximate Distance – 234 KM, Vehicle Number - KA12AB9999

e-way Generation Bill through SMS – Transporter : Generation of new E-Way Bill Number from the E-Way Bill system through SMS by the Transporter

Format of SMS request : EWBT TranTypeSupp GSTINRec GSTIN Del Pin CodeInvNoInv DateTotal ValueHSNCodeApprDist Vehicle (there must a between the parameters)

Explanation of Parameters

– **EWBT** - e-Way Bill Generate Key Word :   It is fixed for generation (so every SMS for e-way bill generation by Transporter must start with this word)

– **TranType** - Transaction Type : 4 character Transaction Code as per list

– **SuppGSTIN** – 15 character Supplier GSTIN (URP for UnRegistered Person)

– **DelPinCode** – 6 digit PIN Code of Place of Delivery of Goods

– **InvNo** - Invoice or Bill Number of the document of supplier of goods

– **InvDate** - Invoice or Bill Date of the document of supplier of goods, in DD/MM/YYYY format

– **TotalValue** - Total Value of goods (in Rs.) as per Invoice/Bill document

– **HSNCode** - HSN Code of the first Commodity

– **ApprDist** - Approximate distance in KMs between consignor and consignee

Example:

SMS : EWBT OSUP 29AXYCX1234K1ZK 29AABCX0892K1ZK 560025 605 20/09/2017 80000.00 1005 250 KA12AB5678

The SMS would generate following e-way Bill :

Outward Supply, Supplier GSTIN - 29AXYCX1234K1ZK, Pin Code of Place of Delivery – 560025, Invoice No – 605, Invoice Date : 20/09/2017, Total Invoice Value Rs 80000.00, HSN Code of first commodity – 1005, Approximate Distance – 250 KM, Vehicle Number - KA12AB5678

Update Vehicle details through SMS

Format of SMS request : EWBV EWB_NO Vehicle ReasCode

Explanation of Parameters

– **EWBV** – e-Way Bill Vehicle Updating Key Word. It is fixed for vehicle updation (so every SMS to update Vehicle details in e-way bill must start with this word)

– **EWBNo** - 12 digits E-Way Bill for which the vehicle details to be updated

– **Vehicle** - Vehicle number for the movement of goods

– **ReasCode** – 3 character Reason Code for adding vehicle (as per list).

List of 3 character Reason Code

FST – First Vehicle, BRK – Break Down, TRS – Transshipment, OTH - Others

Example

SMS : EWBV 120023450123 KA12BA1234 BRK

The SMS would update e-way Bill as follows

Update e-way Bill No. 120023450123, Vehicle No. KA12BA1234, Reason – Break Down

Cancel E-WayBill

Format of SMS request : EWBC EWB_NO

Explanation of Parameters

- EWBC – E-Way Bill Cancellation Key Word. It is fixed for Cancellation (so every SMS for e-way bill Cancellation must start with this word)

- EWBNo - 12 digits E-Way Bill Number, which has to be cancelled

Example

EWBC 120023450001

The SMS would cancel the e-way Bill No 120023450001.

PART 3
GST ACCOUNTING USING TALLY.ERP 9

GST Activation for Composition Dealer

GST Set up in Tally ERP9

We now discuss about Accounting for GST, for organsiations registered under GST rules.

First, activate GST for organisation registered under GST rules, in Tally.ERP 9 system. You should set up GST for only for such Company, in which GST is applicable. For example, if you have created 3 Companies in Tally. First Business Company for your business in which GST is applicable. Second Business Company in which GST is not applicable, and a third Personal Accounts Company in which GST is not applicable, then you do not need to set up GST only for First Company in which GST is applicable, but need not set up GST for 2nd & third Company for which GST is not applicable.

Now, we discuss about the exclusive additional points regrading activation, set up, Accounts & Inventory masters, Transaction entries, Reports relating to maintenance of GST, uploading to GST portal.

GST Composition set up for Company

Now, we will discuss GST Set Up for the Company in Tally.ERP9, who has been registered as Composition Dealer and GSTIN has been allotted.

At Gateway, Press *F11:Features* to get Company Features Menu (F-1A). Select *Statutory & Taxation* (or GoT>F11:Features>F3) to get *Statutory & Taxation* screen (F-2A).

At *Statutory & Taxation screen* (F-2A), set as follows:

− At *GST Activation*, set Yes at *Enable Goods & Services Tax (GST)* to activate GST.

− At *PAN / Income Tax No*, enter the PAN of the organisation.

− In case of Company, at *Corporate Identity No (CIN),* enter the CIN of the Company (otherwise leave blank).

− At *Set / Alter GST details*, set *Yes* to get GST Details entry screen (F-3A). Even having Set Yes and having set the GST details, this option would get set to *No* automatically. So, don't get confused or worried. You have to set *Yes* each time, to view / change the set up.

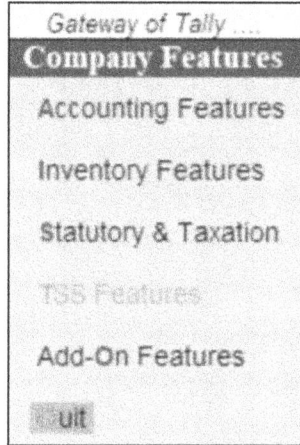

F-1A: Company Features Menu

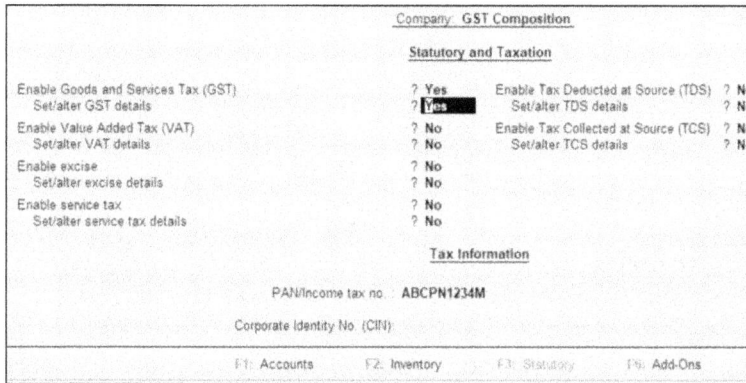

F-2A: GST activation at Statutory & Taxation set up

GST Details entry at Statutory & Taxation screen

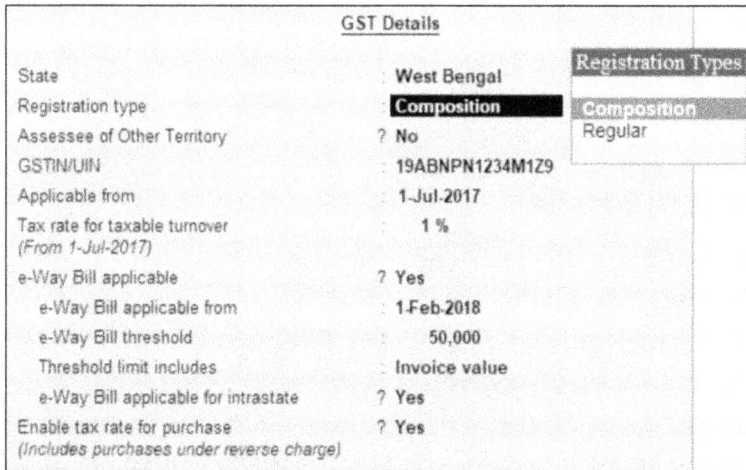

F-3B: GST set up for Composition Dealer

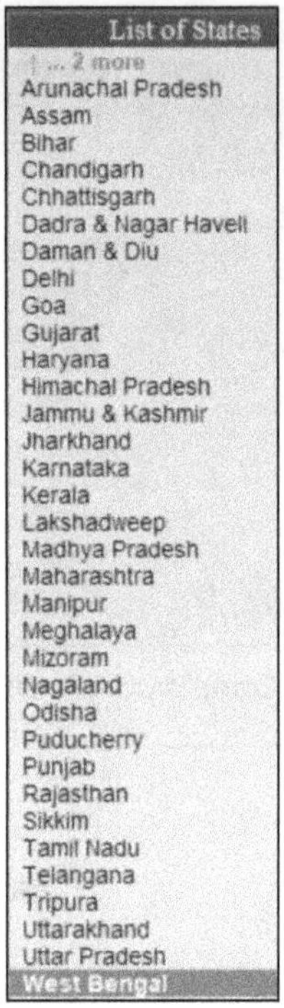

F-3C: List of States

At *GST Details* entry screen (F-3A), enter as follows:

– **State** : At *State*, the State as selected at Company creation screen appears as default, otherwise select the State / UT, from the *List of States* (F-3C), in which the company is registered with GST

– **Registration Type** : At *Registration Type*, select Composition from list

– **Assessee of Other Territory** : Set *Yes* if your business unit in located in the Exclusive Economic Zone (other territory), else Set *No*.

– **GSTIN/UIN** : At *GSTIN/UIN*, correctly enter the complete 15 digit State /UT GSTIN allotted.

  If you are working for Test Company for learning, or the Registration Number is not yet allotted, but you want to go ahead for working, you may enter any imaginary Registration in valid structure, as explained next, and proceed further.

– **Date of Applicability :** At *Applicable from*, normally enter the date of applicability of GST in India (i.e 1 July 2017). For new applicants, enter the Date from which GST became applicable in your organisation. GST will not be applicable for vouchers earlier to this date and such transactions will not be included in any GST report.

– **Tax Rate for Taxable Turnover** : Enter the Tax Rate (2% for Manufacturer, 1% for Trader, 5% for Restaurant not serving alcoholic drinks), which would be considered for Tax Liability computation in GSTR-4 Return.

– **E-way Bill Applicability** : At *E-way Bill Applicable?* set *Yes* if e-way Bill is applicable, else set *No*. If set Yes, then further set up the following options.

    o **E-way Bill ApplicabilityDate :** At*E-way Bill Applicable from,* enter the date of e-way Bill applicability.

    o **E-way Bill Threshold Amount** : At *E-way Bill Threshold* enter the minimum value above which e-way Bill is mandatory (e.g Rs 50000).

    o *E-way Bill Intra State Applicability* : At *E-way Bill Applicable for Intra state,* set *Yes* if e-way Bill is mandatory for Intra State Transaction also beyond the threshold limit, else set *No.*

– **Enable Tax Rate for Purchase :** Set *Yes*to enter the GST rate in the ledgers and stock items which is carried in vouchers (preferred), set No to enter GST rate in each voucher entry. It is preferred to set Yes so that you may sent GST rates in Stock item and applicable ledger Accounts avoiding GST rate entry repeatedly in Invoice, for faster and accurate voucher entry.

GST Set Up for Regular Dealer

GST Set Up for a Company

Now, we will discuss GST Set Up for the Company in Tally.ERP9, enrolled as Regular Dealer, whom GSTIN has been allotted.

First,activate GST for organisation registered under GST rules, in Tally.ERP 9 system. You should set up GST for only for such Company, in which GST is applicable. For example, if you have created 3 Companies in Tally. First Business Company for your business in which GST is applicable. Second Business Company in which GST is not applicable, and a third Personal Accounts Company in which GST is not applicable, then you do not need to set up GST only for First Company in which GST is applicable, and need not set up GST for 2nd& third Company for those Company in which GST is not applicable.

At Gateway, Press *F11:Features* to get Company Features Menu (F-1A). Select *Statutory & Taxation* (or GoT>F11:Features>F3) to get *Statutory & Taxation* screen (F-2A).

At *Statutory & Taxation screen* (F-2A), set as follows:

– At *GST Activation*, set Yes at *Enable Goods & Services Tax (GST)* to activate GST.

– At *PAN / Income Tax No*, enter the PAN of the organisation.

– In case of Company, at *Corporate Identity No (CIN),*enter the CIN of the Company (otherwise leave blank).

– At *Set / Alter GST details*, set *Yes* to get GST Details entry screen (F-3A). Even having Set Yes and having set the GST details, this option would get Set to No automatically. So, don't get confused or worried. You have to set Yes each time, to view / change the set up.

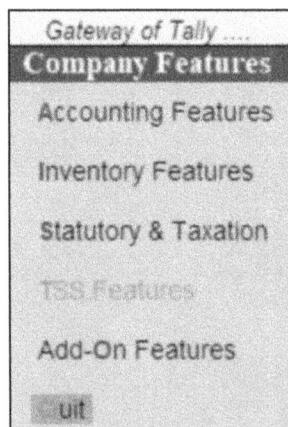

F-1A: Company Features Menu

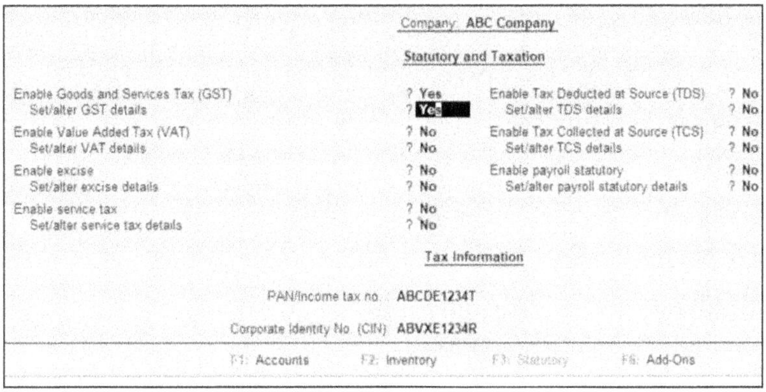

F-2A: GST activation at Statutory & Taxation set up

GST Details entry at Statutory & Taxation screen

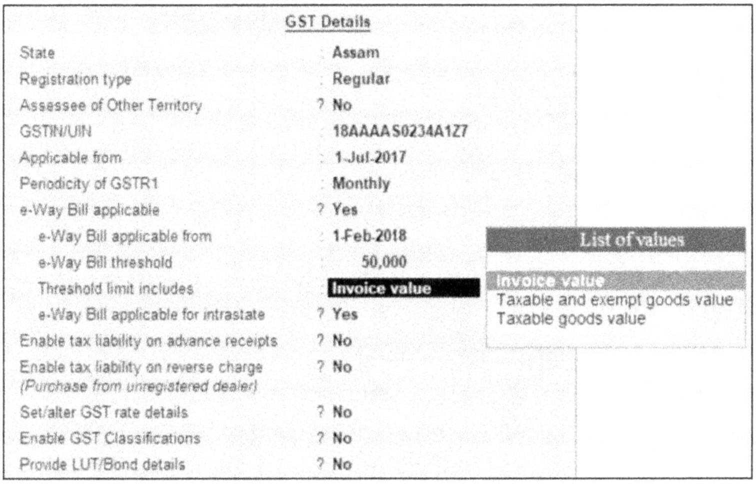

F-3A: GST set up for Registered Dealer

At *GST Details* entry screen (F-3A), enter as follows:

– **State** : At *State*, the State as selected at Company creation screen appears as default, otherwise select the State / UT, from the *List of States* (F-3C), in which the company is registered with GST

– **Registration Type** : At *Registration Type* Select the Registration Type from list (Regular / Composition),as applicable

– **Assessee of Other Territory** : Set *Yes* if your business unit in located in the Exclusive Economic Zone (other territory), else Set *No.*

– **GSTIN/UIN** : At *GSTIN/UIN*, correctly enter the complete 15 digit State /UT GSTIN allotted.

If you are working for Test Company for learning, or the Registration Number is not yet allotted, but you want to go ahead for working, you may enter any imaginary Registration in valid structure, as explained next, and proceed further.

- **Date of Applicability :** At *Applicable from*, normally enter the date of applicability of GST in India (i.e 1 July 2017). For new applicants, enter the Date from which GST became applicable in your organisation. GST will not be applicable for vouchers earlier to this date and such transactions will not be included in any GST report.

- **Periodicity of GSTR**-1 : Select the periodicity of GSTR-1, Monthly / Quarterly, as applicable (in case of Regular Registration), as applicable to you. Business with Turnover upto 1.5 crore may submit Quarterly GSTR-1 Return.

- **E-way Bill Applicability :** At *E-way Bill Applicable?* set *Yes* if e-way Bill is applicable, else set *No*. If set Yes, then further set up the following options.

    o **E-way Bill ApplicabilityDate :** At*E-way Bill Applicable from,* enter the date of e-way Bill applicability.

    o **E-way Bill Threshold Amount :** At *E-way Bill Threshold* enter the minimum value above which e-way Bill is mandatory (e.g Rs 50000).

    o **Threshold Amount computation :** At *Threshold limit includes,* select the method in which Threshold value is computed for e-way Bill, from the list

    o *E-way Bill Intra State Applicability* : At *E-way Bill Applicable for Intra state,* set *Yes* if e-way Bill is mandatory for Intra State Transaction also beyond the threshold limit, else set *No*.

- **Enable Tax Liability on Reverse Charge** : Set No, if Reverse charge Tax liability for purchase from Unregistered dealer is not applicable.

- **GST Rate Details Activation :** At *Set / Alter GST rate Details* set *Yes* if only SAME GST Rate is applicable for all Items.

We recommend to set *No* so that you may set different GST rate for Items / Item Groups at lower level, as discussed later). Otherwise, you may Set Yes to get *GST Details entry* screen to set Tax Details, as explained next. Even if currently only single Rate GST is applicable for all products, at *Set / Alter GST rate Details* it is recommend to set *No*. If you set *No*, it would be easier to set GST Rate for any new Item with different GST Rate (discussed later)

- **GST Classification Activation** : At *Enable GST Classification Yes* to activate entry of GST Classification Masters, and set GST rates in Classification, instead of Stock Item. Otherwise, Set *No* to set GST Rates at Stock Item as explained later. We recommend to set *No* to keep things simpler. We will explain about GST Classification later on.

- **LUT / Bond Details** : LUT / Bond is applicable for certain Importers / Exporters only. At *Provide LUT/ Bond details*, set *Yes* if applicable, else set *No*. When you set Yes, you get *LUT/ Bond Details* screen to enter the LUT / Bond Number (F-4A). You get another screen to enter the validity period (From & To). On enter of validity period, it is reflected at *LUT/ Bond Details* screen (once the period is entered, the period entry screen cannot be accessed any more to edit).

GST Rate Details entry at Company level

When you set *Yes* at *Set / Alter GST rate Details*, you get GST Details entry screen (F-4A), to enter GST Rate applicable for the Company. This is useful when a single GST Rate is applicable for all products the Company. Now set as follows:

o **Taxability** : At *Taxability*, select the Taxability option from the list.

o **Tax Rate** : At *Rate* column, at *Integrated Tax Rate*, enter the GST Rate.The Rate entered here would be carried as default and you need not enter GST rates in individual Stock Items.

Entry of GST Rates : At *GST Details* entry screen (F-4A), you may enter either Integrated GST rate (IGST), or separate Rate split up for CGST & SGST. The rates of CGST and SGST will be auto computed as half of the rate for IGST. Single IGST rate is easier &simpler.

To enterGST rate details shown separately for IGST, CGST & SGST, at Tax details entry screen (F-4A), click *F12:Configure*to get *Configuration* screen (F-4C). At *Show all GST Tax Types* (F-4C), set *Yes* to get the screen showing input fields for all the 3 types of GST (F-4B), else set *No* to get only IGST field (F-4C), as applicable.

Enter the Rate for *Integrated Tax* (IGST) only (F-4A / F-4B). Half of the rate as entered for IGST, is auto filled at Central Tax (CGST) and State Tax (SGST) fields (F-4B).

F-4A: GST rate entry (combined rate), at Company level

F-4B: GST rate entry (separate rate), at Company Level

```
                    Configuration
    Allow HSN/SAC details              ?  No
    Enable reverse charge calculation  ?  No
    Set ineligible input credit        ?  No
    Select valuation type              ?  No
    Show all GST tax types             ?  Yes
```

F-4C: GST Rate configuration

GST Rate Activation: The decision to activate GST rate at Company level is very important at the beginning stage. At *Set / Alter GST Rate* details :

– **Single GST rate for all Products** : Set *Yes* only if same GST rate is applicable to all Products

– **Different GST rates**: If different GST rates applicable, set *No*. In that case, you will enter the *GST Details* at lower level masters (like Stock Group / Stock item), as discussed next.

We recommend to set *No* (always) to this option, so that in future if any product with different GST rate is added, you can easily set the different Rates at Product level. You get complete flexibility for future additions of all sorts of Items and change rate as per law and notifications.

GST Classification Activation: The decision to activate GST Classification Master is very important at the beginning stage. You must understand the implications of this option and decide properly, according to variety of GST rates for products dealt and the number of products bearing same GST Rate.

At *Enable GST Classification* :

– **Few Products with same GST Rate** : If you have a few Products only with same GST rates, you may set *No* at this option. In that case, you will enter the GST details at lower level masters (like Stock Group / Stock item), as discussed next.

– **Many Products with same GST rate** : If you have large number of different products (or different variations of same product like design, size, model, brand etc. which are treated as different Stock Items in Inventory System), but having same GST rate, you may set *Yes* at Activate GST Classification. Consequently, you can create GST Classification Master at *GoT>Accounts Info>Statutory Info>GST Classification*, as explained later.

– **Implication of GST Classification** : On creating GST Classification, you do not have to repeat same GST details in each Stock Item. Just link (select) the respective GST Classification Master with the Stock Item. The Item creation would be quicker and error free.

However, when you link an Item with GST Classification code, you will not be allowed to enter or modify GST details at lower level (like in Stock Group or Stock Item level). So, though GST Classification apparently may lure you to save rate entry time, it hides the applicable rate for the Item from view and

Tax rate is internally pulled up (automatically) during Invoice entry. So, decide yourself, depending on your way of working and Item / rate structure. Tally provides several options

GSTIN Structure

The entire GSTIN (Goods & Services Tax Identification Number) is a unique 15 letter code (2 digit State Code+ 10 letter PAN+ 1 digit Serial Number + 1 letter dummy (any letter) + 1 letter Check digit) allotted to each Registered Dealer, on registration under GST rules.

By GSTIN, the organisation is uniquely identified. This ID must be used in every document or anything related to GST matter.

– **State Code (1-2)** : First 2 digits of the GSTIN / UIN code refers to the code allotted for each State / UT. So, the code must match with the State selected at the Company Creation screen.

Tally verifies the State Code (first 2 digits of the GSTIN entered) with State as entered, and reports error if these do not match.

– **PAN (3-12)**: The next 10 letters are the PAN of the organisation, as it is. The first 5 letters of the 10 digit PAN is alpha, the next 4 digit is numeric and the last digit of PAN is alpha.

– **Serial Number (13)** : The next digit is normally 1 (indicating the first registration number for the PAN). If the organisation have multiple registration under same PAN (for example in different types of business) within the State, then the digit for the successive units would be 2, 3 etc**)**.

An organisation, having same PAN, would have different registration for each State & Vertical Businesses. Assuming that the 13 the digit may be a numeric or Alpha, an organisation with a specific PAN can have maximum (theoretically), 9+26=35 different GSTIN.

– **Dummy (14)**: The next digit may be anything (it is Z by default). It is left unspecified for future use.

– **Check Digit (15)** : The last digit indicates the check digit, which is derived by applying some mathematical formula (checksum) on the first 14 digits, to ensure correct entry of the GSTIN.

If any digit in typing the first 14 letters in wrong (or transposed), the check digit won't match and the entry would be trapped as error. So, errors in typing GSTN are trapped.

GSTIN : 19ADPEG2345K1Z4

Details	2 digit State Code (1-2)		10 letter PAN (3-12) : 5 alpha (3-7)+ 4 numeric (8-11)+ 1 alpha (12)										1 digit serial no (13)	1 Undefined, any letter (14)	1 Check digit (15)
GSTIN	1	9	A	D	P	E	G	2	3	4	5	K	1	Z	4
Position	(1)	(2)	(3)	(4)	(5)	(6)	(7)	(8)	(9)	(10)	(11)	(12)	(13)	(14)	(15)

So, if an organisation having PAN such as ABPDE1234V will have GSTIN such as follows:

08ABPDE1234V1Z4 for Delhi

04ABPDE1234V1Z3 for Chandigarh

09ABPDE1234V1Z2 for Kanpur

09ABPDE1234V2Z6 for Lucknow

In Uttar Pradesh, it has 2 offices, the 13th letter is 1 for Kanpur, 2 for Lucknow. If it opens any more branch in UP, it will have 3 as 13th letter, but the first 2 digits & next 10 digits would be same (like 09ABPDE1234V3Z8)

GST State / UT Code : The first 2 letters of GSTIN represent State / UT code (allotted as per Indian Census 2011), as follows:

01: Jammu & Kashmir, 02 : Himachal Pradesh, 03 : Punjab, 04* : Chandigarh, 05:Uttaranchal, 06 : Haryana, 07* : Delhi, 08 : Rajasthan, 09 : Uttar Pradesh, 10 : Bihar, 11: Sikkim, 12 : Arunachal Pradesh, 13 : Nagaland, 14 : Manipur, 15 : Mizoram, 16 : Tripura, 17 : Meghalaya, 18 : Assam, 19 : West Bengal, 20 : Jharkhand, 21: Odisha, 22 : Chhattisgarh, 23 : Madhya Pradesh, 24 : Gujarat, 25* : Daman & Diu, 26* : Dadra & Nagar Haveli, 27 : Maharashtra, 28 : Andhra Pradesh, 29 : Karnataka, 30 : Goa, 31* : Lakshadweep, 32 : Kerala, 33 : Tamil Nadu, 34*: Pondicherry, 35* : Andaman & Nicobar Islands, 36 : Telangana

[Note: Union Territories (UT) Codes are marked with *]

Summary : Click *F11:Compnay Features* to get Company Features Menu (F-1A). Select *Statutory & Taxation* to get Statutory & Taxation screen (F-2A). Set Yes at *GST Details* to enter GST Details (F-3A)

Recommendation: It is advisable to set Yes at *Set Alter Rate GST Details* (F-3A) only if single Tax Rate is applicable for all Products dealt with by the organisation, otherwise set *No* (recommended). Similarly, you should seriously think and plan whether you need to create GST Classification. Set *No* at *Enable GST Classification* (recommended). These two aspects are explained in details in next chapter (you may change these options later at any time). So, you may leave *No* at these 2 options, for the time being (and change later as required).

Masters Entry & Set Up

GST Masters

Having activated GST for the Company, you first set up required options for in Accounts & Inventory Masters. You may set up Accounts & Inventory Masters in 2 ways :

- **Direct Entry** : Create masters first, through Master records entry (the usual way of Masters entry, referred as primary entry method). During Voucher entry, select the desired master from the list of Masters.

- **Indirect Entry** : Instead of creating Masters from Master records entry, directly Start Voucher Entry. During Voucher Entry, you may create missing master (Master record not created earlier) from within the Voucher entry (also referred as secondary entry method).

If number of Masters are quite few (normally in small organisation, where one person handles all aspects of accounting job), you may go for Secondary entry method, creating Master as and when necessary, whenever a transaction involving the Master arises. This way, you can quickly start the system. But for larger organisation involving lot of Masters, go for Direct Entry Method, which is more logical and organised way of working.

Here we discuss about the Direct Entry (primary entry) method of GST set up in Accounts Masters and Inventory Masters, that are affected by GST related transactions.

Some Masters are created exclusively for GST (like GST Tax Ledger Accounts, GST Classification etc), while in most of the Masters, you need to set up additional fields for GST.

Accounts Masters
- Party Ledger Accounts (Customer / Supplier Ledger)
- Sales / Purchase Ledger Accounts
- GST Ledger Accounts (CGST, SGST, IGST)
- Other Ledger Accounts transacted in Sales Purchase Invoice / Debit Credit Notes (like Packing charges, Freight etc)
- Other GST Ledger Accounts transacted in Payment / Receipt Voucher (like Advance, Penalty, Interest on delayed payment etc)
- Income / Expenses Accounts Taxable under GST

Inventory Masters
- Stock Group
- Stock Item

GST Masters

– GST Classification

Planning for GST Rate & HSN Code set up

For each Item, GST rate is to be specified. Similarly HSN Code is also be specified for each Item. These two properties are directly linked with Stock Item. So, normally, these are specified in Stock Item master creation. However, there are several alternative features to set up these 2 attributes to multiple Stock Items in one shot, instead of specifying for each Item in Item master

However, unless set up in proper methodical way, conflict, confusion and even Tax computation mistake are likely to crop up.

We explain the process of set up of GST rates and HSN Code, in Stock Item Master (at Individual Stock Level) and in higher levels impacting multiple Stock Items

GST Rates Set Up : GST Rates are to be set for each Item. For quicker set up, some alternate short cut methods are also available to set up Rates for multiple Items at a time, like :

– **Company level Set Up** : Set up the GST Rates at *Statutory & Taxation* feature, as explained in earlier chapter. The GST rate set up at Company Level would be applicable to all Items for which GST is activated.

– **GST Classification** : You may create GST classification Master and set GST rates for each Classification. On linking Stock Item with GST Classification, the GST rates would be carried from GST Classification. In such case, GST Rate is not to be entered at individual Stock Item Master.

– **Stock Group** : GST Rates may also be set up at Stock Group. In such case, GST Rates would be carried from Stock Group and GST Rate is not to be entered at individual Stock Item Master.

– **Purchase Ledger Account** : GST Rates may also be set up at Purchase Ledger Account. In such case, GST rates in the Purchase Invoice would be carried from selected Purchase Ledger in the Invoice.

– **Sales Ledger Account** : GST Rates may also be set up at Sales Ledger Account. In such case, GST rates in the Purchase Invoice would be carried from selected Sales Ledger in the Invoice.

– **Income / Expenses Account** : GST rates may be specified in Income / Expenses Ledger Account.

HSN / SAC Code Set Up : In the same way as GST Rate, HSN / SAC Code may also be set up at GST Classification, Stock Group, Stock Item, Income / Expenses Ledger Accounts.

Now with so many options to set up GST rates, you must make proper plan for entry of GST Rates & HSN / SAC, so that no conflict arises in case of transaction and the rates are picked up from ONE specified record only.

Unless you understand the implications properly and carefully enter GST rates at higher level, desist from the lure of advantage of entering GST rates at higher level. It is highly recommended that you set up GST Rates and HSN / SAC Codes in Stock Item (Inventory level) and in case of Income / Expenses Accounts (Accounts Level) only and no where else.

Consequences of Conflict

- **Conflict in GST Rate** : In case of conflict in GST rate (if specified at multiple places), wrong rate may be applied in Invoice. Return may be wrong

- **Conflict in HSN / SAC Code** : HSN / SAC Code may not be printed in Invoice / GST related reports, or may be wrongly printed.

GST Classification

GST Classification represent unique identification for same type of Products. For example, the organisation may be producing / dealing with various types of GI Pipes (Galvanised Iron Pipes) of different diameter / length, brand, description, having same Classification / HSN. In that case, it is convenient to create Classification Master and link the Stock Item to respective classification.

In such case, it may be seem to be convenient to create GST Classification and link Stock Item / Stock Group, with the respective Classification. The GST details (GST Rates etc) as entered in Classification Code would be carried into the Stock Item Master, from the Classification Code (no need to enter the details in Stock Item / Stock Group master).

Normally Classification Master are created for each Tax rate and then linked to Stock Item so that Tax rate need not be entered for each Stock Item, individually.

However, it is recommended NOT to create Classification Master. Enter GST rate directly into Stock Item, to avoid conflict and complications arising form change in rate in Items in subsequent period, due to government notifications.

To avoid complexity & conflicts arising from rates specified in Classification, you may not activate Classification in *Statutory & Taxation Features* set up for the Company, as explained earlier.

However, we explain the steps of Classification, for those who might still find it useful.

GST Classification Master creation : At Gateway of Tally, select *Accounts Info>Statutory Info>GST Classification>Create* (or *Inventory Info>Statutory Info>GST Classification>Create*) to create GST Classifications (F-1A & F-1B). Now enter as follows :

- **Classification Name** : At *Name*, enter Classification Name. You may link specific tax rate for each Classification, create a classification for each applicable rate.

- **Transaction Nature** : At *Nature of Transaction*, select the applicable nature from the list (F-1D), or specify *Unknown* (in that case, nature of transaction would be specified at Invoice / Ledger Accounts entry)

- **Taxability** : Select the *Taxability* from the list (F-1C). Select Taxable or Nil Rates, as the case may be.

- **GST Rate** : At Integrated Tax, enter the GST rate. Enter zero for Nil Rated classification.

- **Cess** : Enter Cess Rate, if applicable

F-1A : GST Classification F-1B : GST Classification

F-1C : Taxability list   F-1D : Trasnaction Nature

Configuration Set Up : At Classification entry / alteration screen, click *F12 : Configure* to get Configuration screen (F-3A) to set up set up GST Configuration. You may set the options to show the relevant info in entry / edit screen, as required.

Configuration	
Allow HSN/SAC details	? Yes
Set type of goods	? Yes
Enable reverse charge calculation	? Yes
Set ineligible input credit	? Yes
Select valuation type	? Yes
Show all GST tax types	? Yes

F-2A : GST Configuration

F-3A : Consolidated Tax Rate entry   F-3B : Individual Tax Rate entry

GST Rates components : You may enter consolidated GST rate (Integrated Tax) or individual component (State Tax & Central Tax). At Configuration screen (F-2A), at *Show all GST Types*, set as follows :

–   **Consolidated Rate entry** : Set *No* to enter consolidated rate at Integrated Tax. 50% of the rate specified at Integrated Tax would be automatically set internally at State tax and Central Tax (F-3A) each.

–   **Individual Rate entry** : Set *Yes* to show individual rates for CGST, SGST, IGST, on entering the consolidated tax rate at Integrated Tax (F-3B).

It is recommended to set *No* at the option *Show all GST Types* and enter only Integrated tax (F-2C). The rates for State tax and Central Tax would be automatically set.

Other Info : You may also set up like Reverse Charge (*Enable Reverse Charges Calculation*), Input Tax Credit eligibility (*Set ineligible Input Credit*) etc. but it is better to specify them at Voucher level, instead of setting at Classification level.

Linking any Master with Classification : Having set Classification masters, you may link Classification at any Stock Master (Stock Group / Stock Item). The GST details would then be carried form the linked Classification Master to the linked Master.

Stock Group set up

The Stock Group are used to group similar items, based on some attributes, as per convenience of the user (like use, nature, supplier, buyer, locality etc). of the Items. So, all the Items under a Stock Group may or may not carry same rate of GST, depending on how the Item groups are organised.

If GST rates of all Items of any Stock Group are same, then you may specify GST Rates at Stock Group, for convenience. The GST Rate as entered at Stock Group would be carried at all the Stock Items placed under the Stock Group. Otherwise, do not specify GST Details for the Stock (specify GST Rate at Stock Item level), described next.

To avoid complexity & conflicts arising from rates specified in Stock Group, do not specify GST details at Stock Group Master. However, we explain the steps of GST set up at Stock Group, for those who might still find it useful.

Stock Group GST details entry

To set up GST Rates for Stock Groups, at Gateway, select *Accounts Info>Stock Group* and then select *Create* (to create a new Sock Group) or *Alter* (to enter GST Rate details for the Stock Group) to get Stock Group Entry / Alteration screen (F-4A).

At Group entry / alteration screen (F-4A), at *Set / Alter GST Details*, set *Yes* to get *GST Details* entry screen, to enter GST Rates for the Stock Group (F-5A), else set No (and enter the details at Stock Item level)

F-4A : Stock Group Entry / Alteration

Stock Group GST Rate entry : At *GST Details* entry screen (F-5A), enter GST details for the related Stock Group, as follows :

– **Taxability** : Select the GST Taxability as applicable for the Stock Group from the drop down list. Select *Taxable* for Taxable Items (Tax not zero), *Exempt* for Exempted Items, and *Nil Rated* for Zero rated items (*Exempt* and *Nil Rated* are different, though no Tax is chargeable for both of them. Be careful!).

– **Tax Rate** : Enter the Tax Rate for Taxable Stock Groups (these fields do not appear for *Nil Rated* and *Exempted* Stock Groups) :

    o **Integrated Tax Rate** : If all the Stock Items under the Stock Group bear same GST rate, enter the total GST rate

    o **Cess** : Enter Cess Rate if applicable, other wise leave zero.

F-5A : Stock Group GST rate Entry

F-5B : Stock Group GST rate Entry with additional details

F-5C : GST Configuration for Stock Group

Other Info : By setting respective options at Configuration (F-5C), you may also set up like Reverse Charge (*Enable Reverse Charges Calculation*), Input Tax Credit eligibility (*Set ineligible Input Credit*) etc. (F-5B), but it is better to specify them at Voucher level, instead of setting at Classification level. When you set yes at Select valuation Type, the columns valuation Type is displayed showing Based on value. However, this is only for info and you cannot set the Valuation Type at Masters like *Classification Master* or *Stock Group* Master.

Linking of Classification with Stock Group : If *Classification* is activated, as explained, at *Classification* (F-5B), you may select Classification (or press Alt+ C at Classification, to create new Classification), if all the Stock Items placed under Stock Group relate to same GST Rate as per selected Classification (GST details will be internally carried from Classification, you do not have to enter them), otherwise select *Undefined* at Classification (set GST rate details at Stock Item level, as explained).

Other details : You may set other details, as per Configuration options set, as discussed, like HSN/SAC Details etc (or set them at Item Level)

Stock Item set up

An organisation registered under GST must set up *GST Details* for each Stock Item, irrespective of the fact whether the Item is Taxable or Non Taxable (even for Zero Rate, Exempted Items or Non GST Items).It is recommended NOT to set up GST Rate at any place, other than Stock Item.

At Gateway, select *Accounts Info>Stock Item* and then select *Create* (to Create a new Stock Item) or *Alter* (to enter GST Rate details for existing Stock Item) to get Stock Item Creation / Alteration screen (F-6A).

F-6A : Stock Item creation / alteration screen

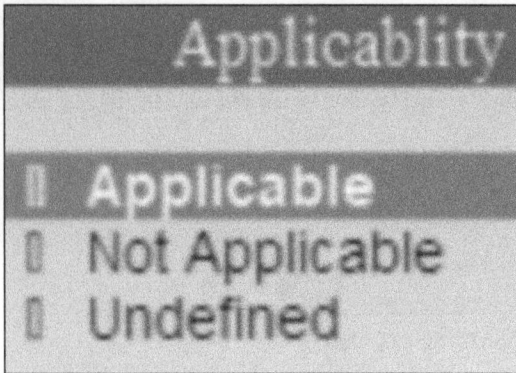

F-6B : GST Applicability List   F-6C : Supply Type List

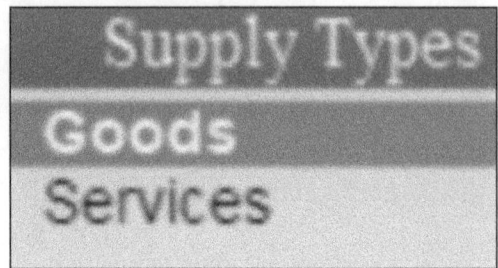

At *Stock Item Creation / Alteration* screen (F-6A), under *Statutory Information* section, set as follows :

– **GST Applicable** : Select the *Applicability* from the list. Select *Applicable*, even if the Item is Exempt, NIL rated or Non GST (Items out of scope of GST). In GST returns, you have to file details of sales of NIL rated, Exempt and Non GST Items.

– **GST Rate Details** : At Items for which you have set GST Applicable, at *Set / Alter GST* details, set *Yes* to get *GST Details* screen (F-7A), to enter GST rate details for the Stock Item.

– **Type of Supply** : Select Goods / Service (F-6C) as applicable from Supply Type list.

– **Rate of Duty** : This is not relevant for GST Rate. So do not enter GST Rate here. GST rate should be entered at GST Details screen.

Stock Item GST Rate entry

At *GST Details* entry screen (F-7A), enter the Stock Item GST Rate, as follows :

– **Calculation Type :** At *Calculation Type*, select the applicable Type from the list.

   o **On value :** Select on value when GST is computed at specified rate on Value (Normally, GST is applicable on sale value (select *On value*) of the Item). So, On Valu is applicable for most of the Item

   o **On Item rate** : Select it when GST Rate is applicable depending on price range (like Footwear). In such case, you need to specify Range of price and GST rate (explained next)

– **Taxability :** Select *Taxability* from the list (F-7B) :

   o **Taxable :** Select Taxable for Items on which GST is charged. Most of the goods / services are Taxable

   o **NIL rated :** Select Nil Rate for Item on which GST Rate is zero (like Meat)

   o **Exempt :** Select Exempt for Item which are exempt from GST (like Cereals) & Non GST Item (like Petrol / Alcohol)

– **Tax Rate** : As explained for Stock Group, for Taxable Stock Items, enter the Tax Rate for the Stock Item as follows (these fields do not appear for *Nil Rated* and *Exempted* Stock Groups) :

  o **Integrated Tax Rate** : Enter the total GST Rate (e.g 12%). 50% (i.e 6%) is shared by State (SGST/ UTGST) and 50% (i.e 6%) is shared Centre (CGST).

  o **Cess** : Enter Cess rate if applicable, otherwise leave zero.

  To enter individual rates for CGST, SGST, IGST, at Configuration screen (F-5C), set *Yes* at *Show all GST Types*, set *No* to show only Integrated Tax (F-5A). Half of rate specified at *Integrated Tax* would be automatically allotted to CGST and SGST each, no need to enter rates separately).

F-7A : Stock Item GST rate details entry F-7B : Taxability Type List

Exempted & NIL Rated Goods

Form point of view of customer, exempted &zero rated goods are same for GST, as GST is not charged in either exempted goods nor in NIL rated goods. However, Suppliers of *NIL-rated* goods and / or services can still reclaim all their input GST, but the suppliers of *exempt* goods are either not registered for GST, or if they are, they cannot reclaim their input GST.

NIL Rate is used to reduce the price of a good. Governments commonly use NIL-rated goods to lower the tax burden on low-income households by zero-rating essential goods.

Other Info : You may also set up like Reverse Charge (*Enable Reverse Charges Calculation*), Input Tax Credit eligibility (*Set ineligible Input Credit*) etc. but it is better to specify them at Voucher level, instead of setting at Stock Item level

GST Computation on Price Range (Slab Rates)

For some Items (like Shoes) and services (hotel tariff), variable GST rate is applied, depending on Price range. For such Items, at *Calculation Type*, select *On Item Rate* (F-7C). Consequently, you get a screen to set Variable GST rate on price slabs, for the Stock Item (F-7D).

Under rate column, enter the price range (at Greater than & Upto) and the corresponding Tax Rate & Cess rate (if any). To charge Tax on additional charges also linked with the Stock Item, set *Yes* at Consider Additional Expenses / Income ledger for slab rate calculation (F-7D), else set No (additional Expenses will not be included).

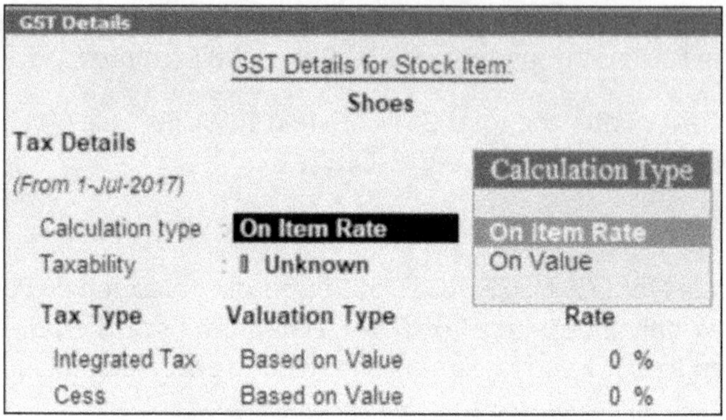

F-7C : GST rate on price

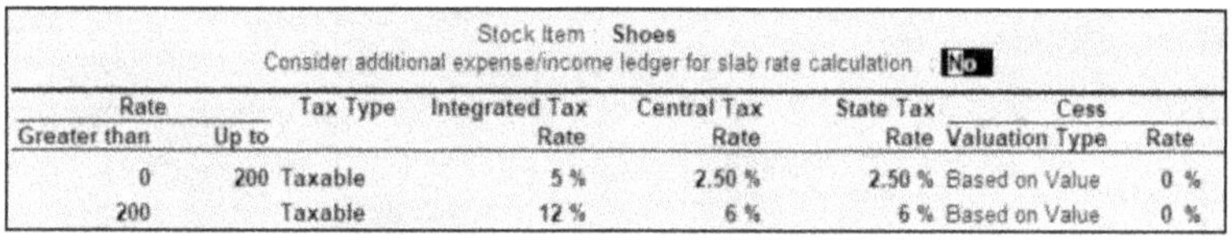

F-7D : Price Range GST rate set up

GST Rate set up : To set / modify GST rate of any Item / Group select *GoT>Inventory Info> Tax rate set up >GST* to get GST Rate set up screen showing the details of Tax rated of Items / groups (F-7E). Select The Item / Group and click *S : Set Tax rate* button (F-7G) to get the GST details screen. Now enter / modify Tax details as explained.

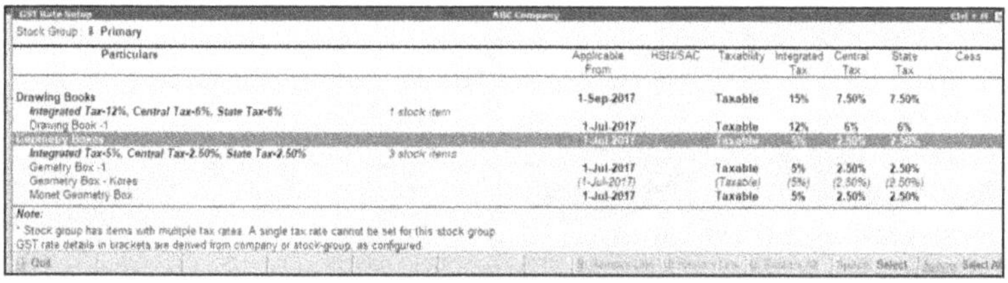

7E : GST Rate set up / alteration

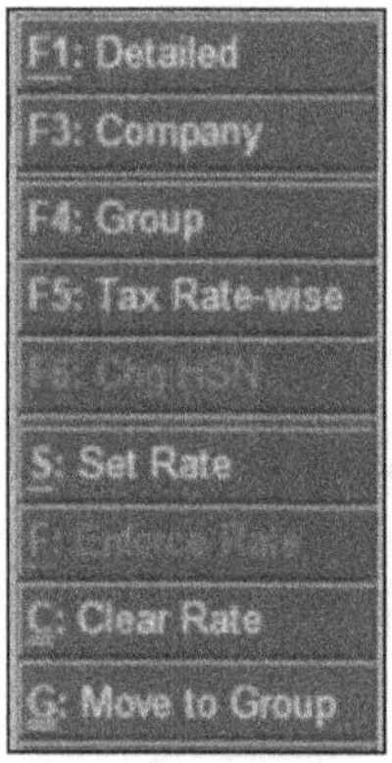

7G : Buttons

GST Rate Change : To modify Tax Rate of a Stock Item (if entered wrong or GST rate is altered subsequently by government notification), select *GoT>Inventory Info>Stock Item>Alter* and them select the Stock Item to get Stock Item alteration screen. At *Set / Alter* GST details, set *Yes* to get GST details screen. Now modify the details. If you change the Tax rate, you will get another prompt to enter the date from which the revised Tax is effective. At Applicable from, enter the revised date

Tax Rate History									
Applicable From	Description	HSN/SAC	Is Non-GST Good(s)?	Nature of Transaction	Nature of Goods	Taxability	Is Reverse Charge Applicable?	Is Ineligible for Input Credit?	Set/Alter Tax Details?
1-Jul-2017			No	Not Applicable		Taxable	No	No	Yes
1-Sep-2017			No	Not Applicable		Taxable	No	No	No

F-7H : Tax Rate History

Revised Applicability

Applicable from : **1-Sep-2017**

F-7I : Effective Date entry

L: Tax Rate History

F-7J : Buttons at GST

To see the Tax rate History of any stock Item, at GSR details entry screen, click L : Tax Rate History button to get the Datewise Tax Rate, showing all the Tax rates set up from the beginning and changed subsequently, in chronological order.

HSN / SAC

HSN / SAC are unique codes used for identification of Goods & Services, irrespective of different nomenclature used at different countries, places and trade.

– **HSN** : HSN (Harmonized System of Nomenclature) is a multipurpose international product nomenclature for products, developed by the World Customs Organization (WCO), and adopted by Customs Tariff Act 1975. HSN Codes are divided into 21 Sections, 99 Chapters. For example, HSN Code for Plastic Material are classified through 3900 00 00 to 3914 00 00)

– **SAC** : Service Accounting Codes, as were being used in Service Tax, for Services. It is 8 digit code (for example, 00440014 is the SAC for Courier Services for the purpose of Tax collection)

Entry of HSN / SAC details for Products

Like GST Rates, you may optionally enter HSN / SAC Codes, at the entry screen for respective Stock Master (GST Classification, Stock Group or Stock Item). Toenter HSN for the Stock Group, Stock Item, click *F12 : Configure* to get *Configuration Screen*. At *Configuration*, set *Yes* at *Allow HSN / SAC details* and enter HSN/ SAC details (HSN Description & HSN Code) also (F-8A).

F-8A : HSN / SAC details in Masters

Sales & Purchase Ledger Accounts planning for GST

Instead of setting GST rate in Inventory master (Classification, Stock Group, Stock Item), you may set up GST details in Ledger Accounts (Sales / Purchase Ledger). First plan the structure of Sales / Purchase Ledger Accounts. You may create one Sales Ledger Account / Purchase Ledger for all types of sales / purchase, separate Account for Intra State / Inter State transactions, and further separate Sales / Purchase Accounts for each GST Rate (to reconcile GST & Accounts Reports properly).

Depending on the plan, enter GST rates in Sales Accounts, only when you create separate sales Accounts for each Tax rates, otherwise, do not enter GST rates at Sales Accounts. The Rates would be picked up from rates specified in Stock items.

It is recommended to create separate Sales & Purchase ledger account for Intra State, Inter State & International (Export / Import) transactions.

Sales Ledger Account set up

At Gateway, select Accounts Info>Ledgers . Now select *Create* to get Ledger creation screen (F-9A), or select *Alter* and select the Sales ledger to get Sales Ledger Alteration screen (F-9A) .

F-9A : sales Ledger Activation

F-9B : Applicability List   F-9C : Supply Type List

At Sales Ledger creation / alteration screen (F-9A), at *Inventory values are affected*, set *Yes*. Under *Statutory Information* section, set GST details as follows :

– **GST Applicability** : At *Is GST Applicable*, select GST Applicability from the *Applicability* list.

– **GST Rate Activation** : At *Set / Alter GST details*, set Yes to get *GST Details* screen (F-10A) to enter GST details (F-10A) for Sales Ledger Account related with a specific GST rate, otherwise set *No* (consequently, GST details entry screen (F-10A) will not appear).

– **Type of Supply** : Select Goods / Service, as applicable, as explained for Stock Item (F-9C)

GST Details entry

Having set *Yes* at *Set / Alter GST details* (F-9A), at *GST Details* entry screen (F-10A), enter as follows :

– **Transaction Nature** : At *Nature of Transaction*, select the transaction nature from the list (F-10B).

– **Tax Details** : At *Taxability*, select the Taxability from List.

– **Tax Rates** : Enter the GST Tax Rates

F-10A : Sales GST rate set up

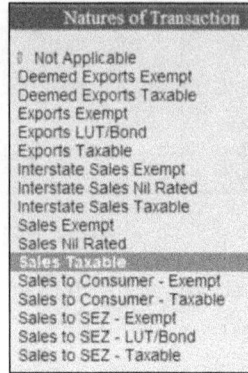

F-10B : Transaction Nature list

Similar to Stock Item, you may view GST Rate History (press At+L) and set up GST Configuration (press F12 : Configure).

Purchase Ledger Account Set Up

Set up GST details in Purchase Ledger. At Gateway, select *Create* to get Ledger creation screen (F-9A), or select *Alter* and select the Purchase ledger to get Purchase Ledger Alteration screen (F-11A)

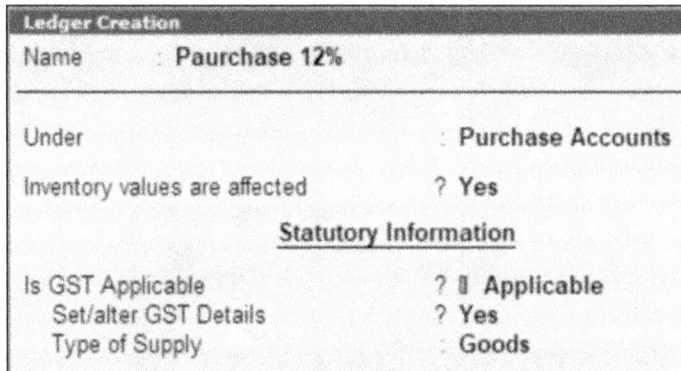

F-11A : Purchase Ledger Activation

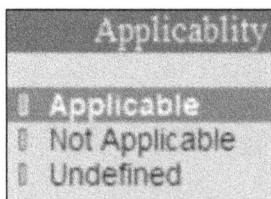

F-11B : Applicability List   F-11C : Supply Type List

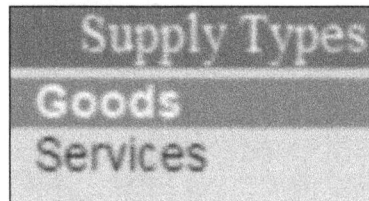

At Purchase Ledger creation / alteration screen (F-11A), at *Inventory values are affected*, set *Yes*. Under *Statutory Information* section, set GST details as follows :

– **GST Applicability** : At *Is GST Applicable*, select GST Applicability from the Applicability list (as explained for Sales Ledger).

- **GST Rate Activation** : At *Set / Alter GST details*, set *Yes* to get GST Details screen (F-12A) to enter GST rates for Purchase Ledger Account related with a specific GST rate (i.e different Sales Ledger for each Tax rate), otherwise set *No* (consequently, GST details entry screen (F-12A) will not appear).

- **Type of Supply** : Select Goods / Service, as applicable, as explained for Stock Item

Purchase GST details entry

At *GST Details* entry screen (F-12A), enter as follows :

- **Transaction Nature** : Select the transaction nature from the list (F-12B).

- **Tax Details** : Set the Tax details, as explained for Stock Item.

GST Details	Natures of Transaction
Tax Rate Details	E Not Applicable
Nature of transaction : **Purchase Taxable**	Imports Exempt
Tax Details	Imports Taxable
(From 1-Jul-2017)	Interstate Purchase Exempt
Taxability : Taxable	Interstate Purchase From Unregistered Dealer - Exempt
Tax Type Rate	Interstate Purchase From Unregistered Dealer - Taxable
Integrated Tax 12 %	Interstate Purchase Nil Rated
Cess 0 %	Interstate Purchase Taxable
	Purchase Exempt
	Purchase From Composition Dealer
	Purchase From SEZ - Exempt
	Purchase From SEZ - Taxable
	Purchase From Unregistered Dealer - Exempt
	Purchase From Unregistered Dealer - Taxable
	Purchase Nil Rated
	Purchase Taxable

F-12A : Purchase GST rate set up   F-12B : Transaction Nature list

Similar to Stock Item, you may view GST Rate History (press At+L) and set up GST Configuration (press F12 : Configure).

GST Details in Sales / Purchase Ledger Accounts

If you Yes at *Set / Alter GST details* in Sales / Purchase Ledger, you need to specify Tax rates and Classification for Sales Purchase Ledger Account. In that case, you will need to create separate Sales / Purchase Account for each *Tax Rate* and *Nature of Transaction* at Tax Rate details screen (F-12A). This would create complication in Voucher Entry for Sales / Purchase and adjustment of Tax. In fact, Tax Rate should be specified at Stock Item and Nature of Transaction Should be specified in in Voucher. So, set *No* at *Set / Alter GST details* in Sales / Purchase Ledger, to keep your system simple

GST Set up for other Ledger Accounts

Sometimes, Revenue Accounts (Expenses / Income) / Other Non revenue Accounts are added in sales / Purchase Invoice, on which GST is charged. For such Accounts, you have to set up GST details so that GST is computed on the amount on such ledger accounts in Sales / Purchase voucher.

Revenue Ledger Set Up

Create Expenses Ledger as usual (*GoT>Accounts Info>Ledger>Create*) to get Ledger creation screen (F-12C). Enter Ledger Account Name, at *Under* select Account Group (Direct / Indirect Expenses or any sub group). At *Type of Ledger*, select *Not Applicable*, At Is GST Applicable, select *Not Applicable*, At Set *Alter GST Details*, set *No*. At Include for Assessable Value for GST, select GST from list. At *Appropriate to*, select Goods / Services / Both (select Both for combination of Goods & Services), as the case may be.

At method of Calculation, select *Based on Quantity / Based on Value* as the case may be. Such Expenses ledger would be used in Purchase Invoice / Sales Invoice of Purchase of Goods, Services or combined Goods & Services, with appropriate set up.

```
┌─────────────────────────────────────────────────────────────┐
│ Ledger Creation                                               │
├─────────────────────────────────────────────────────────────┤
│ Name          : Packing Expenses                             │
│                                                               │
│ Under                              : Direct Expenses          │
│ Inventory values are affected      ? No                       │
│ Type of Ledger                     ? ▌ Not Applicable         │
│                   Statutory Information                        │
│                                                               │
│ Is GST Applicable                  ? ▌ Not Applicable         │
│   Set/alter GST Details            ? No                        │
│ Include in assessable value calculation for: GST              │
│   Appropriate to                   : Goods                    │
│   Method of Calculation            : Based on Value           │
└─────────────────────────────────────────────────────────────┘
```

F-12C : GST set up for Expenses Ledger to be included in Purchase Invoice

```
┌─────────────────────────────────────────────────────────────┐
│ Ledger Alteration                                             │
├─────────────────────────────────────────────────────────────┤
│ Name          : Packing Expenses                             │
│                                                               │
│ Under                              : Indirect Incomes         │
│                                                               │
│ Inventory values are affected      ? No                       │
│ Type of Ledger                     ? ▌ Not Applicable         │
│                   Statutory Information                        │
│                                                               │
│ Is GST Applicable                  ? ▌ Not Applicable         │
│   Set/alter GST Details            ? No                        │
│                                                               │
│ Include in assessable value calculation for: GST              │
│   Appropriate to                   : Goods                    │
│   Method of Calculation            : Based on Value           │
└─────────────────────────────────────────────────────────────┘
```

F-12D : GST set up for Income Ledger to be included in Sales Invoice

Non Revenue Account GST Set Up

Create Expenses Ledger as usual (*GoT>Accounts Info>Ledger>Create*) to get Ledger creation screen (F-12E). Click F12 : Configure and set Yes at *Allow GST for Non Revenue* Accounts.

Enter Ledger Account Name, at *Under* select Account Group (e.g Current Assets / Fixed assets or any sub group).

F-12E : GST Set Up – Non Revenue Account

F-12F : GST Details Set Up – Non Revenue Account

At Is GST Applicable, set Yes to get GST Details screen (F-12F) and set the GST Rates.

GST on Additional charge

Sometimes, additional GST chargeable expenses are added in Invoice (like Freight). In sales Invoice, the charge is made for expenses incurred by the supplier. So, in Sales Invoice it is additional revenue added in the Bill (like an Income Account). For buyer, who enters such Invoice with additional charge as Purchase Invoice, the additional charge is Expense. So, create such additional charge as Expense Account (to be included Purchase Invoice) and Income Account (to be included in Sales Invoice)

GST Additional charge in Sales Invoice : Sometimes, additional GST chargeable expenses are added in Invoice. Even if you charge to realise for some expenses (like Freight, handling Charges, Delivery Charges, Packing Charges etc) which has been incurred by you, you must treat such additional amounts charged in Sales Invoice, as Income (not as expenses). In PL Statement, you may adjust such Income against the related Expenses (or treat them as Miscellaneous Income), like you adjust the amount collected as

Freight from Buyers against the expenses incurred for Outwards Freight, or treat income of Outwards Freight realised in Sales Bill as Miscellaneous Income.

However, GST is charged separately as per applicable GST rate set up for the Ledger Account.

F-12G : Additional Taxable Charges ledger account

F-12H : GST details of Additional Taxable Charges ledger account

Now in sales Invoice, GST would be charged on the ledger amount, at rate specified in the Ledger Account master. In the same way, you should create Expense Ledger Account to be selected in Purchase Invoice.

Dual way of Additional Charges GST treatment

We have explained additional Ledger Account for Revenue Accounts, in 2 ways, which are included in Sales / Purchase Bills of Tradable Items

– **Ledger Account with specified GST Rate** : Ledger Account in which GST is applicable at specified rate. In such account, *Is GST Applicable* is set to *Applicable*, *Set / Alter GST* is set to Yes (F-12G), and GST rate is set in the ledger account (F-12H). In Invoice, GST is charged according to tax Rate specified in Ledger Account.

–   **Ledger Account with unspecified GST Rate** : Ledger Account which amount is apportioned to Items in the Invoice and GST charged as per Item rate, to which the Ledger amount is apportioned. In such case, *Is GST Applicable* is set to *NotApplicable*, *Set / Alter GST* is set to *No* (F-12E / 12F). At *Include In Assessable Value for Calculation of*, select *GST* from the list. In Invoice, apportioned expense amount is adjusted with Item value and GST is charged as per GST rate applicable for the Item. In such case, the ledger amount get apportioned to the Item, as per apportionment rule specified, and becomes part of the Item value

Tax Ledger Account Creation

Now create GST Ledgers for Integrated Tax (IGST) for Inter State transactions; Central Tax (CGST) & State / UT Tax (SGST/UTST) for Intra-State transactions and Cess Ledger Accounts.

You may create separate Tax Ledger Accounts for each Tax Type, for Output GST (for Sales Invoice) and for Input GST (for Purchase Invoice), for better control and accounts reconciliation with GST Reports. In that case, you will select Output GST Ledger Accounts in Sales Invoice, and Input GST Accounts in Purchase Invoice.

At Gateway, select *Accounts Info>Ledger* and create the Tax Ledger Accounts for Output Tax (F-13A to F-13C) and Input Tax (F-13E to F-13G)

Tax Ledger Account Name : At *Name*, enter the Tax Ledger name

–   **Parent Group** : At *Under*, select Duties & Taxes at Parent Group

–   **Type of Tax / Duty** : At *Type of Tax / Duty*, select GST

–   **Tax Type** : At Tax Type, select the Tax type applicable from the list (F-13D), for the Tax Ledger

This way, create a Tax Ledger for each Tax component of GST.

F-13A : Output IGST Ledger Account

F-13B : GST Ledger Account

```
Ledger Alteration
Name        : Output SGST

Under                          Duties & Taxes
                                  (Current Liabilities)

Currency of ledger             : ₹
Type of duty/tax               : GST
   Tax type                    : State Tax
Maintain balances bill-by-bill ? No

Inventory values are affected  ? No
Use For Payroll                ? No
Cost centres are applicable    ? No
Activate interest calculation  ? No
Percentage of calculation      ? 0 %

Rounding method                : Normal Rounding
   Rounding limit              : 0
```

```
Tax Types
Central Tax
Cess
Integrated Tax
State Tax
```

F-13C : Output SGST Ledger Account   F-13D : tax Type list

At percentage of Calculation, enter 0% as the Tax rate would be specified at Stock Item. If you create separate Tax Account for each Tax rate, then you may create separate Tax Account for each Tax Type (IGST/CGST/SGST) and specify Tax rate, However, that would create too much complications.

```
Ledger Creation
Name        : Input IGST

Under                          : Duties & Taxes
                                  (Current Liabilities)

Currency of ledger             : ₹
Type of duty/tax               : GST
   Tax type                    : Integrated Tax
Maintain balances bill-by-bill ? No

Inventory values are affected  ? No
Use For Payroll                ? No
Cost centres are applicable    ? No
Activate interest calculation  ? No
Percentage of calculation      ? 0 %

Rounding method                : ⸱ Not Applicable
```

```
Ledger Creation
Name        : Input CGST

Under                          : Duties & Taxes
                                  (Current Liabilities)

Currency of ledger             : ₹
Type of duty/tax               : GST
   Tax type                    : Central Tax
Maintain balances bill-by-bill ? No

Inventory values are affected  ? No
Use For Payroll                ? No
Cost centres are applicable    ? No
Activate interest calculation  ? No
Percentage of calculation      ? 0 %

Rounding method                : Normal Rounding
   Rounding limit              : 0
```

F-13E : Input IGST Ledger Account   F-13F : Input CGST Ledger Account

```
Ledger Creation
Name        : Input SGST

Under                          : Duties & Taxes
                                  (Current Liabilities)

Currency of ledger             : ₹
Type of duty/tax               : GST
   Tax type                    : State Tax
Maintain balances bill-by-bill ? No

Inventory values are affected  ? No
Use For Payroll                ? No
Cost centres are applicable    ? No
Activate interest calculation  ? No
Percentage of calculation      ? 0 %

Rounding method                : Normal Rounding
   Rounding limit              : 0
```

F-13G : Input SGST Ledger Account

Cess Ledger Account Creation

If Cess is applicable on products dealt with by you, then you have to create a cess account also, in the same way as GST Accounts. In case of Tax Type, select Cess from the list. At Valuation Type, select as follows :

– **Based on Quantity** : If the Cess is charged based on Quantity for all products dealt with by you

– **Based on Value** : If the Cess is charged based on Value for all products dealt with by you

– **Any** : If Cess is charged on different methods for various products, like based on Value for products, based on Quantity for products some products, and also based on Value & Quantity on some products

Ledger Creation	
Name	: Cess
Under	: Duties & Taxes (Current Liabilities)
Currency of ledger	: ₹
Type of duty/tax	: GST
Tax type	: Cess
Valuation type	: ▯ Any
Maintain balances bill-by-bill	? No
Inventory values are affected	? No
Use For Payroll	? No
Cost centres are applicable	? No
Activate interest calculation	? No
Percentage of calculation	? 0 %
Rounding method	: Normal Rounding
Rounding limit	: 0

F-13H : Cess Ledger Account

List of Valuation Types

▯ Any
Based on Quantity
Based on Value

F-13I : Valuation Type for Cess

GST activation for Party Ledger

Set up GST details of all Parties, i.eCustomer & Suppliers (whether registered under GST or not). You may enter the details individually (F-14A / F-14B) in each Ledger Account (useful for new edger creation) or enter for Multiple Ledger Accounts (F-15A/ F-15B) under a Group (convenient for quick entry of GST details, for already created Ledger Account Masters).

GST set up in individual Party Ledger Account : At Gateway, select *Accounts Info>Ledgers*. Now select *Create* to get Ledger creation screen, or select *Alter* and select the Party ledger to get Ledger Alteration screen (F-14A)

− **State :** At ledger creation / alteration screen (F-14A), at *State*, select the State at which the Party is registered under GST.

− **GST Details activation :** At *Set/ Alter GST details* (F-14A), set Yes to get GST Details screen to enter GST details of the Part Ledger Account (F-14B)

The Mailing Details / Tax Registration Details at the right part of Ledger Account screen is available only when you have set Yes at

F-14A : GST Activation for Party Ledger Accounts

F-14B : Party Ledger Account GST details entry

F-14C : Party Type List

GST Details entry for Party Ledger : At *GST details* screen of the Party Ledger Account (F-14B), enter as follows :

- **Registration Type** : At *Registration Type*, select the appropriate type from the list. Select *Regular* for Registered B2B parties (registered Parties who buys for resale). Select *Consumer* (Customers who buy for Consumption) for B2C parties, Unregistered for Parties who are not Registered under GST (normally for Suppliers).

- **GSTN / UIN** : Enter the 15 digit GSTIN of the Party correctly. The first 2 digits of the GSTIN (representing State Code) must match with the State selected at Party Leger screen (F-14A).

- **Party Type** : Select Party Type form the Party Type list (F-14C) (select *Not Applicable* for Parties other than Export / SEZ/ Embassy/ UN Body/Government Entity). So, for most commercial parties, at *Party Type*, you will select *Not Applicable*.

- **E-commerce Operator** : At *Is e-commerce operator*, set Yes if the Party is e-commerce operator, otherwise set *No*.

- **Transporter** : At Is a Transporter, set *Yes* for Transporter, else set *No* (for Non Transporter)

GST set up for Multiple Party Ledger Accounts : To quickly enter the GST details for multiple parties in one screen, at Gateway, select *Display>Statutory Reports>GST>Update Party GSTIN*, select the desired Account Group (F-15A) to get *Update Party GSTIN screen* (F-15B), showing Ledger Accounts of selected Account Group. Now enter the data in blank fields (or modify data) of GST Particulars of the Parties (F-15B). At respective columns (like State, Registration Type), select from the list as explained. At GSTIN, enter the GST Registration of the Party correctly.

F-15A : Multiple Party GSTN

Sl. no	Particulars	Address	Country	State	Registration Type	Other Territory	E-commerce operator	Party Type	GSTIN/UIN
1	ABC Traders	Address Line 1 Address Line 2 Address Line 3	India	West Bengal	Regular	No	No	Not Applicable	
2	DEF Traders		India	Bihar	Regular	No	No	Not Applicable	
3	LMN Supplier		India	West Bengal	Regular	No	No	Not Applicable	
4	XYZ Traders		India	West Bengal	Regular	No	No	Not Applicable	19ABCDE1234A1Z5

F-15B : Multi party GSTN / UIN updation screen

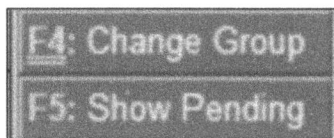

F-15E : Buttons

Pending GSTIN List : Click Show pending / Show all toggle button to show list of all Ledger Accounts under the selected Group, or show only Ledger Accounts for which GSTIN / UIN is pending (not entered).

Address : To show the Address details also (complete address of multiple lines : F-15B), in the report screen click *F12 : Configure* button and set Yes at *Show Party Address*, else set *No* (address column will not be shown)

Consistency of GST Details

You have seen that GST Rates may be entered at various levels, like at Company level (at GST activation), at Classification, at Stock Group and finally at Stock Item (the lowest level). You should ensure that the Rates (and other info) do not conflict. If you enter rates at any higher level, then do not enter rate at lower level. The Rates at the lower level would be carried from higher level, as follows :

- **Company level** : Rates entered at Company level (Statutory Features), would be carried to all Items in the Company.

- **Classification level** : Rates entered at Classification level, would be carried to all Stock Items to which the classification is linked.

- **Stock Group level** : Rates entered at Stock Group level, would be carried to all Stock Items under the Stock Group

- **Stock Item level** : This is the lowest level for specifying GST rates. The rates specified would be applicable when no Rates are specified at any higher level.

To avoid rate conflict at various levels, the safest method is to specify GST Rates only at Stock Item Level and skip GST Rate details at all higher levels.

Multiple Item GST Rate set up

To view / enter / edit GST details of Items in one shot, from one screen, select *GoT>Inventory Info> Tax Rate Set Up>GST* to get the list ((F-16A) of Groups & underlying Stock Items (with filled up GST details, if any).

F-16A : GST Rate set up

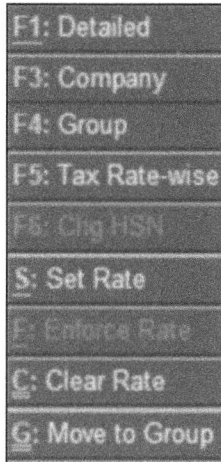

F-16B : GST rate set up buttons

All the Stock Groups / Stock Items would be listed in hierarchical structure of Stock Groups. Now you can set unfilled data in respect of GST as explained earlier, very quickly. Select the Stock Group / Item (place the cursor on the line and press space bar, the line will turn green on selection).

Now click *S : Set Rate* button to get GST details entry screen, as explained, to enter / edit the GST details (GST Rates and other info).

From the buttons at the right side button bar, you may filter the list for specific tax rate (*F5 : Tax Rate* wise), initialize (make zero) the GST Rates (*C : Clear Rate*) for all Stock Items under a Stock Group, etc.

Cess Rate Set Up

Having entered the GST Rate at Stock Item master (F-17A), at Cess rate, select Valuation Type from the list as follows :

– **Based on Value :** Select *Based on Value* and enter the Cess Rate. Cess would be computed on Taxable Value of the Item

– **Based on Value & Quantity :** Select *Based on Value& Quantity* and enter the Cess Rate in % (e.g 5%) and also Cess Rate per unit (e.g 2/ unit). Cess would be computed in parts. The first part of the Tax would be computed on % of Value at the specified Rate. The second part of the Tax would be computed on Quantity (Units) at the specified Rate / unit. These two components would be added and the Total amount of cess would be charged.

– **Based on Quantity :** Select *Based on Quantity* and enter the Cess Rate per unit (e.g 2 /unit)

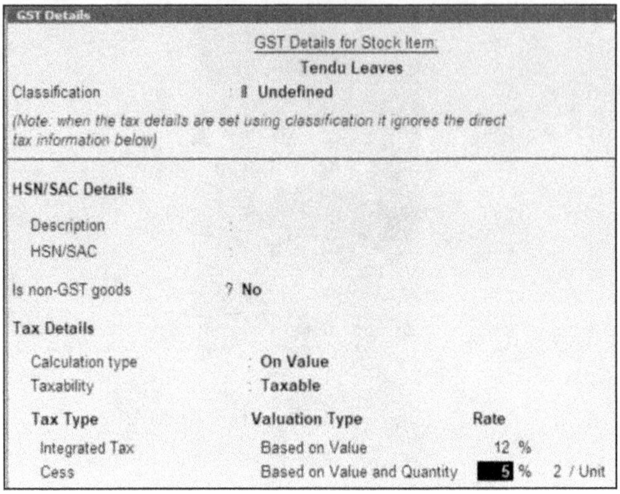

F : 17A : Cess rate set up

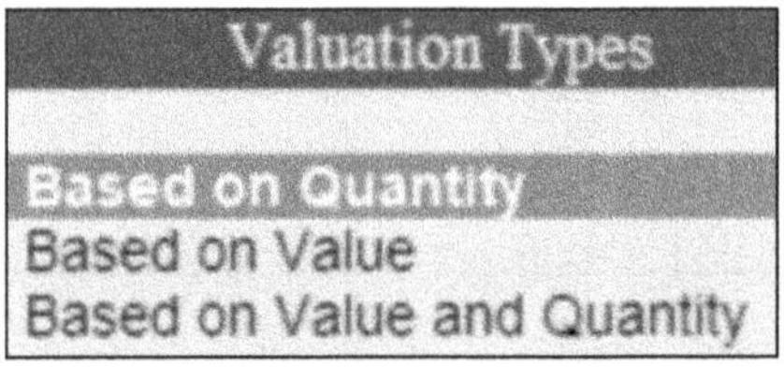

Cess rate Valuation Type

We have explained set up of GST Rates for individual Stock Item, Stock Group, Classification for understanding the organisation and method of GST details set up, for academic purpose (useful for students and organisations with few Stock Items). However, for organsiations with large number of Stock Items, GST set up through Multiple screen may be much quicker & easier.

MRP Rate set up at Item Master

Create *Stock Item Master* as usual (*GoT>Inventory Info>Stock Item>Create*) to get Stock Item entry screen (F-18A). Enter Item Name, UoM. At Stock Item entry screen (F-18A), click *F12 : Configure* button to get *Stock Item Configuration* screen (F-18D).

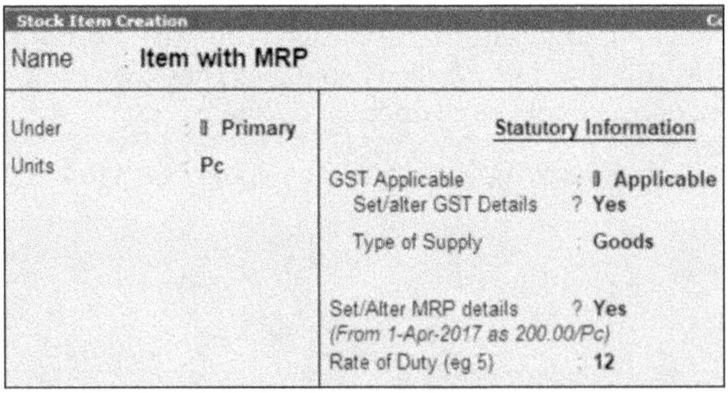

F-18A : Stock Item master with for MRP based GST

F-18B : MRP based Stock Item master GST Rate Set Up

F-18C : Stock Item master MRP Set Up

F-18D : Stock Item Configuration

- At *Stock Item Configuration* screen (F-18D). set Yes at Allow MRP Marginal for Stock Items. Consequently, you will get additional option *Set / Alter MRP details* at Stock Item master screen (F-18A).

- At *Set / Alter MRP details* (F-18A), set *Yes* to get *MRP Details* screen (F-18C). At *MRP Details* screen (F-18C), set as follows :

  - At *Allow MRP Modification*, set *Yes* to allow modification of MRP Rate / unit at Invoice level (during Invoice entry), else set *No* to prevent change of MRP at Invoice entry).

- At Consider MRP rate for Calculation of GST rate in slab rate, set Yes to set Rate as per price slab, as explained (F-7C / F-7D)

Under GST, Tax is computed on supply value, irrespective of MRP. So, MRP is not of much relevance in GST, as were in earlier regime (where Tax were charged on MRP on some Items). But in Tally, features have been carried from earlier regime (for compatibility)

Service Item GST Set Up

The set up is similar to Stock Item as explained. Select *GoT>Inventory Info>Create* to get Stock Item creation screen (F-19A). At *Units*, select *Not Applicable*, At *Type of Supply*, select Services. At *Set Alter GST Details,* set Yes to get *GST Details screen* (F-19B). Set the Calculation Type & GST Tax rates, as applicable (F-19B).

F-19A : Service Item GST Set Up

F-19B : Service Item GST Details

Goods & Services under Reverse Charge

Some goods and services are classified as reverse charge (Buyer liable to Pay GST). So, GST is not charged in Invoice, but GST Liability for Buyer is created (and reported in GSTR-1)

Sales Ledger Account GST Set up for Reverse Charge : Create Accounts Ledger (for Sales Ledger Account) as usual. Select *GoT>Accounts Info>Create* to get Ledger Account creation screen (F-20A). At Under, select the Account Group, At *Type of Ledger*, select *Not Applicable*, At Is GST Applicable, select *Applicable*, At Set / Alter GST Details, set Yes to get GST Details screen (F-20B). At *Type of Supply*, select Goods / Services as applicable. At GST Details screen (F-20B), select the Nature of Transaction from list. Set the applicable Tax Rate (chargeable as Reverse Charge).

Ledger Creation

Name	:	Transport Charges

Under   : **Sales Accounts**

Inventory values are affected   ? **No**

Type of Ledger   ? ▊ **Not Applicable**

Statutory Information

Is GST Applicable   ? ▊ **Applicable**

     Set/alter GST Details   ? **Yes**

     Type of Supply   : **Services**

F-20A : Reverse Charge GST Set up for service sales account

GST Details

GST Details for Ledger:

Trasnsport Charges

Is non-GST goods   ? **No**

Nature of transaction   : **Sales Taxable**

Tax Details

   Taxability   : **Taxable**

     Is reverse charge applicable   ? **Yes**

Tax Type	Valuation Type	Rate
Integrated Tax	Based on Value	5 %
Cess	Based on Value	▊0 %

F-20B : Reverse Charge GST details for service sales account

Discount Ledger

Discount may be allowed at Item Level (separately for each item in the Invoice), or Invoice Level (common discount on the whole Invoice).

– **Item level Discount set Up :** For Item level Discount, select *GoT>F11 : Fetaures>Inventory Feature* to get Inventory Features screen. Now set *Yes* at *Use Separate column in Discount*, as usual. Consequently, in Invoice entry, you get a separate column for Discount to enter Discount Rate. The Discount is reduced from Sales Value. GST would be computed on Sales Value net of Discount. So, no separate Discount Ledger is needed. So, no separate set up for GST is needed. You create invoice with Discount column as usual.

– **Invoice Level Discount set up** : To allow Discount at Invoice Level (as expense / income), you have to create a separate Expense Ledger for Discount Allowed on sales, a separate Income Ledger for Discount Received on Purchase, and set up GST for such ledger accounts, so that GST is computed after reducing the Discount from Item Value. In case of multiple Item Invoice, the Discount is apportioned to each Item as per apportionment rules as set up in the Discount Ledger. GST is computed as per applicable Rate for each item after reducing the apportioned amount of Discount from Item Value.

Creation of Discount Ledger Account

Create a Discount Ledger Account as usual (*GoT>Accounts Info>Ledger>Create*) to get Ledger Creation screen (F-21).

```
┌─────────────────────────────────────────────────┐
│ Ledger Alteration                                │
│ Name          : Trade Discount                   │
│                                                  │
│ Under                         : Direct Expenses  │
│ Inventory values are affected ? No               │
│ Type of Ledger                ? ▯ Not Applicable │
│                                                  │
│              Statutory Information               │
│                                                  │
│ Is GST Applicable             ? ▯ Not Applicable │
│   Set/alter GST Details       ? No               │
│                                                  │
│                                                  │
│ Include in assessable value calculation for: GST │
│   Appropriate to               : Goods           │
│   Method of Calculation        : Based on Value  │
└─────────────────────────────────────────────────┘
```

F-21 : Discount Ledger Account GST Set up

As Discount amount is charged to separate Ledger Account, it is treated like an Expense (not reduction from sales). We have already explained Revenue Ledger Account creation enabling for GST. As Invoice Level Discount is also treated as Expense, set up GST in the same way as explained for GST enable Revenue Account.

At Under, select Expenses Group (e.g Direct Expenses), to place Discount Account under Expenses Group. At *Type of Ledger*, select Not Applicable (do not select *Discount*). At *Is GST Applicable*, set *Not Applicable*, At *Set Alter GST Details*, set *No* (as you do not need to set up GST rates for Discount Account). At method of Calculation, select Based on value / based on Quantity as applicable. In case of multiple Item Invoice, the Discount would be reduced proportionately from the Item value.

For Invoice level Discount allowed on Sales, you should create Discount Allowed on Sales as Expense Account (under Direct Expense). Similarly, For Invoice level Discount received on Purchase, you should create Discount Received on Purchase as Income Account. The GST setting should be set in way.

Summary

Inventory Set Up

– **GST Classification** : If Classification is activated for the Company, create Classification for each type of GST Rate. Link the Classification with respective Stock Groups / Stock Items

– **Stock Group Set Up :** Set UpGST info for Stock Group. Unless Classification is linked for the Stock Group, set up GST rates for the Stock Group, if Stock items under the Stock Group bear same GST rate, otherwise, do not set GST Rates for Stock Groups.

– **Stock Item Set Up :** Set up GST set up for each Stock Item, whether taxable or not. Unless the Stock item is linked with Classification or Stock Group, for which GST rates are specified, you have to set GST rates for each Item.

GST details may be quickly set for many Items from one screen, instead of setting for individual Stock Items / Stock Groups. This mode is very useful for organisations to set up GST details for all Items quickly,

Ledger Accounts Set Up

–   **Sales / Purchase ledger Account Set Up :** It is recommended to create separate Sales & Purchase Accounts for Inter State, Intra-State & International Transactions (Export / Import). If there are numerous transactions with various GST rates, it may be useful to create separate sales / Purchase Account for each type of GST rate, for easier reconciliation and reporting. Normally, you should not set up GST rates in Sales / Purchase Ledger Accounts (GST rates would be carried from Stock items transacted in the Sales / Purchase Voucher).

–   **Tax Ledger Account Set Up :** Create separate GST Ledger Accounts for IGST, CGST & SGST. Normally, you should not set up GST rates in Tax Ledger Accounts (unless only a single Tax rate is applicable for all Stock Items.

–   **Party Ledger Account Set Up :** Set up for GST details for Party Account Master. Set the State of Registration of the Party, Registration Type and GSTIN of the Party correctly. Alternatively, through Multiple Party entry screen, you may set up the GST details of many Parties, very quickly, from one screen

Sales Invoicing for Composition Dealer

Composition Dealer cannot charge GST in sales Invoice. They should issue bill of Supply, as Sales Invoice (cannot issue Tax Invoice).

Sales Ledger Creation : Create Sales Invoice (GoT>Accounting invoice>F8:Sales) to get sales Invoice entry screen (F-1A).). At *Type of ledger*, select *Not Applicable* (F-1B) from the list of Types of Ledger (as it is not for Tax, Discount or Rounding Off). At *Is GST Applicable*, set *No* (as GST is not chargeable for Composition Dealer in Sales Invoice)

```
Ledger Alteration
Name          :  Sales

Under                            :  Sales Accounts
Inventory values are affected    ?  Yes
Type of Ledger                   ?  ▌ Not Applicable

                  Statutory Information

Is GST Applicable                ?  ▌ Applicable
   Set/alter GST Details         ?  No
   Type of Supply                :  Goods
```

F-1A: Sales ledger

```
Type of Ledger
▌ Not Applicable
Central Tax
Cess
Discount
Integrated Tax
Invoice Rounding
State Tax
```

F-1B: Ledger Type List

Sales Invoice Entry : Select GoT>Accounting Invoice>F8:Sales to get sales Invoice entry screen (F-2A). Select Customer ledger, Select item, Quantity & rate as usual. Value is computed and displayed. Enter other ledger account, if any. No tax is charged.

F-2A: Sales Invoice entry for Composition Dealer

Sales Invoice Printing: Having completed the Invoice entry, click *P:Print* button to get Invoice Printing screen. Set the following options:

– **Invoice Printing Configuration** : Click *F12: Configure* to get Sales Invoice Printing Configuration screen (F-3A). Set the Title of Document (as Bill of Supply) and Sub Title as desired.

– **Invoice Title** : At Sales Invoice printing screen (or at Sales Invoice Printing Configuration screen (F-3A)), click *T: Title* button to get *Report Title Screen* (F-4A). Set the Title, Sub Title (the values set are displayed at Report Printing screen) and other option.

F-3A: Sales Invoice Configuration

F-4A: Invoice Title set up

The options and values as set at Report Title screen (F-4A) would be printed in Invoice. So, Title & Sub Title as set at Report Titles (F-4A) would be printed (not the Title set at Invoice printing Configuration screen-F-3A)

Having set the *Configuration* options (F-3A) and *Invoice Title* (F-4A), type Yes at Print Yes / No box, to print the Invoice (F-5A).

F-5A: Sales Invoice of Composition Dealer

Effect in GSTR: Select GoT>Display>Statutory Reports>GST>GSTR-4 to view GSTR-4 in which Sales by Composition Dealer would be reflected at Turnover of Taxable Sales, showing the Taxable Value & Tax Amount (F-6A).

GSTR-4			1-Jul-2017 to 30-Sep-2017
Returns Summary			
Particulars	Voucher Count	Taxable Value	Tax Amount
Outward Supplies			
Turnover of Taxable Sales @ 1%	1	3,000.00	30.00
Total	1	3,000.00	30.00

F-6A: Invoice reflected in GSTR-4 Report

Additional Charges in Sales Invoice

For additional charges in Sales Invoice, create Ledger Account for Additional Charges as Income Account (F-7A). Now create sales Invoice as usual. Include the additional charges (F-8A). The Tax liability would be computed including the Taxable Additional Charges (F-9A), as shown in GSTR-4.

```
Ledger Creation
Name          : Delivery Charges

Under                                    : Indirect Incomes
Inventory values are affected         ? No
Type of Ledger                        ? ▌ Not Applicable
                    Statutory Information
Is GST Applicable                     ? ▌ Applicable
   Set/alter GST Details              ? No
   Type of Supply                        Services
```

F-7A: Income Ledger Account to be included in sales Invoice

```
Accounting Voucher Creation                              Ctrl + M
    Sales         No. 2                              1-Sep-2017
Reference no.                                            Friday

Party A/c name   : Customer 1 URD

Sales ledger     : Sales
Name of Item              Quantity     Rate  per  Disc %   Amount
Item 1                    100 Pcs   300.00 Pcs   10 %    27,000.00
Item 1                     20 Pcs   300.00 Pcs            6,000.00
                                                        33,000.00
Delivery Charges                                         3,500.00
Narration:                120 Pcs                       36,500.00
```

F-8A: Composition Dealer Sales Invoice with Additional Charges.

```
GSTR-4                                    1-Sep-2017 to 31-Oct-2017
Returns Summary
  Particulars         Voucher Taxable Value        Tax Amount
                      Count
Outward  Supplies
  Turnover of Taxable Sales @ 1%  1       36,500.00          365.00
Total                             1       36,500.00          365.00
```

F-9A: Effect in GDTR-4 Report

Sales Invoice for Composition Dealer for Taxable & Non-Taxable Goods

The Tax on Turnover for Composition Dealer would be computed on total sales (irrespective Create Stock Item ledger for Nil rated, Exempt &Non GST Goods) in the Invoice.

F-8A: Nil Rated Item

F-9A: Exempted Item

F-10A : Non GST Goods

Stock Items creation : Create Stock Item (*GoT>Inventory Info>Stock Item>Create*) to get Stock Item entry screen. At *GST details* screen, set the options for NIL rated (F-8A), Exempted (F-9A) &Non GST Items (F-10A).

Invoice Entry : Create Sales Invoice (Got>Accounting Vouchers>F8:Sales) to get sales Invoice entry screen (F-11A). Enter data for Items (Nil rated, Exempt & Non GST Goods) and also including Additional Charges.

```
┌──────────────────────────────────────────────────────────────┐
│ Accounting Voucher Creation                    Ctrl + M  ☒    │
│      Sales        No. 3                          1-Oct-2017    │
│  Reference no.:                                      Sunday    │
│                                                                │
│  Party A/c name   : Custmer 2 Regd                             │
│                                                                │
│  Sales ledger     : Sales                                      │
│  Name of Item           Quantity    Rate  per  Disc %  Amount  │
│                                                                │
│  Item 1                 10 Pcs  300.00  Pcs           3,000.00 │
│  Item 2 Nil Rated       10 Pcs  200.00  Pcs    5 %    1,900.00 │
│  Item 3 Exempted        10 Pcs  400.00  Pcs    5 %    3,800.00 │
│  Item 4 Non GST         10 Pcs   50.00  Pcs   10 %      450.00 │
│                                                       ──────── │
│                                                       9,150.00 │
│  Delivery Charges                                       200.00 │
│ Narration:                      40 Pcs                9,350.00 │
└──────────────────────────────────────────────────────────────┘
```

F-11A: Composition Dealer Invoice

GSTR-4: Tax Liability for the seller would be computed on Total sales of all sorts of Goods (Taxable, Nil Rated, Exempted, Non GST), as reflected in GSTR-4 Report (F-12A)

```
┌──────────────────────────────────────────────────────────────┐
│ GSTR-4                                  1-Oct-2017 to 31-Oct-2017 │
│ Returns Summary                                                │
│   P a r t i c u l a r s    Voucher  Taxable Value   Tax Amount │
│                            Count                               │
│ O u t w a r d   S u p p l i e s                                │
│   Turnover of Taxable Sales @ 1%  1    9,350.00         93.50  │
│ Total                             1    9,350.00         93.50  │
└──────────────────────────────────────────────────────────────┘
```

F-12A: Effect in GDTR-4 Report

So, Composition Dealer cannot charge GST in Sale Bill, but has to pay GST on his own, at specified Rate, on sales of all Types of Goods (Taxable, Nil Rated, Exempted, Non GST), to any type of Customer (Regular, Unregistered, Composition Dealer).

Taxability of Non Taxable Charges : Tax Liability is computed on total turnover. However, tax is computed on taxable Other charges included in Invoice but not charged on Non taxable other charges as shown in next 2 examples. We have created a Rounding Off Ledger (F-13A), setting Invoice Rounding at Type of Ledger. It is set as Non taxable (the option *Is GST Applicable* is set as *Not Applicable*)

F-13A: Non taxable Ledger

The Invoice created includes Taxable &Non Taxable Item, taxable & Non Taxable Other charges (F-14A).

F-14A: Invoice with Taxable &Non Taxable Charges

The GSTR-4 Report (F-15A) shows the amount of Non Taxable Ledger Account is not inlcuded for Computaion of Tax Liabilty.

F-15A: GSTR-4 Report

Another Non Taxable Expenses Ledger is created (F-16A). The option Type of Ledger is set to Not Applicable. The option *Is GST Applicable* is set as *Not Applicable*.

```
Ledger Creation
Name          :  Expenses (Non Taxable)

Under                                    Indirect Expenses
Inventory values are affected         ?  No
Type of Ledger                        ?  ▯ Not Applicable

Method of appropriation in purchase invoice ▯ Not Applicable

                    Statutory Information

Is GST Applicable                     ?  ▯ Not Applicable
    Set/alter GST Details             ?  No


Include in assessable value calculation for: ▯ Not Applicable
```

F-16A: Non taxable ledger

```
    Sales      No. 4                         1-Feb-2018
Reference no.:                               Thursday
Party A/c name    Cash

Name of Item          Quantity    Rate  per  Disc %    Amount

Item 1 @12%             13 Pcs   100.35 Pcs   5 %      1,239.32
Item 2 Nil Rated        3 Pcs    176.50 Pcs             529.50
Item 3 Exempted         1 Pcs    100.57 Pcs             100.57
Item 4 Non GST          1 Pcs     44.51 Pcs              44.51
                                                      ─────────
                                                      1,913.90

Delivery Charges                                         57.50
Expenses (Non Taxable)                                  107.90
Rounding Off  (Non Taxable)                               0.70

Narration:            18 Pcs                          2,080.00
```

F-17A: Sales Invoice

The Invoice created includes Taxable &Non Taxable Item, Taxable & Non Taxable Other charges (F-14A).

The detailed drilled down report at GSTR-4 Report (F-18A) shows the amount of Non Taxable Ledger Account is not inlcuded for Computaion of Tax Liabilty

Vouchers of	Turnover of Taxable Sales @ 1%					For 1-Feb-2018	
Particulars	GSTIN/UIN	Vch Type	Invoice No.	Invoice Date	Total Invoice Value	Total Taxable Value	
Cash		Sales	4	1-2-2018	2,080.00	1,971.40	
Grand Total					2,080.00	1,971.40	

F-18A: GSTR-4 Report

Sales with Discount

We now show Sales Invoicing allowing Discount and the Tax Liability computation on such Sales.

Discount Ledgers : When Item level Discount is allowed, Discount amount is reduced from Sales Value. So, No Discount Ledger need to be created. However, when Discount is allowed on Invoice level, you need to create Discount Ledger Account.

Create Ledger Account (GoT>Accounts Info>Discount) for Discount as (i) Discount Type Ledger (*Type of Ledger* is set to *Discount*: F-19A) and as (ii) Indirect Expenses Ledger (F-19B). The Discount Leger would be considered as Non-Taxable as Tax Liability would not be considered on Discount Allowed (i.e Discount would be reduced from Turnover to compute Tax Liability)

19A: Discount as Expense

F-19B: Discount ledger

Invoice allowing Discount : To understand the implication of both type of Discount, we create an Invoice (F-20A), including both the Discount Ledgers as created above.

Sales	No. 4				1-Feb-2018
Reference no :					Thursday
Party A/c name : Cash					

Name of Item	Quantity	Rate	per	Disc %	Amount
Item 1 @12%	13 Pcs	100.35	Pcs	5 %	1,239.32
Item 2 Nil Rated	3 Pcs	176.50	Pcs		529.50
Item 3 Exempted	1 Pcs	100.57	Pcs		100.57
Item 4 Non GST	1 Pcs	44.51	Pcs		44.51
					1,913.90
Delivery Charges					57.50
Discount (Non Taxable Expense)					(-)107.90
Trade Discount					(-)100.50
Narration:	18 Pcs				1,763.00

F-20A: Invoice with Discount

GSTR-4							For 1-Feb-2018
Particulars	Voucher Count	Taxable Value	Integrated Tax Amount	Central Tax Amount	State Tax Amount	Cess Amount	Total Tax Amount
Outward Supplies							
Turnover of Taxable Sales @ 1%	1	1,971.40		9.86	9.86		19.72
Total	1	1,971.40		9.86	9.86		19.72

F-21A: GSTR-4 Report

Vouchers of	Turnover of Taxable Sales @ 1%					For 1-Feb-2018
Particulars	GSTIN/UIN	Vch Type	Invoice No.	Invoice Date	Total Invoice Value	Total Taxable Value
Cash		Sales	4	1-2-2018	1,763.00	1,971.40
Grand Total					1,763.00	1,971.40

F-21B: Invoice wise details of GSTR-4

However, in GSTR-4 (F-21A / F-21B), the Tax Liability is computed without deducting the Discount Value.

Purchase Entry for Composition Dealer

Purchase Ledger Set up

A Composition Dealer buys goods from Unregistered or Composition Dealer, without paying GST, but they pay GST when buying from Registered Supplier. However, the GST charged in Purchase Bill, if any, on purchasing from regular dealer, is to be borne by the Composition Dealer, as its own cost, as Composition Dealer cannot claim Input Tax Credit on purchases. So, Accounting Treatment and Tax Ledger set up for Composition Dealer would be bit different.

F-2A: Purchase Ledger

Tax Ledger Set Up

GST paid in purchase invoice for goods purchased from registered dealer, is to be treated as expenses as Composition dealer is not entitled to claim ITC.

F-1A: GST ledger as Expenses

F-1B: Ledger Type List

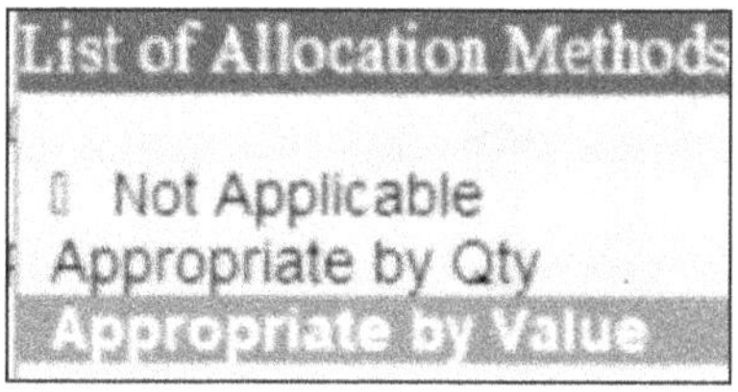

F-1C: Allocation methods list

At Accounts Ledger creation / alteration (GoT>Accounts Info>Ledger), at *Under*, select Direct Expenses (NOT Duties & Taxes) to treat the Tax as Expense Accounts (F-1A). At *Type of ledger*, select *Not Applicable*(F-1B) from the list of Types of Ledger (as it is not Tax, Discount or Rounding Off).

To allocate the Tax (CGST / SGST / IGST) as the case may be to Item Value (to know the actual purchase cost of the respective Item), at the respective ledger accounts, click *F12:Configure* and set Yes at *Allow method of appropriation (used in purchase invoice)*(F-2A).

Consequently, you will set the Method of Appropriation to allocate the amount of the ledger to respective stock Item. At *method of appropriation in Purchase Accounts*, select the method from the list of allocation methods (F-1C)

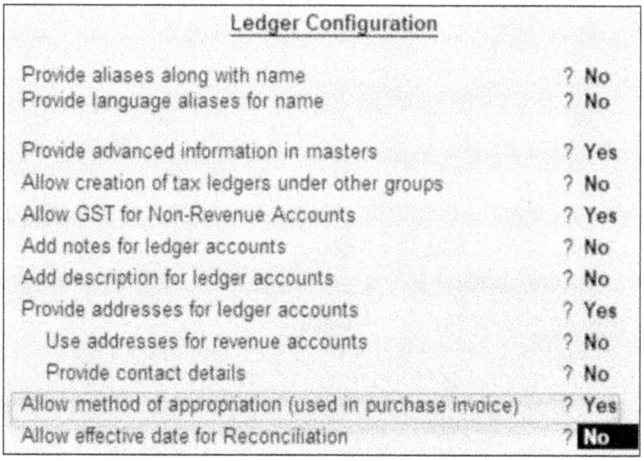

F-2A: Account Ledger Configuration option for

Purchase Cost allocation

This way, create ledger accounts for all the Tax Accounts (CGST/SGST/UTGST/IGST).

Purchase Voucher : Registered Dealer would be charging GST for sales to Composition Dealer. So, in the Purchase Invoice for purchases from Registered Dealer, Composition Dealer would pay SGST / UTST / CGST (for Intra State Purchase) and IGST (on Inter State Purchase).

Accounting Voucher Creation					Ctrl + M
Purchase No. 1					1-Aug-2017
Supplier invoice no.:					Tuesday
Party A/c name : **Supplier Regd**					
Purchase ledger : **Purchase**					
Name of Item	Quantity	Rate	per	Disc %	Amount
Item 1 @12%	200 Pcs	100.00	Pcs	5 %	19,000.00
Item 2 Nil Rated	50 Pcs	100.00	Pcs		5,000.00
Item 3 Exempted	40 Pcs	200.00	Pcs		8,000.00
Item 4 Non GST	10 Pcs	400.00	Pcs		4,000.00
					36,000.00
SGST					1,140.00
CGST					1,140.00
Narration:	300 Pcs				*38,280.00*

F-3A: Purchase Invoice by Composition Dealer

Stock Summary			Ctrl + M
		Inwards	
	Quantity	Rate	Value
Item 1 @12%	200 Pcs	101.02	20,203.34
Item 2 Nil Rated	50 Pcs	106.33	5,316.66
Item 3 Exempted	40 Pcs	212.67	8,506.66
Item 4 Non GST	10 Pcs	425.33	4,253.34
Grand Total	**300 Pcs**		**38,280.00**

F-4A: Stock Summary with showing allocated purchase cost

Enter Purchase Voucher as usual (Got>Accounting Voucher>F9:Purchase to get Purchase Voucher entry screen (F-3A). Enter Item details. Select the Tax Account and enter the Amount (F-3A). Select the Items, enter Quantity,Rate, Discount Rate (if any). After all the Items are entered, select the SGST/ UTGST and CGST or IGST, as the case may be, and enter the Amount.

Cost Allocation : The Tax Amount would be allocated to item as cost of purchase, on the basis of Allocation option (F-1C), selected for Tax Ledger Accounts (F-1A).

In case of multi rate tax invoice of purchase (F-3A), Tax amount would be correctly allocated to Items in the Purchase Invoice if all the Item bear same Tax rate. Otherwise the allocation would not be correct (F-4A). The Tax would be allocated uniformly among all Item on the basis of allocation (Value/ Quantity), without any regard to Tax rate charged on the Item.

Purchase under Reverse Charge

In case of Purchase of Service under Reverse charge (like Transport Charges etc), the Composition Dealer has to pay Tax as per Normal rates applicable.

Creation of Expense Ledger : Create a Ledger Account (*GoT>Accounts Info>ledger > Create*) to get Ledger entry screen (F-5A). At *Set / Alter GST Details*, set *Yes* to get GST Details screen (F-5B). Select *Services* at *Type of Supply*. At *GST Details* screen (F-5B), set *Yes* at *Is Reverse Charge Applicable*. Enter the normal Tax rate applicable for the Service (Tax liability on Reverse Charge would be computed at this Rate)

```
Ledger Alteration

Name            : Transport Expenses (Reverse Charge)

Under                                        : Indirect Expenses
Inventory values are affected                ? No
Type of Ledger                               ? ▌ Not Applicable

Method of appropriation in purchase invoice  ▌ Not Applicable
                        Statutory Information

Is GST Applicable                            ? ▌ Applicable
   Set/alter GST Details                      ? Yes
   Type of Supply                            : Services
```

F-5A: Service Ledger Account under Reverse Charge

```
GST Details

                          GST Details for Ledger:
                    Transport Expenses (Reverse Charge)

HSN/SAC Details

   Description              : Transport Charges
   HSN/SAC                  : 12345678

Is non-GST goods            ? No

Tax Details
(From 1-Jul-2017)
   Taxability               : Taxable
   Is reverse charge applicable  ? Yes

   Tax Type              Valuation Type            Rate
   Integrated Tax        Based on Value            5 %
   Cess                  Based on Value            0 %
```

F-5B: GST Details of Expenses Account under Reverse Charge

Supplier Ledger Creation : Create a Ledger Account (*GoT>Accounts Info>ledger > Create*) to get Ledger entry screen (F-6A). At State, select the State of the supplier. At *Set / Alter GST Details*, set *Yes* to get GST Details screen (F-6B). At GST Details screen (F-6B), at *Registration Type*, select the Registration Type from list. Enter GSTIN for Registered Supplier.

Ledger Alteration				Composition
Name	: **Supplier Regd**			
				Mailing Details
Under	: Sundry Creditors (Current Liabilities)	Name	: **Supplier Regd**	
		Address	:	
Maintain balances bill-by-bill	? Yes			
Default credit period	:			
Check for credit days during voucher entry	? No	Country	: India	
Inventory values are affected	? No	State	: Assam	
		Provide bank details ? No		
				Tax Registration Details
		PAN/IT No.	: ABCPE1234N	
		Set/alter GST details ? Yes		

F-6A: Supplier Ledger Account

GST Details		Registration Types
		I Unknown
Registration type	Regular	Composition
		Consumer
Assessee of Other Territory	? No	**Regular**
GSTIN/UIN	18AAAAS0234A1Z7	Unregistered
Is a transporter	? Yes	

F-6B: Supplier Ledger Account GST Details

Purchase Invoice Entry : Create Purchase Invoice (GoT>Accounting Voucher>F9:Purchase to get Purchase Voucher entry screen. Click *I:Accounting Invoice* button to get Accounting Invoice entry Format (F-7A). Select the Ledger Account and enter Amount (F-7A).

Purchase	No. 2			1-Feb-2018
Supplier invoice no. : **12**		Date : **1-Feb-2018**		Thursday
Party A/c name	: **Supplier Regd**			
Particulars			Rate per	**Amount**
Transport Expenses (Reverse Charge)				2,000.00
Narration:				2,000.00

F-7A: Purchase Invoice for Service under Reverse Charge

GSTR-4 Report : Select *GoT>Display>Statutory Reports> GST>GST Reports>GSTR-4* to get GSTR-4 Report (F-8B), showing the Tax Liability of Purchase under Reverse Charge, computed at Normal rate as specified for the Ledger Account (F-5B). Drill down to get Invoice Details showing the Tax component for the Purchase Invoice (F-8B)

GSTR-4							For 1-Feb-2018
Returns Summary							
Particulars	Voucher Count	Taxable Value	Integrated Tax Amount	Central Tax Amount	State Tax Amount	Cess Amount	Total Tax Amount
Outward Supplies							
Turnover of Taxable Sales @ 1%	1	1,971.48		9.86	9.86		19.72
Inward Supplies							
Purchases Attracting Reverse Charge	1	2,000.00					100.00
Interstate Purchase Taxable @ 5%		2,000.00	100.00				100.00
Total	2	3,971.48	100.00	9.86	9.86		119.72

F-8A: GSTR-4 Report

Vouchers of	Interstate Purchase Taxable @ 5%										For 1-Feb-2018
Supplier Name	GSTIN/UIN	Vch Type	Invoice No.	Invoice Date	Total Invoice Value	Place of Supply	Total Taxable Value	Integrated Tax Amount	Central Tax Amount	State Tax Amount	Cess Amount
Supplier Inc	08AAAAV0516A1ZE	Purchase	48	8-2-2018	2,000.00	Punjab	2,000.00	100.00			
Grand Total					2,000.00		2,000.00	100.00			

F-8B: Invoice wise details of GSTR-4

The Composition Dealer has to pay total tax liability while filing GSTR-4 for the specified Return period.

Sales Invoicing for Regular Dealer

Invoice Entry

Having activated GST features and having set required GST related info in all the Masters, you now enter details of Sales &Purchase transactions. We have already explained sales Invoice entry. We describe additional details exclusively related to GST registered Regular Dealer.

Sales Invoice Entry

Enter Sales Invoice as usual. Select *GoT>Accounting Voucher*, Click *F8:Sales* to get *Sales Voucher* entry screen (F-1A) . Now enter Sales Invoice data as explained earlier. We describe here entry of GST specific details only.

Invoice Header : Enter *Invoice Date*. Select *Customer Ledger*. Select *Sales Leger*, as usual.

Intra State (Same State) Sales Invoice Entry : In Local Sales, the customer is registered in the same state in which the Company is registered:

– **State**: So, same State must be selected in *State* field in *Statutory & Taxation* Details of the Company, and the State field in GST Details of the Customer Master, as explained earlier.

– **State Code part in GSTIN**: The first 2 digit of GSTIN, representing the State Code as entered at GST details for the Company, and Customer, must be same.

Item Details : Enter the details of Item sold (Item Name, Quantity, Rate, Value), as usual (F-1A).

Sales	No. 07/00001/17-18			1-Jul-2017
Reference no.:				Saturday
Party A/c name	Customer 1 - Kol 19			
Sales ledger	: Sales			
Name of Item	**Quantity**	**Rate**	**per**	**Amount**
Item 1 @5%	100 Pc	50.00	Pc	5,000.00
Output CGST				125.00
Output SGST				125.00
Narration:	100 Pc			5,250.00

F-1A: Local sales Invoice

F-1B: Tax Analysis of Local sales Invoice

GST Accounts : Now enter the GST Account details as follows (F-1A):

In Local Sales Invoice (the first 2 digits of GSTIN of the Company and the Customer is same) select *Output* SGST and *Output CGST* (F-1A). The Total GST amount computed as per applicable GST Rate for each Item, is equally divided into both the Tax Accounts (Central Tax – CGST & State Tax – SGST). At Invoice entry screen (F-1A) Click *A:Tax Analysis* button to get the details of Tax Analysis (F-1B)

As illustration, we have used separate GST Accounts like, Output CGST/ Output SGST / Output IGST for outward transactions (Sales) and Input CGST/ Input SGST / Input IGST for inward transactions (Purchase), for better control & reconciliation of huge transactions. But you may use common GST Ledgers for both inwards & Outwards transactions, like CGST/ SGST / IGST.

Multiple Items Invoicing with different Tax Rates

Sometimes, one Sales Invoice may contain multiple Items with Different Tax rates. The invoicing process is same. Just select the Stock Items and enter the details for each Stock Item, one by one (F-2B).

Next select the Tax Accounts (Output CGST and Output SGST) one by one. The Tax would be computed for each Item as per applicable rate and the total tax amount for each rate would be shown against the respective Tax Account.

The details of computation of Tax in respect of each tax account for each Stock item would be shown in Tax Analysis Statement.

F-2A: Local B2B Sales Invoice for Multiple Rate Stock Items

F-2B: Tax Analysis for Sales Invoice for Multiple Rate Stock Items

The amount of Tax would be rounded off as per Rounding Off option set in respective Tax Ledger Account (CGST, SGST, IGST), as explained in Accounts Master Chapter.

Interstate Sales Invoice Entry

In Inter State (Outside State) Sales, the customer is registered in different state in which the Company is registered:

- **State**: So, Different State would be selected in *State* field in *Statutory & Taxation* Details of the Company, and the *State* field in *GST Details of the Customer Master*, as explained earlier.

- **State Code part in GSTIN**: The first 2 digit of GSTIN, representing the State Code as entered at GST details for the Company, and Customer, would be different.

- **Item Details** : Enter the details of Item sold (Item Name, Quantity, Rate, Value), as usual (F-3A).

In Interstate Sales (F-3A), select *Integrated Tax* (instead of CGST& SGST).

F-3A: Inter State sales Invoice

F-2B: Tax Analysis of Inter State Sales Invoice

GST Accounts : For Inter State sale, select Integrated Tax (IGST) Ledger Account. Total GST amount computed as per applicable GST Rate for each Item, is shown against Integrated Tax Account). At Invoice entry screen (F-3A),click *A:Tax Analysis* button to get the details of Tax Analysis (F-3B). As illustration, we have used separate GST Accounts like, Output CGST/ Output SGST / Output IGST for outward transactions (Sales) and Input CGST/ Input SGST / Input IGST for inward transactions (Purchase), for better control & reconciliation of huge transactions. But you may use common GST Ledgers for both inwards & Outwards transactions, like CGST/ SGST / IGST.

Multiple Rate Items : If Multiple Items are entered in Invoice, having different Tax rates, the GST would be computed as per applicable Tax rate for the respective Item and the total GST for each Tax Account (IGST, CGST& SGST) would be shown against the respective account in Invoice entry screen.

Tax Computation Details : To view Tax Details breakup for each Tax Account, in respect of each rate / Item, at Invoice entry (F-1A, F-2A, 3A), click *A:Tax Analysis* button to get Tax Analysis screen (F-1B, F-2B, F-3B). At Tax Analysis screen, click *F1:Detailed/* Condensed toggle button to get details /summary of Tax.

Sales Invoice Printing

To instantly print the invoice after entry, at Invoice entry screen, at top button bar, Click *P:Print* button to get Invoice printing screen and then type *Yes* to print Invoice (F-3A), as per current configuration set. To set configuration, click *F12:Configure* to get Invoice Printing Configuration options (F-3B).

F-3A : Sales Invoice in print

```
                        Standard Sales Configuration

           Title of Document       : Tax Invoice
              (for optional vouchers)  PROFORMA INVOICE
           Sub Title (if any)       :

                General                         Order And Despatch Details

  Print in simple format            ? No    Print order details              ? Yes
  Print Customer's Signature        ? No    Print terms of payment and Delivery ? Yes
  Print Address in a continuous line ? No   Print despatch details           ? Yes
  Print Bank Details                ? No
                                                    Statutory Details
                Item Details
                                          GST
  Print quantity column             ? Yes
  Print alternate quantity          ? No    Print Company GSTIN Number       ? Yes
     Print as separate column       ? No    Print Buyer's GSTIN Number       ? Yes
  Print actual quantity column      ? No    Print Item-wise GST details      ? No
  Print rate column                 ? Yes   Print GST Analysis of Items      ? Yes
  Print Additional Description(s) for Item Name ? No  Print HSN/SAC details  ? Yes
                                          Print GST % column                 ? Yes
             Registration Details         Print HSN/SAC column               ? Yes
                                          Print MRP/Marginal Column          ? No
  Print Company's PAN / Income Tax No. ? No  Print State Name & State Code   ? Yes
  Print Company's Tax Regn. Numbers  ? Yes  Print Place of Supply            ? No
  Print Party's PAN / Income Tax No. ? No   Print Tax Invoice in Base Currency ? No
  Print buyer's tax regn. number     ? Yes  Print Tax amount for Export Invoice ? No
  Print Buyer's CST Regn. Number     ? No   Print e-Way Bill No.             ? Yes


           Jurisdiction                Kolkata

           Generated by      This is a Computer Generated Invoice

                       Press F12 for more options
```

F-3B: Invoice printing Configuration options

```
                        Advanced Sales Configuration
                             Measurements

           Height of normal invoice(inches)    10       Simple: 10
           Width of normal invoice(inches)     7.50     Simple: 7.50
           Margin on top (default 0.25)        0.25     Simple: 0.25
           Margin on left (default 0.5)        0.50     Simple: 0.50

                General                            Statutory Details

  Print Prepared/Verified initials   ? No    Print Item Taxable Values        ? No
  Print voucher reference            ? Yes   Print Declaration                ? Yes
  Print serial number                ? Yes   Print rate of duty with items    ? No
  Print add. description(s) for ledger name ? No
  Print narration                    ? No
  Print narration for each entry     ? No
  Print sub-totals after each line   ? No
  Print Bill-wise Details            ? No
  Print Base Currency Symbol for Total ? Yes
                Item Details

  Print batch details                ? No
  Print godown name                  ? No
     Print godown address            ? No
  Print part number                  ? No


           Format to use for stock item    ? Name Only
           Method to use for Party Name      Name Only
```

F-3C: Invoice printing Advanced Configuration options

Setting Invoice Printing options

At *Invoice Printing* screen (when you click *P:Print* button at top of Invoice entry screen) you may use the buttons (F-4A) to set up Invoice Printing options. Mostly used Invoice printing options are explained below:

- **Invoice Title** : Click *T:Titling* button to get *Title Set Up* screen (F-4B).

  - **Title** : At *Title*, the default Title appears as per current Report Type. You may re-set the Title. Title is printed as Invoice Header at the top, in all pages of the Invoice. The Title setting is reflected in Invoice Printing screen for reference.

  - **Sub Title** : Similarly, at *Sub Title*, you may re-set the Sub Title (Sub Title is printed below the Title in first page of Invoice only).

- **Number of Copies :** Click *C:Copies* button to get *Number of Copies* screen (F-4C). At Number of Copies, enter the number of Copies to the printed. At Type of copy, select All (to print all the copies). To re-print any specific copy, select the specific copy from the list. At the Invoice header, the copy Mark is printed at the top right hand corner of Invoice (1st Copy- Original For Recipient, 2nd Copy- Duplicate for Transporter, 3rd Copy - Triplicate for Supplier, 4th& subsequent copies – Extra Copy). The Copy markers are system fixed, you cannot change it.

L: Print Language		Report Titles	
I: No Preview			
T: Titling		Title : **Invoice cum Bill of Supply**	
G: Page Nos.		Sub-title : **Tax Invoice**	
R: Pre-Printed		**Additional Information**	
F: Print Format		Print with Company Name ? **Yes**	
C: Copies		Print with Company Address ? **Yes**	
S: Select Printer		Print with Company CIN ? **No**	
		Print with Company Phone No. ? **Yes**	
		Print with Company Website ? **No**	
F12: Configure		Print Date Range of Report ? **No**	
		Print Page Numbers in Report ? **No**	

F-4A: Invoice printing options   F-4B: Invoice Title printing options

Number of Copies

	Print
	All
	Not Applicable
Number of Copies : **4**	Duplicate
	Extra copy
	Original
Type of Copy : **All**	Quadruplicate
	Triplicate

F-4C: Number of Copies printing options

```
                          Advanced Configuration

Reduce space between address and item name/particulars      ? Yes
(Enabling this option will not print the contact details of the party
in pre-printed format.)

Retrieve paper size for non-standard printers               ? No

Enable bitmap mode of printing                              ? No
(Set to Yes, in case of overlapping text in the printout)
```

F-4D: Advanced Printing Configuration

Additional Advanced Printing Configuration : Apart from Invoice printing Configuration and Advanced printing Configuration available from Invoice Printing screen (F-3B & F-3C), you may select *GoT>F12:Configure>Printing> Advanced Configuration* to get Advanced Printing Configuration screen (F-4D) to further tune up Invoice Printing Configuration as per your requirement.

– **Inter Item line Space** : Set Yes At *Reduce space between address and item name/particulars?* to reduce the space between Party Name and Item Description for printing on A4 size pre-printed format.

– **Non standard Printer** : For non-standard printer (narrow width paper / paper rolls), normally used in Cash counters, you find the option *Retrieve paper size for non-standard printers* useful.

– **Bitmap printing Mode :** Set the option *Enable bitmap mode of printing*, when some longer names overlap.

Additional Info in GST Invoices

We have explained the Configuration options for Invoice Printing. We summa rise below the various additional Info that may be printed in Invoice /Order / Delivery Note etc, by setting respective Invoice Configuration Options

– **Company GSTIN** : After the Company name / Company Address Details

– **Consignee Details** : State Name, State Code, GSTIN, after Consignee Name / Consignee Address

– **Buyer Details** : State Name, State Code, GSTIN, after Buyer Name / Buyer Address

– **HSN / SAC Details** : Additional column for HSN / SAC Code for each Stock / Service Item and Tax rate

– **GST Tax Columns** : Additional column (Rate & Amount) for GST Accounts

– **GST Analysis** : Tax Analysis section with various GST Details break up

Invoicing for Tax on MRP

As per s.15 of the CSGT act, the value of a supply of goods or services or both shall be the transaction value, which is the price actually paid or payable for the said supply of goods or services or both where the supplier and the recipient of the supply are not related and the price is the sole consideration for the supply.

So, GST would be charged on Sales Value (irrespective of MRP price). However, printing of MRP may be required under some law. For such Items, the MRP may be set and printed in the Invoice. However, tax would be computed on actual sales value (not on MRP rate)

MRP Based Item Master Creation : Select *GoT>Inventory Info>Stock Item>Create* to get Stock Item creation screen (F-5A).

GST Details entry : At *Stock Item creation* screen (F-5A), at *Set Alter GST details*, set *Yes* to get *GST Details* entry screen (F-5B), At *GST Details* entry screen (F-5B), set the GST Rates.

MRP Details entry : At *Stock Item creation* screen (F-5A), at *Set Alter MRP details,* set *Yes* to get *MRP Details* entry screen (F-5C), At *MRP Details* entry screen (F-5B), enter the MRP Rate.

F-5A: MRP based Item creation

F-5B: GST Details set up

F-5C: MRP details set up in Stock Item Master

MRP Based Invoice Entry : At *GoT>Accounting Voucher*, Click *F8:Sales* to get *Sales Voucher* entry screen (F-5D) . Now enter Sales Invoice data like Invoice Date, Customer Ledger as usual.

Select Stock Item for which MRP rate is specified in Stock Item Master.

Invoice Configuration : At Invoice entry screen, click *F12:Configure* to get *Invoice entry configuration screen* (F-5E). At *Invoice entry configuration screen* (F-5B), at *Allow MRP Modification in Voucher*, set as follows:

- **Modification of MRP rate Allowed in Voucher Entry**: Set *Yes* to get MRP Modification screen during voucher entry showing the MRP rate as entered in the selected Stock Item Master (F-5F). Now you may change the MRP rate, which would be shown in current voucher.

- **Modification of MRP rate Allowed in Voucher Entry** : Set *No* (MRP rate would be carried from Stock Item Master (no change in MRP rate would be allowed during Voucher entry).

Accounting Voucher Creation (Secondary)				Ctrl + M ☒
Sales No. 07/00011/17-18				31-Jul-2017
Reference no.:				Monday
Party A/c name : **Cash Customer**				
Name of Item	Quantity	Rate	per	Amount
Item with MRP	10 Pc	180.00	Pc	1,800.00
MRP / Marginal: 200.00/Pc				
Item with MRP	10 Pc	250.00	Pc	2,500.00
MRP / Marginal: 200.00/Pc				
				4,300.00
Output CGST				258.00
Output SGST				258.00
Narration:		20 Pc		4,816.00

F-5D: MRP Based Invoice entry

Sales Invoice Standard Configuration	
General Options	
Enable supplementary details	? No
(Address details, despatch details, etc.)	
Print default name and address of party	? No
Allow separate buyer and consignee names	? No
Use common ledger account for item allocation	? No
Use defaults for bill allocations	? Yes
Use voucher no. as bill ref. no. for bill allocations	? Yes
Provide additional descriptions for stock item name	? No
Provide additional descriptions for ledger name	? No
Warn if voucher number exceeds 16 characters	? Yes
Statutory Options	
Allow entry of rate inclusive of tax for stock item	? No
Calculate tax on current sub-total	? No
(else calculations are on inventory total only)	
Allow MRP modification in voucher	**Yes**
Allow modification of tax details for GST	? Yes
Other Options	
Warn on negative stock balance	? No

F-5E: Invoice entry Configuration

MRP / Marginal : **220.00/Pc**

5F: MRP modification during Invoice entry

F-5G: Tax Analysis of MRP Based Invoice

Having set the MRP value in Invoice (where changed), the MRP rate is reflected just below the selected Stock Item in Invoice entry screen (F-5D). This way, enter the details of all the Items, as usual

Now select the Tax Accounts as usual. The Tax would be computed on Sales Value.

Invoice printing with MRP details : To print MRP Value also in Invoice separately (F-5H), at *Invoice Printing Configuration* (click F12:Configure at Invoice Printing screen), set *Yes* at *Print MRP / Marginal* Column

F-5H: Invoice showing MRP Column

Invoicing with Over riding GST /Cess Rates

To change the GST rate / Cess rate in specific Invoice, at Sales Invoice Entry, press *F12:Configure* to get Sales Invoice Configuration screen. Set *No* at *Use common ledger account for item allocation* (so that you may override the Tax rates for each Item in the Invoice). Set *Yes* at *Allow modification of tax details* for GST (to change Tax rate at Invoice entry level)

F-6A: Tax rate change during Invoice entry

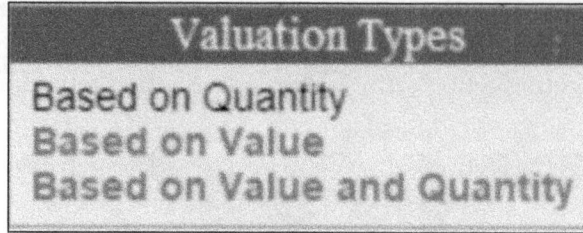

F-6B: Tax Computation method selection

After Stock Item selection in Invoice entry (F-6C), you get Tax rate change screen (F-6B). Now you may change the Tax rate (GST / Cess), as per your wish.

Now select the Tax Accounts in Invoice entry. The Taxes (GST / Cess) are computed on the basis of changed rate. Click *A:Tax Analysis* button to get the Tax Analysis Screen, showing the details of Computation of Tax with revised rate (F-6D). In the *Tax Analysis* screen, a message Value overridden by User is also displayed in screen for information.

F-6C: Voucher entry with Tax rate change

F-6D: Tax Analysis

When you type Yes at Accept to save the Invoice, a warning message appears reminding you modification of Tax (F-6C). Now type as follows to save the Invoice (F-6C) :

- Type Y to accept the Invoice (and resolve the conflict later on).

- Type O to override finally accepting the overridden rate (no conflict resolution later).

- Type N to go back to the voucher to review if you want the change in rates and make changes as necessary.

This way, you may change any rate / Valuation Type at Invoice level and create Invoice in your own way. However, this option should be sparingly used (as Tax rates are statutorily fixed) and should be used with caution, keeping in mind the legal aspects.

Sales Voucher with Additional Expenses

Sometimes, additional accounts are included in Sales / Purchase Voucher on which GST is charged. When you charge to realise for some expenses (like Freight, handling Charges, Delivery Charges, Packing Charges etc) which has been incurred by you as expense, you must treat such additional amounts charged in sales Invoice, as Income (not as expenses). In PL Statement, you may adjust such Income against the related Expenses (or treat them as Miscellaneous Income), like you adjust the amount collected as Freight from Buyers against the expenses incurred for Outwards Freight, or treat income of Outwards Freight realised in Sales Bill as Miscellaneous Income.

We have already discussed GST Set up for such ledger Accounts. Consequently, when such GST enabled ledger Accounts are included in Sales / Purchase Voucher, GST is computed on the amount of such Ledger Accounts in the Voucher.

At GoT>Accounts Voucher, Click *F8:Sales* to get Sales Invoice entry screen. Enter Voucher Date, select Party Account, Stock Item as usual. Now select the GST enabled Expenses Ledger Account and enter the amount. Now select the applicable GST Ledger Accounts. GST would be computed including the amount of GST enabled Ledger Account. Click *A:Tax Analysis* to view the details of GST Computation (F-7B).

Sales Invoice entry with additional charges : Sometimes, taxable additional charges are added in Invoice. GST is charged on such additional charges as usual like Taxable Item

Additional Charges (Indirect Income) Ledger Account creation

Create Ledger Account as Income Account, as usual and set GST details like Taxable Item (F-7A) and enter the GST details (F-7B).

F-7A: Additional Taxable Charges ledger account.

F-7B: GST details of Additional Taxable Charges ledger account.

Sales Invoice Entry with Taxable additional charges

Enter Sales Invoice as explained (F-7C) and view Tax Analysis (F-7D).

F-7C: Sales Invoice with additional charges

F-7D: GST details of Sales Invoice with additional charges

Automatic Rounding Off of Invoices

You may create a Ledger Account (say Round Off), as additional expenses, into which the odd fractional figure of the Invoice gets auto posted to make the Invoice Rounded off. The steps are explained below

Creation of Round Off ledger Account : Select *Gateway of Tally >Accounts Info. >Ledgers >Create* to get Ledger creation screen (F-7D). At *Type of Ledger*, select *Invoice Rounding* from the list. Select the *Rounding Method* and *Rounding Limit*, as desired.

```
Ledger Creation                                                      Con
Name            Invoice Round Off

Under                              : Indirect Expenses  Name
                                                          Type of Ledger
Inventory values are affected      ? No                 ▯ Not Applicable
Type of Ledger                     ? Invoice Rounding     Discount
                                                         Invoice Rounding
Rounding method                    : Normal Rounding
  Rounding limit                   : 1
                  Statutory Information               Provide bank details

Is GST Applicable                  ? ▯ Not Applicable
  Set/alter GST Details            ? No
                                                        PAN/IT No
Include in assessable value calculation for  ▯ Not Applicable
```

F-7D: Invoice Round off ledger

Entry of Sales Invoice with Rounding off : Having created the Ledger Account (with Rounding Off parameters set the Ledger Account), in Voucher Entry (F-7E), select the *Rounding off Ledger Account* after entry of all other Ledger Accounts. The fractional figure of the Net Invoice Amount would be auto computed (as negative or positive figure), as per Rounding Off parameters set in the Rounding Off Ledger account. Such auto computed amount of Rounding Off would be auto carried against the Round Off Ledger Account and included in the Invoice (as addition or reduction). Consequently the Net Invoice Amount would become rounded off (F-7E) as per Rounding Parameters.

```
Accounting Voucher Creation                          Ctrl + H ⊠
     Sales       No. 07/00007/17-18              2-Mar-2018
Reference no.:                                        Friday
Party A/c name    : Customer 1 - Kol 19

Name of Item               Quantity    Rate  per    Amount

Item 2 @12%                13 Pc  195.50  Pc      2,541.50

CGST                                                152.49
SGST                                                152.49
Invoice Round Off                                   (-)0.48

Narration:                       13 Pc           2,846.00
```

F-7E: Sales Invoice with Rounded off figure

```
                          Tax Analysis
, Particulars                    Taxable Value  Tax rate   Duty/Tax Value

GST Details

Sales Taxable                      2,541.50                    304.98
  Item 2 @12% (1235)                2,541.50                    304.98
    Item Value ( Sales Value 2,541.50 )  2,541.50
    Central Tax                                  6%            152.49
    State Tax                                    6%            152.49
                                              Total           304.98
```

F-7F: Tax Analysis of Rounded Invoice

Sales Invoice Entry with Item allocable additional charges

We have shown additional charges on which GST is charged on such additional charges as per rate specified in the Master. However, sometimes, no GST rate is specified for additional charges. The amount is allocated to Items in the Invoice and GST charged in Item value together with allocated expenses. The GST set up for such additional expenses is shown.

Ledger Account Creation : Create Ledger Account for such Additional Expenses (*Gateway of Tally >Accounts Info. >Ledgers >Create)*to get Ledger creation screen (F-7G).

F-7G: Item allocable Expense ledger

Sales Invoice Entry : Create Sales Invoice with such additional charges (F-7H). The *Tax Analysis*(F-7I) shows the inclusion of Additional charges with Taxable Value.

F-7H: Sales Voucher with Additional Revenue Account

F-7I: GST Details with Additional Expenses

Slab Based Sales Invoice entry

We have explained GST set up for Slab based GST set up for Stock Item Master. We now explain the Invoice entry for Slab based Items.

Stock Item Mastercretaion: Select Stock Item Master (GoT>Inventory Info>Stock Item>Create) to get stock Item master screen (F-8A). Set the Stoc Item GST Details (F-8B) and set the slabwise GST Rate (F-8C).

F-8A: Slab based Item Master set up

F-8B: Slab based Item Master GST set up

F-8C: Item Master Slab Rate set up

Invoice Entry : At GOT>Accounts Voucher, Click *F8:Sales* to get Sales Invoice entry screen (F-8D). Enter Voucher Date, select party Account, Stock Item as usual.

Now select the applicable GST Ledger Accounts. GST would be computed including the amount of GST enabled Ledger Account. Click *A:Tax Analysis* to view the details of GST Computation (F-8E).

F-8D: sales Invoice with slab based Items

F-8E: Slab based Invoice Tax Analysis

Sales Invoice for Goods & Services Combined

We have explained GST Set up for Goods Items and Service Item. Now explain entry of Invoice involving Goods & Service in one Invoice.

F-9A: GST Invoice for Goods & Service combined

F-9B: GST Details for Goods & Service combined Invoice

At GoT>Accounts Voucher, Click *F8:Sales* to get Sales Invoice entry screen (F-9A). Enter Voucher Date, select party Account, Stock Item as usual.

Now select the GST taxable Ledger Account and enter the Amount. Select applicable GST Ledger Accounts. GST would be computed including the amount of GST enabled Ledger Account. Click *A:Tax Analysis* to view the details of GST Computation (F-9B).

Sales under Reverse Charge

Some goods and services are classified as reverse charge (Buyer liable to Pay GST). So, GST is not charged in Invoice, but GST Liability for Buyer is created (and reported in GSTR-1)

We have already explained GST set up for such Sales ledger Accounts chargeable under Reverse Charge, at Accounts Master chapter.

At GOT>Accounts Voucher, Click *F8:Sales* to get Sales Invoice entry screen (F-10A). Click *V: As Voucher* button to get to get Accounting Voucher entry screen. Enter Voucher Date, select party Account. Select the Reverse Charge set up Ledger Account. On selection of Reverse Charge activated Ledger Account, the Tax Liability is internally computed and you cannot select any GST Account (as GST is not chargeable in Invoice).

F-10A : Reverse Charge Sales Invoice entry

F-10B : Reverse Charge Sales Invoice Tax Liability details

Click *A:Tax Analysis* button to get the Tax Analysis screen showing the Tax Liability for the recipient (F-10B). A message Amount of Tax subject to Reverse charge appears on the Tax Analysis Report for Information

F-10C: Reverse Charge Sales Invoice

Click P:Print to print the Invoice (F-10C) as per configuration set. In the Invoice, a note *Amount of Tax Subject to Reverse Charge* is printed.

Sales with Item level Discount

For Item level Discount, select *GoT>F11:Fetaures>Inventory Feature* to get Inventory Features screen. Now set *Yes* at *Use Separate column in Discount*, as usual. Consequently, in Invoice entry, you get a separate column for Discount to enter Discount Rate. The Discount is reduced from Sales Value. GST would be computed on Sales Value net of Discount. So, no separate Discount Ledger is needed. So, no separate set up for GST is needed. You create invoice with Discount column as usual.

At *GoT>Accounts Voucher*, Click *F8:Sales* to get Sales Invoice entry screen (F-11A). Enter Voucher Date, select Party Account. Select Item. At *Discount* column, enter Discount rate. Net value after Discount is shown in Amount column.

F-11A : Sales Invoice with Item level Discount

F-11B : Sales Invoice Tax Analysis

Now select the GST ledger Accounts. GST would be computed on value after Discount is shown in Amount column in the Invoice. Click *A:Tax Analysis* to view the GST computation details (F-11B).

You may selectively enter Discount rate for each Item (with different discount rates). To allow fixed amount Discount, just override the Net Amount after Discount at Amount column. So, it is extremely flexible to allow Discount with % or fixed amount. No additional Ledger Account is necessary for Discount Account.

F-11C: Invoice with Item Level Discount

Print the sales Invoice with Item level discount.

Sales with Invoice level Discount

In case of Invoice Level Discount, the allowed Discount is not reduced from Item Value, but is treated as Expense. So, create Discount account (F-12A) as allocable Revenue Expense and set the options, as explained.

– **Expense Group** : At Under, select Expense group.

– **Assessable Value** : At Include in Assessable Value calculation, set Yes to deduct the allocated portion of Discount in Assessable Value

– **Appropriation Method** : At Appropriate to, select *Goods* (in case of services invoice, select Services. In case of composite Invoice including Goods as well Services, select Both)

– **Method of Appropriation of Discount** : Select based on value / Based on Quantity as applicable. The Amount of Discount is apportioned to the Item Assessable value (the computation details are shown in Tax Analysis)

F-12A: Invoice Level Discount (value allocable to Items)

At *GOT>Accounts Voucher*, Click *F8:Sales* to get Sales Invoice entry screen (F-12B). Enter Voucher Date, select Party Account. Select Item. This way enter details of all the Items in Invoice.

F-12A: Sales Invoice with Invoice Level Discount

F-12B: Sales Invoice with Invoice level Discount

After entry of Item details, select Discount Account and enter the Amount (in negative figure for deduction in Invoice Value)

Select Tax Account. The Tax would be computed after deducting the apportioned amount of Discount for each item.

Invoice Printing

Click *P:Print* and print the Invoice (F-13A).

F-13A; Invoice with Invoice level Discount

Voucher Class for Automated Voucher entry

To automate Sales / Purchase Tax Ledger Accounts and Tax account s for regularly used Invoices, you may create Voucher Classes for frequently used transaction types, like Taxable sales, Exempted sales, Inter state sale, Local sales, Tax Inclusive Rates etc. and set up the Ledger Accounts in Voucher Class. During Invoice entry the ledger Accounts are auto selected as set in the respective Voucher Class

Create a Voucher Class for sales Voucher class (*GoT>Accounts Info>Voucher Type>Alter*), select Sales from Voucher Type to get Voucher Type Alteration screen. Enter the Name of Voucher class at Class name to get Voucher Class entry screen (You may create multiple voucher class for sales and set Ledger Accounts accordingly for each Voucher Class

Comp Kol 19					
Class: Tx Inv					

If you wish to restrict the groups to which this class can be used, specify them here.

Exclude these Groups			Include these Groups		
▮ End of List			▮ End of List		

Default Accounting Allocations for all items in Invoice (except for the items specified below)

Ledger Name	Set/Alter Tax Class?	Percentage %	Rounding Method	Rounding Limit	Override using Item Default ?
Taxable Sales	**No**	100 %			No

Additional Accounting Entries (e.g. Taxes / Other charges) to be added in Invoice

Ledger Name	Type of Calculation	Value Basis	Rounding Method	Rounding Limit	Remove if Zero ?
Output CGST	GST				Yes
Output IGST	GST				Yes
Output SGST	GST				Yes
Trade Discount	As User Defined Value				Yes
Packing Expenses	As User Defined Value				Yes

F-14A: Voucher Class entry for sales Invoice

Under default Accounting Allocation, select the Sales Leger Account (for Sales Voucher Class) or Purchase Ledger Account (for Purchase Voucher Cass) and set the % allocation

Accounting Voucher Creation	Comp Kol 19			Ctrl + M ☒
Sales No. 07/00002/17-18 *Voucher class:* **Tx Inv**				1-Sep-2017 Friday
Reference no.				
Party A/c name **Customer Cuttack -21**				
Name of Item	Quantity	Rate per	Disc %	Amount
Item 1 @5%	10 Pc	270.00 Pc		2,700.00
Item 2 @12%	10 Pc	300.00 Pc		3,000.00
Item 3 Nil Rate	10 Pc	200.00 Pc		2,000.00
				7,700.00
Output CGST				
Output IGST				544.50
Output SGST				
Trade Discount			10	770.00
Packing Expenses				
Narration:	30 Pc			9,014.50

F-14B: Sales Invoicing using Voucher Class

Tax Analysis	Comp Kol 19		Ctrl + M ☒
Tax Analysis			
Particulars	Taxable Value	Tax rate	Duty/Tax Value
GST Details			
Interstate Sales Nil Rated	2,200.00		
Item 3 Nil Rate (12345678)	2,200.00		
Item Value (Sales Value 2,000.00) 2,000.00			
Trade Discount (770.00 / 7,700.00 * 2,000.00) 200.00			
Interstate Sales Taxable	6,270.00		544.50
Item 1 @5% (1234)	2,970.00		148.50
Item Value (Sales Value 2,700.00) 2,700.00			
Trade Discount (770.00 / 7,700.00 * 2,700.00) 270.00			
Integrated Tax		5%	148.50
Item 2 @12% (1235)	3,300.00		396.00
Item Value (Sales Value 3,000.00) 3,000.00			
Trade Discount (770.00 / 7,700.00 * 3,000.00) 300.00			
Integrated Tax		12%	396.00
		Total	544.50

F-14C: Tax Analysis

At Other Accounts, select all the ledger accounts applicable for the sales Invoice of the Voucher Class (F-14B). You may select all the tax Accounts and Ledger Accounts. The auto computed amount of Tax would be displayed as per transaction type. Similarly, amount of other ledger accounts would be auto computed as per specification in Ledger Accounts (or to be input in voucher entry for User Defined Amounts). This way, you can quickly and correctly enter voucher. The Tax Analysis shows the details of Tax Computation of applicable Taxes.

Tax Inclusive Invoicing

For quick invoicing and avoiding with rounded off invoice value for easier cash transaction, retailers normally fix up rates inclusive of GST. The Sales value is split into Taxable value and Tax Amount automatically and posted into Statutory Returns

If Inclusive GST Value is regularly used, then it is recommended to create a Voucher Class for Inclusive Value Invoice, for quick invoicing and automated Tax computation & allocation.

Computation of Rate : The Amount of Tax Inclusive Value would be split to Taxable value (sales value) and Tax Amount (F-15A). You should create separate Voucher class for Inter state (allocating Tax to IGST) and for Intra State (allocating Tax to CGST and SGST).

For example, the amount of Tax inclusive Value (tax @12%- CGST-@6% and SGST @6% for Intra state sale) would be split to Taxable Amount – 89.286% [(100/112) x 100%], CGST – 5.357 % [(6/112) x 100%] & SGST – 5.357% [(100/112) x 100%].

Compute allocation rates for each Tax rates. However, Voucher class is useful only when a single Tax rate is applicable in one Invoice for all Items. Multi Tax rate Inclusive Invoice cannot be created with Voucher Class.

F-15A: Voucher Class for Tax Inclusive sales Invoice

Voucher Class for Invoicing with Additional Charges

If other accounts (like Packing Charges, Delivery Charges are also applicable in Invoice), these can be added under Additional Accounting Entries

Class: LocInc					
If you wish to restrict the groups to which this class can be used, specify them here.					
Exclude these Groups			Include these Groups		
ll End of List			ll End of List		
Default Accounting Allocations for all items in Invoice (except for the items specified below)					
Ledger Name	Set/Alter Tax Class?	Percentage %	Rounding Method	Rounding Limit	Override using Item Default ?
Sales	No	89.286 %	ll Not Applicable		No
Output IGST	No	10.714 %			
Additional Accounting Entries (e.g. Taxes / Other charges) to be added in Invoice					
Ledger Name	Type of Calculation	Value Basis	Rounding Method	Rounding Limit	Remove if Zero ?
Packing Expenses	As User Defined Value			Yes	
Freight Charges Taxable @ 18%	As User Defined Value			Yes	

F-15B: Voucher Class for Invoicing including additional charges

Invoice Entry : Having created the Voucher class, create Tax inclusive Invoice using the Voucher Class.

Accounting Voucher Creation	Comp Kol 19	Ctrl + M
Sales No: 07/00001/17-18 *Voucher class:* LocInc		1-Sep-2017 Friday
Reference no.:		
Party A/c name : Customer 1 - Kol 19		

Name of Item	Quantity	Rate per Disc %	Amount
Item 2 @12%	100 Pc	300.00 Pc	30,000.00
Packing Expenses			**200.00**
Freight Charges Taxable @ 18%			
Narration:	100 Pc		30,200.00

F-15C: Inclusive Tax sales Invoice using Voucher Class

Tax Analysis	Comp Kol 19		Ctrl + M
Tax Analysis			
Particulars	Taxable Value	Tax rate	Duty/Tax Value
GST Details			
Sales Taxable	26,985.80		3,238.30
Freight Charges Taxable @ 18% (3456)			
Sales Value			
Central Tax		9%	
State Tax		9%	
Item 2 @12% (1235)	26,985.80		3,238.30
Item Value (Sales Value 26,785.80)	26,785.80		
Packing Expenses (200.00 / 30,000.00 * 26,785.80)	178.57		
Central Tax		6%	1,619.15
State Tax		6%	1,619.15
As per Calculation			3,238.30
As per Transaction			3,214.20

F-15D: Sales Invoice Tax Analysis

Now create sales Invoice using Voucher Class, as usual. At *GOT>Accounts Voucher*, Click *F8:Sales* and select the Voucher Class to get Sales Invoice entry screen. Enter Voucher Date, select Party Account. Select Item. Enter Tax Inclusive item rate, for each Item entered. You do not have to select Tax Ledger Accounts (as Tax is included in Price)

Having entered Item details, enter amount for Additional ledger Accounts. The Tax Analysis (F-15D) shows the computation of Tax included in Invoice value

Invoice Printing : Click print button to print the Invoice. Though Tax details are not shown in entry screen, Tax details are printed in Invoice (F-16A). The Tax are posted in respective GSTR for supplier (for Tax Liability) and buyer (for Input Tax Credit).

F-16A: Tax Inclusive sales Invoice

Purchase from Registered Dealer

A Registered Dealer, purchasing tradable goods from Registered dealer, is eligible for ITC on GST paid.

Purchase Invoice Entry

Enter Purchase Invoice as usual. Select *GoT>Accounting Voucher*, Click *F9:Purchase* to get *Purchase Voucher* entry screen (F-5A) . Now enter Purchase Invoice data as explained earlier. We describe here entry of GST specific details only.

Intra State Purchase from Registered Dealer

Having entered the Party and Item details (item name, Quantity, Rate, Value etc) of all the Items in the Invoice, enter the details of Item purchased (Item Name, Quantity, Rate, value), as usual.

Purchase No. 1				1-Jul-2017
Supplier invoice no.: 12	Date : 1-Jul-2017			Saturday
Party A/c name : **Supplier -1 Kol 19**				
Purchase ledger : **Purchase**				
Name of Item		**Quantity**	**Rate per**	**Amount**
Item 1 @5%		10 Pc	50.00 Pc	500.00
Item 2 @12%		50 Pc	40.00 Pc	2,000.00
Item 3 Nil Rate		100 Pc	25.00 Pc	2,500.00
				5,000.00
Input CGST				132.50
Input SGST				132.50
Narration:		160 Pc		5,265.00

F-1A: Taxable Local Purchase entry

Tax Analysis	Comp Kol 19			Ctrl + H
Tax Analysis				
Particulars		Taxable Value	Tax rate	Duty/Tax Value
GST Details				
Purchase Nil Rated		2,500.00		
Item 3 Nil Rate (12345678)		2,500.00		
Item Value (Purchase Value 2,500.00)	2,500.00			
Purchase Taxable		2,500.00		265.00
Item 1 @5%		500.00		25.00
Item Value (Purchase Value 500.00)	500.00			
Central Tax			2.50%	12.50
State Tax			2.50%	12.50
Item 2 @12%		2,000.00		240.00
Item Value (Purchase Value 2,000.00)	2,000.00			
Central Tax			6%	120.00
State Tax			6%	120.00
			Total	265.00

F-1B: Purchase Invoice Tax Details view

In Local Purchase Invoice from Registered Party (F-1A), select *Input CGST* and *Input SGST*. The amount is equally divided into both the Tax Accounts. To view Tax Details, click *A:Tax Analysis* button to get Tax

Analysis screen (F-1B). Click F1:Detailed / Condensed toggle button detailed / summary get details.

Interstate Purchase from Registered Party

In Interstate Purchase from Registered Party (F-2A), select Integrated Tax (instead of Local and Central Tax).

To view Tax Details, click *A:Tax Analysis* button to get Tax Analysis screen (F-2B). Click F1:Detailed / Condensed toggle button detailed / summary get details.

F-2A: Taxable Interstate Purchase entry

F-2B: Purchase Invoice Tax Details

Computation Difference : Purchase Invoice is normally entered from the Invoice of the supplier. So, sometimes there may be some computation difference in Item value or Tax due to rounding off difference, method of computation etc. You may change the Tax amount during entry (F-2A). If the computed Tax amount and the Tax amount entered as per supplier invoice differ, then both the values are shown in the Tax Analysis report (F-2B).

Purchase of Fixed Assets

The ITC paid on Fixed Asset Purchase are to be spread over multiple years. This requires some adjustment in respect of ITC and carry forward to subsequent years.

Fixed Asset Ledger Account : For Fixed Asset, you have to set up GST features in Fixed Asset Ledger Account *(GoT>Accounts Info>Ledger>Create)* to get Ledger Accounts creation screen. Set *Yes* at *GST Applicable*. Select the Nature of Transaction (you cannot leave it as Not Applicable) and then select Type of Supply (Goods / Services).

F-3A: Fixed Asset ledger creation

F-3B: GST set up for Fixed Asset ledger

Purchase Invoice Entry : Create a Purchase Voucher as usual (GoT>Accounts Vouchers>F9:Purchase). Click *V:As Voucher* toggle button, to get entry screen in Accounting voucher mode (F-4B).

At Purchase Voucher entry (F-4B), click *F12:Configure* to get Purchase Configuration screen. Again press *F12:Configure* to get *Advanced Purchase Configuration* screen. At *Allow Expenses / Fixed Asset* for Accounting Allocation (F-4A) to enable Fixed Assets ledger entry in Purchase Voucher.

F-4A: Purchase Voucher Configuration for Fixed Asset entry

At Purchase Voucher entry screen (F-4B),select Supplier Ledger Account and enter the total amount of the supplier. Select GST Ledger Account (CCGST/SGST or ITGST) and enter the amount. Enter other expenses ledger accounts and amount, if any.

F-4B: Fixed Asset Purchase from Registered Dealer

F-5A: Effect in GSTR-2 Report

The Fixed Asset Purchase voucher has no Input Tax implication. So when you click *A:Tax Analysis* button in Voucher entry screen, you get a message *This Voucher has no Tax implications / Tax Analysis is not supported.* Capital Goods Purchase from registered dealer would be reflected in GSTR-2 Report (F-5A) under Table B2B Invoices, Table 3, 4A

ITC Adjustment Journal Voucher for Fixed Asset Purchase

However, you can claim ITC on Capital Goods in equal instalments over a period of 5 years, only if the Capital Goods is used for business purpose. So, in the financial year of purchases, you can claim only 1/5th of the GST paid. Balance 4/5th would be claimed in 4 subsequent years (1/5th in each Financial Year)

So, you have to create a Journal voucher to provide for 1/5th amount as ITC in current year and transfer the balance 4/5th, in an asset account, to be adjusted in subsequent financial year.

Deferred ITC ledger Account : Create a Ledger account (*GoT>Accounts Info>Ledger Create*), *Deferred ITC on Capital Goods* to keep the balance 4/5th amount to be adjusted in subsequent Year (F-6A).

F-6A: Deferred ITC Ledger Account

ITC Adjustment Journal : Create a Journal Voucher (GoT>Accounts Vouchers>F7:Journal). At Journal Voucher screen, click *J:Stat Adjustment*button (F-7C) to get Stat Adjustment screen (F-7B).

Adjustment Details : At *Stat Adjustment* screen (F-7B), at *Type of Duty / Tax*, select GST. At *Nature of Adjustment*, select *Reversal of Input Tax Credit*. At *Additional Details*, select *Not Applicable*. Having entered the details at Stat Adjustment screen (F-7B), you get back to Journal Voucher entry main screen (F-7A).

Accounting Voucher Creation		Ctrl + N
Journal No. 8		**2-Nov-2017** Thursday
Particulars	**Debit**	**Credit**
Dr **Deferred ITC on Capital Goods**	9,600.00	
Cr **Input IGST**		9,600.00
Narration:	9,600.00	9,600.00
Prvion of deferred ITC to be claimed in subsequent years		

F-7A: Journal Voucher for Deferred ITC adjustment

Stat Adjustment

Type of duty/tax	:	**GST**
Nature of adjustment	:	**Reversal of Input Tax Credit**
Additional Details	:	**Ⅱ Not Applicable**

F-7B: Stat Adjsutment for Deferred ITC adjustment

F4: Contra
F5: Payment
F6: Receipt
F7: Journal
F8: Sales
F8: Credit Note
F9: Purchase
F9: Debit Note
J: Stat Adjustment

F-7C: Voucher Buttons

Ledger Account details : At Voucher entry main screen (F-7A), select Deferred ITC ledger account and enter the total of ITC to be carried forward, to be claimed in subsequent years (Total GST – 1/5th of GST, i.e 4/5th of GST charged) in debit column. Now select the GST Account (IGST or CGST& SGST) and enter the respective amount (full amount for IGST or 50% of the amount to CGST & UTGST, as the case may be) in credit column.

In case of Capital Goods purchased solely for Business Use, to produce only Taxable Goods, GST paid can be fully claimed as ITC, like other inputs purchased to produce taxable goods. However, apportionment / deferment is applicable for common use of Capital Goods purchased for Business / Non Business and for production of Taxable / Exempted Goods, and in some special circumstances, as specified under CGST rules 42,43

Expenses Entry for payments to Registered Dealer

Like goods Purchased from Registered dealer, ITC may be claimed on GST paid for Taxable Business Expenses paid to Registered Dealer.

Expenses Ledger creation : Select *GoT>Accounts Info>Ledger>Create* to get Accounts Ledger creation screen. At *Under*, select a Group under *Expenses*. Set *Yes* at *Set / Alter GST* and set the Tax Rate.

F-8A: Expenses Ledger creation

F-8B: Expenses Ledger - GST Set Up

Supplier Leger creation : Select *GoT>Accounts Info>Ledger>Create* to get Accounts Ledger creation screen. At *Under*, select a Group under *Sundry Creditors*. Set *Yes* at *Set / Alter GST* and set the GST details of the supplier. Select *Regular* at *Registration Type*, Enter *GSTIN*.

F-9A : Registered Service Provider Ledger Account

F-9B : Registered Service Provider Ledger GST details

Voucher for Taxable Expenses incurred : You may book the expenses in following alternate ways:

- Purchase / Journal / Payment Voucher

    o   Create Purchase Voucher, or

    o   Create Journal Voucher

    o   and then a Payment Voucher for payment

- Create Payment voucher directly to book and pay for the expenses incurred

We now explain voucher creation in each of the cases

Purchase Voucher Entry : Select *GoT>Accounting Voucher>F9:Purchase* and then select *I:Accounting Invoice* to get Purchase Voucher entry screen (F-10A). Select the supplier Ledger Account. Now select Expenses Ledger and enter the amount (if you do not get Expenses ledger in Ledger list then Click *F12:Configure* and then set Yes at *Allow Fixed Asset / Expenses in Purchase Voucher – F-4A*). Select the Tax Classification at Tax Classification screen (if you do not get the screen then Click *F12:Configure* and set *Yes* at *Override GST in voucher entry*) and select Tax Classification from *Nature of Transaction* list.

Next select the Tax Ledger Accounts (the amount would be auto computed and carried). Click *A:Tax Analysis* to get Tax Analysis screen showing the Taxable & Tax Amount.

F-10A: Purchase Voucher Entry for Taxable Expenses provided by Registered Supplier

F-10B: Tax Classification Details

F-10C: Tax Analysis

Journal Voucher Entry : Alternatively, you may create a Journal Voucher to record the expenses. Select *GoT>Accounting Voucher>F7:Journal* to get Journal Voucher entry screen (F-11A). Select the Expenses Ledger Account enter the amount in Debit column. Select the Tax Classification at tax Classification screen (if you do not get the screen then Click *F12:Configure*and set Yes at *Override GST* in voucher entry) and select Tax Classification from *Nature of Transaction* list (F-11B).

Next select the Tax Ledger Accounts and enter the amount in Debit Column. Select the supplier account and enter the amount in Credit column (F-11A).

F-11A: Journal voucher booking expenses with GST

F-11B: Tax Classification

Payment Voucher after booking Expenses : Having booked the expenses through Purchase Voucher or Journal Voucher, you will make payment to the supplier of the expenses bill booked. Select *GoT>Accounting Voucher>F5:Payment* to get Journal Voucher entry screen (F-12A). In Payment Voucher, the supplier account would be Debited and Cash / Bank account would be credited. There would be no entry for Tax Ledger Accounts as Tax ledger Accounts have already been charged in earlier Purchase Voucher / Journal Voucher.

F-12A: Payment Voucher after booking expenses thru Journal / Purchase Voucher

Direct Payment Voucher Entry : Instead of booking the expenses with Tax Accounts through Purchase Voucher (F-10A) / Journal Voucher (F-11A) and subsequent Payment Voucher (F-12A), you may make payment through Payment Voucher booking the expenses and Tax Accounts.

Select *GoT>Accounting Voucher>F5 : Payment* to get Payment Voucher entry screen. Select the Expenses Ledger Account enter the amount in Debit column. Select the *Tax Classification* at tax Classification screen (if you do not get the screen then Click *F12:Configure* and set Yes at *Override GST* in voucher entry) and select Tax Classification from *Nature of Transaction* list (F-13C).

At Voucher entry screen (F-13A), select the Tax Ledger Accounts and enter the amount in Debit Column.

Select the Cash / Bank account and enter the amount in Credit column. At Party details pop up screen(F-13B), at Party Name, enter Party Name, address, Registration Type, GSTIN) etc (or select supplier ledger account, if created and get enter the details carried from Party Ledger Account).

Accounting Voucher Creation		Ctrl + M
Payment No. 1		**1-Aug-2017** Tuesday
Particulars	Debit	Credit
Dr Telephone Charges	2,000.00	
Dr CGST	50.00	
Dr SGST	50.00	
Cr Cash		2,100.00
Narration	2,100.00	2,100.00
Telephone Bill payment		

F-13A: Direct payment voucher booking expenses with GST

Party Details	
Party Name	BSNL
Address	
State	Assam
Registration Type	Regular
GSTIN/UIN	18ABNPN1234M1Z7

F-13B: Party details

Tax Classification Details	
Classification/Nature	**Purchase Taxable**

F-13C:

Effect of Expenses entry in GSTR-2 : The Taxable expenses paid to registered supplier are reflected in GSTR-2.

Purchase from Unregistered Dealer

When a registered buyer purchases taxable goods / services from unregistered seller (who do not charge Tax in the invoice, as he is unregistered), the registered buyer would pay the Tax under Reverse, on such purchase and would be entitled to claim Input Tax Credit on the Tax so paid.

Deferment of Reverse Charge on purchase from unregistered dealer : A registered buyer has to pay Reverse Charge on Purchase from Unregistered Dealer. However, from 13th October 2017, the reverse charge is deferred till 30st Sep 2018. Purchase from Unregistered Dealer from 13th October onwards would be reflected as *Not relevant for Reports* in GSTR-2 & GSTR-3B.

Reverse Charge is applicable on purchases from unregistered dealer, during applicable period (i.e 1st July to 12th October). Liability for such transactions would be reflected under Reverse Charge supplies in GSTR Reports.

GST Set up for the for Reverse Charge Liability : At GoT, click F11:Feature>Statutory Feature to get Statutory Features set up screen (F-1A). At *Enable Tax Liability under Reverse Charge* (Purchase from Registered Dealer), set *Yes* to enable Reverse Charge for Purchase from Registered Dealer.

	GST Details
State	: Assam
Registration type	: Regular
Assessee of Other Territory	? No
GSTIN/UIN	: 18AAAA S0234A1Z7
Applicable from	: 1-Jul-2017
Periodicity of GSTR1	: Monthly
e-Way Bill applicable	? Yes
e-Way Bill applicable from	: 1-Feb-2018
e-Way Bill threshold	: 50,000
e-Way Bill applicable for intrastate	? Yes
Enable tax liability on advance receipts	? Yes
Enable tax liability on reverse charge (Purchase from unregistered dealer)	? Yes
Set/alter GST rate details	? No
Enable GST Classifications	? No
Provide LUT/Bond details	? No

F-1A: Company Features Statutory details set up

Stock Item Master : Create Stock Item Master as usual, setting the GST Rates. For Taxable Items, select Taxable and enter the Tax rate. (F-2A/ F-2B). Enter Cess Rate if applicable.

F-2A: F-Stock Item Master (main screen)

F-2B: Tax Chargeable Stock Item master Set Up (tax rates)

F-3A: Stock Item Master (main screen)

F-3B: NIL rated Stock Item Master Set Up

For NIL rated Items, select NIL rated at Taxability (F-3A / F-3B).

In case of Items under reverse charge, at GST details screen (F-2B / F-3B), set Yes at 'Is Reverse Charge Applicable.

Supplier Ledger Account set up : Create Ledger Account of unregistered supplier (GoT>Accounts Info>Ledger>Create). At *State*, select the State of the unregistered party (F-4A / F-4C).

F-4A: Unregistered Party (within State) Ledger Creation

F-4B: GST details of Unregistered Party Ledger

GST details screen, at *Registration Type*, select *Unregistered* (F-4B)

F-4C: Unregistered Party (Outside State) Ledger Creation

Purchase Ledger Account

Create of Purchase Ledger Account (GoT>Accounts Info>Create) to get Ledger Account screen (F-5A). At *Under*, select Purchase Account.

F-5A: Common Purchase Ledger creation

Statutory Information set up for Purchase Ledger Account : You may set a common Purchase Ledger Account for Purchase from Registered or Unregistered Party, within or Outside state, to keep the Ledger Accounts fewer and simpler.To use such common Purchase Account, at Purchase Ledger Account creation screen (F-5A), set *No* at *Set Alter GST details*. Consequently, you will not set up GST GST details (Nature of Transaction, Taxability or GST Rate) at purchase ledger account (such info will be set up at Stock Item / Invoice). This will reduce the number of Ledgers and transaction entry would be simple and uniform.

Still, if you set Yes at set *Yes* at *Set Alter GST details,* at GST details screen (F-5B), at Nature of transaction (F-5B), set *Not Applicable* from the list (F-5C). Consequently, during Purchase Voucher entry, you will need to select the Nature of Transaction (F-6D), as explained later.

F-5B: GST details for common Purchase ledger

Natures of Transaction
▮ **Not Applicable**
Branch Transfer Inward
Imports Exempt
Imports Taxable
Interstate Purchase Exempt
Interstate Purchase Nil Rated
Interstate Purchase Taxable
Purchase Exempt
Purchase From Composition Dealer
Purchase From SEZ - Exempt
Purchase From SEZ - Taxable
Purchase From Unregistered Dealer - Exempt
Purchase From Unregistered Dealer - Taxable
Purchase Nil Rated
Purchase Taxable

F-5C: Common Purchase ledger Account set up

Invoice entry for Purchase from Unregistered Dealer

Accounting Voucher Creation				Ctrl + M ▨
Purchase No. 3				1-Jul-2017
Supplier invoice no.: 123		Date : 1-Jul-2017		Saturday
Party A/c name : Supplier -1 URD Kol 19				
Purchase ledger : Purchase				
Name of Item		**Quantity**	**Rate** per	**Amount**
Item 1 @5%		10 Pc	200.00 Pc	2,000.00
Item 2 @12%		50 Pc	200.00 Pc	10,000.00
Item 3 Nil Rate		20 Pc	50.00 Pc	1,000.00
				13,000.00
Narration:		80 Pc		*13,000.00*

F-6A: Purchase from local unregistered dealer

Tax Analysis		Comp Kol 1S		Ctrl + M ▨
		Tax Analysis		
Particulars		**Taxable Value**	**Tax rate**	**Duty/Tax Value**
GST Details				
Purchase From Unregistered Dealer - Exempt		1,000.00		
Item 3 Nil Rate (12345678)		1,000.00		
Item Value (Purchase Value 1,000.00)	1,000.00			
Purchase From Unregistered Dealer - Taxable		12,000.00		1,300.00
Item 1 @5%		2,000.00		100.00
Item Value (Purchase Value 2,000.00)	2,000.00			
Central Tax			2.50%	50.00
State Tax			2.50%	50.00
Item 2 @12%		10,000.00		1,200.00
Item Value (Purchase Value 10,000.00)	10,000.00			
Central Tax			6%	600.00
State Tax			6%	600.00
Note: Amount of tax subject to reverse charge				
		As per Calculation		1,300.00
		As per Transaction		

F-6B: Tax details of Purchase from local unregistered dealer

If Nature of Transaction is not specified at GST Details screen in the selected Purchase Ledger, specify the type of transaction in Purchase Voucher entry. To get the Classification pop up screen at Purchase Voucher entry screen,

Click *F12:Configure* and set *Yes* at *Allow Modification of Tax details* for GST. Consequently, a pop up screen will appear (F-6D) to select *Classification / Nature* of transaction during voucher entry to properly reflect the transaction in GSTR reports and placed under the respective subheads. On selection of Tax Classification, at *Tax Details are modified* message, type Y to accept the entry (F-6E), to avoid conflict to be resolved before GSTR Return filing.

```
                 Purchase Standard Configuration
                        General Options

   Enable supplementary details                  ?  Yes
   Use Cr/Dr instead of To/By during entry        ?  Yes
   Warn on negative cash balance                  ?  No
   Show inventory details                         ?  Yes
   Show table of bills for selection              ?  No

   Show bill-wise details                         ?  Yes
      Expand into multiple lines                  ?  No
   Show current balances of ledgers               ?  No
                        Statutory Options
   Allow modification of tax details for GST      ? Yes
   Allow tax difference up to                     :  10
      Actual tax versus computed tax              :  Greater or Lesse
                  Press F12 for more options.
```

F-6C: Purchase Voucher Configuration

```
                   Tax Classification details

   Classification/Nature :  Purchase From Unregistered Dealer - Taxable
```

F-6D: Tax Classification set up in Voucher

```
           The tax details are modified.

   Y  Accept   (accept with conflicts and resolve later)
   O  Override (accept without conflicts)
   N  Back     (go back to the voucher)
```

F-6E: Voucher Message

Though no tax entry has been entered in the Invoice (as the Invoice has been raised by Unregistered Dealer), tally senses the type of Purchase from the GST details of supplier (Registration type & State), and classified the transaction accordingly. Tax is internally computed showing the applicability of Reverse charge at Tax Analysis details.

However, Tax liability is not reflected in Balance Sheet, but reflected in GSTR-2 (F-7A), as per details shown in Tax Analysis (F-6B), after Purchase Voucher entry.

F-7A: Purchase Details showing the Reverse Charge Tax liability in GSTR-2

As the Purchase is from unregistered dealer, there would be no tax charged in the Invoice. However, the Tax Analysis (Click *A:Tax Analysis*) would show Tax details and a note that the Tax is under Reverse charge (F-6B). This would be shown in GSTR-3B as Liability created, yet to be booked.

As per notification dt 29 June, 2018, reverse charge on Purchases from Unregistered Parties u/s 9(4) is deferred till 30th Sep 2018. However, Reverse Charge on specified Goods & Services u/s 9(3) are still applicable.

Reverse Charge Liability creation

On purchase from unregistered dealer, a liability for Reverse Charge is to be created.

Create Ledger Account for Tax on Reverse Charge & then a Journal Voucher to make adjustment entry to create the Reverse Charge Liability

Reverse Charge Ledger Account : Create Reverse Charge liability Ledger Account (GoT>Accounts Info>Ledger>Create) under Current Asset (F-8A). It is used to create the liability of Reverse Charge and then subsequently relinquished on adjustment of input credit. Finally, the balance of this account would be Nil when the Reverse Charge is paid to the Government and the corresponding input credit is adjusted

F-8A: Reverse Charge Ledger Account creation

Journal Voucher for Reverse Charge Liability creation

Having created the Purchase voucher, create a Journal Voucher in usual way (GoT>Accounting Voucher> F7:Journal), to create Reverse Charge Liability (F-9A).

At Journal Voucher (F-9A), select Tax on Reverse Charge ledger account and enter the GST Reverse Charge amount in Debit column and credit the respective Tax Accounts (CGST/SGST or IGST as the case may be), as per GSTR-3B report. Enter the *Rate* & *Taxable Value* in pop up screen and then enter the amount in main voucher (the computed amount as per Taxable Value & Rate is not carried in the voucher and you have to type it).

F-9A: Journal Voucher entry for Reverse Charge liability creation

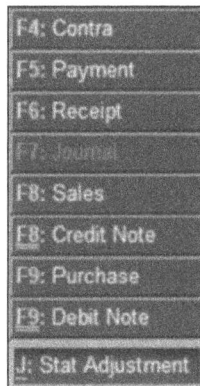

F-9B: Buttons

At Journal Voucher entry screen (F-9A), click *J:Stat Adjustment* button (F-9B) to get Stat Adjustment screen (F-10A).

F-10A: Stat Adjustment for Reverse Charge

At Stat Adjustment entry screen, at *Type of Duty / Tax*, select GST. At *Nature of Adjustment*, select Increase of Tax Liability and Input Tax Credit. At Additional Details, select Purchase from Unregistered Dealer.

F-10B: Nature of Adjustment list in Stat Adjustment

F-10C : Additional Details list in Stat Adjustment

Alternatively, At GSTR-3B Report Click *S:Stat Adjustment* to get Statutory Adjustment screen and Journal Voucher creation screen, as described.

This Journal Voucher would be reflected in GSTR-3B as Eligible Input Credit

Effect of Purchase entry in GSTR & in Accounts :

– **Effect in GSTR-3B Report** : This would be reflected in GSTR-3B, under List of Purchases from Unregistered Dealer, as Liability to be booked.

– **Effect in Balance Sheet**: At this stage, in Balance Sheet (*GoT>Balance Sheet*), only the Sundry Debtors is reflected in Accounts, without reflecting any liability for reverse charge.

The creation of Tax Liability is would be reflected in GSTR-3B report

F-11A: Tax Liability on Reverse Charge in GSTR-3B

You can drill down to lower level to view the list of vouchers leading to such Reverse Charge.

F-11B: Reverse Charge liability details for Inward supply

Note: In Tally Rel 6.4, you may create a single Journal Voucher in place of Journal Voucher F-9A and F-13A, debiting and crediting The Tax Accounts (CGST / SGST), as explained in Chapter Reverse Charge Mechanism. In that case, at Stat Adjustment (F-10A), at Nature of Adjustment, select Increase of Tax Liability & Input Tax Credit, and at Additional Details, select Purchase from Unregistered Dealer. The single voucher would make adjustments for creation of Liability (F-9A) and also Input tax Credit (F-13A).

Payment of Tax Liability on Reverse Charge

Now the liability has to be extinguished by paying the Tax to Government. Create a Payment Voucher (*GoT>Accounting Voucher>F5:Payment*) for Payment of Reverse Charge Tax Liability (F-12A).

F-12A: Reverse Charge Tax Payment Voucher

F-12B : Stat payment details for
Reverse Charge Tax Payment Voucher

F-12C: Bank Derails for Tax Payment

Click *S:Stat Payment* button to get Statutory Payment screen (F-12B). Now enter as follows :

– **Tax Type** : At Tax Type select GST

– **Period** : At period, enter the Range of Accounting Month period for which Tax is being deposited (irrespective of Date of Payment).

– **Payment Type** : Select *Recipient Liability* for payment of Reverse charges on account of purchase from Unregistered Dealer.

Now you get back to the main voucher screen (F-12A). At *Provide GST Details*, type *Yes* to get Bank Details screen (F-12C). Enter the respective details as available. Write Narration and save the voucher

Journal Entry for Input Credit

Having paid the Tax for Reverse Charges, create a Journal Voucher to avail the Input Credit. This entry would be reverse to Journal Voucher for creation of ITC liability, discussed earlier (F-9A).

F-13A: Input Credit Adjustment Voucher for Reverse charge

F-13B: Stat Adjustment for Reverse Charge on Purchase from URD

Select the Tax Accounts and enter the amount in debit columns. Select Tax on Reverse Charge Account and enter the amount in credit columns.

The balance of the Tax Accounts and the Tax on Reverse Charge Ledger Account created for the purpose, would become *Nil* when all adjustments are complete.

F-13C: List of Nature of Adjustment for URD Purchase

F-13D: Additional Details for URD Purchase Adjustment

Click *A: Stat Adjustment* button to get Stat Adjustment screen (F-13B). At *Type of Tax*, select *GST*. At *Nature of Adjustment*, select *Reversal of Input Credit* from the list (F-13C). At Additional details, select Purchase from Unregistered Dealer (F-13D).

Purchase from Composition Dealer

When a regular dealer buys form Composition dealer (who do not charge GST and do not give Tax Invoice), there is no Tax Accounts or ITC involved for the buyer.

Supplier Ledger set up : Create supplier leger (GoT>Account Info>Ledger>create) as usual (F-1A).

– **State** : At State, select the State of the Composition dealer supplier (F-1A). Composition dealers are normally allowed to sell only within same state (Intra State sale). So, the State selected would be same as the State of the Company (Bury Company)

– **GST Details** : At Composition supplier ledger account entry screen (F-1A), set *Yes* at *Set / Alter GST details* to get GST details screen (F-1B). At supplier ledger GST details screen (F-1B), at *Registration Type*, select *Composition* from the list. At *GSTIN/ UIN*, enter the GSTIN of the supplier (The 1st two digit of GSTIN should be according to the State selected).

F-1A: Composition Supplier Ledger

F-1B: Composition Supplier GST details

Voucher entry for Purchase from Composition Dealer: Crate a Purchase Voucher entry (*GoT>Accounting Voucher>F9:Purchase*) to get Purchase voucher entry screen. Click *F12:Configure* and set Yes at *Allow Modification for Tax details for GST* (to set up the proper classification) of the transaction during voucher entry at Tax Classification details.

F-2A: Purchase from Composition Dealer

F-2B: Tax Analysis

F-2C: Tax Classification entry

Enter Voucher date, Select Supplier Ledger, Select Purchase Account. At *Tax Classification* details pop up screen, the Tax Classification (F-2C), *Purchase from Composition Dealer* would be auto selected by default (select it if necessary from Nature of Transaction list).

Enter the Item details (Quantity, Rate, discount if any) for each Item purchased. There would be no GST charged in the Invoice. Click *A: Tax Analysis* to get Tax Analysis screen (F-2B) showing the Taxable Value (No Tax amount would be displayed). Enter Narration (if any) and save the voucher (F-2A).

GSTR Reports : Purchase from Composition Dealer (both Inter State and Local) would be reflected as *NIL Related Income- Table 7* in GSTR-2 and under Table 5 of GSTR-3B (F-3A).

GSTR-2					Ctrl + M
GSTIN/UIN : 18AAAAS0234A1Z7					1-Oct-2017 to 31-Oct-201
Particulars	No. of Invoices	Taxable Value	Total Tax	Total ITC Available	Reconciliation Status
To be reconciled with the GST portal					
B2B Invoices - 3, 4A					
Credit/Debit Notes Regular - 6C					
To be uploaded on the GST portal					
B2BUR Invoices - 4B					
Import of Services - 4C					
Import of Goods - 5					
Credit/Debit Notes Unregistered - 6C					
Nil Rated Invoices - 7 - (Summary)	1	7,000.00			
Advance Paid -10A - (Summary)					
Adjustment of Advance - 10B - (Summary)					
Total Inward Supplies		7,000.00			
ITC Reversal/Reclaim - 11 - (Summary)					
Total No. of Invoices	1				
Reverse Charge Liability to be Booked					
Reverse Charge Inward Supplies					0.0
Import of Service					0.0

F-3A: GSTR-2 : Purchase from Composition Dealer

GSTR-3B	GST Co. Assam 18		Ctrl + M
GSTR-3B		1-Oct-2017 to 31-Oct-2017	
Table No.	Particulars	Taxable Value	Tax Amount
3.1	Outward supplies and inward supplies liable to reverse charge		
3.2	Of the supplies shown in 3.1 (a) above, details of inter-state supplies made to unregistered persons, composition taxable persons and UIN holders		
4	Eligible ITC		
5	Value of exempt, nil rated and non GST inward supplies	7,000.00	
5.1	Interest and Late fee Payable		
	Reverse Charge Liability to be booked		
	Reverse Charge Inward Supplies		0.00
	Import of Service		0.00

F-3B: GSTR-3B : Purchase from Composition Dealer

Invoice Reconciliation

GSTR-2A

GSTR-2A is an auto-populated statement viewed by Recipient, showing all the inward supplies reported by counterpart supplier in their GSTR-1 (and also in GSTR-5, GSTR-7& GSTR-8).

The details may be directly viewed in the GST Portal, or GSTR-2A downloaded and viewed in the offline utility tool. Invoices / records up to 500 can be viewed online for a table / section in Form GSTR-2A. In case, if invoices are more than 500, generate the GSTR-2A file and use the offline utility tool (GST Portal > Services > Return > Prepare Offline > Download Tab > Generate File) available on the portal for viewing the invoice details.

GSTR-2

GSTR-2 is a statement in which a regular dealer needs to capture all the inward supplies made during the month. Broadly, all the inward supplies from registered businesses (B2B), including the supplies on which tax needs to be paid on reverse charge are required to be captured at the invoice level. In addition to inward supplies, you also need to declare the details of advances paid on supplies liable for reverse charge, and the advance amount on which tax was paid in the earlier return period but the invoice has been received in the current reporting period. The last date to submit the GSTR-2 for the month of July 2017 is 31st October, 2017.

Based on the details submitted in GSTR-2, the eligible ITC will be determined and accordingly it will be credited to your e-credit ledger on a provisional basis.

'GSTR-2 vis-à-vis GSTR-2A'

There is no need to enter all inward invoices details in GSTR-2. Most of the details in GSTR-2 is auto-populated, based on the outward supplies declared by counter party suppliers in their returns. The auto-populated details of inward supplies shown in GSTR-2A, are also shown in GSTR-2. In other words, GSTR-2A will be an exact replica of GSTR-2 containing only the details declared by your counter party suppliers in their GSTR-1.

Therefore, you need to reconcile the details of inward supplies available in GSTR-2A, with your books of accounts and accordingly figure out the additions, modifications and deletion of invoices shown in GSTR-2A.

The form GSTR-2A is just a read-only document. Therefore, any action on inward supplies shown in GSTR-2A, is to be done in GSTR-2 only.

So, any omission or correction not actioned as per the statement in GSTR-2A with inward supplies register (in the books), will impact input tax credit eligibility, as reflected in GSTR-3B.

Identifying Mismatch in GSTR-2 / GSTR-2A

- **Download JSON form Portal** : Download GSTR-2A JSON file of the required tax period from the GST portal .

- **Load JSON File into Tally for Comparison** : GoT> Display > Statutory Reports > GST > GSTR-2 . Select the period as per the GSTR-2A JSON file. At GSTR-2 report screen, click *L : Load File* button and load the GSTR-2A JSON file (for comparison only). Successful File Loading message appears. Type No (not to update as you have loaded only for Comparison)

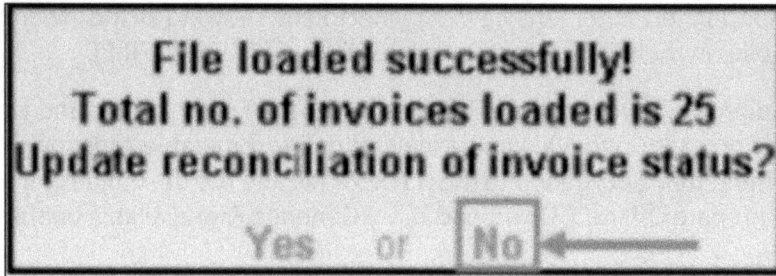

F-1A : JSON file Loading message

Compare Data : Now compare the data recorded in your Book (in Tally) and uploaded in GST Portal

- Records in Blue show details as per the downloaded GSTR-2A JSON file. This includes the details of invoices submitted by the supplier, and the invoices that you have manually uploaded on the portal.

- Records in Black show details of invoices *As per Books* .

Click *A:View Statuswise* button to show the records according to Status of the Invoice. It shows records classified as:

- **Fully Matched** : Invoices recorded in Books (in Tally) match with the records in Portal. No action is needed

- **Partially Matched**: Some info not matched between invoices available in the books with invoices available on the GST portal.

- **Available only in Books**: Inward Invoices recorded in books (Tally) by you, but supplier has not uploaded the invoices.

- **Available only in Portal**: If you have not recorded the transaction in your books but your supplier has uploaded the same

Resolving Mismatch : Drill down through *Partially Matched* item in the report (Click *F1:Detailed*) to list the Invoices and note down the differences. If any amendment done by the counterparty in GSTR-1, it is also reflected in your GSTR-2A. These invoices may not be available in your books. Check your book information across return periods for further action.

Similarly, Drill down through *Available in Portal* item. Based on the differences observed, you or your counterparty should record appropriate entries in the current return period, to correct the books.

To avoid mismatches in input tax credit as per books and GSTR-2A, you may download and compare GSTR-2A to match the details of input tax credit for the previous and upcoming return periods. This helps to ensure correctness of input tax credit claimed.

Mismatch between GSTR-3B & GSTR-2A

Consolidated value of inward supplies are filed in GSTR-3B returns. The suppliers have uploaded their sales invoices in GSTR-1, based on which counter party inward supplies get auto populated in GSTR-2A.

Any difference in values between inwards supply details (furnished in GSTR-3B) and outwards supply details uploaded by respective counter party suppliers (available on GST portal as GSTR-2A) may lead to loss in the claimed Input Tax Credit (ITC).

Possible Reasons of Mismatch

- Supplier has not uploaded the invoices for which you have already claimed Input Tax Credit.

- Values in the supplier's invoices are not matching with values available in your books.

- You might have missed out recording any Purchases or Debit Notes (Purchase Returns) resulting reduced Input Tax Credit.

Resolving Mismatch between GSTR-3B & GSTR-2A

- Compare purchases recorded in books (in Tally) with GSTR-2A (available on GST Portal) of the respective return period and identify the mismatch invoices.

- Having identified mismatch / missing invoices, contact the respective supplier asking him to either upload the related invoice in his latest return which is yet to be filed, or amend the invoice details at the time of filing his returns.

- On the other hand, you check the physical copies of respective purchase invoices and correct your purchase data (in Tally), and accordingly make corrections in your latest GST returns which are yet to be filed (you may need to reverse ITC)

Advance Receipt & Adjustment

Advance Receipts against Supplies

A supplier has to pay tax on receipt of advance for supplies to be made in future, if the turnover of the buyer in previous year is more than 1.5 crores.

- **Suppliers with Turnover not exceeding 1.5 crores in previous year** : So, for suppliers having Turnover upto 1.5 crores there would be no Tax liability for parties receiving advance. They would create receipt voucher for Advance received from customers as usual, without any effect for GST. In GST returns (GSTR-1 & GSTR-3B), these transactions would be reported under the section *Not Relevant for Returns* section

- **Suppliers with Turnover exceeding 1.5 crores in previous year** : Suppliers having turnover more than 1.5 crores in previous Financial Year need to set up relevant options for GST Liability on Advance Received. As per notification dt 15 Nov 17, no GST is payable on advance received against supply of goods (irrespective of turnover). However, this relief is not available to Composition Dealer and in case of Supply of Services.

- **Tax Liability on Advance Receipt option set up**: At *Statutory & Taxation* screen (*GoT>F11 Features>Statutory & Taxation*), set *Yes* to get Company GST set up screen. Set yes at Set / Alter GST Details to get GST Details screen (F-1A). At GST Details screen (F-1A), set *Yes* at *Enable Tax Liability on Advance Receipts*, to enable GST Liability on Advance Receipt.

GST Details	
State	: West Bengal
Registration type	: Regular
Assessee of Other Territory	? No
GSTIN/UIN	: 19AMAPS5106K1ZV
Applicable from	: 1-Jul-2017
Periodicity of GSTR1	: Monthly
e-Way Bill applicable	? Yes
e-Way Bill applicable from	: 1-Feb-2018
e-Way Bill threshold	: 50,000
Threshold limit includes	: Invoice value
e-Way Bill applicable for intrastate	? Yes
Enable tax liability on advance receipts	? **Yes**
Enable tax liability on reverse charge (Purchase from unregistered dealer)	? Yes
Set/alter GST rate details	? No
Enable GST Classifications	? No
Provide LUT/Bond details	? No

F-1A: Tax Liability on Advance receipt option Set up

Receipt Voucher Entry for Advance Received

At *GoT>Accounting Vouchers*, click F6: Receipt button to get Receipt Voucher entry screen to record receipt of Advance (F-2A). At Receipt Voucher entry screen (F-2A), click *V:Advance Receipt* button (F-2B) to mark the Voucher as Advance Receipt (the Mark appears in the receipt voucher entry screen).

F-2A: GST chargeable Advance receipt

F-2B: Buttons

- **Cash / Bank Account** : At *Account*, select Cash / Bank Account, as the case may be.

- **Party Details** : At *Particulars*, Select Party Ledger Account to get Party Details pop up screen (F-3A). The details of Party (Address, GSTIN etc are carried from Party master) is carried.

- **Advance Receipt details** : You get Advance Receipt details screen (F-3B). At particulars column, select the Item / Service for which Advance is received. Enter the amount of Advance received against the supply. According to the tax rate applicable for the selected Item / Service, the Amount would be split into Taxable value and tax (CGST+SGST or IGST as per nature of supply (Inter State / Intra State). The total of Taxable Amount and Tax would be equal to Amount Received.

- **Bill Allocation Details** : You get back to main voucher screen (F-3A) and get Bill Allocation screen (F-3C). Set the Refence at Bill Allocation screen to get back to the main voucher screen.

Enter Voucher Narration (F-2A). Save the Voucher.

F-3A: Party Details

F-3B: Tax details for Advance Receipt

F-3C: Bill Allocation for Advance receipt

Receipt Voucher Printing : To print Receipt, at Receipt Voucher screen (F-2A), click *P:Print* button to get Voucher Printing screen. Set Yes at *Print GST Advance Receipt* to print Advance Receipt Voucher with GST details (F-4A)

F-4A: Advance Receipt with GST details

Creation of GST Liability on Advance Receipt

Entry of Receipt Voucher just affects the Accounting System. Though you enter GST details, the GST system does not automatically get updated (GST Liability not created on its own). If the Sales Bill is not created in the same month and the Advance not fully adjusted against the Sales Bill, you have to create the GST liability for the month, through a Journal Voucher. However, if sales Bill is created in the same month and advance adjusted, you do not need to create the Journal Voucher for creation of Tax Liability.

Tax on Advance Ledger Account : When the receipt of advance and adjustment of advance (on creation of sales bill) happen in different Return period, you have to first create a liability for the Tax Payable in the Tax Return period in which Advance is received. In later Tax filing period, when Advance is adjusted against Sales Invoice, the Tax liability entry is reversed, and the balance in the Tax Liability is squared off.

Create a temporary intermediate ledger account (e.g Tax on Advance) to record the Tax liability entry without setting any GST parameters. This is an intermediary account which would ultimately be squared on adjustment of Advance & Tax on Advance

Select *GoT>Accounts Info>Ledger>Create* to get Leger Entry screen (F-5A) to create the Ledger Account. Select *Current Asset* at *Under*. Set *No* at *Inventory Values are affected*. Set *Not Applicable* at *Is GST Applicable*. Set *No* at *Set/ Alter GST details*. This Ledger Account would be used in Journal Voucher only, to create and adjust the GST Tax liability, in respective Return filing period.

F-5A: Tax on Advance Ledger Account creation

Journal Voucher to create Liability for GST on Advance : If Advance not adjusted in the same Tax Return period in which advance is received, GST Tax Liability on Advance received, is to be created, as shown in the *Advance Receipt Details* in Receipt Voucher (F-3B). Select *GoT>Accounting Voucher>F7:Journal* to get Journal Entry screen (F-6A), to create a Journal Voucher for GST liability on Advance received.

F-6A: Journal Voucher for Tax on Advance Receipt Liability creation

At Journal Voucher entry screen (F-6A), select Tax on Advance Account and enter the amount of Total Tax Liability on Advance as per Receipt Voucher, in Debit Column. Select the Tax Accounts and enter the Amount of Tax in Credit Column, as per Receipt Voucher.

Statutory Adjustment Details : Journal Voucher entry screen (F-6A), Click *J:Stat Adjustment* button to get *Stat Adjustment* screen (F-7A) to enter the GST Adjustment details :

– At Type of Duty / Tax, select GST

– At *Nature of Adjustment*, select *Increase in Tax Liability*

– At Additional details, select On Account of Advance Receipts

The options selected are reflected in the main voucher screen for info.

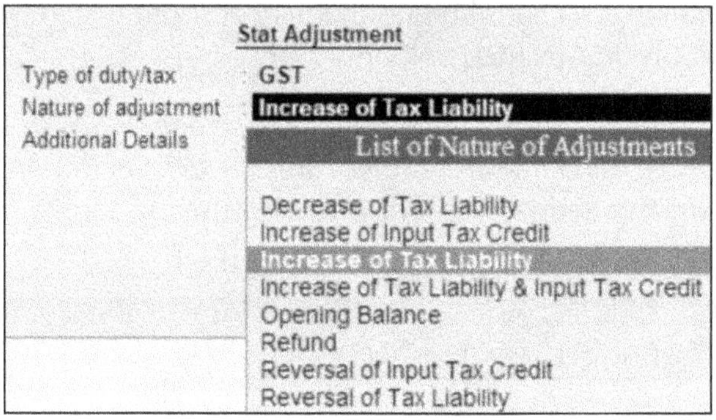

F-7A: Stat Adjustment screen

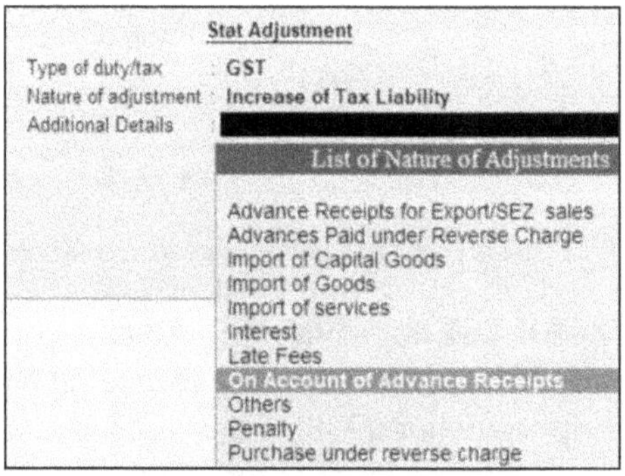

F-7B: Nature of Adjustment selection

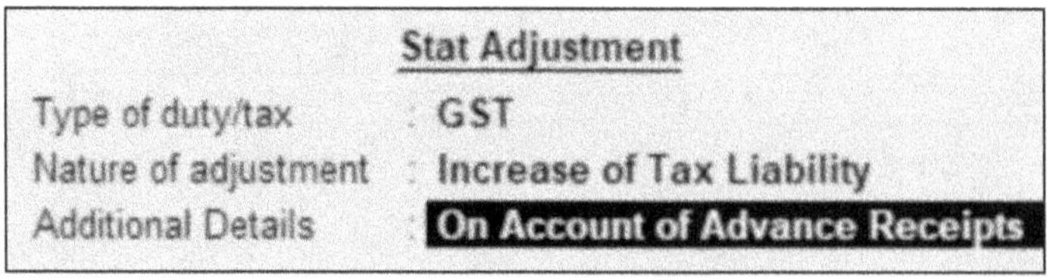

F-7C: Additional Details

GST Details: At voucher main screen, set *Yes* at *Provide GST Details*, to get *Advance Details screen*. At *Ledger Name*, select Party Ledger Account from the list of Ledger Accounts. Details of the Ledger Account (Place of Supply, Registration Type, Party Type & GSTIN) are auto filled from the selected Ledger Account Master

Advance Details

Ledger Name	: Customer 1 - Kol 19
Place of supply	: West Bengal
Registration type	: Regular
Party type	: Not Applicable
GSTIN/UIN	: 19ABCDE1234V1Z1

F-8A: Advance details

Creation of Sales Invoice

On supply of materials / service, create the sales Invoice, as usual (F-9A). Enter Voucher Date, select Party Ledger Account, Enter Item details (in Item Invoice) or Ledger Accounts (in Accounting Invoice). Select the Tax Accounts. The Tax amount would be auto computed in respective heads. Enter Other Ledger Accounts and amount, if any.

Accounting Voucher Creation — Ctrl + M

Sales No. 07/00001/17-18 — 1-Oct-2017, Sunday

Reference no.:

Party A/c name : Customer 1 - Kol 19

Sales ledger : Taxable Sales

Name of Item	Quantity	Rate	per	Disc %	Amount
Item 2 @12%	50 Pc	300.00	Pc		15,000.00
Output CGST					900.00
Output SGST					900.00
Narration:	50 Pc				16,800.00

F-9A: sales Invoice

Bill-wise Details for : **Customer 1 - Kol 19**
Upto: **₹ 16,800.00 Dr**

Type of Ref	Name	Due Date, or Credit Days (wef: 1-Oct-2017)	Amount	Dr/Cr
Advance	1		10,000.00	Dr
New Ref	07/00001/17-18		6,800.00	Dr
			16,800.00	Dr

F-9B: Bill Allocation

Tax Analysis			Ctrl + M ☒
Particulars	Taxable Value	Tax rate	Duty/Tax Value
GST Details			
Sales Taxable	15,000.00		1,800.00
Item 2 @12% (1235)	*15,000.00*		*1,800.00*
Item Value (Sales Value 15,000.00)			
Central Tax		6%	*900.00*
State Tax		6%	*900.00*
		Total	1,800.00

F-9C : Tax Analysis

– **Bill Allocation details** : At Bill Allocation screen, enter Bill details at as usual (F-9B)

– **Tax Analysis** : Click *A:Tax Analysis* to get Tax Analysis screen view Tax Details (F-9C).

Sales Invoice Printing : To print the Sales Invoice, at Sales Voucher entry screen (f-9A), click *P:Print* button and print the Sales Invoice, as usual.

Adjustment of Advance & Reversing the Tax Liability on Advance

Now create another Journal Voucher to reverse the Tax Liability created earlier at the time of receipt of Advance. Select (*GoT>Accounting Voucher- F7:Journal*) to get Journal Voucher entry screen (F-10A). Select the Tax Accounts and enter the Amount of Tax at Debit column as per Receipt Voucher. Select Tax on Advance Account and enter the amount of Total Tax Liability on Advance at Credit column, as per Receipt Voucher. This Journal Voucher (F-10A) would be just reverse of the Journal Entry for creation of Tax Liability in earlier Tax Return Period

Accounting Voucher Creation	Comp Kol 19		Ctrl + M ☒
Journal No. 5			31-Oct-2017 Tuesday
	Used for: Decrease of Tax Liability *(Additional Details: Sales against Advance Receipts)*		
Particulars		**Debit**	**Credit**
Dr **Output CGST**		535.71	
Dr **Output SGST**		535.71	
Cr **Tax on Advance**			1,071.42
Narration: Reversal of Tax on Advance		1,071.42	1,071.42

F-10A: Journal Voucher for Reversing Tax on Advance liability

Statutory Adjustment Details : At Journal Click *J:Stat Adjustment* button to get *Stat Adjustment* screen to enter the GST Adjustment details (F-10B):

– At Type of Duty / Tax, select GST

– At *Nature of Adjustment*, select *Decrease in Tax Liability*

– At Additional details, select *Sales Against Advance Receipts*

The options selected are reflected in the main voucher screen for info (F-10A).

F-10B: Stat Adjustment

GST Details : At voucher main screen, set *Yes* at *Provide GST Details*, to get *Advance Details screen* (F-10C). At *Advance receipt number*, enter the reference of Advance as entered in earlier Receipt voucher. At *Advance receipt date*, enter the date of earlier Receipt voucher. At *Ledger Name*, select Party Ledger Account from the list of Ledger Accounts. Details of the Ledger Account (Place of Supply, Registration Type, Party Type & GSTIN) are auto filled from the selected Ledger Account Master

F-10C: Advance details

You should create the Reversal Journal to the extent of Advance Adjusted against sales Invoice. If the Tax in sales Invoice is lower than the Tax in Advance received (because sales Bill is lower than the amount of Advance received), then you should reverse the Tax amount to the extent of Tax charged in sales Bill. The balance amount would be adjusted against subsequent Invoice, or the Balance Advance is to be refunded (if not further sales Bill is to be prepared).

Refund of Advance

Sometimes Advance may have to be returned in full (if the supply is cancelled or for some other reason). Sometimes, the supply may be for lesser amount than advance received. In that case, balance amount of unadjusted Advance is to be refunded. In such case, GST on Advance and Tax Liability of Advance is also to be adjusted.

The cycle of vouchers related to Advance are :

– Receipt Voucher for receipt of Advance (F-11A to F-11C)

– Journal Voucher for creation of Liability of GST on Advance received (F-12A to F-12D)

– Refund Voucher for refund of Advance received (F-13A to F-13D)

– Journal Voucher for reversal of GST on advance (F-14A to F-14D)

All the vouchers in the chain are shown next, to explain the complete process related to Advance Receipt, Tax Adjustments & Refund of Advance.

Receipt Voucher creation : On receipt of advance received from customer, create a Receipt Voucher (*GoT>Accounting Voucher>F6:Receipt*) to get Receipt Voucher entry screen. The steps of entry of Receipt Voucher for receipt of advance has been explained earlier.

Accounting Voucher Creation (Secondary)	Comp Kol 19	Ctrl + M ☒
Receipt No. 2		**2-Oct-2017**
		Monday
	Used for: Advance Receipt	
Account : **Cash**		
Particulars		**Amount**
Customer Cuttack -21		8,000.00
Narration:		8,000.00
Advance received from Customer		

F-11A: Receipt Voucher for Advance receipt

The voucher entry for receipt of advance and the inner details are shown for reference

	Advance Receipt Details					
Particulars	Advance Amount	Taxable Value	Integrated Tax		Cess	
			Rate	Amount	Rate	Amount
Item 1 @5%	8,000.00	7,619.05	5 %	380.95		
	8,000.00	7,619.05		380.95		

F-11B: Tax details entry of Advance Receipt

Bill-wise Details for : **Customer Cuttack -21** Upto : ₹ 8,000.00 Cr			
Type of Ref	Name	Due Date, or Credit Days (wef: 2-Oct-2017)	Amount Dr/ Cr
Advance	2		8,000.00 Cr
			8,000.00 Cr

F-11C: Bill allocation details of Advance receipt.

Journal Voucher for creation of Liability : The Journal Voucher for creation of Liability on GST for Advance received is shown. The entry process of creation of liability for receipt of advance have been explained earlier.

Select *GoT>Accounting Voucher- F7:Journal* to get Journal Voucher entry screen(F-12A). At Journal Voucher entry screen (F-12A), select *Tax on Advance Account* and enter the amount of Total Tax Liability on Advance as per Receipt Voucher in Debit Column. Select the Tax Accounts and enter the Amount of Tax in Credit column, as per Receipt Voucher.

F-12A: Journal Voucher for creation of liability for
Advance Receipt

F-12B: Advance Receipt details entry

F-12C: Buttons

Statutory Adjustment Details : At Receipt Voucher screen (F-12A), click *F:Refund of Advance* button (F-12C) to get *Stat Adjustment* screen (F-12D) to enter the GST Adjustment details :

– At Type of Duty / Tax, select GST

– At *Nature of Adjustment*, select *Increase of Tax Liability*

– At Additional details, select *On Account of Advance Receipts* from the list

The options selected are reflected in the main voucher screen for info.

Stat Adjustment

Type of duty/tax	: GST
Nature of adjustment	: **Increase of Tax Liability**
Additional Details	: **On Account of Advance Receipts**

F-12D: Stat Advance details of Tax liability of Advance receipt

GST Details : At voucher main screen (F-12A), set *Yes* at *Provide GST Details*, to get *Advance Details screen* (F-12B). At *Ledger Name*, select Party Ledger Account from the list of Ledger Accounts. Details of the Ledger Account (Place of Supply, Registration Type, Party Type & GSTIN) are auto filled from the selected Ledger Account Master

Payment Voucher for Refund of Advance

To refund the Advance receipt, select *GoT>Accounting Voucher- F5:Payment to* create a Payment Voucher (F-13A). At Payment Voucher(F-13A), select Party ledger Account and enter the Amount of Refund.

Click *F:Refund of Advance Recd* button

Payment No. 2		1-Nov-2017
		Wednesday
	Used for: Refund of Advance Receipt	
Account : **Cash**		

Particulars		Amount
Customer Cuttack -21		8,000.00
New Ref 2	8,000.00 Dr	
Provide GST details	Yes	
Narration:		8,000.00
Refund of Advance for cancellation of order		

F-13A: Payment Voucher for Advance Refund

Bill-wise Details for : **Customer URD - Cuttack 21**
Upto: ₹ 8,000.00 Dr

Type of Ref	Name	Due Date, or Credit Days (wef: 1-Nov-2017)	Amount Dr/ Cr
Agst Ref	2	30 Days (1-Dec-2017)	8,000.00 **Dr**
			8,000.00 Dr

F-13B: Bill Allocation details

Select the Party ledger Account and enter the amount of Refund. Click *F:Refund of Advance Received* to get Refund details screen (F-13A). Select the Item. Enter Refund Amount. The tax details are auto populated. At main voucher screen (f-13A), set Yes at provide GST details to get Original Receipt details screen 9f-13D). Enter the details of original receipt voucher for receipt of advance (which is being refunded now). At Bill allocation screen (F-13B), select *Against Ref* at Type of Reference and select the reference of original advance receipt to square off the Advance)

Particulars	Refund Amount	Taxable Value	Integrated Tax		Cess	
			Rate	Amount	Rate	Amount
Item 1 @5%	8,000.00	7,619.05	5 %	380.95		
	8,000.00	7,619.05		380.95		

F-13C: Refund Details

Original Receipt Details

Receipt No. : **2**   Date : 2-Oct-2017

F-13D: Original Advance Receipt Details

Printing of Refund Voucher : At payment Voucher screen (F-13A), click P:Print to get Refund Voucher printing screen. Set Yes at *Print Refund Voucher*. The refund voucher is printed as per printing configuration set (F-13E).

F-13E : Refund Voucher printing

Journal Voucher to reverse GST Liability on Advance Refund

On Refund of Advance, on which you earlier created Tax Liability, you have to again create a Journal Voucher to reverse the Tax Liability.

Particulars	Debit	Credit
Dr **Output IGST**	380.95	
Cr **Tax on Advance**		380.95
Provide GST details: **Yes**		
Narration:	380.95	380.95
Adjustment of Tax on Advance Refund		

Accounting Voucher Creation (Secondary)   Comp Kol 19   Ctrl + M
Journal   No. 7   2-Nov-2017 Thursday
Used for: Decrease of Tax Liability
(Additional Details: Cancellation of Advance Receipts)

F-14A: GST reversal Journal Voucher on Refund of Advance

```
                          Advance Details

Advance Receipt Number  : 2
Advance Receipt Date    : 2-Oct-2017
Refund Voucher Number   : 2
Refund Voucher Date     : 1-Nov-2017
Ledger Name             : Customer Cuttack -21
Place of supply         : Odisha
Registration type       : Regular
Party type              : ▯ Not Applicable
GSTIN/UIN               : 21ABCDE2222M1Z1
```

F-14B: Adjustment details on Refund of Advance

Select *GoT>Accounting Voucher- F7:Journal* to get Journal Voucher entry screen (F-14A). Select the tax Account and enter the Tax Amount of Refund of Advance in Debit column. Select Tax on Advance Account and enter the Tax Amount under Credit column.

```
                        Stat Adjustment

Type of duty/tax     : GST
Nature of adjustment : Decrease of Tax Liability
Additional Details   : Cancellation of Advance Receipts
```

F-14C: Stat Adjustment option selection on Refund of Advance

```
                    Stat Adjustment

Type of duty/tax     : GST
Nature of adjustment : Decrease of Tax Liability
Additional Details   :

                    List of Nature of Adjustments
        Adjustment Against Credit
        Cancellation of Advance Payments under Reverse Charge
        Cancellation of Advance Receipts
        Cancellation of Advance Receipts for Exports/SEZ sales
        Purchase against Advance Payment
        Sales against Advance Receipts
        Sales against Advance Receipts for Export/SEZ sales
```

F-14D: Stat Adjustment additional details on Refund of Advance

Stat Adjustment : Click *J:Stat Adjustment* button to get Stat Adjustment screen (F-14C). At *Type of Duty / Tax*, select GST. At *Nature of Adjustment*, select *Decrease of Tax Liability*. At Additional details, select *Cancellationof Advance Receipts* from the list (F-14D). The options selected are reflected in the main voucher screen for info (F-14A).

Advance received for Supply under Reverse Charge

For Advance Received by the supplier, from the customer, for supply of Goods / Services subject to RCM, you have to create Liability for RCM and also Liability for Advance Received. Both the concepts have been explained earlier. Here we explain the entries for Advance Received from Customer against supply of Goods / Service under RCM.

RCM option set up : For Supply under Reverse Charges, set the RCM option at the respective Ledger Account for Service (F-15A) / Stock Item. Set Yes at Set / Alter GST Details (F-15A) to get GST Details screen (F-15B). At GST Details screen (F-15B), set *Yes* at *Is Reverse Charge Applicable*, t activate the RCM option for the Service purchase.

F-15A: Ledger Account creation for Service under RCM

F-15B: RCM option set up and Service under RCM ledger Account

Creation of Receipt Voucher for Advance Receipt

Select *GoT>Accounting Voucher>F6:Receipt*) to get Receipt Voucher entry screen (F-16A) to make entry for Advance received, in same way explained earlier. Click *V:Advance received* button.

F-16A: Advance receipt for reverse charge supply

F-16B: Bill allocation details for Advance receipt

Select Cash / Bank Account. Select Party Ledger. Enter Amount received (including GST) to get *Advance Receipt details* screen (F-16D).

F-16C: Party Details for Advance receipt

F-16D: GST details of Advance Receipt

Advance Receipt Details : At *Advance details* screen (F-16D), select Stock Item / Ledger Account (to get list of Ledger Account, press Alt+L at Advance ReceiptDetails screen, if you do not get the Ledger Account selection list).

Enter the amount of advance received (including the Tax Amount). The amount is split up into Advance Amount, Taxable Value and Tax Amount against the applicable Tax Ledger Account and displayed. A note *Amount subject to Reverse Charge* appears at the bottom of the screen, for info

F-16E: Advance Receipt printing

Printing of Advance Receipt : To print Advance Receipt, at Receipt Voucher screen (F-16A), click *P:Print* button to get Receipt Printing screen. Set *Yes* at Print GST Advance receipt to print the Advance Receipt (F-16E) as per Configuration option set, as explained earlier. The printed receipt voucher also contains a note *Amount subject to Reverse Charge.* Save the Voucher.

Creation of Sales Invoice for supply against Advance Received

On supply, create Sales Invoice (GoT>Accounting Invoice- F8:Sales) as usual to get sales Invoice entry screen (F-17A).

F-17A: Sales Invoice for supply against Advance received

F-17B: Bill allocation for adjustment of Advance

F-17C: GST details on Advance received against Reverse Chargeable supply.

Select Party Ledger Account. Select the sales Account (Reverse Chargeable) and enter the Amount.

- **Advance Adjustment** : At Bill allocation screen (F-17B), select the Advance Reference and enter Advance adjusted. The balance would be allocated to the Bill Reference as New Reference.

- **Tax Analysis** : Click *A:Tax Analysis* to view the Tax Analysis details (F-17C). A note *Amount is subject to Reverse Charge* appears in the Tax Analysis screen for info.

Reverse Charge Mechanism

Normally the Seller is liable to collect tax from buyer and deposit with government. Here we discuss instances where Buyer be liable to pay tax to the Government (referred as RCM- Reverse Charge Mechanism)

We have already explained Reverse Charge on Purchase from unregistered dealer, effective till 12th October 2018.Here we discuss about Reverse Charge applicable on purchase of Specified Goods and Services.

Purchase of Services under Reverse Charge : Certain Services like Road Transport Charges, services by Advocate are under Reverse charge, where recipient to Service are to pay the GST under Reverse Charges. The supplier does not charge GST in their supply Bill. So, the purchase Invoice do not contain GST but a liability to pay GST is created on entry of such purchases.

Expenses Ledger Account creation : Create Ledger Account (*GoT>Accounts Info>Ledger>Create*) for Expenses under Reverse Charge(F-1A). At GST Applicable, set yes. At *Set/Alter GST*, set Yes to get GST Details screen (F-1B). At *Type of supply*, select Services (Expenses / Services) / Goods (for Purchase Ledger Account for Purchase of Goods under Reverse Charge).

F-1A: Expenses Ledger under Reverse Charge

F-1B: GST set up forExpenses Ledger under Reverse Charge

F-1C: GST Details configuration

Reverse Charge Option set up at GST ledger Details screen : At Ledger Account GST Details screen (F-1B), at *Is Reverse Charges Applicable*, set yes. If you do not get the option, at GST Details screen (F-1B), click F12:Configure to get *GST Details Configuration* screen (F-1C). Set Yes at Enable Reverse Charge Calculation.

Purchase Voucher entry for purchase of Reverse Chargeable Services

Create Purchase Voucher (GoT> Accoung Voucher>F9:Purcahse) to get Purchase Voucher screen (F-2A). Click *V:As Invoice* toggle button to get the Voucher in Accounting Invoice mode. Select Service supplier Ledger Account

F-2A: Purchase of Services under Reverse Charge

Tax Analysis			
Particulars	Taxable Value	Tax rate	Duty/Tax Value
GST Details			
Purchase Taxable	18,000.00		900.00
Road Transport Charges	18,000.00		900.00
Purchase Value	18,000.00		
Central Tax		2.50%	450.00
State Tax		2.50%	450.00
Note: Amount of tax subject to reverse charge			
		As per Calculation	900.00
		As per Transaction	

F-2B: Tax Analysis

Select the Service Ledger Account and enter the Amount. Select other ledger accounts, if any, and enter the amount. Enter Narration. Click *A:Tax Analysis* button to view the Tax Analysis screen (F-2B). Though no Tax amount has been entered in the voucher, the Tax Payable under Reverse Charge is internally computed and shown, A note *"Amount of Tax is subject to Reverse Charge"* is also shown in Tax analysis screen (F-2B)

Effect in GST Reports

The Reverse Charge Tax Liability is reflected in GSTR-3B Report (F-3A / F-3B).

F-3A: GSTR-3B: Purchase of Service under Reverse Charge

F-3B: GSTR-3B: Reverse Charge Liability for Purchase of Service

Journal Voucher for Reverse Charge Liability

To adjust and reflect ITC & Reverse Charge liability, create a Journal Voucher debiting & crediting the Tax Accounts (no effect in Accounts). Enter the Rate & taxable Value to compute Tax Amount (F-4C). Enter the Tax Amount (the computed Tax amount is not auto carried in Amount column).

Click *J:Stat Adjustment* to get *Stat Adjustment screen* (F-4B). At *Stat Adjustment* screen (F-4B), at *Nature of Statement*, select *Increase of Input Tax & Input Tax Credit* from the list. At *Additional Details*, select *Purchase under Reverse Charge.*

F-4A: Journal Voucher for Reverse Charge Liability & Input Tax eligibility

F-4B: Stat Adjustment details

F-4C: Tax rate & Taxable Value entry

The Journal voucher is reflected in GSTR-3B report under Tax Liability Booked column (F-5B).

F-5B: GSTR-3B: Reverse Charge Liability booked

Payment of Reverse Charge Liability

Now create a Payment voucher to make Tax Payment. Select *GoT>Accounting Voucher>F5:Payment*to get Payment Voucher screen (F-6A). Enter the Tax Ledger and amount in Debit column.

Statutory payment Details : Click *S:Stat Payment* to get Statutory payment screen (F-6B). At *Tax Type*, select GST. At *Period from & To enter* the period for which the Reverse Charge payment is being made. At *Payment Type*, select *Recipient Liability*.

F-6A: Payment Voucher for Recipient Liability Payment

F-6B: Statutory details of Recipient Liability Payment

F-6C: Bank details of Recipient Liability Payment

Payment Details : At *Provide GST Details*, set Yes to get Bank Details screen (F-6C). Enter the details.

Ineligible Input Tax Credit

Normally GST paid for taxable expenses for business purposes are eligible for Input Credit. However, in some case, even business related expenses are not eligible for Input Credit (like Leave Travel / Home Travel benefits / concession to Employee, Club / Heath/ Fitness centre membership / Rent a cab, life/ Health Insurance to employees, Goods lost / damaged/ stolen / written off / given free as gift or samples / food, beverages, outdoor catering etc.). We explain below the entry of Ineligible ITC through illustration of Car for Personal use. Similar treatment would be made for all types of Ineligible ITC expenses / payments

Car used for Non Business Purpose

Business enterprise may avail ITC paid on purchase of Car for Trade (Dealer of Motor Vehicle - as Goods), Transportation of Passengers / own goods (Transporter - as Fixed asset), training in own driving school (Motor Training school - as Fixed asset). ITC will not be available for personal use of Car or for nonbusiness purpose. We will explain entry of Car purchase where ITC on GST paid on purchase of Car will not be available.

Ledger Account : Select GoT> Accounts Info>Ledger>Create) to get Ledger creation screen to create Ledger Account for Ledger Account subject to ineligible ITC (F-1A).

Enter Account Name, Parent Group (at Under). At *Is GST Applicable*, select Applicable. At Set / Alter GST details, set Yes to get *GST Detail* screen to set the GST details (F-1B)

Ledger Creation	
Name	: **Motor Car - Non Business**
Under	: **Fixed Assets**
Inventory values are affected	? **No**
Statutory Information	
Is GST Applicable	? **▮ Applicable**
Set/alter GST Details	? **Yes**
Type of Supply	: **Goods**

F-1A: Ineligible ITC Ledger Account

F-1B: GST details for Item of ineligible Input Credit

F-1C: GST details option configuration

GST Details set up : At *GST Details* screen (F-1B), set as follows :

–   At *Is Non GST Goods*, set *No*.

–   At *Nature of Transaction*, select *Not Applicable* (Nature of Transaction would be specified in Voucher)

–   At *Taxability*, select *Taxable*

–   At *Is ineligible for Input Credit*, set *Yes*. If you do not see the option in the GST details screen, click F12:Cofigureto get Configuration screen (F-1C) and set Yes at Set Ineligible Input Credit.

–   At *Tax Type*, enter the Tax Rate.

Purchase Voucher Entry : Select *GoT>Accounting Voucher>F9:Purchase* to get Purchase Voucher entry screen. Click *V: As Voucher & I: Accounting Invoice* to get Accounting Invoice format.

At Tax Analysis pop up screen, select Tax Classification from the list. Click *F12:Configure* to get Configuration screen and then again click *F12:Configure* to get *Purchase Advanced Configuration* screen (F-2C). Set *Yes* at *Allow expenses / Fixed Asset in Purchase Voucher,* to enable entry of Fixed Asset Ledger Account in Purchase Voucher.

```
Purchase    No. 3                                           1-Oct-2017
Supplier invoice no : 25          Date : 1-Oct-2017            Sunday

   Particulars                              Debit            Credit

Cr  Customer 4 RG (Cuttack -21)                            6,40,000.00
Dr  Motor Car - Non Business              5,00,000.00
Dr  IGST                                  1,40,000.00
                                        ┌─────────────────────────────┐
                                        │     This voucher has        │
                                        │ no tax implications/Tax Analysis │
                                        │    is not supported!        │
Narration:                              │                             │
Purchase of Motor Ca for non Business Purpose    (press any key)      │
                                        └─────────────────────────────┘
```

F-2A: Purchase Invoice

Tax Classification Details

Classification/Nature : **Interstate Purchase Taxable**

F-2B: Tax Classification

Purchase Advanced Configuration

General Options

Skip Date field during creation for faster entry	? No
Allow expenses/fixed assets in purchase vouchers	? **Yes**
Show Bank Allocation details	? No
Confirm each cheque before print	? No

F-2C: Configuration option for Fixed Asset
ledger set up in Purchase Voucher

Ledger Accounts entry in Purchase Voucher : At Purchase Voucher entry screen (F-2A), select Customer Account and enter the amount of Bill (including Tax) at credit column. Select Fixed Asset Ledger account (specified for Ineligible ITC) and enter the value in Debit column. Select GST Accounts an enter the amount of GST in Debit Column. Save the voucher.

Tax Analysis : When you click A:Tax Analysis to view the Tax details, a message "This voucher has no Tax Implications / Tax Analysis is not supported" is displayed in the voucher screen (F-2A)

You may even record the Purchase Transaction in *Journal Voucher*, instead of Purchase Voucher. The effect would be same.

Effect in GSTR Reports

In GSTR-2, such Purchases are reflected in B2B Invoices (F-3A). In GSTR-3B, it is reported as Ineligible supplies (F-3B).

Particulars	No. of Invoices	Taxable Value	Total Tax	Total ITC Available	Reconciliation Status
To be reconciled with the GST portal					
B2B Invoices - 3, 4A	1	5,00,000.00	1,40,000.00		
Credit/Debit Notes Regular - 6C					

F-3A: Effect in GSTR-2

GSTR-3B	1-Oct-2017 to 31-Oct-2017	
Particulars	Taxable Value	Tax Amount
Inward Supplies		
Local Purchase	7,000.00	
Exempted	7,000.00	
Ineligible Supplies	(5,00,000.00)	(1,40,000.00)
Total Inward Supplies	5,07,000.00	1,40,000.00
Total Input Tax Credit	7,000.00	

F-3B: Effect in GSTR-3B

Ineligible Expenses

We now explain entry of Ineligible ITC expenses incurred by Registered Dealer.

Ineligible Expenses Ledger set Up : Create Ledger Account Master for Ineligible ITC Expenses, and make necessary set up for GST implication, in the Ledger Account Master.

Select *GoT>Accounts Info>Ledger>Create* to get Ledger creation screen (f-4A). Create Ledger Account as usual. Set as follows:

– **GST Applicability** : At *GST Applicable*, set Yes

– **GST Details activation** : At Set Alter GST details, set *Yes* to get the GST details set up screen

– **Nature of Supply** : At *Type of Supply*, select Services

F-4A: Ineligible Expenses Ledger Account

F-4B: Ledger Account GST screen

At *GST Details* screen (F-4B), set as follows:

– **Nature of Transaction** : At nature of Transaction, set *Not Applicable*. The nature of Transaction would be set at Voucher entry

– **Taxability :** At *Taxability*, select Taxable. The expense is Taxable and the registered supplier would charge GST in their Invoice (the GST has to be paid but ITC would not be available).

– **ITC Applicability** : At *Is ineligible for Input Credit*, set Yes (if this option does not appear in the GST details screen , click *F12:Configure* to get *Configuration* screen and set *Yes* at *Set Ineligible Input Credit*.

– **Tax rate** : Enter the Tax Rate applicable for such expenses.

At *GST Details* screen (F-4B), click *F12:Configure* and set Yes at *SetIneligible Input Credit* (F-1C)

Ineligible Expenses Voucher Entry

To enter such expenses, create a Purchase Voucher (*GoT>Accounting Voucher>F9:Purchase*),as usual (F-5A). Click *I:Accounting Invoice* (or press Alt+I) to get Accounting invoice mode (to enter expenses ledger account).

At Purchase Voucher entry screen (F-5A), at Party Name, select the Party (supplier of service). At Particulars, select the Expenses Ledger (Ineligible ITC). Next select the Tax Ledgers as usual. At Tax Classification Details pop up screen, select Classification from the list (F-5B)

F-5A: Ineligible Expenses entry

F-5B: Tax Classification

F-5C: Tax Analysis

Click *A:Tax Analysis* button to view the Tax details (F-5C).

Effect in GSTR : Select *Display>Statutory Reports>GST* Reports.

– Select *GSTR-2* to view the GSTR2 Report. The purchase is reflected in *B2B Invoice* (F-6A).

– Select *GSTR3B* to view GSTR-3B (Click *F1:Details* to get details and scroll down), where it will be reflected as Ineligible ITC (F-6B).

F-6A: GSTR-2 Report

GSTR-3B		1-Dec-2017 to 31-Dec-2017
Particulars	Taxable Value	Tax Amount
Inward Supplies		
Ineligible Supplies	(12,000.00)	(3,360.00)
Total Inward Supplies	12,000.00	3,360.00
Add/Less: GST Adjustments		(-)3,360.00
Total Input Tax Credit		(-)3,360.00

F-6B: GSTR-3B Report

Effect in Balance Sheet : However, in Balance Sheet, the Tax paid for Ineligible ITC would be reflected under Duties &Taxes, apparently implying that this would available as Input Credit. However, this need to be adjusted through Journal Voucher (both for Ineligible ITC for Motor car Purchase as Fixed Assets as well as for Ineligible Expenses (like Club Expenses), explained next.

Adjustment for Reversal of Input Credit

Since input credit is not available for such expenses, create Journal Voucher (GoT>Accounting Voucher> F7:Journal) to reverse the Input Credit entry from accounts (F-7A).

At Journal Voucher entry screen (F-7A), select Ineligible Expenses ledger Account and enter the Tax Amount. The Tax amount gets charged to expense account. Select Tax Account.

At Tax Amount pop up screen (F-7B), enter the Tax rate and taxable Amount. Enter the Tax Amount in Credit Column. This way the Tax Account gets adjusted and the ITC amount is charged to expenses Account.

Stat Adjustment : At Journal Voucher screen (F-7A), click *J:Stat Adjustment* to get Stat Adjustment screen (F-7C). Set as follows:

– **Tax Type :** At *Type of Tax*, select *GST*

– **Nature of Adjustment :** At *Nature of Adjustment*, select *Reversal of Input Credit*, from the *List of Nature of Adjustment*.

– **Additional Details :** At Additional Details, select

– **Additional Details :** At*Additional Details*, select*Ineligible Credit,*from the *List of Nature of Adjustment*.

Accounting Voucher Alteration (Secondary)	Comp Kol 19		Ctrl + M
Journal No. 11			1-Dec-2017 Sunday
	Used for: Reversal of Input Tax Credit (Additional Details: Ineligible Credit)		
Particulars		Debit	Credit
Dr Ineligible ITC Expenses		3,360.00	
Cr CGST			1,680.00
Cr SGST			1,680.00
Narration		3,360.00	3,360.00
Reversal of Input Credit on Ineligible expenses			

F-7A: Reversal of ineligible ITC

F-7B: Tax Amount entry

F-7C: Stat Adjustment – Nature of Adjustment

F-7C: Stat Adjustment – Additional Details

Now in Balance Sheet, under Duties & Taxes, the amount would be adjusted (shown NIL).

With this entry, the expenses account in P L Statement would include total cost including the GST.

Eligible ITC at the time of Purchase, Ineligible later on

Let us assume Purchase is made for 10 Boxes of Goods valued Rs 10000 (tax @12%). For this create a regular Purchase Voucher as explained. ITC of Rs 1200 would be available on the Purchase. Assume that later One Box is lost. Now ITC would not be available on the value of 1 Box and ITC (Rs120) is to be reversed as Ineligible ITC, through Journal Voucher, as explained above (F-7A)

Delivery Challan

Delivery Challan is a document of movement of goods, without Invoice being created. *Delivery Out* (popularly known as Delivery Note) is created by the supplier of goods while *Delivery In* (popularly known as Goods Receipt Note or GSN) is created by receiver of goods

Under GST rules, it is necessary to issue Invoice at the time of movement of Goods. However in some cases, e.g delivery to job workers, sale on approval etc. goods may be delivered without issuing Invoice. Even in case of delivery for supply, Delivery challan are used where invoice could not be issued for some reason but the Invoice is subsequently issued to cover the Delivery challan (Delivery Out). Sometimes, one combined Invoice is created against multiple Delivery Notes issued in a Tax period.

The Delivery Challan looks similar to Invoice. Normally Value is not included. Tax is not included. The delivery challan updates the Stock but does not update accounts (even if amount is entered in Delivery Challan).

Sometimes, goods are received back (delivery In Challan) against the earlier delivery out challan through which goods were sent out. In such case, a delivery In Challan is created in reference to the earlier delivery out.

You should create Delivery Challan in Tally ERP9 as usual. However, we briefly explain the salient points of creation of Delivery Challan under GST regime.

Company Features set up for Delivery Challan

Click *GoT>F11:Features>F2:Inventory* to get *Inventory Features* set up screen.

–   Under *General section*, set *Yes* at *Enable Zero Valued transaction* to enable entry of only Quantity details, without materials value (zero materials value).

–   Under *Other Features* section, set *Yes* at *Use Tracking Numbers (enables Delivery & Receipt Notes)*. Consequently, relevant buttons and options related to Delivery Challans (Delivery Notes & Receipt Notes) get activated.

Inventory Features			
General		**Invoicing**	
Integrate accounts and inventory	? Yes	Enable invoicing	? Yes
Enable zero-valued transactions	? Yes	Record purchases in invoice mode	? Yes
Storage and Classification		Use debit and credit notes	? Yes
Maintain multiple Godowns	? No	Record credit notes in invoice mode	? Yes
Maintain stock categories	? No	Record debit notes in invoice mode	? Yes
Maintain batch-wise details	? No	Use separate discount column in invoices	? No
Set expiry dates for batches	? No	**Purchase Management**	
Use separate actual and billed quantity columns	? No	Track additional costs of purchases	? No
Order Processing			
Enable purchase order processing	? No	**Sales Management**	
Enable sales order processing	? No	Use multiple price levels	? No
Enable job order processing	? No	**Other Features**	
(Enables the options Maintain multiple godowns and Use material in and out vouchers)		Use tracking numbers (enables delivery and receipt notes)	? **Yes**
		Use rejection inward and outward notes	? Yes
		Use material in and out vouchers	? No
		Use cost tracking for stock item	? No

F-1A: Activation of Delivery Challans at Inventory Features screen

Receipt Notes

When you receive materials under Delivery Note of the supplier (without Invoice), select (*GoT>Inventory Vouchers>F9:Receipt Note*) to get *Receipt Note* entry screen to create Receipt Note (F-2A).

F-2A: Receipt Note entry

F-2B: Tracking Number in Receipt Note

F-2C: Item allocation in Receipt Note

Enter details as usual, like Purchase Invoice entry :

– **Receipt Note details** : Enter Date of Receipt note (date when materials is received by receiver of goods). At Ref No, enter the reference number of delivery Challan of supplier and date of delivery Challan of supplier (F-2A). Select Party from whom material received (F-2A)

– **Item details** : Now select the Item. At Tracking Number subscreen (F-2B), select the Reference number of current Delivery Note from the list of Tracking Number. At *Quantity* column, enter the quantity received. At *Rate* column, enter ZERO. The Amount would be zero (DO NOT enter any value in *Rate* or *Amount* column). The *Amount* should be ZERO (F-2B).

The Item entered is listed in the main voucher screen. This way, enter details of all the items received, one by one, with value zero for each Item.

– **Tax Analysis** : When you click A:Tax Analysis, no Amount figures are shown

Stock Report: The receipt note would be reflected in Stock Inwards as per date of Receipt Note and would increase the Stock In hand

Receipt Note Printing : Click *P:Printing* button to get printing screen. You may click relevant button (at right side button bar) to set the respective Printing option. You may click *F12:Configure* to set the Receipt Note printing Configuration. Type *Y* to print Receipt Note as per options set (F-3A).

F-3A: Receipt Note in print

Purchase Invoice against Receipt Note

On receiving the materials, select *GoT>Accounting Vouchers>F9:Purchase* to get Purchase Invoice entry screen (F-4A), to create a Purchase Invoice, against the Receipt Note.

Name of Item	Quantity	Rate	per	Amount
Item 3- 12%	100 Pcs	120.00	Pcs	12,000.00
IGST				1,440.00
Narration:	100 Pcs			13,440.00

Purchase No. 4 — 2-Oct-2017
Supplier invoice no.: 15 — Date : 2-Oct-2017 — Monday
Party A/c name : Customer 2 RG(Kolkata - 19)

Purchase Invoice entry against Receipt note

Tax Classification Details

Classification/Nature : Interstate Purchase Taxable — (Interstate Purchase Taxable)

F-4A: Tax Classification Details

F-4B: Tracking Number selection

F-4C: Item Rate entry

F-4D: Tax Analysis of Purchase Invoice

At Item allocation screen, the Purchase Invoice is linked to earlier Receipt Note (F-4B / F-4C). The Tax Analysis (F-4D) displays the ITC.

GSTR Report : Now the Purchase Invoice has same effect in GSTR-2 and eligible for ITC (F-5A)

F-5A: GSTR-2 : Purchase Invoice

Stock Report: The Reference of Purchase Invoice would be reflected against Receipt Note entry already captured as per Receipt Note entered earlier. There would be no further impact on Stock for entry of Purchase Invoice (as Stock was already updated on entry of Receipt Note).

Rejection Note

If the goods received under Receipt Note are Returned (not accepted) or Goods Delivered under Delivery Note are Returned, then you will create a Rejection Voucher - *Rejection Out Note* against the Receipt Note / *Rejection In Note* against the Delivery Note to nullify the effect of Receipt / Delivery note.

Rejection Note activation :   To activate *Rejection Note* (Rejection Out & Rejection In), select *GoT>F11:Fetaures>Inventory Features*. Under *Other Features*, set *Yes* at *Use Rejection Inward &Outward Notes* to activate Reject Notes (F-1A) to record of Goods returned which were earlier recorded under Delivery Note / Receipt Note, to adjust the stock.

You should not create a Delivery Note for goods returned against earlier Receipt note. Similarly, you should not create a Receipt Note for Goods received back against earlier Delivery Note issued. If you create a new delivery note / Receipt Note in such cases,, these will remain unadjusted for linking with Invoice and create accounting complications.

−   If the goods are returned against earlier Receipt Note, create a Rejection Out Note.

−   If the goods are received against earlier Delivery Note, create a Rejection In Note.

Creation of Rejection Out Note for goods returned against earlier Receipt Note

On returning the Goods received earlier under Receipt Note, select *GoT>Inventory Voucher>F6:Rejections Out* to get *Rejections Out* entry screen (F-6A)

F-6A: Rejection Out Note

F-6D: Day Book

F-6B: Tracking Number selection

F-6C: Item Allocation

Enter following details:

– **Party Ledger** : At ledger Account, select the Party ledger whom the materials are returned to. The name of Party & Address is displayed (which you may change in the Rejection Note, if required).

– **Item details** : Now select the Item. At Tracking Number subscreen, select the Reference number of the original Receipt note against which the materials are returned under current Rejection Note (F-6B). At *Quantity* column, enter the quantity returned. At *Rate* column, enter ZERO. The Amount would be zero (DO NOT enter any value in *Rate* or *Amount* column). The *Amount* should be ZERO (F-6C). The Item entered is listed in the main voucher screen (F-6A). This way, enter details of all the items received, one by one, with value zero for each Item.

However, when the entire quantity of goods received under Receipt Note are returned through Rejection Note, the stock is nullified. In such case, neither the Receipt Note nor the Rejection Note is displayed in Stock Summary (they are completely hidden in Stock Summary).

Delivery Notes

When you deliver materials (without Invoice), select (*GoT>Inventory Vouchers>F8:Delivery Note*) to get *Delivery Note* entry screen to create a Delivery Note (F-7A).

F-7A: Delivery Note entry

F-7B: Tracking Number selection

F-7C: Item allocation

Enter details as usual, like Sales Invoice entry :

- **Delivery Note details** : Enter Date of Delivery note. At Ref No, you may enter any other reference number. Select Party to whom the material is delivered.

- **Item details** : Now select the Item. At Tracking Number subscreen (F-7B), select the Delivery Note number of current Delivery Note from the list of Tracking Number. At *Quantity* column, enter the quantity Delivered. At *Rate* column, enter ZERO. The Amount would be zero (DO NOT enter any value in *Rate* or *Amount* column). The *Amount* should be ZERO (F-7C).

  The Item entered is listed in the main voucher screen (F-7A). This way, enter details of all the items received, one by one, with value zero for each Item.

Stock Report: The Delivery note would be reflected in Stock Outwards as per date of Delivery Note and would decrease the Stock In hand

Delivery Note Printing : Click *P:Printing* button to get printing screen. You may click relevant button (at right side button bar) to set the respective Printing option. You may click *F12:Configure* to set the Delivery Note printing Configuration. Type *Y* to print Delivery Note (F-8A) as per options set.

F-8A: Delivery Note in print

Sales Invoice against Delivery Note

To create Sales Invoice against Delivery Note, select *GoT>Accounting Vouchers>F8:Sales* to get *Sales Invoice* entry screen.

F-9A: Sales Invoice

F-9B: Tracking Number selection

F-9C: Item details entry

F-9D: Tax Classification

Enter details as usual in Sales Invoice entry :

– **Invoice details** : Enter Date of Sales Invoice. At Ref No, you may enter any other reference number. Select Party to whom the material is delivered.

– **Item details** : Now select the Item. At Tracking Number subscreen, select the Delivery Note number (from the list of Tracking Number), against which you are creating the current sales Invoice. At *Quantity* column, enter the quantity Delivered. At *Rate* column, enter Rate. The Amount would be displayed. The Item entered is listed in the main voucher screen. This way, enter details of all the items received, one by one, with value for each Item.

– **Tax Classification** : At Tax Classification pop up screen, select the Tax Classification from the list (F-9D)

– **Tax Accounts** : At main voucher screen (F-9A) Select the Tax Accounts. The amount is auto computed

– **Tax Analysis** : Click A:Tax Analysis to get the Tax Analysis screen showing details of Taxable Amount and Tax (F-9A).

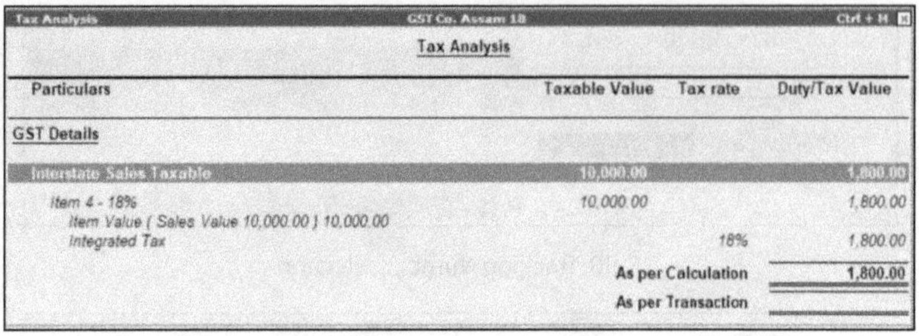

F-9E: Tax Analysis

Sales Invoice Printing : Click *P:Printing* button to get printing screen. You may click relevant button (at right side button bar) to set the respective Printing option. You may click *F12:Configure* to set the sales Invoice printing Configuration. Type *Y* to print Sales Invoice (F-9F) as per options set.

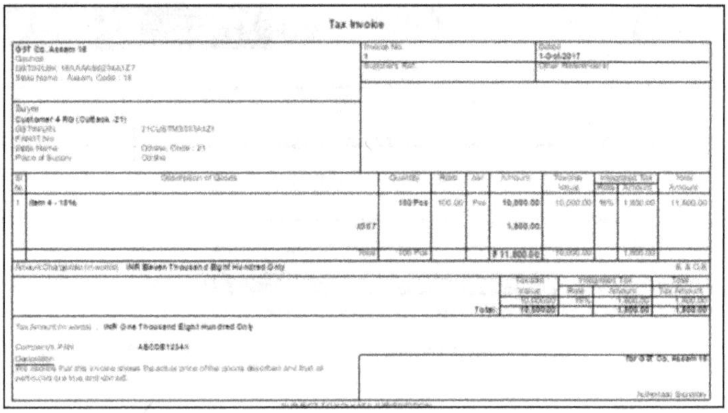

F-9F: Sales Invoice in Print

Creation of Rejection In Note for goods returned against earlier Delivery Note

On getting the Goods received back against Goods delivered under Delivery Note earlier, select *GoT>Inventory Voucher>F6:Rejections In* to get *Rejections In* entry screen (F-10A)

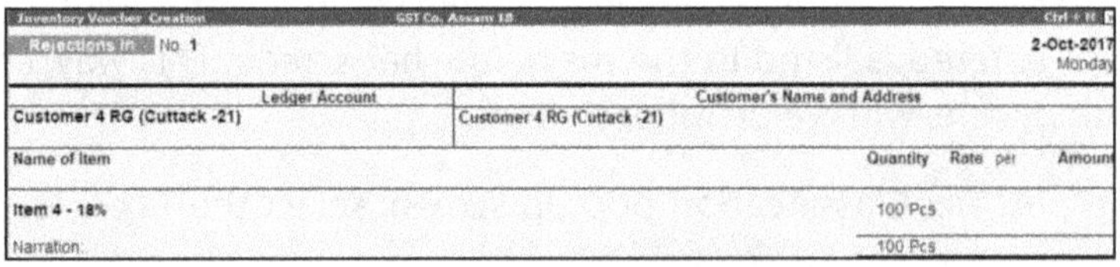

F-10A: Rejection In Note

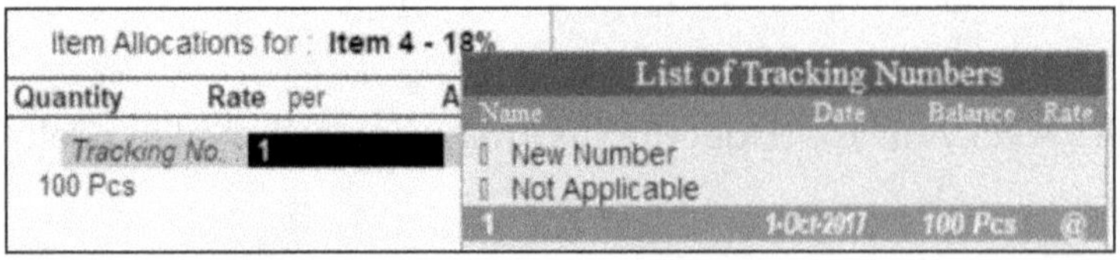

F-10B: Tracking Number selection

F-10C: Item Allocation

Enter following details:

- **Party Ledger** : At ledger Account, select the Party ledger whom the materials are returned to. The name of Party & Address is displayed (which you may change in the Rejection Note, if required).

- **Item details** : Now select the Item. At Tracking Number subscreen, select the Reference number of the original Delivery note against which the materials are returned under current Rejection Note (F-10BO. At *Quantity* column, enter the quantity returned. At *Rate* column, enter ZERO. The Amount would be zero (DO NOT enter any value in *Rate* or *Amount* column). The *Amount* should be ZERO (F-10C).

  The Item entered is listed in the main voucher screen (F-10A). This way, enter details of all the items received, one by one, with value zero for each Item.

Day Book : At Day Book (GoT>Display>Day Book), the vouchers created (Receipt Note, Delivery Note, Rejection In Note, Rejection out Note etc) are displayed along with other types of vouchers, as usual. In case of Accounting Vouchers the Amount is shown in Debit / Credit column. In case of Inventory Voucher like Rejection In, Rejection Out etc., the quantity (with UoM) is shown in positive (Delivery Note / Rejection Note) / negative quantity (Rejection In / Rejection Out) in respective Inwards / Outwards column.

Day Book				1-Oct-2017 to 31-Oct-2017	
Date	Particulars	Vch Type	Vch No.	Debit Amount	Credit Amount
				Inwards Qty	Outwards Qty
1-10-2017	Item 4 - 18%	Delivery Note	1		100 Pcs
1-10-2017	Item 3- 12%	Receipt Note	1	100 Pcs	
2-10-2017	Item 3- 12%	Rejections Out	1	(-)100 Pcs	
2-10-2017	Item 4 - 18%	Rejections In	1		(-)100 Pcs

F-11A: Day Book

e-way Bill

E-way bill (stands for Electronic Way Bill) is a unique Way Bill number to be generated mandatorily for specific consignment involving the movement of goods in motorized vehicle, for a consignment value exceeding Rs 50000. Even in case of inward supply of goods from unregistered person, E-Way Bill is applicable.

We have explained the process of registration, generation & printing of e-way Bill from GST on-line portal. Here we explain the features available in Tally, in respect of e-way Bill

Most of the States have implemented e-way bill for Intra State (within State) from 1st Feb 2018.Generation of e-way bill for Intra State (within State) is mandatory for all states w.e.f 1st June 2018

GST Statutory Features Set up : At Statutory Features screen *(GoT>F11:Features>Statutory Features)*, set *Yes* at *Set Alter GST Details* to get GST details screen to set up options for e-way Bill (F-1A)

– **e-way Bill applicability** : Set *Yes* at *e-way Bill applicable*. You may then further set up following e-way bill options:

– **e-way Bill applicability date** : At *Enter the date from* enter the date which you start implementing e-way Bill in the system

– **e-way Bill threshold** : At *e-way Bill threshold,* enter the minimum Bill amount above which e-way bill is mandatorily issued.

– **Threshold limit computation rule** : At *Threshold limit includes*, select from the list (Invoice Value, Taxable & Exempt Goods value, Taxable Goods value)

– **Intra State applicability** : At *e-way Bill applicable Intra state*, set *Yes* if e-way Bill to be issued for Intra State transaction also, else set *No*, to issue e-way Bill only for Inter State Transactions.

F-1A: e-way Bill options set up Statutory Features

In Tally.ERP 9, e-Way Bill details can be entered when Inventory is activated and Stock Item Masters are created. e-Way Bill options are not available in accounting invoice mode, and in companies enabled to *Maintain only accounts*

Transporter Ledger Account

In e-way Bill, you have to submit Transporter details. So, create a Ledger Account *(GoT>Account Info>Ledger> Create)* to get Ledger Account creation screen (F-2A). Enter the Transporter details in Transporter Ledger Account (f-2B). These details would be pulled from Transporter Ledger Account to the e-way Bill and you will not have to enter the details in each e-way Bill.

F-2A: Transporter Ledger Account

F-2B: Transporter Ledger Details of Registered Transporter

At Transporter Ledger Account screen (F-2A), enter the complete address including PINCode. Select the State of the Transporter. At Set / Alter GST details (F-2A) to get GST details screen (F-2B). At *Registration Type* select the Registration type from the list (F-2B). Enter GSTIN for Registered Transporter. At *Is a Transporter*, set *Yes.*If the Transporter is registered, The GSTIN/UINis considered as the transporter ID and Transporter ID is not to be entered (F-2B). If the Transporter is unknown or unregistered, enter the Transporter ID (F-2C).

F-2C: Transporter Ledger Details of Unregistered Transporter

Sales Invoice Entry

Select GoT>Accounting Voucher>F8:Sales>Create to get sales Voucher entry screen (F-3A).

Accounting Voucher Creation			Ctrl + M
Sales No 07/00001/17-18			1-Mar-2018
Reference no.			Thursday
Party A/c name : Customer 1 - Kol 19			

Name of Item	Quantity	Rate per	Amount
Item 1 @5%	100 Pc	400.00 Pc	40,000.00
Item 2 @12%	50 Pc	200.00 Pc	10,000.00
Item 3 Nil Rate	100 Pc	100.00 Pc	10,000.00
			60,000.00
CGST			1,600.00
SGST			1,600.00
Provide GST/e-Way Bill details : **Yes**			
Narration:	250 Pc		63,200.00
eway Bill Number 191234567890 dt 1.3.18			

F-3A: Sales Invoice with e-way Bill details

Order Details

Other Reference(s)   :

Buyer's Details

Buyers	: Customer 1 - Kol 19
Address	: 19 Park Street
	9th Floor. Suite 910
Country	: India
State	: West Bengal
Place of Supply	: West Bengal
GSTIN/UIN	: 19ABNPN1234M1Z9

F-3B: Supplementary Details

Tax Classification Details

Classification/Nature : **Sales Taxable**   (*Sales Taxable*)

F-3C: Tax Classification

Invoice Configuration : At Invoice entry screen, Click F12:Configure to get Invoice Configuration screen (F-3D). At Invoice Configuration screen, set as follows:

– **Supplementary Details**: Set *Yes* at *Enable Supplementary Details* to get *Supplementary Details* screen to enter Buyer / Despatch details.

– **e-way Bill JSON file conversion** : Set Yes at *Export e-way bill details from Invoice after saving*, to enable e-way Bill details entered in Invoice, exported to JSON file.

– **Tax Difference tolerance** : At *Allow Tax Difference upto,* set the amount upto which Tax Difference may be allowed (zero means no difference allowed). Having set up non zero value, next you may further set up option for the difference amount type

– **Actual Tax versus Computed Tax** : Having set up non zero value at the Tax Difference option, you may further select the allowable difference type option from the list.

```
                    Sales Invoice Standard Configuration
                              General Options

     Enable supplementary details                    ? Yes
        (Address details, despatch details, etc.)


     Allow separate buyer and consignee names        ? No
     Use common ledger account for item allocation   ? No
     Use defaults for bill allocations               ? No
     Use voucher no. as bill ref. no. for bill allocations  ? Yes
     Provide additional descriptions for stock item name    ? No
     Provide additional descriptions for ledger name        ? No
     Warn if voucher number exceeds 16 characters    ? No
                              Statutory Options
     Allow entry of rate inclusive of tax for stock item    ? No
     Calculate tax on current sub-total              ? No
        (else calculations are on inventory total only)
     Allow MRP modification in voucher               ? Yes
     Allow modification of tax details for GST        ? Yes
     Export e-Way Bill details from invoice after saving  ? Yes
     Allow tax difference up to                       : 10
        Actual tax versus computed tax               : Greater or Less
                              Other Options
     Warn on negative stock balance                  ? No

                    Press F12 for more options.
```

F-3D: Sales Invoice configuration

Invoice Entry

– **Invoice Details** : Select Customer name (F-3A). Enter Buyers details in supplementary details subscreen (F-3B). The Buyers detail from master are carried, which you may change. Enter other relevant details as applicable.

– **Item Details** : At main voucher entry screen (F-3A), enter Item details (Quantity, rate, value). Select sales Ledger Account of the Item (unless Common Ledger account set at Voucher entry configuration).

– **Tax Classification** : At Tax Classification pop up screen, select Tax Classification for the Invoice (F-3C).

– **Tax Details** : Select the applicable Tax Ledger Accounts (F-3A). The amount is auto computed as per Tax rates specified in Item Master.

– **e-way Bill Details** : At Invoice entry screen, at *Provide GST/e-way Bill details*, set *Yes* to get e-way Bill details screen (F-4A). Enter the relevant details. At e-way Bill details entry screen:

 o **Transporter Details** : Click Transporter Details button (F-4B) to enter Transporter Details (F-4C)

 o **E-way Bill Details** : Click e-way Bill Details button (F-4B) to enter e-way Bill Additional Details (F-5A)

F-4A: e-way Bill details in sales Invoice

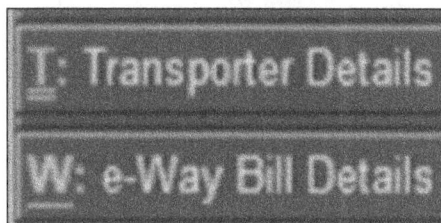

F-4B: e-way Bill details buttons

Narration ; You may enter e-way Bill at Narration if you like, for your record and printing in Invoice.

Invoice Saving & Printing : Save the Sales Invoice. you may print the Invoice, if you like as described next, before saving the Invoice.

e-way Bill Additional Details : You may enter additional details through the buttons at e-way bill details entry screen (F-4A)

- **Multiple Transporter Details** : If goods are transported in different modes or vehicles, at e-way Bills detail screen, click *T: Tranporter detail* (F-4B) button (or press Ctrl+T) to get Transporter detail for e-way Bill to enter the e-way Bill details (F-4C). You may enter multiple lines for each mode, transporter, vehicle number etc. At *Modes*, column (F-4C), select the Transport Mode from *Modes* list (F-4D). At *Reason* column (F-4C), select the Reason from *Reasons* list (F-4E).

Mode	Distance (in KM)	Name	Transporter ID	Vehicle Number	Doc/Lading/RR /Air Way No.	Date	Place of Change	State of Change	Reason	Remarks
Road	100	ABC Trasporter	19ABCPC1234B1Z7	WB02V1234	1234	1-Mar-2018	Madhyamgram	West Bengal	Due to Transhipment	

F-4C: Transporter Detail for change in vehicle or multiple vehicle

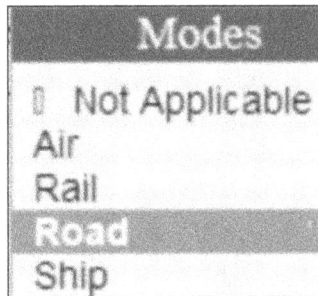

F-4D: Transporter Detail for change in vehicle or multiple vehicle

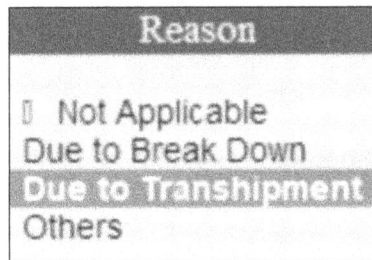

F-4E: Reasons list

- **Multiple e-way Bills (Consolidated e-way Bill) Details** : At e-way bill additional details screen (F-4A), click *W : e-Way Bill Details* button (F-4B) or press Alt+W, to enter the details of multiple e-Way Bills (consolidated e-way Bill) generated for a single transaction (F-5A). Enter a line for each e-way Bill and respective details. At *Sub Type* column (F-5A), select Supply Type from list of Sub Type (F-5B). At *Document Type* column (F-5A), select Document Type from list of Document Type (F-5C). At *Status of e-way Bill* column (F-5A), select Status Type from Status list (F-5D).

e-Way Bill No.	Date	Consolidated e-Way Bill No.	Date	Sub Type	Document Type	Update Consignor Details	Update Consignee Details	Update Transporter's Details	Status of e-WayBill
1912345667890	1-Mar-2018	192345678900	1-Mar-2018	Supply	Tax Invoice	No	No	No	Generated by me
193456789012	1-Mar-2018		1-Mar-2018	For Own Use	Tax Invoice	No	No	No	Generated by me

F-5A: e-way Bill details

Option list of various columns of e-way Bill Details report

Sub Type
▯ Not Applicable
Exhibition or Fairs
Export
For Own Use
Job Work
Lines Sales
Others
Recipient Not Known
SKD/CKD
Supply

F-5B: Sub Type list

Document Type
▯ Not Applicable
Bill of Entry
Bill of Supply
Challan
Credit Note
Others
Tax Invoice

F-5C: Document Type list

Status
▯ Not Applicable
Cancelled by me
Generated by me
Generated by other party on my GSTIN
Rejected by me
Rejected by other party

F-5D: e-way Bill Status list

e-way Bill printing

You may print e-way Bill from Portal, through Tally in 2 methods.

– Individual e-way Bill from Invoice entry screen at the time of entry.

– e-way Bill for Multiple saved Invoices

In both the cases, export the data in a JSON file and upload on the e-Way Bill Portal to generate your e-Way Bill.

e-Way Bill Number (EBN) is shown for each e-way Bill generated. Type the EBN in corresponding invoice, and print Invoice with EBN

Exporting Invoice to JSON file : To enable JSON file generation for Invoice, at Invoice Configuration screen (F-3D), set Yes at *Export e-way bill details from Invoice after saving* (F-6A), as explained.

− **JSON file creation for current invoice during Invoice entry** : After entry of Invoice, *Export Details for e-Way Bill*screen appears (F-6A). Enter the JSON file name and save the JSON (by default, JSON file is saved under filename e-waybill followed by GSTIN, Invoice Date & Invoice Number for easy identification). Now use the JSON file at e-way Bill Portal to generate e-way Bill

− **JSON file creation for saved Invoices :** Select *Display>Statutory Reports>GST>e-way Bill>Exportfor e-way Bill* to get the status list of e-way Bills (F-8A). Drill down through the item *Invoices Ready for Export* (F-8A) to get list of Invoices for which e-way Bill has not been generated (F-9A). Select the Invoices for which JSON file to be created (you may select multiple Invoice using the spacebar).

F-6A: JSON file creation for e-way Bill Generation

Uploading JSON to portal

− At e-waybill Portal (*ewaybillgst.gov.in*) [or click gst.gov.in, click e-Way Bill System >Click here to go to e-Way Bill Portal]**.** Login and select **:**

o e-Waybill >Generate Bulk

o Consolidated EWB >Generate Bulk

Click *Choose File > select the JSON > click Upload & Generate*. The e-Way Bill gets generated

e-way Bill Menu

Select *GoT>Display>Statutory Report>GST Reports >e-way Bill* to get e-way Bill Menu (F-7A).

F-7A: e-way Bill menu

F-8A: e-way Bill Status Report

F-8B: e-way Bill export configuration

e-way Bill Status Report: At e-way Bill menu, select *Export for e-way Bill* to get *Export for e-way Bill* report (F-8A) showing the number of Bill for each Status (e-way Bill Status Report).

– **e-way Bill status report Configuration**: Click F12:Configure button to get *e-way Bill export configuration* screen (F-8B). Set the configuration options as desired.

– **Resolving Mismatch / Incomplete records**: To resolve Incomplete / Mismatch, if shown in the e-way Bill Status Report, click on the line under *Invoices with Incomplete / Mismatch in information* section (F-8A), to get details of mismatch to be resolved. Edit the offending Invoice and resolve the mismatch issue

– **Exporting ready Invoices to create JSON file** : Drill down from the Item Invoices Ready for Export (F-8A) to get e-way Bill ready for Export list (F-9A). Select the line Invoices ready for Export for which you may create JSON file, as explained next.

F-9A: e-way Bill ready for export list

F-9B: e-way Bill report Configuration

F-9C: e-way Bill report Buttons

e-way Bill Generation at Portal

– **E-way Bill report Configuration** : At e-way Bill report (F-9A), click *F12:Configure* to get e-way Bill Configuration screen (F-9B), to set the Configuration options.

– **Exporting e-way Bill Report to JSON file :** At e-way Bill Report (Invoice ready for export), click *E:Export for e-way Bill*(F-9C) button (or press Ctl+E) to get *Export Details for e-way Bill* screen (F-10A), to generate JSON file. The default export location file and output JSON file name are displayed. Press Y to create the default named JSON file as shown in the screen, else Type N and change the Export Location & Output file name. Then type Y to create JSON file at specified location.

– **Upload JSON file at Portal :** In the GST Portal (www.gst.gov.in) click *e-Way Bill System >Click here to go to e-Way Bill Portal* (F-11A). Click PROCEED. Select the link (e-way Bill Generate Bulk or Consolidate de-way Bill > Generate Bulk). Click *Choose file* and select the saved JSON file. Click Upload and Generate to generate the e-way Bill.

– **Generate e-way Bill at Portal :** To generate the e-Way Bill, choose the required links *(e-Waybill >Generate Bulk/ Consolidated EWB >Generate Bulk).* Click *Choose File,* select the saved JSON file. Click Upload & Generate. The e-Way Bill gets generated.

F-10A: JSON export file for e-way Bill

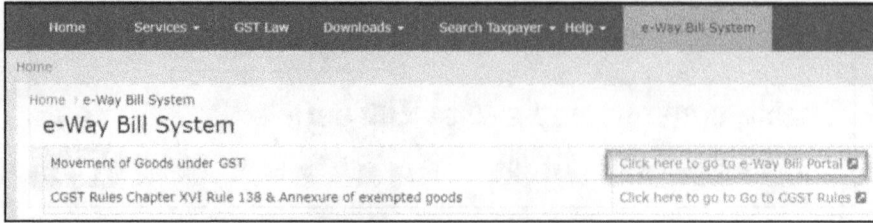

F-11A: e-way Bill system at GST Portal

Update e-way Bill Number in Invoice in Tally : To print Invoice with e-way Bill Number, first update the e-way Bill Number in respective Invoice record in Tally. At e-way Bill Report (Invoice ready for export), click *I:Update e-way Bill Info* button (or press Ctrl+I) to get Update e-way Bill details screen (or select Update e-way Bill information at e-way Bill menu). Select the Party and enter the date range to get the list of invoices, select the Invoice and enter / update the details.

Invoice Printing with e-way Bill Number

– **Invoice printing Configuration** : Click *F12:Configure* to get *Printing* Configuration screen (F-12A). Set *Yes* at *Print e-way Bill Number* to get printed invoice with e-way Bill Number shown beside the Invoice Number. Set Other Configuration options as desired.

– **Invoice printing Advanced Configuration**: At *Invoice printing Configuration* screen (F-12A), further click *F12:Configure* to get Invoice *Advanced Configuration* screen (F-12B). Set the options as desired.

F-12A: Sales Invoice Configuration

F-12B: Sales Invoice Advanced Printing Configuration

Invoice Printing : Having updated the e-way Bill in the Invoice, select Invoice from Reports like Day Book (GoT>Display>Day Book) etc, to get the Invoice in Alteration mode. Click *P:Print* button to get Invoice printing screen. Set the printing options through buttons available, as required, and type Y to print the Invoice (F-13A).

F-13A: Invoice with e-way Bill Number

e-way Bill report

At e-way Bill Menu (F-7A), select *e-way Bill Report* to get the list of Invoices having e-way Bill numbers. Drill down through any Invoice to get the Invoice in Edit Mode. Now you may update Invoice data as desired.

F-14A: e-way Bill Report

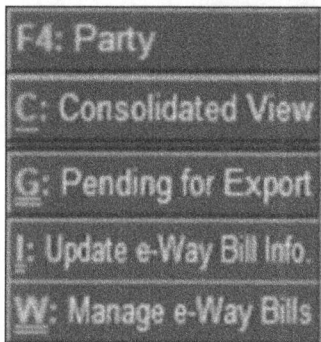

F-14B : Buttons at e-way Bill Report

Buttons at e-way Bill Report : You may update / export / manage e-way bills form various buttons (F-14B) available ate-way Bill Report (F-14A) :

– **F4:Party** - To select a party to list e-way Bills for selected Party

– **C:Consloidated View** – To get list of e-way Bills grouped on mode, vehicle number, place and state.

– **G:Pending for Export** – Bills which have not been exported to JSON file

– **Update e-way Bill Info** : Select party, period to get list of Invoices. Select the Invoice and update e-way Bill details in the Invoice.

– **W:Manage e-way Bills** : To get the entry screen of e-way Bill to view / update e-way Bill details

GSTR-1 Return Filing from Tally.ERP9

We have explained GSTR-1 Return direct entry in GSTN Portal and GSTR-1 Return filing from offline tool, in separate chapters.

In this chapter, we describe GSTR-1 Return Filing using GSTR-1 Report from Tally.ERP 9 system. This entails export of Tally.ERP system produced GSTR-1 Return into JSON Format directly, or into Excel / CSV Format intermediary format and then export such Intermediary file JSON format, and finally uploading JSON file into GSTN portal to file GSTR-1 Return

GSTR Reports Data Validation

After all transaction data entry, Sales, Purchase, Payments etc, you should print and review the GST Statutory Reports before filing with the authorities within specified period.

Tally.ERP 9 first validates the GST data for data consistency. Any data anomalies, are first shown in the GSTR reports, Report (F-1A to F-1C).

Mismatch & Exception Resolution

At the top of the report, the Details of data anomalies, are indicated. The figures of records having any error are not included main part of the report. These are included only when the inconsistencies are resolved.

F-1A: GSTR-1 – Monthly report showing mismatch data

Click on the line showing Incomplete / Mismatch records to view reason wise statistics (number of Vouchers) of mismatch (F-1B).

Now edit the record and resolve mismatch

List of Exceptions	Total Vouchers
No. of vouchers with incomplete/mismatch in information	11
UoM(s) not mapped to Unit Quantity Code(UQC)	11
Country, state and dealer type not specified	2

GSTR-1 — Vouchers with incomplete/mismatch in information — 1-Jul-2017 to 31-Jul-2017

F-1B: Reasonwise details of Mismatch

The reasonwise number of mismatch record are shown.

F-2A: UoM / UQC Mismatch records resolution

F-2B: UQC updation for mismatch UoM

F-2C: UQC set up for mistach UoM

Click on the respective reasonwise mismatch record and to resolve mismatch for each type (F-2A to F-2C for UoM/UQC Mismatch, F-3A for Country, State & Dealer type. The records are to be edited to resolve the anomaly.

F-3A: List of mismatch Dealer records

After making rectification, the corrected records are shown, for final review (F-4A)

F-4A: Updated dealer record after mismatch resolution

On resolution of errors, the respective figures for each part of Table would be shown in GSTR-1

Status Reconciliation

GSTR-1 is a report of Outwards supplies, which must be accepted by counter Party (Receiver), through a reconciliation process (involving Acceptance, Rejection, Pending etc) :

– Supplier upload details of outward supplies in GSTR-1.

– Buyers receiving the supply view details in their GSTR-2A.

– Buyer approve, reject, modify or add supply details and file GSTR-2.

– Supplier approve (or reject) the modified supply details in GSTR-1A.

All the approval, rejection, or modification is done on the GST portal. The GSTR-1 report enables to reconcile and mark the status of each transaction based on the online status, allowing to track the status of all transactions uploaded without having to login to the portal.

Status Reconciliation Report

Select *GoT>Display >Statutory Reports >GST >GSTR- 1.* to get *GSTR-1 Report.* Click U : Status Reconciliation. to get Status Reconciliation screen..

F-4B: Status Reconciliation- Status View

F-4C: Buttons

Click F5 button (F-4C) to toggle between Status View (F-4B) and Return View (F-4D) of Status Reconciliation screen.

F-4D: Status Reconciliation- Return View

The Return View of Status Reconciliation screen (F-4D) shows a Table showing number of Vouchers under following columns :

- **Activity Status:**

    o **To Be Uploaded** : Number of vouchers yet not exported (to be exported) to GSTR-1 return file.

    o **Uploaded** : Number of vouchers exported (automatically updated when a voucher is exported to GSTR-1 return file).

    o **Rejected by GST** : Number of vouchers marked as Rejected by GST (when GST rejects voucher for reasons such as, duplicate invoice, reference of original transaction is not found in case of debit/credit note, GSTIN of any user being suspended, and so on), mark the Vouchers as Rejected by GST.

    o **Accepted** : Number of vouchers marked as *Accepted.* Mark the status as accepted when input tax claim made by the buyer in the GSTR-1A.

    o **Rejected** : Number of vouchers marked as *Rejected.* Mark the status as rejected when the buyer rejects the voucher details in GSTR-1A.

- **Reconciliation Status**

    o **Not Reconciled** : Number of vouchers marked as *Not Reconciled.* Mark the status as *Not Reconciled* when the details in the online portal do not match with your books.

    o **Reconciled** : Number of vouchers marked as *Reconciled.* Mark the status as *Reconciled* when the details in the online portal match with your books.

Status Reconciliation Report Configuration : At Status Reconciliation (F- 4B/F-4D), click F12:Configure to get *Status Reconciliation Report Configuration* screen (F-4E).

F-4E: Status Reconciliation Report Configuration

– At *Show uncertain transaction,* set Yes to view the number vouchers that are not included in the returns due to incomplete information or mismatch.

– At *Show Status for,* Select option to show specific columns or all columns in the Report

Status Set Up

Drill down from any Item in Status Reconciliation – Return View (F-4D) to get Voucher Register showing the list of Vouchers in respective of the Table in GSTR-1 (F-4F)

F-4F: Voucher list for Status set up

Select one or multiple vouchers (using space bar) and click S:*Set Status* button to get Set Status Screen (F-4F). Select the appropriate *Activity Status* & *Reconciliation Status* for the selected Voucher, based on the GST portal details and press <enter>.

F-4G: Status Set Up

GSTR-1

GSTR-1 has to be filed by a taxable person registered under GST (other than compounding taxpayer and ISD). GSTR-1 includes the details of all outward supplies of B2B invoices, B2C invoices, adjustments to sales made in debit/credit notes, exports, nil rated invoices, advances received with tax adjustments.

GSTR-1 is to be filed monthly, for tax payers having aggregate turnover exceeding Rs. 1.5 crores. However, Tax payers having aggregate turnover upto Rs. 1.5 crores need to file the Return Quarterly

At Gateway, select Display>Statutory Reports>GST>GSTR-1 to get GSTR-1 report. It may be viewed in 2 alternate formats.

– **Return Format** : It shows the details break up as per Table of GSTR-1 Report uploaded in Portal (F-5A). Click *F12:Configure* to get GSTR-1 Return Format Configuration screen (F-5B).

– **Summary Format** : It shows a snapshot of Business Operations during the Return period

F-5A: GSTR-1 after error resolution (Return Format)

F-5B: Return Format report Configuration

Click *V:View Return Format / View Summary* to toggle between alternate formats (Return Format & Summary Format) of the Report

F-6A: GSTR-1 Report of outward supplies (Summary Format)

Buttons : The report provides buttons (F-6B) for various task like *V: View Return Format / Summary toggle button* (to view Report in alternate formats), *U: Status Reconciliation* (Status wise position of various stages), *A: View Accepted* as, for performing subsequent steps, view various components and details of the report, *J:Stat Adjustment* (for accounting adjustments of credit / reversals), *E: Export GSTR-1* (to Export GSTR-1 data to upload in Portal), *O: Open GSTN Portal* (to access GST Portal directly from within Tally GSTR Report screen)

Report Configuration : Click *F12:Configure* to get Configuration screen (F-2C).

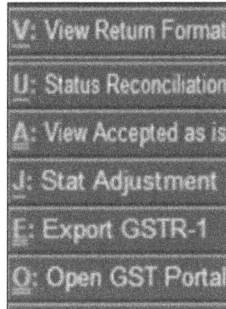

F-6B: Buttons

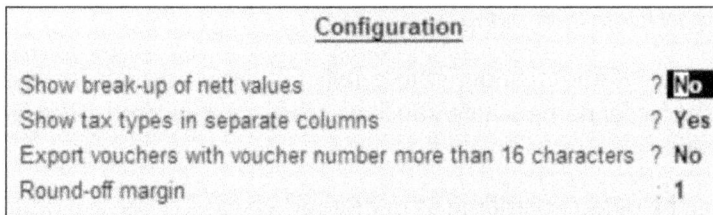

F-6C: Summary Format Report Configuration

Mode of Filing of GSTR-1 Return

- **Filing Directly into GSTN Portal without using Tally GSTR-1 Report :**

  - Uploading GSTR-1 data created offline, and uploading to GSTN Portal, using the GST Offline tool

  - Filing Returns directly on the GST portal

  These methods have been explained earlier in separate chapters.

- **Filing of GSTR-1 Return from Tally GSTR-1 Report** : GSTR-1 may be filed in following methods:

  - Generating JSON from GSTR-1 Report from Tally.ERP 9 and uploading JSON into GSTN Portal.

  - Exporting GSTR-1 Report from Tally.ERP 9 to Excel / CSV file and then creating JSON file therefrom.

  These 2 methods are now explained in this chapter

Exporting GSTR-1 Report of Tally ERP 9 into JSON Format

First Generate JSON file from tally ERP to be uploaded in GST Portal.

Select *GoT>Display >Statutory Reports >GST >GSTR-1*, to get GSTR-1 Report screen. Click *E:Export GSTR-1* button (or Press Ctrl+E) to get Exporting GSTR-1 screen (F-7A).

```
                          Exporting GSTR-1
                      (1-Mar-2018 to 31-Mar-2018)
        Language                      : Default (All Languages)
        Format                         JSON (Data Interchange)
        Export Location              , C:\Program Files\Tally\Tally.ERP9
        Output File Name               GSTR-1_19AMAPS5106K1ZV_March_2017.18.json
        Open Exported File           ? Yes
        Export HSN/SAC details even if UQC is not available  ? Yes
        Export HSN/SAC details not included for other reasons  ? Yes
        Export document summary      ? No

Note:
* Tax values in the exported file are based on taxable value and tax rate as the portal accepts only the exact tax amount.
* Add details of Nil Rated Invoices and Document Summary tables directly on the portal. Click H: Help for details.
```

F-7A: Exporting GSTR-1 into JSON Format for uploading

At *Export GSTR-1* screen (F-7A), set as follows:

− At Format, select *JSON (Data Interchange)*.

− At *Export Location*, the default location (where Tally ERP application is installed) appears. You may change and enter the folder name where you like to save the Exported JSON file (or keep the default location as displayed).

− At *Output file name*, the default filename as per Report Name, GSTIN and period is shown. You may change the filename as desired. You should keep distinct filename for report of each period to avoid conflict / overwriting (or keep the default filename as displayed).

If the option at GSTR-1 Configuration (F-5B), the option *Show HSN/SAC Summary?* is set to Yes, at GSTR-2 Export screen (F-7A), you may further set up following options (if *Show HSN/SAC summary* is set to *No*,HSN summary of the exported output file will be blank):

− **Export HSN/SAC details even if UQC is not available** : Set *Yes*, to export transactions where UQCs are not available. Later on, you have to map the units of measurement of the stock items to related UQCs.

− **Export HSN/SAC details not included for other reasons :** Set *Yes* to export transactions not included in the *HSN/SAC Summary*due to various reasons. You have to enter this data directly on the portal).

The JSON file as per specified name would be saved at the specified location.

Uploading JSON file to Portal.

At GSTR-1 Return statement, clickK̲Q̲:Open GSTR-1 Portal (or press Ctl+O). Log in to the GST portal with your credential (Username / Password). Select *Services>Returns >Returns Dashboard* to get File Returns screen. Select the option for Period (Monthly – for Turnover exceeding 1.5 crores / Quarterly – for Turnover upto 1.5 crores. Select the Return filing period. Click SUBMIT. Click PREPARE OFFLINE under the GSTR-1 tile. To get Offline Upload / Download of GSTR-1 screen. Click Choose file ans elected the saved JSON file to upload. On successful upload, a message would be displayed. Verify details of uploaded file (after specified time).

Manual Entry : Now manually enter the details of NIL rated supply and Documents Issued, as shown in the respective Table of GSTR-1 Return (as Tally ERP 9 cannot upload these details in GSTR-1 portal).

–   **Manual Entry of NIL rated supply :** At GSTR-1 Return, select Table 8A, 8B, 8C, 8D Nil rated supplies. Enter the details as described in off line Return filing

–   **Manual Entry of Documents Issued :** At GSTR-1 Return, select Table, select Table 13 : Documents Issued and enter the details in the Portal Form

Accounting Adjustment of Liabilities &Credits : To make adjustment of various liabilities & credits, At *GSTR-1* report, click *J:Stat Adjustment* button, to get *Stat Adjustment* screen. Select the desired option from the respective list.

```
                    Stat Adjustment
Type of duty/tax      : GST
Nature of adjustment  : Decrease of Tax Liability
                    Additional Details
Additional Details    :  ████████████████████████████

                    List of Nature of Adjustments

                    Adjustment Against Credit
                    Cancellation of Advance Payments under Reverse Charge
                    Cancellation of Advance Receipts
```

F-8A: Stat Adjustment screen

```
            List of Nature of Adjustments

Decrease of Tax Liability
Increase of Input Tax Credit
Increase of Tax Liability
Increase of Tax Liability & Input Tax Credit
Opening Balance
Refund
Reversal of Input Tax Credit
Reversal of Tax Liability
Reversal of Tax Liability & Input Tax Credit
```

F-8B: Adjustment Nature list

On selecting the options, you get a Journal Voucher screen to make necessary accounting adjustments.

Status set up : At *GST Status reconciliation* report (Click *U:Status Reconciliation* button at GSTR-1 report), drill down through respective entries to get Voucher Register containing the filtered Invoices (F-9A). At Voucher Register, select the desired Invoice record (click or press space bar on the Invoice record line and click *S:Status* button to get Status Set up screen (F-9B). Set the status for the selected (F-9B / F-9C). This update the Status for unreconciled records.

F-9A: Status set up

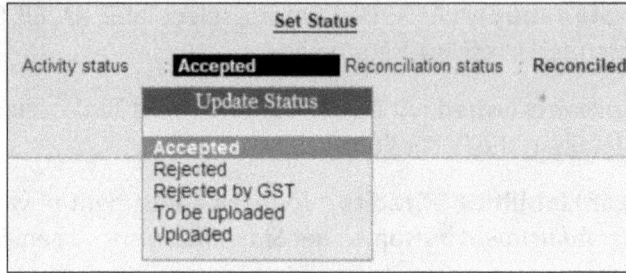

F-9B: Records Status Update

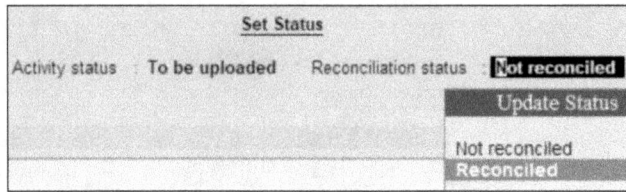

F-9C: Reconciliation Status Update

Exporting GSTR-1 report from Tally into Excel File

Select *GoT> Display > Statutory Reports > GST > GSTR-1* and set the period to get GSTR-1 Report for the specified period. Click E:Export GSTR-1 Button (or press Ctl+E)to get Exporting GSTR-1 screen (F-10A).

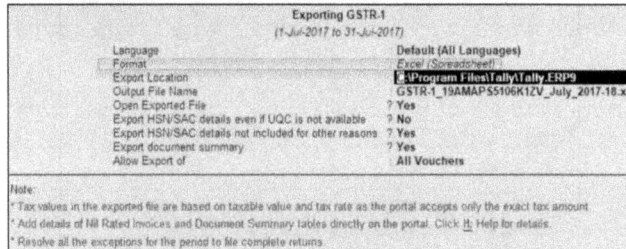

F-10A: Exporting GSTR-1 e-return in Excel Format

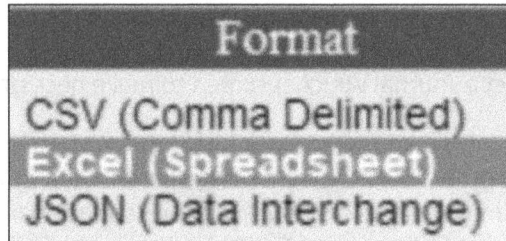

F-10B: Data Format selection list

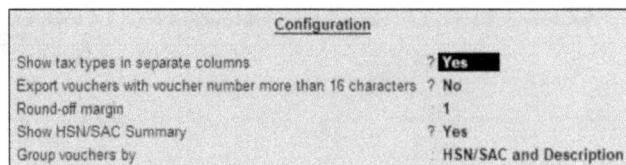

F-10C: GSTR-1 Configuration

[Before exporting GSTR-1, If any adjustments (like advance receipts etc) must be adjusted first, using Stat Adjustment button (on the right side) and pass the adjustment voucher entry to be reflected in GSTR 1 report].

At Exporting GSTR-1 screen (F-10A), set as follows :

- At Format, select Excel (Spreadsheet) (F-10B).

- Export Location &Filename : The default File location and filename of the exported File is displayed.

- You may change the location and filename if you like. The exported file would be save as per specified filename at specified location.

- HSN/SAC Code : When you have set *Yes* at *Show HSN Summary* at GSTR-1 Configuration (F-5B), set the following options regarding HSN/SAC Code

  - At *Export HSN/SAC details even if UQC is not available,* set *Yes* to export transactions where UQCs are not available. For such transactions, you have to map the units of measurement of the stock items to related UQCs in the MS Excel or CSV file.

  - At *Export HSN/SAC details not included for other reasons,* set *Yes* to export transactions that are not included in the *HSN/SAC Summary* due to various reasons. You have to enter this data directly on the portal.

- At *Allow Export of*, select :

  - *All Vouchers* to export all the transactions that have been already filed on the GST portal.

  - *Only New Vouchers* to export the transactions that are not filed on GSTN portal. To avoid overwriting the existing files with the new transactions, use a different Excel file name.

Press *Enter* to export. If $ symbol appears in the data exported to MS Excel, generate your data in the CSV format (to continue in the MS Excel format, go to the *Trust Center Settings* in MS Excel, and add the location where Tally.ERP 9 is installed on your computer)

Exporting GSTR-1 report from Tally in CSV Format

To export data in CSV Format, at Exporting GSTR-1 screen (F-10A), at *Format*, select *CSV (Comma Delimited)*. Separate CSV file would be created for each table in GSTR-1, which are to be imported into the *GST Offline Tool*.

Resolving Internal error

Sometimes error *Internal Error Report GSTR 1 Export File* appears (for Capsule Files under Multi User version). Close the Server & Client instances. Open capsule Folder in Server & Client and delete the Capsule File (.cap) for which error message was displayed. Reload Tally ERP connecting to Internet. The deleted capsule file would be recreated again and the error is expected to be resolved.

Creation of JSON file from Tally Exported GSTR-1 File :

- **Import data and generate the JSON file from Excel File :** Open the latest version of *GST Offline Tool*. Click *NEW.* Enter the required details (Select GSTR-1 Return, Enter GSTIN, Financial Year, Tax period, Aggregate Turnover in preceding Financial Year, Aggregate Turnover in April to June 17 (for

July 17 / July Sep Quarter). SEZ Taxpayer option. Click IMPORT FILES button. Click Import Excel and select the saved Excel File.

- **Import data and generate the JSON file from CSV File :** The process is similar to import from Excel file described above. In place of the Excel File, you have to select the name of the Table of the Return file and select the corresponding CSV file (and click Import CSV) to import. This way, you have to import for each table section of the report.

JSON File Generation : Click *YES*on the warning message, and click *VIEW SUMMARY.* Click GENERATE FILE., to Generate JSON file. The Generated JSON file is to be uploaded into GSTN Portal to upload GSTR-1 Return, as explained.

Contents of Exported GSTR-1 Excel File

We now describe the contents of GSR-1 Excel File Format. The first sheet contains Help and instructions about the Excel Sheet

All the transactions that are displayed under *Included in returns* section in *GSTR-1* report in Tally ERP 9, will be exported to the Excel File format.

The e-return created on export of GSTR-1 is in line with the format prescribed by the department. The file can be imported to the offline utility tool. This tool then creates the JSON file that can be uploaded on the GST portal.

The data of *exemp* (NIL rated) *&docs* (Document Details) will not be carried to JSON file. You will have to enter these data directly into the Portal as per the respective table in GSTR-1.

The e-Return in the portal contains fields for taxable value and Tax Rate but not the Tax Amount. So, the Tax Amount is not exported from Tally to the e-Return file. Tax value in the e-return file is auto computed in the portal based on Tax Rate, Taxable Value and Place of Supply.

Section Sheets ofGSTR-1 Excel File** : The Tally exported Excel file is comprised of following sheets, containing the data in respect of each element of GSTR- Form.

Sheet B2B

The Tab B2B in the exported Excel Sheet displays the details of vouchers captured in the Table 5 - B2B Invoices, showing the following columns :

- **GSTIN/UIN** : GSTIN/UIN of the buyer selected in the sales transaction, as recorded in the GSTIN/UIN field of GST Details screen in party ledger or in GSTIN/UIN field in the Party Details screen of the voucher.

- **Invoice Number** : Invoice number of the outward supply transaction

- **Invoice Date** : Date of the outward supply transaction (default format, dd-mmm-yyyy format, like 12-Jul-17)

- **Total Invoice Value** : Total value in the invoice including tax and cess (the amount debited to Customer Ledger Account).

- **Place Of Supply** : State code & Sate name of the buyer's location (like 21-Odisha).

- **Reverse Charge** : Shows value Y if the transaction is reverse charge transaction, else N.

- **Provisional Assessment** : Shows value Y if the transaction requires provisional assessment, else N.

- **E-Commerce GSTIN** : GSTIN/UIN of the e-commerce operator if the buyer is an e-commerce operator.

- **Category** : Shows value G if the Type of Supply selected is goods and S if it is Services.

- **HSN/SAC of Supply** : HSN/SAC of the item/service selected in the outward supply transaction.

- **Total Taxable Value** : Taxable value in the invoice on which tax is calculated.

- **IGST Rate** : Integrated tax rate levied in the voucher, in case of interstate transaction.

- **IGST Amount** : Integrated tax amount levied in the voucher, in case of interstate transaction.

- **CGST Rate** : Central tax rate levied in the voucher, in case of local transaction.

- **CGST Amount** : Central tax amount levied in the voucher, in case of local transaction.

- **SGST Rate** : State tax rate levied in the voucher, in case of local transaction.

- **SGST Amount** : State tax amount levied in the voucher, in case of local transaction.

- **CESS Rate** : Cess rate levied in the voucher, where cess is applicable.

- **CESS Amount** : Cess amount levied in the voucher, where cess is applicable

Sheet B2Ba

The Tab B2Ba in the exported Excel Sheet displays the details of amendments of vouchers reported in B2B ofearlier period

o Reference of *Original Invoice* of earlier period, which is being amended in the current period.

   o **Original Invoice Number** : Invoice number of the outward supply transaction of previous period which is being amended in the current period.

   o **Original Invoice Date** : Invoice date of the outward supply transaction of previous period which is being amended in the current period.

o Details of *Amended Invoice* in the current period, similar to columns in Tab B2B, as explained

   o **Revised Invoice Number** : Invoice number of the outward supply transaction recorded in the current period for amending a previous period transaction.

   o **Revised Invoice Date** : Invoice date of the outward supply transaction recorded in the current period for amending a previous period transaction.

   o **Total Invoice Value** :   Total value in the invoice including tax and cess.

   o **Place Of Supply** : State code of the buyer's location.

o **Reverse Charge** : Shows value Y if the transaction is reverse charge transaction, else N.

o **Provisional Assessment** : Shows value Y if the transaction requires provisional assessment, else N.

o **E-Commerce GSTIN** : GSTIN/UIN of the e-commerce operator if sold through e-commerce operator.

o **Category** : Shows value G if the Type of Supply selected is goods, S if it is Services.

o **HSN/SAC of Supply** : HSN/SAC of the item/service selected in the outward supply transaction.

o **Total Taxable Value** : Taxable value in the invoice on which tax is calculated.

o **IGST Rate** : Integrated tax rate levied in the voucher, if it is an interstate transaction.

o **IGST Amount** : Integrated tax amount levied in the voucher, if it is an interstate transaction.

o **CGST Rate** : Central Tax Rate levied in the voucher, if it is a local transaction.

o **CGST Amount** : Central tax amount levied in the voucher, if it is a local transaction.

o **SGST Rate** : State tax rate levied in the voucher, if it is a local transaction.

o **SGST Amount** : State tax amount levied in the voucher, if it is a local transaction.

o **CESS Rate** : Cess rate levied in the voucher, if cess is applicable.

o **CESS Amount** : Cess amount levied in the voucher, if cess is applicable

Sheet B2CL

The Tab **B2CL** in the exported Excel Sheet displays the details of vouchers captured in the Table 6 - B2CL Invoices, in respect to Inter State Sales to Consumers exceeding Rs 2,50,000, showing the following columns:

– **Recipient State Code** : State code of the buyer's location.

– **Recipient Name** : Name of the buyer selected in the transaction, as the name specified in the ledger master.

– **Invoice Number** : Invoice number of the outward supply transaction.

– **Invoice Date** : Invoice date of the outward supply transaction.

– **Total Invoice Value** : Total value in the invoice including tax and cess, payable by buyer

– **Place Of Supply**: State code of the buyer's location.

– **Provisional Assessment** : Shows value Y if the transaction requires provisional assessment, else N.

– **E-Commerce GSTIN** : GSTIN/UIN of the e-commerce operator if sold through an e-commerce operator.

- **Category** : Shows value G if the Type of Supply selected is goods and S if it is Services.

- **HSN/SAC of Supply** : HSN/SAC of the item/service selected in the outward supply transaction.

- **Total Taxable Value** : Displays the taxable value in the invoice on which tax is calculated.

- **IGST Rate** : Integrated tax rate levied in the voucher, in case of interstate transaction.

- **IGST Amount** : Integrated tax amount levied in the voucher, in case of an interstate transaction.

- **CGST Rate** : Central tax rate levied in the voucher, in case of local transaction.

- **CGST Amount** : Central tax amount levied in the voucher, in case of local transaction.

- **SGST Rate** : State tax rate levied in the voucher, if it is a local transaction.

- **SGST Amount** : State tax amount levied in the voucher, if it is a local transaction.

- **CESS Rate** : Cess rate levied in the voucher, if cess is applicable.

- **CESS Amount** : Cess amount levied in the voucher, if cess is applicable

Sheet B2CLa
The Tab B2CLa in the exported Excel Sheet displays the details of amendments of vouchers reported in B2CL ofearlier period

- **Recipient State Code** : State code of the buyer's location.

o   Reference of original Invoice which is being amended in the current period.

   o   **Original Invoice Number** : Invoice number of the outward supply transaction of previous period which is being amended in the current period.

   o   **Original Invoice date** : Invoice date of the outward supply transaction of previous period which is being amended in the current period.

o   Details of *Amended Invoice* in the current period, similar to columns in Tab B2CL, as explained

   o   **Recipient Name** : Name of the buyer selected in the transaction, as the name specified in the ledger master.

   o   **Revised Revised Invoice Number** : Invoice number of the outward supply transaction.

   o   **Invoice Date** : Invoice date of the outward supply transaction.

   o   **Total Invoice Value** : Total value in the invoice including tax and cess, payable by buyer

   o   **Place Of Supply**: State code of the buyer's location.

   o   **Provisional Assessment** : Shows value Y if the transaction requires provisional assessment, else N.

   o   **E-Commerce GSTIN** : GSTIN/UIN of the e-commerce operator if sold through an e-commerce operator.

- o **Category** : Shows value G if the Type of Supply selected is goods and S if it is Services.

- o **HSN/SAC of Supply** : HSN/SAC of the item/service selected in the outward supply transaction.

- o **Total Taxable Value** : Displays the taxable value in the invoice on which tax is calculated.

- o **IGST Rate** : Integrated tax rate levied in the voucher, in case of interstate transaction.

- o **IGST Amount** : Integrated tax amount levied in the voucher, in case of an interstate transaction.

- o **CGST Rate** : Central tax rate levied in the voucher, in case of local transaction.

- o **CGST Amount** : Central tax amount levied in the voucher, in case of local transaction.

- o **SGST Rate** : State tax rate levied in the voucher, if it is a local transaction.

- o **SGST Amount** : State tax amount levied in the voucher, if it is a local transaction.

- o **CESS Rate** : Cess rate levied in the voucher, if cess is applicable.

- o **CESS Amount** : Cess amount levied in the voucher, if cess is applicable

Sheet B2CS

The Tab **B2CS** in the exported Excel Sheet displays the details of vouchers captured in the Table 7 - B2CS Invoices, in respect to Sales to Consumers upto Rs 2,50,000, showing the following columns :

- **Type** : Shows value *ecom* for sale through e-commerce operator, *non-ecom* for others.

- **Category** : Shows value G if the Type of Supply selected is goods and S if it is Services.

- **HSN/SAC of Supply** : HSN/SAC of the item/service selected in the outward supply transaction.

- **Recipient State Code** : State code of the buyer's location.

- **Total Taxable Value** : Total value in the invoice including tax and cess.

- **IGST Rate** : Integrated tax rate levied in the voucher, if it is an interstate transaction.

- **IGST Amount** : Integrated tax amount levied in the voucher, if it is an interstate transaction.

- **CGST Rate** : Central tax rate levied in the voucher, if it is a local transaction.

- **CGST Amount** : Central tax amount levied in the voucher, if it is a local transaction.

- **SGST Rate** : State tax rate levied in the voucher, if it is a local transaction.

- **SGST Amount** : State tax amount levied in the voucher, if it is a local transaction.

- **CESS Rate** : Cess rate levied in the voucher, if cess is applicable.

- **CESS Amount** : Cess amount levied in the voucher, if cess is applicable

- **Provisional Assessment**: Shows value Y if the transaction requires provisional assessment, else N.

- **E-Commerce GSTIN** : GSTIN/UIN of the e-commerce operator if the buyer is an e-commerce operator.

Sheet B2CSa

The Tab B2CSa in the exported Excel Sheet displays the details of amendments of vouchers reported in B2CS ofearlier period

- Details of Original Invoice of earlier period being amended in current period :

  o **Month** : Month in which the original invoice that is being amended was recorded.

  o **Original HSN** : HSN/SAC of the item/service selected in the original outward supply transaction.

  o **Original Category** : Shows value G if the Type of Supply selected is goods, S if it is Services in the original outward supply transaction.

  o **Original State Code** : State code of the buyer's location in the original Invoice.

- Details of Invoice amended in current period :

  o **Type** : Shows value *ecom* for e-commerce party and *non-ecom* for others.

  o **Revised HSN** : HSN/SAC of the item/service selected in the revised outward supply transaction.

  o **Revised Category** : Shows value G for Goods, S for Services, in the revised transaction.

  o **Recipient State Code** : State code of the buyer's location in the revised transaction.

  o **Total Taxable Value** : Total value in the invoice including tax and cess.

  o **IGST Rate**: Integrated tax rate levied in the voucher, for interstate transaction.

  o **IGST Amount** : Integrated tax amount levied in the voucher, for interstate transaction.

  o **CGST Rate** : Central tax rate levied in the voucher, for local transaction.

  o **CGST Amount** : Shows central tax amount levied in the voucher, for local transaction.

  o **SGST Rate** : State tax rate levied in the voucher, for local transaction.

  o **SGST Amount** : State tax amount levied in the voucher, if it is a local transaction.

  o **CESS Rate** : Cess rate levied in the voucher, if cess is applicable.

  o **CESS Amount** : Cess amount levied in the voucher, if cess is applicable

  o **Provisional Assessment** : Shows value Y if the transaction requires provisional assessment, else N.

  o **E-Commerce GSTIN** : GSTIN/UIN of the e-commerce operator if sold through e-commerce operator

Sheet CDNR

The Tab CDNR in the exported Excel Sheet displays the details of Debit & Credit notes issued to Registered Dealers

- **GSTIN/UIN** : GSTIN/UIN of the buyer, as recorded in the GSTIN/UIN field of GST Details screen in party ledger or in GSTIN/UIN field in the Party Details screen of the voucher.

- **Note Type** : Shows value credit for credit note and debit for debit note.

- **Reason For Issuing Note** : Reason for issuing the debit note as selected in the voucher.

- **Debit Note Number** : Invoice number of the debit note transaction.

- **Debit Note Date** : Invoice date of the debit note transaction.

- **Invoice Number** : Invoice number of the transaction against which debit note is recorded, as recorded in the Original Invoice no. field in the voucher.

- **Invoice Date** : Invoice date of the transaction against which debit note is recorded, as recorded in the Original Invoice Dt. field in the voucher.

- **Total Differential Value**: Total value in the debit note including tax and cess.

- **IGST Rate** : Integrated tax rate levied in the voucher, if it is an interstate transaction.

- **IGST Amount** : Integrated tax amount levied in the voucher, if it is an interstate transaction.

- **CGST Rate** : Central tax rate levied in the voucher, if it is a local transaction.

- **CGST Amount** : Central tax amount levied in the voucher, if it is a local transaction.

- **SGST Rate** : State tax rate levied in the voucher, if it is a local transaction.

- **SGST Amount** : State tax amount levied in the voucher, if it is a local transaction.

- **CESS Rate** : Cess rate levied in the voucher, if cess is applicable.

- **CESS Amount** : Cess amount levied in the voucher, if cess is applicable

- **E-Commerce GSTIN** : GSTIN/UIN of the e-commerce operator if transacted through e-commerce operator.

Sheet CDNRa

The Tab CDNRa in the exported Excel Sheet displays the details of amendments of vouchers reported in CDNR ofearlier period.

- Details of earlier Debit note being amended in this month

    o **GSTIN/UIN** : GSTIN/UIN of the buyer recorded in earlier note being modified in this month

    o **Original Debit Note Number**: Displays the invoice number of the original debit/credit note of previous period which is being amended in the current period.

- o **Original Debit Note Date** : Displays the invoice date of the original debit/credit note of previous period which is being amended in the current period.

- Details of amended Debit / Credit note in this month

- o **Revised Debit Note Number** : Invoice number of the revised debit/credit note, amending a previous transaction.

- o **Revised Debit Note date** : invoice date of the revised debit/credit note, amending a previous transaction.

- o **Note Type**: Shows value Debit for debit note, Credit for credit note.

- o **Reason For Issuing Note** : Reason for issuing the debit note

- o **Invoice Number** : Invoice number of the transaction against which the original debit note was recorded

- o **Invoice date** : Invoice date of the transaction against which the original debit note was recorded

- o **Total Invoice Value** : Total value in the revised debit note including tax and cess.

- o **IGST Rate** : Integrated tax rate levied in the voucher, if it is an interstate transaction.

- o **IGST Amount** : Integrated tax amount levied in the voucher, if it is an interstate transaction.

- o **CGST Rate** : Central tax rate levied in the voucher, if it is a local transaction.

- o **CGST Amount**: Central tax amount levied in the voucher, if it is a local transaction.

- o **SGST Rate** : State tax rate levied in the voucher, if it is a local transaction.

- o **SGST Amount** : State tax amount levied in the voucher, if it is a local transaction.

- o **CESS Rate** : Cess rate levied in the voucher, if cess is applicable.

- o **CESS Amount** : Cess amount levied in the voucher, if cess is applicable

- o **E-Commerce GSTIN** : GSTIN/UIN of the e-commerce operator if the buyer is an e-commerce operator.

Sheet AT

The Tab AT in the exported Excel Sheet displays the details of Advance Received for which Tax Liability is to be created during this month.

Customer GSTIN/UIN/Name : GSTIN/UIN of the buyer, as recorded in the GSTIN/UIN field of GST Details screen in party ledger.

- **Recipient State Code** : State code of the buyer's location.

- **Document Number** : Invoice number of the receipt transaction.

- **Document Date** : Date of the receipt transaction.

- **Total Invoice Value** : Total value in the receipt voucher including tax and cess.

- **Category** : Shows value G for goods, S for Services.

- **HSN/SAC of Supply** : HSN/SAC of the item/service.

- **Total Taxable Value** : Displays the taxable value in the receipt voucher on which tax is calculated.

- **IGST Rate** : Displays the integrated tax rate levied in the voucher, if it is an interstate transaction.

- **IGST Amount** : Displays the integrated tax amount levied in the voucher, if it is an interstate transaction.

- **CGST Rate** : Displays the central tax rate levied in the voucher, if it is a local transaction.

- **CGST Amount** : Displays the central tax amount levied in the voucher, if it is a local transaction.

- **SGST Rate** : Displays the state tax rate levied in the voucher, if it is a local transaction.

- **SGST Amount** : Displays the state tax amount levied in the voucher, if it is a local transaction.

- **CESS Rate** : Displays the cess rate levied in the voucher, if cess is applicable.

- **CESS Amount** : Displays the cess amount levied in the voucher, if cess is applicable

In rel 6.1 onwards, the AT and ATAdjust Tab contains only the following columns

A. Place Of Supply

B. Rate

C. Gross Advance Adjusted

D. Cess Amount

Sheet ATa

The Tab ATa in the exported Excel Sheet displays the details of amendments of vouchers reported in AT ofearlier period.

Details of original receipt voucher being amended now :

- **Original Customer GSTIN/UIN/Name** : GSTIN/UIN of the buyer in the original receipt being amended now.

- **Original Document Number** : Voucher number of the original receipt of earlier period, being amended now.

- **Original Document Date** : Date of the original receipt transaction being amended now.

Details of amended receipt Voucher :

- **Revised Customer GSTIN/UIN/Name** : GSTIN/UIN of the buyer selected in the revised receipt transaction

- **Revised Document Number** : Displays the invoice number of the revised receipt transaction recorded for amending the earlier transaction.

- **Revised Document Date** : Date of the revised receipt transaction amending the earlier transaction.

- **Recipient State Code** : State code of the payer's location in revised voucher

- **Total Invoice Value** : Total value in the revised receipt voucher including tax and cess.

- **Category** : Shows value G for Supply, S for Services.

- **HSN/SAC of Supply** : HSN/SAC of the item/service selected in the receipt transaction.

- **Total Taxable Value** : Taxable value in the revised receipt voucher on which tax is calculated.

- **IGST Rate** : Integrated tax rate levied in the amended voucher, for interstate transaction.

- **IGST Amount** : Integrated tax amount levied in the amended voucher, for interstate transaction.

- **CGST Rate** : Central tax rate levied in the amended voucher, for local transaction.

- **CGST Amount** : Central tax amount levied in the amended voucher, for local transaction.

- **SGST Rate** : State tax rate levied in the amended voucher, for local transaction.

- **SGST Amount** : State tax amount levied in the amended voucher, for local transaction.

- **CESS Rate** : Cess rate levied in the amended voucher, if cess is applicable.

- **CESS Amount** : Cess amount levied in the amended voucher, if cess is applicable

Sheet ATAdj

The Tab ATadj in the exported Excel Sheet displays the details of Invoice against which earlier advance is adjusted, as recorded in Table 12 during this month.

- **Invoice Number** : Invoice number of the outward supply transaction against which previous advance received is adjusted now.

- **Invoice Date** : Date of the outward supply transaction against which advance recorded against advance received in previous period.

- **GSTIN/UIN** : GSTIN/UIN of the buyer as recorded in sales Invoice

- **Document Number** : Voucher number of the earlier advance receipt transaction against which the supply is adjusted.

- **Document Date** : Date of the advance receipt transaction against which current Invoice is adjusted

- **Total Invoice Value** : Total value in the invoice including tax and cess.

- **Type** : ecom for transaction through e-commerce, non-ecom for a others.

- **IGST Rate** : Integrated tax rate levied in the voucher, for interstate transaction.

- **IGST Amount** : Integrated tax amount levied in Invoice, for interstate transaction.

- **CGST Rate** : Central tax rate levied in Invoice, for local transaction.

- **CGST Amount** : Central tax amount levied in Invoice, for local transaction.

- **SGST Rate** : State tax rate levied in Invoice, for local transaction.

- **SGST Amount** : State tax amount levied Invoice, for local transaction.

- **CESS Rate** : Cess rate levied in Invoice, if cess is applicable.

- **CESS Amount** : Cess amount levied in Invoice, if cess is applicable.

Sheet Exp

The Tab Exp in the exported Excel Sheet displays the details of Export Invoices recorded in Table 10 during this month.

- **Export Type** : Export type based on the type of export transaction.

- **Invoice Number** : Invoice number of the export transaction.

- **Invoice Date** : Date of the export transaction.

- **Total Invoice Value** : Total value in the invoice including tax and cess.

- **Ship Bill Code** : NA

- **Ship Bill Number** : Shipping bill number recorded in the GST Provide Details screen of the voucher.

- **Ship Bill Date** : Shipping bill Date recorded in the GST Provide Details screen of the voucher.

- **Provisional Assessment** : Shows value Y if the transaction requires provisional assessment, else N.

- **Category** : Shoes G Goods, S for Services.

- **HSN/SAC of Supply** : HSN/SAC of the item/service exported

- **Total Taxable Value** : Taxable value in the invoice on which tax is calculated.

- **IGST Rate** : Integrated tax rate levied in the voucher, if it is an interstate transaction.

- **IGST Amount** : Integrated tax amount levied in the voucher, if it is an interstate transaction.

- **CESS Rate** : Cess rate levied in the voucher, if cess is applicable.

– **CESS Amount** : Cess amount levied in the voucher, if cess is applicable

Sheet EXPa

The Tab EXPa in the exported Excel Sheet displays the details of amendments of Export Invoices reported in EXP of earlier period.

– **Export Type** : Displays the export type based on the type of export transaction.

Orginal Invoice details

– **Original Invoice Number** : Displays the invoice number of the original export transaction that is being amended.

– **Original Invoice Date** : Displays the date of the original export transaction that is being amended.

Revised Invoice Details

– **Revised Invoice Number** : Displays the invoice number of the revised export transaction.

– **Revised Invoice Date** : Displays the date of the revised export transaction.

– **Total Invoice Value** : Displays the total value in the invoice including tax and cess.

– **Ship Bill Code** : NA

– **Ship Bill Number** : Displays the shipping bill number recorded in the GST Provide Details screen of the voucher.

– **Ship Bill Date** : Displays the shipping bill Date recorded in the GST Provide Details screen of the voucher.

– **Provisional Assessment** : Displays Y if the transaction requires provisional assessment, else N.

– **Category** : Displays G if the Type of Supply selected is goods and S if it is Services.

– **HSN/SAC of Supply** : Displays the HSN/SAC of the item/service selected in the outward supply transaction.

– **Total Taxable Value** : Displays the taxable value in the invoice on which tax is calculated.

– **IGST Rate** : Displays the integrated tax rate levied in the voucher, if it is an interstate transaction.

– **IGST Amount** : Displays the integrated tax amount levied in the voucher, if it is an interstate transaction.

– **CGST Rate** : Displays the central tax rate levied in the voucher, if it is a local transaction.

– **CGST Amount** : Displays the central tax amount levied in the voucher, if it is a local transaction.

– **SGST Rate** : Displays the state tax rate levied in the voucher, if it is a local transaction.

– **SGST Amount** : Displays the state tax amount levied in the voucher, if it is a local transaction.

- **CESS Rate** : Displays the cess rate levied in the voucher, if cess is applicable.

- **CESS Amount** : Displays the cess amount levied in the voucher, if cess is applicable

Sheet HSN

The Tab *HSN* in the exported Excel Sheet displays the details of HSN Code as per Table 12

Sheet Docs

The Tab *docs* in the exported Excel Sheet displays the details of various documents issued as per Table 13

Troubleshooting

GSTR-1 contains maximum data. So, it is likely that you may encounter several errors during uploading / filing. Here we discuss some common problems encountered and workaround to resolve the issues.

- **HSN Code - HSN Description :** When the combination of HSN code and its description is not unique, an error appears on the GST Offline Tool and GST portal, showing the offending HSN Codes in the error message. This may occur when multiple UQCs are being used for a single HSN, and *HSN Code - HSN Description* combination is not unique for each UQC for a given HSN code.

  Workaround : If multiple UQCs are used for a single HSN, modify the descriptions and keep the *HSN Code - HSN Description* combination unique for each UQC for a given HSN code.

  Open the Excel sheet or the CSV exported from Tally.ERP 9. Search for these HSN Codes either by using filters on Excel or through manual search on the CSV. Modify the description (add some extra identifier) and make the HSN Code – Description combination unique. Remove the filters and save the Excel sheet or CSV file. Delete all data on the GST Offline Tool, a fresh import is done. Import the modified/corrected excel sheet or CSV file in the offline tool.

- **Invoices contain invalid inputs :** Error message shows " Do enter correct invoice date. Invoice date needs to be earlier than today and from the same financial year".

  This error occurs in the CDNR /CDNUR section when sales return is recorded for a sales recorded before 1st July 2017 (i.ebefore GST was introduced).

  Workaround : Import the same data into the GST offline tool using MS Excel or CSV

- **Unable to map UOM to the UQC list.** : When some UQC is missing.

  Workaround : Manually make changes in the exported Excel or CSV, and correct the quantity specified against a UQC on the HSN Summary sheet. For example, if Litre is missing in the UQC list, you may use kilolitres for UQC mapping. Later in the exported data, you have to divide the quantity by 1000 before importing it into the GST Offline Tool for JSON creation. Similarly, you can convert units like inches and feet.

- **Negative Quantity cannot be entered** (but negative values can be entered) : Manually enter the negative quantities in the *HSN Summary* on the portal.

GST Offline Tool Troubleshooting

- **SEZ supplies** : In CSV format under the B2B section, the details of the invoice types *SEZ supplies with payment* and *SEZ supplies without payment* do not get imported to the GST Offline Tool.

  Workaround : In the exported CSV files, if the "s" (in "supplies") is in lower case in the invoice types SEZ supplies with payment and SEZ supplies without payment, then the details of these invoice types do not get imported. Change the "s" to upper case before importing the CSV files to the GST Offline Tool.

GSTR-1 Filing on Portal Troubleshooting

- **Unable to download :** On clicking Generate error report , the error Unable to download appears, and the report does not get downloaded.

  Workaround : Click Generate error report again after sometime.

- **Errors encountered while uploading the files :** Error occurs while uploading the JSON file to the portal using Internet Explorer browser.

  Workaround: Try using a different browser (like Google Chrome), to upload the file to the GSTN portal.

- **File could not be Uploaded**: This error appear while uploading the JSON file to the GST portal. Some of the possible reasons and the corresponding solutions are listed below

    o *HSN description is captured with more than 30 characters* : It my occur when you manually entered data in CSV or Excel File.

    o Invoice numbers are not maintained for purchases from unregistered dealers or sales, and the JSON file is generated with document summary from Tally.ERP 9.

  Workaround : Correct the data before uploading it to the GST Offline Tool for JSON creation. Delete specific transactions from CSV or Excel sheets before uploading them to the GST Offline Tool for JSON creation. Manually enter these transactions on the GST Portal.

- **Unable to enter data in GST Portal** : This happens when you have more than 500 records in a Table.

  Workaround : Download the invoice data from the portal. View data in GST Offline Tool and make the required modifications. Generate a fresh JSON from the GST Offline Tool. Re Upload the data to GSTN Portal.

- **Prepare Online : Invoice count is not updated**, when an Invoice is added.

  Workaround : To view the updated invoice count, you have to go back to the Returns menu, select the Return Filing Period, and click *Prepare Online*

- **Not able to Work Offline.** Internet 11 not installed.

  Workaround : Install Chrome and make it your default Browser.

GSTR-2 filing from Tally.ERP9

We have already explained the contents of GSTR-2 and how to upload GSTR-2 online, review of GSTR-2A, making additions / modification in GSTR-2 Return in GSTN portal.

GSTR-2 report includes the details of all inward supplies made in the given period.

> The GST council deferred filing of GSTR-2 returns until 31st March 2018. Accordingly, the uploading, saving, and submitting of GSTR-2 are temporarily suspended on the GST portal.

The inward supply details include B2B invoices to registered and unregistered dealers, import of goods and services, adjustments to purchases in debit/credit notes, nil rated invoices, advances paid and adjusted, and tax credit reversed or re-claimed

GSTR-2 Return

Select *GoT>Display >Statutory Reports >GST >GSTR–2* to get GSTR-2 Report (F-1A)

GSTR-2					Ctrl + H
GSTIN/UIN : 19AMAPS5106K1ZV					1-Mar-2018 to 31-Mar-2018
Particulars	No. of Invoices	Taxable Value	Total Tax	Total ITC Available	Reconciliation Status
To be reconciled with the GST portal					
B2B Invoices - 3, 4A					
Credit/Debit Notes Regular - 6C					
To be uploaded on the GST portal					
B2BUR Invoices - 4B					
Import of Services - 4C					
Import of Goods - 5					
Credit/Debit Notes Unregistered - 6C					
Nil Rated Invoices - 7 - (Summary)					
Advance Paid -10A - (Summary)					
Adjustment of Advance - 10B - (Summary)					
Total Inward Supplies					
ITC Reversal/Reclaim - 11 - (Summary)					
Total No. of Invoices					
HSN/SAC Summary - 13					
Reverse Charge Liability to be Booked					
URD Purchases					0.00
Reverse Charge Inward Supplies					0.00
Import of Service					0.00
Advance Payments					
Amount Unadjusted Against Purchases					
Purchase Against Advance from Previous Periods					

F-1A: GSTR-2 Report

GST Return sections : The Tally GSTR-2 Return contains following major sections (F-1A)

– **Returns summary** : Summary break up of number of vouchers.

– **Particulars** : Table wise details as per Statutory GSTR Format

The vouchers are shown under heads *To be Reconciled* and *To be Uploaded* head, according to their Status.

Reconciliation Overall Status : The *Reconciliation Status* column (F-1A) indicates overall status of the table based on the invoice matching.

– **Completed :** When status is set for all the vouchers in the table.

– **Not Complete :** When status is not set for any/multiple/all the invoice(s).

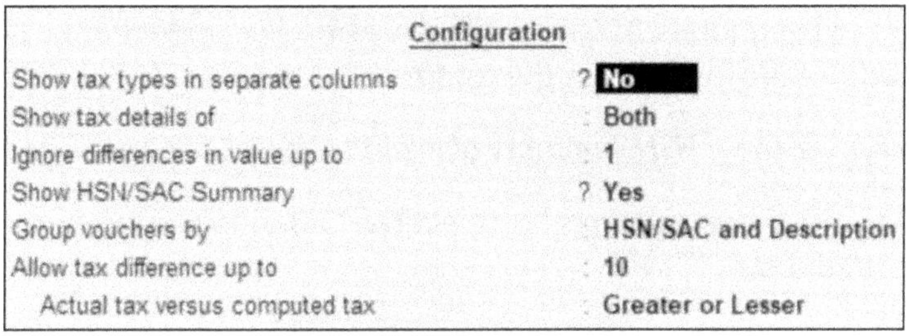

F-2A: GSTR-2 Configuration

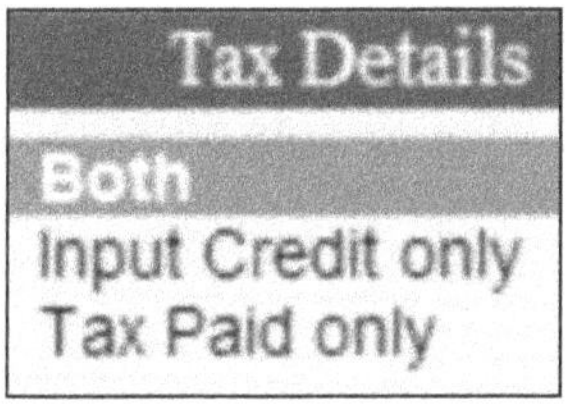

F-2B: Tax Details selection list

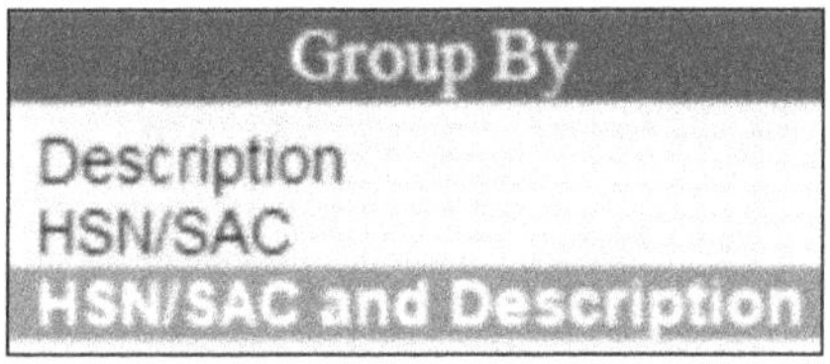

F-2C: Gropu by selection list

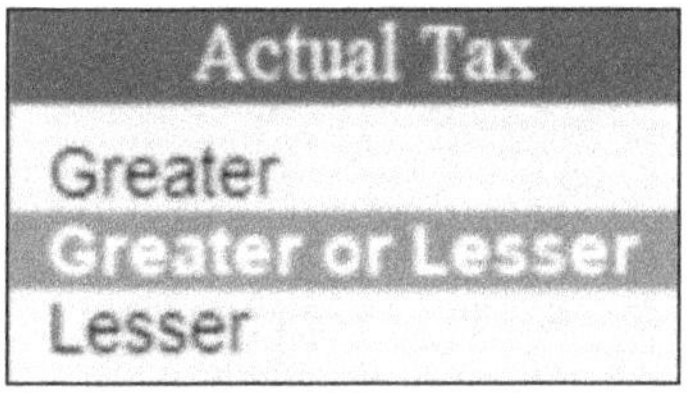

F-2D: Tax comparation otions

GSTR-2 Configuration : AtGSTR-2 Return, click *F12:Configure* to get *Configuration screen* (F-2A) to set the report options, as follows :

– **Tax types in separate columns :** Set *Yes* at *Show tax types in separate columns* to view all GST tax types in separate columns, else set No to display all Taxes in a single column without the central tax, state tax and integrated tax break-up.

– **Tax details** : At *Show tax details of*, select the option from list as follows (F-2B):

o   Select *Input Credit Only* to view only the tax credit claimed.

o   Select *Tax Paid Only* to view the tax amount paid.

o   Select *Both* to view the tax paid and the tax credit claimed.

−   **Invoice Amount Difference** : The difference in Invoice value appearing in GSTR-2 file of portal and Tally.ERP 9 is set to 1 to be ignored. At *Ignore differences in value up to* change it as required to ensure the relevant transactions are included in the returns.

−   **HSN/SAC Summary** : To show *HSN Summary of inward supplies,* set *Yes Show HSN/SAC Summary*

−   **Vouchers Grouping :** At *Group vouchers by,* select the Ordering Option from the list(F-2C) to show the vouchers in desired order.

−   **Tax difference up to** : At *Allow tax difference up to, set the value to allow Tax Difference* to ensure the transactions having allowable difference are included in the returns.

o   **Tax Difference Type :** Having set the allowable tax difference as above, at Actual Tax versus Computed Tax is, select the type of allowable difference from the list (F-2D):

−   **Greater** : Vouchers with actual (transaction) value greater than the computed value are included in the returns.

−   **Greater or lesser** : Vouchers with actual (transaction) value greater or lesser than the computed value are included in the returns.

−   **Lesser** : Vouchers with actual (transaction) value lesser than the computed value are included in the returns.

Voucher Statistics Summary

The Return Summary section at the top part shows summary of all transactions recorded in the reporting period (F-3A). Drill down on each row to view the details

Returns Summary	
Number of vouchers for the period	55
Included in returns	8
Invoices ready for returns	4
Invoices with mismatch in information	4
Not included in returns due to incomplete information	5
Not relevant for returns	42

F-3A: Voucher Statistics Summary

Voucher Type wise Details : Drill down from Number of Vouchers for the period to get the Voucher Statistics, showing Number of Vouchers for each Voucher type for the Report Period.

•   **Included Vouchers** : Drill down form Included in returns to get the Voucher Type wise number of Vouchers that has been considered in compiling of GSR-2 Return

- **Excluded Vouchers :** Drill down from *Not relevant for returns* to view the *Summary of Excluded Vouchers* report, with the transaction type-wise voucher count

  Other transaction types that can appear under excluded vouchers:

  - **Excluded by User** : Manually excluded by you from the list of included or uncertain transactions. Drill down and use I : Include Vouchers, if required . Based on the information in the voucher it will move to either included or uncertain.

    Number of each Voucher type wise and vouchers and number of each Voucher Type that do not have any GST implication (No GST Implications).

  - **Non GSTR-2 Transactions :** The transactions which are part of other returns having no implication on GSTR–2.

  Based on the voucher type used and the exclusions specified, the relevant categories appear with the voucher count.

- **Not included in returns due to incomplete information :** Displays number of all vouchers for which tax type/tax rate not specified, vouchers have incomplete/incorrect adjustment details, and UQC is not selected. Rectify the vouchers before exporting GST returns. If the computed tax is not equal to the tax entered in the invoice, the transaction appears under *Incomplete/Mismatch in information (to be resolved)*. Set the tax difference that you want to allow, as explained under Configuration options of the Return.

Invoices with mismatch in information : Displays the count of all vouchers for which information required for filing returns is missing in the invoice. You can correct exceptions in the vouchers before exporting GST returns.

The exceptions are listed in the order of priority, based on the importance of the information for generating returns. Update the missing information and resolve the mismatches to include them in the Returns.

Resolving Mismatch Invoices

Drill-down through *Invoices with mismatch in information of GSTR-2.* Press *Enter* at *No. of vouchers with incomplete/mismatch in information* to view the complete list of transactions. Drill down through any row to get the voucher in *Alteration* screen. Enter / update the required details in the *Voucher Alteration* screen, to resolve the mismatch, as follows:

- **Incomplete information :** Drill-down through *Not included in returns due to incomplete information in GSTR-2.*Enter the missing information as reported at Type of Mismatch / Incomplete info column

- **UoM not mapped to Unit Quantity Code (UQC)** .: Select the *UoM Symbol.*

  o **Exclude from Summary :** Click <u>X</u>*: Exclude from Summary* to exclude the transactions involving these unit of measurements from the *HSN/SAC Summary* report. These transactions will appear under the *Not included in HSN/SAC Summary (UQC not available)* section of *HSN/SAC Summary* report. The transactions will get included in the relevant sections of the GST return

o **Mapping with UQC from the report :** Click $\underline{S}$: *Map with UQC,* select the *UQC* and press *Enter* .

o **Selecting UQC in the stock item master :** Press *Enter* on the selected *UoM Symbol* and select the *Unit Quantity Code (UQC)*

– **Country, state and dealer type not specified :** Select the state, specify the GSTIN and select dealer type for each transaction.

– **Tax rate/tax type not specified :** Displays the count of transactions for which the rate or tax type is not selected in the item/ledger master. Select the Nature of Transaction, Enter the Tax Rate for respective Tax Type.

– **Nature of transaction, taxable value, rate of tax modified in voucher :** Select the offending voucher. Click $\underline{R}$: *Resolve* to select *Nature of transaction* and enter other details manually, or click $\underline{A}$: *Accept as is* to accept the voucher as is (a confirmation message for acceptance is displayed), type Yes to accept.

– **Incorrect tax type selected in Tax Ledger :** Select the applicable GST Tax ledger in Voucher

– **Mismatch due to tax amount modified in voucher :** Depending on the mismatch you may resolve in any of the following ways:

o **Resolve :** Click $\underline{R}$: Resolve, enter the tax value at *As per transaction* column of the voucher, and press Ctrl+A to accept.

o **Accept as it is :** Click $\underline{A}$: Accept as is , and press **Enter** to confirm acceptance.

o **Recompute :** Click F5:Recompute to recompute the Tax amount and press *Ctrl+A*to accept.

– **Voucher with incomplete/incorrect adjustment details:** At *Nature of adjustment* and at *Additional details,* select the proper applicable option for each voucher

– **Information required for generating table-wise details not provided :** Displays Voucher excluded from GSTR-2 due to incomplete information. Select *Information required for generating table-wise details not provided.* Select voucher displaying Table wise Exception screen. Enter / Update missing info and get back to Exception Resolution screen.

Click *Exception Type* and resolve Party Ledger / Voucher level inconsistencies from one place.

o **Party Level Exception :** Select *Party Ledger Level Corrections* at *Select Exception Resolution Type*screen. Enter Party GSTIN at *Party Ledger Level correction*

o **Voucher level exceptions :** Select *Voucher Level Corrections* at *Select Exception Resolution Type*screen. Enter the details in listed vouchers.

This way, drill down form any row to resolve the inconsistencies. Having done the update, press *Enter* to save the changes

Filter for Item level and Ledger level exceptions : Exceptions of incomplete/mismatch information are listed voucher-wise. To view the exceptions Master wise (item master-wise or ledger-wise), filter the exceptions caused by an item / ledger to resolve from a single screen.

- **Resolve exception at master level**

  o **Item Exception :** Click *L: Item Exceptions* Button at Button Bar. Select the required exception type from *Total Masters* column to display *Multi Stock Alteration* screen. Enter *HSN/SAC*, *Tax Rate*. Select *Taxability* and enter the *Effective Date*

  o **Ledger Exception :** Click *L: Ledger Exceptions*. Select exception type from *Total Masters* column to display *Multi Ledger Alteration* screen. Select / Enter relevant details.

- **Resolve exception at voucher level**

  o **Item Exception** : Click *L: Item Exceptions*. Button at Button Bar. Select required exception type from *Total Masters* column to display *Exception Resolution* screen. Select Nature of Transaction. Enter Tax Rate.

  o **Ledger Exception :** Click *L: Ledger Exceptions*. Select required exception type from *Total Masters* column to display *Exception Resolution* screen. Select / Enter relevant details.

GSTR -2 Return Table Details : In GSTR-2 (F-1A) drill down from any Item under the Heads To be Reconciled with GST Portal, and To be uploaded to GST Portal, you get Tables corresponding to Tables in GSTR-2 Portal, described in another chapter.

URD Purchases : On drill down form URD Purchases in GSTR-2 Report (F-1A), you get the URD Purchases Report (for Reverse Charges Liability) showing Invoice details with taxable amount and tax value for URD purchases only for the days on which the set threshold limit (the Threshold limit may be set through F12:Configure option) is exceeded (default value of Rs. 5000).

GSTR-2 Return Filing from Tally

Having resolved all the issues in GSTR-2 Return in Tally ERP9, you are now ready to file the GSTR-2 Return from Tally, in following steps

- Download JSON file from GST Portal

- Load the JSON File and reconcile Transactions

- Generate the GSTR-2 Return in JSON Format

- File the GSTR-2 Return in GSTN Portal

Download GSTR-2 file from the GST portal

Log in to the GST portal. Select *Services >Returns >Returns Dashboard. Select period.* Select the Return filing period, Click *SEARCH.* At *Inward supplies received by taxpayer GSTR2*tile, click *PREPARE ONLINE.* Click *GENERATE GSTR2 SUMMARY* button and click *PREVIEW* button to view the transactions submitted by supplier on GSTN portal. Click *BACK* to return to the dashboard. At *Inward supplies received by taxpayer GSTR2*, click *PREPARE OFFLINE.* At *Download* tab, click *GENERATE FILE.* The file will be generated. Click the link *Click here to download* to download the GSTR-2 JSON file. Copy the ZIP/extracted JSON file in the folder to your computer.

Load the downloaded JSON file from GSTN Portal in Tally

Select *Gateway of Tally >Display >Statutory Reports >GST >GSTR-2* to get GSTR-2 Return. Click *L : Load File* button to get *Load File* screen.

In *Load File* screen, at *File Location*, enter the pathname where the downloaded JSON file is placed. At *Filename*, select the JSON filename from list(The ZIP/JSON file will be listed only if the return period in the GSTR-2 report and company GSTIN/UIN matches). Message of successful file load specifying the number of Invoices, is displayed. Type *Yes* to update the invoice status, else type *No* to load the file, without updating Invoice status.

Downloaded GSTR-2 file : Blue colour lines show the details as per the downloaded GSTR-2 file (details of invoices submitted or saved by the supplier & Invoices manually uploaded on the porta0. Black colour lines show the details of invoices *As per books*.

The status displayed for *B2B Invoices - 3, 4A and Credit/Debit Notes Regular - 6C* are:

− **New** : Set the status of invoices *Available only in Books* as *New* and upload them to portal as new claims. This will reflect in GSTR-1A for the counter party to act on.

− **Accepted** : Set the status as *Accepted* when the invoices in Tally.ERP 9 are fully matching with the invoices in the GSTR-2 file (downloaded from portal).

− **Modified** : Set the status as *Modified* when the invoices in Tally.ERP 9 are partially matching with the invoice details in the portal. This will reflect in GSTR-1A for the counter party to act on.

− **Pending** : Set the status as *Pending* to put the invoice on hold. For example, the invoice is available in books or in portal but the goods have not been delivered during the return period. You can accept, reject or modify the invoice in the next return period based on the transaction status.

− **Rejected** : Set the status as **Rejected** when:

   o   An unknown invoice is available on the portal.

   o   The purchase invoice is created but the actual delivery of goods or rendering of services has not happened during the return period.

The rejected invoice appears for the counter party in GSTR-1A to accept or reject.

− **Rejected by GST** : Set the status as *Rejected by GST* when:

o There is duplication of invoice.

o The reference of original invoice is not found for debit or credit note.

o GSTIN of the party has been suspended

Reconcile Invoice status in GSTR-2 file

Select **B2B Invoices - 3, 4A** .

- **Status not Updated** : Displays the party-wise details of transactions for which status is not set.

- **Status Updated** : Displays the party-wise details of transactions for which status is set.

- **Saved Transactions (Create if not available in books)** : Displays the transactions which the counter party has submitted but not filed as part of GSTR-1 returns.

- **Available Only in Books (Can mark as 'New' when exporting)** : Displays transactions which are available only in Tally.ERP 9. While exporting the data to JSON format, you can set the status as New and export it to JSON file.

Invoice-wise Match Status : Click *F5: Invoice-wise)* to displayt list of transactions made with all the parties, grouped into the following categories.

- **Matched but Status not Updated** : Select the status *Accepted* , *Accepted with Ineligible ITC* , *Modified, Pending* , or *Rejected* .

- **Partially Matched** : Select the *status* Accepted , Accepted with Ineligible ITC, Modified , Pending , or Rejected.

- **Available Only in Portal (Set status or create voucher in book)** : Click <u>A</u> : *Add Voucher* to create the transaction in Tally.ERP 9.

- **Status Updated** : Set the status to be uploaded as *Accepted* , *Accepted with Ineligible ITC* , *Modified* , *Pending* , or *Rejected* .

- **Available Only in Books (Can Mark as 'New' when exporting)** : While exporting the data to JSON format, set the status as *New* and export it to JSON file.

- **Saved Transactions (can mark as 'New' when exporting)** : Displays the transactions which the counter party has submitted but not filed as part of GSTR-1 returns.

Voucher Register : From *Party Register* , drill down on a Party ledger to view the *Voucher Register* showing the Invoices of selected Party. Click <u>S</u> : *Set Status* to get Set Status screen. *At Activity Status* field, select the status as per books and as per GSTR-2 file, from the list of Status, for each Transaction.

- Invoices with Status selected as *Accepted, Pending* , or *Rejected* moves to *Status Updated* section.

- Invoices for with Status selected as *Accepted with Ineligible ITC,* the Edit Information screen appears. Set the option *ITC Ineligible* to *Yes* and save.

- *Modified-* the *Edit Information* screen appears. Modify the details as required and save

Credit/Debit Notes : Select *Credit/Debit Notes Regular - 6C.* Reconcile the transactions as per the procedure explained for *B2B Invoices - 3, 4A*.

To clear the status set, go to *Voucher Register*, select the transaction (press *Spacebar* for one transaction or *Ctrl + Spacebar* for multiple transactions) and click *R : Clear Status*

Progressive Reconciliation at Regular Interval

The GSTR-2 transactions may be huge for a large business organisation. Instead of waiting till the period end to reconcile all invoices in one shot, which may be difficult to do within such short period, you may progressively reconcile the Invoices in stages. After having reconciled the first set of transactions, load the saved JSON file to continue the reconciliation for the next set of transactions. Check the date and time of the file before loading, to ensure the file has updates as per last changes made.

The overall reconciliation status of B2B invoices and credit/debit notes of regular tables appear as *Not Completed*. Continue reconciliation process from where ended last time. Set Yes at the configuration option 'Save Transactions available only in the book with the Status New'.

Click *S: Save Return* before exiting from the GSTR-2 report of Tally.ERP 9

After all the transaction statuses are reconciled, you may proceed to generate the return in JSON format and file the return.

Generating GSTR-2 in JSON format

Load the JSON file. At *GSTR-2* report, click *F12: Configure*. Set *Yes* at '*Export a separate file for CDNR & CDNUR tables*' (F-4A). Click E:Export button and set Yes at 'Export Transactions available only in the book with the Status New' (F-4B).

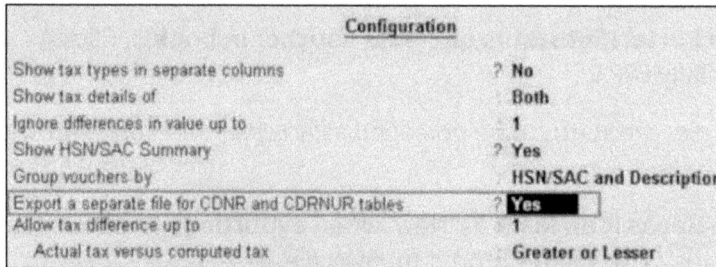

Configuration	
Show tax types in separate columns	? No
Show tax details of	Both
Ignore differences in value up to	1
Show HSN/SAC Summary	? Yes
Group vouchers by	HSN/SAC and Description
Export a separate file for CDNR and CDRNUR tables	? **Yes**
Allow tax difference up to	1
Actual tax versus computed tax	Greater or Lesser

F-4A: JSON File Generation Configuration

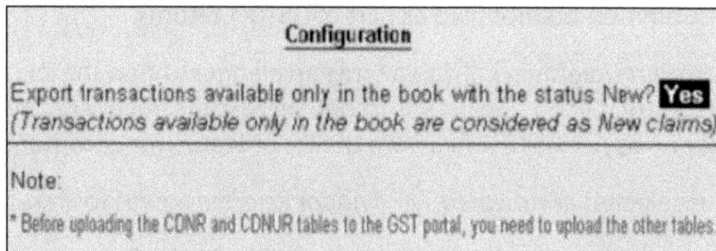

Configuration
Export transactions available only in the book with the status New? **Yes**
(Transactions available only in the book are considered as New claims)
Note:
* Before uploading the CDNR and CDNUR tables to the GST portal, you need to upload the other tables.

F-4B: File Export option set up

The files will be exported in JSON format in the *FiletoUpload* folder (in the path from where the GSTR-2 file downloaded from portal, was loaded in GSTR-2 report of Tally.ERP 9). The status of transactions which are available only in the books will be marked as *New* and exported to JSON file.

If the data is exported without setting Yes at *Show HSN/SAC summary?* GSTR-2 report configuration screen of the GSTR-2 report, the HSN section of the exported output file will be blank.

Filing GSTR-2 Return in GSTN Portal

At GSTN Portal, Click *Services > Returns > Returns Dashboard* . Select the *Return Filing Period*, click *SEARCH*. Click *PREPARE OFFLINE > UPLOAD* tab. Click *CHOOSE FILE* to import the GSTR-2 file in JSON format. First upload the file for all tables other than *CDNR-CDNUR* and then upload *CDNR-CDNUR* . After the JSON files are uploaded successfully, success message would be displayed,

Click *BACK* to return to the dashboard.. Under *Inward supplies received by taxpayer GSTR2* Tile, click *PREPARE ONLINE* . Click *SUBMIT* , and *FILE RETURN* . The *GSTR-2* will be filed electronically, as usual.

Upload GSTR-2 New Data from Tally Exported File using offline tool

You may use the GSTR-2 file downloaded from the portal for filing the complete GSTR-2 return using the offline tool, through the following Steps :

– Download the GSTR-2 file from portal

– Import the GSTR-2 file in the offline tool, reconcile transactions, and generate JSON

– Upload the JSON file on the portal and file your returns

Use the MS Excel file generated from Tally.ERP 9 for uploading new claims of GSTR-2. The generated Excel file includes only the invoices with the status *New* or blank.

– Export GSTR-2 from Tally.ERP 9 in Excel format.

   o   Open GSTR-2 report, and press *Ctrl+E (Export Return)*.

   o   *Select Excel (Spreadsheet)* .

   o   Set Yes at Export unreconciled invoices to mark the status of unreconciled invoices as *New* .

– Import the Excel file to the offline tool, and generate the JSON file.

– Upload the JSON file to the portal, reconcile your invoices with that of your counter party, and file your returns.

The status updates done in Tally.ERP 9 for the invoices seen on the portal will not be included in the MS Excel file. In case of NO NEW claims, the Excel file created will be blank.

The MS Excel file provided by GST as a part of the Offline tool processes the invoice statuses for B2B Invoices and Credit/Debit Notes Regular.

GSTR-2 filing from Portal

Log in to the GST Portal (www.gst.gov.in). Select *Services > Returns > Returns Dashboard*. Select the Return filing period. click *SEARCH* . At *Inward supplies received by taxpayer GSTR2* tile, click *PREPARE ONLINE*. Click *Generate GSTR2 Summary* to view the transactions submitted by the supplier on GSTN portal.

Click *BACK* to return to the dashboard. At *Inward supplies received by taxpayer GSTR2* tile, click *PREPARE OFFLINE* . At *Download* tab, click *GENERATE FILE* . The file will be generated. At *Click here to download* link, click to download the GSTR-2 file at specified folder in the computer.

Import JSON file in offline tool and reconcile

Open**GST***Offline Tool* . Click *OPEN* under *Open Downloaded Return file*from GST portal. Select the *ZIP* file of JSON downloaded from portal. Click *PROCEED.* Compare the invoice details with the details available in Tally.ERP 9.   Reconcile the transactions *Uploaded by Supplier* with the transactions available in Tally. ERP 9 (press **Alt+tab** to compare). Select desired transaction (one, multiple, or all transactions) displayed in a page. Based on the transaction status, click *ACCEPT, REJECT* or *PENDING* button.

New Claims : Add the details of new claims, if any (add only one invoice at a time). Alternatively, export all NEW claims in MS Excel format from Tally.ERP 9 (Set Yes at *Export unreconciled invoices*) .

Click *IMPORT FILES*toImport the MS Excel file in the offline tool. Click SAVE button.

Having added all the claims, click *BACK* > *PROCEED* > *GENERATE FILE* > Save to save the file. Upload the file to the portal, as explained next

Uploading JSON in portal and Return filing

At GSTN Portal, Click *Services* > *Returns* > *Returns Dashboard*. Select the *Return Filing Period* , click *SEARCH*. Click *PREPARE OFFLINE*. Click *Choose File* and select JSON file to import. A message follows on successful uploading of JSON file.

At *Inward supplies received by taxpayer GSTR2* tile, click *PREPARE ONLINE.* Click *SUBMIT* and*FILE RETURN*button to file GSTR-2 Return.

Troubleshooting

We now discuss about some common errors encountered during Filing of GSTR-2 and workaround to resolve / overcome the problems / errors

– **Error in JSON Structure Validation** : This error may occur when uploading JSON File on GST Portal.

  Workaround : Download latest GSTR-2 (not GSTR-2A) from the Portal and use it.

– **Negative Quantity in HSN Summary :** In the GST Offline Tool, Negative Quantity cannot be entered while negative values can be entered

  Workaround : Manually enter negative quantity in GSTN portal directly.

GSTR-3B Filing from Tally.ERP9

GSTR-3B is an interim Return form (in addition to GSTR-3), to be submitted when Return Filing Due Date of GSTR-1 & GSTR-2 is extended. GSTR-3 is then to be filed as per notification. GSTR-3B Return contains summary of Outward Supplies, Inward Supplies, Advance receipts & adjustment thereof, Input Tax Credit & Tax Payments, for the selected Return filing period

Filing of GSTR-3B

GSTR-3B can be filed in following methods

- **File GSTR-3B from Tally by exporting in Offline Utility :** Export GSTR-3B in the MS Excel Offline Utility tool. Login to the GST portal, download the GSTR-3B Offline Utility and save it in your computer. Provide this same location path in Tally. ERP 9. Tally will export GSTR-3B in the Offline Utility Excel file. Although Tally. ERP 9 already validates the information, you should recheck the information again. This has already been explained in another chapter.

- **File GSTR-3B from Tally by printing GSTR-3B Report :** Print GSTR-3B which is in line with format of GST portal. Then login to the portal and manually enter the details, as explained in another chapter.

- **File GSTR-3B from Tally by exporting data in JSON format :** Export GSTR-3B directly in JSON format which can then be uploaded on the GST portal . This is the easiest and fastest ways to file GSTR-3B using Tally, as described in this chapter.

- **File GSTR-3B from Tally by exporting data in Excel format :** Export GSTR-3B in Excel format. Export the Excel File into JSON Format and then upload the JSON file to GST portal, as explained in this chapter.

GSTR-3B Report in Tally ERP.9

Select GoT >*Display* >*Statutory Reports* >*GST* >*GSTR-3B* to get GSRT-3B Report (F-1A).

Return Format: Click *V: View Return Format* toggle button to view the Report in Return Format, in line with the GST 3B Return Form, segregated into following Tables (F-1A). The components of each section are explained in details, in another chapter.

The column Taxable Value includes Value of Debit / Credit Note, Advance liabilities, excluding Tax

Table section 3 :

- Table 3.1 shows the break up of Outwards supplies subject to Reverse Charge.

- Table 3.2 shows the figures of Inter State supplies to Unregistered, Composite & UIN Holders, included in Table 3.1

F-1A: GSTR-3B : Table section 3

Table section 4 : Shows break up of Ineligible ITC (F-2A)

F-2A: GSTR-3B : Table section 4

Table section 5 : Shows break up of Composition Scheme, Exempt & Nil Rated. It also shows the Interest & Late fees payable (F-3A)

F-3A: GSTR-3B : Table section 5

Table Section- RCM & Advance : Shows the break up of Reverse Charge Liability to be booked, Advance Receipt & Advance Payments (F-4A).

F-4A: GSTR-3B : Table – RCM & Advance

GSTR-3B – Return Format Configuration

At GSTR-3B - Return Format screen, click *F12:Configure* to get GSTR-3B – Return Format Configuration screen (F-5A), to set the Configuration options as follows:

- **Tax Type Columns**: At *Show tax type in separate columns?,* set *Yes* to view the breakup of tax amount.

- **Allowable Tax Difference :** At *Allow tax difference up to,* Enter the value upto which Tax Difference in Return is allowable (default set to Zero).

  – **Actual vs Computed Tax Difference :** Having set value for Allowable Tax Difference at above option, based on the tax difference value allowed, you set following option to include vouchers with following difference types vouchers.

    o **Greater :** Vouchers with actual (transaction) value greater than the computed value are included in the returns.

    o **Greater or lesser :** Vouchers with actual (transaction) value greater or lesser than the computed value are included in the returns.

    o **Lesser :** Vouchers with actual (transaction) value lesser than the computed value are included in the returns.

F-5A: GSTR-3B – Return Format Configuration

GSTR-3B – Summary Format : Click *V : View Summary* toggle button to view the Report in Summary Format (F-6A), showing tax computation details with the taxable value and tax break-up for local and interstate supplies under taxable, exempt, and nil-rated categories.

– **Outward Supplies :** Local & Inter State outward supplies (including Reverse Charge Supplies, Ineligible Supplies & Non GST Supplies) & Adjustments thereof

– **Inward Supplies:** Local & Inter State Inward Supplies (including Reverse Charge Supplies, Ineligible Supplies & Non GST Supplies) & Adjustments thereof

GSTR-3B	1-Jul-2017 to 31-Mar-2018	
Particulars	Taxable Value	Tax Amount
Outward Supplies		
Local Sales	4,14,540.00	29,450.80
Taxable	3,83,790.00	29,450.80
Exempted	30,750.00	
Interstate Sales	3,84,620.00	32,495.02
Taxable	3,79,020.00	32,495.02
Exempted	5,600.00	
Reverse Charge Supplies	10,000.00	1,540.00
Total Outward Supplies	8,09,160.00	63,485.82
Add/Less: GST Adjustments		3,700.00
Total Liability	7,99,160.00	65,645.82
Inward Supplies		
Local Purchase	1,20,000.00	12,000.00
Taxable	1,20,000.00	12,000.00
Ineligible Supplies	(17,000.00)	(4,760.00)
Total Inward Supplies	1,37,000.00	16,760.00
Add/Less: GST Adjustments		(-)960.00
Total Input Tax Credit	1,20,000.00	11,040.00

F-6A: GSTR-3B: Summary View

GSTR-3B – Summary Format Configuration : At GSTR-3B Summary Format screen (F-6A), click *F12:Configure* to get GSTR-3B Summary Format Configuration screen (F-6B), to set the Configuration options.

Printing of GSTR-3B Report

At GSTR-3B Report display screen (return Format or Summary Format, as needed, as explained), click P: Print Button to print the Report.

Generating JSON file from Tally.ERP 9

At GSTR-3B Report (*GoT>Display >Statutory Reports >GST >GSTR-3B),*Click *E:Export* button at top button bar (or press Alt+E), or click E: Export Return button (or press Crl+E) at right side button bar to get Exporting GSTR-3B screen (F-7A)

F-7A: Exporting GSTR-3B into JSON file

At *Exporting GSTR-3B* screen (F-7A), at *Format* select *JSON (Data Interchange)*. At *Export Location*, the default location is shown which you may change. At *Output filename*, the default filename as per GSTIN is shown (which you may change). Press **Enter** to export GSTR-3B data. As per the e-filing requirements, negative net values will be exported with a negative sign. Now upload the JSON file to the portal for filing returns.

Submitting and filing GSTR-3B Return from JSON file

– **Uploading JSON File :** Log in to GST Portal (www.gst.gov.in). Select Dashboard >Return Dashboard**.** Select Return filing period. Click *SEARCH* button. At *Monthly Return GSTR3B*tile**,** click *PREPARE OFFLINE >UPLOAD* tab. click *CHOOSE FILE* to import the GSTR-3B JSON file generated from Tally. ERP 9. Successful uploading is indicated by a message (Status column shows *Procssed*, Error Report column shows NA)

– **Return File**Preview : Click *BACK >Monthly Return GSTR3B*, click *PREPARE ONLINE*. The values get posted in the relevant tables of GSTR-3B. Click *SAVE GSTR3B*buttonto save the details. Click *PREVIEW DRAFT GSTR-3B*to preview or download the form, check the details (and rectify as needed)

– **Input Tax Credit Adjustments :** Having checked the Report, click *PROCEED TO PAYMENT* buttonto view the available input tax credit (modify values if required). Confirm the input tax credit, to offset against the payable value.

- **Payment & Challan Preparation** : For the balance amount payable, challan gets generated automatically with the relevant details, and payment options appear. After making online payment, the payments table appears.

- **Return Filing** : Click *PROCEED TO FILE* button. Select the authorised signatory and *SUBMIT* with EVC or DSC.

After submission of GSTR-3B, it cannot be revised.

Exporting GSTR-3B returns from Tally ERP9 to Excel template

First, download of line Excel Utility from GSTN portal, as explained in another chapter.

At Exporting GSTR-3B screen (F-7A), at *Formats* elect Excel Spreadsheet to export file in Excel Template (instead of JSON Format) as explained. At Export location enter the folder name where the Excel template downloaded from GSTN, has been saved. At *Output filename*, enter the name of the Excel Template file (if the specified Excel file is not found at the folder specified at Export Location, an error message is displayed). If there are negative net values in the return, a message appears. Such values will not be exported to the Excel template.

Now the Excel template opens with the data updated in the relevant fields. In the template:

- Click *Validate* to view the status of the sheet. If validation fails, correct the errors mentioned in the template, and then click *Validate*, as explained in another chapter.

- Click *Generate File* to generate and save the JSON file on the desktop.

Submitting and filing GSTR-3B Return from JSON file : Upload the JSON file, submit & file return as explained above

GSTR-4 Filing from Tally.ERP9

GSTR-4 Return contains details of Taxable outward supplies and inward supplies under reverse charge, made by a GST composition dealer. To file GSTR-4, a JSON file is to be created, either exporting from GSTR-4 Report from Tally.ERP9, or using the GST Offline tool.

Here we explain the method of generating GSTR-4 JSON file from Tally ERP and uploading in GST Portal. The alternate method of generating GSTR-4 JSON file using GST offline tool has been explained in another chapter.

Generating JSON from Tally.ERP 9

Tally.ERP 9 allows to generate JSON file, which may be uploaded in GST portal. It is a simple convenient method to file GSTR-4

Generate GSTR-4 returns in the JSON format: Select *GoT>Display>Statutory Reports>GST>GSTR-4* to get GSTR-4 Report (F-1A). Set the period (click F2: Period) for which GSTR-4 Return is to be filed.

GSTR-4			1-Jul-2017 to 31-Mar-2018
Particulars	Voucher Count	Taxable Value	Tax Amount
Outward Supplies			
Turnover of Taxable Sales @ 1%	4	50,821.40	508.22
Inward Supplies			
Purchases Attracting Reverse Charge	1	2,000.00	100.00
Interstate Purchase Taxable @ 5%		2,000.00	100.00
Total	5	52,821.40	608.22

F-1A: GSTR-4 Return

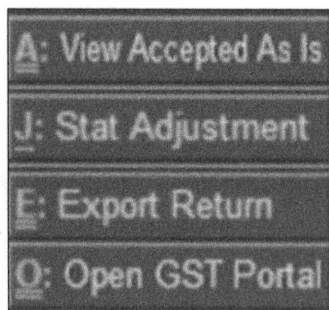

A: View Accepted As Is
J: Stat Adjustment
E: Export Return
O: Open GST Portal

F-1B: GSTR-4 Return Buttons

GSTR-4 Configuration : At GSTR-4 Report (F-1A), click F12:Configure to get GSTR-4 Configuration screen (F-2A)

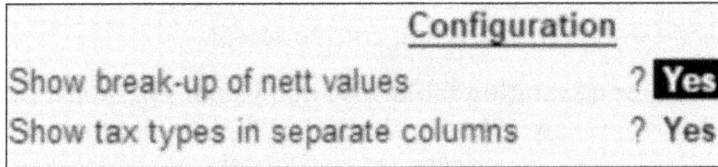

```
                      Configuration
Show break-up of nett values              ? Yes
Show tax types in separate columns        ? Yes
```

F-2A: GSTR-4 Configuration

Contents of GSTR-4 Return in Tally.ERP9 : The GSTR-4 Return contains 2 major sections

- **Voucher Summary Statistics** : This section of GSTR-4 Return contains break up of the number of vouchers for the Return period. Drill down from respective line to get the list of related vouchers

- **GSTR-4 Report**: This section of GSTR-4 Return shows the figures of Outward Supplies, Inward Supplies, Advance received and adjustments thereof. The Tax is to be paid as per figures in the Return.

Summary Statistics Details : On drill down from Summary Report lines (F-1A), you get following details

- **Total number of vouchers for the Period :** Drill-down from the line Total number of vouchers for the period shows the Voucher Statistics report, listing number of vouchers of each Voucher Type

- **Included in Returns :** Drill down from *Included in returns* line to get the *Summary of Included Vouchers* report, showing Number of vouchers for each Voucher types considered in the current GSTR-4 Return being shown

- **Not relevant for returns :** Drill down from *Not relevant for returns* row to view the *Summary of Excluded Vouchers* report, showing Number of vouchers for each Voucher types NOT considered in the current GSTR-4 Return being shown.

Other transaction types under excluded vouchers:

- **Excluded by User** : Displays transactions manually excluded from the list of included or uncertain transactions. Drill down and click *I: Include Vouchers*, if required. Based on the information in the voucher, the voucher will move to either included or uncertain.

- **No GST Implications** : Displays the number of receipts, payments, and journal vouchers that do not have any GST implication.

- **Non GSTR-4 Transactions** : Displays the transactions which are part of other returns (like GSTR – 1, GSTR-2 or GSTR-3B etc.) not have any implication on GSTR-4.

Incomplete/Mismatch information

Drill down from respective rows under *Incomplete / Mismatch in information (to be resolved),* to view vouchers for which information required for filing returns is missing in the invoice. The mismatches are to be resolved by rectifying / updating the data in respective voucher.

- **Taxability, Reverse charge applicability, Taxable value, Rate of tax modified in voucher :** Drill down to get list of offending vouchers. Select the offending voucher. Click R: *Resolve* to select from the list of options, and enter other details manually. Alternatively, you may click A: *Accept as is* if you do not want to change any information. Press *Enter* to accept.

- **Information required for generating table-wise details not provided** : Drill down to get list of vouchers excluded from Table wise format due to incomplete information. Click *Exception Types* button (or press Ctrl+E). Select *Information required for generating table-wise details not provided.* Select voucher to display the *Exceptions as per Return Tables*. Enter the missing information or update the incorrect details.

This way, resolve for all vouchers for Incomplete / Missing information to be included in return. The exceptions are listed in the order of priority, based on the importance of the information to generate the returns. Update the missing information and resolve the mismatches

GSTR-4 Export to JSON Format

Having resolved all the Mismatch missing info you are ready to export GSTR-4 File. At GSTR-4 Report (F-1A), Click *E: Export Return* button (F-1B),to get GSTR-4 Export screen (F-3A). At *Format*, select *JSON GSTR-4 (Data Interchange)*. At *Export Location*, the default location of Exported Excel file to be saved in displayed. You may change it. At *Output File* name, the default output Excel Filename is shown. You may change it.

F-3A: Exporting GSTR-4 into JSON

The JSON file is downloaded as per specified *Output File Name*, in the specified *Export Location* Folder. Now Upload the JSON file generated from Tally.ERP 9 to the portal for filing returns, as explained.

File GSTR-4 returns in GST Portal uploading the JSON file

Log in to the GST portal (www.gst.gov.in) with username password credentials. Click *Services* > *Returns* > *Returns Dashboard* to get Returns Dashboard screen. Select the *Return Filing Period* and click *SEARCH* button. Click *PREPARE OFFLINE at GSTR4* tile.

Click *Choose File* and select the saved JSON file generated from Tally.ERP 9. A successful message is shown (else Error message is shown if error encountered and JSON file is not uploaded). Verify the uploaded details after the specified time. Submit your returns and e-sign.

PART 4
ASSIGNMENTS

Assignments

Having read the book, you are now quite familiar and knowledgeable person in GST. So, it is time to test your knowledge, to get the concepts correct and clear. To assist you assess yourself, 4 sets of assignments for self-evaluation are included in this Part.

- **Quiz** : The GST topics have been divided in 5 major sections. Quiz (Multiple Choice Questions) are included for each Section. The Questions are graded in 4 different level of difficulty (Level 1 being simplest and level 4 as most difficult). Questions under each section are uniquely numbered for reference. Just tick mark against the right answer. Answers are not included. You should try yourself. However, you may e-mail us to std@etallyguru.com, for assistance/ guidance.

- **Test** : A set of short questions are set, divided into various topics. Just write a short answer within 2-3 sentences, with key points only.

- **GSTN Projects** : A few practical projects of uploading data and GST Returns filing are included. Just explain the steps of data input, data upload and Returns Filing into GSTN Portal.

- **GST with Tally ERP9 Projects**: Some practical projects of transaction involving GST are included. Create a Company using Tally.ERP9, create Masters & Vouchers. Explain the steps of data input and appropriate options set up. Explain the steps of relevant GST Returns printing and uploading the Returns into GSTN portal.

These assignments will help you clear your concepts, improve your understanding and skills of working & problem solving: as Business user, as Accountant in the organisation you are working, and as job seeker to get employment in Accounts Department of various organisations, highly demanded in present market scenario.

So, go ahead and complete the assignments. Its exciting, challenging &rewarding !

Quiz GST - General

The GST topics have been divided in 5 major sections. Write the Answer of the Quiz sets (Multiple Choice Questions). The Questions are graded in 4 different level of difficulty (Level 1 being simplest and level 4 as most difficult). Questions under each section are uniquely numbered for reference. Just tick mark against the right answer. Answers are not included. You should try yourself. However, you may e-mail us to std@etallyguru.com, for assistance / guidance.

Quiz # GST-GEN -1-01
Level -1

Q#01 : India has chosen _____ model of dual-GST?

a. Canadian b. Cuba c. Belize d. Nicaragua

Q#02 : What is Integrated Goods and Services Tax?

a. Tax imposed on imported goods and services. b. Tax imposed on value additions to exports c. Tax imposed on interstate trade d. Tax on international trade

Q#03 : GST on services can be levied by

a. Centre b. States c. Centre and States both d. None of the above

Q#04 : Which of the following is statement is not correct about GST?

(a) GST is like a last-point retail tax, to be collected at point of Sale. (b) GST will abolish all the direct tax levied in India (c) It will be implemented from 1 July, 2017 throughout the country. (d) It will create unified tax structure in India

Q#05 : Which of the following tax is abolished by the GST?

(a) Service Tax (b) Corporation tax (c) Income Tax (d) Wealth Tax

Q#06 : What is CGST?

(A) Center Goods and Service Tax (B) Capital Goods and Service Tax (C) Capacity Goods and Service Tax (D) Central Goods and Service Tax

Q#07 : What is SGST?

(A) State Goods and Service Tax (B) Special Goods and Service Tax (C) Statutory Goods and Service Tax (D) None of these

Q#08 : What is IGST?

(A) Integrated Goods and Service Tax (B) Indian Goods and Service Tax (C) Initial Goods and Service Tax (D) None of these

Q#09 : The headquarters of GST council is located at :

(A) New Delhi (B) Lucknow (C) Ahmadabad (D) Mumbai

Q#10 : Which of the following tax will be abolished by the GST?

(A) Service Tax (B) Corporation tax (C) Income Tax (D) Wealth Tax

Q#11 : What is Integrated Goods and Services Tax?

(A) Tax imposed on imported goods and services B) Tax imposed on value additions to exports

(C) Tax imposed on interstate trade (D) Tax on international trade

Q#12 : GST will be levied on–

(A) Manufacturers (B) Retailers (C) Consumers (D) All of the above

Q#13 : What kind of Tax is GST?

(A) Direct Tax (B) Indirect Tax (C) Depends on the type of goods and services (D) None of the above

Q#14 : IGST is charged by .... Government.

(A) Central (B) State (C) Concerned department (D) Both A and B

Q#15 : GST is a .... based tax on consumption of goods and services.

(A) Origin (B) Destiny (C) Development (D) Destination

**Q#16 : The Central Board of Excise and Customs (CBE(C) announced that every year ....
will be considered as GST Day.**

(A) April 1 (B) March 1(C) June 1 (D) July 1

Q#17 : What is Integrated Goods and Services Tax

(A) Tax on international trade (B) Tax imposed on interstate trade (C) Tax imposed on value additions to exports (D) Tax imposed on imported goods and services

Q#18 : GST is _____

a) a value added tax b) tax on goods and services c) tax on consumer goods and services d) none of the above

Quiz # GST-GEN -1-02

Level -2

Q#01: Which article spells formation of GST Council?
a. 270 , b. 246A (2), c. 269A (1), d. 279A

Q#02 : Which of the following is/are true?
a. Both the State and Centre will have power to make laws on taxation of goods and services.
b. Parliament's law will not override a state law on GST. c. Both (a) and (b) d. Neither (a) nor (b)

Q#03 : Who of the following will be the members of the GST Council?
a) Union Finance Minister & Chief Ministers of States b) Union Finance Minister & Union Minister of State in charge of Revenue or Finance c) Union Minister of State in charge of Revenue or Finance & Chief Ministers of States d) Union Finance Minister, Union Minister of State in charge of Revenue or Finance & Chief Ministers of States

Q#04 : GST will be levied on.....................
(a) Manufacturers (b) Retailers (c) Consumers (d) All of the above

Q#05 : Which of the following good will not be covered under the GST bill?
(a) Cooking gas (LPG) (b) Liquor (c) Petrol (d) All of the above

Q#06 : Combined Stake of Central and State Government in GSTN is
(A) 20% (B) 25% (C) 49% (D) 51%

Q#07 : What is location of supply in case of import of goods?

A Customs port where the goods are cleared B Location of the importer C Place where the goods are delivered after clearance from customs port D Owner of the goods

Q#08 : Which state became the first state of India to ratify GST bill?

(A) Bihar (B) Telangana (C) Assam (D) Andhra Pradesh

Q#09 : In which year concept of GST was first introduced by Indian Government?

(A) Atal Behari Bajpayee in 2000 (B) Vijay Kelkar in 2004 (C) P Chidambarm in 2005 (D) Finance Minister in Feb 2006

Q#10 : Who is the chairman of GST council?

(A) RBI Governor (B) Prime Minister (C) Finance secretary (D) Union Finance Minister

Q#11 : A special purpose vehicle .... has been launched to cater the needs of GST.
(A) GSTS (B) GSTR (C) GSTM (D) GSTN

Q#12 :Input Means:

A) Any Goods Excluding Capital Goods B) Any Goods including Capital Goods C) Capital Goods Only D) Capital goods used for the furtherance of the Business

Q#13 : The last date for the filing of GSTR-9 for FY 17-18 (y/e 31.3.18)

A) 30.6.18, B) 30.9.18, C) 31.12.18 D) 31.7.18

Q#14 : Are Supplies to UN Agencies taxable under GST?

A) Yes B) Taxable at Supply Point and Refundable on submission of Purchase statement C) Both (A) and (B) D) GST not applicable for supplies to UN Agencies

Q#15 : The normal nature of assessment in GST is:

A) Self assessment B) Provisional Assessment C) Best Judgment Assessment D) Protective Assessment

Q#02 : Minimum notice period for conducting departmental audit

A) 7 working days B) 15 working days C) 21 working days D) No minimum period specified.

Q#16 : From the date of the commencement of departmental audit, it should normally be completed by:

A) 12 Months B) 9 Months C) 6 Months D) 3 Months

Q#17 : Inter-state supplies means:

A) Any-supply where the location of the supplier and the place of supply are in the same state
B) Any supply where the location of supplier and the place of supply are in different states
C) Any supply where location of the supplier and place of supply are outside the country
D) Any supply where location of the supplier or place of supply are outside the country

Q#18 : Place of supply of goods under GST means?

A) location of the goods at the time at which the movement of goods terminates for delivery to the recipient
B) location of the goods at the time at which movement of goods commences for delivery to the recipient
C) location of the principle place of business of the supplier
D) location of the principle place of business of the recipient

Q#19 : Place of supply where the goods are assembled or installed?

A) Place of supplier B) Place of recipient C) Place where materials for assembling or installation are delivered to the recipient D) Place of the such assembly or installation

Q#20 : The default rule of place of supply of services made to a registered person shall be ....?

A) Location of recipient B) Location of service provider C) Location where service is provided D) Location where agreement for rendering of service is executed

Q#21 : The default place of supply of services made to any person other than a registered person if address on record exist, shall be ....?

A) Location of service provider B) Location where service is rendered C) Location where agreement for rendering of service is executed D) Location of the recipient

Q#22 : Compensation to states under GST (Compensation to States) Act , 2017 is paid by

a) Central Government from consolidated fund of India b) Central Government from GST compensation fund of India c) Central Government directly from the collection of compensation cess d) GST Council under Constitution of India.

Q#23 : The first committee to design GST model was headed by

a) Vijay Kelkar b) P Chidambaram c) Asim Das Gupta d) None of the above

Q#24 : Works contract under GST is goods used in work relating to

a) Immovable property b) Both movable and immovable property c) Immovable property treated as supply of service d) Immovable property treated as supply of goods

Q#25 : IGST deals with

a) Composition scheme b) Time of supply c) Service tax on imported services d) None of the above

Q#26 : Full-fledged GST was recommended by

a) Raja Chellaiah committee b) GST Council c) Vijay Kelkar Task Force d) Man Mohan Singh Commission

Q#27 : One of the following taxes is subsumed under GST

a) Tax on motor spirit c) Luxury Tax b) Tax on production of alcohol d) Tax on electricity

Q#28 : One of the following taxes is not subsumed under GST

a) Octroi by local authorities b) Entry tax by State Governments c) Entertainment tax by local authorities d) Tax on lottery by State Governments

Q#29 : President of India gave assent to the Central GST Law on:

a) 18th April 2014 c) 22nd April 2015 b) 5th April 2017 d) 12th April 2017

Q#30 : GST Council constituted on

a) 12th September 2016 c) 13th September 2015 b) 20th September 2014 d) 16th September 2016

Q#31 :Which of the following is subsumed under Central GST?

a) Central Sales Tax c) Central Excise Duty b) Service Tax d) all of the above

Q#32 : Which of the is excluded from the definition of goods / services

a) securities and money c) Only Securities b) Only Money d) None of the above

Q#33 : ITC respect to goods lost, stolen, destroyed or written off, gifted, given as free samples are:

a) 100% Allowed, b) 50% Allowed, c) Not Allowed. D) None of the above

Q#34 : Which of the following taxes leviable on Imports?

a) CGST b) IGST c) SGST d) all of the above

Q#35 : Who is called a Deemed Supplier of Services?

A) Job Worker B) ISD C) Agent D) Sister Concern

Q#36 : Both Central and State Governments have simultaneous power to levy GST on :

A) Intra-State Supplies Only B) Interstate Supply Only C) Import D) Both Intra-State and Inter-State Supply

Quiz # GST-GEN -1-3
Level 3

Q#01: Which of the following country is first to implement GST?

(A) USA (B) France (C) China (D) Switzerland

Q#02: The country with highest GST Rate in the world is :

(A) USA (B) India (C) China (D) Greece

Q#03: GST comes under which amendment bill?

(A) 101 (B) 120 (C) 122 (D) 115

Q#04: GSTN is formed under which Act?

(A) Banking Regulation Act 1949 (B) RBI Act 1934 (C) Indian Partnership Act, 1932 (D) Companies Act, 2013

Q#05: The recommendation of the GST Council will be

A) Mandatory B) Only Advisory Power C) Mandatory and sometimes Advisory D) Mandatory on States only

Q#06: The decision of the GST Council should be taken based on majority votes not less than

A) ½ of the weighted votes B) 2/3rd of the weighted votes C) 1/3rd of the weighted votes D) 3th of the Weighted Votes

Q#07: The weigh tage of the votes of the Central Government in GST Council Decision will be

A) ½ of the votes B) 2/3rd of the votes C) 1 /3rd of the votes D) 3/4th of the Votes

Q#08: The quorum required for a meeting of the GST Council will be

A) ½ of the members B) 2/3rd of the members C) 1/3rd of the members D) 3/4th of the members

Q#09: A special Audit is conducted by :

A) The CGST Officials B) The SGST Officials C) CA or Cost Accountant nominated by the Commissioner D) Practicing CA appointed by Taxpayer

Q#10: The expenses for conducting a special audit are borne by:

A) The Government alone B) The Dealer alone C) As per order of the government D) Equally shared by Government & Dealer

Q#11: Maximum permissible Adjournment in GST for personal hearing:

A) 1 Adjournment B) 2 Adjournments C) 3 Adjournments D) Any number of Adjournments within 5 years, as necessary

Q#12: Under GST, in case of goods delivered to transporter, Place of supply means where the goods are supplied on board for conveyance (such as vessel, an aircraft, a train or motor vehicle).

A) Location of supplier B) Location of recipient C) Location at which such goods are taken on board D) Registered office of carrier

Q#13: Which one of the following shall not be treated as supply;

A) Rental B) Lease C) Actionable claim D) License

Q#14: Which one of the following items are taxable under GST

A) Aviation fuel B) Liquefied petroleum Gas

C) Natural Gas D) High Speed Diesel oil

Q#15: Works contract is :

A) Supply of goods B) Supply of services C) Supply of Goods and Services D) None of the above

Q#16: Roll out of GST requires constitutional amendment because

a) existing laws were cascading b) the powers to levy were exclusive i.e. the state had power to tax the goods but not services and centre had power to tax services and levy on goods c) there are separate laws for goods and services d) All of the above

Q#17: Under GST, Aggregate Turnover does not include

a) Exempt supplies b) export of goods and/ or services c) All taxable supplies d) value of inward supplies on which tax has been paid under reverse charge

Q#18: In a Supply of Goods, possession of the goods are transferred. But, the title on the same will be transferred at a future date. It is considered as :

A) Normal Sale of goods B) Sales on Approval Basis or Hire Purchases C) Rent a Car D) None of the Above

Quiz # GST-GEN -1-4
Level -4

Q#01: After SCN (Show Cause Notice) for short / irregular tax payment without any fraud, what is the option available to the dealer?

A) Compounding of the Offence B) Remittance of Tax and interest, within 30 days of the receipt of the SCN C) Remittance of Tax, interest and 25% of the tax as penalty, within 30 days of the receipt of the SCN D) Remittance of Tax, interest and 50% of the tax as penalty, within 30 days of the receipt of the SCN

Q#02: Place of supply of services in relation to mobile connection for pre-paid customers through sale of vouchers shall be ....?

A) Location of supplier B) Location of recipient C) Location where such pre-payment is received by local seller D) None of these

Q#03: Mr. A of Ahmedabad, is constructing a house in Mumbai and appoints Mr D of Delhi to provide architectural services with regard to proposed construction of house located in Mumbai. The place of supply would be :

a) Ahmedabad b) Delhi c) Mumbai d) Any of them

Q#04: B of Bangalore, conducts training for employees of Software Ltd, of New Delhi, registered under GST, in Resort located in Shimla, the place of supply would be:
a) Bangalore b) New Delhi c) Simla d) Any of them

Q#05: B of Bangalore, conducts training for employees of Software Ltd, of New Delhi, not registered under GST, in Resort located in Shimla, the place of supply would be:
a) Bangalore b) New Delhi c) Simla d) Any of them

Q#06: Mr. M of Mumbai (not registered under GST), purchases air ticket from Airlines Ltd, of Chennai, for travel from New Delhi to NEW YORK via Dubai. The place of supply would be
(a) Mumbai (b) Chennai, (c) New Delhi, (d) New York

Q#07: Mr. M of Mumbai, an employee of G & Co, registered in Kolkata, purchases air ticket from Airlines Ltd, of Chennai, for business travel from New Delhi to NEW YORK via Dubai. The place of supply would be
(a) Mumbai, (b) Chennai, (c) New Delhi, (d) Kolkata

Quiz GST- Registration

Quiz # GST- REG -1-01
Level -1

Q#01: Which one of the following is true?

A) A person can collect tax only if he is registered
B) Registered person not liable to collect tax till his aggregate turnover exceeds threshold limit
C) A person can collect the tax during the period of his provisional registration
D) None of the above

Q#02: Which form is to be used for registration?

A) Form GSTR -1A . B) Form GSTR – 2 C) Form GST REG-01 D)Form GST REG

Q#03: Minimum Registrable Turnover Limit in GST

A) Rs.4Lakhs B) Rs.1.5 Crores C) Rs.10Lakhs D) Rs.19Lakhs

Q#04: Under GST, Alcoholic Liquor for industrial and other usages is

A) Non Taxable B) Taxable C) Exempted D) Zero rated

Q#05: Taxable Minimum Turnover Limit in GST (other than NE & Special Areas)

A) Rs.9 Lakhs B) Rs.1.5 Crores C) Rs.5 Lakhs D) Rs.20 Lakhs

Q#06: Aggregate Turnover Limit for Opting Composition Scheme (other than NE Region)

A) Rs.60 Lakhs B) Rs.50 Lakhs C) Rs.1 Crore D) Rs.1.5 Crore

Q#07: The Number of Digits in the PAN based GSTIN registration Number will be

A) 10 Digits B) 12 Digits C) 14 Digits D) 15 Digits

Quiz # GST- REG -1-02
Level -2

Q#01: What is the time period to give clarification in respect of the GST REG-03 from the part of the applicant of the registration?

A) Online submission of GST-REG-04 within 3 common working days from the receipt of GST REG-03
B) Online submission of GST-REG-04 within 5 common working days from the receipt of GST REG-03
C) Online submission of GST-REG-04 within 7 common working days from the receipt of GST REG-03.
D) Online submission of GST-REG-04 within 10 common working days from the receipt of GST REG-03

Q#02: A registered taxable person is liable to show his GSTN number :

A) Tax Invoice B) Name plate of Principal Place and additional place of business C) Tax Invoice and also at Name plate of Principal Place and additional place of business D) Tax Invoice and also at Name plate of Principal Place

Q#03: On crossing 90% of the threshold limit, a dealer has to get his business unit registered under GST within:

A) 10 Days B) 15 Days C) 30Days D) 90 Days

Q#04: To get final registration certificate, Provisional registration certificate holders has to e-file online registration application with the prescribed scanned documents within

A) 1 months from the appointed day B) 2 months from the appointed day C) 3 months from the appointed day D) 6 months from the appointed day

Q#05: A person having multiple businesses require

a) Single registration for all businesses owned by him b) One registration for each State c) each business separately d) none of the above

Quiz # GST- REG -1-03

Level 3

Q#01: The Items which will be taxable both under current Central Excise Law and new GST even after the implementation of the GST Act.

A) Motor Spirit B) Alcoholic Liquor for Human Consumption C) Tobacco and Tobacco Products
D) Natural Gas

Q#02: The Dealers who are not eligible for any Threshold Limit in the minimum Registrable Turnover?

A) Casual Dealers and Non-Resident Taxable Persons B) Input Service Distributors and Dealers making supply through Electronic Commerce Operator. C) Dealers making interstate Supplies and those having Reverse tax Liability D) All of the Above

Q#03: Head Office of a Business group enter into a centralised service contract in respect of its subsidiary units or branch business places and wants to distribute IPT among them and that dealer also conducts normal taxable business activities. The type of Registration required to that Head Office will be :

A) ISD Registration Only B) Normal SGST-CGST and IGST Registration Only C) Both ISD Registration and Normal SGST-CGST & IGST RegistrationD) No registration Required

Q#04: One Business Group has 35 Business Verticals within a state and has to take separate GST Registration under the same PAN. How many Online Registration applications with scanned documents have to be filed by that Business Group?

A) 35 Separate Applications in GST REG-01 B) Only One Registration Application incorporating the entire business verticals in One Go C) Either of the above at the option of the Business Group D) Either of the above at the discretion of the Proper Office

Q#05: If the proper officer needs any clarification in the REG-01 filed by a dealer, what will be the option available to him?

A) Online issuance of GST REG-03 within 3 common working days from the receipt of the GST REG-01
B) Make field visit C) Either a) or b) D) Provisional issuance of the registration certificate

Q#06: The proper officer is not satisfied with the clarification given by the appellant. What will be the fate of such registration application?

A) The Registration application will be rejected by issuing GST REG-05 B) Provisional registration will be granted C) Either a) or b) D) The same will be kept pending for field enquiry

Q#07: What is the prescribed time period to apply for GSTN by a non-resident taxable person?

A) Within 5 days from the crossing of the threshold limit B) Within 7 days from the commencement of business C) Within 30 days from the commencement of business D) At least 5 days prior to the commencement of business

Q#08: A goods vehicle contains 10 consignments having a total value of Rs. 4 Lakhs. However, the individual value of each consignment is less than Rs.50,000. The goods vehicle should carry prescribed documents (like e-way bill) :

A) 11 e-generated prescribed documents from the common portal for transportation B) Only One e-generated prescribed document in respect of the entire consignment C) 10 e-generated documents for each consignment D) No e-generated Document needed

Q#09: A goods vehicle contains 10 consignments having a total value of Rs.5 Lakhs. Out of the above 2 consignments are of a transactions value of Rs.60, 000 and 70,000, while individual value of the remaining 8 consignments are less than Rs.50,000. It should carry e-generated documents.

A) 10 e-generated prescribed documents from the common portal for transportation B) 2 e-generated prescribed document in respect of all consignments C) 2 e-generated documents in respect of the consignment having transaction value of more than Rs.50,000. D) No E-generated Document needed

Q#10: A supplier (in other than special category states) is liable to get registered under GST only if his aggregate turnover in a financial year crosses Rs. 20 lakh, if he is

a) an interstate supplier b) an intra-state supplier c) Electronic commerce operator d) Person liable to pay GST under reverse charge

Q#11: Which of the following is not eligible for Composition Scheme

a) Inter-state supply of goods b) manufacture of notified goods c) Person supplying goods through e-commerce sector d) All of the above

Q#12: Who of the following require mandatory registration irrespective of threshold value?

a) Casual taxable person c) non-resident taxable person b) Input service distributor d) all of the above

Q#13: All Registered Dealers under earlier laws will be automatically migrated in to GST on provisional basis except:

A) Local VAT Dealer B) Dealer having both VAT and CST C) Manufacturing Units availing Cenvat D) ISD

Quiz # GST- REG -1-04
Level 4

Q#01: A dealer crossed the registrable limit on 30-09-2017. But, he applied for GST registration on 25-10-2017 and he was granted GST registration on 28-10- 2017. What will be his effective date of registration?

A) 30-09-2017 B) 01-10-2017 C) 25-10-2017 D) 28-10-2017

Q#02: A Dealer applied for Registration and crossed the taxable limit before getting GSTIN. How can the recipient of supplies can avail Input Tax Credit on purchases from such a dealer?

A) By Receiving Revised Tax Invoice from the supplier B) By Receiving Credit Notes C) By Receiving Debit Notes D) No Option to avail Input Tax Credit at all.

Q#03: In GST Input Tax will be allowed only on the basis of Matching Principles. It allows Input Tax Credit on Manual Basis only in the case of :

A) ISD B) New Registrants who had crossed taxable limits even before getting GSTIN due to delay from the part of the department C) Job Worker D) Exporter

Q#04: The dealers liable to make estimated Advance Tax Remittance to obtain GST Registration are:

A) ISD B) Dealers having Business Verticals C) Casual Dealers and Non-Resident Taxable Person D) E-Commerce Operator and Aggregator of Branded Services

Q#05: If a Registration is cancelled, the Electronic Credit Ledger or Electronic Cash Ledger are debited by

A) ITC availed on Stock, Semi-Finished Goods or finished Goods and Capital Goods B) Output Tax payable on Such Goods C) ITC availed on Stock, Semi-Finished Goods , finished Goods and Capital Goods or Output Tax payable on Such Goods whichever is Higher D) No Tax Liability on Cancellation of Registration

Q#06: A dealer has been issued Provisional Registration Certificate, but is not liable for registration under GST (due to the below registrable limit or items not liable to tax under GST). In the provisional registration period, the dealer may

A) Apply for the cancellation of the provisional registration B) Wait for the completion of the provisional registration period of 6 months C) Apply for Cancellation only after One year from the appointed day D) Not needed to take any action

Q#07: If any actions are instituted against the admissibility of ITC under earlier law, under GST it will be treated as:

A) Collected as a tax arrears under earlier law B) Collected as a tax arrears in GST C) Actions under earlier law will get nullified. D) None of the Above

Q#08: A manufacturer was not liable to get registered in the earlier law (because he was manufacturing exempted goods under earlier law), but now became taxable under GST. How the tax element involved in his raw material stock or semi-finished goods or finished goods on the appointed day will be treated in GST?

A) Refunded under earlier laws B) Allowed as ITC in GST C) Refunded under GST law D) No ITC Credit

Quiz GST- ITC & Tax

Quiz # GST-ITC-1-01
Level -1

Q#01 : CGST and SGST will be levied on

A) Intra-state supply B) Inter-state supply C) Import D) Export

Q#02 : The Tax applicable to interstate supplies will be:

A) SGST Only B) CGST Only C) IGST Only D) CGST + IGST

Q#03 : The Tax which are levied on an intra-state or Local supply of goods and / or Services

A) SGST Only B) CGST Only C) Both SGST and CGST D) IGST Only

Q#04 : The person in charge of the conveyance carrying any consignment of goods exceeding the value of _____, shall carry prescribed documents (EWaybill)

A) Rs.50,000 B) Rs.1,00,000 C) Rs. 10,000 D) Rs. 100 lakhs

Quiz # GST-ITC-1-02
Level 2

Q#01 : The permissible order of cross utilisation of IGST credit over the tax liabilities

A) SGST, CGST and IGST B) IGST, CGST and SGST C) CGST, IGST and SGST D) CGST, SGST and IGST

Q#02 : Electronic Credit Ledger is Credited by

A) Cash Deposit towards Tax remittance B) Input Tax on IGST,CGST and SGST C) Cash Deposit towards Fees, Fine, Interest and Penalty D) Advance tax Remittance

Q#03 : Electronic Cash Ledger is Credited by

A) Cash Deposit towards Tax remittance, Fine, Interest and Penalty B) IPT on IGST,CGST and SGST C) Cash Deposit towards Fees, Fine, Interest and Penalty Only D) Advance tax Remittance Only

Q#04 : The Tax Liability of a person receiving the goods instead of the person supplying the goods will be knows as:

A) Purchase Tax B) Reverse Tax C) Reverse Charge D) Supply Tax

Q#05 : All pending Refunds, Appeals, Revision & Review related to earlier enactment will be disposed in GST regime as per:

A) respective Earlier Law B) GST Law C) Either earlier Law or GST law, at the option of the dealer D) Either earlier Law or GST law, at the option of the proper officer

Q#06 : Inspections can be conducted at the business places of, _____

A) Taxable persons B) Transporter of goods C) Owner or Operator of Godowns/Ware house D) All of the above

Q#07 : Input tax credit as per the VAT law will be carried forward as

A) CGST B) SGST C) IGST D) Not allowed under GST

Q#08 : Input tax credit is not available on ....?

A) Goods used for personal use B) Trading goods C) Capital goods D) None of the above

Q#09 : When does the liability to pay tax on goods arise?

a) at the time of supply b) at the time when goods reach supplier c) at the time of preparing invoice d) None of the above

Q#10 : Credit of CGST can be utilised for the payment of:

a) SGST b) UTGST c) IGST d) none of the above

Q#11 : Limit of OTC payment through challan in Bank by cash, cheque or demand draft :

a) Ten thousand rupees b) Two thousand rupees c) One thousand rupees d) No limit

Q#12 : Zero rated supply includes supplies made

a) By SEZ unit in India b) by SEZ in India or to SEZ in India c) to SEZ unit in India d) None of the above

Quiz # GST-ITC-1-03
Level 3

Q#01 : The TDS Remittance of the Deductor will be shown in the :

A) Electronic ITC Ledger of the Deductor B) Electronic ITC Ledger of the Deductee

C) Electronic Cash Ledger of the Deductor D) Electronic Cash Ledger of the Deductee

Q#02 : ITC on Capital Goods used for Business dealing with Taxable Goods will be allowed in GST in :

A) 3 Monthly Instalments B) 12 Monthly Instalments C) 36 Monthly Instalments D) Full amount on Purchase

Q#03 : Whether Taxi aggregators like Ola, Uber, etc. (not owning cars or not employing drivers) are Liable to Pay Tax In GST

A) Yes B) No C) Liability to Pay Tax is on the Actual Service Providers D) Exempted

Q#04 : The Unadjusted Cenvat Credit under earlier law will be transferred and credited to

A) IGST ITC B) CGST ITC C) SGST ITC D) Any of the Above

Q#05 :For a dealer defaulter of non-payment of some Tax dues :

A) Refund is adjusted over arrear dues B) 80% of the Refund is allowed on a Provisional basis. C) Refund Application is withheld D) 20% of the Refund is allowed on a Provisional basis

Q#06 :Refund amount due is less than Rs.1000

A) Full Amount is allowed within 3 working days without any document verification B) 80% of the Refund is allowed on Provisional basis. C) Refund Application is Rejected. D) Refund Application is Withheld

Q#07 : The Tax wrongly paid under IGST instead of CGST/ SGST. The adjustment would be through

A) Refund of Tax paid B) Automatic System Adjustment C) IGST may be adjusted against CGST / SGST due D) Any of the Above.

Q#08 : In case of delayed refunds, the tax payer is eligible to interest

A) 1 Month After the date of receipt of the refund Application B) 2 Months After the date of receipt of the refund Application C) 3 Months After the date of receipt of the refund Application D) Not eligible to any Interest .

Q#09 : The Time Period for completing Job Work on Capital Goods to avail Input Tax Credit on inputs sent for Job Work will be:

A) 90 Days B) 180 Days C) 1 Year D) 2 Years

Q#10 : The TDS deduction details will be auto populated from GSTR-7 and will be shown as a credit in the Electronic cash Ledger of :

A) TDS Deductor B) TDS Deductee C) Either of the Above as per the Option of the Deductor D) None of the Above

Q#11 : What will be the amount carried forward as CGST/SGST from the earlier law and shown in the return filed for the period ending as on appointed date?

A) No amount will be carried forward from the earlier law B) Amount which is admissible under earlier law but may not be admissible under GST C) Amount which is admissible under GST but may not be admissible under earlier law D) Amount which is admissible under both the GST and earlier law

Q#12 : To avail credit of tax on inputs held in stock by a dealer who was exempted from payment of tax as per earlier law, the said inputs may be used for making :

A) Taxable supplies under GST B) Exempt supplies C) Either taxable or exempt supplies D) Both taxable and exempt supplies

Q#13 : A taxable person shall not be entitled to take input tax credit in respect of any goods services to him after the expiry of .... from the date of tax invoice related to such supply?

A) One month B) Six months C) One year D) Two years

Q#14 : ITC is allowed on tax paid on capital goods used to produce taxable goods for business purpose, in .... instalments in GST

A) 12 B) 5 C) 60 D) 1

Q#15 : Tax is paid on which value?

a) Transaction value c) manufacturing cost b) MRP d) MRP or Transaction value whichever is higher

Quiz # GST-ITC-1-04
Level 4

Q#01: One Dealer has a credit of Rs.5 Lakhs in his Electronic ITC Ledger. That dealer has Interest arrears dues of 6 Lakhs and Penalty Dues of Rs.2 Lakhs. How much, he has to deposit to settle all Dues?

A) Rs.3/-Lakhs B) Rs.6/-Lakhs C) Rs.2/-Lakhs D) Rs.8/-Lakhs

Q#02: GST of Rs.3 Lakhs is levied on an Unregistered Dealer for some default. What will be the mode of Tax remittance by such unregistered dealer?

A) Manual Challan Remittance B) Direct Cash Remittance to the concerned Head of Account C) E-Payment by logging in to the Temporary Registration No. D) Any of the Above

Q#03: Goods are sent for Job Work before 1ˢᵗ July 2017, and the same were not received back within 6 months and even after the time extension period. What will be its effect in GST?

A) Deemed Supply of the Registered Dealer who sent the goods for Job Work B) Deemed Supply of Job Worker C) No Taxable Event D) Either of the Party Liable to Pay GST

Q#04: Goods are sent for Job Work before 1ˢᵗ July 2017, and the same were not received back within 6 months but returned within the 2 months of extended period allowed. What will be its effect in GST?

A) Exempted Supply B) No Taxable Event C) Sales Return of the Registered Dealer D) Deemed Supply of the Registered Job Worker

Q#05: Following Free Supply of Goods and Services considered is / are considered as Taxable Supply in GST.

A) Free Transfer of Business Assets to some one else or Assets retained after De-Registration B) Temporary Application of Business Asset for a non-business needs or self supply of goods or Services C) Stock/ Branch Transfer Out to another State D) All of the Above

Q#06: A Dealer has SGST Credit of Rs.3 Lakhs in his ITC Ledger and at the same time, he has a CGST liability of Rs.2 Lakhs. What amount should be deposited by that dealer to his Electronic Cash Ledger maintained in GSTN Portal to file a Valid return

A) No Deposit is Required as full liability can be adjusted B) Rs.2 Lakh C) Rs.3 Lakh D) Rs.5 Lakh

Q#07: One Dealer has an IGST Credit of Rs.4 Lakhs in his ITC Ledger and the same time he has an IGST Liability of Rs.2 Lakhs, CGST Liability of Rs.3 Lakhs and SGST Liability of Rs.5 Lakhs. What amount that dealer should have to deposit to his Electronic Cash Ledger to discharge his tax liability and to file a Valid return

A) Rs.6 Lakhs (Rs.1 Lakh to CGST and Rs.5 Lakh to SGST) B) Rs.6 Lakhs (Rs.1 Lakh to SGST and Rs.5 Lakh to CGST) C) Rs. 6 Lakhs (Rs.1 Lakh to IGST and Rs.5 Lakhs to SGST) D) Rs.6 Lakhs (Rs.2 Lakhs to IGST and Rs.4 Lakhs to SGST)

Q#08: The unutilized ITC in the electronic ITC Ledger will be allowed to a new entity on business as a whole transfer, merger, demerger, amalgamation and on lease if the transfer deed provides for:

A) Transfer of all the Assets of the Existing Business Concern B) Transfer of all the Liabilities of the Existing Business Concern C) Transfer of both Assets and Liabilities of the existing business concern including credit on Electronic Cash Ledger D) Unutilized ITC will not be transferred to new entity in any case.

Q#09: One Dealer paying tax under Normal Scheme switch over in to Composition Scheme. What will be the fate of his already ITC availed on existing stock and Credit balance on Electronic ITC Ledger?

A) Reversal of ITC on Existing Stock by Debiting the Electronic ITC Ledger and Electronic Cash Ledger B) The balance ITC Ledger after Reversal of ITC on Stock will be lapsed C) Both (A) and (B) above D) No Reversal of ITC

Q#10: On 20-12-2017, One Supplier / Recipient detected some omission of invoices related to the return period of June, 2017. What will be their option to incorporate such supply or receipt in their self-assessment returns?

A) To add such invoices in the amendment table in respect of the return period of June, 2017 by revising the return. B) To add Such invoices in the amendment table in respect of the return period of September,2017 C) To add Such invoices in the amendment table in respect of the return period of December,2017 D) To add Such invoices in the amendment table in respect of the return period of January,2018

Q#11: Which ledgers are available in dashboard of the dealer in GSTN Portal

Ledger showing GST Tax Liabilities Only based on the self assessment returns B) Ledger showing GST Tax, Interest, Fine, Fee, and Penalty based on the self assessment returns. C) Ledger showing all Tax Liabilities including self assessment, best judgment Assessment and Appellate Orders, interest, Fine, Fee and Penalties. D) Ledger showing all Tax Liabilities including self assessment and best judgment Assessment, interest, Fine, Fee and Penalties (excluding that as per the Appellate Orders)

Q#12: On 24-06-2017, B, the Buyer remitted an Advance Amount of Rs10 Lakhs towards the total order value of 50 Lakhs to Supplier S. The Actual Supply of the goods and the issuance of the invoice will take place only in the month of December, 2017. In which Month, the supplier has to remit tax on the Advance Receipts? In which month, the dealer who remitted advance can take ITC credit on the same?

A) By 20th of July, 2017. But No ITC Credit to other Party for the month of June, 2017 B) By 20th of January, 2017 on full amount with ITC Credit to other Party C) Both (A) and (B) Above D) None of the Above

Q#13: The provisional ITC credit of Rs.50,000 -was auto reversed in absence of any matching invoice and tax remittance from the part of the selling dealer and added back to the tax liability for the succeeding month with interest. On taking up the issue, the supplier realised the omission and declared the same in subsequent return period and remitted tax on the same. Consequently:

A) Electronic Cash Ledger of the Supplier of the Goods will be credited with the ITC B) Electronic Cash Ledger of the Recipient of the Goods will be credited with the ITC C) Electronic Cash Ledger of the Supplier of the Goods will be credited with the ITC with interest remittance D) The Electronic Cash Ledger of the Recipient of the Goods will be credited with the ITC with interest remittance

Q#14: A dealer issued a tax invoice showing more taxable value or charging more tax than the actual. What is the remedy?

A) Seller to issue a Credit Note on Buyer for the excess taxable value/tax on or before 30th September or the date of the filing of the Annual Return whichever is earlier B) Buyer to issue a Debit Note for the excess taxable value/tax on or before 30th September or the date of the filing of the Annual Return whichever is earlier C) Seller to issue a Credit Note for the excess taxable value /tax within 30 days of such detection D) Buyer to issue a Debit Note for the excess taxable value /tax within 30 days of such detection

Q#15: A dealer issued a tax invoice showing less taxable value or charging more tax than the actual. What is the remedy for the Seller?

A) To issue a Credit Note for the excess taxable value/tax on or before 30th September or the date of the filing of the Annual Return whichever is earlier B) To issue a Debit Note for the excess taxable value/tax on or before 30th September or the date of the filing of the Annual Return whichever is earlier C) To issue a Credit Note for the excess taxable value /tax within 30 days of such detection D) To issue a Debit Note for the excess taxable value /tax within 30 days of such detection

Q#16: Where the goods sold paying VAT within 6 months prior to the appointed day are returned by an unregistered person within 6 months from the appointed day, the registered person can,

A) Re sale the goods without paying GST B) The VAT paid will be lost C) Claim for refund of VAT under VAT rules D) Pay tax on reverse charge basis

Quiz # GST-ITC-1A-01
Level -1

Q#01 : Which Return contains details outward supplies of goods / services

(a) GSTR-1, (b) GSTR-1A, (c) GSTR-1A, (d) GSTR-2A,

Q#02 : Which Return contains details of inward supplies of goods / services

(a) GSTR-2, (b) GSTR-3, (c) GSTR-4, (d) GSTR-6,

Q#03 : GSTR2A Contains auto-drafted communication in respect of

(a) goods and services procured by it and uploaded by the supplier. (b) distribution of credit by Input Service Distributor in FORM GSTR-6 (c) tax deducted at source from the payments to the receiver based on FORM GSTR-7 of the deductor (d) All of the above

Q#04 : Which Monthly return is filed after finalization of outward supplies and inward supplies

(a) GSTR-1, (b) GSTR-3 (c) GSTR-6, (d) GSTR-7

Q#05 : Which Monthly Return to be filed in lieu of GSTR-3 when the due date for filing FORM GSTR-1 and FORM GSTR-2 has been extended

(a) GSTR-1, (b) GSTR-3B (c) GSTR-6, (d) GSTR-7

Q#01 : Which Return is filed by a registered taxable person under composition scheme

(a) GSTR-1, (b) GSTR-1A, (c) GSTR-3, (d) None of the above

Q#06 : Which Return is filed by a registered taxable person under composition scheme

(a) GSTR-1, (b) GSTR-4, (c) GSTR-9, (d) Both (b) & (c)

Q#07 : Which Return is to be furnished by nonresident taxable person

(a) GSTR-1, (b) GSTR-5, (c) GSTR-3, (d) None of the above

Q#08 : Details uploaded by the supplier in GSTR-1 would be communicated to the receiver by:

(a) Part A of FORM GSTR-2A auto-drafted form (b) Part B of FORM GSTR-1A auto-drafted form,
(c) Part A of FORM GSTR-3B, auto-drafted form (d) None of the above

Quiz # GST-ITC-1A-02
Level 2

Q#01 : GSTR2A Contains auto-drafted communication in respect of

(a) goods and services procured by it and uploaded by the supplier. (b) distribution of credit by Input Service Distributor in FORM GSTR-6 (c) tax deducted at source from the payments to the receiver based on FORM GSTR-7 of the deductor (d) All of the above

Q#02 : Examples for Deemed Supply of Services

A) Renting of Immovable Property and Temporary Transfer of Intellectual Property Right

B) Works contract C) Services of Aggregators D) All of the Above

Q#03 : One dealer has sent some goods to another dealer for Sales on Approval Basis. In absence of any confirmation even after 6 months, it will be treated as :

A) Sales Return B) Deemed Supply of Goods C) Purchase return D) None of the Above

Q#04 : Valuation of the supply of Goods for GST is computed on:

A) Market Value B) MRP price C) Transaction Value D) MRP price or Transaction value whichever is higher

Q#05 : In the case of all Zero Rated Export and Deemed Export, the GSTR-1 must contain :

A) 4 digit HSN Code for Goods only B) 4 Digit HSN Code for Goods and Accounting Code of Services C) 8-Digit HSN Code for Goods and Accounting Code of Services along with Shipping /Bill of Export Number D) HSN Code is optional.

Q#06 : In case of Export and Import, it is mandatory to quote HSN Code in invoice:

A) 2 Digits Level of HSN Code B) 4 Digits Level of HSN Code C) 6 Digits Level of HSN Code D) 8 Digits Level of HSN Code

Q#07 : The dead line for making amendments (in respect of the already filed returns) in subsequent return period is :

A) September, 30th of the Next Financial Year B) December,31st of the Next Financial Year

C) September, 30th of the Next Financial Year or Date of filing of the Annual Return whichever is earlier

D) No Such Dead Line

Q#08 : In an interstate B2C Supplies, a Supplier is liable to report the invoice wise sales or supplies details with specific state code as place of supply in the case of Supplies of value above

A) Rs.5000/- B) Rs.25,000/- C) Rs.1.5/-Lakhs D) Rs.2.5/-Lakhs

Q#09 : In case of Mismatched invoices the correction are permitted

a. At any later stage up to 30th September of the next financial year through: A) Credit Note B) Debit Note C) Amendment Table D) Any of the Above

Q#10 : The GST Returns defaulters will be issued notices by

A) SGST Officials B) CGST Officials C) System generated by GSTN through e-mail/SMS D) Any of the Above

Q#11 : If case of any duplication in the entries in the GSTR-2, then the GSTN will communicate the same to:

A) Both the Supplier and Recipient B) Recipient Only C) Supplier Only D) Either of the above

Q#12 : GSTR-1 should contain details of :

A) All Taxable outward Supplies, including Zero Rated Supply, Export and Interstate Supplies along with supplementary invoice details B) Purchase Return (Being a Deemed Sales) C) Debit Notes/Credit Notes D) All of the Above

Q#13 : GSTR-2 should contain:

A) All Taxable Inward Supplies, Import and Interstate Inward Supplies along with supplementary invoice details B) Sales Return (Being a Deemed Inward Supply) C) Debit Notes/Credit Notes D) All of the Above

Q#14 : Any Rectification of error or omission is to be incorporated in any subsequent return up to the return for the month of

A) March of the same financial year B) April of the subsequent financial year C) September of the subsequent financial year D) December of the subsequent financial year

Quiz # GST-ITC-1A-03
Level 3

Q#01 : Tasks of filing of the GSTR2 involve

A) Verify, validate, modify or delete the supplies along with the debit note and credit notes reported by the supplier in his GSTR-1 B) Make additional entries in respect of the supplies along with the debit note and credit notes details which failed to be reported by the supplier in his GSTR-1 C) Both a) and b) Above D) Individual Inward Supply entry uploading by the recipient

Q#02 : Time period allowed for issuance of a Debit/Credit Note in respect of a Financial Year

A) Within 31st March of the current financial year B) Within 30th April of the succeeding financial year C) Within 30th September of the succeeding financial year D) Within 31stDecember of the succeeding financial year

Q#03 : One dealer has two business verticals at Kozhikode dealing with Computer Systems and another at Palakkad dealing with Iron and steel items. If he makes a purchase of computer items from Kozhikode unit to Palakkad, how that supply will be treated in GST?

A) No Supply invoice and No GST B) At the discretion of the dealer C) Supply invoice should be issued and GST has to be remitted like normal trade transaction D) None of the Above

Q#04 : If any dealer fails to give satisfactory explanation to a Show Cause Notice on Return scrutiny, it may result in

A) Departmental Audit B) Special Audit C) Inspection, Search/Seizure D) Any of the Above

Q#05 : A dealer failed to file return in time. The proper officer completed best judgment assessment. To get the best Judgment deemed to be withdrawn, the dealer may file Return within

a) 7 days of receipt of the best judgment assessment order.b) 15 days of receipt of the best judgment assessment order.c) 30 days of receipt of the best judgment assessment order.d) 60 days of receipt of he best judgment assessment order.

Q#06 : For dealer defaulter of return :

A) Refund would be made on the basis of best judgment by the officer, after adjusting tax liability B) 80% of the Refund is allowed on a Provisional basis. C) Refund Application is withheld D) 20% of the Refund is allowed on a Provisional basis.

Q#07 : In case of B2C interstate supplies where the supply value of less than Rs.2.5-Lakhs, which details are reported in GSTR-1

A) Invoice wise Details B) Tax Rate Wise Aggregate Taxable Value of all the B2C invoices C) Date Wise Details of Aggregate Taxable Value of all the B2C invoices D) Aggregate Taxable Value of all the B2C invoices with Aggregate Tax Figure

Quiz # GST-ITC-1A-04
Level 4

Q#01 : In a B2C supplies for Rs.5 Lakhs from Telungana to Kerala, the State of recipient is not recorded. the tax share will goes to

A) CGST and Telungana SGST (Considering it as a Local Supply) B) CGST and Kerala SGST
C) Full Tax to CGST D) Full Tax to Telungana SGST

Q#02 : One Supplier omitted to report one Supply Transactions in his GSTR-1. But, the Recipient of the Supply uploaded the same being a missing entry in the auto populated inward supply list generated from GSTR-1. If the Supplier admits such an omission, what a course action will be required from the part of the supplier within the permitted period of statement revision?

A) Make separate Uploading of the missing invoices in to GSTR-1 B) View the invoice from the GSTR-2 and confirm the same by ticking C) Insert the missing invoice in to the amendment table D) None of the Above.

Q#03 : After freezing the outward and inward supply list on 18th June, 2017, One dealer realised that in month of May, 2017, 3 sales (outward) transactions were omitted in his GSTR-1. What course of action be taken to incorporate the above outward supply to his return?

A) To revise the monthly return for May, 2017 and incorporate the above transactions

B) To add the above transactions in to the Annual Return for the year of 2017- 18

C) To insert the above transactions in the amendment table for the month of June,2017 at the time of filing GSTR-1 between 01-07-2017 to 10-07-2017

D) None of the Above

Q#04 : One Supplier invoiced for 100 kgs of taxable goods .But, there were delivery of 60 kgs for some reasons. In GST, how this Quantity Variations are adjusted?

A) By Issuing Credit Note by the Supplier and uploading the same in his GSTR1 without correlating the Original Invoice Number B) By Issuing Debit Note by the Supplier and uploading the same in his GSTR1 without correlating the Original Invoice Number C) By Issuing Credit Note by the Supplier and uploading the same in his GSTR1 showing the corresponding Original Invoice Number D) By Issuing Debit Note by the Supplier and uploading the same in his GSTR1 showing the corresponding Original Invoice Number.

Q#05 : A Recipient of inward Supply can avail and utilise ITC on his declared Inward Supplies irrespective of the same declared in the GSTR-1:

A) As and when GSTR-2 is submitted with necessary addition or modifications B) As and when GSTR-3 is submitted with necessary addition or modifications C) On a Provisional Basis for 2 month from the last date of the monthly return period D) Any of the Above

Quiz GST- Miscellaneous

Quiz # GST-MIS-1-01
Level -1

Q#01 :Which of the following Acts were passed and received the President's assent on 12th April, 2017

(a)The Central Goods and Service Tax Act, 2017(CGST), (b) The Integrated Goods and Service Tax Act, 2017(IGST), (c) The Goods and Service Tax (Compensation to States) Act, 2017(Compensation Cess) (d) All of the above

Q#02 :All the states (except J & K) passed their respective SGSTAct by

(a) 30th June, 2017 (b) 1st July 2017 (c) 1st April 2017 (d) None of the above

Q#03 :Jammu & Kashmir passed their SGST Act on

(a) 5th July, 2017 (b) 1st July (c) 1st April 2017 (d) J & K did not pass the SGST Act

Q#04 :Goods and Service Tax(GST) to mean a tax on

(a) supply of goods or services, or both (b) on sale of goods or services or both (c) sale of goods only (d) supply of services only

Q#05: Items not chargeable under GST

(a) Alcoholic Liquor for human consumption (b) Petroleum crude, natural gas and aviation turbine fuel (c) Electricity (d) All of the above

Q#06:Items not chargeable under GST

(a) Alcoholic Liquor for human consumption (b) Tobacco & Tobacco Products (c) Electricity (d) All of the above

Quiz # GST-MIS-1-02
Level -2

Q#01 : Validity of the regular registration certificate?

(a) 1 year (b) 2 years (c) Till end of next financial year (d) Until Cancelled.

Q#02 : State which one is true

GST is payable on chargeable Inter-state stock transfers and branch transfers of same Company (same PAN) (b) GST is payable on Stock Transfers where taxable person has multiple GST registration within the State (with same PAN) (c) No GST is payable on Stock Transfers within the State with single GST registration (d) All of the above

Q#03 : On FREE supplies / samples

(a) GST will be payable on FREE supplies to related persons. (b) No GST will be payable on free gifts / samples to unrelated person, but input tax credit availed in respect of such goods, will have to be reversed. (c) both (a) & (b) (d) None of the above

Q#04 : The details submitted by the outward supplier in Form GSTR 1 shall be furnished to the recipient regular dealer in form

(a) GSTR 4A (b) GSTR 5A (c) GSTR 2A (d) GSTR 6A

Q#05 : The details submitted by the outward supplier in Form GSTR 1 shall be furnished to the recipient composition dealer in form

(a) GSTR 4A (b) GSTR 5A (c) GSTR 2A (d) GSTR 6A

Q#06 : The details submitted by the outward supplier in Form GSTR 1 shall be furnished to the ISD in form

(a) GSTR 4A (b) GSTR 5A (c) GSTR 2A (d) GSTR 6A

Q#07 : Any modification / deletion done by the recipient to the details contained in Form GSTR 2 shall be communicated to the supplier in:

(a) Form GSTR 1A (b) Form GSTR 3A (c) Form GSTR 6A (d) Form GSTR 2A

Q#08 : Which of these registers / ledgers are maintained online?

(a) Tax liability register (b) Credit ledger (c) Cash ledger (d) All of them

Q#09 : Payment made through challan will be credited to which registers/ledgers?

(a) Electronic Tax liability register (b) Electronic Credit ledger (c) Electronic Cash ledger (d) All of them

Balance in electronic credit ledger can be utilized against

(a) Output tax payable (b) Interest (c) Penalty   (d) All of them

Q#10 : A registered person may claim refund of balance in electronic cash ledger after :

(a) Application for refund (b) Annual Return (c) Returns filed at the end of tax periods (d) None of the above

Q#11 : The following Tax amounts due cannot be paid through installments

(a) Self-assessed tax shown in return (b) Short paid tax for which notice has been issued(c) Arrears of tax (d) All of the above

Q#12 : Who is liable to pay the tax in case of Agency?

(a) Principal (b) Agent (c) Both Principal & Agent jointly and severally (d) Jointly

Q#13 : When two or more companies are amalgamated, the liability to pay tax on supplies between the effective date of amalgamation order and date of amalgamation order would be on :

(a) Transferee; (b) Respective companies; (c) Any one of the companies; (d) None of the above

Q#14 : Time limit for issue of order in case of fraud, misstatement or suppression?

(a) 30 months (b) 18 months (c) 5 years (d) 3 years

Q#15 : Time limit for issue of order in case of other than fraud, misstatement or suppression?

(a) 30 months (b) 18 months (c) 5 years (d) 3 years

Quiz # GST-MIS-1-03
Level -3

Q#01 : Which of the following is an intrastate supply?

(a) Supplier of goods located in Delhi and place of supply of goods SEZ located in Delhi (b) Supplier of goods located in Delhi and place of supply of goods in Jaipur (c) Supplier of goods located in Delhi and place of supply of goods in Delhi (d) All the above

Q#02 : Which of the following transaction is inter-state supply of goods involving movement of goods?

(a) Location of supplier is in Bangalore and location of recipient is in Mumbai (b) Location of supplier is in Bangalore and place of supply is Mumbai (c) Location of supplier and place of supply is Bangalore (d) None of the above

Q#03 : Place of supply in case of installation of Generator is

(a) Where the movement of Generator commences from the supplier's place (b) Where the delivery of Generator is taken (c) Where the installation of Generator is made (d) Where address of the recipient is mentioned in the invoice

Q#04 : 'Zero Rated Supply' means

Supplies made to SEZ units / developers, or exports of goods / services. (b) Items not subject to GST (c) Items taxed at "0" (Zero or NIL) Rate (d) All of the above

Q#05 : In the hands of the supplier, supply of goods to SEZ unit is treated as

(a) Exempt Supply – Reversal of credit (b) Deemed Taxable Supply – No reversal of credit (c) Export of Supplies (d) Non-Taxable Supply – Outside the Scope of GST

Q#06 : Any amount of tax collected shall be deposited to the credit of the Central or State Government:

(a) Only when the supplies are taxable (b) Regardless of whether the supplies in respect of which such amount was collected are taxable or not (c) Only when the supplies are not taxable (d) None of the above

Q#07 : Where business are situated in multiple places within a state specified in the Registration Certificate, the books and Accounts shall be maintained at

(a) Each place of business (b) Place where the books of accounts are maintained for all places situated within a state (c) At principal place of business mentioned in the Registration Certificate for all places of business in each state (d) Any of the above

Q#08 : Details of Inward supplies shall include

(a) Inward supplies of goods and services communicated in Form GSTR 2A (b) Inward supplies in respect of which tax is payable under reverse charge mechanism (c) Inward supplies of goods and services not declared by suppliers (d) All the above

Q#09 : If Input credit claimed by recipient is more than the output tax declared by the supplier or if the supplier has not declared the outward supply, then

(a) The excess amount claimed as input is added to the output tax liability of the recipient in the return of succeeding month (b) The discrepancy is communicated to both the supplier and receiver (c) The excess amount claimed as input is added to the output tax liability of the supplier (d) The supplier is given an opportunity of being heard

Q#10 : Who will notify the rate of tax to be levied under CGST?

(a) Central Government suo moto (b) State Government suo moto (c) GST Council suo moto (d) Central Government as per the recommendations of the GST Council

Q#11 : Which of the following services are covered under Reverse Charge Mechanism under Section 9(3) of CGST Act, 2017

(a). Legal Consultancy (b) Goods Transport Agency (c). both (a) and (b) (d). Rent-a-Cab

Q#12 : Which one of the following is true?

(a) Entire income of any trust is exempted from GST (b) Entire income of a registered trust is exempted from GST (c) Incomes from specified/defined charitable activities of a trust are exempted from GST (d) Incomes from specified/defined charitable activities of a registered trust are exempted from GST

Q#13 : Services to a single residential unit is, exempted if:

(a) It is pure labour service only (b) It is works contract only (c) It is a part of residential complex only (d) It is on ground floor without further super structure

Q#14 : Which of the following is exempted from GST

(a) Letting out any immovable property (b) Letting out any residential property for use as residence (c) Letting out any residential property irrespective of its use (d) None of the above

Q#15 : Can a registered person opt for composition scheme only for one out of his 3 business verticals, having same Permanent Account Number?

(a) Yes (b) No (c) Yes, subject to prior approval of the Central Government (d) Yes, subject to prior approval of the concerned State Government

Q#16 : Transportation of passengers exempted if :

(a) It is by air-conditioned stage carriage (b) It is by air-conditioned contract carriage (c) By non-air conditioned stage carriage for tourism, charter or hire (d) None of the above

Q#17 : Transportation of passengers is exempted :

(a) In an air conditioned railway coach (b) In a vessel for public tourism within India (c) In a metered cab/ auto rickshaw / e rickshaw (d) No exemption for any Transportation service

Q#18 : Transportation of goods is not exempted :

(a) by a goods transport agency / courier agency (b) by inland waterways (c) by an aircraft from a place outside India upto the customs station of clearance in India (d) by all the above

Q#19 : Transportation of agricultural produces, milk, salt and food grain including flour, pulses and rice, 'relief materials meant for victims of natural or man-made disasters, calamities, accidents or mishap', newspaper or magazines registered with the Registrar of Newspapers - is exempted

(a) If it is by a goods transport agency (b) If it is by rail - within India (c) If it is by a vessel - within India (d) all of the above

Q#20 : What is time of supply of goods, in case of forward charge?

(a) Date of issue of invoice (b) Due date of issue of invoice (c) Date of receipt of consideration by the supplier (d) Earlier of (a) & (b)

Q#21 : What is time of supply of goods, in case of supplier opting for composition levy

(a) Date of issue of invoice (b) Date of receipt of consideration by the supplier (c) Latter of (a) & (b) (d) Earlier of (a) & (b)

Q#22 : What is time of supply of goods liable to tax under reverse charge mechanism?

(a) Date of receipt of goods (b) Date on which the payment is made (c) Date immediately following 30 days from the date of issue of invoice by the supplier (d) Earliest of the above

Q#23 : What is date of receipt of payment by Cheque

(a) Date of entry in the books (b) Date credited into bank account (c) Date of posting the cheque by payer. (d) Earlier of (a) and (b)

Q#24 : Deductions allowed in computation of transaction value

(a) Discounts offered to customers, subject to conditions (b) Packing Charges, subject to conditions (c) Amount paid by customer on behalf of the supplier, subject to conditions (d) Freight charges incurred by the supplier for CIF terms of supply, subject to conditions

Q#25 : Input tax credit on capital goods and Inputs can be availed in :

(a) 36 installments (b) 12 installments (c) 1 installment (d) 6 installments

Q#26 : Time limit to pay the value of supply with taxes to avail the input tax credit?

(a) 3 months (b) 6 Months(c) 180 days(d) Till the date of filing of Annual Return

Q#27 : ITC should be availed on

(a) Receipt of goods (b) Receipt of Documents (c) Receipt of goods and Receipt of Documents (d) Either receipt of documents or Receipt of goods

Q#28 : Inputs sent for job work shall be treated as supply if goods are not returned within

(a) One year (b) Five years (c) Six months (d) 2 years

Q#29 : Principal entitled to ITC on Inputs sent for job work if goods are returned within

(a) One year (b) Five years (c) Six months (d) 2 years

Q#30 : Principal entitled to ITC on Capital Goods sent for job work if goods are returned within

(a) 1 year (b) 5 years (c) 6 months (d) 3 years

Q#31 : Distributor of ISD and recipient

(a) must have same PAN (b) May have different PAN in same State (c) May have different PAN in different State (d) None of the above

Q#32 : A person should apply for registration :

(a) Within 60 days from the date he becomes liable for registration. (b) Within 30 days from the date he becomes liable for registration. (c) No Time Limit (d) Within 90 days from the date he becomes liable for registration

Q#33 : The books and other records U/S 35 are to be maintained at

(a) Place where the books and accounts are maintained (b) Place of address of the Proprietor/ Partner/ Director/Principal Officer (c) Principal place of business as mentioned in the Certificate of Registration (d) Any of the above

Q#34 : On what value TDS needs to be deducted?

(a) Contract value (b) Contract value excluding tax (c) Invoice value including tax (d) Invoice value excluding tax

Q#35 : Retiring partner should intimate the retirement to

(a) Department (b) Government (c) Commissioner (d) All of the above

Q#36 : Validity of registration certificate issued to casual taxable person and non-resident taxable person?

(a) 90 days from the effective date of registration (b) Period specified in the application for registration (c) Earliest of (a) or (b) above (d) 180 days from the effective date of registration

Q#37 : The applicant is not required to furnish documentary evidence if the amount of refund claimed is less than Rupees:

(a) 6 lacs (b) 2 lacs (c) 10 lacs (d) 20 lacs

Q#38 : Maximum amount of demand for which the officer can issue an order u/s 73 (other than fraud, misstatement or suppression)

(a) Amount of tax + interest + penalty of 10% of tax (b) Amount of tax + interest + penalty of 10% of tax or Rs. 10,000/- whichever is higher (c) Rs. 10,000/- (d) Amount of tax + interest + 25% penalty

Q#39 : Maximum amount of demand for which the officer can issue an order u/s 74 (fraud, misstatement or suppression)

(a) Amount of tax + interest + penalty of 15% of tax (b) Amount of tax + interest + penalty of 25% of tax (c) Amount of tax + interest + penalty of 50% of tax (d) Amount of tax + interest + penalty of 100% of tax

Quiz # GST-MIS-1-04
Level 4

Q#01 : In case of amalgamation between two companies, such companies shall be treated as two distinct companies till :

(a) Till the date of the Court order (b) Till the effective date of merger (c) Till the date of cancellation of registration (d) None of the above

Q#02 : If intimation of Retirement of Partner the Commissioner is delayed, then the retiring partner is liable to pay tax, interest or penalty till:

(a) The intimation of the date of retirement of partner is received by the Commissioner (b) Till the date of acceptance of intimation by the Department (c) Till the date of retirement (d) Till the date of show cause notice

Q#03 : Sponsorship services provided by Mr. A to M/s AB Ltd., liability to pay GST is on:

a) Mr. A (b) M/s AB Ltd. (c) Both (d) None of the above

Q#04 : GST on Renting of land, inside an Industrial estate, by State Government to a private manufacturing company

(a) Exempted (b) Applicable under Normal Charge (c) Applicable under Reverse Charge (d) None of the above

Q#05 : GST on Services by an Insurance Agent to ABC Insurance Co. Ltd., is to be paid by:

(a) Insurance Agent (b) ABC Insurance Co. Ltd. (c) Both (d) None of the above

Q#06 : Liability for GST payment on sitting Fees received by director of XYZ Ltd. Is on

(a) Director (b) XYZ Ltd (c) Both of above (d) None of the above

Q#07 : Liability for GST payment on Services provided by a Recovery Agent to ZZZ bank Ltd., is on

(a) ZZZ bank Ltd. (b) Recovery Agent (c) Both the above (d) None of the above

Q#08 : Silk yarn procured by ABC Silks Ltd. from a Trader, GST is payable by

(a) Trader (b) ABC Silks Ltd (c) Both the above (d) None of the above

Q#09 : Lottery procured from State Government by a lottery distributor, GST is payable by:

(a) Lottery Distributor (b) State Government (c) Both the above (d) None of the above

Q#10 : PQR Ltd. has availed rent-a-cab service from ABC Travels (unregistered). GST would be payable by

(a) ABC Travles (b) Reverse charge is applicable (c) No GST payable (d) None of the above

Q#11 : Banking services provided by Department of Post

(a) Taxable & Reverse Charge Mechanism is applicable (b) Taxable & Normal Charge is applicable (c) Exempt from GST(d) None of the above

Q#12 : Which of the following persons can opt for composition scheme?

(a) Person making supply of goods which are not leviable to tax under GST (b) Person making any inter-State outward supplies of goods; (c) Person effecting supply of goods through e-commerce operator liable to collect tax at source (d) None of the above

Q#13 : Rate of CGST to a registered person being a hotelier (providing accommodation also) under composition scheme?

(a) 1% (b) 0.5% (c) 2.5% (d) Not eligible for composition scheme, thus liable to pay normal tax

Q#14 : Which of the following will be excluded from the computation of 'aggregate turnover'?

(a) Value of Taxable supplies (b) Value of Exempt Supplies (c) Non-taxable supplies (d) Value of inward supplies on which tax is paid on reverse charge basis [after considering NN38 and NN32]

Q#15 : A registered person opting to pay taxes under composition scheme during the year 2017-18 crosses threshold limit?

(a) He can continue under composition scheme till the end of the financial year (b) He will be liable to pay tax at normal rates of GST on the entire turnover for the financial year 2017-18 (c) He will cease to remain under the composition scheme with immediate effect (d) He will cease to remain under the composition scheme from the quarter following the quarter in which the aggregate turnover exceeds threshold limit

Q#16 : Services by a hotel, inn, guest house, club or campsite are exempted for residential / lodging purposes, if declared tariff for a unit of accommodation is below:

(a) Rs 10,000 (b) Rs. 1,000 (c) Such accommodation is always taxable (d) Rs 5000

Q#17 : Which of the following services is exempted

(a) Loading, unloading, packing, storage or warehousing of rice (b) Loading / unloading of jute (c) Packing and storage or warehousing of rubber (d) None of the above

Q#18 : Core services of which organization is not exempted

(a) Services provided by the Insurance Regulatory and Development Authority of India to insurers

(b) Services provided by the Securities and Exchange Board of India (c) Services by Port Trusts (d) Services by the Reserve Bank of India

Q#19 : Which of the following leases is exempted?

(a) All kinds of long term (30 or more years) leases of industrial plots (b) Long term (30 or more years) leases of industrial plots or plots for development of infrastructure for financial business by State Government Industrial Development Corporations or Undertakings, to industrial units (c) Short term (up to 30 years) leases of industrial plots by State Government Industrial Development Corporations or Undertakings to industrial units (d) All kinds of short term (up to 30 years) lease of industrial plots

Q#20 : Which of the following business exhibition is exempted from GST

(a) All business exhibition (b) A business exhibition in India (c) A business exhibition outside India (d) None of the above

Q#21 : Which of the following is not exempted

(a) Health care service to human beings by authorized medical practitioners / para medics (b) Health care services to Animals/Birds (c) Slaughtering of animals (d) Rearing horses

Q#22 : Which of the following are exempted services?

(a) Services by an artist by way of a performance in folk or classical art forms of music/ dance / theatre for consideration upto Rs. 1 lakh (b) Services by an artist by way of performance in folk or classical art forms of music/ dance for consideration upto Rs. 2 lakh (c) Services by an artist by way of a performance in folk or classical art forms of music/ dance / theatre for consideration upto Rs. 1.5 lakh (d) Services by an artist as a brand ambassador by way of a performance in folk or classical art forms of music/ dance / theatre for consideration upto Rs. 1.5 lakh

Q#23 : A composition dealer, supplies goods worth Rs. 24,300 to Mr. B and issues an invoice dated 25.12.2017 for Rs. 24,300. Mr. B pays Rs. 25,000 on 1.01.2018 against such supply of goods. The excess Rs. 700 is adjusted in the next invoice for supply of goods issued on 5.01.2018. Identify value of supply and time of supply:

(a) Rs. 25,000 – 1.01.2018 (b) For Rs. 24,300 – 25.12.2017 and for Rs. 700 – 1.01.2018 (c) For Rs. 24,300 – 25.12.2017 and for Rs. 700 – 5.01.2018. (d) (b) or (c) at the option of the supplier.

Q#24 : What is the time of supply of service in case of reverse charge mechanism?

(a) Date of payment as entered in the books of account of the recipient (b) Date immediately following 60 days from the date of issue of invoice (c) Date of invoice (d) Earlier of (a) & (b)

Q#25 : There was increase in tax rate of certain service from 12% to 18% w.e.f.1.02.2018. Which of the following rate is applicable when services are provided in February 2018, but invoice issued and payment received, in January, 2018

(a) 12% (lower of the two) (b) 18% (higher of the two) (c) 12% as invoice issued and payment were received prior to rate change (d) 18% as the supply was completed after rate change

Q#26 : There was decrease in GST rate from 18% to 12% w.e.f. 1.02.2018 in respect of some goods. Which of the following rate is applicable if Goods removed goods from supplier's factory in Delhi on 31.01.2018 and delivered to Buyer in UP on 2.02.2018. Supplier issues Invoice on 31.01.2018 and payment is received on 4.02.2018.

(a) 12% as it is lower of the two (b) 18% as date of invoice and dispatch of goods from factory, has happened before change of rate (c) 12% as both payment and completion of supply, has happened after change of rate. (d) 18% as it is higher of the two

Q#27 : The value of supply includes

(a) Any non-GST taxes, duties, cess, fees charged by supplier separately (b) Interest, late fee or penalty for delayed payment of any consideration for any supply of goods or services (c) Subsidies directly linked to the price except subsidies provided by the Central and State Government (d) All of the above

Q#28 : Rule 30 of the CGST Rules inter alia provides value of supply of goods / services based on cost shall be ....% of cost of production or manufacture or the cost of acquisition of such goods or the cost of provision of such services

(a) 100 (b) 10 (c) 110 (d) 120

Q#29 : B & Co Purchases 1000 Pcs of an Item from S & Co at highly discounted rate of 40 /pc (though market rate of similar quality of the Item is Rs 50). S & Co charges Rs 5000 as freight. The value of supply would be

(a) Rs 45000 (b) Rs 40000, (c) Rs 50000 (d) Rs 55000

Q#30 : Supplier issued Invoice and deposited the taxes but receiver has not received the documents. Is receiver entitled to avail credit?

(a) Yes, it will be auto populated in recipient monthly returns (b) No as one of the conditions of s.16(2) is not fulfilled (c) Yes, if the receiver can prove later that documents are received subsequently (d) None of the above

Q#31 : Can the recipient avail the Input tax credit on part payment to the supplier within 180 days

(a) Yes, on full tax amount (b) No, until full amount is paid to supplier (c) Yes, but proportionately to the extent of value and tax paid (d) None of the above

Q#32 : Depreciation on tax component of capital goods permissible for ITC Credit

(a) Yes (b) No Depreciation allowed on Capital Goods to avail ITC (c) Input tax credit is eligible if depreciation on tax component is not availed (d) None of the above

Q#33 : Is Input tax to be reversed in case of disposal of capital goods

(a) Yes fully (b) No (c) Yes, to extent of credit taken as reduced by prescribed percentage or tax on transaction value, whichever is higher (d) Yes, to the extent of transaction value of such goods

Q#34 : In case of ISD, credit applicable to more than one recipient shall be distributed

(a) Equally among the recipients (b) Proportionate to aggregate turnover of such recipients (c) cannot be distributed to multiple recipients (d) As per Adhoc pre fixed Ratio decided by the ISD.

Q#35 : Input Tax credit as credited in Electronic Credit ledger can be utilized for

(a) Payment of Interest (b) Payment of penalty & Fine (c) Payment of Taxes (d) All of the above

Q#36 : E-commerce operator

(a) Must get registered irrespective of any threshold limit (b) Required to register only if turnover exceeds threshold limit. (c) Not required to get registered if located in North Eastern states. (d) None of the above

Q#37 : Consequences of obtaining registration by misrepresentation?

(a) Liable to cancellation of registration by proper officer. (b) Fine upto Rs. 1 Lakh (c) Imprisonment form 6 months to 3 years. (d) Fine upto Rs. 1 Lakh and Imprisonment upto 3 years.

Q#38: Business having centralized registration under erstwhile Act.

(a) Shall obtain a centralized registration under GST Law. (b) Shall obtain separate registration in each state from where it is making taxable supplies (c) Shall obtain registration on temporary basis. (d) No need to apply for registration under GST.

Q#39 : An invoice must be issued:

(a) At the time of removal of goods (b) On transfer of properties of the goods to the recipient (c) On receipt of payment for the supply (d) Earliest of the above dates.

Q#40 : On receipt of advance payment in respect of supply of goods or services:

(a) Proforma invoice to be issued (b) A receipt voucher for amount received to be issued (c) Invoice for the value of advance received to be issued (d) None of the above

Q#41 : For an increase in the tax/ taxable value, under GST rule:

(a) A Debit Note should be issued by the supplier on the Buyer (b) A Credit Note should be issued by the Buyer in favour of the supplier (c) A Credit Note should be issued by the supplier in favour of the Buyer (d) A Debit Note should be issued by the Buyer on the supplier

Q#42 : What should the taxpayer do if he pay's the wrong tax i.e. IGST instead of CGST/SGST or vice versa?

(a) Remit tax again and claim refund (b) It will be auto-adjusted (c) It will be adjusted on application/ request (d) None of the above

Q#43 : What is the time limit to receive back the tools and dies or jigs and fixtures sent to jobworker's place?

(a) 1 year (b) 3 years (c) 5 years (d) No time limit specified under GST

Q#44 : Which of the following is an inter-State supply?

(a) Supplier of goods located in Delhi and place of supply of goods SEZ located in Delhi (b) Supplier of goods located in Delhi and place of supply of goods in Jaipur (c) Supplier of goods located in Delhi and place of supply of goods SEZ located in Chandigarh (d) All the above

GST – Tests

Write the answer of following questions, within 2-3 sentences, with key points only.

T-GST-1-01 : What is the taxability on transfer of goods to another branch

T-GST-1-02 : What is the taxability on gifts given by employer to employee

T-GST-1-03 : What is the taxability on Artworks supplied to Art Galleries

T-GST-1-04 : What are implications if recipient refuses to pay tax on reverse charge?

T-GST-1-05 : Is GST wrongly paid by supplier [In case of Reverse Charge] available as Input Tax Credit (ITC) to recipient?

T-GST-1-06 : Is GST on reverse charge basis payable even if payment to supplier is not made?

T-GST-1-07 : What is the Taxability on immovable Property?

T-GST-1-08 : What is the taxability on lease of exempt goods ?

T-GST-1-09 : X, the supplier of goods, receives payment from customer by Cheque on 12 Jan, deposits the cheque on 15th Jan and records in the books on that day, the amount is credited to his bank account on 17th Jan. What would be the date of receipt of payment.

T-GST-1-10 : X appoints auditor Y on terms that all out of pocket expenses related to audit work incurred by auditor (like Travel expenses etc) is reimbursable. Auditor pays for flight ticket. Should Y, the CA include the cost of Flight Ticket in their service bill ?

T-GST-1-11 : X supplies goods to Y on Ex Factory terms, and incurs expenses for transportation and loading charges on behalf of Y. How the supply value should be computed in respect of such expenses incurred by X.

T-GST-1-12 : Quantity discounts are not recorded on the face of the invoice. Can the Quantity discounts be claimed as deduction while computing GST?

T-GST-1-13 : Buyer pays after deducting Cash Discount from the Invoice value, if the payment is made within 7 days. What would be the implication of GST on the Cash Discount deducted by Buyer

T-GST-1-14 : Will GST be applicable on interest charged by supplier for delayed payment made by buyer ?

T-GST-1-15 : Will the out-of-pocket expenses charged by professionals to claim reimbursement of expenses incurred by them for rendering services to their clients be included in the transaction value?

T-GST-1-16 : Will the Customs duty paid by Customs House Agent on behalf of the client also be required to be included in the transaction value?

T-GST-1-17 : What will be the value of supply of person dealing in second-hand goods?

T-GST-1-18 : Whether Input tax credit on Inputs and Capital Goods is allowed in one installment?

T-GST-1-19 : Invoice not paid by recipient within 180 days. What would be the implication for ITC

T-GST-1-20 : Capital Goods purchased @ Rs 20000 + GST @12% 2400. Total value Rs 22400. Depreciation @10% provided on 22400. Compute eligible ITC

T-GST-1-21 : Capital Goods purchased @ Rs 20000 + GST @12% 2400. Total value Rs 22400. Depreciation @10% provided on 20000. Compute eligible ITC.

T-GST-1-22 : Whether input tax credit is allowed on inputs which become waste and is sold as scrap?

T-GST-1-23 : Whether Input tax credit is available in respect of Input tax paid on use of mobile phones/ laptops/as given to employees?

T-GST-1-24 : What is aggregate turnover?

T-GST-1-25 : Can unregistered person (turnover below threshold limit) buy goods from other states without being liable for registration.

T-GST-1-26 : S supplies Stationery to B on regular basis and issues invoice on quarterly basis on 15th of the following month of each quarter end, on submission of statement of accounts, instead of issuing Invoice on each supply.

T-GST-1-27 : Annual return for the year 2017-18 is not yet filed. Can I issue a credit note in respect of supplies made during the year 2017-18, on 1st October2018.

T-GST-1-28 : Annual return for the year 2017-18 has been filed 0n 30th August. Can I issue a credit note in respect of supplies made during the year 2017-18 on 1st October 2018.

T-GST-1-29 : When I reject an inward supply, can I issue a Debit Note?

T-GST-1-30 : A shop has 3 sales counters issuing Tax Invoice and receiving payments. How should the Invoice be numbered.

T-GST-1-31 : Passenger Transportation Service issue a Ticket. Is it mandatory to issue Invoice also ?

T-GST-1-32: A Registered person supplies Taxable as well as Exempted goods / services. What type of Invoice should be issued ?

T-GST-1-33: Can I start a fresh series of serial number for my 'invoice' or 'bill of supply' every day, e.g., 20160401/001, 20160401/002 for April 1st and 20160402/001, 20160402/002 for 2nd April?

T-GST-1-34: X. having several places of Can X, maintain accounts & records only at principal place of business?

T-GST-1-35: The recipient finds the details reflected in GSTR-2A incorrect 'How he should correct it ?'

T-GST-1-36: Supplier raises an invoice on 30.08.2017 and discloses the same in FORM GSTR-1 for August 2017. Recipient receives the goods and records the inward supply in his books of account on 01.09.2017. How the transaction would be reflected in the GSTR of the respective parties in Aug & Sep in their GSTR-1 / GSTR-2 Returns

T-GST-1-37: X was liable to get registered from July 15, 2017, but got registration on August 16, 2017. How should X disclose the details of supplies effected during the period July 15, 2017 to August 16, 2017?

T-GST-1-38: Can ITC be used for payment of tax under reverse charge basis?

T-GST-1-39: Can CGST, IGST, UTGST and SGST be paid separately in different challans?

T-GST-1-40: The Contract Value was for Rs 2,25,000 plus applicable GST @ 18%. Whether TDS would be deducted by the deductor.

GSTN Projects

Explain the steps of data input, data upload and Returns Filing into GSTN Portal of the following Practical Projects.

P-GSTN-1-1

X owns 3 proprietary business units B-1, B-2 & B3,of different verticals, in 3 different places, in West Bengal. The turnover of FY 16-17 of these 3 Business were :

- B1:5 lakhs – Exempted items, 7 Lakhs – Taxable Items, both Intra State & Inter State outwards transactions
- B2: 5 Lakhs, all Non Taxable Items, only Intra State outwards transactions
- B3: 3 Lakhs - Non Taxable Items, 4 Lakhs – Taxable Items, both Intra State & Inter State outwards transactions

State the liability of X regarding Registration under GST in FY 17-18, for each of these Business units.

X proposes to start another business in BIHAR, in Aug 2017. State the registration liability of the proposed new business.

State the process of registration. Explain the key steps, right from filing the Application till securing registration certificate for the business units to be registered. No need to give details of info to be provided, Clearly explain the operational steps.

P-GSTN-1-2

X owns 3 proprietary business units B-1, B-2 & B3,of different verticals, in 3 different places, in West Bengal. The turnover of FY 16-17 (no Inter State outward transactions in any of the unit) :

- B1:5 lakhs – Exempted items, 7 Lakhs – Taxable Items
- B2: 5 Lakhs, all Non Taxable Items
- B3: 3 Lakhs - Non Taxable Items, 8 Lakhs – Taxable Items.

Is X liable to register as Composition Dealer in FY 17-18. If so, Explain the key steps, right from filing the Application to get registration certificate for the business units to be registered. No need to give details of info to be provided, Clearly explain the operational steps.

P-GSTN-1-3

S of West Bengal (WB), a registered dealer, issues Invoice as follows (RG means registered, URG Means Unregistered Party).

Inv #	Inv Dt	Customer name	State	Reg Type	Total Tax rate	Supply Value
1	1.8.17	C-1-RG-WB	WB	RG	12%	10000
2	1.8.17	C-2-RG-WB	WB	RG	0%	2500
					5%	2000
					12%	2600

3	2.8.17	C-1-RG-WB	WB	RG	5%	2377
					EX	2000
4	2.8.17	C-3-URG-WB	WB	URG	12%	4000
					0%	1000
5	2.8.17	C-4-RG-BR	BR	RG	12%	3500
6	2.8.17	C-5-URG-BR	BR	URG	12%	4500
7	31.8.17	C-1-RG-WB	WB	RG	12%	3000
					5%	2000

The details of all invoices uploaded, except Invoice #3 & # 7 were found to be Ok by buyers and the buyers approved them. In Invoice #3, The supplier charged GST @ 5% on 2377 as Rs 118.85, but the Buyer entered the Tax amount rounded as 119, and kept the Invoice as pending, informing the discrepancy to the supplier on 3.8.17. Buyer revised the Invoice accordingly, charging GST 119.00 on 28.8.17, but GSTR-1 was already filed by Supplier on 20.8.17. The Buyer approved the Invoice on 2.9.17.

The materials of Invoice Number 7 were received by Buyer on 2.9.17 and was included as Inwards return for Sep 17.

Explain how these transactions would appear in GSTR reports of seller and buyer for the Returns submitted for Aug & Sep. 17

P-GSTN-1-4

S(a registered dealer of WB) supplies 15 units of Goods @ 100 on 1 Aug 17 to B(a registered dealer of WB). S issues Invoice # 3 charging 12% GST (SGST + CGST) on 1 Aug 17. B& Co received only 14 units of Goods on 2 Aug and informed S of the short supply. B & Co did not approve the Invoice # 3, and issued a Debit Note # 5, on S on 31 Aug for short supply. S issued a Credit note # 8, on 2 Sep 17 for short supply against original Invoice #3. On 2.9.17, B& Co approved the Credit Note# 8 dt 2.9.17for returned goods and Invoice # 3 dt 1.8.17 of for original supply.

On 2nd Sep 17, the proprietor of B & Co used 1 unit of Goods for personal purpose. On 1st October 17, 1 unit of Goods was given as sample Free of Cost to a prospective buyer. On 2nd October 17, 1 unit was destroyed by Fire.

Explain how these transactions (and applicable GST / ITC) would appear in GST reports of seller and buyer, for the Returns filed by S and B & Co, for Aug, Sep & Oct 17.

P-GSTN-1-5

B & Co (a registered dealer) buys 100 Pcs of Mobiles Phones @ 6000 per Pc + GST @12% on 1.8.17. It distributes 60 Pcs of Phones to its clients for promotion of their products and 20 Pcs of Phones to employees for performing their duties in Aug. The remaining 20 Pcs were lying with B & Co.

Explain how the purchase transaction, GST / ITC would appear in respective GST reports of Aug 17

P-GSTN-1-6

S & Co of Kolkata, West Bengal, delivers Goods worth Rs.90000 (Taxable @ 12%) through a Transporter for exhibition in Siliguri of West Bengal, on 1st Aug. In the exhibition, goods of value 25000 were sold during 3rd to 7th Aug at Rs 35000 + Tax. Goods valued Rs 5000 were lost / destroyed in Exhibition. The remaining goods were booked back to Kolkata through Transporter on 8th Aug 17, which due to some reasons, delivered by Transporter in Kolkata on 2nd Sep 17.

Explain how the transactions & GST would appear in their respective GSTreports of Aug & Sep 17

P-GSTN-1-7

S & Co (a registered dealer in WB) entered into Contract supply of goods to B & Co(a registered dealer in Bihar) for Rs 1 Lakh on 1st Aug 17[Item of value 50000 each of Item -1 (GST @ 12%) & Item - 2 (GST @18%)]. B & Co paid Advance of Rs 15000 against supply of Item-1 and Rs 10000 against supply of Item-2, to S & Co on 2 Aug 17.Later on, there was shortage of Item-2 in market.So, S & Co told they would supply Item 2 only to the extent available in their stock and would supply Item 1 in place of Item-2, to which B & Co agreed. On 2 Sep, S & Co supplied Item -1 of value 40000, Item -2 of value 8000 and issued Final Invoice to B & Co. The balance quantity of order was mutually canceled and not to be delivered. B &Co paid the balance due amount of Invoice dt 2 Sep, on 31.10.17, adjusting the Advance paid.

State how the transactions of Advance paid, Issue of Invoice and adjustment would be reflected in respective GSTR returns of S& Co and B & Co for Aug, Sep & Oct 17

P-GSTN-1-8

B & Co (Unregistered Party of WB) paid Rs 10000 (lump sum) as advance to S & Co (Registered Party of Bihar) to execute a service job of value Rs 30000 (+Tax @ 12%) on 2.9.17. S & Co did part job (of value Rs 6000) and supplied Invoice dt 1.10.17 for the part Job done (6000+Tax @12%). The engineer of S & Co fell ill. So, S & Co asked B & Co, to terminate the contract. B & Co asked for refund of Advance. S & Co, refunded the balance of advance to B & Co, after deducting the Invoice value (including Tax) on 31.10.17. It was received by B & Co and recorded in their books on 1.11.17

State how the transactions of Advance received, Tax Liability and Tax Payment on Advance Received, Issue of Invoice, Adjustment of Advance & Refund would be reflected in respective GST returns of S& Co for Sep, Oct & Nov 17

P-GSTN-1-9

S & Co sold TV set @ 25000 (+GST @ 18%) to X and similar TV set @ 20000 (+ 18% GST) to Y (who returned an old TV). How these sales and GST would be reflected in Tax Returns of S & Co.

P-GSTN-1-10

B & Co buys goods worth Rs 50000 (+ GST @12%) on 1.8.17. Goods worth Rs 10000 (+Tax) retuned to supplier on 10.8.17. B & Co made Payment of Rs 25000 on 1.9.17. Supplier issued credit note for Returned Goods on 1.11.17. B& Co made balance payment due on 1.2.18. Show respective GST reports of B & Co for Aug 17 to Feb 18, showing ITC eligibility.

P-GSTN-1-11

(a) S & Co supplied a Boiler of Rs 2 Lakh + Tax @12%, to B & Co under Invoice # 5 Dt 1.8.17. C & Co provided installation service to install the boiler at Rs 30000 (+ Tax @18%) and supplied service Invoice # 15 dt 1.9.17. on B & Co. B & Co paid lump sum payment of Rs 100000 on 1.12.17 to S & Co and balance (including Tax) on 31.1.18. B & Co paid full amount of Invoice # 15 on 31.10.17.

State how the transactions of Purchase & ITC reflected in respective GSTR of B & Co in respective period of Aug 17 to Jan 18.

(b) Assuming that B & Co provided depreciation @ 10% on Boiler in books, on 31.3.18

(i) on Rs 2,00,000 on Boiler (ii) 2,00,000 on Boiler + 30,000 on Installation (iii) 2,24,000 for Boiler & 35,400 for Installation Charges

State how the transactions of Purchase of Boiler & Installation Charges & ITC availed would be reflected in Annual Return of B & Co for FY 17-18.

P-GSTN-1-12

(a) B & Co purchased Machinery of Rs 1 Lakh (+ GST @ 12%) on 1.8.17 from a registered dealer. It purchased inputs for Rs 1 Lakh (+ 5% GST) on 1.9.17. It uses Machine and Inputs to produce Taxable & Exempted Goods. The turnover of Taxable Goods in FY 16-17 was Rs 3 Lakhs and that of Exempted Goods were Rs 50,000 during FY 16-17.

Show how the transactions of Purchase of Machine & Inputs and eligible ITC thereon would be reflected in respective GSTR of B & Co in each monthly Return from Aug 17 to Mar 18 in FY 17-18

(b) B & Co sold the Machine on 1.12 18 @ 40000 + GST @12%. Show how the sale of machine &ITC would be reflected in GST Returns of Dec 18.

P-GSTN-1-13

B & Co purchased a Motor Car on 1.8.17 for Rs 3 Lakh (+GST 18%). It pays for Driver to Manpower Agency @Rs 15000 (+GST @ 18%) at end of each month, from October 17. It paid for repairs of Rs 15000 (+GST 12%) on 1.12.17. The proprietor of B & Co uses the Motor Car for Business use (50%) and Personal use (50%).

Show how the transactions of Purchase of Car & eligible ITC on Car and Expenses would be reflected in respective GSTR of B & Co in each monthly Return from Aug 17 to Mar 18 in FY 17-18

P-GSTN-1-14

S & Co (Registered Dealer) supplied to B & Co (Unregistered Dealer), 5 items (sale price 5000 each + GST @12%) under Sale on Approval basis on 1.7.17. On 1.8.17, B & Co informed that one Item has been accepted by them (5000+Tax). On 31.8.17, B & Co returned one Item. On 1.9.17, B & Co informed that 2 Items are accepted by them at an agreed price of Rs 4800 each + tax. B & Co did not report anything about one Item lying with them.

Explain various documents would be prepared by S & Co for delivery of goods to B & Co, Return of Goods from B & Co, and Invoice to B & Co, and how these transactions would be reflected in relevant Returns for the respective months.

P-GSTN-1-15

P & Co (registered in WB) supplied goods valued Rs 95000 (applicable GST @12%) to J & Co (unregistered Jobber in Bihar) for Job work on 1.11.17. J & Co returned the jobbed goods on 31.12.17 along with surplus items not consumed in the Job. It was found that Goods worth Rs 20000 was consumed by J & Co for their own use, Goods worth Rs 5000 were damaged (due to negligence of J & Co) and Goods worth Rs 3000 were stolen at the premises of J & Co. J & Co issued Invoice of Rs 21000 to P & Co., as Jobbing Charges on 1.1.18

Explain the various documents to be issued by P & Co and relevant GST Returns of P & Co, for each month from Nov 17 to Jan 18.

GST Projects using Tally.ERP9

Work out the following practical projects of transaction involving GST. Create a Company using Tally. ERP9. Create Masters & Vouchers. Explain the steps of data input and appropriate options set up. Explain the steps of relevant GST Returns printing and uploading the Returns into GSTN Portal.

P-Tally-1-1

(a) Create Company (enter your Name & Address at Company Name & postal address, e-mail id, mobile number in the Company particulars). Set up GST details as Regular Registered Company, giving a valid GSTIN.

(b) Create following Stock Items, Classification – Undefined. UOM – Nos. Assume other info as necessary.

Item Name	Tax Type / Rate	Opening Stock	Standard Sale price	Standard Pur-chase price
Item-1 5%	5%	112	18	16
Item -2 12%	12%	62	68	60
Item-3 18%	18%	12	530	501
Item -4 28%	28%	21	1255	1203
Item -5 NIL	NIL	263	252	203
Item -6 EXEMPT	Exempt	156	48	40
Item – 7 Non GST	Non GST	76	59	51
Capital Goods	18%	-	-	-

Compute Opening Stock Value, as per Standard Purchase Price less 10%.

(c) Create following Customers. Assume Info as necessary. Enter valid GSTIN as per State, where applicable.

Customer Name	Type	State
Cash Customer – URD-WB	Unregistered	WB
Cash Customer – URD -Bihar	Unregistered	Bihar
Customer -1 – RG- WB	Registered	WB
Customer -2 – URG - WB	Unregistered	WB
Customer -3 – RG-BR	Registered	Bihar
Customer -4 – URG - BR	Unregistered	Bihar
Customer 5 – Comp- WB	Composite	WB
Customer 6 - Comp - BR	Composite	Bihar

(d) Create following Supplier. Assume Info as necessary. Enter valid GSTIN as per State, where applicable.

Supplier Name	Type	State
Cash Supplier – URD-WB	Unregistered	WB
Supplier -1 – RG- WB	Registered	WB
Supplier -2 – URG - WB	Unregistered	WB
Supplier -3 – RG-BR	Registered	Bihar
Supplier -4 – URG - BR	Unregistered	Bihar
Supplier 5 – Comp- WB	Composite	WB
Supplier 6 - Comp - BR	Composite	Bihar

(e) Enter the following Purchase Voucher, at Standard Purchase Price.

Supplier Name	Supplier Invoice #	Supplier Invoice Date	Purchase Voucher Date	Item	Quantity
Cash Supplier	12	1.7.17	1.7.17	Item -1 Item -5	12 23
Supplier -1	28	2.7.17	2.7.17	Item -1 Item -6	34 33
Supplier -2	45	1.8.17	2.8.17	Item -2 Item -7	32 11
Supplier -3	61	2.8.17	2.8.17	Item -3 Item -5 Item -6 Item -7	3 16 18 32
Supplier -4	14	31.8.17	1.9.17	Item -4 Item -5 Item -6 Item -7	15 11 14 8
Supplier 5	34	1.9.17	2.9.17	Item -5 Item -7	31 32
Supplier 6	46	31.7.17	2.8.17	Item -4 Item -5	12 14

Supplier 1 makes normal rounding off each GST Account of to paise, while Supplier 3 makes makes normal rounding to higher Rupee, in their Invoice. But the Company enters GST rounded off to nearest Rupee. As a rule, mismatch is to be resolved by modifying the Purchase Voucher as per Invoice issued by the supplier.

(e) Enter the following Sales Voucher, at Standard sales Price.

Supplier Name	Supplier Invoice #	Supplier Invoice Date	Item	Quantity
Cash Customer -A	12	1.7.17	Item -1 Item -5 Item -6	11 21 9
Cash Customer -B	13	1.7.17	Item -3 Item -5 Item -6 Item -7	1 3 11 21
Customer -1	28	2.7.17	Item -1 Item -6	33 31
Customer -2	45	1.8.17	Item -2 Item -7	31 9
Customer -3	61	2.8.17	Item -3 Item -5 Item -6 Item -7	3 15 17 31
Customer -4	14	31.8.17	Item -4 Item -5 Item -6 Item -7	15 11 13 7
Customer 5	34	1.9.17	Item -5 Item -7	31 29
Customer 6	46	31.7.17	Item -4 Item -5	11 11

Company enters GST rounded off to nearest Rupee, in Sales Invoices.

(e) Resolve Incomplete / Mismatch issues before printing any GST Reports (it should show zero number of mismatch voucher). Create voucher to deposit Tax Payable.

(f) Save GSTR-1, GSTR-2 and GSTR-3B for July, Aug & Sep 17, in PDF. Create JSON file for GSTR-1 for Jul – Sep 17, for upload. Explain the steps of uploading JSON, adjustment of ITC, creation of Tax Challan, and filing GSTR-1 for the Quarter Jul to Sep 17.

P-Tally-1-2

Continue working in the Company created and vouchers entered for Project 1

(a) The Company paid advance of Rs 4000 to Supplier-1, for supply of 6 units of Item -4 on 31.7.17. The Company further paid Advance of Rs 3000 for supply of 50 units of Item -2 on 2.8.17. As Item-4 was not available with the supplier, the supplier supplied 8 units of Item 3 on 1.9.17. The Company adjusted the amount of advance received against the Bill and refunded the excess amount on 1.10.17. Create the necessary vouchers for these transactions

Compute the GST liability on receipt of Advance. Show the relevant sections of GSTR reports for the months of Jul, Aug, Sep & Oct in respect of GST liability on Sale & Advance received and adjustment of GST on Advance.

(b) On 1.8.17, 2 units of Item 4, 1 unit of Item -5, 1 units of Item 6 and 1 unit of Item 7 were destroyed by Fire. The Company gave 5 units of Item-2 and 2 units of Item 3 as FREE sample to prospective customers on 2.9.17. Create vouchers for these transactions and show the relevant sections of respective GSTR returns for Aug & Sep.

(c) on 1.7.17, the Company delivered 20 Pcs of Item 4 to Customer 1 under Sale on Approval scheme. On 31.7.17, Customer 1 reported sale of 2 Pcs. On 1.8.17 they returned 5 Pcs back to the Company. On 31.8.17, they reported loss of 2 Pcs in their place, and sale of 9 Pcs. After that they did not convey anything, nor returned the unsold Items. Enter the necessary vouchers and show the relevant portion of GST reports affected.

(d) on 1.1.2018, the Company bought Capital Goods (Machinery) to produce Taxable, Non Taxable& Exempted Goods, @ 60000 + GST 12% from Supplier 3. During previous accounting year, it sold goods of Rs 1,00,000 Taxable, 20,000 Exempted Goods. On 31.3.18, it provided deprecation @10% on Machinery on value Rs 60000. Show the voucher entries. Show the portion of relevant GST reports related to ITC claim and reversals for Jan to Mar 18. It sold the Machine on 30.6.18 @ Rs 30000+ GST 12%. Show the portion of relevant GST reports related to Sale & ITC reversals for 'Jan 18 to Mar 18 & Apl 18 to Jun 18'.

(e) The Company paid Rs 2000 to an advocate for legal matters on 1.8.17. The advocate submitted Bill for Rs 5000 for the services on 1.9.17. The Company paid the bill on 2.9.17, after adjusting the advance. Create the necessary Ledger Accounts and make Voucher entries for the transactions. Show the portion of relevant GST reports related to ITC on Advance paid, Adjustments, Reverse Charges.

Index

W-Z

References

GST is a new Tax implemented from 1ˢᵗ July. Many experts in fields of Taxation & Digital Accounting have contributed in form of Books, Articles, Blogs, Videos etc, in print and digital media. There are lots of contribution in Digital media, which are easily accessible, FREE of cost, on the NET.

For benefit of Readers, I am appending references of some popular materials (Blogs, Videos, PDF etc), which I found to be informative. You will get topic wise compiled best materials so far published, instantly, which no book or any other resources would provide.

I hope, all readers, Students, Accountants, Business owners, will find it helpful. You need not buy dozens of books, spend time in searching Internet, or consult experts. You will have authentic and updated information from highly reputed experts of the country, at your fingertips, instantly, FREE of COST.

To access the resources, you need to type the cryptic URL in your device. It is often difficult (for long URL), error prone and time consuming. To get updated document (PDF) containing a comprehensive links of the URL, readers may mail the author (*aknadhani@gmail.com*). Just click on the relevant link in the document (PDF)

Contributors of Blogs, Videos, may send their URL with brief description of the contents and the contributor. Their refences, if found useful, will be added in the PDF (and also in next edition of the book).

PART-I : GST Overview
01: General Overview of GST

http://www.cbic.gov.in/htdocs-cbec/gst/index

https://www.gst.gov.in/help/helpmodules/

http://icmai.in/TaxationPortal/GST/index.php

https://gst.caknowledge.com/

https://cleartax.in/s/gst-law-goods-and-services-tax

http://www.gstindia.com/category/download/

https://services.gst.gov.in/services/gstlaw/gstlawlist

http://www.gst.gov.bz/downloads/gst303_preparingreturn.pdf

https://cbec-gst.gov.in/pdf/03062017-return-formats.pdf

https://www.jiogst.com/home

https://gst.taxmann.com/

https://cleartax.in/s/gst-guide-introduction?ref=navbar_static_overlay

https://www.legalraasta.com/gst/

https://www.profitbooks.net/gst/
https://www.zoho.com/in/books/help/gst/
https://cbec-gst.gov.in/
https://gst.caknowledge.com/
http://www.eximguru.com/gst/default.aspx
https://www.exactlly.com/blog/
https://www.youtube.com/channel/UCDy5n4YEOg6daXPT-P-eESA/playlists

02 Transition to GST

https://cleartax.in/s/transition-to-gst
https://vakilsearch.com/advice/gst-transition-input-credits/

03:Types of GST

http://howtoexportimport.com/Types-of-GST-in-India-4189.aspx
https://cleartax.in/s/what-is-sgst-cgst-igst
http://www.profitbooks.net/gst-registration-process-india/

04:GST Registration

https://cleartax.in/s/gst-registration
https://cleartax.in/s/how-to-register-for-gst/
https://cleartax.in/s/cancellation-gst-registration/
https://cleartax.in/s/voluntary-registration-gst
https://cleartax.in/s/uin-unique-identification-number/
https://cleartax.in/s/change-gst-registration-details/
https://cleartax.in/s/gst-number-verification/
https://cleartax.in/s/gst-registration-for-ecommerce/
https://cleartax.in/s/process-of-migration-to-gst/
https://cleartax.in/s/non-resident-taxable-person-gst/
https://cleartax.in/s/aggregate-turnover-under-gst-for-registration/
https://cleartax.in/s/gst-jammu-kashmir/
http://incometaxmanagement.com/Pages/GST/GST-India.html
https://gst.registrationwala.com/gst-forms/gst-registration-forms/form-gst-reg-01
https://www.zoho.com/in/books/gst/how-to-register-for-gst.html
https://services.amazon.in/resources/seller-blog/how-to-register-for-gst.html
https://www.legalraasta.com/gst-registration/
https://www.indiafilings.com/learn/online-gst-registration-guide/
https://www.webtel.in/Image/GST_REG_01.pdf

https://youtu.be/W0LQhnppBfU
https://youtu.be/amdGfHTdVw4
https://youtu.be/IFtuuY3jvRk
https://youtu.be/80VCKv2n4kM
https://youtu.be/m1pdyv4gjxM

05:Supply of Goods & Services

https://cleartax.in/s/place-of-supply-gst
https://cleartax.in/s/place-of-supply-of-goods
https://cleartax.in/s/time-supply-goods-gst
https://www.avalara.com/in/en/blog/2017/06/time-supply-goods-gst.html
https://taxmantra.com/meaning-of-supply-of-goods-and-supply-of-services-under-gst/

06:Composition Scheme

https://cleartax.in/s/gst-composition-scheme
https://cleartax.in/s/composition-scheme-under-gst/
https://cleartax.in/s/gst-cmp-04-filing/
https://www.legalraasta.com/gst/composition-scheme/

07:e-commerce

https://cleartax.in/s/impact-of-gst-on-e-commerce-marketplace-sellers
https://cleartax.in/s/tds-and-tcs-under-gst
https://www.profitbooks.net/gst-impact-on-ecommerce-business/
https://www.legalraasta.com/gst/impact-of-gst-on-e-commerce/
https://www.indiafilings.com/learn/gst-ecommerce/
https://blog.capitalfloat.com/implication-gst-e-commerce-sellers/

08: Tax Invoice

https://www.profitbooks.net/gst-invoice/
https://cleartax.in/s/gst-invoice
https://taxguru.in/goods-and-service-tax/tax-invoice-gst.html
https://tallysolutions.com/gst/gst-invoice/
https://www.indiafilings.com/learn/gst-invoice-format-rules/
https://gst.caknowledge.com/gst-invoice-rules-gst-tax-invoice/
https://www.legalraasta.com/gst/gst-invoice/
https://www.mastersindia.co/gst/gst-invoicing-rules

09 Input Tax Credit

https://cleartax.in/s/input-tax-credit-under-gst

https://cleartax.in/s/what-is-input-credit-and-how-to-claim-it

https://www.profitbooks.net/input-tax-credit-under-gst/

http://www.charteredclub.com/gst-input-tax-credit/

https://www.legalraasta.com/gst/input-tax-credit-under-gst/

https://studycafe.in/2017/10/ineligible-input-tax-credit-or-block-credits-under-gst.html

https://youtu.be/HZw6GR_HovU

https://youtu.be/y-bDVMVEv1E

10:Reverse Charge Mechanism

https://cleartax.in/s/reverse-charge-gst

https://www.profitbooks.net/reverse-charge-gst/

https://www.legalraasta.com/gst/reverse-charge/

https://blog.saginfotech.com/reverse-charge-mechanism-under-gst

https://www.zoho.com/in/books/gst/reverse-charge-mechanism-gst.html

http://www.charteredclub.com/gst-reverse-charge/

https://studycafe.in/2017/06/reverse-charge-gst.html

https://youtu.be/d0zOgRYlGCE

https://youtu.be/hM61r7xTV2s

https://youtu.be/V-XVV_lgC2w

https://youtu.be/xwRWQ0UBrdk

https://youtu.be/vcV73TufX604

https://youtu.be/jG_VMWpX4Pc

11: Advance Receipt

https://cleartax.in/s/advance-received-under-gst

https://www.caclubindia.com/articles/gst-on-advances-31705.asp

12: Tax Payments & Refunds

https://www.profitbooks.net/tax-payments-under-gst/

https://www.profitbooks.net/gst-refund-process/

https://cleartax.in/s/gst-payments-and-refunds

https://cleartax.in/s/gst-payments-and-refunds#what

http://www.gstindia.com/refund-in-gst-goods-and-services-tax/
http://vikaspedia.in/social-welfare/financial-inclusion/faqs-on-gst-1/gst-payment-of-tax

13: Returns Filing
https://cleartax.in/s/gst-returns#what
https://www.legalraasta.com/gst-return/
https://www.profitbooks.net/gst-returns/
https://www.bankbazaar.com/tax/gst-returns.html
https://www.indiafilings.com/gst-return-filing
https://www.reachaccountant.com/erp-software-pos-software-blog/file-gst-returns-india/

14 Movement of Goods
https://www.indiafilings.com/learn/gst-delivery-challan-format/
https://cleartax.in/s/impact-stock-transfer-gst
https://www.gstkeeper.com/blog/gst/how-will-gst-impact-stock-transfer-between-branches
http://blogs.tallysolutions.com/gst-branch-stock-transfer/
https://www.exactlly.com/blog/index.php/impact-of-gst-on-stock-transfer-between-branches/
https://dailytally.in/branch-transfer-outward-inward-in-tally
http://blogs.tallysolutions.com/gst-calculation-branch-transfers/
http://thevistaacademy.com/interstate-and-intra-state-stock-transfer-in-gst-regime-in-tally/
http://tally9book.com/Pages/Quick-Help/Stock%20Transfer-in-Tally9.html
http://164.100.80.180/ewbnat9/Documents/usermanual_ewb.pdf
https://cleartax.in/s/eway-bill-gst-rules-compliance
https://cleartax.in/s/generate-gst-eway-bills/
https://cleartax.in/s/gst-eway-bill-registration
http://www.gstindia.com/e-way-bill-under-gst/
https://blog.saginfotech.com/gst-e-way-bill-how-generate
http://www.charteredclub.com/e-way-bill/

https://youtu.be/80MOT0DKJAs
https://youtu.be/8hNejeWuKl4
https://youtu.be/_1Fea56XlOw
https://youtu.be/GSxMapU1rck
https://youtu.be/zuebaPA4lqU
https://youtu.be/YD41h7iElqw
https://youtu.be/dmpNSLaZ6ko
https://youtu.be/dmpNSLaZ6ko

15 Input Service Distributor

https://cleartax.in/s/input-service-distributor-under-gst

https://www.legalraasta.com/gst/input-service-distributor/

https://www.taxmanagementindia.com/visitor/detail_article.asp?ArticleID=6345

https://taxguru.in/goods-and-service-tax/input-service-distributor-isd-gst.html

https://www.gstindia.com/input-service-distributor-in-gst/

https://www.indiafilings.com/learn/gst-input-service-distributor/

https://www.hrblock.in/earlygst/input-service-distributor/

16 Import & Export

https://www.indiafilings.com/learn/gst-applicable-imported-goods/

https://gstindiaguide.com/gst-vessel-freight/

https://cleartax.in/s/itc-rules-capital-goods-gst

https://taxmantra.com/faqs-on-exports-under-gst/

https://thegstindia.com/gst-export-goods-services/

17 Books of Accounts

https://gst.caknowledge.com/gst-accounts-records/

https://cleartax.in/s/cgst-rules-chapter-7-accounts-and-records

https://taxguru.in/goods-and-service-tax/accounts-records-goods-services-tax-gst.html

http://taxadda.com/gst/accounts-and-records-to-be-maintained/

18 Audit

https://cleartax.in/s/audit-under-gst

http://www.charteredclub.com/gst-audit/

https://www.legalraasta.com/gst/special-audit/

https://gst.caknowledge.com/gst-audit-formats/

https://www.icsi.edu/portals/2/PPT/Pavan%20GST%20AUDIT.pdf

https://gst.registrationwala.com/gst-forms/gst-audit-forms

https://www.gstbazaar.com/gst-forms/gst-audit-forms

19 Assessment

https://cleartax.in/s/assessment-gst

https://cleartax.in/s/gst-procedure

https://www.legalraasta.com/gst/gst-assessment/

https://taxguru.in/goods-and-service-tax/assessment-gst-laws.html

https://taxguru.in/goods-and-service-tax/assessments-gst.html

https://taxmantra.com/assessments-and-audit-under-gst/
https://taxmantra.com/assessments-and-audit-under-gst/
https://www.indiafilings.com/gst-portal/cgst-act/summary-assessment
https://www.hrblock.in/earlygst/best-judgement-assessment-gst/

https://youtu.be/_iRJ3IY-pWY

20 Demands & Recovery

https://taxguru.in/goods-and-service-tax/important-points-demand-recovery-gst.html
https://cleartax.in/s/gst-demand
https://cleartax.in/s/cgst-rules-chapter-18-demands-and-recovery
https://gstindiaguide.com/demand-and-recovery/
https://home.kpmg.com/content/dam/kpmg/pdf/2016/07/tnf-india-gst-jul19-2016.pdf
https://gstindia.net/topic/cgst73/
http://www.eximguru.com/gst/faqs-gst-demands-recovery.aspx
https://taxguru.in/goods-and-service-tax/important-points-demand-recovery-gst.html
http://gstportal.in/demand-and-recovery-process-under-gst/
https://centrik.in/blogs/demands-and-recovery-under-gst/
http://www.sircofical.org/downloads/cpe-materials/SIRC_Demand_recovery_10082017.pdf
https://www1.avalara.com/in/en/blog/2017/09/faqs-gst-refunds-demand-recovery.html
https://gst.caclub.in/demands-and-recovery-under-gst-faqs-by-cbec/
https://thegstindia.com/demands-recovery-provisions-gst-law/
https://www.itrtoday.com/demand-and-recovery-under-gst-a-quick-walk-through/
https://www.indiafilings.com/learn/gst-show-cause-notice/

21 Penalties & Prosecution

https://cleartax.in/s/offences-and-penalties-gst
https://cleartax.in/s/prosecution-under-gst
https://cleartax.in/s/gst-penalties-and-appeals
https://www.hrblock.in/earlygst/guide-category/gst-law-and-rules/
https://gst.caclub.in/offences-penalties-prosecution-and-compounding-under-gst-faqs-by-cbec/
https://www.reachaccountant.com/erp-software-pos-software-blog/offences-and-penalties-under-gst/
https://www.profitbooks.net/offenses-penalties-appeals-gst/
http://www.cutmytax.com/offences-penalties-prosecution-under-gst/
https://www.legistify.com/blogs/view_detail/149-offences-and-penalties-under-gst
https://www.itrtoday.com/offences-and-penalties-under-gst-an-overview/

https://thegstindia.com/prosecution-compounding-gst-law/

https://taxmantra.com/inspection-search-demand-penalties-and-compounding-under-gst/

http://www.gstgovt.in/20-offences-and-penalties-prosecution-and-compounding/

http://gstpanacea.com/services/penalties-proposed-under-gst/

https://www.coniferlabs.in/gstdocs/penalities.html

http://www.saitaxonline.in/faq-on-offences-penalties-and-prosecution/

http://www.gsthelplineindia.com/blog/2017/07/21/gst-offences-penalties-and-appeals/

https://gst.registrationwala.com/article/gst-penalties-and-appeals

22:Appeals

https://cleartax.in/s/gst-appeals

https://cleartax.in/s/appeals-under-gst-first-appellate

https://www.profitbooks.net/offenses-penalties-appeals-gst/

http://www.gsthelplineindia.com/blog/2017/07/21/gst-offences-penalties-and-appeals/

https://gst.registrationwala.com/article/gst-penalties-and-appeals

https://cleartax.in/s/appeals-gst-court

https://www.indiafilings.com/gst-portal/gst-model-law/appeal-the-high-court

https://integrabooks.co/appeal-under-gst/

23:Advance Ruling

https://cleartax.in/s/advance-ruling-gst

http://www.gstcouncil.gov.in/advance-rulings

https://www.hrblock.in/earlygst/advance-ruling-under-gst/

http://www.eximguru.com/gst/faqs-gst-advance-ruling.aspx

https://taxguru.in/goods-and-service-tax/gst-advance-ruling.html

https://www.legalraasta.com/gst/advance-ruling/

PART-II : GSTN Portal

https://tutorial.gst.gov.in/userguide/returns/

01: On line GST Registration

https://gst.caknowledge.com/gst-new-registration/

https://services.gst.gov.in/services/quicklinks/registration

https://cleartax.in/s/how-to-register-for-gst/

http://dvat.gov.in/website/GST.htm

https://aagst.com/

https://thegstindia.com

http://incometaxmanagement.com/Pages/GST/GST-India.html

https://gst.caknowledge.com/gst-new-registration/

https://services.gst.gov.in/services/quicklinks/registration

https://cleartax.in/s/how-to-register-for-gst/

http://dvat.gov.in/website/GST.htm

https://aagst.com/

https://thegstindia.com

http://incometaxmanagement.com/Pages/GST/GST-India.html

https://youtu.be/m1pdyv4gjxM

https://youtu.be/wD0Q-fJ1SK0

https://youtu.be/W0LQhnppBfU

https://youtu.be/ft8qGWoCYj0

https://youtu.be/3x7QZ8xFlE8

https://youtu.be/o700WtbBTrw

https://youtu.be/owY4oVmX1qU

https://youtu.be/W0LQhnppBfU

https://youtu.be/ft8qGWoCYj0

https://youtu.be/3x7QZ8xFlE8

https://youtu.be/o700WtbBTrw

https://youtu.be/owY4oVmX1qU

02 User Account Management

http://taxin.in/gst/how-to-create-a-username-and-password-of-gst-goods-and-service-tax-common-portal/

http://howtoexportimport.com/Step-by-step-procedures-to-create-username-and-pas-4541.aspx

https://cleartax.in/s/cleartax-guide-on-gst-portal

https://cleartax.in/s/how-to-register-as-gst-practitioner

http://taxin.in/gst/how-to-create-a-username-and-password-of-gst-goods-and-service-tax-common-portal/

https://gst.caknowledge.com/gst-login/

https://vakilsearch.com/advice/gst-enrollment/

https://www.zoho.com/in/books/gst/how-to-register-for-gst.html

http://www.howtoexportimport.com/How-to-retrieve-user-name-under-GST-registration-o-4514.aspx

https://taxguru.in/goods-and-service-tax/retrieve-forgotten-username-gst-portal-website.html

https://www.knowyourgst.com/question/forgot-gst-user-id-and-password/88/

https://filegst.com/retrieve-login-username-under-gst/

https://gstindia.net/password-reset/

https://www.indiafilings.com/learn/solved-gst-provisional-id-not-generated-or-not-working/

https://thegstindia.com/existing-taxpayers-register-gst-process/

https://www.caclubindia.com/forum/gst-user-name-change-394194.asp

http://blogs.tallysolutions.com/how-to-change-mobile-number-and-email-id-in-gst/

https://comtaxappl.uk.gov.in/Migration_FAQ.PDF

https://gst.caknowledge.in/register-update-digital-signature-gst-portal/

https://www.emsigner.com/

https://www1.avalara.com/in/en/blog/2017/04/digital-signing-gst-returns.html

http://www.consultease.com/taxation/gst-in-india/use-e-sign-gst-enrolment/

https://esign.cdac.in/

https://youtu.be/ZnXOQzt_-4o

https://youtu.be/cn6yf0Sr3O8

03:GSTR-1: Outwards Supplies Physical Form

https://cleartax.in/s/gstr-1

https://cleartax.in/s/guide-to-gstr1-filing

https://www.profitbooks.net/gstr-1-return-filing/

https://tallysolutions.com/gst/gstr1-filing-format-due-date/

https://blog.saginfotech.com/gstr-1-online-return-filing

https://youtu.be/C_z6HFODm0A

https://youtu.be/udhNUKOzqqM

https://youtu.be/BZkFyti-fU4

https://youtu.be/93-xsjM1uLw

https://youtu.be/Enel24GPo80

https://youtu.be/bd2Jw9-wu1w

https://youtu.be/tw3tb8RNp38

https://youtu.be/U7yoqbryx_s

https://youtu.be/9sqXkEnYcHE

https://youtu.be/9sqXkEnYcHE

https://youtu.be/WRl8s7pXhS0

https://youtu.be/mT3Jv7gOOLk

https://youtu.be/8zwCDs6Flws

https://youtu.be/5KarM8yJ2gQ

https://youtu.be/F8wAimtS-yE

https://youtu.be/C_z6HFODm0A

04:GSTR-1: Outwards Supplies off-line upload

https://tutorial.gst.gov.in/downloads/invoiceuploadofflineutility.pdf
https://cleartax.in/s/download-gstr-1-make-changes
http://comtax.up.nic.in/GSThome/Traingmaterial/gstr%201.pdf
https://taxguru.in/goods-and-service-tax/17-steps-prepare-gstr1-offline-tool.html

05:GSTR-1: Outwards Supplies On-line entry

http://blogs.tallysolutions.com/guide-to-file-gstr-1/
http://eicbma.com/gst2017/gst-tax-invoice-debit-credit-notes-with-form-050617.pdf
https://cleartax.in/s/gst-hsn-lookup
https://cleartax.in/s/debit-note-credit-note-and-and-how-to-revise-gst-invoices
https://cleartax.in/s/cgst-rules-chapter-6-tax-invoice-credit-and-debit-notes
http://eicbma.com/gst2017/gst-tax-invoice-debit-credit-notes-with-form-050617.pdf
https://cbec-gst.gov.in/pdf/cgst-rules-01july2017.pdf

https://youtu.be/udhNUKOzqqM
https://youtu.be/93-xsjM1uLw
https://youtu.be/tw3tb8RNp38
https://youtu.be/XGNj_NdEgL4
https://youtu.be/5PQdNFU0Grl
https://youtu.be/xVQyjq_58T0
https://youtu.be/eG5Sez6Liec
https://youtu.be/-n2xhXp0vfY
https://youtu.be/o3R8hWou6lo
https://youtu.be/Lo9xurf2BuM
https://youtu.be/96syx8ALfcg
https://youtu.be/ml4lbUVSs1c
https://youtu.be/iWg8svOCQlU
https://youtu.be/0AYzihctkC4

06:GSTR-2: Inwards Supplies Off line upload

https://www.indiafilings.com/learn/file-nil-gstr2-return/
https://taxguru.in/goods-and-service-tax/step-step-guide-prepare-gstr2-offline-filing.html
https://www.gstindia.com/steps-to-file-gstr-2/
https://studycafe.in/2017/09/how-to-file-gstr-2.html

https://gstindiaguide.com/gstr-2-offline-version-2-1-gst-offline-utility/

http://www.gstindiaonline.com/pages/downloads/doc/GST-GSTR%202-Guidelines.pdf

https://youtu.be/4sYysZ1eW3A

https://youtu.be/DvL9VD3_cFM

https://youtu.be/R3EcvpBDZYM

https://youtu.be/PPyGU6DWbe4

https://youtu.be/R3EcvpBDZYM

https://youtu.be/8ANAxK1rnq4

https://youtu.be/TO6IzJxhwOw

07:GSTR-2: Inwards Supplies On line Entry

https://tutorial.gst.gov.in/userguide/returns/Creation_of_Inward_Supplies_Return.htm

https://www.legalraasta.com/gst/gstr-2-return/

https://cleartax.in/s/gstr2

https://cleartax.in/s/guide-on-gstr-2-filing-on-gst-portal

https://www.profitbooks.net/gstr-2-return-filing/

https://www.indiafilings.com/learn/gstr-2-filing/

https://www.zoho.com/in/books/gst/how-to-file-gstr-2.html

https://youtu.be/-mFw1SARQjk

https://youtu.be/IveXN7CKhes

https://youtu.be/8vsqIAWzIXc

https://youtu.be/L0B4PSfbyaE

https://youtu.be/AOe8FxFVD6M

https://youtu.be/SjdLZ6PdzHk

https://youtu.be/V0uewHRDDnl

https://youtu.be/UmhKYm1ffww

https://youtu.be/Oyq0bzVd56Q

https://youtu.be/nBEN8-F9jng

https://youtu.be/SzHm5OWmUxE

https://youtu.be/V9MJz5mZ5oA

https://youtu.be/tft73Ey6yy0

https://youtu.be/vEl80ojgztQ

https://youtu.be/NQFrJQ5cKP8

https://youtu.be/PeP6nbQY4NA

https://youtu.be/hOz9XyKXaaE

08 :GSTR-2A Sales Purchase Matching
https://www.profitbooks.net/invoice-matching-in-gst/
https://cleartax.in/s/invoice-matching-under-gst
https://studycafe.in/2018/05/matching-purchases-and-input-tax-credit-through-gstr-2a.html
https://taxguru.in/goods-and-service-tax/semi-finals-gst-starts-match-purchases-gstr-2a.html
http://icmai.in/TaxationPortal/upload/IDT/Article_GST/11.pdf
https://www.legalraasta.com/gst/gstr-2a-return/
https://www.zoho.com/in/books/gst/how-to-file-gstr-2a.html#gstr2a-contents
https://www.zoho.com/in/books/gst/how-to-file-gstr-1a.html
https://cleartax.in/s/gstr2
https://cleartax.in/s/gstr-2a
http://www.profitbooks.net/gstr-2-return-filing/
https://www.indiafilings.com/learn/file-gstr-2-return-online/
https://taxguru.in/goods-and-service-tax/semi-finals-gst-starts-match-purchases-gstr-2a.html

https://youtu.be/X1CSpLDy9W0
https://youtu.be/IveXN7CKhes
https://youtu.be/AydsfYXDsiI
https://youtu.be/TO6IzJxhwOw
https://youtu.be/rRAnvtg2-N4
https://youtu.be/8vsqlAWzlXc
https://youtu.be/tft73Ey6yy0
https://youtu.be/_hRDgzZBynU
https://youtu.be/RMEF3JSzj-o
https://youtu.be/jcfDNFwEGR4
https://youtu.be/PeP6nbQY4NA
https://youtu.be/tHpVlG4lhus
https://youtu.be/za9GDk4sXag
https://youtu.be/bLyO3QLc-cl
https://youtu.be/R25_mFIXG-w
https://youtu.be/zqEnT_C-tH8
https://youtu.be/IveXN7CKhes

09:GSTR-3 Monthly Tax Return
https://gst.caknowledge.com/file-gstr-3-gst-monthly-return/
https://cleartax.in/s/gst-return-gstr3
https://tallysolutions.com/gst/gstr3-filing-format-due-date/

https://www.legalraasta.com/gst/gstr-3-return/
https://www.hrblock.in/earlygst/guide-on-gstr3/
https://www.mastersindia.co/gst/gstr-3-format-filing-procedure-file-gstr-3/
https://blog.saginfotech.com/gstr-3-filing-guide
https://www.indiafilings.com/learn/gstr-3-return-filing/
https://www.greengst.com/how-to-file-gstr-3/

https://youtu.be/MjJDu0AMNtU
https://youtu.be/gOeNFJHmtl8
https://youtu.be/05XU5wSIa0E
https://youtu.be/PeP6nbQY4NA
https://youtu.be/TsDhfhCEuSE
https://youtu.be/AOq3F2sFySs
https://youtu.be/PeP6nbQY4NA
https://youtu.be/ZiH5qMgUy5o
https://youtu.be/9sqXkEnYcHE
https://youtu.be/buPEW_3eqSg
https://youtu.be/PriTvjgvdi4

10 :GSTR-3B Monthly Tax Return Off line filing
https://tutorial.gst.gov.in/downloads/gstr3bofflineutility.pdf
https://cleartax.in/s/gst-excel-templates
https://blog.saginfotech.com/gstr-3b-return-filing-procedure-guide
https://www.profitbooks.net/gstr-3b-format/
https://octabits.in/gstr3b-view-upload/
https://gstindianews.info/gstr-3b-offline-tool-download-free/

https://youtu.be/dgYIcaJWcnY
https://youtu.be/3Nd-j7HG9Jo
https://youtu.be/kt1Z5L0MG4k
https://youtu.be/MGCFv5DfXpU
https://youtu.be/HViPoWySPe4

11:GSTR-3B Monthly Tax Return On- line filing
https://taxmantra.com/how-to-file-gstr-3b-step-by-step-guide/
https://cleartax.in/s/file-gstr-3b-gst-portal-guide
https://tutorial.gst.gov.in/userguide/returns/Create_and_Submit_GSTR3B.htm

https://www.jiogst.com/documents/20182/459320/GSTR-3B+Return+Filing
https://www.indiafilings.com/learn/gstr-3b-return/
https://blog.saginfotech.com/gstr-3b-return-filing-procedure-guide
https://www.hrblock.in/earlygst/gstr-3b/
https://www.zoho.com/in/books/gst/how-to-file-gstr-3b.html

https://youtu.be/nBEN8-F9jng
https://youtu.be/rplJ94s94io
https://youtu.be/xqXXBElqLKE

12:GSTR-4 Composition Dealer Return

https://blog.saginfotech.com/gstr-4-online-return-filing
https://www.indiafilings.com/learn/gstr-4-return/
https://cleartax.in/s/gstr4-composition-dealer-gst-return

https://youtu.be/gALI9v4Gl7Q
https://youtu.be/f_hM35_ZKD0
https://youtu.be/e4DXDBiTjkQ
https://youtu.be/OchGdAPR5Yc
https://youtu.be/5-3REunJu6g
https://youtu.be/wZnhTK3Sm3c
https://youtu.be/RQ9Y7XLModl
https://youtu.be/Cp2ABAdLooQ
https://youtu.be/18OzLlRsRwM
https://youtu.be/0VeLKJBke6k
https://youtu.be/AHisx_ku0Kc

13:GSTR-5 Non-Resident Return Physical Form

https://cleartax.in/s/gst-registration-process-for-nri/
https://cleartax.in/s/gst-return-gstr5
https://www.legalraasta.com/gst/gstr-5-return/
http://www.caalley.com/gstforms/gstr05.pdf
https://www.greengst.com/gstr-5-return-filing-for-non-resident-foreign-taxpayers/
http://www.gsthelplineindia.com/blog/2017/07/31/gstr-5/
https://tutorial.gst.gov.in/userguide/returns/index.htm#t=GSTR-5.htm
https://www.hrblock.in/earlygst/gstr5-return-under-gst/

https://www.gsthelplineindia.com/blog/2017/07/31/gstr-5/
https://youtu.be/93aG8Vled08

14:GSTR-5 Non-Resident on-line Return Filing
https://taxguru.in/goods-and-service-tax/all-about-gstr-5-return-filing-with-faqs-filing-procedure.html
https://www.dailypioneer.com/impact/gstr-5-is-now-available-for-filing-at-gst-portal.html
https://enterslice.com/learning/gstr-5-under-gst-for-foreigners/

15:GSTR-5A OIDAR Return
https://tutorial.gst.gov.in/userguide/returns/index.htm#t=GSTR-5A.htm
https://cleartax.in/s/place-of-supply-for-oidar
https://www.taxmann.com/blogpost/2000000312/oidar-services-in-gst.aspx
https://www.indiafilings.com/learn/oidar-services-under-gst/
https://www.indiafilings.com/learn/examples-of-oidar-services-under-gst/
https://www.mastersindia.co/gst/oidar-online-information-database-access-retrieval-services/
https://www.gstreporting.com/2017/07/21/all-about-oidar-services/
https://www.caclubindia.com/articles/oidar-services-in-gst-31516.asp

16:GSTR-6 ISD Return
https://cleartax.in/s/gst-offline-tool-excel-utility
https://gstlatest.com/gstr-6-offline-tool-download-excel-utility-for-isd-return-filing/
https://cleartax.in/s/gstr-6-gst-return
https://cleartax.in/s/gstr-06-filing/
https://tutorial.gst.gov.in/userguide/returns/index.htm#t=GSTR-6.htm
https://www.hrblock.in/earlygst/gstr6-return-under-gst/
https://tallysolutions.com/gst/gstr6-filing-format-due-date/
https://www.mastersindia.co/gst/gstr-6-return
https://blog.saginfotech.com/gstr-6-form-filing-online
https://www.webtel.in/Image/Form%20GSTR_6_New.pdf
http://www.udyogsoftware.com/gstr-6-filing-guidelines-and-format/
https://taxguru.in/goods-and-service-tax/gstr6-latest-frequently-asked-questions-faqs.html

https://youtu.be/XtYN7ui4Bkc
https://youtu.be/7pXxmbUVX5E
https://youtu.be/GPn95P13S90
https://youtu.be/u7g4JP7Z740
https://youtu.be/X5Vvf4uz-lQ

https://youtu.be/CPRos_eTX48
https://youtu.be/T5v-t154Oxk
https://youtu.be/X5Vvf4uz-lQ
https://youtu.be/JC7xAgnv7M8

17: GSTR-7 TDS Return
https://cleartax.in/s/gstr-7-gst-return
https://www.legalraasta.com/gst/gstr-7-return/
https://www.hrblock.in/earlygst/guide-on-gstr7/
https://blog.saginfotech.com/gstr-7-form-filing
https://taxguru.in/goods-and-service-tax/gstr7-tds-return.html
https://www.webtel.in/Image/Form%20GSTR_7_New.pdf
https://blog.saginfotech.com/gstr-7-form-filing
https://tallysolutions.com/gst/gstr7-filing-format-due-date/

https://youtu.be/aPp3S8TaUpM
https://youtu.be/JD5g1krpsHM

18: GSR-8 TCS Return
https://cleartax.in/s/gstr-8-gst-return
https://taxguru.in/goods-and-service-tax/tcs-tax-collected-source-gst.html
https://www.zoho.com/in/books/gst/how-to-file-gstr-8.html
https://tallysolutions.com/gst/gstr8-filing-format-due-date/
https://blog.saginfotech.com/gstr-8-form-filing
https://www.indiafilings.com/learn/gstr-8-filing/
https://www.legalraasta.com/gst/gstr-8-return/
https://www.gsthelplineindia.com/blog/2018/03/29/gstr-8-return-guide/

https://youtu.be/ectM7v9MYYw
https://youtu.be/ulERZJT_d1Q

19:GSTR-9 Annual Return
https://cleartax.in/s/gstr-9-annual-return
https://blog.saginfotech.com/gstr-9-online-return-filing
https://tallysolutions.com/gst/gstr9-filing-format-due-date/
http://gstblog.i-tax.in/Forms/Return/GSTR-9.pdf
https://studycafe.in/2018/05/annual-return-in-gst-act-2017-all-about-gstr-9.html

https://www.indiafilings.com/learn/gstr-9-filing/

https://taxheal.com/gst-anuual-return.html

https://www.gsthelplineindia.com/blog/2018/05/10/gstr-9-annual-return-filing/

https://www.greengst.com/how-to-file-gstr-9-annual-return/

https://www.zoho.com/in/books/gst/how-to-file-gstr-9.html

https://youtu.be/XFPoJuLa0zo

https://youtu.be/50adt-QhZ00

https://youtu.be/4m1QacznPVl

20: Electronic Ledgers

https://www.gst.gov.in/help/ledgers

https://cleartax.in/s/e-ledgers-under-gst

https://www.hrblock.in/earlygst/e-ledgers-under-gst/

https://www.indiafilings.com/learn/gst-ledgers/

https://taxguru.in/goods-and-service-tax/electronic-credit-ledger-gst.html

https://www.hostbooks.com/in/blog/gst/various-types-electronic-ledgers-gst/

https://www.legalraasta.com/gst/gst-electronic-ledger-working/

https://studycafe.in/2017/11/how-to-use-electronic-cash-ledger-and-itc-ledger.html

https://quickbooks.intuit.com/in/resources/gst-center/gst-e-ledgers-accounting/

https://www.profitbooks.net/tax-payments-under-gst/

http://www.nimsme.org/ranzo/uploads/articles/payment-gst-rules.pdf

https://integrabooks.co/electronic-ledgers-under-gst/

https://www.zoho.com/in/books/gst/gst-accounting.html

https://youtu.be/omHVQdjqbco

https://youtu.be/J3dEQn_oGEk

https://youtu.be/UFpNk2JrptM

21 : Utilisation of Cash & ITC

https://tutorial.gst.gov.in/userguide/ledgers/index.htm#t=UtilizingCashmanual.htm

https://tutorial.gst.gov.in/userguide/ledgers/index.htm#t=UtilizingCashfaq.htm

https://www.mastersindia.co/gst/set-off-liability-form-3b/

https://www.greengst.com/how-to-set-off-input-tax-credit-in-gst-regime/

https://sahigst.com/knowledge/t/set-off-utilization-of-input-tax-credit-under-gst-in-india/734

https://blogs.tallysolutions.com/how-to-set-off-input-credit-against-liability-in-gst/

http://tallyerp9book.com/Pages/Web-Page/GST/Adjustment-Set-Off-The-Liability-Of-GST(Tax)Credit-in-TallyERP9.html

https://youtu.be/Z_lxibivtzA
https://youtu.be/5GNfhj8ONAo
https://youtu.be/WATCFLIE2BU

22: Tax Payments

https://cleartax.in/s/gst-payment
https://cleartax.in/s/gst-payments-and-refunds
https://www.profitbooks.net/tax-payments-under-gst/
http://vikaspedia.in/social-welfare/financial-inclusion/faqs-on-gst-1/gst-payment-of-tax
http://taxadda.com/gst-payment-and-interest-late-payment/
https://tallysolutions.com/gst/gst-payment-rules-process-form/

https://youtu.be/yxHJ1RzP5lk
https://youtu.be/nBEN8-F9jng
https://youtu.be/HIE6Mn86YCl
https://youtu.be/GxAU-NusxmE
https://youtu.be/pwZRRrHvyts
https://youtu.be/QtVFrt7KvXk
https://youtu.be/trpR7G6KbLc
https://youtu.be/jZvOZ8EMiCs
https://youtu.be/jZvOZ8EMiCs
https://youtu.be/_aXLQQlLqw0
https://youtu.be/OaANtDnbfJM
https://youtu.be/__e8CGYTdlQ
https://youtu.be/v-OVGQwzdQA
https://youtu.be/sfqOF-j-luk
https://youtu.be/Yz4FSC56mX0
https://youtu.be/m9cbE2ExBtc
https://youtu.be/r_iE4oiWWVk
https://youtu.be/9IBAv-GJcLk
https://youtu.be/QvDWZ6RvlnA
https://youtu.be/KVM7xnvqs50
https://youtu.be/UFdmq4fSkEQ
https://youtu.be/10X14kKS38k

https://youtu.be/dtxYJMo913c

https://youtu.be/SoEbh70K6CI

https://youtu.be/89Ux4b_Iosw

https://youtu.be/tz0GibIF_Ow

https://youtu.be/hOhwHdoP-F8

https://youtu.be/NtRFQu2mcxY

https://youtu.be/ps_3c508yTY

23 :Refunds

https://www.gst.gov.in/help/refund

https://www.gstindia.com/refund-in-gst-goods-and-services-tax/

https://www.profitbooks.net/gst-refund-process/

https://www.mastersindia.co/gst/claim-refund-of-excess-balance-in-electronic-cash-ledger/

https://www.legalraasta.com/gst/tax-refund-gst/

https://cleartax.in/s/refund-claims-under-gst-for-tax-and-itc

https://cleartax.in/s/refund-process-under-gst

https://www.profitbooks.net/gst-refund-process/

https://www.legalraasta.com/gst/tax-refund-gst/

https://www.indiafilings.com/learn/unutilised-input-tax-credit-refund-under-gst/

https://www.gstindia.com/refund-in-gst-goods-and-services-tax/

https://www.hrblock.in/earlygst/refund-under-gst/

https://www.charteredclub.com/gst-refund/

https://www.charteredclub.com/gst-refund/

https://youtu.be/W2izR9merIM

https://youtu.be/7Tzjau9JrDM

https://youtu.be/kUWNSg1WerE

https://youtu.be/LDdH3d4gGbE

https://youtu.be/a7vbKdF9Q8c

https://youtu.be/4WGzTrehZxY

https://youtu.be/SBHuin8VmpY

https://youtu.be/7Tzjau9JrDM

https://youtu.be/U2qgZU0merA

24:e-signature

https://www.gst.gov.in/help/loginanddsc

http://www.consultease.com/taxation/gst-in-india/use-e-sign-gst-enrolment/#.Wvl6cIiFPIU

https://www.consultease.com/gst-compliances-in-india/use-e-sign-gst-enrolment/#.W3F_L-gzblU

http://www.efilingworld.com/2017/11/25/guide-to-install-emsigner/

https://www.hrblock.in/blog/can-e-sign-gst-returns/

https://blogs.tallysolutions.com/difference-between-dsc-e-sign-and-evc-in-gst-portal/

https://www.indiafilings.com/learn/signing-gst-documents-requirement-digital-signature/

https://taxguru.in/goods-and-service-tax/faqs-on-login-dsc-registration-e-sign-and-evc-on-gst-portal.html

https://taxguru.in/goods-and-service-tax/esign-gst-enrollment-application-aadhar-number.html

https://youtu.be/YcUZ0TCWNbk

https://youtu.be/PlHmsVXo6og

https://youtu.be/xJhCvwYNMwY

25:e-way Bill On-line

https://ewaybill.nic.in/

https://ewaybillgst.gov.in/ewb.html

https://services.gst.gov.in/services/ewaybill/ewaybillsystem

https://www.profitbooks.net/eway-bill/

http://blogs.tallysolutions.com/bulk-consolidated-eway-bill-generate-cancel-update/

https://tallysolutions.com/gst/e-way-bill-under-gst/

https://www.charteredclub.com/e-way-bill/

https://www.hrblock.in/earlygst/gst-e-way-bill-rules/

https://www.gstindia.com/50-practical-issues-possible-solutions-on-e-way-bills-under-gst/

https://www.zoho.com/in/books/gst/e-way-bill.html

https://www.caclubindia.com/articles/complete-guide-to-e-way-bill-under-gst-31892.asp

https://afleo.com/learn/eway-bill-gst

http://pib.nic.in/newsite/PrintRelease.aspx?relid=178856

https://cleartax.in/s/generate-gst-eway-bills

https://cleartax.in/s/generate-gst-eway-bill-via-sms

https://cleartax.in/s/generate-gst-consolidated-eway-bill

https://cleartax.in/s/e-way-bill-transporter-rules-compliances

https://cleartax.in/s/eway-bill-gst-rules-compliance

https://youtu.be/MviRTqkrifw

https://youtu.be/E8ZgybiPtUI

https://youtu.be/MviRTqkrifw

Part 3 : GST Accounting using Tally.ERP 9

General Guide on GST Accounting using Tally.ERP9

https://tallysolutions.com/gst/

https://cleartax.in/s/basic-guide-to-use-tally-erp-9-release-6-for-gst

http://tallyerp9book.com/Pages/Web-Page/GST/GST-Home.html

http://www.tallyerp9tutorials.com/tally-erp-9/taxation/gst-tally/

http://www.tallyerp9gst.com/Index.html

01:GST Set up for Composition Dealer

http://www.tallyerp9tutorials.com/taxation/gst-tally/activate-gst-tally-erp-9/

https://help.tallysolutions.com/article/Tally.ERP9/Tax_India/gst/activating_gst_for_your_company.htm

https://www.tallyschool.com/set-gst-details-in-tally/

http://tallygame.com/tally-erp-9/statutory-taxation/gst/how-to-activate-gst-in-tally-erp-9/

https://youtu.be/cnMkhhZXWOE

https://youtu.be/Y_Nw01HCoyM

https://youtu.be/Y88ojKO3F5I

https://youtu.be/Prrzj6UBAIA

https://youtu.be/zc6BALZdnAE

https://youtu.be/Bs6vvTCJQMQ

02:GST Set up for Regular Dealer

http://www.tallyerp9tutorials.com/taxation/gst-tally/activate-gst-tally-erp-9/

https://help.tallysolutions.com/article/Tally.ERP9/Tax_India/gst/activating_gst_for_your_company.htm

https://www.tallyschool.com/set-gst-details-in-tally/

http://tallygame.com/tally-erp-9/statutory-taxation/gst/how-to-activate-gst-in-tally-erp-9/

https://youtu.be/cnMkhhZXWOE

https://youtu.be/Y_Nw01HCoyM

https://youtu.be/Y88ojKO3F5I

https://youtu.be/Prrzj6UBAIA

https://youtu.be/zc6BALZdnAE

https://youtu.be/Bs6vvTCJQMQ

03 : Masters Entry & Set Up

https://help.tallysolutions.com/article/te9rel64/Tax_India/gst/an_overview_of_gst_in_tallyerp_9.htm

http://www.tallyerp9gst.com/Pages/Setup-GST/GST-Setup-Using-TallyERP9.html

http://www.tallyerp9gst.com/Pages/Setup-GST/Managing-HSN-Codes-SAC-and-Tax-Rates-in-TallyERP9.html

http://www.tallyerp9tutorials.com/tally/gst-masters/

http://www.tallyerp9tutorials.com/taxation/gst-tally/updatecreate-sales-purchase-ledgers-gst-compliance/

https://youtu.be/70ioQWssR8k

https://youtu.be/F7Yd31yiYqM

https://youtu.be/Eh0JNxqcJBM

https://youtu.be/XwYv3QOHmI4

https://youtu.be/zvLzgRWh2TM

https://youtu.be/0qdWkrf6GfI

https://youtu.be/lOJLWIXOa4I

https://youtu.be/rBCiFovw5BU

https://youtu.be/gp9lwm7Y2l0

https://youtu.be/sGxyHWlHE98

https://youtu.be/XzoFnpNqQBQ

https://youtu.be/V65zS7ZrHpQ

https://youtu.be/nK_QFmcpPuQ

https://youtu.be/hWq5YqmTf9U

04 :Sales Invoicing for Composition Dealer

http://www.tallyerp9tutorials.com/taxation/gst-tally/create-bill-supply-composition-scheme-gst-tally-erp-9/

https://cleartax.in/s/how-to-create-sales-invoice-in-tally-erp-9-release-6-for-gst

https://www.tallyschool.com/create-gst-invoice-tally-erp-9/

http://www.tallyerp9tutorials.com/taxation/gst-tally/enter-sales-voucher-gst-printing-invoice-format-tally-erp-9/

https://blogs.tallysolutions.com/generating-gst-bill-gst-invoice-in-tally-erp-9/

https://help.tallysolutions.com/article/Tally.ERP9/Tax_India/gst/recording_gst_sales_and_printing_invoices.htm

https://youtu.be/J113SJo4kU4

https://youtu.be/VbiuD1v_GDc

05 :Purchase Entry for Composition Dealer

http://www.tallyerp9tutorials.com/taxation/gst-tally/enter-purchase-gst-tally-erp-9/

https://help.tallysolutions.com/article/Tally.ERP9/Tax_India/gst_composition/purchase_gst_composition.htm

https://youtu.be/J113SJo4kU4

https://youtu.be/VbiuD1v_GDc

https://youtu.be/Y88ojKO3F5I

https://youtu.be/KwkE_npVCfs

https://youtu.be/4jSJ0cY29cw

https://youtu.be/Prrzj6UBAIA

https://youtu.be/w6AvyYCnje8

https://youtu.be/zc6BALZdnAE

https://youtu.be/p1DNJEkP0js

https://youtu.be/u2AqK7hCEck

https://youtu.be/txMBugG4ojg

06 :Sales Invoicing for Regular Dealer

http://www.tallyerp9tutorials.com/taxation/gst-tally/create-bill-supply-composition-scheme-gst-tally-erp-9/

https://cleartax.in/s/how-to-create-sales-invoice-in-tally-erp-9-release-6-for-gst

https://www.tallyschool.com/create-gst-invoice-tally-erp-9/

http://www.tallyerp9tutorials.com/taxation/gst-tally/enter-sales-voucher-gst-printing-invoice-format-tally-erp-9/

https://blogs.tallysolutions.com/generating-gst-bill-gst-invoice-in-tally-erp-9/

https://help.tallysolutions.com/article/Tally.ERP9/Tax_India/gst/recording_gst_sales_and_printing_invoices.htm

http://blogs.tallysolutions.com/generating-gst-bill-gst-invoice-in-tally-erp-9/?utm_source=subs_16Oct1&utm_medium=blog&utm_campaign=generate_invoice

https://youtu.be/J113SJo4kU4

https://youtu.be/VbiuD1v_GDc

https://youtu.be/-VxUdQA2Mxg

https://youtu.be/zuebaPA4lqU

https://youtu.be/w6AvyYCnje8

https://youtu.be/VdbF5xwH5Jg

https://youtu.be/7Pt5WU-9uB0

https://youtu.be/7Pt5WU-9uB0

https://youtu.be/CrUSMIRTXDg
https://youtu.be/IjtWCE6TeTU
https://youtu.be/Gs7tgmHQwsY

07 :Purchase from Registered Dealer
http://www.tallyerp9tutorials.com/taxation/gst-tally/enter-purchase-gst-tally-erp-9/
https://cleartax.in/s/how-to-create-purchase-invoice-in-tally-erp-9-release-6-for-gst
http://thevistaacademy.com/gst-tally-erp-9/
https://cleartax.in/s/itc-rules-capital-goods-gst

https://youtu.be/yi5mxRY-GnY
https://youtu.be/YVi5S0-1fHk
https://youtu.be/WWMcL1U6sLA

https://youtu.be/fTsgpAO8VCQ
https://youtu.be/VQKPuNlfu-8
https://youtu.be/hEKwfctFDf4

08:Purchase from Unregistered Dealer
https://help.tallysolutions.com/article/Tally.ERP9/Tax_India/gst/acctng_inward_supply_urd_gst_6_0_3.htm
http://www.tallyerp9tutorials.com/taxation/gst-tally/record-gst-purchase-unregistered-dealer/
http://www.tallyerp9gst.com/Pages/Purchase-GST/Purchase-from-Unregistered-Dealers-under-Reverse-Charge-in-GST-in-TallyERP9.html
http://thevistaacademy.com/purchase-from-unregistered-dealers-reverse-charge-in-tally/
http://blogs.tallysolutions.com/managing-reverse-charge-gst/
https://blogs.tallysolutions.com/gst-reverse-charge-purchases-from-unregistered-dealers-in-tally-erp-9-release-6/
https://cleartax.in/s/reverse-charge-buying-from-unregistered-dealers
http://blogs.tallysolutions.com/handling-reverse-charge-scenario-of-import-supplies-in-gst-ready-software/

https://youtu.be/fTsgpAO8VCQ
https://youtu.be/EWP2lDYu92U
https://youtu.be/5EG6P6sVsU8
https://youtu.be/p2eWqPfsf_s
https://youtu.be/28elYVG7t4M

https://youtu.be/JS1odsxMO9Y
https://youtu.be/vcV73TufX60
https://youtu.be/M3WA7ggSK_Q
https://youtu.be/4jSJ0cY29cw
https://youtu.be/ccdFTRQrkFI
https://youtu.be/jfvj0ifN1NU
https://youtu.be/pN5jCIqixo4
https://youtu.be/QVKLrKwhA9w
https://youtu.be/YJbJlQA6z-0
https://youtu.be/_s0DDkDyaMo
https://youtu.be/dfrCvOiNJZE
https://youtu.be/gz5pb6gaKFE
https://youtu.be/p2eWqPfsf_s
https://youtu.be/3iUtxrahGzs
https://youtu.be/j3oJcar-YSM
https://youtu.be/8k9klAABmVo
https://youtu.be/wfj2drbMAQo
https://youtu.be/ykHRW_xvsOI

09:Purchase from Composition Dealer

https://www.legalraasta.com/gst/composition-scheme/

https://youtu.be/ccdFTRQrkFI
https://youtu.be/4jSJ0cY29cw
https://youtu.be/3sZdBv93jMo
https://youtu.be/jfvj0ifN1NU
https://youtu.be/QVKLrKwhA9w
https://youtu.be/o7B-kRt734o
https://youtu.be/u2AqK7hCEck
https://youtu.be/1twiuK1m-bc
https://youtu.be/Prrzj6UBAIA

10: Invoice Reconciliation

http://blogs.tallysolutions.com/what-is-gstr-2-and-gstr-2a/
https://help.tallysolutions.com/article/Tally.ERP9/Tax_India/gst/mismatch_in_input_tax_credit.htm

https://youtu.be/Ry5yRhY4wQ8
https://youtu.be/fLsT5h_t6aM
https://youtu.be/PGCPBjuU8l0
https://youtu.be/xenL9Rzl37U
https://youtu.be/ycxlg9cat3c
https://youtu.be/TO6IzJxhwOw
https://youtu.be/J113SJo4kU4
https://youtu.be/ze7hYvzDkRc
https://youtu.be/2fVe8N_WIi8

11: Advance Receipt & Adjustment

https://help.tallysolutions.com/article/Tally.ERP9/Tax_India/gst/gst_advance_receipts_from_customers.htm
http://www.tallyerp9tutorials.com/taxation/gst-tally/record-advance-receipt-customers-gst-taxation/
https://tallyhelp.com/pdf/Advance_Receipt_Entry.pdf
http://www.tallyknowledge.com/2017/07/how-to-do-advance-receipt-gst-voucher.html
http://thevistaacademy.com/advance-receipt-customer-gst-tally/
http://thevistaacademy.com/journal-entry-advance-receipt-payment/
http://www.tallyerp9help.com/Pages/CHM-Help/GST/GST-Advance-Receipts-from-Customers-under-GST-in-TallyERP9.html
https://help.tallysolutions.com/article/Tally.ERP9/Tax_India/gst/tax_liability_-_Adv_Rcpts.htm

https://youtu.be/kb9zK_JiEq0
https://youtu.be/r6rZj9H2vOE
https://youtu.be/QaJTndiAruY
https://youtu.be/kP0nV2L7tQg
https://youtu.be/r9IFCLBcN_U
https://youtu.be/-TNo7skJT_A
https://youtu.be/NBv8tKlZrkE
https://youtu.be/TyWoz1tAmlc
https://youtu.be/JK-B8VP9Vx4
https://youtu.be/-AJC9uLawdI
https://youtu.be/Naqpw8aSlWg
https://youtu.be/vSPnQRakbu0
https://youtu.be/7iDcWAVUoDI
https://youtu.be/BCrAqWOuKyw
https://youtu.be/TfIfc7A3lQw

https://youtu.be/i4XTAbgKvSA

https://youtu.be/O5C5o1T2fJw

https://youtu.be/ZpChJzFNM3I

12: Reverse Charge Mechanism

https://tallysolutions.com/gst/reverse-charge-mechanism-in-gst/

https://help.tallysolutions.com/article/Tally.ERP9/Tax_India/gst/reverse_charge_on_sales.htm

https://help.tallysolutions.com/article/Tally.ERP9/Tax_India/gst/acctng_inward_goods_services_rc_gst_6_0_3.htm

https://blogs.tallysolutions.com/managing-reverse-charge-gst/

http://www.tallyknowledge.com/2017/09/how-to-create-reverse-charge-gst.html

http://www.tallyknowledge.com/2017/12/solution-of-gst-reverse-charge.html

https://youtu.be/eppzCZmZr6k

https://youtu.be/8quU1ZNRBB8

https://youtu.be/m9Mz5TevfRk

https://youtu.be/qkDQnr_gxXI

https://youtu.be/JPCebTt5hg4

https://youtu.be/3WWa8zXTmMs

https://youtu.be/p2eWqPfsf_s

https://youtu.be/4oUZDJztYK8

https://youtu.be/P7Nh-uVJWrI

https://youtu.be/82tCZ2dg2sE

https://youtu.be/3VOY-1_Bg5k

13 : Ineligible Input Tax Credit

https://help.tallysolutions.com/article/Tally.ERP9/Tax_India/gst/gst_accounting_for_ineligible_itc.htm

https://taxguru.in/goods-and-service-tax/items-eligible-input-tax-credit-gst.html

https://cleartax.in/s/gst-cases-where-input-tax-credit-is-unavailable

https://studycafe.in/2017/10/ineligible-input-tax-credit-or-block-credits-under-gst.html

https://www.meteorio.com/ineligible-input-tax-credit-itc-under-gst/

https://taxguru.in/goods-and-service-tax/input-tax-credit-not-allowed-gst-175-cgst-act-blocked-credit.html

https://www.hrblock.in/earlygst/section-17-5-gst/

https://help.tallysolutions.com/article/Tally.ERP9/Tax_India/gst/gst_accounting_for_ineligible_itc.htm

https://blog.saginfotech.com/list-goods-services-not-eligible-input-tax-credit

https://www.profitbooks.net/input-tax-credit-under-gst/

https://www.profitbooks.net/input-tax-credit-gst-india/
http://www.tallyknowledge.com/2018/01/how-to-enter-ineligible-input-tax.html
https://taxmantra.com/purchases-availingnot-availing-input-tax-credit/

https://youtu.be/YFWl7MCumME
https://youtu.be/yV63aMHb1Vk
https://youtu.be/qB3QUD-yhaE
https://youtu.be/_H6Sl93P-gA
https://youtu.be/a49k1LuhUCA
https://youtu.be/wBlQGqMXkgQ
https://youtu.be/fZlQpit9_rM
https://youtu.be/VdbF5xwH5Jg
https://youtu.be/yxCXxr1fl_A
https://youtu.be/cKlrxBFnaY0
https://youtu.be/ke0gJDja_lo
https://youtu.be/_H6Sl93P-gA
https://youtu.be/aci0keMJp6o
https://youtu.be/JC7xAgnv7M8
https://youtu.be/EdL4KhYYel0

14 :Delivery Challan

http://thevistaacademy.com/what-is-delivery-challan-in-tally-under-gst-regime/
https://blogs.tallysolutions.com/transport-of-goods-without-invoice-under-gst/
https://www.indiafilings.com/learn/gst-delivery-challan-format/

https://youtu.be/GSxMapU1rck
https://youtu.be/aCW1Vjn9bj8
https://youtu.be/qwN6vpBwi5E
https://youtu.be/80MOT0DKJAs

15 :e-way Bill

https://docs.ewaybillgst.gov.in/Documents/usermanual_ewb.pdf
https://cleartax.in/s/eway-bill-gst-rules-compliance
https://cleartax.in/s/generate-gst-eway-bills
https://cleartax.in/s/modify-gst-eway-bills
https://cleartax.in/s/generate-gst-consolidated-eway-bill

https://www.profitbooks.net/eway-bill/
https://www.charteredclub.com/e-way-bill/

https://help.tallysolutions.com/article/Tally.ERP9/Tax_India/gst/eway_bill.htm
https://blogs.tallysolutions.com/e-way-bill-for-multiple-vehicles/
https://tallysolutions.com/gst/eway-bill-generation-using-tally/
https://tallysolutions.com/gst/e-way-bill-under-gst/
http://blogs.tallysolutions.com/eway-bill-generation-for-transactions-recorded-in-tally/
https://cleartax.in/s/generate-gst-eway-bill-via-sms

https://youtu.be/gZGpzzOEXn8
https://youtu.be/b6tULtfVPgI
https://youtu.be/1H7bbLRRKf0
https://youtu.be/pPezinc_hYI
https://youtu.be/MjKumImGjzk
https://youtu.be/FZ-UQiWP0kE
https://youtu.be/MviRTqkrifw
https://youtu.be/M0_CkqNZlvo
https://youtu.be/N_GFf3iOiBg

16 :GSTR-1 Filing from Tally.ERP9

https://cleartax.in/s/file-gstr-1-using-tally-erp-9-release-6
https://help.tallysolutions.com/article/Tally.ERP9/Tax_India/gst/filing_gstr1.htm
https://tallysolutions.com/gst/gstr1-filing-format-due-date/
https://blogs.tallysolutions.com/gstr1-filing-using-tally-erp9/
https://help.tallysolutions.com/article/Tally.ERP9/Tax_India/gst/gstr-1.htm
https://help.tallysolutions.com/article/Tally.ERP9/Tax_India/gst/gst_issues_offline_portal.htm
http://blogs.tallysolutions.com/file-gstr-1-using-tally-erp-9/
https://help.tallysolutions.com/docs/te9rel61/Tax_India/gst/filing_gstr1.htm
https://cleartax.in/s/file-gstr-1-using-tally-erp-9-release-6
http://www.tallyerp9tutorials.com/taxation/gst-tally/export-gstr-1-excel-format-return-filing-uploading-gst-portal/
http://www.tallyerp9tutorials.com/taxation/gst-tally/gstr-1-view-gstr-1-report-tally-erp-9/
http://www.tallyerp9gst.com/Pages/Generate-GSTR-1-Returns-Reports-under-Tally-ERP9.html
https://twitter.com/hashtag/gstr1
https://www.reachaccountant.com/erp-software-pos-software-blog/tally-latest-version/
https://help.tallysolutions.com/docs/te9rel61/Tax_India/gst/exporting_gstr-1.htm

https://youtu.be/SzHm5OWmUxE
https://youtu.be/Xc3j9OALD20
https://youtu.be/SzHm5OWmUxE
https://youtu.be/B7Trqh4pUOk
https://youtu.be/SzHm5OWmUxE
https://youtu.be/oTnhZwh-5YI
https://youtu.be/tglj43bKPI0
https://youtu.be/vlgR5hjJ004
https://youtu.be/97B3FYr6pic
https://youtu.be/GlmBNEQ6cF0
https://youtu.be/8J7TgcNBYP0
https://youtu.be/Xc3j9OALD20
https://youtu.be/8ICDWEPvesg
https://youtu.be/crgNffcHi1c
https://youtu.be/fot6NCeZ60o
https://youtu.be/WWommFVT9D8
https://youtu.be/7ifAG-xUhrA
https://youtu.be/UZPaBJ_Lxa0
https://youtu.be/CCeo-sjux7Y
https://youtu.be/eT11KDvvOEk
https://youtu.be/pUrTCvn9G7I
https://youtu.be/gjDPmQFTzEw
https://youtu.be/-E8tOrW1qKY

17:GSTR-2 Filing from Tally.ERP9

https://help.tallysolutions.com/article/Tally.ERP9/Tax_India/gst/file_gstr2_from_rel_6_2.htm
https://tallysolutions.com/gst/gstr2-filing-format-due-date/
https://help.tallysolutions.com/article/te9rel60/Tax_India/gst/status_reconciliation_gstr2.htm?refer=https://www.google.com/
https://help.tallysolutions.com/article/Tally.ERP9/Tax_India/gst/gstr_2.htm
https://blogs.tallysolutions.com/gstr2-filing-using-tally-erp9/

http://blogs.tallysolutions.com/uderstanding-gstr-2-part1/
http://blogs.tallysolutions.com/uderstanding-gstr-2-part2/
http://blogs.tallysolutions.com/uderstanding-gstr-2-part3/
http://blogs.tallysolutions.com/uderstanding-gstr-2-part4/
http://blogs.tallysolutions.com/uderstanding-gstr-2-part5/

http://blogs.tallysolutions.com/uderstanding-gstr-2-part6/
http://blogs.tallysolutions.com/uderstanding-gstr-2-part7/
http://blogs.tallysolutions.com/uderstanding-gstr-2-part8/
http://blogs.tallysolutions.com/uderstanding-gstr-2-part9/

https://youtu.be/za9GDk4sXag
https://youtu.be/nfqJMx3fJg8
https://youtu.be/r5pZP63ihbg
https://youtu.be/pOX5qdo76UE
https://youtu.be/pzgQsbLczUU
https://youtu.be/BeZzLnSsHDo
https://youtu.be/4D2533apE9s
https://youtu.be/7oJjRH-DmX0
https://youtu.be/CcXXye7c_z0
https://youtu.be/5EbyYjilF64
https://youtu.be/mfs7Cf2vM10
https://youtu.be/mfs7Cf2vM10
https://youtu.be/tHpVlG4lhus
https://youtu.be/KweGgiqEwhg
https://youtu.be/tHpVlG4lhus
https://youtu.be/-E8tOrW1qKY

18:GSTR-3B Filing from Tally.ERP9

https://cleartax.in/s/file-gstr-3b-tally-guide
http://www.tallyerp9tutorials.com/taxation/gst-tally/form-gstr-3b-generate-gstr-3b-file-return-tally-erp-9/
http://tallyerp9book.com/Pages/Web-Page/GST/Filing-GSTR-3B-Report-from-TallyERP9-in-Govt-GST-Portal.html

http://www.tallyerp9gst.com/Pages/GSTR-3B/Generating-Form-GSTR-3B-on-TallyERP9.html
http://www.tallyerp9gst.com/Pages/GSTR-3B/Filing-GSTR-3B.html
http://www.tallyerp9gst.com/Pages/GSTR-3B/Login-and-Navigate-to-GSTR-3B%E2%80%93GST-Return.html
http://www.tallyerp9gst.com/Pages/GSTR-3B/Details-in-Section-3-1(GSTR-3B-Return).html
http://www.tallyerp9gst.com/Pages/GSTR-3B/Details-in-Section-3-2(GSTR-3B%20Return).html
http://www.tallyerp9gst.com/Pages/GSTR-3B/Enter-ITC-Details-in-Section-4(GSTR-3B-Return)Eligible-ITC.html

http://www.tallyerp9gst.com/Pages/GSTR-3B/Enter-Details-in-Section-5-1(GSTR-3B-Return)Interest-and-Late-Fee.html

http://www.tallyerp9gst.com/Pages/GSTR-3B/Preview-Draft-GSTR-3B-Return-under-GST-Portal.html

http://www.tallyerp9gst.com/Pages/GSTR-3B/Payment-Details-in-Section-6-1(GSTR-3B-Return)Payment-of-Tax.html

http://www.tallyerp9gst.com/Pages/GSTR-3B/File-GSTR-3B-Return-under-GST-Portal.html

http://www.tallyerp9gst.com/Pages/GSTR-3B/Download-Filed-GSTR-3B-Return-under-GST-Portal.html

http://www.tallyerp9gst.com/Pages/GSTR-3B/Filing-of-NIL-GSTR-3B-Return-under-GST-Portal.html

http://www.tallyerp9gst.com/Pages/GSTR-3B/FAQ-on-GSTR-3B-under-GST.html

https://tallysolutions.com/gst/file-gstr3b-from-tally-erp9/

https://help.tallysolutions.com/article/Tally.ERP9/Tax_India/gst/Form_GSTR-3B.htm

https://tallysolutions.com/gst/file-gstr3b-from-tally-erp9/

http://blogs.tallysolutions.com/file-gstr3b-from-tally-erp9-export-gstr3b-using-tally/

https://youtu.be/laqcr2e3rkY

https://youtu.be/JYda3gn4l1w

https://youtu.be/UVm0amSghOo

https://youtu.be/3Qg1jKLje9I

https://youtu.be/ZiK9LPWRSV0

https://youtu.be/rOWoAtYwebs

https://youtu.be/NUcImKsfZO0

https://youtu.be/PcSarJormX8

https://youtu.be/L1RlagsplOY

https://youtu.be/cAaWnMeZ38M

https://youtu.be/VZu-qspqQ6U

https://youtu.be/paqSfgAvXxE

https://youtu.be/UGoLkxaG8wA

https://youtu.be/nBEN8-F9jng

19: GSTR-4 Filing from Tally.ERP9

https://cleartax.in/s/guide-on-filing-gstr4-on-portal

https://help.tallysolutions.com/article/Tally.ERP9/Tax_India/gst_composition/gstr4_gst_composition.htm

https://tallysolutions.com/gst/gstr4-filing-format-due-date/

https://help.tallysolutions.com/article/Tally.ERP9/Tax_India/gst_composition/file_gstr4.htm

https://tallysolutions.com/gst/gstr4-filing-using-tally-erp9/

https://youtu.be/QB3uOLjVxTw
https://youtu.be/acjiVr2GIEM
https://youtu.be/zc6BALZdnAE
https://youtu.be/YKckdl44lCw
https://youtu.be/SzHm5OWmUxE
https://youtu.be/0bCs60rdZvA
https://youtu.be/WVlg-ZqufWw
https://youtu.be/AJlQJg-HPjM
https://youtu.be/x6BluwUJEZY
https://youtu.be/9zUkZBUbpTA
https://youtu.be/xs-axdnXH60
https://youtu.be/Prrzj6UBAIA
https://youtu.be/p1DNJEkP0js
https://youtu.be/kUn7rDOl6tg
https://youtu.be/J1DbnWZfGFs
https://youtu.be/pXzlHL5r6Vw

www.ingramcontent.com/pod-product-compliance
Lightning Source LLC
Chambersburg PA
CBHW080343220326
41598CB00030B/4587